Privacy Protection Measures and Technologies in Business Organizations:

Aspects and Standards

George O.M. Yee
Aptus Research Solutions Inc., Canada & Carleton University, Canada

Managing Director:	Lindsay Johnston
Senior Editorial Director:	Heather Probst
Book Production Manager:	Sean Woznicki
Development Manager:	Joel Gamon
Development Editor:	Myla Harty
Acquisitions Editor:	Erika Gallagher
Typesetters:	Milan Vracarich, Jr.
Print Coordinator:	Jamie Snavely
Cover Design:	Nick Newcomer, Greg Snader

Published in the United States of America by
Information Science Reference (an imprint of IGI Global)
701 E. Chocolate Avenue
Hershey PA 17033
Tel: 717-533-8845
Fax: 717-533-8661
E-mail: cust@igi-global.com
Web site: http://www.igi-global.com

Library of Congress Cataloging-in-Publication Data

Privacy protection measures and technologies in business organizations: aspects and standards / George O.M. Yee and Aptus Research Solutions Inc., editors.
     p. cm.
  Includes bibliographical references and index.
  Summary: "This book is a collection of research on privacy protection technologies and their application in business organizations"--Provided by publisher.
  ISBN 978-1-61350-501-4 (hbk.) -- ISBN 978-1-61350-502-1 (ebook) -- ISBN 978-1-61350-503-8 (print & perpetual access) 1. Business--Data processing--Security measures. 2. Computer security. 3. Data protection. 4. Privacy, Right of. I. Yee, George. II. Aptus Research Solutions.
  HF5548.37.P755 2012
  658.4'78--dc23
                          2011038433

British Cataloguing in Publication Data
A Cataloguing in Publication record for this book is available from the British Library.

All work contributed to this book is new, previously-unpublished material. The views expressed in this book are those of the authors, but not necessarily of the publisher.

Table of Contents

Section 1
Privacy Protection Technology Applicable to Business

Martin Gilje Jaatun, SINTEF ICT, Norway
Inger Anne Tøndel, SINTEF ICT, Norway
Karin Bernsmed, SINTEF ICT, Norway
Åsmund Ahlmann Nyre, SINTEF ICT, Norway

Antonio F. Gomez-Skarmeta, University of Murcia, Spain
Alejandro Perez Mendez, University of Murcia, Spain
Elena Torroglosa Garcia, University of Murcia, Spain
Gabriel Lopez Millán, University of Murcia, Spain

Anna Antonakopoulou, National Technical University of Athens, Greece
Georgios V. Lioudakis, National Technical University of Athens, Greece
Fotios Gogoulos, National Technical University of Athens, Greece
Dimitra I. Kaklamani, National Technical University of Athens, Greece
Iakovos S. Venieris, National Technical University of Athens, Greece

Section 3
Privacy Related Analyses and Evaluations

Detailed Table of Contents

Section 1
Privacy Protection Technology Applicable to Business

Chapter 1
    Martin Gilje Jaatun, SINTEF ICT, Norway
    Inger Anne Tøndel, SINTEF ICT, Norway
    Karin Bernsmed, SINTEF ICT, Norway
    Åsmund Ahlmann Nyre, SINTEF ICT, Norway

This chapter begins by providing background information on the value of personal information and the privacy regulation approaches in use today. It then describes the challenges and market opportunities of Privacy Enhancing Technologies (PETs). A survey of PETs suitable for business organizations is presented, including a study on the Platform for Privacy Preferences (P3P). The chapter concludes with the authors' conviction of what businesses have to do to promote privacy.

Chapter 2
    Antonio F. Gomez-Skarmeta, University of Murcia, Spain
    Alejandro Perez Mendez, University of Murcia, Spain
    Elena Torroglosa Garcia, University of Murcia, Spain
    Gabriel Lopez Millán, University of Murcia, Spain

This chapter is concerned with Identity Management (IdM). It describes what IdM is, why it is important, and how it can be useful for both users and business organizations. The chapter begins with background and definitions of terminology. It then discusses the general IdM architecture and standards, and overviews a number of existing IdM systems. An analysis of how IdM can be introduced into organizations is given, along with business opportunities arising from IdM.

Chapter 3

Anna Antonakopoulou, National Technical University of Athens, Greece
Georgios V. Lioudakis, National Technical University of Athens, Greece
Fotios Gogoulos, National Technical University of Athens, Greece
Dimitra I. Kaklamani, National Technical University of Athens, Greece
Iakovos S. Venieris, National Technical University of Athens, Greece

Access control is fundamental for security. Privacy-aware access control is fundamental to privacy protection. This chapter concerns itself with the legal and technical requirements of privacy-aware access control in business environments and provides a study of the proposed solutions in the literature. The latter includes access control models that incorporate privacy policy enforcing features that account for the purpose of the access, privacy obligations, and other contextual constraints.

Chapter 4

Anne V. D. M. Kayem, University of Cape Town, South Africa
Patrick Martin, Queen's University, Canada
Selim G. Akl, Queen's University, Canada

This chapter discusses privacy and access control in a business context and describes how access control models have been extended in recent years to protect privacy on the Web. It considers the advantages of self-protecting Cryptographic Access Control (CAC) models over standard models in privacy enforcement, and postulates that self-protecting CAC schemes need to be supported by fault tolerance. The authors show how this support can be achieved using ideas from the autonomic computing paradigm.

Chapter 5

Xiaoxun Sun, Australian Council for Educational Research, Australia
Min Li, University of Southern Queensland, Australia

Protecting anonymity when publishing microdata (data at the individual level such as age and home address) is always a problem due to linking attacks that can identify the individual owner of the data. k-anonymity is a technique that prevents linking attacks by generalizing or suppressing portions of the released microdata so that no individual can be uniquely distinguished from a group of size k. This chapter investigates a practical full-domain generalization model of k-anonymity and presents an efficient privacy hash table structure to compute a minimal k-anonymous solution.

Chapter 6

Alfonso Rodríguez, University of Bio-Bio, Chile
Eduardo Fernández-Medina, University of Castilla-La Mancha, Spain
Mario Piattinim, University of Castilla-La Mancha, Spain

Business processes describe the set of activities that enterprises perform to reach their objectives. Security and privacy are essential elements in competitiveness. This chapter proposes a model-driven approach for the development of secure (and privacy protecting) business processes. The secure processes also provide artifacts, including security artifacts, useful for software development. The proposal is proved in a case study, verifying its pertinence and validity.

This chapter by the originator of the "Privacy by Design (PbD)" concept describes the origins and meaning of PbD, and traces its evolution in terms of information technologies, universal principles to guide the design for privacy, and the work of the Information and Privacy Commissioner of Ontario, Canada, in supporting Privacy by Design. The chapter also outlines the recognition for PbD and the challenges ahead.

Section 2
Privacy Protection in Specific Business Domains

Electronic Health Record (EHR) systems are powerful tools for both healthcare providers and patients. Unfortunately, EHR systems also result in new threats to patient privacy. The inclusion of medical images in patient records poses unique challenges, since such images may reveal a patient's identity or medical condition. This chapter gives an overview of EHR systems, and discusses how privacy challenges from EHR systems and medical images may be mitigated, by combining technology, policy, and legislation aimed at reducing the risk of re-identification.

Chapter 9

A wellness cloud is an instance of cloud computing. A wellness cloud is an integrated, interconnected and intelligent collection of healthcare processors processing data from wellness devices, whose purpose is to help users achieve their wellness goals. This chapter describes the issues and solutions surrounding the privacy protection of healthcare data, as the data resides on the devices, as it travels to the cloud, and as it is processed in the cloud and used by analytic services.

Chapter 10

In recent years, video surveillance technology has come into vogue for general law enforcement and public safety. However, such technology raises issues with privacy protection, lawful evidence enforcement, and content confidentiality, among others. This chapter presents an innovative network-based digital video surveillance solution that meets security and privacy requirements, ensuring that the recorded data will be only accessible to a subset of authorities.

Chapter 11

Social network analysis (SNA) is becoming an important tool in investigative organizations such as the police. However, privacy legislation often prevents the free sharing of information needed in SNA. This chapter presents two protocols that allow for the selective disclosure of information needed in SNA. The authors have implemented one of the protocols in a commercial enterprise system used in criminal investigations, showing that SNA can be applied in a privacy-preserving manner.

Chapter 12

This chapter presents a model for assisting user decision making with regard to managing privacy risks associated with pervasive computing. The model brings into alignment four aspects: business, regulation, technology, and user behaviour, and is able to achieve compliance with privacy policies within a dynamic and context-aware risk management situation. The authors describe a small middleware implementation of the model along with the outcomes of the implementation.

Section 3
Privacy Related Analyses and Evaluations

Chapter 13

This chapter examines various aspects of harm mitigation from the release of personal identity information, using a real life example involving the release of social security numbers, along with names and addresses. Questions dealt with include: What are the harms associated with a data breach of this nature? How can these harms be mitigated? What are, or should be, the costs and consequences to the organization releasing the data? The authors propose the use of a statistical model to estimate the likely financial repercussions for individuals and organizations.

Chapter 14
Faye Fangfei Wang, Brunel University, UK

Technological change seems always to be ahead of governing legislation. In the case of automated information systems, personal information can be collected from individuals with very little human interaction, raising serious concerns over data privacy. This chapter evaluates whether current EU legislation is sufficient to ensure that future automated information systems will be designed and built to protect privacy. It also discusses the impact of the legislation on business organizations and suggests solutions for enhancing privacy protection from a legal point of view.

Foreword

With the advent of the World Wide Web, social networks, and the abundance of data mining and analysis tools, privacy violations have become a major threat to society. While individuals are giving out more and more personal information about themselves on social networking sites, data mining tools can analyze this information and extract highly private and sensitive data about these individuals, completely unknown to them. One of the reasons for the privacy challenges is that there is no universal definition of privacy. For example, different communities have different notions of privacy. In the case of the medical community, privacy is about a patient determining what information the doctor should release about him/her. Typically, employers, marketers, and insurance corporations may seek information about individuals. It is up to the individuals to determine the information to be released about them. In the financial community, a bank customer determines what financial information the bank should release about him/her. In addition, retail corporations should not be releasing sales information about individuals unless the individuals have authorized the release. In the case of the government community, privacy may take a whole new meaning. For example, the FBI may determine what information about a US citizen it can release, to say the CIA. That is, the FBI has to ensure the privacy of US citizens. Therefore, what are needed are standards for privacy.

Various types of privacy problems have been studied by researchers. Here is a list of the various problems and the solutions proposed. (i) Problem: Privacy violations that result due to data mining. In this case the solution is privacy-Preserving Data Mining. That is, we carry out data mining and give out the results without revealing the data values used to carry out data mining. (ii) Problem: Privacy violations that result due to the inference problem. Note that inference is the process of deducing sensitive information from the legitimate responses received to user queries. The solution to this problem is privacy constraint processing. (iii) Problem: Privacy violations due to un-encrypted data. The solution to this problem is to utilize encryption at different levels. (iv) Problem: Privacy violation due to poor system design. Here, the solution is to develop methodology for designing privacy-enhanced systems.

While books on privacy are emerging, these books address a specific type of privacy solution such as privacy-preserving data mining or encryption for privacy. Furthermore, while researchers have stated that privacy is not just a technological problem and that we need technologists, standards organizations, and policy makers to work together, very little work has been done on this interdisciplinary area of privacy. To date, there is no comprehensive book that addresses multiple aspects of privacy. I believe that this book, titled *Privacy Protection Measures and Technologies in Business Organizations: Aspects and Standards*, edited by Dr. George Yee, is the first such book. It not only discusses privacy technologies, but also heavily emphasizes the applicability to the business environment. In particular, it describes privacy aspects in domains such as healthcare, social networks, surveillance, and pervasive computing. It also discusses the risks involved and addresses legislative issues.

This book is a must for anyone who wishes to conduct research in privacy. It is also an excellent reference book on privacy that could be taught in multiple colleges including computer science departments, business schools, and social science departments. It will also serve as a guide to business organizations who wish to introduce privacy policies and determine the technologies to utilize. Finally, government agencies such as the Department of Homeland Security, who are very concerned about individual privacy being violated through data mining, will benefit from the various solutions proposed in this book. In summary, I would highly recommend this book to anyone who is interested in conducting research on privacy, getting educated on privacy, or who wishes to enforce privacy policies.

Bhavani Thuraisingham
June, 2011

Bhavani Thuraisingham is the Louis A. Beecherl, Jr. I, Distinguished Professor in the Erik Jonsson School of Engineering and Computer Science at the University of Texas at Dallas (UTD) since September 2010. She joined UTD in October 2004 as a Professor of Computer Science and Director of the Cyber Security Research Center which conducts research in data security and privacy, secure networks, secure languages, secure social media, data mining, and semantic web. Dr. Thuraisingham is an elected Fellow of four prestigious organizations: the IEEE (Institute for Electrical and Electronics Engineers, 2003), the AAAS (American Association for the Advancement of Science, 2003), the BCS (British Computer Society, 2005), and the SDPS (Society for Design and Process Science, 2011). She is the recipient of numerous awards including (i) the IEEE Computer Society's 1997 Technical Achievement Award for "outstanding and innovative contributions to secure data management," (ii) the 2010 Research Leadership Award for "Outstanding and Sustained Leadership Contributions to the Field of Intelligence and Security Informatics" presented jointly by the IEEE Intelligent and Transportation Systems Society Technical Committee on Intelligence and Security Informatics in Transportation Systems and the IEEE Systems, Man and Cybernetics Society Technical Committee on Homeland Security, (iii) the 2010 ACM SIGSAC (Association for Computing Machinery, Special Interest Group on Security, Audit and Control) Outstanding Contributions Award for "seminal research contributions and leadership in data and applications security for over 25 years," and (iv) AFCEA (Armed Forces Communication and Electronics Association) 2011 Medal of Merit for service to the Association and sustained professional excellence in communications, electronics, intelligence and information systems. She is a Distinguished Scientist of ACM, was an IEEE Distinguished Lecturer between 2002 and 2005, and was also featured by Silicon India magazine as one of the seven leading technology innovators of South Asian origin in the USA in 2002. Her full biography may be found at: http://www.utdallas.edu/~bxt043000/

Preface

Business and political realities make privacy harder.
> — *Bruce Schneier in "Architecture of Privacy" (Schneier, 2009)*

This book arises from the need to ensure that business leaders and others understand the importance of privacy and have the necessary tools to build privacy into their business processes. Why is privacy important to business? Karen Curtis, the former Privacy Commissioner of Australia, claimed in a keynote address that good privacy is good business, and gave a number of compelling reasons in support of her claim (Curtis, 2006). Among her top reasons are that bad privacy can lead to:

1. Damages to brand and reputation
2. Loss of customers and business partners
3. Loss of valuable information to competitors or malicious individuals

Other reasons (Curtis, 2006) include:

- Business pragmatism: providing good privacy will reduce (or at least not increase) the amount of regulation to which businesses must comply.
- Avoiding legal costs and penalties: businesses do not in general like to be involved in litigation as a result of a privacy breach.
- Improved staff morale: an organization that has respect for privacy embedded in its culture will enjoy a happier and more productive work force.
- Corporate social responsibility: leading businesses take this responsibility to heart, operating in a manner that meets or exceeds the ethical, legal, commercial and public expectations that society has of business.

Why are tools needed to build privacy into business processes? As in most endeavors, tools can help, and in an application area where, for example, privacy may be resisted in favor of the fallacious argument of higher profits, tools are needed. Most professionals have heard of the Privacy Impact Assessment (Warren et al., 2008). This is a tool that evaluates the impact to privacy of a proposed change to business practice. Prior to the introduction of this tool, such impacts to privacy were either done in an ineffective way or not even considered.

Tools are built on technology. Privacy tools are built on privacy technology. A well-known example of privacy technology is the Privacy Enhancing Technology (PET). An example of a PET is the AT&T

Privacy Bird (Cranor, Arjula, & Guduru, 2002), which is a browser plug-in that automatically retrieves privacy policies from service providers and compares these with the user's specified privacy preferences. Another example of privacy technology is privacy-aware access control. PETs and other privacy technologies are described in this work. The typical business may not have the resources to directly work with some of the more technical privacy technologies, but all privacy technologies can be incorporated into privacy tools by businesses that build the tools. The typical business can then directly make use of these tools.

CURRENT SITUATION WITH BUSINESS PROTECTION OF PRIVACY

The current state of privacy protection in business organizations is far from good. In many organizations, privacy protection is non-existent. Consider the serious privacy breaches that have been recently reported in the news, the latest of which at the time of this writing is the "Sony breach." In this breach (Akkad, 2011), an attacker stole names, addresses, and other personal data belonging to about 77 million Sony PlayStation Network accounts. Consider also, that it is only the more sensational breaches that are reported in the news. There are many breaches that go unreported.

Most businesses today only pay lip service to privacy requirements by making available their privacy policy. Such a policy is useless unless there are foolproof safeguards that ensure that the policy is followed. In the case of e-commerce, it is next to impossible to tell if the privacy policy is followed. For privacy policies that are posted on e-commerce websites, this editor wrote in (Yee, 2006): "Merely the posting of the website's privacy policy and requesting consumers to read it is tantamount to a joke. It is more a legalistic self-protection action rather than one that has the consumer's best interest at heart. First of all, most consumers will not bother to read it – who would? - there are many other more pressing (and perhaps more interesting) things to do. Second, and more importantly, the posted provisions do not speak to the consumer's personal privacy needs, only the provider's needs. Everyone is different and have different privacy needs. The expectation of one provider policy fitting everyone's needs is ridiculous." It has been 5 years since this was written, and sadly, ensuring that web posted privacy policies are followed has not measurably improved. About the only areas that have improved in the last 5 years are: a) public awareness of the potential loss of their privacy – this puts more pressure on business to protect consumer privacy, b) increasing awareness by business of the need to comply with privacy regulation, but far more awareness is needed, and c) educational programs are producing more security and privacy professionals.

CHALLENGES AND OPPORTUNITIES

In the coming years, the need for privacy protection in business organizations will only increase. In the past, the rapid growth of the Internet, together with increases in computerization, accompanied by soaring deployments of client-related business applications, resulted in more and more consumer personal information in the possession of business organizations. The Internet is still expanding. Computerization and use of client-related business applications are still growing. In fact, these rates of growth may increase as the world's economies shift from being based on manufacturing to being based on information. Some of the challenges and opportunities that lie ahead for ensuring effective privacy protection in business organizations are:

- Business organizations need to be aware of the need to protect privacy, and the consequences of not protecting privacy.
- Business organizations need to be aware of what actions they need to take to protect privacy, including what tools are available, and carry out those actions.
- Protective foolproof measures must be in place to guard against potential privacy breaches, including safeguards for ensuring privacy policy compliance.
- Privacy legislation needs to be reviewed regularly against changing technology and business practices to ensure that they are adequate, and updated if they are not.
- Penalties for privacy breaches need to be sufficient to persuade business organizations to install privacy protective measures.
- Business privacy practices need to be audited on a regular basis. If such practices are found to be inadequate, the business should be required to upgrade them.
- Government privacy commissioners should have their powers increased and their staff expanded, so that they can participate in auditing business privacy practices, and prosecute violators who refuse to comply.

This work addresses the first four points. As an example of the third point on the need for protective foolproof measures, consider that business communication and collaboration include content sharing and email. How can these be safeguarded against the leakage of consumer personal information? As another example, internal business systems comprise workflows that handle and process client personal information. What measures are needed to avoid inadvertently and illegally revealing this information? What standards can be followed to reduce this risk?

ORGANIZATION OF THIS BOOK

This book reports on the latest advances in privacy protection technologies and their application in business organizations. It is organized into 3 Sections and 14 chapters. A brief description of each chapter follows.

I. Privacy Protection Technology Applicable to Business

This section presents a collection of chapters on privacy protection technology that can be applied to business activities.

Chapter 1: "Privacy Enhancing Technologies for Information Control"

This chapter begins by providing background information on the value of personal information and the privacy regulation approaches in use today. It then describes the challenges and market opportunities of Privacy Enhancing Technologies (PETs). A survey of PETs suitable for business organizations is presented, including a study on the Platform for Privacy Preferences (P3P). The chapter concludes with the authors' conviction of what businesses have to do to promote privacy.

Chapter 2: "User-Centric Privacy Management in Future Network Infrastructure"

This chapter is concerned with Identity Management (IdM). It describes what IdM is, why it is important, and how it can be useful for both users and business organizations. The chapter begins with background and definitions of terminology. It then discusses the general IdM architecture and standards, and overviews a number of existing IdM systems. An analysis of how IdM can be introduced into organizations is given, along with business opportunities arising from IdM.

Chapter 3: "Leveraging Access Control for Privacy Protection: A Survey"

Access control is fundamental for security. Privacy-aware access control is fundamental to privacy protection. This chapter concerns itself with the legal and technical requirements of privacy-aware access control in business environments and provides a study of the proposed solutions in the literature. The latter includes access control models that incorporate privacy policy enforcing features that account for the purpose of the access, privacy obligations, and other contextual constraints.

Chapter 4: "Self-Protecting Access Control: On Mitigating Privacy Violations with Fault Tolerance"

This chapter discusses privacy and access control in a business context and describes how access control models have been extended in recent years to protect privacy on the Web. It considers the advantages of self-protecting Cryptographic Access Control (CAC) models over standard models in privacy enforcement, and postulates that self-protecting CAC schemes need to be supported by fault tolerance. The authors show how this support can be achieved using ideas from the autonomic computing paradigm.

Chapter 5: "Privacy Hash Table"

Protecting anonymity when publishing microdata (data at the individual level such as age and home address) is always a problem due to linking attacks that can identify the individual owner of the data. k-anonymity is a technique that prevents linking attacks by generalizing or suppressing portions of the released microdata so that no individual can be uniquely distinguished from a group of size k. This chapter investigates a practical full-domain generalization model of k-anonymity and presents an efficient privacy hash table structure to compute a minimal k-anonymous solution.

Chapter 6: "Developing Secure Business Processes: A Model Driven Approach"

Business processes describe the set of activities that enterprises perform to reach their objectives. Security and privacy are essential elements in competitiveness. This chapter proposes a model-driven approach for the development of secure (and privacy protecting) business processes. The secure processes also provide artifacts, including security artifacts, useful for software development. The proposal is proved in a case study, verifying its pertinence and validity.

Chapter 7: "Privacy by Design: Origins, Meaning, and Prospects for Assuring Privacy and Trust in the Information Era"

This chapter, by the originator of the "Privacy by Design (PbD)" concept, describes the origins and meaning of PbD, and traces its evolution in terms of information technologies, universal principles to guide the design for privacy, and the work of the Information and Privacy Commissioner of Ontario, Canada, in supporting Privacy by Design. The chapter also outlines the recognition for PbD and the challenges ahead.

II. Privacy Protection in Specific Business Domains

This section is a collection of chapters exploring privacy issues and proposing privacy protection techniques in specific business domains.

Chapter 8: "Privacy Considerations for Electronic Health Records"

Electronic Health Record (EHR) systems are powerful tools for both healthcare providers and patients. Unfortunately, EHR systems also result in new threats to patient privacy. The inclusion of medical images in patient records poses unique challenges, since such images may reveal a patient's identity or medical condition. This chapter gives an overview of EHR systems, and discusses how privacy challenges from EHR systems and medical images may be mitigated, by combining technology, policy, and legislation aimed at reducing the risk of re-identification.

Chapter 9: "Privacy Protection Issues for Healthcare Wellness Clouds"

A wellness cloud is an instance of cloud computing. A wellness cloud is an integrated, interconnected and intelligent collection of healthcare processors processing data from wellness devices, whose purpose is to help users achieve their wellness goals. This chapter describes the issues and solutions surrounding the privacy protection of healthcare data, as the data resides on the devices, as it travels to the cloud, and as it is processed in the cloud and used by analytic services.

Chapter 10: "Ensuring Privacy and Confidentiality in Digital Video Surveillance Systems"

In recent years, video surveillance technology has come into vogue for general law enforcement and public safety. However, such technology raises issues with privacy protection, lawful evidence enforcement, and content confidentiality, among others. This chapter presents an innovative network-based digital video surveillance solution that meets security and privacy requirements, ensuring that the recorded data will be only accessible to a subset of authorities.

Chapter 11: "Protecting Privacy by Secure Computation: Privacy in Social Network Analysis"

Social network analysis (SNA) is becoming an important tool in investigative organizations such as the police. However, privacy legislation often prevents the free sharing of information needed in SNA. This chapter presents two protocols that allow for the selective disclosure of information needed in SNA. The authors have implemented one of the protocols in a commercial enterprise system used in criminal investigations, showing that SNA can be applied in a privacy-preserving manner.

Chapter 12: "A Dynamic Privacy Manager for Compliance in Pervasive Computing"

This chapter presents a model for assisting user decision making with regard to managing privacy risks associated with pervasive computing. The model brings into alignment four aspects: business, regulation, technology, and user behaviour, and is able to achieve compliance with privacy policies within a dynamic and context-aware risk management situation. The authors describe a small middleware implementation of the model along with the outcomes of the implementation.

III. Privacy Related Analyses and Evaluations

This section presents chapters that provide analyses and evaluations on specific privacy situations, namely harm mitigation for a privacy breach, and the sufficiency (or insufficiency) of privacy legislation to cope with technological change.

Chapter 13: "Harm Mitigation from the Release of Personal Identity Information"

This chapter examines various aspects of harm mitigation from the release of personal identity information, using a real life example involving the release of social security numbers, along with names and addresses. Questions dealt with include: What are the harms associated with a data breach of this nature? How can these harms be mitigated? What are, or should be, the costs and consequences to the organization releasing the data? The authors propose the use of a statistical model to estimate the likely financial repercussions for individuals and organizations.

Chapter 14: "Consumer Privacy Protection in the European Union: Legislative Reform Driven by Current Technological Challenges"

Technological change seems always to be ahead of governing legislation. In the case of automated information systems, personal information can be collected from individuals with very little human interaction, raising serious concerns over data privacy. This chapter evaluates whether current EU legislation is sufficient to ensure that future automated information systems will be designed and built to protect privacy. It also discusses the impact of the legislation on business organizations and suggests solutions for enhancing privacy protection from a legal point of view.

CONCLUSION

This book collects together material that addresses the first four points in the Challenges and Opportunities section above. The first point on business awareness of the need to protect privacy is clearly imparted to readers by all chapters, but especially by chapter 13 on the mitigation of harm. The second point on what actions to take to protect privacy is again covered by all chapters, both from a technology point of view (Section I) and a technology applications point of view (Section II). The third point on foolproof measures is covered by all chapters in Sections I and II. The fourth point on regularly reviewing privacy legislation to ensure adequacy is addressed by chapter 14, which provides an assessment of the sufficiency of privacy legislation to cope with ever changing technology. In addition, this book will provide insights and will support professionals concerned with the management of expertise, knowledge, information, and organizational development in different types of business organizations and environments.

The target audience for this book is composed of business professionals and researchers working in the field of privacy protection in various disciplines, e.g. business sciences and management, information and communication sciences, library, education, sociology, computer science, computer engineering, and information technology.

REFERENCES

Akkad, O. (2011, April 28). Sony data breach fuels privacy concerns. *The Globe and Mail*. Retrieved May 14, 2011, from http://www.theglobeandmail.com/news/technology/tech-news/sony-data-breach-fuels-privacy-concerns/article2001228/

Cranor, L. F., Arjula, M., & Guduru, P. (2002). *Use of a P3P user agent by early adopters*. Paper presented at the 2002 ACM Workshop on Privacy in the Electronic Society.

Curtis, K. (2006). *Good privacy is good business*. Keynote address to the New Zealand Privacy Issues Forum. Retrieved May 14, 2011, from http://privacy.org.nz/good-privacy-is-good-business-karen-curtis

Schneier, B. (2009). *Architecture of privacy*. IEEE Security & Privacy, January/February 2009. Retrieved May 14, 2011, from http://www.schneier.com/essay-253.html

Warren, A., Bayley, R., Bennett, C., Charlesworth, A., Clarke, R., & Oppenheim, C. (2008). Privacy impact assessments: International experience as a basis for UK guidance. *Computer Law & Security Report, 24*(2008), 233-242. Retrieved May 14, 2011, from www.colinbennett.ca/Recent%20publications/AWetal_CLSR_0508.pdf

Yee, G. (2006). *Privacy protection for e-services*. Hershey, PA: Idea Group Publishing.

Acknowledgment

First and foremost, I would like to thank all the authors for their excellent contributions to this book.

My heartfelt gratitude goes to all the reviewers who provided insightful and constructive comments, in particular to Carlisle Adams of the University of Ottawa, Jose Delgado of Universidade Técnica de Lisboa, Martin Jaatun of SINTEF ICT, Norway, Steve Marsh of the Communications Research Centre Canada, Siani Pearson of HP Labs, UK, Ed Simon of XMLsec Inc., Canada, and Ronggong Song of Defense Research and Development Canada.

A special note of thanks goes to Myla Harty at IGI Global. Her guidance and answers to questions throughout the process made it easier.

George O.M. Yee
Aptus Research Solutions Inc., Canada & Carleton University, Canada

Section 1
Privacy Protection Technology Applicable to Business

Chapter 1
Privacy Enhancing Technologies for Information Control

Martin Gilje Jaatun
SINTEF ICT, Norway

Inger Anne Tøndel
SINTEF ICT, Norway

Karin Bernsmed
SINTEF ICT, Norway

Åsmund Ahlmann Nyre
SINTEF ICT, Norway

ABSTRACT

Privacy Enhancing Technologies (PETs) help to protect the personal information of users. This chapter will discuss challenges and opportunities of PETs in a business context, and present examples of currently available PETs. We will further study the Platform for Privacy Preferences (P3P), and discuss why it so far has failed to deliver on its promise. Finally, we provide our advice on further research on privacy preferences, and conclude with our conviction that businesses need to take a progressive stance on providing privacy to their customers.

INTRODUCTION

Privacy is a fuzzy concept with many definitions, one of which is "the right to be let alone" (Warren & Brandeis, 1890). This particular definition seems to have lost much of its validity, however, as we in modern society base so much of our existence on interaction with others over the internet. This is in particular true for us as consumers, as increasingly businesses assume that we will use the internet for both purchases and user support.

Privacy Enhancing Technologies (PETs) comprise a broad collection of tools and processes that help protect the privacy of end-users. PETs range from mechanisms that prevent disclosure of personal information, via ways of hiding location information, to methods for anonymous communication.

To the casual observer it might seem that most businesses have been more interested in privacy-

DOI: 10.4018/978-1-61350-501-4.ch001

invasive technologies than privacy-enhancing technologies, in that businesses have wanted to learn as much as possible about their (potential) customers, in order to deploy more targeted advertisements, sales projections and production planning. On the "dark side" of the business spectrum, this has led to the development of spyware that monitors individual computer users, but retailers have also looked into the possibility of exploiting RFID tags on merchandise to harvest information on their customers (CASPIAN, 2006).

To this day, most consumers seem oblivious to privacy concerns, and their behavior is usually not motivated by such concerns; to the contrary, most people seem overly free with their personal information, particularly in the context of online social networks such as Facebook (2011) and LinkedIn (2011). However, as advances in data mining techniques are progressing, the vast amounts of data available to businesses are bound to be recognized as a concern by consumers, and a backlash is imminent.

It has been said that online businesses instead of establishing a trust relationship with their customers, rather focus on avoiding *distrust* (Clarke, 2008), and that this is mainly achieved through how they treat the personal data of their customers – in many cases, the more personal data a business demands from a customer, the more the distrust increases. In this context, it would seem that organizations that facilitate the use of Privacy Enhancing Technologies in their interactions with their customers should have a business advantage. Many businesses tend to collect personal information about their customers as a matter of course, regardless of whether they actually need this information. This could potentially end up as a liability for a business, since in many jurisdictions, storing personal information requires informed consent, and forces the business to abide by privacy legislation.

The obligation to inform users of privacy practices is commonly resolved by using a comprehensive and high-level description of an organization's privacy policy (Guarda, 2009). In the digital world, privacy policies have become the main instrument for service providers to explain how users' personal data are collected, used, disclosed, and managed. Unfortunately, due to their complexity, difficult language and sheer length, users tend to neither read nor understand the policies prior to acceptance (Berendt, Günther, & Spiekermann, 2005). Vila et al. (2003) show that market forces are actually counter-productive to use of privacy policies when effort is required by users to verify a policy. This is an argument for more automated processes.

As the 20th century was drawing to a close, the Platform for Privacy Preferences (P3P) (W3C, 2006) emerged as an innovative privacy-enhancing concept, based on the transformation of textual privacy policies into machine-readable instructions for computers. A main motivation for the P3P project was to make it easier for users to understand privacy policies and make well-informed decisions on how to interact with services that collect personal data (Argyrakis, Gritzalis, & Kioulafas, 2003). Central to its vision was the privacy agents that allowed the user to specify what was acceptable and not, in terms of information sharing, and let the agent compare the user's privacy restrictions with the intentions of the web site that he was visiting. P3P is considered one of the most significant efforts to help web users control the sharing of their personal information. Later on in this chapter we will discuss its background, history and uptake, criticisms and technical obstacles, and explain the main reasons for its failure.

Strictly speaking, one may be reluctant to categorize approaches such as P3P as PETs, since they are more concerned with informing users about how their personal information will be (ab)used than actually protecting the users (often against themselves). It is important to consider P3P as a concept, however, as it primarily has relied on individual websites (i.e. businesses) for deployment, and the current verdict is that for the most part, this must be considered a dismal failure.

This chapter thus explores the failure of P3P based on a motivation to determine how future PET deployments for business organizations may avoid the same fate.

In this chapter we will explore Privacy Enhancing Technologies (PETs) that focus on active information gathering (Lioudakis, et al., 2007). We thus do not consider passive or semi-passive information gathering, which in turn means that mechanisms such as onion routing or other anonymisation efforts are beyond the scope of this chapter. For most users, privacy is really about *information control*, since we intuitively want to restrict who has access to our personal information. In practice, however, users find it difficult to live by the privacy rules they make for themselves, and PETs represent one way of balancing the scales in this respect.

Note also that this chapter takes a business perspective. The objective of the chapter is to present Privacy Enhancing Technologies that are suitable for deployment by businesses for the protection of their customers' privacy, and outline how PETs could be wielded as a competitive advantage by discerning businesses. Though we acknowledge that businesses are of various types and have varying needs for personal information, we do not go into these differences in this chapter. This also means that we do not put particular emphasis on, e.g., the special needs of social network providers. In most cases, we will refer to the business as a *service provider* and the customer as a *user*, but sometimes we will explicitly highlight the business/customer relationship.

The chapter is structured as follows. First, the chapter provides background information on the value or personal information and on the privacy regulation approaches that are in use today. Then, it describes the market opportunities of PETs, addressing both the potential problems that can be encountered as well as the opportunities that can be realized. An overview is provided of some existing PETs as well as research prototypes, followed by a discussion of P3P and the reasons for its failure.

Based on the business needs and corresponding problems of P3P that are identified, we point at some important areas for future research.

BACKGROUND

In this section we have a look at some of the important characteristics of privacy and personal information as seen by different stakeholders; the businesses, the users and the society. First, we outline the main rationale for businesses to collect personal information from users. Next, we identify the motivation for users to share their personal information, before we give an overview of society's view on privacy through providing a summary of regulatory efforts to protect privacy.

The Value of Personal Information

Odlyzko (2003) argues that the main motivation for businesses to use personal information is to perform effective price discrimination. The idea is that the more the business knows about their consumers, the more accurately they can determine the price they are willing to pay. Hence, consumers willing to pay more are also charged more than other consumers for the exact same product, such that the charge on the entire customer base reaches its potential maximum. In an ideal world, everyone would be satisfied with price discrimination, since the idea is that you are charged the amount you are willing to pay for a service. However, it is a dangerous strategy that is likely to cause outrage if the discrimination is too blatant (Acquisti, 2002).

A variant of this motivation is the targeted offerings or advertisements that seem to interest businesses. Based on purchase history, ratings, demographic information and personal likings, potential customers may be offered to buy products that are likely to be interesting to them (Acquisti, 2002). Despite the obvious benefits for both users and service providers; e.g. users are to a greater extent only presented with advertisements for products they are interested in, and advertisers experience greater impact of each presented advertisement; customers tend to disapprove of targeted advertising (CASPIAN, 2006). This may possibly be due to the discomfort users are experiencing when realizing the amount of information available on them. As we will see in the next section, people tend to not act rationally when it comes to privacy.

Most businesses will claim that their use of personal information is mainly motivated by improved customer experience. The ability to adapt to the various needs of consumers is fundamental to provide value-added features such as auto completion, location-based services, translations, etc, which in turn require collection, storage and use of personal information. One may of course argue that the underlying motivation is to increase profit, not to improve customer experience. However, as with conventional retailers, online businesses have a motivation for keeping their customers happy.

Using consumer information for these purposes is not new; it has been done for quite some years already. However, previously such information was used in a generalized manner mostly for market segments, geographic regions, or other particular user groups. A common example is the use of student discounts, or regional special offers or targeted advertising for readers of a magazine, issues that normally not constitute a threat to privacy. The difference today is that the information is not generalized in any way, instead it is used on an individual basis, not targeting groups of users but rather specific users. Evidently, this new approach to an old phenomenon will introduce added challenges.

Users' Attitude

Users are generally concerned about their online privacy and therefore initially reluctant to share personal information. However, research shows that this is not reflected through their actions, resulting in what is termed the *privacy paradox*;

user behavior does not match their stated preferences (Berendt, et al., 2005; Jensen, Potts, & Jensen, 2005). There may be various reasons for the privacy paradox, one of them is that users do not care about privacy after all, another that users lack the knowledge and understanding needed (Flinn & Lumsden, 2005) to make privacy decisions that are according to their principles. Studies also suggest that users have a tendency of forgetting their privacy principles once interacting with services on the web (Spiekermann, Grossklags, & Berendt, 2001).

Privacy Regulations

Although privacy by many is regarded as a fundamental human right, it is not something you can expect as an automatic feature. In the following we will discuss how privacy is regulated through self-regulation, third parties and legislation.

Self-Regulation

Traditionally, industry players in the U.S. have been wary of new government rules and regulations, and this has also had consequences for American privacy legislation (or the lack of same). In the U.S., privacy is assumed to be handled through self-regulation. That is, the market mechanisms (buyer and supplier) should ensure a proper level of privacy protection for end-users. The guiding principles are set forth by the Federal Trade Commission (FTC) and labeled the *fair information principles* (Vila, et al., 2003). These principles comprise:

- **Notice/awareness:** Consumers should be given notice of an entity's information practices before any personal information is collected from them.
- **Choice/consent:** Giving consumers options as to how any personal data collected from them may be used.

- **Access/participation:** An individual has the right to view data collected about him/her and to contest the accuracy of that data.
- **Integrity/security:** Data must be accurate and protected against loss or unauthorized access.
- **Enforcement/redress:** Effective privacy protection requires some means to ensure that these principles are applied.

The self-regulation approach encourages the use of third-party providers to mediate and ensure privacy.

Third Parties

Privacy seals have emerged as means to convey trust between service providers and users. The idea is that a trusted third party can certify that a service provider follows a set of privacy requirements, which subsequently should induce trust in the service provider. For this setup to work, the user must first trust the third party certifier, and second acknowledge the requirements it has set forth. The first assumption may turn out to be problematic since most of these third parties are relatively new to users, and furthermore they always require a fee for issuing a seal. Clearly, there may thus be a conflict of interest when judging whether a site should be accepted or not, since rejected candidates do not generate revenue for the third party. The second assumption is perhaps more subtle, since the requirements set forth by the third party may be inappropriate, insufficient or ineffective in capturing what assurance the user actually needs. If the "privacy approved"-seal only verifies that the site has a privacy policy that contains all the required parts, a user may falsely assume that the actual policy has been approved. So, if the user has substantially different privacy requirements than the third party, the seal does not convey any particular trust. This assumption is often also misunderstood for other security evaluations,

such as the Evaluation Assurance Levels (EALs) of the Common Criteria (Information technology -- Security techniques -- Evaluation criteria for IT security -- Part 1: Introduction and general model 2009). The assurance (expressed through seven EALs) is only concerned with verifying a match between the requirements for the product (as given by the developer) and the actual implemented product (as provided by the developer). So in essence, a Common Criteria EAL states how sure you can be that the product does what it says it does, and is not a ranking of security products (such that EAL4 products necessarily are better than EAL3 products).

The TRUSTe privacy seal (Benassi, 1999; TRUSTe) is one of the prominent examples of such privacy seal programs. TRUSTe uses its own set of requirements that are based on the Federal Trade Commission's Fair Information Principles. Although there are some specific requirements (e.g., Secure Socket Layer (SSL) required for transferring personal information, and presence of dispute resolution), most of them are more focused on the presence of certain aspects of the privacy policy and adherence to these aspects. Hence, the seal does not imply any qualitative assessment of the policy itself, but rather that the policy contains all the parts it should. A more thorough approach is the European Privacy Seal, or EuroPriSe (2010), which covers certification of all computerized systems and products. The European Privacy Seal indicates that the product (or web site) has been certified to adhere to European regulations on privacy protection (EU, 2002). Therefore, the requirements imposed on the web site operator are much more stringent than those of TRUSTe. The process to obtain a Seal resembles that of a Common Criteria evaluation for security products, and is also similar in choices of words. Assurance is only given in binary form, either the product is certified or it is not. Currently, there are only a handful of services that have received the EuroPriSe, presumably due to its extensive nature.

Legislation

Meeting government requirements is central to any service provider on the Internet, including with respect to privacy. The European Union member states have ratified the directive on protection of personal information (EU, 2002) and thereby committed themselves to laws on privacy protection that are at least as strict as the directive. By adopting and extending the fair information principals, the European privacy legislation is among the strictest. Particularly, the directive states detailed requirements on the third country legislation required for it to allow transfer of personal information to a company governed by that legislation. In fact, this initially excluded U.S. companies from exchanging personal information with European partners, but was solved later on by the introduction of the *safe harbor program* (US, 2011), a program designed to let U.S. companies voluntarily subject themselves to terms and conditions (not a law as such) laid down by the commission on how to handle personal information.

While it may seem that the legislative approach should require anyone to implement appropriate privacy measures, the fundamental problem is the lack of enforcement. There are few, if any, being prosecuted for not adhering to the statutory demands of the law. Although the law should protect users' privacy, it may seem that it is not capable of such. One reason may be disputes regarding which country's rules actually govern the service.

Whether to address the business motivation, user motivation, legislative demands or self-regulation, it is evident that all parties' could benefit from Privacy Enhancing Technology.

MARKET OPPORTUNITIES FOR PETS

In this section we discuss the main market opportunities of supporting PETs, and also the main reasons for not doing so. We focus on five different activity goals where privacy can be used as an opportunity: Building of reputation and trust, keeping customers happy, establishing a competitive advantage, reducing risk of privacy compromises, and making users share more information. For each of the activity goals we describe problems and opportunities, Problems constitute arguments for not investing in PETs and can e.g. describe uncertainties regarding the benefits that will be achieved or potential obstacles businesses should be aware off. Opportunities describe positive gains that can be achieved if managing to use PETs effectively.

Reputation and Trust

Businesses are expected to show corporate responsibility in a number of areas, including privacy. In addition businesses are dependent on customer trust, and privacy can be one important piece that needs to be addressed in order to gain more trust. Trust is however characterized by the long time it takes to earn it and the short time in which it can be broken. Loss of business and damage to brand has been suggested as one of the prominent risks of a privacy breach (Borking, 2009).

Trust is a very complex term that can take on very different meanings in various contexts. Here, we use trust to denote the level of confidence one part has that the other part will behave as expected. More specifically, how can a user be sure that the service provider actually lives up to its stated policy?

Problem – limited risk of getting caught: On the one hand, there is the risk of a privacy breach, and on the other, the risk of getting caught. Nehf (2007) points at two fundamental accountability problems: First, users seldom know about privacy breaches that occur, and second, if breaches are detected it may be near impossible to trace them to a particular source. In general, the majority of data collection occurs outside public view. Personal information is present in countless databases, and it is difficult for users to have any overview of how this information is shared and sold, as this is often not detailed in the privacy policy (Gomez, Pinnick, & Soltani, 2009). When users experience harm because of data breaches, they are therefore in most cases not able to put the blame on one specific business.

Problem – consequence of privacy breach may increase: To benefit from PET investments, businesses will likely rely on an increased focus on privacy among their (potential) customers. Such an increased focus on privacy will, for most companies, be an opportunity but at the same time a bit risky. Odlyzko claims that when it comes to privacy, companies "tend to hide what they do, most likely because of the implicitly understood fear of consumer backlash, and potential government intervention." (Odlyzko, 2007) With increased focus on privacy comes a possible increase in the risk related to privacy breaches, as the consequences of a breach may increase. Promoting the use of PETs does not remove the risk of privacy breaches for own business. In the event that companies only seemingly promote trust, there may be a tremendous penalty for not following up.

Problem – costs vs. benefits: If businesses are to succeed in using privacy to build trust and reputation, they must expect to make investments both to improve their privacy (e.g. invest in PETs) but also to get the message through. The costs to do this are certain. The benefits are however not quite clear as the relation between privacy and trust is not yet fully understood. Industry often promotes the model of self-regulation for privacy. This model builds on the assumption that if consumers really care about privacy they will be offended by privacy invasive practices. As a consequence, companies having such practices will suffer a repudiation loss. When this has not happened so far, businesses have reason to believe that privacy is not that important anyway.

Opportunity – signals that there is nothing to hide: In terms of trust building, setting the stage for privacy can have a huge impact on consum-

ers' trust in a business. By promoting privacy enhancing technology, a company is signaling that it has nothing to hide, which in turn may build consumer trust significantly faster than through positive experience. Since PETs are not normally supported by today's businesses, those that choose to support PETs have a better chance of being perceived as someone who is leading the way when it comes to privacy.

Opportunity – more privacy-aware future users: A lack of actual privacy concern is not the only possible explanation for the limited consumer demand for privacy. As also explained in the background section, several studies have shown that when it comes to privacy, users in generally do not act according to their principles (Ackerman, Cranor, & Reagle, 1999; Berendt, et al., 2005; Jensen, et al., 2005). The model of self-regulation, on the other hand, assumes that they do (Greenstadt & Smith, 2005). And although today's users' behavior related to privacy is best described by the privacy paradox, this may not be the case for future users. As users share more and more data, the risk of privacy breaches increases, and with it the potential media attention related to privacy. As users become more aware of the potential privacy problems of sharing their information with a variety of services, they may raise their demands for privacy. If the future brings an increasing awareness of privacy issues, businesses will benefit from being ready when the shift occurs.

Keeping Customers Happy

For any business it will be important to take good care of existing customers. An important part of this is to handle their customers' personal information in a responsible way.

Problem – future users may be less privacy concerned: As explained above, future users may demand better privacy. But there is also another possibility; users may simply become less privacy concerned. Currently, the popularity of blogging and social media services more generally suggest that people are freely sharing a lot of information about themselves. When so much personal information is available on the Internet anyway, then why should companies invest in privacy protection? As pointed out by Odlyzko: "privacy technologies languish because practically no one bothers to use them, and often intimate information is given out for very little or no monetary reward."(Odlyzko, 2007) Privacy concerns are in many cases also associated with conspiracy theorists and those with "something to hide" (Wilton, 2009).

Problem – whether improved privacy will be appreciated: Businesses are unlikely to have knowledge of whether their customers will appreciate improved privacy and support for PETs. Existing customers have already some minimum level of trust in the company, and are willing to use its services with the current trust level. They have directly or indirectly accepted the current privacy policy, potentially also stating that the privacy policy can be changed at any time without notification. If positive changes in privacy management are to have any effect on the existing customers, they must be made aware of the changes. Though many customers will probably appreciate the improved practices, some may find it annoying and others may become suspicious – why are they introducing this now, have they had a privacy breach that we are not aware of...? In addition there is the risk that increased focus on privacy can make current (unfortunate) practices more easily understandable, and therefore easier to react to.

One of the main problems with privacy is that the users in fact have no means to verify or enforce any of the agreed policies. Hence the service provider has no incentives of making privacy understandable and improving their privacy, other than avoiding a publicly known privacy breach.

Opportunity – meet legislative requirements: Though users may not care about their privacy, legislation will in many cases put requirements on how personal information should be treated. These requirements need to be addressed independently of whether the customers care or not. PETs can help in addressing some of the legislative requirements (Szeto & Miri, 2007).

Opportunity – signal that the business cares for their customers' well-being: Businesses have no reason to simply assume their customers do not care about privacy because they do not experience strong demands for improved privacy. A large amount of users claim to be concerned about their privacy, though their current actions do not necessarily imply so. Convincing current users that their privacy is taken well care of may pay off, as it shows customers that the business cares about their well-being. Customers wishing to get services from a competitor can also become more aware of the privacy implications of doing so (since users then have to share information one more time).

Competitive Advantage

If users take privacy into account when choosing services, privacy can be seen as a competitive factor where businesses with good privacy practices get a market advantage.

Problem – investments needed: Any business that decides to use PETs will need to spend money and resources on new technology and/or modification of existing systems. In addition, internal processes will probably also need to be updated. To be able to do this, businesses will need access to necessary expertise, not only on the technology itself, but also on legal and organizational issues. As PETs are not that commonly used today, there is a lack of experience and research that can give concrete guidance to businesses that consider implementing PETs. Businesses are unlikely to have the necessary competence in-house, and it may also be scarce among external consultants (Borking, 2009). It is also worth noting that many PETs, e.g. user agents such as AT&T Privacy Bird (introduced later in this chapter), will only be of interest to users when they are supported by a relatively large number of providers (Wilton, 2009).

Problem – visibility of privacy: Currently we do not see a lot of competition or differentiation among organizations when it comes to privacy protection. Use of PETs does not result in social recognition. Usually privacy is mainly seen as a negative driver, where avoidance of privacy breaches is the most important. It is not common to view privacy as a positive driver that can result in market advantage (Borking, 2009). For privacy to become a competitive factor, users need to take privacy into account when selecting services. Currently this is not the case (ref. the privacy paradox). One reason may be the visibility of privacy and PETs, and specifically the availability of privacy information. Companies commonly use privacy policies in order to inform users of their privacy practices. These privacy policies are usually time consuming and difficult to read and understand. In addition they often can be changed without notice and are generally not believed by customers. As a consequence, they are not a good basis for users to make decisions as to whether to share information. It is also important to remember that when users interact with a service online, privacy is not in the forefront of the customers mind – "they're not buying privacy, they're buying some other thing" (Greenstadt & Smith, 2005). As data handling is tightly bundled with some good or service, people tend to forget privacy, and if they manage to keep privacy focus, there are often no good privacy choices available that will allow them to acquire the goods or services they want. As a result, consumers do not know about nor believe in good privacy practices, and businesses as a consequence have no incentive to create any (Greenstadt & Smith, 2005).

Problem – human factors that influence decision making: Businesses wanting to compete on privacy need to take into account how human factors influence decision making. Nehf (2007) describes the decision making goals of users as *accuracy of decisions*, *cognitive ease* and *emotional comfort*. People do not necessarily strive towards optimal solutions. Rather they seek satisfactory solutions that can be reached with a minimum of effort. As a result, some factors may be left out. Since the consequences of sharing information with a particular site are not clear to most users, privacy is a potential candidate for exclusion.

Since users strive for cognitive ease, they prefer alternatives that are easy to evaluate. As a consequence, service providers should not make it too complicated to choose their particular service. Forcing users to delve into privacy policies (e.g. by having them press an "I agree" button) in order to use a service is probably not a good idea, as this will increase the effort required to use the service. Unless the privacy policy is really superior, users will be likely to choose other easier available services instead.

If forced to make difficult trade-offs, users can experience negative emotions. People seek to minimize such discomfort in their selection of decision strategies. As a result important factors may be excluded from the decision base. It is difficult to put a price on privacy or compare its value towards other benefits. Users will also in many cases consider privacy as a protected value that should not be prized and traded away. As a result people may tend to avoid making privacy comparisons.

Nehf also describes other factors that influences decisions:

- *Inferences*: If an important attribute is not easy to evaluate, people may infer a value based on what they already know, e.g. that it is similar across brands.
- *Framing effects:* The way information is presented influences the decisions. In particular, users evaluate the cost of digging deeper into the subject against the cost of accepting it as is.
- *The availability heuristic*: People commonly over-respond to risks that they are

well aware of, and may underestimate risks that do not often come to their attention.

Inferences may result in difficulties of making privacy a competitive factor. Users may simply assume that the privacy policies of similar sites are also similar. Businesses wanting to stand out as strong on privacy will have to put effort into making this message come through. This can however result in increasing the cognitive effort of users and forces them to make more emotionally-laden comparisons. As a result the site may be seen as less appealing. The framing effect makes it possible to look privacy conscious without actually being that. The mere presence of a policy or a privacy seal may give users the impression that privacy is taken care of, and few users will study the details and discover the facts. Because of the availability heuristics users may underestimate privacy risks. Though privacy breaches gain some publicity, there is seldom much focus on what are the consequences experienced by users of the weak privacy practices of providers, and as users have little knowledge about what information is collected and with whom it is shared, it is difficult to couple the risks with actual businesses.

Opportunity – ability to support privacy concerned customers without bothering the other customers: Though there are problems with making privacy a competitive factor, PETs can actually reduce some of the problems. Many current PETs come in the form of user agents that user have to download and install themselves. Businesses in many cases just need to support these PETs, e.g. by making their privacy policy available in a proper machine-readable form. Thus, by publishing machine-readable policies businesses can support those users that are privacy concerned without troubling less interested users with privacy information that forces them to make difficult and emotionally laden trade-offs.

Opportunity – adapt to users' privacy preferences: Businesses also have the potential to offer more advanced privacy services to users. Consider the static nature of current online privacy policies that do not fit the otherwise dynamic world of the Internet. Typically, users are forced to either accept the privacy policy in full or reject it entirely; a situation that rarely is the case offline. This is particularly problematic since most web sites only provide a single privacy policy for potentially a myriad of different services. For service providers, the concern is that potential customers may refrain from using their services due to the stated privacy policy, without the provider even knowing about it. One solution to this problem is privacy policy negotiation, where the service provider and user negotiate and agree on a set of privacy rules governing the use of a particular service. For instance the service provider may provide only limited services to users that do not acknowledge a particular rule in the privacy policy. In the event that the particular rule is mandatory for delivering any service to the user, the service provider at least gains knowledge on the particular rule causing the problem. The irony is that by employing a negotiation strategy, the service provider may actually end up with more information than before. The obvious benefit of such an approach is that customers originally rejecting the privacy policy may now use the services offered by the provider, though with potentially reduced functionality. Additionally, service providers have the option to change their privacy policies (and implementation) based on the rules users are unwilling to accept.

Reduce Risk of Privacy Compromise

Businesses trusted with personal information always face the risk of privacy breaches. PETs can influence this risk, both positively and negatively.

Problem – uncertain costs of privacy breaches: There is currently a lack of empirical data on what privacy breaches cost and how likely they are. It is not possible based on current research and experience to say what damage should be expected in case of a major privacy breach. Research and experience often show conflicting results, and trust is difficult to verify (Borking, 2009). As mentioned earlier, users experiencing problems that can be related to a privacy breach are often unable to trace the source of the problems. Thus, businesses have a quite good chance of not getting caught (Nehf, 2007). Still, regulations such as the Data Protection Directive in the European Union, and the Health Insurance Portability and Accountability Act (HIPAA) in the United States put requirements on how personal information should be treated. Often such legislation is general and quite abstract, and it can be difficult for organizations to understand what they actually require them to do. They also put no direct pressure to invest in PETs (Borking, 2009), but probably as important, "there is nothing to stop anyone from breaking these laws except the fear of getting caught." (Greenstadt & Smith, 2005) Since there up till now have been relatively few investigations and penalties, it is likely that the consequences of not complying with privacy laws are not considered that important (Borking, 2009).

Problem – consequence of privacy breach may increase: As also mentioned earlier, an increased focus on privacy does not eliminate the risk of experiencing privacy breaches. Though the likelihood of a privacy breach may be reduced by increasing organizational awareness of privacy, the consequences of a breach may increase as users have higher privacy expectations.

Opportunity – more holistic privacy management: As businesses collect more and more personal information about their customers, the risk of privacy breaches are likely to increase unless measures are taken to protect privacy. Investments in PETs will likely influence also the existing routines and technology related to handling of personal information. Thus it brings with it an opportunity to handle privacy more holistically. As will be seen in the next section on existing PETs, many PETs are concerned about making the privacy policy more understandable to users. A side-effect of such PETs will be that the privacy policy is also easier accessible to manag-

ers, developers and others dealing with personal information within the organization. Thus it can be an important part in building privacy awareness among own employees, and as a result reducing the likelihood of privacy breaches.

Users Will Share More?

From the customers' point of view, improved privacy can be achieved by sharing less information, with the result that many services cannot be used. Privacy can however also be improved by businesses taking better care of the personal information they are trusted with. Businesses that are considered trustworthy when it comes to privacy may therefore find that users are willing to trust them with more information, and more correct information, than other businesses.

Problem – privacy consciousness of users: We have already identified a number of problems with using privacy as a competitive factor; users may not care about privacy, may forget about it, and dislike privacy trade-offs because of lack of understanding of the issues and the emotional implications. In order for users to take privacy into account, they have to somehow get an idea of how different businesses handle privacy issues. A main challenge in this respect is the lack of visibility of privacy in today's Internet services.

Opportunity – quality of information: Personal information, and especially correct personal information, is of high value to businesses. Experiments have shown that when users get explanations on why certain information is collected they are more willing to share information (Kobsa & Teltzrow, 2005). Improved privacy is likely to further increase users' willingness to share information about themselves.

Summary

As can be seen from our discussion, with every problem there is an accompanying opportunity for businesses to capitalize on users' need of privacy. Especially since privacy awareness and protection is rather scarce, one need not do very much in order to convince users that privacy is taken seriously and thereby get a competitive advantage. However, the fundamental problem of privacy in business is the uncertainty when it comes to predicting user behavior and acceptance. It is therefore extremely difficult to calculate the benefit (for a business) of implementing privacy enhancing measures to ensure a reasonable return on investment. That being said, there are several measures to be taken that are relatively inexpensive and at least are assumed to comfort the most privacy conscious users.

A SURVEY OF PETS SUITABLE FOR BUSINESS ORGANIZATIONS

The foundation for most PETs dealing with information control is the privacy policies of service providers. Privacy policies are the most common way of explaining to users how data is collected, used, stored and shared. Privacy policies are however usually difficult to understand for the users (Cranor, Guduru, & Arjula, 2006). A common approach among existing PETs is, in varying ways, to make the content of privacy policies more accessible to users. To do this, the form in which policies are presented is important.

In this section we start describing the different shapes PETs may take. Then we give an introduction to P3P, before we provide an overview of a number of different PETs that are available either as products or as research prototypes – many of which build on P3P.

Different Shapes of PETs

PETs for information control differ in their sources of information, the actions they take and in where they are implemented. Below we give an overview of the main options available.

Sources of Privacy Information

Privacy related information can be made available to users and presented in various ways. Below we present the main alternatives. It should be noted that they can be used in combination; a business can for instance create a machine-readable policy that is based on the textual policy, and make both available to their users. In addition third parties can create additional sources of privacy information, e.g. through communities.

The most common way of presenting privacy policies is to publish them in textual form on the web site. Several surveys however show that few users actually bother to read such policies (Jensen, et al., 2005). There have been various surveys of the content of privacy policies. One such example is the study by Pollach (2007) of 50 policies belonging to popular web sites from various business areas. This study found that the policies were of varying length (the longest was more than ten times longer than the shortest one), and that the language of the policies is used actively to highlight positive aspects of privacy practices, and put more negative aspects in the background. Actually, the word "may" was found to be fourth most frequently used non-grammatical word! In addition, many, if not most, policies lack information that users care about.

The varying quality and accessibility of current privacy policies, and the fact that users do not bother to read them calls for other ways to present privacy policies in order for the message to come through. Several initiatives have worked on defining privacy icons (Hansen, 2009) so that users can get important privacy information by just taking a quick look at the icons – if familiar with the icons' uses.

Privacy policies can also be provided in machine-readable form so that PETs can use them in providing services to users. The most common example of such machine-readable policies is P3P.

Privacy information can also be provided without involving the service provider. One option is to have third parties offering information to users on the privacy policies of popular service providers. The offering of privacy seals can be considered a special type of such service where some third party verifies that basic privacy issues are taken care of. Another commonly suggested approach is to have community services, e.g., where users can rate privacy policies of a business, and provide their own experiences when it comes to privacy.

PET Actions Taken

PETs related to information control can take on different task in order to provide support for users. First, PETs can present privacy information to users in a more easily understandable form than what is commonly available. As an example, PETs can interpret machine-readable policies and use them to extract parts that the PET's users are likely to care about. Then this information can be presented to the user. PETs can also retrieve information from privacy communities, and present information to users that is relevant for the site the user is currently visiting. However, PETs have the potential to move beyond simple information presentation. A very common type of functionality is matching of user preferences towards privacy policies of service providers. With such an approach users are expected to explain their privacy preferences to the agent, which in turn warns users in cases where the preferences and the privacy policy do not match. It will also be possible for PETs to block user behavior, if this is desirable.

A more advanced type of functionality that also can be supported by PETs is that of negotiating privacy terms associated with a service. Today, the common approach is for service providers to state their privacy terms, and users accept by using the service. It is however possible to envision that the privacy terms are negotiable, and that PETs can negotiate automatically on behalf of users based on knowledge of users' privacy preferences.

Some PETs also keep track of which information has been shared with the different service providers. Thus users are better able to exercise rights of access to, and eventually correction or deletion, of information concerning them.

PET Implementation

PETs also vary in who install or implement them into their systems. Service providers can implement PETs that e.g. make privacy policies more understandable for users. Users can install PETs, e.g. in form of browser plug-ins. Such user agents are typically running during all web interactions, and can assist with real-time evaluation of possible information disclosure as it is being performed by the user. To support agents, businesses do not necessarily have to make changes to their systems, other than for instance providing machine-readable policies if the PETs rely on their availability. PETs can also require third-party support, e.g. in the form of community services. But there are also more complex PETs available that take the form of middleware that needs to be supported by both users and service providers.

The Platform for Privacy Preferences (P3P)

P3P (W3C, 2006) is a standard that enables service providers to communicate the privacy policies of web sites to their clients. P3P provides both a standardized format for privacy policies and a protocol that enables web browsers to read and process the privacy policies automatically. P3P was developed by the World Wide Web Consortium (W3C) and was the first privacy policy language to be standardized by the W3C. The latest specification for P3P is version 1.1, which was finalized in 2006.

P3P is an XML-based language that allows service providers to express privacy policies in a machine understandable way. By using P3P, service providers can specify rules that include the type of data, the type of use, the user of the data, the purpose of the use and how long the data will be retained. User agents can then fetch P3P policies, interpret them and present them to the end-user in order to assist the end-users in determining whether a particular service provider's published privacy policy matches the user's individual privacy preferences. The user agent can also warn the user in the case of a mismatch between the privacy policy and the user's preferences. Such user agents can be built into web browsers, browser plug-ins or proxy servers. They can also be implemented as a part of electronic wallets, form-fillers or any other user data management tool. Users therefore do not need to read the privacy policies at every site they visit or for every service they access.

P3P-Enabling a Website

To P3P-enable a web site, the service provider translates the privacy policy for the site into one or more P3P policy files. The policy files are then made available to the user, either by storing them in a well-known location (/w3c/p3p.xml), or by embedding information in the HTML response (directly in the header or by using link tags) (Cranor & Lessig, 2002). The policy file will then be collected by the client when visiting the web site, and read and processed by the client computer.

The P3P Specification

The P3P data scheme consists of a set of data elements, sets and structures. Data elements are individual pieces of data, for example first name or telephone number. Data sets are used to combine data elements into groups; For example, the home postal address data set contains data elements for street address, city, state, postal code and country. Data structures can be used to create templates which can be reused with multiple data sets (Cranor & Lessig, 2002).

The P3P specification defines two types of P3P policies; full policies and compact policies. The full policy is written in a XML format based on the P3P vocabulary and data scheme. The compact policy is used to describe the privacy practices related to the use of cookies. According to the P3P specification, a compact policy is required to have a corresponding full P3P privacy policy.

A full P3P policy is written as a sequence of STATEMENT elements, which includes several sub-elements:

- PURPOSE: The purpose for information collection. The P3P specification contains 12 pre-defined values, for example "current" (to complete and support the activity for which the data was provided) and "pseudo-analysis" (to infer e.g. habits and interests of individuals without identifying specific individuals).
- RECIPIENT: The intended user of the information. The P3P specification contains 6 pre-defined values, for example "ours" (ourselves) and "same" (legal entities following our practices).
- RETENTION: the duration that the collected information will be kept. The P3P specification contains 5 pre-defined values, for example "stated-purpose" (discard information at the earliest time possible) and "indefinitely".
- DATA-GROUP: lists the individual data items that will be collected for the stated purpose

A simple example of a full P3P policy is the privacy policy for the P3P handbook website (http://p3pbook.com/). The human-readable privacy policy looks like this:

This is the web site for the book Web Privacy with P3P by Lorrie Faith Cranor. We do not currently collect any information from visitors to this site except the information contained in standard web server logs (your IP address, referrer, information about your web browser, information about your

HTTP requests, etc.). The information in these logs will be used only by us and the server administrators for website and system administration, and for improving this site. It will not be disclosed unless required by law. We may retain these log files indefinitely. Please direct questions about this privacy policy to privacy@p3pbook.com.

The corresponding machine-readable P3P policy file looks like this:

```
<POLICIES>
<POLICY discuri="http://p3pbook.com/privacy.
    html" name="policy">
<ENTITY>
<DATA-GROUP>
<DATA ref="#business.contact-info.online.
    email">privacy@p3pbook.com </DATA>
<DATA ref="#business.contact-info.online.
    uri">http://p3pbook.com/
</DATA>
<DATA ref="#business.name">Web Privacy With
    P3P</DATA>
</DATA-GROUP>
</ENTITY>
<ACCESS>
<nonident/>
</ACCESS>
<STATEMENT>
<CONSEQUENCE>
Our Web server collects access logs containing
    this information.
</CONSEQUENCE>
<PURPOSE>
<admin/>
<current/>
<develop/>
</PURPOSE>
<RECIPIENT>
<ours/>
</RECIPIENT>
<RETENTION>
<indefinitely/>
</RETENTION>
```

```
<DATA-GROUP>
<DATA ref="#dynamic.clickstream"/>
<DATA ref="#dynamic.http"/>
</DATA-GROUP>
</STATEMENT>
</POLICY>
</POLICIES>
```

A compact P3P policy contains a set of tokens that represents the following elements from the P3P vocabulary: ACCESS, CATEGORIES, DISPUTES, NON-INDENTIFIABLE, PURPOSE, RECIPIENT, REMEDIES and RETENTION. The vocabulary is designed to reduce the number of bytes transferred within a HTTP response header. An example of a P3P compact policy is

CP="NOI DSP COR NID ADM DEV PSA OUR IND UNI PUR COM NAV INT STA"

where for example "PSA" and "OUR" represent the <pseudo-analysis/> and <ours/>" value in the PURPOSE and RECIPIENT element respectively (i.e. in this simple example these two tokens mean that the site will use the collected data only for themselves, in order to infer, e.g., habits and interests of individuals without identifying specific individuals).

APPEL: User Preferences

The creators of P3P also designed the P3P preference language (APPEL), which is a standard for encoding the user's privacy preferences in a machine-readable way. Similarly to P3P, an APPEL preference file therefore consists of a set of machine-readable rules. The primary goal when developing APPEL was to simplify the sharing and installation of user preferences in terms of machine-readable rule-sets. By storing privacy preferences in a file, the preferences can be shared amongst users with similar privacy principles and easily transferred between different devices. The APPEL rule set is composed of patterns that can be matched against P3P policies, and specifies action that will be taken is case the policy does not match the preferences. The syntax is very similar to the P3P policy syntax. APPEL is further described in (Cranor, Langheinrich, & Marchiori, 2002).

P3P User Agents

A P3P user agent is capable of matching privacy policies to stated user preferences autonomously. Such user agents can be implemented in web browsers, electronic wallet, ISP proxies etc. The basic concept is as follows: Whenever a user makes a service request, the user agent will retrieve the privacy policy of the service and compare it to the user preferences. Depending on the capabilities of the agent and languages used for specification, the agent may enter a negotiating phase, initiate mitigating measures, block access to the service or simply issue a warning that the policy does not match the user's preferences. Microsoft's Internet Explorer 6 (IE6) was one of the first P3P user agents available on the market. It contains built-in support for fetching and displaying full P3P policies in a human-readable format, and to match user preferences with P3P compact policies (concerning the use of cookies). Examples of stand-alone P3P user agents will be presented later in this chapter; the most well-known being the AT&T Privacy Bird (Cranor, Arjula, & Guduru, 2002).

The user agent was considered a crucial part of the P3P project. The P3P specification therefore includes guiding principles, which are specific recommendations for P3P user agent software design. The guiding principles include advice on how the users should be informed, and how the software should be configured by default.

P3P Policy and Preferences Tools

The goal of the P3P project was twofold. It allows service providers to formulate and present their privacy policies in standardized, easily-located, machine-readable manner. It also provides the users with a mechanism to understand how their personal data will be collected and used. However, the syntax of both P3P and APPEL makes it very difficult for human beings to correctly specify their intentions, both regarding privacy policies and privacy preferences. Especially, writing a P3P policy can be a tedious procedure, just look at the simple example provided above. Several tools have therefore been developed to facilitate this process. An example is the IBM P3P policy editor (Bergmann, Rost, & Pettersson, 2006) that was developed to assist the service providers in translating their privacy policy into the P3P format.

Most of the existing P3P user agents contain support for preference generation. For example, the AT&T Privacy Bird contains a graphical user interface that allows the user to specify preferences based on a subset of the P3P vocabulary (Cranor, Arjula, et al., 2002).

Examples of PETs

Below we briefly describe a number of existing PET solutions and research prototypes for improved information control. We give an overview of their main idea and solution, and explain what information source they rely on, what actions they take, and where they are implemented. An overview of the PETs is given in Table 1.

P3P User Agents: AT&T Privacy Bird, Integrated Privacy View

The AT&T Privacy Bird (Cranor, Arjula, et al., 2002) is an early P3P user agent, which was implemented as a browser helper object for Internet Explorer. A graphical window allows the user to set up his/her privacy preferences, based on a subset of the P3P specification vocabulary. The AT&T Privacy Bird then automatically retrieves privacy policies from service providers and compares these with the user's specified privacy preferences. The user is warned of any mismatches, and can also access a summary of the P3P policy.

Table 1. Overview of existing PETs

PET	Information source	Actions taken	Implementation
AT&T Privacy Bird	P3P policy	Match and present	Browser plug-in
Integrated Privacy View	P3P extension, edit HTML	Match	Browser add-on
Privacy and Identity Management for Europe (PRIME)	Service provider	Manage credentials, control interactions, present, match, negotiate	Needs to be supported by both users and service providers
Collaborative privacy	Community	Match and present	Browser plug-in
Web of trust	Community	Present	Browser add-on
PIPWatch toolbar	Community	Match with legislation	Web browser add-on
Privacy panel	Service provider	Provide access to privacy information and functionality	Service provider; web site and underlying system
Privacy nutrition label	P3P policy	Present	Not specified
Privacy finder	P3P policy	Present	Online search engine

Another example of a user agent that utilizes P3P policies is the Integrated Privacy View (IPV) (Levy & Gutwin, 2005). Where standard P3P operates on a page level, IPV considers each input field separately. This is possible through an extension of P3P that makes it possible to link policy statements directly to HTML elements. IPV can thus present how an individual piece of information is handled, and whether or not this matches the user's preferences.

The potential of Privacy Bird has been shown in several user studies (Cranor, et al., 2006). In practice however, its usefulness has turned out to be very limited. A major reason is that the agent is dependent on the availability of P3P privacy policies, and that few service providers have published such policies. IPV similarly relies on the availability of P3P policies, and in addition service providers need to make changes to their HTML code.

Privacy Management: Privacy and Identity Management for Europe (PRIME)

Privacy agents such as Privacy Bird only deal with a limited part of privacy management. The PRIME project is an example of a more comprehensive

privacy solution that has the potential of offering better privacy, but at a higher cost. The PRIME architecture (Andersson, et al., 2005; Camenisch, et al., 2005; Pettersson, et al., 2005) brings different PETs together, in order to protect and improve Internet users' privacy. Their goals include

- to achieve user informed consent and control related to all disclosure of personal data,
- to allow privacy negotiations in order to come to agreements with service providers on how personal data should be handled,
- to provide solutions for data minimization so that only the necessary information is collected and that it is deleted when no longer needed,
- to develop solutions for user controlled identity management,
- to allow a spectrum of anonymity services, ranging from the use of anonymous communication channels to the use of identity proofs issued by third parties, and
- to ensure accountability for anonymous users.

Note that the three latter goals strictly speaking fall outside the scope we are considering in this chapter.

PRIME services involve three main parties: the users, the service providers and a certification authority. Users and service providers share essentially the same architecture. Both hold a database with certificates and declarations of the party, default policies for handling of data, and logs of previous interactions with other parties. Service providers in addition hold data collected from other parties. Access to this database is controlled by the access control component, identity control component and the graphical user interface. Service providers also have an obligation management component. PRIME offers the possibility to include components that assure policy compliance.

For service providers, support of PRIME requires modifications to their systems. It is however possible to start supporting parts of the PRIME solution and then to gradually include more and more privacy support. One particularly interesting feature of PRIME is the possibility to assess the trustworthiness of service providers. This feature makes it easier for smaller companies to gain trust more quickly than what is common today.

Communities: Collaborative Privacy Management, Web of Trust, PIPWatch Toolbar

Because of the lack of availability of P3P policies, it may be – at least in the near future – that PETs are more likely to be successful if they rely less on service providers, instead of putting more requirements on them, as is done with PRIME. Kolter et al. (2010) uses similar arguments as a basis for suggesting collaborative privacy management. Their tool consists of four parts; a privacy preference generator, a privacy agent, a data disclosure log and a browser plug-in. The basic concept is similar to that of e.g. Privacy Bird; users specify preferences that are matched with the published P3P policies of service providers. The major dif-

ference is that the tool is not dependent on support from the service providers. Rather than convincing the service providers to implement and update their privacy policies, the tool relies on support from an online privacy community that will contribute to privacy related information on service provides by using a Wiki-like Web front-end. Examples of information that can be provided include general information on the service provider, the amount of data that is required, information on who the service provider shares data with, explanations of the textual privacy policy, historical policies, information on whether or not the service providers adhere to their policy and individual experiences with this service provider when it comes to privacy.

A simpler but already up and running approach is the Web of trust (http://www.mywot.com/) add-on where users can share information relevant for trust through a community. Users can rate websites based on their own experiences, and can in turn get information on the trustworthiness, vendor reliability privacy and child safety of a web site. For privacy the add-on can provide information on whether or not the site has a privacy policy and the privacy implications of the practice stated in this policy.

Another community based browser add-on is the PIPWatch Toolbar (Clement, et al., 2008) that helps the users to interpret whether the privacy policies of the websites they visit comply with the Canadian private-sector privacy legislation. The PIPWatch toolbar is not based on any privacy policy language. Instead users are expected to contribute with information on the website by using functionality embedded in the toolbar. This includes filling out basic information on the website and to send email to privacy officers, asking them to fill out a questionnaire. The responses will be stored at a central server and used by the toolbar to evaluate to what degree the site fulfils the users' privacy expectations and the privacy legislation.

The community based PETs do not put requirements on service providers, and can therefore be considered of little direct relevance for businesses. Businesses should however care about what is registered about them in various privacy communities. Privacy communities are in many ways a reaction to the lack of useful privacy information available from today's businesses. As businesses do not provide what users need to make privacy decisions, users have to provide it themselves, but then businesses have no guarantee that what is published about them is indeed correct.

Policy Presentation: Privacy Nutrition Label, Privacy Panel

Some PETs focus mainly in policy presentation, in order to make privacy information more available and understandable to users. We have already mentioned the concept of privacy icons. Another example is the Privacy Nutrition Label (Kelley, et al., 2009), which is a design approach to improve the visual presentation of privacy policies to end users. The design was inspired by nutrition facts panel on food products in the United States, hence the name. The Privacy Nutrition Label is a refinement of its predecessors; the Expendable Grid (Reeder, et al., 2008), which implemented the entire P3P specification and thus turned out be very hard to read and comprehend; and the Simplified Label, which the authors considered to be *too* simple (Kelley, et al., 2009). The Privacy Nutrition Label uses a combination of symbols and color codes to illustrate how the user's personal data will be treated. The data is organized according to what type of information it represents, how it will be used by the service provider itself and whether it will be shared with 3rd party service providers. The terminology used in the Privacy Nutrition Label is derived from the P3P specification, but simplified in order to fit into a one-page summary. The design has been evaluated by a laboratory study that compared how end-users perceived the difference between ordinary textual-based privacy policies and privacy policies presented as Privacy Nutrition Labels. The results indicate that privacy policy information is easier to find and more enjoyable to read when presented as a Privacy Nutrition Label (Kelley, et al., 2009).

Where the Privacy Nutrition Label is mainly concerned with visualizing the content of the policy, the privacy panel proposed by Schunter and Waidner (2007) is more concerned with how users can easily access important privacy information on a website. They suggest a panel that consists of four icons: one for access to the privacy policy, one for access to the stored data about oneself, one to block identity and another to delete identity. Schunter and Waidner propose that this panel can be standardized and used at all participating web sites, such that the users will have a common way to control their data. The main contribution of Schunter and Waidner's paper is not the design of the quite simple user interface, but rather the formalization of the underlying protocol mechanisms that handles how privacy controls are implemented and used both locally and across multiple organizations.

Policy presentation is relevant for businesses that want to make their privacy policy more available. The Privacy Nutrition Label is based on P3P and can be used by e.g. user agents to provide presentations of various site policies, but businesses can also use this visualization on their own web site. The privacy panel is however something that must be included on the website, and supported in the underlying systems.

Search-Based Approaches: Privacy Finder

Search-based approaches can be especially useful when users are considering whether or not to conduct business with a particular provider. An example of such an approach is the privacy-enhanced online search engine Privacy Finder (http://www.privacyfinder.org/) developed and operated by the CyLab Usable Privacy and Security Laboratory (CUPS) at Carnegie Mellon University. Privacy Finder orders search results according to their

P3P privacy policies. A "privacy meter" next to the search result indicates whether a P3P policy exists, and to what degree the policy corresponds with a list of preset privacy preferences. Clicking on the privacy meter will open up more detailed a privacy report on the site.

Like for the other PETs that are based on P3P policies, businesses that want to be evaluated on privacy by Privacy Finder need to make their policy available in P3P. The incentives for doing so will depend on the popularity of such search engines, and the action taken if a P3P policy is not available (e.g., if the site is then given the lowest score).

CASE STUDY: THE RISE AND FALL OF P3P

The work on P3P started in the 1990ies, and represents a great step forward in the quest of automating the process of communicating data management practices. However, its history has been controversial and the standard has been subject to numerous disputes. In this section we discuss the background of P3P and point out some of its technical limitations and obstacles, before touching upon the P3P uptake and summarizing the main reasons for its failure.

Background and History

P3P was developed over several years. Early work started in 1995 when three associates at the Center for Democracy and Technology (CDT) discussed the idea of using the Platform for Internet Content Selection (PICS) (W3C, 1997) for protection of Internet user privacy. The idea was then further explored by the Internet Privacy Working Group (IPWG) who developed a draft privacy vocabulary (a standard set of terms for web sites to describe their privacy practices), which eventually was named the Platform for Privacy Preferences (P3P) (Cranor & Lessig, 2002; W3C, 2006). P3P was

officially launched as a W3C project in May 1997. The development process was initially projected in an 18-month period but turned out to continue through the next three years. The details of the specification were changed a number of times during this period. Initially automatic data transfer mechanisms were proposed as a part of the P3P specification, but were later removed. Negotiation of privacy policy was also considered to be a part of the P3P protocol and vocabulary, but never made it into the final specification. The P3P 1.0 specification was eventually released as a "candidate recommendation" in late 2000 (Cranor & Lessig, 2002). The relatively long development process was explained by the P3P developers to be caused by the "deliberative and thoughtful process" behind P3P (Cranor, Schwartz 1999), which amongst other things included revision of the specification based on feedback from the European Commission (Cranor & Lessig, 2002).

Criticisms

The P3P specification has been heavily questioned, already from the beginning. Large parts of the critique against P3P as a privacy protection mechanism is based its limited scope. P3P was a U.S. initiative and has its roots in the U.S. Federal Trade Commission (FTC) privacy model (Hochheiser, 2002). As described earlier in this chapter, the FTC privacy model consists of five parts: Notice/awareness, choice/consent, access/participation, integrity/security and enforcement/redress.

As can be seen, the P3P specification only covers the two first parts: notice/awareness (fetching and displaying electronic policy files) and choice/consent (specifying user preferences and matching them with privacy policies); it does not attempt to cover any of the other three parts. Probably the most fundamental problem is that P3P does not comprise enforcement. P3P in itself does not provide any mechanism for making sure service providers act according to their stated policies.

Hence, the technology involves a risk that the user may be mislead into believing that if a privacy policy matches the stated privacy preferences, it will be safe to proceed. Critics such as Coyle (Coyle, 2000) therefore argue that P3P fail to address privacy since it will never be able to provide general privacy protection for Internet users. This view is shared by Catlett (Catlett, 2000) who states that "P3P is not going to protect privacy, and the public shouldn't continue to be told it will".

The above criticism mainly applies to the U.S. (Hochheiser, 2002). Many countries have laws that protect the individual's privacy. As an example, the EU privacy directive (2002) puts strong restrictions on the use of personal data. To comply with the privacy principles stated in the EU privacy directive, organizations must, amongst other things, inform their users about the use of their personal data. For example, organizations need to get informed consent from data subjects before processing personal data (the principle of consent). Moreover, the directory states that data subjects shall be able to check and influence the processing of their data (the principle of data subject control). In addition, organizations are not allowed to process data in a way that is incompatible with the stated purpose of collection. The EU privacy directive is therefore considerably stricter that the FTC privacy model, which is more ambiguous in several respects. Non U.S. Internet users, such as EU citizens, may therefore find P3P useful as a complement to already existing legal requirements that limits the collection of personal information (Hochheiser, 2002).

Other critics are based on the political context surrounding P3P. In the middle of the 90ths several workshops and reports from the FTC promoted self-regulation as the preferred approach to privacy protection (Hochheiser, 2002). However, many privacy activists rejected the idea of self-regulation and privacy. Catlett compared privacy in the U.S. context with copyright in the music industry to motivate why privacy preferences and "promises" (i.e. policies) is a model ill-suited

to protect consumer privacy (Catlett, 2000). He stated that clearly a law is a necessity to protect the privacy of American consumers. Also Coyle (1999) argued that since the U.S does not have data protection laws, a possible breach of the privacy agreement stated in a P3P policy will not have any negative consequences whatsoever for the company in question. A common argument articulated by privacy activists was therefore that the large corporation support of P3P is an attempt to avoid privacy legislation. Similarly privacy activists also maintained that the slow development pace of the standard was a mean to delay or avoid regulatory actions (Hochheiser, Catlett).

Technical Limitations and Obstacles

There has also been heavy criticism regarding the technical limitations of P3P. Hochheiser (2002) identified the limited scope (only web sites), lack of limitations on personal data collection and the restricted vocabulary as the main areas of technical criticism against the P3P specification. Particularly the precision of terms is said to be sub-optimal, which for example makes it difficult for service providers to express conformance to privacy legislation. While extensions may be developed to answer several of these shortcomings, this would conflict with the P3P intention of being simple and easy to use.

On the other hand, Catlett argued that the P3P vocabulary was unnecessary complex, since "the core of consumers' desires for privacy are simple and easily stated, but unpalatable for marketers: consumers don't want their personal information sold, shared, or reused for secondary purposes" (Catlett, 2000). His view was shared by Coyle, who stated that collection of personal data is only necessary when purchasing a product online (Coyle, 2000).

Service providers also experienced practical difficulties when attempting to translate to textual policies to the P3P format, something that contributed to the large number of erroneous policies that can be found online. Moreover, P3P lacks support for stating that accepting the current policy also implies accepting any future versions of the policy.

Also APPEL has its limitations, as pointed out by e.g. Agrawal et al. (2003). They state that simple preferences are surprisingly hard to express in APPEL and that writing the preferences is an error prone procedure. In addition, APPEL suffers from some serious problems that arise from the fundamental interactions between P3P and APPEL. In particular, they point out that with APPEL users can only specify what is unacceptable, not what is acceptable. Another problem with APPEL is that its limited expressiveness makes it difficult to translate real human intentions to a set of machine-readable preferences, even with support from a user agent with a graphical interface.

P3P Uptake

To achieve its goal, the P3P concept relied on support from both the client and the server side. On the client side, P3P support had to be built into the browsers, as core functionality or as browser add-ons. Additionally, the users, who access P3P enabled web sites using their browsers, had to understand and accept the technology in order to install and configure the P3P preferences settings. On the server side, the service providers had to encode their privacy policies in the P3P format, maintain them, and make them available to the P3P user agent.

Even though there have been occasional reports of increasing rates of P3P adoption amongst service providers, especially for e-commerce sites (Egelman et al. (2006) showed that out of a sample of e-commerce websites, 21% contained a P3P policy), it seems like adoption of the specification is doomed to fail. A study performed in 2005 showed that although 28% of the 75 most popular domains (the most clicked on domains from America Online search results) have P3P policies, only 9% of the sites of a random selection were P3P enabled (Cranor, et al., 2008). The study

also revealed that a majority of the P3P policies contained syntax errors. After what seems to be the peak in 2005, the number of P3P enabled sites has been steadily decreasing. A simple sample performed at the time of writing revealed that large service providers, such as Google.com and Apple.com, currently do not provide P3P privacy policies at all. The same is true for social networking sites such as Facebook.com and LinkedIn.com.

After the launch of P3P in early 2000, Microsoft has been an avid supporter of the technology, to the extent that Internet Explorer version 6 (IE6) and its successors (IE7 and IE8) provide the ability to display P3P privacy policies and to compare the policies with the user's privacy preferences settings. However, the support is quite limited, in that only a subset of the specification has been implemented in the conformance checking; namely the compact P3P policy, which covers the use of cookies. IE will not alert the user if the web site violates the privacy preferences regarding any other personal information, such as user-provided data. IE uses the P3P compact policy, which is transmitted in the HTTP headers, to make cookie blocking decisions. If the cookie policy of the service provider does not match the user's preferences, IE will display an eye covered by a do-not-enter sign in the browser frame.

The release of the P3P-enabled IE6 by Microsoft in 2001 was probably the most important factor for the large number of websites that adopted P3P in the following years. Service providers quickly found out that supporting P3P was necessary for their web sites to function properly when viewed using this browser (Cranor & Lessig, 2002). IE6 employed a fairly strict privacy policy regarding cookies. As previously discussed, IE looked for P3P compact policies; however, in addition to warning the user, IE6 also automatically blocked third-party cookies if a compact policy could not be found. This lead to a situation where sites that were not P3P enabled, but employed targeted advertising, page counters, etc. (that rely on 3rd part cookies), did not work in IE6, and its subsequent versions (P3P user agents based on compact policies were also implemented as a part of Mozilla Firefox and Netscape web browsers in early 2000, however, the functionality has since then been removed).

At its birth, P3P was praised by the Internet community and widely believed to be the keystone to resolving large privacy issues on the web. In practice, the specification has never been widely adopted, something that by some was predicted already early in the project (Catlett, 2000). In 2006, the work on P3P was officially suspended by the specification group due to the "insufficient support from current browser implementers" (W3C, 2007). In an interview from 2009 one of the W3C spokespersons on privacy stated the main reason for the P3P failure was that they "did not manage to convince the browsers" (Out-Law, 2009). Even though P3P policies were implemented and made available by the service providers, transparency was never really achieved because the client side did not utilize all the privacy information (i.e. P3P policies) that was actually out there.

Reasons for Failure

There are several reasons why P3P never became a success in the market. In hindsight, we are here able to point out some of the most obvious ones.

P3P's dependence on service providers to declare their privacy policy using the P3P policy language is one of the factors explaining why it never reached critical mass of adoption (the stage where adoption becomes self-reinforcing). Some have asserted that P3P suffered from the "chicken and egg" problem (Schwartz, 2009). The problem is that with few P3P compliant web sites, the user demand for P3P user agents is low, which in turn reduces the usage of P3P-declared policies. And if no one is using the P3P policies, why should service providers bother providing them? Reaching the critical mass is what turns this around to a positive reinforcement, rather than a negative one.

It has been said that many of the service providers who were early P3P adopters supported the technology to show their customers that they respected their privacy and to demonstrate a voluntary step to address privacy concerns (Cranor & Lessig, 2002). On the contrary, service providers currently have little or no incentive to implement or facilitate the use of machine-readable privacy policies such as P3P. From the service providers' perspective, information gathering is extremely important; however, there is a trade-off between obtaining as much information about the users a possible, while still preserving their trust. If service providers are to implement privacy enhancing measures, there will have to be a very concrete and measurable upside - fuzzy concepts such as "community spirit" and "doing the right thing" are unlikely to carry the day. In our opinion, for a user agent to become useful in practice, convincing the service providers to adopt the concept is the key to success. P3P never represented a competitive advantage for the service providers in this respect.

Even though the P3P vocabulary may have its limitations, its specification was by many considered as far too complex. There was never any user interface that could use all the metadata in the specification; most of the tools implemented only a subset of the specification. P3P was therefore never fully implemented, as the creators had hoped (Schwartz, 2009).

Microsoft did it best to push the usage of P3P by forcing web site developers to create P3P compact policies to be able to use third-party cookies. However, the result was not as intended. Many developers chose a "quick fix" by simply looking for P3P policies and compact policies on random Web sites and copying them onto their own sites (Cranor, 2002). Even though Microsoft's effort contributed to the increased number of P3P-enabled sites, the result was not as expected. A P3P policy is considered a contract and must therefore be consistent with the web site's human readable policy. The large number of random (and often erroneous) P3P compact policies that could be found online did not contribute to its credibility.

As discussed in the previous section, the P3P working group never managed to convince the big browser developers to support the technology (with the exception of Microsoft and its cookie handling in IE6). One of the key concepts of P3P was transparency, i.e. its ability to let the users say what is acceptable and what is not, and be informed of to what degree a particular service provider treats his personal information in ways that he does not like, without any knowledge of the underlying technology. This objective could never be achieved without support from the browser developers. Even though several browser add-ons were developed and distributed (the most well-known being the AT&T Privacy Bird), the lack of built-in P3P support in the browsers meant that the majority of the users were never aware of the technology and its possible implication on their personal data management.

The fact that P3P in its basic form cannot ensure that a service provider conforms to its own privacy policy, contributes to the hesitancy to adopt the technology. Especially browser developers are likely to be reluctant of enabling support for the technology because a P3P policy represents a privacy promise that may not be kept. Supporting P3P may therefore fool the users into believing that their browser will be responsible for handling their private information in the way stated in the users' privacy preferences.

The end-users also represented a huge challenge in the P3P project. The deployment of P3P assumed that the users regarded the privacy policies as trustworthy, and that they would act in accordance with their privacy preferences. Unfortunately, as discussed earlier in this chapter; even though most users claim to be concerned about their privacy, this has little effect on their actual behavior. This implies that most people do not take the time to read through the privacy policy, and those who do probably do not understand it. We also believe that most users do not understand the implications of personal data sharing; they look for short-time benefits rather than long-time consequences. It is also questionable whether users pay attention to, or tinker with, the default settings for any software that is already working. It is therefore highly uncertain whether users will spend time to actively specify their privacy preferences, or even to browse through the P3P summaries presented by the client software. Finally, most Internet users are not technically savvy. It is therefore a challenge to make people play an active role in the protection of their own privacy.

Current Status

P3P is not dead. Creating new user agents or new languages based on P3P is not a waste of time. In fact, in a time when social networking and personal data sharing has become an integrated part of the daily life, tool support to help the users control their privacy is more important than ever before. The concept of machine-readable policies, and preferences, is still considered a very promising approach. We should learn from the P3P creation, deployment and promoting process when building future privacy enhancing technology.

FUTURE RESEARCH DIRECTIONS

The adoption of PETs is currently low. One possible way of increasing adoption is of to push PETs through legislation, forcing businesses to support and provide such technology. Another option is to build PETs that are relevant and beneficial enough to be implemented of own free will. Such new and more relevant PETs need to:

- Constitute a competitive advantage for service providers.
- Be easy and pleasant to use for end users.
- Provide functionality that adequately represents the complexity of the privacy area.

As explained above, P3P fails in all these respects. Service providers that supported P3P early on did not gain a competitive advantage, as the technology was only useful to users when a large portion of the service providers supported the technology, and when proper user agents were available that built on P3P. For end users, the agents that are based on P3P have suffered from usability problems, e.g. when it comes to presentation of policies in an understandable way, and in the support users are given in their preference specification. P3P has also gained critique for shortcomings of the vocabulary.

If service providers are to implement PETs, they will need a clear and positive answer to the question: "What's in it for them?" As previously explained, the motivation for offering and supporting PETs can be to build reputation and trust, to keep their customers happy, to gain a competitive advantage or to reduce the risks associated with privacy compromise. PETs may even result in an increased willingness of users to share personal information. However, the investments that need to be made, both technically and for marketing purposes, and the uncertainty of the effects of these investments are likely to result in businesses investing their money elsewhere. More research is thus needed on the likely effects of using PETs so that businesses can have an improved decision basis.

Current PETs are, like P3P, commonly dependent on a certain level of adoption to be considered useful for end-users. Thus, businesses have little incentives to be first out on PET adoption. New PETs need to solve these problems, so that businesses that are pioneers in implementing PETs, can gain from this investment even though others may not follow them.

If PETs are to be successful, they need to be perceived as useful by the end-users. Users also must be made aware of them. This is challenging as today's Internet users do not spend a lot of time and effort on managing their privacy. Research is needed to improve our knowledge of what privacy support that users actually want. More research is also needed on how to present privacy information in a user-understandable way. But maybe even more important, we need PETs that are useful to users despite users' lack of privacy understanding, and lack of willingness to spend time on privacy. PETs should make the right privacy information and advice available at the right point in time. The Integrated Privacy View solution can be used as a starting point in this respect, as IPV allows users to get easy access to the privacy implications of providing specific information pieces at the point in time when this information is shared. Using PETs should also not be time-consuming and require users to take part in complex setup processes, potentially forcing them to make difficult and emotion-laden decisions regarding what they allow or disallow when it comes to personal information. The privacy paradox aside, users are most frequently put off by lengthy configuration processes for specifying preferences. One way of tackling this challenge may be through machine learning approaches that track user behavior, helping users to behave consistently with respect to privacy (Tøndel, Nyre, & Bernsmed, 2011). An additional challenge here is today's pervasive computing practices, where users access the web through a multitude of devices, many of which are mobile. This also implies that a future "preference generator" will need to take context information such as time and place into account.

Privacy is complex and personal. Individuals may have quite different opinions on what is acceptable and what is not, and what is acceptable may additionally vary between situations. Solutions that take an over-simplistic view of privacy, e.g. by having users specify a set of simple rules that always apply, are likely to be less useful to users, producing advices that do not match the situation the user is facing. Instead, privacy solutions are needed that take into account the complexity of privacy decisions. Especially solutions should acknowledge that privacy decisions are in many ways cost-benefit tradeoffs. Tools that only consider the costs will be less relevant than tools that also consider the benefits involved. Currently PETs in general have only focused on the costs of sharing information, while businesses and end-users are more focused on achieving benefits. These benefits should also be taken into account by PETs.

More research is also needed on the role that third-parties should play in privacy technology. A limitation of the privacy policy approach (e.g. P3P) is the lack of control that companies actually follow what is written in their policies. Stricter privacy legislation is an option, but one could also consider improved privacy seal programs and third-party control, possibly integrated with PET tools.

Participating in social networks while at the same time preserving privacy is currently a challenging task. Neither Facebook nor LinkedIn currently support P3P, and it is not clear how this could be successfully implemented. Privacy in social networks could be a research topic of its own.

In the quest for relevant and useful PETs it will be important to look beyond the common focus on improving presentation and availability of privacy information. Real advantages are likely to be experienced when privacy support is built into the systems, and not only addressed by adding privacy policies. As an example of such a future privacy service, we describe some ideas related to service adaptation (Nyre, Bernsmed, Bøe, & Pedersen, 2011). This type of PET can be useful in cases where collecting personal information is not central to the service to be provided, but still considered by the provider as a nice option. Assuming that a user employs a browser or third-party plug-in that has access to the user's privacy preferences, these can be communicated to the service provider during session initiation. Based on these preferences, the service provider can refrain from asking for information which would violate the user's privacy preferences. This would improve the user experience, saving the user from eschewing a site which is too

noisy, and the service provider would not lose a potential customer because of information that the provider doesn't really need. For other users with more relaxed preferences (or even with no privacy preferences) the service provider can collect more information, possibly in return for more services. For this to work, a universal, standardized format for privacy preference specification is needed. It may even be possible to establish a community portal of privacy preferences, where a simple ID (or URI similar to those provided by http://tinyurl.com) can be used to identify a complex policy. The user (or client) then only needs to communicate the ID to the provider, which can retrieve the full policy from the online repository. Tools for generating privacy preferences would upload complete policies to the repository, but only new unique policies will create a new ID.

To sum up the research challenges, there is a need for improved knowledge and understanding of the likely effects for businesses of supporting or offering PETs, but we also need to develop improved privacy technology. Researchers should learn from the failure of P3P and develop PETs that are better able to meet the requirements of both end-users and businesses, and can thus be used as a business advantage.

CONCLUSION

This chapter has discussed Privacy Enhancing Technologies in a business context, highlighting both challenges and opportunities. One insight that emerges from this work is that the most important part businesses can play is the facilitation of PETs deployed by others; i.e., even if businesses are not pushing PETs at their customers, they should provide foundations and interfaces that cater to the PETs that their customers decide to use. This includes making machine-readable privacy policies available.

Although P3P has failed to deliver on its promise, we maintain that it is important for businesses to be proactive when it comes to PETs. The alternative would be to surrender the playing field to the community-based approaches, and although these can provide a useful service to consumers, the businesses themselves will have few opportunities to influence them with respect to incomplete or erroneous information.

REFERENCES

W3C. (1997). *Platform for internet content selection* (PICS). Retrieved March, 2011, from http://www.w3.org/PICS

W3C. (2006). *Platform for privacy preferences.* Retrieved April, 2011, from http://www.w3.org/P3P/

W3C. (2007). *The W3C privacy page.* Retrieved March, 2011, from http://www.w3.org/Privacy/

Ackerman, M. S., Cranor, L. F., & Reagle, J. (1999). *Privacy in e-commerce: Examining user scenarios and privacy preferences.* Paper presented at the 1st ACM Conference on Electronic Commerce.

Acquisti, A. (2002). *Protecting privacy with economics: Economic incentives for preventive technologies in ubiquitous computing environments.* Paper presented at the Workshop on Socially-informed Design of Privacy-enhancing Solutions in Ubiquitous Computing.

Agrawal, R., et al. (2003). *An XPath-based preference language for P3P.* Paper presented at the 12th International Conference on World Wide Web.

Andersson, C., et al. (2005). *Trust in PRIME.* Paper presented at the Fifth IEEE International Symposium on Signal Processing and Information Technology.

Argyrakis, J., Gritzalis, S., & Kioulafas, C. (2003). Privacy enhancing technologies: A review. In Traunmüller, R. (Ed.), *Electronic government* (*Vol. 2739*, pp. 282–287). Springer. doi:10.1007/10929179_51

Benassi, P. (1999). TRUSTe: An online privacy seal program. *Communications of the ACM, 42*(2), 56–59. doi:10.1145/293411.293461

Berendt, B., Günther, O., & Spiekermann, S. (2005). Privacy in e-commerce: Stated preferences vs. actual behavior. *Communications of the ACM, 48*(4), 101–106. doi:10.1145/1053291.1053295

Bergmann, M., Rost, M., & Pettersson, J. S. (2006). Exploring the feasibility of a spatial user interface paradigm for privacy-enhancing technology. In A. G. Nilsson, R. Gustas, W. Wojtkowski, W. G. Wojtkowski, S. Wrycza & J. Zupancic (Eds.), *Bridging the gap between academia and industry* (pp. 437--448).

Borking, J. (2009). *Organizational motives for adopting privacy enhancing technologies (PETs).* Paper presented at the D 7.3 PRISE Conference Proceedings: Towards Privacy Enhancing Security Technologies - The Next Steps.

Camenisch, J., et al. (2005). *Privacy and identity management for everyone.* Paper presented at the 2005 Workshop on Digital Identity Management.

CASPIAN. (2006). *Metro future store - Special report overview.* Retrieved March, 2011, from http://www.spychips.com/metro/overview.html

Catlett, J. (2000). *Open letter to P3P developers & replies.* Paper presented at the Tenth Conference on Computers, Freedom and Privacy: Challenging the Assumptions

Clarke, R. (2008). Business cases for privacy-enhancing technologies. In Subramanian, R. (Ed.), *Computer security, privacy and politics: Current issues, challenges and solutions* (pp. 135–155). Hershey, PA: IGI Global. doi:10.4018/978-1-59904-804-8.ch007

Clement, A., et al. (2008). *The PIPWatch toolbar: Combining PIPEDA, PETs and market forces through social navigation to enhance privacy protection and compliance.* Paper presented at the Technology and Society, 2008. ISTAS 2008. IEEE International Symposium on, http://dx.doi.org/10.1109/68.593394

Coyle, K. (1999). *P3P: Pretty poor privacy? - A social analysis of the platform for privacy preferences (P3P).* Retrieved April, 2011, from http://www.kcoyle.net/p3p.html

Coyle, K. (2000). *A response to "P3P and privacy: An update for the privacy community" by the Center for Democracy and Technology.* Retrieved April 2011 from http://www.kcoyle.net/response.html

Cranor, L. F. (2002). Help! IE6 is blocking my cookies. Retrieved April 2011 from http://www.oreillynet.com/pub/a/javascript /2002/10/04/p3p.html

Cranor, L. F. (2003). *"I didn't buy it for myself" privacy and ecommerce personalization.* Paper presented at the 2003 ACM Workshop on Privacy in the Electronic Society.

Cranor, L. F. (2008). P3P deployment on websites. *Electronic Commerce Research and Applications, 7*(3), 274–293. doi:10.1016/j.elerap.2008.04.003

Cranor, L. F., Arjula, M., & Guduru, P. (2002). *Use of a P3P user agent by early adopters.* Paper presented at the 2002 ACM Workshop on Privacy in the Electronic Society.

Cranor, L. F., Guduru, P., & Arjula, M. (2006). User interfaces for privacy agents. *ACM Transactions on Computer-Human Interaction, 13*(2), 135–178. doi:10.1145/1165734.1165735

Cranor, L. F., Langheinrich, M., & Marchiori, M. (2002). *A P3P preference exchange language 1.0 (APPEL1.0).* (Working Draft): W3C.

Cranor, L. F., & Lessig, L. (2002). *Web privacy with* (p. 3P). O'Reilly & Associates, Inc.

Egelman, S., Cranor, L. F., & Chowdhury, A. (2006). *An analysis of P3P-enabled web sites among top-20 search results.* Paper presented at the 8th International Conference on Electronic Commerce: The New E-commerce: Innovations for Conquering Current Barriers, Obstacles and Limitations to Conducting Successful Business on the Internet.

EU. (2002). *Directive on privacy and electronic communications.* 2002/58/EC

EuroPriSe. (2010). *Welcome! - EuroPriSe - European privacy seal.* Retrieved March, 2011, from https://www.european-privacy-seal.eu/

Facebook. (2011). *Welcome to Facebook - Log in, sign up or learn more.* Retrieved April, 2011, from http://www.facebook.com

Flinn, S., & Lumsden, J. (2005). *User perceptions of privacy and security on the Web.* Paper presented at the Third Annual Conference on Privacy, Security and Trust (PST 2005)

FTC. (2010). *Protecting consumer privacy in an era of rapid change: A proposed framework for businesses and policymakers.* Federal Trade Commission. Retrieved April 2011 from http://www.ftc.gov/os/2010/12/101201 privacyreport.pdf

Gomez, J., Pinnick, T., & Soltani, A. (2009). *KnowPrivacy.* Retrieved April 2011 from http://www.knowprivacy.org/report/ KnowPrivacy_Final_Report.pdf

Greenstadt, R., & Smith, M. D. (2005). *Protecting personal information: Obstacles and directions.* Paper presented at the Fourth Workshop on the Economics of Information Security (WEIS05)

Guarda, P., & Zannone, N. (2009). Towards the development of privacy-aware systems. *Information and Software Technology, 51*(2), 337–350. doi:10.1016/j.infsof.2008.04.004

Hansen, M. (2009). *Putting privacy pictograms into practice - A European perspective*. Paper presented at the GI Jahrestagung.

Hochheiser, H. (2002). The platform for privacy preference as a social protocol: An examination within the U.S. policy context. *ACM Transactions on Internet Technology*, *2*(4), 276–306. doi:10.1145/604596.604598

IPTF. (2010). *Commercial data privacy and innovation in the internet economy: A dynamic policy framework*: The Department of Commerce, Internet Policy Task Force. Retrieved April 2011 from http://www.ntia.doc.gov/reports/2010/IPTF_Privacy_GreenPaper_12162010.pdf

ISO/IEC 15408-1. (2009). *Information technology -- Security techniques -- Evaluation criteria for IT security -- Part 1: Introduction and general model*. Retrieved April 2011, from http://www.common-criteriaportal.org/files/ccfiles/CCPART1V3.1R3.pdf, Retrieved

Jensen, C., Potts, C., & Jensen, C. (2005). Privacy practices of internet users: Self-reports versus observed behavior. *International Journal of Human-Computer Studies*, *63*(1-2), 203–227. doi:10.1016/j.ijhcs.2005.04.019

Kelley, P. G., et al. (2009). *A nutrition label for privacy*. Paper presented at the 5th Symposium on Usable Privacy and Security.

Kobsa, A., & Teltzrow, M. (2005). *Contextualized communication of privacy practices and personalization benefits: Impacts on users' data sharing and purchase behavior. Privacy Enhancing Technologies* (Vol. 3424, pp. 329–343). Berlin, Germany: Springer.

Kolter, J., Kernchen, T., & Pernul, G. (2010). Collaborative privacy management. *Computers & Security*, *29*(5), 580–591..doi:10.1016/j.cose.2009.12.007

Levy, S. E., & Gutwin, C. (2005). *Improving understanding of website privacy policies with fine-grained policy anchors*. Paper presented at the 14th International Conference on World Wide Web.

LinkedIn. (2011). *Relationships matter*. LinkedIn. Retrieved April, 2011, from http://www.linkedin.com/

Lioudakis, G. V. (2007). A middleware architecture for privacy protection. *Computer Networks*, *51*(16), 4679–4696. doi:10.1016/j.comnet.2007.06.010

Nehf, J. P. (2007). Shopping for privacy on the Internet. *The Journal of Consumer Affairs*, *41*(2), 351–375.

NTIA. (2010). Information privacy and innovation in the internet economy. *Federal Register*. Retrieved April 2011 from http://www.federal-register.gov/articles/2010/12/21/2010-31971/information-privacy-and-innovation-in-the-internet-economy

Nyre, Å. A., Bernsmed, K., Bøe, S., & Pedersen, S. (2011). A server-side approach to privacy policy matching. Paper presented at the Sixth International Conference on Availability, Reliability and Security.

Odlyzko, A. (2003). *Privacy, economics, and price discrimination on the Internet*. Paper presented at the 5th International Conference on Electronic Commerce.

Odlyzko, A. (2007). *Privacy and the clandestine evolution of e-commerce*. Paper presented at the Proceedings of the Ninth International Conference on Electronic Commerce Out-Law. (2009). *Privacy policy tool failed because of browser rejection, says W3C lawyer*. Retrieved March, 2011, from http://www.out-law.com/page-10437

Pettersson, J. S., et al. (2005). *Making PRIME usable*. Paper presented at the Symposium on Usable Privacy and Security.

Pollach, I. (2007). What's wrong with online privacy policies? *Communications of the ACM, 50*(9), 103–108. doi:10.1145/1284621.1284627

Reeder, R. W., et al. (2008). *A user study of the expandable grid applied to P3P privacy policy visualization*. Paper presented at the 7th ACM Workshop on Privacy in the Electronic Society.

Schunter, M., & Waidner, M. (2007). *Simplified privacy controls for aggregated services: Suspend and resume of personal data*. Paper presented at the 7th International Conference on Privacy Enhancing Technologies.

Schwartz, A. (2009). *Looking back at P3P: Lessons for the future*. Retrieved April 2011 from http://www.cdt.org/files/pdfs/P3P_Retro_Final_0.pdf

Spiekermann, S., Grossklags, J., & Berendt, B. (2001). *E-privacy in 2nd generation e-commerce: Privacy preferences versus actual behavior*. Paper presented at the 3rd ACM Conference on Electronic Commerce.

Szeto, M., & Miri, A. (2007). *Analysis of the use of privacy-enhancing technologies to achieve PIPEDA compliance in a B2C e-business model*. Paper presented at the Eighth World Congress on the Management of eBusiness, 2007. WCMeB 2007.

Tøndel, I. A., Nyre, Å. A., & Bernsmed, K. (2011). *Learning Privacy Preferences*. Paper presented at the Sixth International Conference on Availability, Reliability and Security.

TRUSTe. (n.d.). Privacy seals & services. Online Trust & Safety from TRUSTe. Retrieved February 17, 2011, from http://www.truste.org

US. (2011). Welcome to the U.S.-EU & U.S.-Swiss safe harbor frameworks. Retrieved April, 2011, from http://www.export.gov/safeharbor/

Vila, T., Greenstadt, R., & Molnar, D. (2003). *Why we can't be bothered to read privacy policies - Models of privacy economics as a lemons market*. Paper presented at the 5th International Conference on Electronic Commerce.

Warren, S. D., & Brandeis, L. D. (1890). The right to privacy. *Harvard Law Review, 4*(5), 193–220. doi:10.2307/1321160

Wilton, R. (2009). What's happened to PETs? *Information Security Technical Report, 14*(3), 146–153. doi:10.1016/j.istr.2009.10.010

ADDITIONAL READING

Clarke provides a largely non-technical treatise on the business motivations for deploying Privacy Enhancing Technologies (Clarke, 2008). A European perspective on such motivations is provided by Borking (2009), although it should be noted that we have found no independent confirmation of Borking's claim that an organization which is innovative with respect to implementation of advanced Identity and Access Management (IAM), will also be more likely to deploy PETs.

The P3P web site (http://www.w3.org/P3P/) provides a wealth of information on P3P, and also provides links to other P3P documentation. The book "Web Privacy with P3P" (Cranor & Lessig, 2002) explains the working of the P3P protocol in depth. The book is written by Lorrie Faith Cranor who was a co-author of the P3P and APPEL specifications, and who served as chair of the P3P specification working group at the W3C. Lorrie Faith Cranor and colleagues have thus been working with P3P from its inception, and provide an insider view of the technology (Cranor, 2002, 2003; Cranor, Arjula, et al., 2002; Cranor, et al., 2008; Cranor, et al., 2006; Cranor & Lessig, 2002). A more critical view of P3P is offered by Hochheiser (2002). Argyrakis et al. (2003) presents a thorough survey of PETs, which in spite of its age is still surprisingly relevant. For an up-to-date view of US policy work on electronic privacy, see the reports from the U.S. Federal Trade Commission and Department of Commerce (FTC, 2010; IPTF, 2010; NTIA, 2010).

KEY TERMS AND DEFINITIONS

P3P: Platform for Privacy Preferences.

Personal Information: Any information that can be stored, and associated with an identifiable person. Personal data includes, e.g., a person's full name, e-mail address, IP address, credit card number, digital identity, membership in groups, relationships to other people, financial data and purchasing history, and so on. Sometimes, the term "personal identifiable information (PII)" is used instead of personal information.

PET: Privacy Enhancing Technology.

Privacy Paradox: The fact that although most users claim to be concerned with privacy, their actions are usually anything but privacy-preserving.

Privacy Policy: A policy published by a service provider stating how the service provider will use personal information collected from users of the service.

Privacy: The right to be left alone. Can sometimes be achieved through confidentiality, but not always.

Reputation: The opinion or social evaluation of a group toward an entity such as a person, business or organization.

Risk: Probability of (unwanted) incident multiplied by the cost occurred when the incident manifests itself. Cost does not necessarily have to be a monetary value, but in order to simplify calculations, non-monetary costs (such as loss of reputation) are usually assigned a monetary value.

Security: Mechanisms that protect a system from its environment. Composed of the three parts Confidentiality, Integrity and Availability.

Trust: Expecting another party to behave as they say they will.

Chapter 2
User–Centric Privacy Management in Future Network Infrastructure

Antonio F. Gomez-Skarmeta
University of Murcia, Spain

Alejandro Perez Mendez
University of Murcia, Spain

Elena Torroglosa Garcia
University of Murcia, Spain

Gabriel Lopez Millán
University of Murcia, Spain

ABSTRACT

Identity management is becoming more and more important every day. Users need a way to centralize the management of their identity information, such as simplifying the access to services with mechanisms like Single Sign-On. Organizations need a means of obtaining reliable information about users of their services. While this is the main concern for service providers, users are more worried about how their information is treated, what information is provided to what entity, and how privacy is assured in general. IdM provides the means for adequate privacy protection.

While several IdM (Identity Management) solutions that work at Web layer exist, they usually lack integration with network layer services. Future network infrastructures must integrate IdM functionality, in such a way that the user is provided with a unified and simplified vision of his identity, which results in an improved privacy and security protection. The IdM framework defined in the SWIFT (Secure Widespread Identities for Federated Telecommunications) project provides the means for cross-layer identity management as well as a set of advanced identity management concepts allowing improved privacy protection, simplification of user interactions, and extensible architecture.

Finally, it is analyzed how the inclusion of IdM in business organizations can provide economical benefits. These benefits range from a reduction in resource requirements to the increment of potential clients

DOI: 10.4018/978-1-61350-501-4.ch002

thanks to the incorporation of the organization in an identity federation. Special attention is placed on the case where the telecommunications operator is established as the main point of identity providing, as a straightforward result of its already established trust relationships with a wide range of parties (clients and service providers).

INTRODUCTION

The number of users that interact with digital services, as well as the number of services offered, has drastically increased in recent times. Different organizations have found in the Internet a good business opportunity due to the benefits it provides to the user (immediacy, 24/7 availability, access to other countries' companies…) and for the organization itself (easy deployment, low maintenance cost…).

Generally users have one account or profile for each one of the services they use. This presents several drawbacks that limit the usability of this approach. Users need to remember lots of different user names and passwords, especially if they want to preserve their privacy and to prevent their activities being traced. Users are also requested to fill out registration forms for each service they register for, so having to insert again and again their identity information. This may lead to inconsistencies and to out-of-date information.

Thus, for both users and services it is very important to deploy an identity management (IdM) system that allows the same identity information to be shared among the different services. Like this, users only need to remember a small number of credentials, while services will be provided with reliable and up-to-date information. Identity management should be applied in two different planes: horizontal (across domains and services) and vertical (across network layers).

Once identity information is shared among services, it is of paramount importance for the user to control the access to this information, determining by whom, when and how information about himself can be retrieved. So the user has a high control over how his privacy is being preserved. In addition, a user may want to access a service anonymously, just by providing a little information about himself (i.e. he is authenticated and is over 18 years old).

Network connectivity is a primary service that is required for access to this digital world. Therefore, network operators are usually the first place where users have to authenticate prior to accessing any other service. The integration of IdM into network operators is a step that can be done in order to anticipate the user requirements in terms of usability and privacy. Information should be accessed and provided by the network operator from and to other services and providers in a safe, controlled way, with special care with sensitive information (Attribute release policies - ARPs defined by the user in the different information providers will dictate how information is distributed, along with providers' local policies).

This chapter will present the analysis performed within the European research project *SWIFT*, which has its continuity in the *INS* standardization group of ETSI (European Telecommunications Standards Institute). It is divided into the following subsections. The chapter starts with a background where essential identity management terminology and concepts are introduced and some of the most relevant state-of-the-art technologies are briefly introduced. The chapter continues by describing identity management and privacy protection, and what mechanisms the former uses to achieve the latter. Then the chapter provides an overview of the main aspect of the SWIFT identity management framework, including identity aggregation, cross-layer identity management, distributed policies, integration with smart card technology and integration with legacy systems. The chapter goes on to discusses the advantages and business opportunities that appear when integrating identity management in business environments. Finally, some future research directions and business opportunities are provided.

BACKGROUND

Most of the identity management systems share a common base architecture and a set of definitions that must be contextualized for the rest of the chapter. This section will begin by providing the reader with a basic knowledge of identity management, including main definitions, basic architecture and a small state-of-the-art section.

Terminology

An attribute is a piece of information that represents a single property of a principal, for example *age, postal address* or *music preferences.* Attributes can be made up by a single value, like *age,* or by multiple values, like *music preferences.*

A credential is a piece of information that is used for authentication purposes and that allows a principal to demonstrate he/she is who he/she claims to be. Examples of credentials are *passwords, identity cards, certificates, smartcards...*

In the context of IdM, authentication is the process of asserting the identity of a principal in such a way that the *authentication* has no reasonable doubts of its authenticity. To perform authentication the principal is required to present some kind of credential. Depending on the type of the credential, as well as when, by whom and how this credential was issued, the *authenticator* can associate a *Level of Assurance* (or degree of confidence that the principal is who he/she claims to be) to the authentication. The *authentication* may reject authentications that result in an insufficient level of assurance.

In the context of IdM, authorization is the process of determining if an authenticated principal has the proper rights to access a specific service.

Usually, this process is strongly based on the value of a set of attributes regarding the principal that the service provider obtains by means of the IdM system (i.e. age, credit card number...). Additionally, environment variables can be used in the authorization process (for example, access is only granted on Mondays and Wednesdays, from 8.00am to 3.00pm, or when the system load is below a certain threshold).

An identity federation is a set of technologies, standards and use-cases which enable different autonomous security domains to use identity information from other domains. For example, the use of this information allows a user from one organization to be authorized to access a service provided by a different organization, using his/her already defined attributes and credentials.

A policy is a set of rules that control the behaviour of a system. In the context of IdM, and more precisely in the context of access control, a policy indicates the conditions that a principal has to fulfil to be authorized to access a protected resource. For example, a policy may indicate that to access resource X, a principal has to be authenticated in the identity federation, have an attribute called *age*, and that the value of this attribute is over 18.

A pseudonym is a special anonymous identifier that is established between two or more entities in order to identify a principal (usually a user). The aim is to improve privacy by unlinking the use of the pseudonym with the principal's real identity.

Single Sign On (SSO) is the mechanism that allows a principal to reuse the results of an authentication process to simplify (and even to omit) the following authentication processes to the same or another service provider within the identity federation.

General IdM Architecture

Below, we present an architecture that, with minor modifications, can be applied to all the IdM systems. It is lade up of three main components:

Figure 1. General IdM architecture

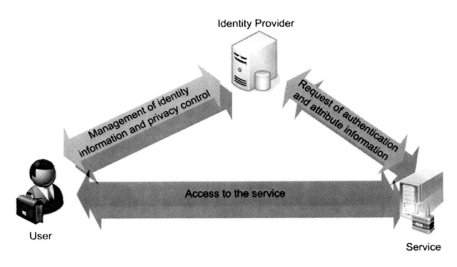

User; Service Provider; and Identity Provider. *Figure 1* depicts this general architecture.

The User (U) is the entity that wishes to access the services within the identity federation using his/her already defined identity information. The user has strong interests in security (information cannot be accessed by unauthorized third parties), privacy (access to identity information is narrowed to the minimum acceptable to provide the service) and usability (the use of the IdM solution does not imply a big effort in time, resources or knowledge by the user).

The Service Provider (SP) is the entity that wants to provide a service to users belonging to the identity federation. The main concerns of service providers are reliability of the received identity information (comes from trusted sources) and security (identity information has not been modified or erroneous information injected).

The Identity Provider (IdP) is the entity that holds the identity information of the principals. Usually there exists one identity provider per organization. The responsibility of the IdP is to provide the identity information to the service providers, taking care in security and privacy protection.

Common Standards

There exist different technologies and solutions for identity management. This section will briefly describe some of the most important ones.

SAML

The Security Assertion Markup Language (SAML) (Cantor, 2005) is a XML-based proposal by the OASIS consortium for the creation and exchange of security information. SAML defines both, the representation of the information and the protocols that are used to exchange this information. SAML defines two main use cases: on the one hand, the Web Single Sign On allows a user to access different web services through a standard web browser, authenticating only once. On the other, the establishment of identity federations allows online services to establish a collaborative environment for their users.

SAML defines assertions as the security statement format to transport information regarding a specific principal. Assertions can be signed by the issuing entity, which must be trusted within the context it is going to be used. Assertions are included in statements, which can be of three different kinds. An a*uthentication statement* asserts that a principal has been authenticated under certain circumstances. An *authorization decision* indicates if a user is authorized to perform an action on a shred resource. Finally, an a*ttribute statement* represents attributes associated to a principal.

To exchange these assertions, SAML defines the use of several query/response protocols, like *Authentication Request Protocol* to request authentication information regarding a principal, *Assertion Query and Request Protocol* to obtain an assertion or *Name Identifier Management Protocol* to change the identifier given to a principal.

The specific mechanisms in terms of communication protocols used to implement these protocols are defined by means of *bindings*. Examples of these bindings are HTTP redirections, HTTP forms or SOAP messages.

Finally, SAML defines the concept of *profile* as the specification of how *assertions, bindings* and *protocols* are used together to solve a specific scenario.

XACML

The eXtensible Access Control Markup Language (Rissanen, 2010) provides an XML-based policy language for specification of access control policies and it provides an XML-based message format for what policy decision requests and responses should look like.

Policies specify the actions that can be performed by the users under specific circumstances. The language is extensible enough to adapt to any scenario where access control is required. A typical XACML scenario is composed of the following entities: *PEP (Policy Enforcement Point)* - the entity that protects the resource: *CH (Context Handler)* - the entity that gathers all the required information to take the authorization decision (like user attributes); *PDP (Policy Decision Point)* - the entity that evaluates the policies and takes the decision based the received information; and

PAP (Policy Administration Point) - the entity that allows the creation and management of policies.

XACML policies are hierarchically structured. A policy starts with a PolicySet, which might contain other PolicySets or particular Policies. A Policy in turn consists of several Rules, which actually specify the outcome of a policy decision, e.g. permit or deny. The hierarchical policy format of XACML is used to concretize the applicability from the top (PolicySet) down to the rule (Policy). Therefore, each part (PolicySet, Policy, and Rule) contains a so called Target section, which specifies the applicability. The target contains statements about the subject, the resource, the action and the environment, which have to be fulfilled tu be applicable.

State of the Art

Shibboleth

Shibboleth (Scavo, 2005) is a web authentication and authorization infrastructure (AAI) based on the use of SAML and web redirections to determine if a user can access a resource through its web browser. This decision is based on the user's information kept in his home institution.

This mechanism enables the definition of identity federations such that the user always authenticates through his home institution, and then the information needed is sent where necessary to authorize him. Shibboleth defines a Service Provider (SP) and an Identity Provider (IdP). The former is at the institution providing resources and the latter is at the institution managing the user's identity. Thus, when the user accesses some protected resource, the SP asks the IdP where the user is from, in order to obtain information about him. If the user was previously authenticated, the IdP returns the needed information, otherwise the user is redirected to the IdP to be authenticated. In this way, web SSO is provided. Moreover, this process is performed transparently to the user by means of web redirections.

Shibboleth defined a new service called WAYF (Where Are You From) to locate the user's IdP with or without user interaction. It is independent of both the SP and the IdP. This element is essentially a proxy for the authentication request passed from the SP to the SSO Service.

OpenID

OpenID (Fitzpatrick, 2007) is a Single Sign-On protocol that solves the problem of having an individual login and password for every web site. Using OpenID-enabled sites, web users do not need to remember traditional authentication tokens such as username and password. Instead, they only need to be previously registered on a website with an OpenID "identity provider" (IdP). Since the protocol is decentralized, any website can employ the software as a way for users to sign in; OpenID solves the problem without relying on any centralized website to confirm digital identity. It therefore removes the need for multiple usernames across different websites, so simplifying surfing the Net. OpenID is an open and free framework, that allows user-centric digital identity and it takes advantage of already existing internet technologies (URI, HTTP, SSL, Diffie-Hellman).

OpenID is still in the adoption phase and is becoming more and more popular, as large organizations like AOL, Microsoft, Sun, Novell, Google, IBM, Verisign, Yahoo, and Orange begin to accept and provide this protocol. In addition, integrated OpenID support has been given high priority in Firefox 3 and it can be used with Windows CardSpace. Today it is estimated that there are over 160-million OpenID enabled URIs with nearly ten-thousand sites supporting these kind of logins.

Besides the obvious benefit of having a single login and password that do not need to be written down anywhere to be remembered, OpenID also has another important security advantage. As the majority of users will only use one OpenID login, the authentication of that login can be made extremely secure. At present, it is expensive for individual web sites to provide their users with extra security features such as client-side certificates, smartcards or SecurIDs. However, with OpenID an Identity Provider might be able to afford to put the time and money into securing a single "front gate" instead of having dozens of sites securing their individual "front gates". This has the potential to greatly increase the security of our everyday logins.

CardSpace

Windows CardSpace (Microsoft Corporation, 2006) is client software that enables users to provide their digital identity to online services in a simple, secure and trusted way. It is what is known as an identity selector: when a user needs to authenticate to a web site or a web service, CardSpace pops up a special security-hardened UI with a set of "information cards" for the user to choose from.

Each card has some identity data associated with it – though this is not actually stored in the card that is either given to the user by an identity provider such as their bank, employer or government or is created by users themselves. Having the user as an identity provider sounds a bit strange on first acquaintance (who would trust the user?) but this is a very common scenario: this is what we do every time we register at a web site.

The CardSpace UI enables users to create Personal cards (aka self-issued cards) and associate a limited set of identity data. It also enables the user to import Managed cards from third party identity providers. When the user chooses a card, a signed and encrypted security token containing the required information (e.g. name and address, employer's name and address, or credit limit) is generated by the identity provider that created the card. The user, in control at all times, then decides whether to release this information to the requesting online service. If the user approves. then the token is sent on to this relying party, where the token is processed and the identity information is extracted.

Higgins

Higgins (Shelat, 2006) is an open source framework for the web that allows users and systems to integrate identity information and profiles, besides information on social relations across multiple systems, applications and devices. The framework supports many identity management systems such as CardSpace (Higgins is a direct free software implementation) and OpenID; in addition, it is in the process of supporting Idemix. Its infrastructure is based on the most popular identity protocols such as WS-Trust [8], OpenID, SAML, XDI (Reed, 2004) or LDAP. The framework offers similar features in the treatment of privacy to CardSpace, with the added benefit of working with open source implementations and the use of standards.

The main advantage of Higgins for developers is that it facilitates the creation of applications and services that work with other identity managers. For the user, Higgins provides a graphical interface, called the Identity Selector, which provides control of digital identity management to the user.

The Higgins project also provides an API and a data model for integration and federation of digital identity and security information from multiple sources. It also offers adapters to enable integration in the framework of various data sources such as directories, communication systems, collaboration systems and databases with different protocols and schemas.

PrimeLife

The research project PrimeLife (Zwingelberg, 2010) is led by IBM and funded by the European Commission's 7th Framework Programme. The goal is to bring the privacy and identity management to the collaborative environments of Internet, allowing people to control personal data trail left behind their navigation. PrimeLife is based on the success of the FP6's PRIME project (Leenes, 2008) which developed a working prototype of an identity management system that improves privacy, while it was also the starting point of the Idemix project.

Idemix (Identity mixer) (Camenisch, 2002) is a suite of cryptographic protocols developed by IBM Research [40] that allows strong authentication while maintaining privacy in identity management. Its operation is based on the use of an anonymous credential system that allows aggregation of attributes from different digital identities and partial disclosure of these.

The project also focuses on the development of new mechanisms to support the online privacy and identity management in order to interact in new ways with the new services that have emerged on the Internet, communities and the Web 2.0. To do this, the project works on the design and the implementation of an appropriate policy language that allows web sites and end users to express their privacy policies and preferences. In turn, it is undergoing a process of analysis and design in order to implement the prototype of a tool that allows users to evaluate the reliability of collaboratively content such as wikis and blogs.

Summary

Identity management systems are focused on enabling the user to manage their digital identity on the network to improve their privacy. OpenID proposes a solution based on a unique identifier to access the services provided by the management, but it also represents a single point to undermine security. Other systems such as CardSpace, Higgins or Shibboleth offer more advanced features such as anonymity and unlinkability. PrimeLife (based on the project Idemix) also provides identity aggregation and complex privacy mechanisms that allow the use of anonymous credentials to enhance privacy. Figure 2 summarizes the different IdM solutions and their features.

Figure 2. Summary of IdM solutions

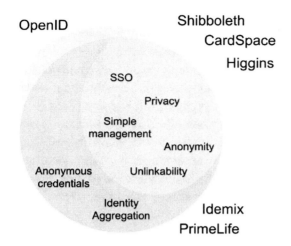

European Data Protection Legislation

The European Union considers the right to privacy a main right of its citizens. The *Data Protection Directive* (Directive 95/46/EC) focuses on the protection of individuals against misuse of their personal information. This directive understands *personal data* as any data that can to be linked to a person (e.g. address, credit card number, criminal records...).

The directive states that data should not be processed, except under specific conditions are met: transparency (who is going to process the data and the purpose of such processing must be clear for the user and authorized third party), legitimate purpose (data cannot be used for a different purpose) and proportionality (the data gathered from a user must be relevant to the purpose of the processing, and must be kept updated)

Identity management works towards privacy protection laws enforcement, making it easier to follow recommendations and directives and providing proper tools to facilitate end user involvement in the process.

PRIVACY IN IDENTITY MANAGEMENT (IDM)

Introduction on Identity Management

We usually give the name *identity management* to the set of processes and functions that deal with user's identity information. This information usually consists of a user name and some credentials that allow this user to authenticate as the legitimate owner of the identity claimed. Additionally, identity information can be completed with additional personal information of the user, like year of birth, nationality, email address, music preferences, etc.

Identity management has been performed for a long time by service providers to directly control access their protected services. Identity information is used to perform authentication and authorization. Authentication consists of determining if the user actually owns the identity claimed, that is, demonstrating that the user knows the credentials associated to that identity. Authorization consists of determining whether an authenticated user can access a service.

Furthermore, services can delegate not only storage capabilities but also some of their identity management functionality to external entities called Identity Providers (IdPs). This allows all the common identity management functionality of the services within an organization to be concentrated in one entity, the IdP, so avoiding replication of functionality and simplifying development of services (developer has no need to worry about identity management). Usually services delegate authentication and attribute storage into the IdP, since these processes are common for all the services, while authorization is performed by the services themselves since it is highly dependent process.

The introduction of IdPs is also interesting from the users' point of view, since using them users can have a centralised control over their identity information within an organization, simplifying coherence maintenance and updating of data.

When several organizations agree on how to perform identity management in such a way that they accept identity information coming from other's IdP it is called an *Identity Federation*. Identity federations allow that users from one organization can access to other organization's services using their already provided identity information (including credentials and attributes).

Privacy Protection and Security

Due to the special sensitivity of the data involved, privacy is a cornerstone of identity management. Users not only want to manage their data in an easy and usable way, but they also require the process to be done securely. This becomes even more important when talking about personally identifiable information (PII), like name, credit card number, phone number, etc. This information must not be revealed to any entity but those authorized to access the information. This section will describe how privacy and security are managed in IdM.

In this *information age*, it is truer than ever that "knowledge is power" (Bacon 1597). Thus, most service providers try to gather as much information of their users as they can, in order to build accurate profiles of them. This information is usually intended to be used to improve their business opportunities. Example of these opportunities would be personalization of contents, market studies, localized advertisements, data mining… Having a good knowledge of the customers may help the SP to provide a service that is more valuable for the user and, thus, they will not go the competition for alternatives.

However, the information gathered by service providers can also be used for undesirable purposes from the point of view of the user. SPs can use this information to deduce new information that may be beyond the acceptable threshold of the user, to the point that the SP knows more about

the user than the user himself. This usually makes the user uncomfortable. A descriptive example is a supermarket that provides some kind of *affinity card* to their customers. When paying with this card the customer may obtain a discount ticket for future shopping that will be valid under certain circumstances (i.e. only for milk or bread, only for purchases over 40€, only within a small time window…). Thanks to the identification of the customer, the supermarket is able to generate a really accurate shopping profile of their customers, knowing what they purchase, when they go shopping and how much money they usually spend. Moreover, and more importantly, the supermarket can try to drive customers' shopping through the discounts and special offers, with the aim of making them spend more. This situation may become much more uncomfortable to the user when several SPs collude to trace user activities across services. This could lead to a very accurate global profile of the user himself as a person, not only as a customer.

SPs could also use the information gathered for indiscriminate advertisement purposes (i.e. SPAM). Contact information could be used to send non requested offers, brochures, and catalogues from companies or products that are not directly related with the company that the user provided the data to in the first place.

Often, to obtain all this valuable information, SPs request more information about the user than what is strictly required for providing the service. The user has no decision power in this; either he accepts the conditions of the SP and provides the information or he cannot access the service.

Privacy protection stands for the set of mechanisms that allow users to protect themselves against the misuse that an authorized party can perform with the identity information received (profiling, spamming, tracing…). These mechanisms can be implemented in a technical way, that is, by secure protocols, pseudonyms, strong cryptography, etc. or they can be implemented in an implicit way, by means of agreements and contracts. While the first approach prevents damage, the second provides a legal protection to be applied if any damage has been suffered. Usually, the more technical the solution, the more attractive it will be to the user. Users will prefer solutions that avoid problems, instead of those solutions that just solve problems, since they would usually imply legal processes, paperwork and bureaucracy that will result in time lost and additional worries.

Since identity information is so important and sensitive, it must also be protected against potential unauthorized third parties that try to access or somehow modify this information. The most usual threat that may occur is eavesdropping on sensitive information. An attacker may listen to communications between honest participants, waiting until identity information is exchanged. This information can then be used to perform some kind of malicious behaviour, ranging from the more or less innocuous spamming, to the very dangerous impersonation of the user.

Another possible attack occurs when the malicious party not only eavesdrops on the communications but also modifies the data. The intention of this modification could be to insert different values that lead the system to grant privileges to the intruder, thinking that it is an honest agent (i.e. impersonation) or just the introduction of junk data, that leads the system to fail, stopping the user accessing the service normally (i.e. DoS attack).

A different attack may affect the physical systems instead of the communications. If an intruder manages to break into an honest system, it could access all the sensitive identity information stored there, including credentials.

Security stands for the set of mechanisms that allow users to protect themselves against the access or modification that an unauthorized party might perform to the identity information managed by honest participants.

Privacy in Identity Management

Identity management aims to provide users with technical mechanisms for security privacy protection, as well as a formalization of what trust relationships must be established between the parties involved, and which ones must be realized by means of contracts or agreements.

As commented above, one cornerstone of privacy protection in IdM is the minimization of disclosed information. The information that a service provider must know about the user should be the minimum required to provide the service. IdM solutions usually try to solve this by decomposition of the identity information into small pieces of data called *attributes* (as seen above). These attributes can be provided independently to the SP, selecting just those that are relevant for the service. This supposes a difference with how *real-life* identity proofs usually work, where for example if a user needs to prove that he/she is over 18 years old, he/she has to present some kind of identity card that will usually contain more information than the birth year (e.g. it usually discloses information such as nationality, postal address, full name...). Hence, thanks to the ability of discomposing identity information into attributes and the possibility of presenting only those attributes that are relevant, IdM allow users to minimize the amount of information disclosed to service providers.

Though attributes allow users to control the granularity of the information provided, users still require mechanisms that allow them to control which of these attributes are actually provided to service providers. IdM solutions provide two different approaches for this. The first places users in the middle of the IdM architecture (i.e. user-centric approach). Thus, users are asked on each identity information transaction about what attributes can be distributed to the service provider. The pros of this approach are that users have the best control over the process, deciding every time the data to be disclosed. On the other hand, there are some cons to be taken into account. It implies a high involvement of the user in the process, which can be annoying for him/her and may be difficult for understand.

In contrast, the IdP could be placed in the middle of the architecture, with the responsibility of deciding which information can be disclosed to the requesting service providers. In order to control how IdP manage identity information, users define attribute release policies (ARPs) (see above). With these policies users can define which services are allowed to access to which data (i.e. attributes) and under which circumstances. For example, a user may forbid a specific service provider to access his credit card number except to Amazon, which he would be allowed to do. The pros of this approach are the low involvement of the user in the IdM. Users just need to define the initial policies and start using services. Policies can be tuned up later when the user detects that they are too restrictive (the service provider will notify the user when some attributes are not accessible). The downside of this approach is the reduction of the control of the process that the user has. The user has to trust the IdP is going to enforce the defined policies correctly. Additionally, the case when a policy is not restrictive enough is not easily detectable, and may lead to situations when information is disclosed to undesired third parties until detected.

In order to protect the identity of the user, IdM solutions usually establish the creation and distribution of pseudonyms (see above) that refer the user between the IdP and one of the different service providers that make use of the identity information. The use of pseudonyms means that two or more service providers cannot determine if two users that are accessing their services actually correspond to the same identity. This behaviour increases unlinkability and avoids traceability and correlation of information between services.

Pseudonyms can be *transient* or *permanent*. Permanent pseudonyms are generated and established the first time they are required, and they are used until they are explicitly deleted or the associated identity expires. Thus, they are used to identify the user between the IdP and a specific SP for different sessions. This type of pseudonym allows a SP to recognize the same user across sessions and thus, the service can be customized. In contrast, transient pseudonyms are generated within the context of a specific transaction and do not allow the user to be recognised across sessions. This type of pseudonym provides a higher level of privacy (anonymity), at the cost of avoiding local customization of the service.

If IdM is applied just in one network layer (for example, for web applications), privacy could be exposed to some attacks since, even though pseudonyms are used, for the other layers of the network stack there could be static identifiers that somehow identify a concrete user (for example, IP address, MAC address...). For instance, if a service provider receives two connections from two different pseudonyms but from the same IP address, the possibilities that those two pseudonyms correspond to the same identity are really high. Thus, it is important for better privacy protection that IdM is applied following a cross-layer approach, with homogeneity at the different layer of the network stack, especially at application and transport layers.

Regarding security, IdM usually implements mechanisms based on cryptography. For the protection of communications, secure channels (e.g. SSL/TLS (Dierks, 2008)) are usually established between honest participants, including encryption to provide confidentiality (avois eavesdropping) and integrity protection to avoid modification of data and assure its authenticity. For the protection of local information stored on the agents, encryption is usually used to protect against thieving, while integrity protection is used to avoid interested modification of data.

USER-CENTRIC PRIVACY MANAGEMENT IN FUTURE NETWORK INFRASTRUCTURE

The European research project *SWIFT* (SWIFT, 2008) defined a user-centric identity management framework. This framework aims to offer solutions for advanced identity management aspects to service providers and users, with a special focus on user-centric privacy. The work carried out in SWIFT has its continuity in the *INS* (INS, 2010) standardization group of ETSI, which aims to adapt the SWIFT solution to future network infrastructure. (Lopez, 2009) describes the identity management framework of SWIFT, including its main components and usage profiles.

Identity Aggregation

As described above, when services and operators require identity information from the user, and they make use of the IdM infrastructure and queries and the user's IdP for this information. However, it is envisioned that in future network infrastructures this identity information will not be contained in a single IdP. Instead, the information can be spread over different IdPs, each managing a part of the user's identity. Furthermore, these partial identities could overlap, providing different values for the same attribute or providing different credentials to authenticate the user. From the point of view of the user, IdPs can play two different roles. If the IdP manages user's attributes, then it can be referred to as an *Attribute Provider*. On the other hand, if the IdP manages user's credentials it can be denoted as an *Authentication Provider*. A single IdP can play both roles simultaneously if required. Future network infrastructure would require that services and operators can access this information in a distributed but transparent way.

This distributed model requires that an entity is able to link these different and dispersed pieces of information and provide them to the different consumers (i.e. services and operators). This en-

tity is called *Identity Aggregator (IdAgg)*, since it *aggregates* identity information from different sources and builds up a new *virtual identity*.

A virtual identity is a partial identity built up based on existing user's identity information from different providers. A virtual identity does not contain data itself, but references to the original source. Virtual identities are used to access services and operators, which will query the Identity Aggregator to retrieve user information as if it was a regular IdP. The Identity Aggregator would then determine which *Attribute Provider* has the required data and will obtain it to forward to the service provider. Virtual identities are associated also with one or more credentials from *Authentication Provider(AuthNP)*. They will be used to authenticate the user when required. Figure 3 depicts an example of identity aggregation, where user *Alice* has aggregated identity information from three different sources *IdP A*, *IdP B* and *IdP C*.

The inclusion of the Identity Aggregator has a great impact on user experience and usability, as well as on privacy protection. On the one hand, users do not need to remember a lot of identifiers and credentials, just those that are aggregated into their virtual identities. Additionally, they are able to *customize* their identity when accessing services, including or removing attributes at will.

Moreover, the inclusion of Identity Aggregator adds a new indirection level to the architecture. This level increases privacy protection, since at each level pseudonyms are used to protect user's identity. Thus, the amount of knowledge the IdP had on previous architecture is now distributed among the IdAgg, Attribute Providers and Authentication Providers. For example, the IdAgg does not know which identifiers the user has on the Attribute and Authentication Providers. This increases privacy, as the user could have more than one virtual identity aggregating data from the same Attribute Provider account, but the IdAgg will never know. On the other hand, the Attribute Provider does not know which services are used

Figure 3. Identity aggregation

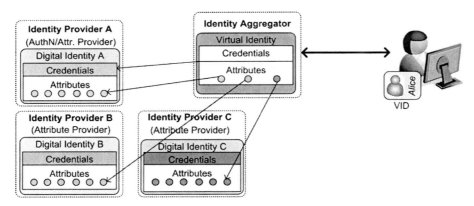

by their users, since this information is managed at IdAgg level.

An alternative model for attribute aggregation and privacy protection is provided by Idemix (Camenisch, 2002). In this solution, users collect a number of credentials from different issuers, each asserting attributes about the principal. Users can create proofs that combine a set of desired attributes from these credentials. Using zero-knowledge proof protocols, users convince consumers (i.e. service providers) that the proof presented is authentic.

End-User Identifiers and Pseudonyms

In the subsection above, the use of different identifiers and pseudonyms to protect end user's privacy has been introduced. The entities in the SWIFT architecture establish a series of permanent and transient pseudonyms to refer to the end user between themselves, so hiding the identifier they are internally using. This serves to avoid correlation between the various providers involved as there is no unique identifier used across them.

Figure 4 depicts the different entities and the identifier they share to refer to the end user.

Identifiers A and B

These identifiers are established between the end user and the Attribute and Authentication Providers before any SWIFT interaction and their management is outside of the scope of SWIFT. These identifiers must never be revealed to other parties.

VID

The VID (Virtual identity IDentifier) is established between the end user and the Identity Aggregator during the creation of a virtual identity and refers to it. It is used by the end user to identify himself to the Identity Aggregator.

Pseudonym (AttrP – IA) and Pseudonym (AuthNP – IA)

These pseudonyms are established during the virtual identity creation process between the specific provider from where the identity information is being aggregated and the Identity Aggregator. These pseudonyms hide internal identifiers (i.e. Identifier A, Identifier B and VID) from external parties.

Figure 4. Different identifiers and pseudonyms of the SWIFT architecture

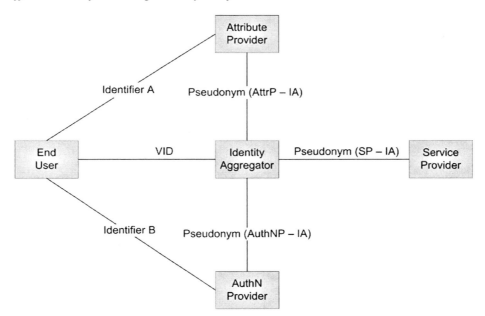

Pseudonym (SP – IA)

This pseudonym is established between a service provider and the Identity Aggregator after a successful end user authentication. It serves to hide the internal permanent identifier (i.e. VID), so avoiding linking of sessions between different SPs, as they would obtain different pseudonyms. If desired by the end user, a SP may obtain different pseudonyms for different application sessions, even if the end user authenticates using the same VID for all of them.

Cross-Layer Identity Management

Current state-of-the-art IdM solutions are mainly focused on the service layer, especially on web services. However, nowadays it is very common that the user has to authenticate to access the network as well, making network connectivity one more service. Network authentication usually requires the use of specific protocols, like 802.1X (P802.1X/D11, 2001), while web service

authentication is performed by HTTP mechanisms and the use of SAML.

This technological difference leads to a gap that avoids users homogeneously using their identities across services provided at different network layers. The user has, then, at least two points of identity management that are unrelated. This obviously leads to usability issues (need to authenticate twice, consistence problems between information from both sources, different privacy policies semantics, etc.). From an operational point of view, IdM functions are replicated at network and service layers, which is completely unnecessary and could be avoided with a cross-layer approach. Hence, future network infrastructure will need to integrate with an IdM system in order to in the first place offering a higher quality experience to end users, and secondly to avoid replication of functionality. If network providers, like any other service provider, can leverage IdM to specialised parties, it would represent a simplification that may help them to put more effort in other aspects of their service. SWIFT defined a cross-layer IdM

Figure 5. Cross-layer identity management and SSO in SWIFT

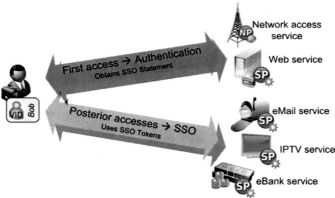

framework that provides a homogeneous IdM API to services no matter what layer they work with.

Once IdM is consistently managed across layers, the second step is to provide single sign on capabilities to the IdM infrastructure in a way that once the user has authenticated the first time (usually, but not necessarily, to access the network service), the results of this authentication can be used to access services within the federation without repeating the process. For example, a user that authenticates in the first place to access the network then should be able to access a mail service without rewriting his/her credentials again. On the other hand, if a user authenticates to access a mail service, he/she should be able to authenticate to access a network service (e.g. hand-over to a UMTS network) without presenting again his/her long-term credentials. Figure 5 shows an example of how cross-layer IdM is performed in SWIFT. On the first access the user *Bob* makes, he is provided with a SSO statement (no matter whether he accessed a web service or the network access service). In the following accesses to services, the SSO statement is used to generate SSO Tokens that are provided to the service providers for authentication.

The use of broadly accepted SSO mechanisms supposes a clear benefit for both users and services. Users are not mandated to write their cre-

dentials again and again, while service overload is at the same time minimized, since re-authentication methods are intended to be much lighter than full authentications.

SWIFT and DAMe (Lopez, 2008) provide cross-layer SSO mechanisms based on SAML assertions. While SWIFT provides a generic solution, that could be instantiated using different protocols and deployments, DAMe is a solution intended to be used on a well-known eduroam environment.

Distributed Policies

Along with user's information, policies play a fundamental role in IdM. They model the expected behaviours of the entities. We are interested in those policies directly involved with user information, that is, attribute release policies and access control policies.

Traditional policy management assumes that the entity that is going to take a decision (usually denoted as PDP) has all the required policies defined in its own domain. In federated environments this may not scale well, since every single organization within the identity federation must have a local copy of the policies. For example, if an organization O_1 would like their users to have limited access to services provided by another

Figure 6. Deductive policy example

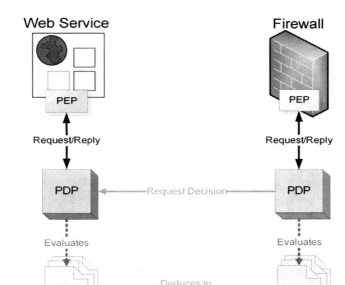

organization O_2, both should agree on the policies that should be defined in O_2 that enforce O_1 preferences. Additionally, O_2 should have access to all the information from O_1 that was required to take the decision. This last requirement may be an inconvenient to organizations that do not wish to disclose internal information about their processes.

Instead, SWIFT defines a distributed and deductive policy framework, which allows distribution of authorization decisions across different domains. The different entities within the federation manage the policies regarding their own domain, but they offer an endpoint for deductive policy decisions. A policy deduction consists of a reference on a local policy that indicates the PDP that, in order to be evaluated, is required to first request a remote decision from a different administrative domain. This solution solves the issues presented in the example above, since O_2 access control policies for O_1's users could include a deduction that refers to an O_1 decision.

To achieve these objectives, the XACML language requires some modifications and extensions as described in (Lischka, 2009), so as to include deductions in the policy structure.

Figure 6 depicts an example scenario where deductive policies are applied. The Firewall Service (O_2) will only allow users to pass through it when they are authorized to access the target Web Service (O_1). To do this, the policies defined in the Firewall service include a reference to the policies in the Web Service. Thus, when a user wants to pass through the firewall, the Web Service's PDP is queried by the Firewall's one to obtain a decision.

Integration with Smart Card Technology

The use of smart card technology can be combined with IdM to provide a higher level of privacy and a better availability of the IdM system (Marx, 2010). The IdP (or Identity Aggregator in the SWIFT architecture) could issue a smart card containing some of the user's credentials and attributes. This way, users can provide service providers with the required identity information, without the interaction with the IdP (or Identity Aggregator) at each access. This improves privacy, since the architecture becomes even more user-centric and the IdP is not involved in the service access process. That is, the IdP does not know which services the user is accessing and thus, even when the IdP has the user information, it does not know how the user is using it.

On the other hand, the IdP is also benefited from this approach. Since each service access process does not involve the IdP, its work load decreases. This would imply a decreased cost for identity providers that could have a positive effect on other areas, if this cost is reinvested in improving the system.

The data included in the card does not need to be a full representation of the user identity and may consist of a subset of the identity information of the user (due to limitations in storage space in the card). This means that a service provider may require an attribute from the user that is not included in the card, and thus not provided by the user. In such a case, the SP will contact the user's IdP to retrieve the remaining information.

User identities are mutable, that is, attributes can be added or removed from an identity. Moreover, attribute values can change (e.g. postal address, phone number...). Hence, this integration of IdM and smart cards requires specific mechanisms to update information stored in the card in a secure way from the IdP (IdAgg). It also requires management of revocation lists and of deprecated information, enabling SPs to verify the reliability of the information received.

Basic Use Cases of the SWIFT Architecture

The bases of the SWIFT architecture are established in five basic use cases that perform the core functionality of the identity management framework. They are the *virtual identity enrol-* *ment, web-based authentication, network-based authentication, single sign on access* and *attribute retrieving.*

This section briefly describes them and provides simplified message flow diagrams to make their behaviour more comprehensible.

Virtual Identity Enrolment

The end user creates a new virtual identity, aggregating authentication credentials from an Authentication Provider, and several attributes from different Attribute Providers. After the process, a new virtual identity is created associated to a VID.

Web-Based Authentication

The end user makes use of one of her virtual identities to get authenticated to access a web service. Through web redirections, the end users end up authenticating with her Authentication Provider and as a result of the process, the SP obtains an *Authentication Statement* that includes a pseudonym to refer to the end user in future interactions with the Identity Aggregator. The end user obtains evidence that will serve as a Single Sign On proof.

Network-Based Authentication

This use case is similar to the web-based one, but in this case the end user desires to get authenticated to access the network. The end user makes use of the same virtual identity as in the web-based authentication (cross-layer authentication). The process is different due to the specific restrictions that the network authentication process imposes, though at the end all the entities obtain the same information as in the web-based use case (i.e. The SP an Authentication Statement and the EU an evidence).

Figure 7. Virtual identity enrolment

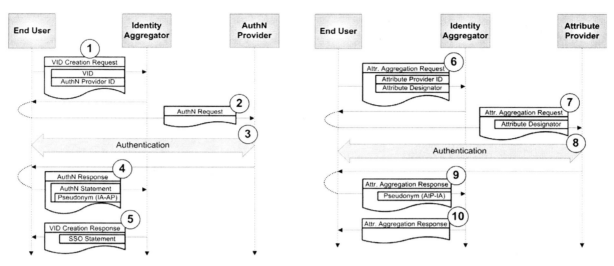

Figure 8. Web-based authentication

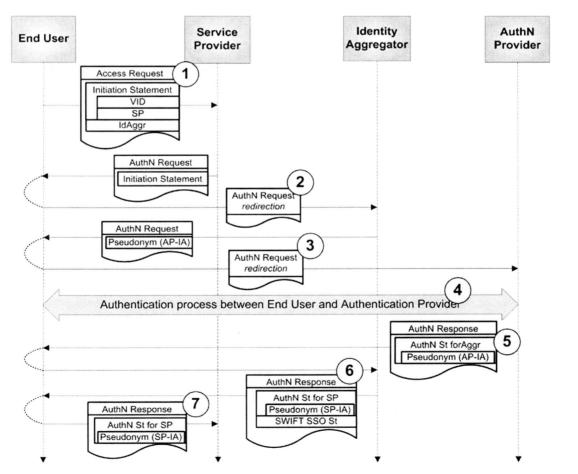

Figure 9. Network-based authentication

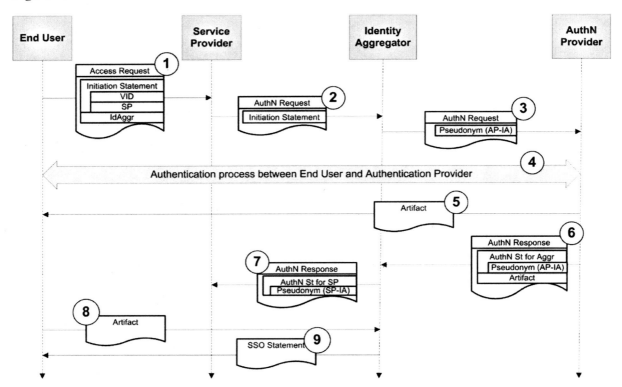

Single Sign On Access

In this use case, the end user already obtained evidence as a result of a previous authentication. Thus, this evidence is provided to the IdAgg as a proof of authentication. This avoids the need to go to the Authentication Provider and perform the whole authentication process again.

Attribute Retrieving

This use case can be executed in any of the authentication or access use cases described above. Once the SP has obtained the Authentication Statement, it can use the provided pseudonym to retrieve further end user's information from the Identity Aggregator. The information will actually be retrieved from their original sources.

INTEGRATION OF IDM IN BUSINESS ENVIRONMENTS

The integration of IdM in business environments opens up new business opportunities to a variety of organizations that can take advantage of the possibilities that IdM brings.

In the first place, IdM provides the required mechanisms to manage identity information in an effective and efficient way within an organization. Instead of spreading all the user information across the different services provided in the organization (as represented in *Figure 12*), IdM allows centralising the storage of this information and the access to it in a distributed way from the different services. The most obvious benefit of this approach is the saving of storage capacity, especially when user profiles contain a high amount of information, though there are other important

Figure 10. Single Sign On access

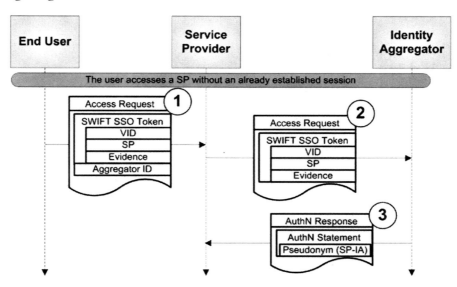

Figure 11. Attribute retrieval

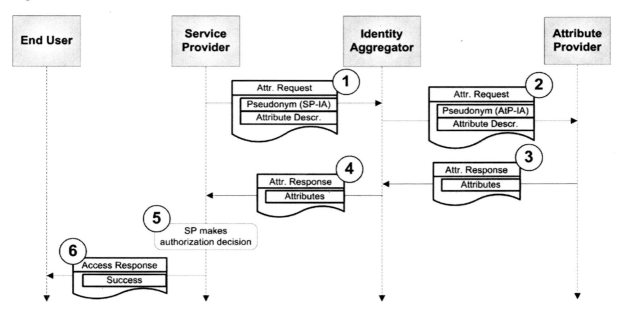

benefits that make the integration of IdM into the organization a good investment.

The protection of private user data becomes easier and more controllable when data storage is centralized. The weakest point of a system determines the whole security level of the system. Thus, if a service managing private data did not

store it properly; complete security of the organization would be compromised. Centralization allows all the effort to be focused on the protection of a single point, making its management simpler and more controllable (e.g. updating encryption keys). Additionally, some countries specify special protection measures that must be

Figure 12. Access to services without IdM

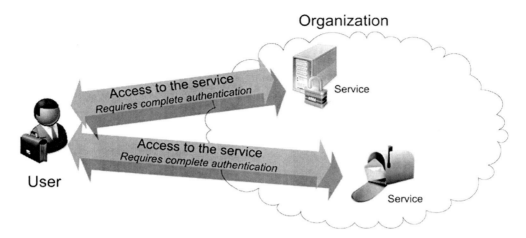

followed when storing certain private user data (like medical records, religion or political affiliations...). Following this centralised approach, this knowledge is not required to be on each server, but with the one that actually stores the data.

The information can be accessed in a distributed way. Services can access identity information by using data query mechanisms (like LDAP or SQL). Again this simplifies maintenance of consistency. When several copies of the same data exist, it is required that mechanisms exist to assure that all these instances are updated consistently when required. If a single copy of such information is managed by the system, there is no need to spend resources on this task.

Furthermore, organizations can delegate not only storage capabilities but also some of their identity management functionality to entities called Identity Providers (IdPs). This allows concentration of all the common IdM functionality required by the services within an organization in one entity - the IdP - so avoiding replication of functionality and simplifying development of new services (developers do not need to worry about IdM functionality). Within the different functionality of IdM, IdPs usually take responsibility for authentication and attribute retrieval, since these

processes are common for all the services. On the contrary, authorization is performed by the services themselves since it depends to a high degree on the service and it does not make much sense to centralise that information. This approach allows easy integration of SSO, since there exists a single point of authentication within the organization. *Figure 13* depicts an example where an organization has deployed an IdP to manage authentication and attribute provisioning for two different services.

Going a step further, organizations can become members of an identity federation, where now the IdP that is responsible for the user authentication and attribute management may not be internal to the organization, but belongs instead to another federation member. Within identity federation some trust relationships are established between the members. These relationships fulfil their requirements in terms of reliability and confidence for the information received from external IdPs.

There exist some business opportunities that are created with this approach. The first one is that business organizations can open their services to a wider range of users (those coming from other organizations within the federation) without an increased cost in resources. All they need to do is to configure their IdM infrastructure to accept

Figure 13. Access to services using IdM within the organization

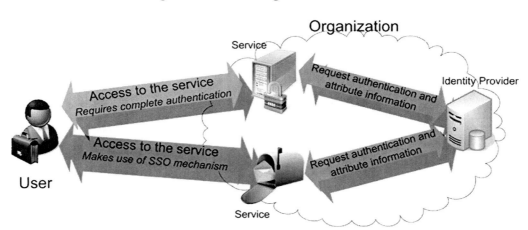

federated users. This obviously is a great opportunity, since the target market for the services is increased.

A second opportunity comes from the possibility that some organizations completely outsource IdM to external IdPs. These organizations do not need to worry about authentication or information storage, since all this functionality is already implemented at the external IdPs. This approach is generally followed by information consuming organizations, for example service providers, which can thus offer their services to the users that belong to an identity federation without having to implement a complete IdM solution. Hence service providers can focus completely on the services they provide, so increasing their quality, interest and value.

Finally, an opportunity appears for those organizations that desire to provide IdM as a service. These organizations are usually primary identity information sources, that is, they have first hand access to some users' information. In general, these organizations have the information due to two main, different, reasons. On the one hand, users themselves have provided it to the organization. The most usual case is when the user has filled out a registration form (e.g. google, flickr, facebook…) or has a formal contract with the orga-

nization (e.g. ISP, TV operators, mobile operators, company where they work…). On the other, the organization has the information because it is the generator of the information (e.g. bank → account number, gmail → list of contacts, telecommunication operator → phone number, government → identity card, etc.). *Figure 14* illustrates an example scenario where two different organizations (Service Provider 1 and Service Provider 2) have their identity management functionality externalized to a third-party IdP. Since from the point of view of the user the authentication point is the same, he/she can benefit from SSO across organizations.

Historically, network operators have required a signed contract with the user. In that contract the user must provide reliable information about himself (full name, postal address, age, nationality, banking information…) along with identity proofs that assert he is who he claims to be (presentation of identity card, manual signature, etc.). Furthermore, network operators have already deployed mechanisms for strong user authentication (e.g. based on SIM card). These preconditions make network operators great candidates for offering IdM services, as they implement strong authentication mechanisms and possess reliable information about the user. They just need to

Figure 14. Access to services using an external IdP

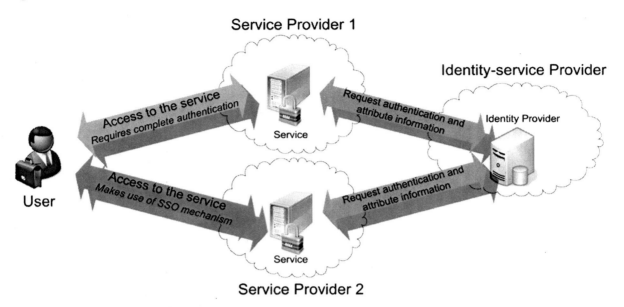

deploy IdPs in their system that will take part of one (or many) identity federation(s). Then, they will be accessible by federation members, acting as intermediaries between the information consumers and the actual information.

When the SWIFT framework is being used, the network operators are perfect candidates to deploy the Identity Aggregator, providing the central point of trust for both, users and services. *Figure 15* illustrates an example scenario where the network operator deploys an Identity Aggregator that acts as an intermediate point between the services and the actual identity providers, providing an additional level for privacy protection, as described earlier.

The implantation of IdM to support privacy in a business organization has a cost, in terms of the deployment of new entities (resource and maintenance costs) and implantation (operational costs). However, the economic benefits envisioned and described above in this subsection make IdM a positive investment for almost any kind of organization, as long as it has a significant

load of identity management functionality implicit in its operations.

Considerations about Disclosed Information

When an organization decides to take part in an identity federation, it agrees to disclose some identity information about its users. This information is usually a subset of the totality of the information the organization manages about its users. In the first place, as described above, a user may restrict the information he/she wants to be disclosed to third parties. Figure 16 shows where attribute release policies will be deployed to provide privacy protection. Selection of which attributes can be disclosed is made by the user from a list of available attributes the organization would accept to disclose. However, this list is not an exhaustive enumeration of the information in the user profile, but a pre-filtered list. Why might an organization want to keep private some data regardimg its users? One reason would be the irrelevancy of some information outside the

Figure 15. Network operator deploys the Identity Aggregator

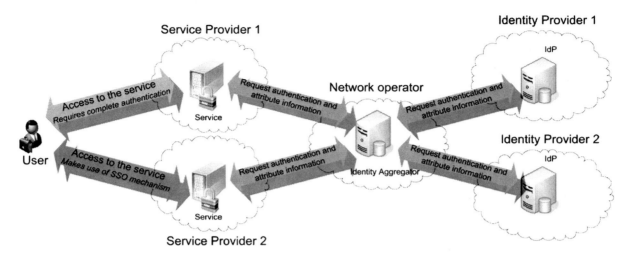

scope of such an organization. For example, the number of emails received in the last two months by a principal is not relevant outside the company. Another reason could be legal issues. Some personal information cannot be provided to third parties under any circumstances.

However, the main reason was given at the beginning of the chapter: the power and value of information. Some of the information that the

organization has about its users may be expensive or difficult to obtain. Once this information is in possession of the organization, it probably may not want to provide this information to other parties so easily. Those parties are potential competitors and the last intention of the organization would be to simplify their task. There is a special relevance here in the profiles generated in an organization after data mining processing. A lot

Figure 16. Policies and their deployment over the infrastructure

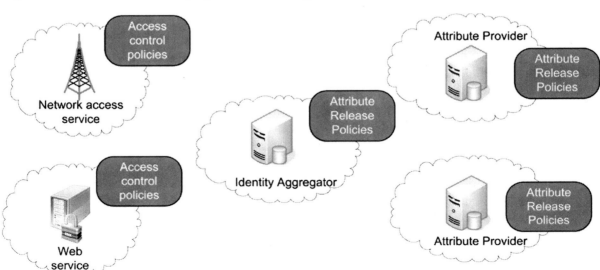

of money, and effort in R&D is usually spent on this kind of processing that converts data (attributes) into valuable information. This information is considered by most organizations as an investment, and they will be unlikely to want to provide it to other organizations.

Even though organizations have the power to decide which set of information they are going to make available to other organizations, it is possible that identity federations include in their requirements a list of minimum information that must be made available by each organization so that interaction is possible. For example, if we think of an education identity federation for universities, minimum information could include *name, home university* and *affiliation*. Hence, visited universities can define their access control policies based on that minimum set, knowing that every user would provide enough information.

Integration of IdM with Legacy Systems

When an organization decides to integrate an IdM system it has to decide if the legacy authentication system will be completely replaced or if some kind of interoperability will be allowed with the new one.

If the organization has few services, it may be simpler to adapt them to accept access requests using the new IdM system. However, if an organization has many services, and they are using a consolidated authentication mechanism already established (e.g. Kerberos, X509 certificates...), then it might not be reasonable to upgrade each single service to support the new IdM system.

To solve this kind of situation and allow a smoother transition from one system to another, SWIFT proposes a security credential bootstrapping mechanism (Gomez-Skarmeta, 2008) that allows a valid credential for the legacy service to be obtained by using the new IdM mechanism. Thus, organization's users can use both the new IdM solution and the legacy alternative to access the services, while users from other organizations within the federation can access through this credential bootstrapping.

Though the security credential bootstrapping mechanism proposed in SWIFT is intended to be used when deploying a SWIFT IdM solution, it provides a generic solution that can be easily adapted to any IdM solution. The solution consists of deploying a new service, called Credential Bootstrapping Service (hereinafter CBS). The CBS requires users to access using IdM authentication mechanisms. Then users are verified to be authorized to obtain credentials for the requested service. If the requesting user is authorized, the CBS will either generate the credential itself (if possible) or request the creation of the credential on behalf of the user (e.g in the case of X509 certificates, it would be requested from the established Certification Authority). Figure 17 depicts the generic interactions that are required to bootstrap a credential based on IdM.

For each kind of credential, it is necessary to define a binding where it is stated how users request these credentials from the CBS (i.e. protocol, data format...) and how they are generated and delivered to the user. Gomez-Skarmeta (2008) provides some example bindings for generating Kerberos tickets and X.509 certificates.

IdM and Network Access

Nowadays, network connectivity is an asset that in the first place must be protected against unauthorized access and in the second must provide accountability. The threats to be avoided are of diverse nature, but most important are unauthorized users making use of the network connectivity of the company for other purposes than organization's objectives, wasting organization's resources and even provoking DoS attacks; and authorized users that perform dishonest actions under the anonymity that a free-for-all connectivity would provide. Hence, it is important for an organization to deploy an IdM system at network layer

Figure 17. Security credential bootstrapping service generic interactions

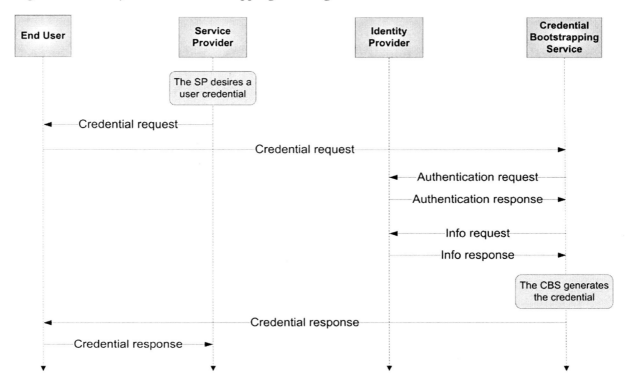

that assures the authentication and authorization of the users.

In a previous section we discussed the importance of establishing a convergence between IdM at network layer and IdM at service layer, and how emerging technologies like SWIFT or DAMe dealt with it. In business environments this convergence provides interesting benefits that should be taken into account when determining the IdM solution to be deployed or the identity federation to be joined.

Users who successfully authenticate at network layer (usually the first authentication that is required) would automatically benefit from either single sign-on or a faster authentication mechanism for subsequent accesses to the services within the organization. This makes IdM more transparent for users that do not need to authenticate twice (for network and for the first service they access).

The extension of the identity federation to the network layer improves mobility of users across organizations within the same identity federation. Users can access the network seamlessly in an authenticated and accountable fashion when they are visiting a different organization (e.g. commercial agents, executive meetings). There is no need for temporal accounts at the visited organizations to provide visitors with connectivity.

Additionally, as network would become just one service more, network providers that are members of the identity federation could provide connectivity to federated users that are authorized by their respective organizations. Nowadays, an organization usually has a pool of corporative hotspot accounts and/or SIM cards that are used by roaming users to connect to the network when they are physically outside the organization. However, having such a pool does not scale, since it has to be large enough to cover high demand periods, while in low demand periods most of them will be unused. Additionally, per-user accountability and accounting is also more difficult. Using the federated approach, an organization could grant a user access to a network provider by just adding an attribute associated to his/her identity. No need of pre-allocated resources is required, so an economical advantage is envisioned.

FUTURE RESEARCH DIRECTIONS

We provide succinctly those issues which in our opinion may become the starting point for new research directions and business models. In particular, we will focus on the following themes.

The Internet of Things

The era of the ubiquitous, the everywhere, anytime and all the time has begun. Devices become smaller, communicate between each other, increase computation and integrate closer to the service. Perhaps they are the service. In all this, managing the associated digital user becomes more important than ever to the point where devices can be shared and the user may not even be aware of their involvement. Privacy is a concern which may well become the deciding factor on how these technologies affect our lives. As part of new business models, objects can be services. In such a case they may need to make use of externalized identity services as a way of reducing their processing and storage requirements, and as a way of becoming accessible to a wider range of users.

Intent Based Communication

Getting connected used to be a cumbersome task. Users would have to ensure they had access to a fixed line, pay their internet provider, dial in, insert passwords and numbers and, many times, repeat the process when it failed. Today getting connectivity can be as simple as noticing a sign on the window that says "Free Wi-Fi", the device will do the rest. Such is the same with many menial tasks associated to the use of services, devices and networks. More and more we see the trend that users want to perform a certain task and not be bothered with the details of how it gets to the laptop, mobile or desktop computer. The service should be there, should be simple and should be consistent amongst devices. Identity management is a core component to achieve this, to identify the user and its preferences, associate the task and allow the services and networks to operate together in an autonomous way to provide the user the desired outcome.

The Future Internet

The Internet was built for devices, nodes, computers, machines. As we evolved this University experiment to what became the fabric of today's digital era, we have lost perspective of us humans. Humans are social beings, they need to communicate, exchange ideas, results; they need to gossip, to be updated on the news of the world, etc. And while the Internet facilitates all that, its nature is still the machine. We argue that people want to talk to people and this should be the true nature of the Internet. Independently of the device, task and service, the user wants to have an easy way to communicate with others. Identity management is paramount to achieve this. The user's digital representation in the digital world must link its actions, its services, its endpoints and its preferences (profile). All this should be available to other providers and users, provided the user allows it to be so. Privacy becomes a concern which guides our design. With all the benefits of having a consistent digital identity, humans need to be able to behave differently depending on the situation and to compartmentalise the different aspects of their being. We propose a path to a Future Internet for the user which elevates and protects the user's digital essence.

Session-Based, Intent-Driven Mobility

A lot work has been done in this area by SWIFT in trying to support the digital identity as a way to provide data for the mobility decision. User preferences may be associated with its profile and provide the means for an informed handover decision. In addition, providing such information in the user profile allows such decisions to be made across devices and to link user actions across platforms. By building on these concepts we can achieve simpler but richer semantics for handover and session establishment. The digital identity acts as the gateway between the services, the devices, the mobility infrastructure and the user profile.

The Cloud

While the word itself means very little, its potential is tremendous. We observe how "cloud" has affected enterprises and telecommunication services, how it impacts web services and the user experience. Without a consistent way to address users, their preferences (including privacy) and authentication, the benefits of "cloud" will be lost. Whether it be SaaS (Software as a Service), PaaS (Platform as a Service) or IaaS (Infrastructure as a Service), this flavour of cloud focuses on the capability for virtualization and distribution of the services in any physical location. In another flavour of "cloud", the services run in the web in cooperation with each other to achieve a richer user experience. It goes without saying that Identity Management can provide the link amongst all these services providing information about the user and protecting its data in a distributed, yet consistent, way.

CONCLUSION

This chapter has described the importance of identity management and how it could be useful for both users and business organizations. Identity management has intrinsically associated the concept of privacy: how is personal information protected? What use is being made with it? How can users control all this without falling into an over-complicated architecture? This chapter has presented these concerns and how identity management mechanisms deal with them.

Next, the reader has been provided with an overview of the work performed within SWIFT regarding the user-centric privacy management in future network infrastructure, including some advanced topics in identity management such as identity aggregation, cross-layer single sign on or distributed policy management.

The chapter continues with an analysis of how identity management can be introduced into organizations, describing the main business opportunities that appear to provide an economical benefit to either the organization that outsources its identity management processes to an external entity and the organization that provides IdM as a service. The chapter concludes that identity management would suppose a good investment for business organizations, which will see how the complexity of their identity management processes are decreased, while deploying new services becomes faster and more secure as access control functionality is centralized. Furthermore, the integration of the organization into an identity federation would open its services to a wider range of clients while, at the same time, the service provided to its own clients would be enriched with the possibility of accessing services from other member organizations.

Additionally, identity management would allow organizations to follow legal directives concerning protection of personal data in an easier and centralized way.

Some considerations must be taken into account when incorporating IdM to the organization. This chapter has analyzed two of the most important ones: what information to disclose to external entities and how to interconnect legacy authentication system with the new IdM solution.

Finally, a brief description of some topics that are interesting for further research has been provided. It is envisioned that these topics will be interesting specially from the point of view of business organizations, as they seem to be in line with the evolution of society and will provide additional business opportunities.

REFERENCES

P802.1X/D11. (2001). *Standard for port based network access control*. LAN MAN Standards Committee of the IEEE Computer Society.

Bacon, F. (1597). *Meditationes Sacræ*. De Hæresibus.

Camenisch, J., & Herreweghen, E. V. (2002). Design and implementation of the idemix anonymous credential system. In V. Atluri (Ed.), *9th ACM Conference on Computer and Communications Security (CCS '02)* (pp. 21-30). New York, NY, USA.

Cantor, S., Kemp, J., Philpott, R., & Maler, E. (2005). *Assertions and protocols for the OASIS security assertion markup language (SAML) V2.0*. Retrieved October 26, 2010, from http://docs.oasis-open.org/security/saml/v2.0 /saml-core-2.0-os.pdf

Dierks, T., & Rescorla, E. (2008). *The transport layer security (TLS) protocol version 1.2*. The Internet Engineering Task Force (IETF) - Network Working Group. Request For Comments (RFC) 5246. Retrieved October 26, 2010, from http://tools.ietf.org/html/rfc5246

Fitzpatrick, B., Recordon, D., Hardt, D., Bufu, J., & Hoyt, J. (2007). *OpenID authentication 2.0 – Final*. Retrieved October 26, 2010, from http://openid.net/specs/openid-authentication-2_0.html

Gomez-Skarmeta, A. F., López, G., Cánovas, O., Pérez, A., Torroglosa, E. M., Gómez, F., et al. (2008). *Identity as a convergence layer*. SWIFT white paper. Retrieved October 26, 2010, from http://www.ist-swift.org/component/option,com_docman/task,doc_download/gid,20/Itemid,37/

INS. (2010). *Identity and access management for networks and services*. Retrieved October 26, 2010, from http://www.etsi.org/website/document/ technologies/leaflets/identity%20and%20access%20management%20for%20networks%20and%20services_2010_02.pdf

Leenes, R., Schallaböck, J., & Hansen, H. (2008). *PRIME white paper*. Retrieved October 26, 2010, from https://www.prime-project.eu/prime_products/whitepaper/PRIME-Whitepaper-V3.pdf

Lischka, M., Endo, Y., & Sanchez, M. (2009, November). *Deductive policies with XACML*. Paper presented at the Workshop on Secure Web Services, co-located with 16th ACM Conference on Computer and Communications Security (CCS-16), Chicago, Illinois, USA.

Lischka, M., Endo, Y., Torroglosa, E., Perez, A., & Gomez-Skarmeta, A. F. (2009, November). *Towards standardization of distributed access control*. Presented at the W3C Workshop on Access Control Application Scenarios, Luxembourg.

Lopez, G., Canovas, O., Gomez-Skarmeta, A. F., & Sanchez, M. (2008). A proposal for extending the eduroam infrastructure with authorization mechanisms. *Computer Standards & Interfaces*, *30*(6), 418–423. doi:10.1016/j.csi.2008.03.010

Lopez, G., Reverte, O. C., Gomez-Skarmeta, A. F., & Girao, J. (2009). A swift take on identity management. *IEEE Computer*, *42*(5), 58–65.

Marx, R., Fhom, H. S., Scheuermann, D., Bayarou, K. M., & Perez, A. (2010). *Increasing security and privacy in user-centric identity management: The IdM card approach.* Presented at the First International Workshop on Securing Information in Distributed Environments and Ubiquitous Systems (SIDEUS 2010), Fukuoka, Japan.

Microsoft Corporation. (2006). *A technical reference for the information card profile V1.0.* Retrieved October 26, 2010, from http://download. microsoft.com/download/ 2/7/c/27c16ebb-bf83-4abd-8002-21fa111ba7ac/infocard-profile-v1-techref.pdf

Reed, D., & Strongin, G. (2004). *The Dataweb: An introduction to XDI.* A White Paper for the OASIS XDI Technical Committee. Retrieved October 26, 2010, from http://www.oasis-open. org/committees/download.php/6434/wd-xdi-intro-white-paper-2004-04-12.pdf

Rissanen, E., Parducci, B., & Lockhart, H. (2010). *eXtensible access control markup language* (XACML) Version 3.0. Retrieved October 26, 2010, from http://docs.oasis-open.org/xacml/3.0/ xacml-3.0-core-spec-cs-01-en.pdf

Scavo, T., & Cantor, S. (2005). *Shibboleth architecture: Technical overview.* Retrieved October 26, 2010, from http://shibboleth.internet2.edu/docs/ draft-mace-shibboleth-tech-overview-latest.pdf

Shelat, A. (2006). *Project Higgins: User-centric identity meta system and privacy.* IBM Research. Retrieved October 26, 2010, from https://www. prime-project.eu/events/standardisation-ws/ slides/Higgins.pdf/download

SWIFT. (2008). *Secure widespread identities for federated telecommunications.* Retrieved October 26, 2010, from http://www.ist-swift.org

Zwingelberg, H., & Storf, K. (2010). *PrimeLife dissemination report V2.* Retrieved October 26, 2010, from http://www.primelife.eu/images/ stories/ deliverables/h3.1.2-primelife_dissemination_report_v2.pdf

ADDITIONAL READING

American National Standard for Information Technology. (2004). *Role-based Access Control.* ANSI INCITS 359-2004

Association, G. S. M. (2007). *White paper on Identity Management Requirements, Issues, and Directions for Mobile Industry.* Retrieved October 26, 2010, from http://www.gsmworld.com/documents/ se4710.pdf

Azevedo, R., Barisch, M., Cleynenbreugel, J., Gómez-Skarmeta, A. F., et al. (2010). SWIFT Evaluation and Impact Report with Outlook on Open Issues. *SWIFT deliverable D208.*

Azevedo, R., Santos, P., Barisch, M., Lutz, D., et al. (2008). Specification of Identity-based Service Architecture with AAA functions. *SWIFT deliverable D402.* Retrieved October 26, 2010, from http:// www.ist-swift.org/component/option,com_docman/task,doc_download/gid,14/Itemid,37/

Azevedo, R., Santos, P., Matos, A., Marques, R., et al. (2010). Final SWIFT architecture. *SWIFT deliverable D207b.*

Barisch, M., Neinert, S., Lischka, M., Girao, J., et al. (2009). Interoperable Information and Data Models. *SWIFT deliverable D206.*

Biskup, J. (2009). *Security in Computing Systems.* New York, NY: Springer.

Canovas, O, Sanchez, M., López, G., Fernandez, L., et al (2007). Deliverable DJ5.3.2 (internal report 2): DAMe Overall Concept Specification. *GN2 JRA5. GEANT 2.*

Chan, K., et al. (2001). COPS Usage for Policy Provisioning (COPS-PR). *The Internet Engineering Task Force (IETF). Request For Comments (RFC) 3084.* Retrieved October 26, 2010, from http://tools.ietf.org/html/rfc3084

Foresti, S. (2011). *Preserving Privacy in Data Outsourcing.* New York, NY: Springer.

Girao, J., Endo, Y., Santos, H., Lischka, M., et al. (2008). First Draft of the Identity-driven Architecture and Identity Framework. *SWIFT deliverable D203*. Retrieved October 26, 2010, from http://www.ist-swift.org/component/option,com_docman/task,doc_download/gid,16/Itemid,37/

Grégoir, S., Scholta, P., Raatz, T., Barisch, M., et al. (2009). SWIFT Mobility Architecture. *SWIFT deliverable D403*.

Hagen, J. M., Sivertsen, T. K., & Rong, C. (2008). Protection against unauthorized access and computer crime in Norwegian enterprises. *Journal of Computer Security.*, *16*(3), 341–366.

International Organization for Standardization. (2006). *ISO/IEC 19785-1:2006 – Information technology – Common Biometric Exchange Formats Framework – Part 1: Data element specification.*

International Organization for Standardization. (2007). *ISO/IEC 19794-1:2006 Information technology – Biometric data interchange formats – Part 1: Framework.*

International Organization for Standardization. (2007). *ISO/IEC 19784-2:2007 – Information technology – Biometric application programming interface – Part 2: Biometric archive function provider interface.*

International Organization for Standardization. (2008). *ISO/IEC WD 24745 Information technology – Biometric template protection.*

International Organization for Standardization. (2008). *ISO/IEC WD 24760 Information Technology – Security Techniques – A Framework for Identity Management.*

International Organization for Standardization. (2008). *ISO/IEC FCD 24761 Information technology – Security techniques – Authentication context for biometrics.*

International Organization for Standardization. (2008). *ISO/IEC WD 29100 Information technology – Security techniques – A privacy framework.*

International Organization for Standardization. (2008). ISO/IEC WD 29101 Information technology – Security techniques – A privacy reference architecture (Under development), March 2008

International Organization for Standardization. (2008). *ISO/IEC WD 29115 Information technology – Security techniques – Entity authentication assurance.*

International Telecommunication Union. (2007). Telecommunication Standardization Sector, Focus Group on Identity Management (FG IdM). *Report on Identity Management Use Cases and Gap Analysis.*

International Telecommunication Union. (2007). Telecommunication Standardization Sector, Focus Group on Identity Management (FG IdM). *Report on Requirements for Global Interoperable Identity Management.*

López, G., Gomez-Skarmeta, A. F., Marín, R., Canovas, O. (2005). A Network Access Control Approach Based on the AAA infrastructure and Authorization Attributes. *Journal of Network and Computer Applications, JNCA*. Elsevier.

Lutz, D., Marx, R., Gruschka, N., Perez, A., et al. (2010). Simulation, Modelling and Prototypes. *SWIFT deliverable D504*.

Marx, R., Azevedo, R., Scholta, P., Lutz, D., et al. (2009). Resource and Name Resolution mechanisms. *SWIFT deliverable D404*.

Marx, R., Barisch, M., Pérez, A., Endo, Y., et al. (2008). Specification of General Identity-centric Security Model that supports user control of privacy. *SWIFT deliverable D302*. Retrieved October 26, 2010, from http://www.ist-swift.org/component/option,com_docman/task,doc_download/gid,17/Itemid,37/

Marx, R., Lischka, M., Torroglosa, E., Lutz, D., et al. (2009). Prototype Specification. *SWIFT deliverable D503*.

Matos, A., Ferreira, R., Girao, J., Lischka, M., et al. (2008). Gap Analysis and Architecture Requirements. *SWIFT deliverable D202*. Retrieved October 26, 2010, from http://www.ist-swift.org/component/option,com_docman/task,doc_download/gid,10/Itemid,37/

Matos, A., Ferreira, R., Lischka, M., Pashalidis, A., et al. (2008). Identifiers and Name Resolution Namespaces, Discovery and Federation. *SWIFT deliverable D204*. Retrieved October 26, 2010, from http://www.ist-swift.org/component/option,com_docman/task,doc_download/gid,13/Itemid,37/

Perez, A., Torroglosa, E., López, G., Gómez-Skarmeta, A. F., et al. (2010). Final SWIFT architecture. *SWIFT deliverable D207a*.

Rajasekaran, H., Girao, J., Perez, A., Torroglosa, E., et al. (2010). Final SWIFT architecture. *SWIFT deliverable D207*.

3rd Generation Partnership Project. (2005). *3GPP TR 23.941: 3GPP Generic User Profile (GUP); Stage 2; Data Description Method (DDM) v6.0.0*.

3rd Generation Partnership Project. (2007). *3GPP TR 32.808, Telecommunication management; Study of Common Profile Storage (CPS) Framework of User Data for network services and management v8.0.0*.

3rd Generation Partnership Project. (2007). *3GPP TS 23.016: Subscriber data management; Stage 2 v7.0.0*.

3rd Generation Partnership Project. (2007). *3GPP TS 23.240: 3GPP Generic User Profile (GUP) requirements; Architecture (Stage 2) v7.0.0*.

3rd Generation Partnership Project. (2007). *3GPP TS 29.240: 3GPP Generic User Profile (GUP); Stage 3; Network v7.0.0*.

3rd Generation Partnership Project. (2007). *3GPP TS 32.140, Telecommunication management; Subscription Management (SuM) requirements v7.0.0*.

3rd Generation Partnership Project. (2007). *3GPP TS 32.171, Telecommunication management; Subscription Management (SuM) Network Resource Model (NRM) Integration Reference Point (IRP): Requirements v7.0.0*.

3rd Generation Partnership Project. (2007). *3GPP TS 32.175, Telecommunication management; Subscription Management (SuM) Network Resource Model (NRM) Integration Reference Point (IRP): eXtensible Markup Language (XML) v8.0.0*.

3rd Generation Partnership Project. (2007). *Generic Authentication Architecture (GAA); Support for subscriber certificates v7.1.0*.

3rd Generation Partnership Project. (2008). *3GPP TS 33.220, Generic Authentication Architecture (GAA); Generic bootstrapping architecture v8.3.0*.

3rd Generation Partnership Project. (2008). *3GPP TS 33.222, Generic Authentication Architecture (GAA); Access to network application functions using Hypertext Transfer Protocol over Transport Layer Security (HTTPS) v8.0.0*.

Scheuermann, D., Fhom, H. S., Pérez, A., Torroglosa, E., et al. (2009). Specification of Identity-centric Security Modules and Cross-layer Interfaces. *SWIFT deliverable D303*.

Torroglosa, E., Foth, G., Marx, R., Marques, R., et al. (2010). Refined SWIFT Scenarios, Use Cases and Business Models. *SWIFT deliverable D505*.

Torroglosa, E., Foth, G., Scholta, P., Steigerwald, W., et al. (2008). SWIFT Scenarios, Use Cases and Business Models. *SWIFT deliverable D502*. Retrieved October 26, 2010, from http://www.ist-swift.org/component/option,com_docman/task,doc_download/gid,15/Itemid,37/

KEY TERMS AND DEFINITIONS

Aggregation: Set of information coming from different sources that correspond to a unique principal.

Anonymity: Entities' ability to hide any kind of personally identifiable information (PII) from specific parties, in order to prevent to be identified.

Business: Activity involving financial, commercial and industrial aspects performed to produce a economical benefit.

Identity: Set of information that represents specific characteristics of a principal that, usually, identifies univocally that principal.

Management: Activity of controlling the direction of something, usually with concrete objectives.

Privacy: Entities' ability to hide part of their identity information from specific parties, in order to prevent it to be disclosed to them.

Security: Only the authorized parties can obtain and manipulate the data exchanged between them.

Chapter 3
Leveraging Access Control for Privacy Protection:
A Survey

Anna Antonakopoulou
National Technical University of Athens, Greece

Georgios V. Lioudakis
National Technical University of Athens, Greece

Fotios Gogoulos
National Technical University of Athens, Greece

Dimitra I. Kaklamani
National Technical University of Athens, Greece

Iakovos S. Venieris
National Technical University of Athens, Greece

ABSTRACT

Modern business environments amass and exchange a great deal of sensitive information about their employees, customers, products, et cetera, acknowledging privacy to be not only a business but also an ethical and legal requirement. Any privacy violation certainly includes some access to personal information and, intuitively, access control constitutes a fundamental aspect of privacy protection. In that respect, many organizations use security policies to control access to sensitive resources and the employed security models must provide means to handle flexible and dynamic requirements. Consequently, the definition of an expressive privacy-aware access control model constitutes a crucial issue. Among the technologies proposed, there are various access control models incorporating features designed to enforce privacy protection policies, taking mainly into account the purpose of the access, privacy obligations, as well as other contextual constraints, aiming at the accomplishment of the privacy protection requirements. This chapter studies these models, along with the aforementioned features.

DOI: 10.4018/978-1-61350-501-4.ch003

INTRODUCTION

The recent technological advances in the data processing and communication capabilities of information technology spur an information revolution that brings significant improvements to the citizens' quality of life and new potentials for business organizations, including operational efficiency, increased quality of products and services, as well as capabilities for innovation. On the other hand, they pose serious risks on privacy, meaning the *"claim of individuals, groups, or institutions to determine for themselves when, how, and to what extent information about them is communicated to others"* (Westin, 1967); the personal data collection scale is augmented, information access, processing, aggregation, combination and linking are facilitated, new types of data are collected and the service provision chain is becoming complex, involving multiple actors exchanging and sharing data. More than a century after the seminal essay identifying that privacy as a fundamental human right was endangered by technological advances (Warren & Brandeis, 1890), citizens have never before in history been so concerned about their personal privacy and the threats posed by emerging technologies (Gallup Organization, 2008).

On the other hand, the protection of privacy has evolved to a salient issue and a business requirement also for organizations that constitute personal data collectors and processors. As trust is spotlighted at the core of social order, the adoption and consumption of their products and services is determined by the perception of risk and benefit on behalf of the potential users. Hence, from the organizations' point of view, the recognition of the importance of privacy protection is motivated by the business losses due to privacy violations and mishaps that support users' mistrust: economy faces setbacks because of the risks to privacy (Acquisti, 2010). Moreover, the privacy domain is a legislated area (Solove, 2006); several countries, e.g., Canada and the members of the European Union, have adopted data protection laws, which generally reflect the fundamental principles, set forth by the Organization for Economic Co-operation and Development in its milestone guidelines (OECD, 1980). Therefore, regulatory compliance and the potential of sanctions constitute the primary reasons to motivate businesses for the adoption of fair business practices with respect to personal information management.

In order for business organizations to engender trust to their customers, as well as to achieve compliance with the privacy legislation, they adopt data management practices that are reflected by privacy policies. Recently, several frameworks have emerged for the formalization of privacy policies specification, while programs of "privacy seals" are frequently joined as confidence-building measures. Nevertheless, privacy policies and seals by themselves are not effective from an operational point of view; a critical challenge concerns the automation of their enforcement or, in other words, their realization by technical means and their integration with the underlying Information and Telecommunication Technology (ICT) systems.

One of the most important technologies enabling the enforcement of fair data practices is access control. In fact, what any privacy violation certainly includes is some access to personal data and, intuitively, access control constitutes a fundamental aspect of privacy protection. Traditional access control models, such as the Discretionary Access Control (DAC) (NCSC, 1987), the Mandatory Access Control (MAC) (Pfleeger, 1997) and the Role-Based Access Control (RBAC) (Ferraiolo et al., 2001; Sandhu et al., 1996) fail to meet the requirements stemming from the fundamental privacy principles (OECD, 1980) that demand the incorporation of different criteria in access control decisions, rather than just *which user*, having *which role*, is performing *which action* on which *data object*. In that respect, the development of access control models specifically tailored towards privacy protection has been the focus of intense research in the last few years.

This trend usually referred to as "privacy-aware access control", typically concerns the enhancement of traditional approaches, in addition with other technologies that have started being applied in access control that are or should be leveraged in combination with privacy-awareness, in order to make access control policies more effective; these include contextual parameters as part of the decision making process, as well as the use of semantic technologies for enhanced expressiveness and reasoning capabilities.

The rest of this chapter is organized as follows: the next section provides some background information, concerning on the one hand the fundamental principles of privacy, as it stems from the legislation, and, on the other hand, some important technical aspects of access control that are either derived from the privacy principles or have been broadly acknowledged as security practices. The chapter then delves into the literature and provides an overview of the most important, characteristic and influential models. Before concluding with a short overview of the current and future research directions, the chapter provides a comparative study of the access control models.

BACKGROUND

Overview of the Legal and Regulatory Framework

The design of a business system or service cannot be considered as a purely technical activity, as it clearly has a considerable societal impact in terms of its implications on personal data protection and the right to privacy. Moreover, public policy and regulatory requirements do significantly affect the technical requirements of such a system. Therefore, the provision of an overview of the underlying principles is deemed necessary. From a philosophical perspective, the notion of privacy has broad historical roots; for instance, consider Aristotle's distinction between the public sphere

Figure 1. OECD privacy principles

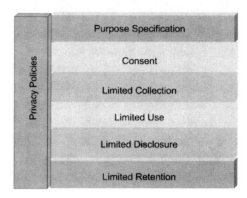

of political activity and the private sphere associated with domestic life, or the Hippocratic Oath, the seminal document on the ethics of medical practice that explicitly included privacy among the medical morals. Nowadays, privacy is recognized as a fundamental human right by the Universal Declaration of Human Rights of the United Nations (1948) and is protected by relevant legislation in all the democratic countries throughout the world.

The first data protection act, adopted in 1970 by the West Germany state of Hesse, set in motion a trend towards adopting privacy legislation. A significant milestone in the privacy literature has been the codification of the fundamental privacy principles (Figure 1) by the Organization for Economic Co-operation and Development (OECD), as this codification lays out the basis for the protection of privacy. The OECD principles are reflected in the European Directive 95/46/EC (European Parliament and Council, 1995), *"on the protection of individuals with regard to the processing of personal data and on the free movement of such data"*. The Directive 95/46/EC enforces a high standard of data protection and constitutes the most influential piece of privacy legislation worldwide, affecting many countries outside Europe in enacting similar laws.

Under Article 2, the Directive 95/46/EC defines personal data as "*any information relating to an identified or identifiable natural person ('data subject'); an identifiable person is one who can be identified, directly or indirectly, in particular by reference to an identification number or to one or more factors specific to his physical, physiological, mental, economic, cultural or social identity*". This definition stresses on the explicit reference to indirect identification data, implying any information that may lead to the identification of the data subject through association with other available information (thus indirectly), that may be held by any third party. The Directive 95/46 EC is further particularized and complemented by other Directives and Decisions; for instance, with reference to the electronic communication sector the Directive 2002/58/EC (European Parliament and Council, 2002) imposes explicit obligations and sets specific limits on the processing of users' personal data by network and service providers in order to protect the privacy of the users of communications services and networks.

In the following, the fundamental legal and regulatory principles and requirements are summarized. The focus is on the legislation of the European Union, since it comprises the most representative, influential and mature approach worldwide, that seems to pull a general framework and has been characterized as an "engine of a global regime" (Birnhack, 2008). For some insights in the frameworks of the U.S. and other countries, the reader is referred to Solove's excellent essay (Solove, 2006).

The legal and regulatory requirements (OECD, 1980; European Parliament and Council, 1995; European Parliament and Council, 2002; Lioudakis et al., 2010) that should be taken under consideration for privacy protection in business environments can be summarized as follows:

- *Lawfulness of the data processing*: The business systems/services should be able to

examine whether the data processing complies with applicable laws and regulations.

- *Purposes for which data are processed*: The business systems/services should provide the means for identifying the data processing purposes, which must be lawful and made explicit to the data subject. Moreover, they should be able to check these purposes to avoid that data processed for a purpose may be further processed for purposes that are incompatible with these for which data have been collected.

- *Necessity, adequacy and proportionality of the data processed*: The business systems/services should be able to guarantee that only the data that are functional, necessary, relevant, proportionate and not excessive with regard to the sought processing purpose are processed.

- *Quality of the data processed*: The business systems/services should provide that the data processed are correct, exact and updated. Inaccurate data must be deleted or rectified; outdated data must be deleted or updated.

- *Identifiable data*: The business systems/services should provide the means for keeping the data processed in an identifiable form only for the time necessary to achieve the sought processing purpose.

- *Notification and other authorizations from competent Privacy Authority*: The business systems/services should be able to monitor compliance with the notification requirement (e.g., Articles 18-21, (European Parliament and Council, 1995)) and with the provisions on the authorizations of competent Privacy Authority. Moreover, the systems/services should provide for means that allow communications between the systems/services and the competent Privacy Authority.

- *Information to the data subjects*: The business systems/services should be able to provide for informing the data subject that the data are processed according to applicable data protection legislation.

- *Consent and withdrawal of consent*: The business systems/services should guarantee that when requested by applicable data protection legislation, the data subject's consent to the data processing is required, and that the data processing is performed according to the preferences expressed by the data subject. Further, withdrawal of consent and an objection to data processing by the data subject should be handled appropriately.

- *Exercising rights of the data subject*: The business systems/services should enable the data subject to exercise the rights acknowledged by applicable data protection legislation in relation to intervention in the data processing (for example the right to access data, to ask for data rectification, erasure, blocking, the right to object the data processing, etc.).

- *Data security and confidentiality*: The business systems/services should be secure in order to guarantee the confidentiality, integrity, and availability of the data processed. Moreover, the systems/services should provide that the listening, tapping, storage or other kinds of interception or surveillance of communications and the related traffic data may be performed only with the data subject's consent or when allowed by applicable legislation for public interest purposes.

- *Traffic data and location data other than traffic data; special categories of data*: The business systems/services should be able to guarantee that the processing of special categories of data (for example traffic or other location data, sensitive and judicial data) is performed in compliance with the specific requirements that the applicable data protection legislation sets forth for said categories of data.

- *Access limitation*: The business systems/services should provide for an authorization procedure that entails differentiated levels of access to the data and also for recording the accesses to the data.

- *Data storage*: The business systems/services should be able to automatically delete (or make anonymous) the data when the pursued processing purpose is reached or in case of elapse of the data retention periods specified under applicable legislation.

- *Dissemination of data to third parties*: When components of the service logic are outsourced to third party providers and, in this context, personal data are disseminated for being processed, the business systems/services should be able to provide certain guarantees that the consequent processing of information complies with the underlying fair data practices and the contract with the data subject.

- *Transfer of data to third countries*: The data dissemination principle described above applies especially when data are transferred to third countries, possibly with essentially different legislation regarding personal data collection and processing. The business systems/services should be able to provide for compliance with the specific provisions ruling on transfer of data. For instance, consider the Safe Harbour Principles regulating data transfer between the European Union and the USA (European Commission, 2000).

- *Supervision and sanctions*: The competent Privacy Authority should be provided with the means for supervising and controlling all actions of personal data collection and processing.

- *Lawful interception*: The competent Privacy Authority should be provided with the means to perform interception only when this is allowed by applicable laws and regulations and according to the conditions therein set forth. The necessary "hooks" for the lawful interception should under no circumstance become available to other unauthorized third parties.

Privacy Enforcement Issues and Requirements

The enforcement of privacy policies for personal data stored by enterprises constitutes a key issue. Personal data modeling along with privacy policies specification and deployment are closely correlated with this issue. As it is already mentioned, current privacy laws require dealing with: limited collection of data; limited use of data; limited disclosure of data; limited retention of data. In this respect, privacy policies should be complex enough to impose several conditions and constraints, dictated by data subjects and legislation, on which personal data can actually be accessed, given a specific context. They must keep into account aspects such as the stated purposes for which these data have been collected, consent given by data subjects, notifications, intents of data requestors as well as other complementary actions. In traditional approaches to privacy enforcement, modified queries of data including constraints based on data subjects' consent and the filtering of data could have been embedded in applications and services: this would work in case of static environments that are not subject to changes. However, in the real world the situation is much more complex, especially for medium-large enterprises that need to run thousands of applications and services, have many customers and need to cope with ever changing business and legal needs.

Consequently, the enforcement of privacy policies must ensure that: the requestor's intent is consistent with the specified data purposes; data subjects' consent is kept into account and enforced along with preferences and constraints.

All these aspects have access control implications. We argue that traditional access control systems are necessary but not sufficient to enforce privacy policies on personal data. Important issues are how to consider all these additional elements and build "privacy extensions" of traditional access control systems to move towards privacy-aware access control systems (Figure 2).

The access control models that will be presented in the next sections provide the most representative and comprehensive frameworks for specification, administering and enforcing both traditional access control and privacy policies exploiting the benefits of the RBAC. The employment of RBAC helps organizations to manage securely the increasingly large numbers of users. It maps intuitively to the way business roles and responsibilities are managed, and therefore it is easy to understand and use. Businesses can group individual users into assigned groups that map their job responsibilities or common security privileges and therefore manage limited numbers in groups as opposed to managing hundreds to millions of individual users. In turn, businesses can pass these roles and security policies to delegated administrators within the company or to their partner organizations, which can efficiently control and manage their own groups of users. Furthermore, RBAC is highly flexible and can have many variants with sophisticated features (e.g. role hierarchies, dynamic separate of duty constraints), making it possible to meet more complex business needs. As a result, users gain access to only that information they need to fulfill their responsibilities, in order for the privacy of data to be protected.

ACCESS CONTROL MECHANISMS

This section provides an overview of the studied models along with each model's specific characteristics concerning privacy oriented aspects as well as the most important non-trivial features

Figure 2. Privacy enforcement

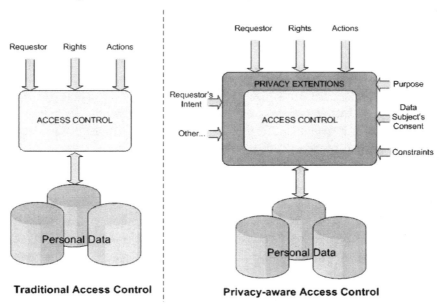

that are met in the state-of-the-art access control models. Each of the following described models is based on RBAC providing well defined privacy-preserving access control mechanisms. However, all these approaches in their perspective to fill specific scientific gaps have their strong points as well as certain limitations. In that respect, a comparative study between the models regarding their features and the importance of their contribution in the field of privacy-aware access control is provided, as a reference for further investigation and research in order for more comprehensive solutions to be specified.

Access Control Aspects and Features

"The machine is the problem: the solution is in the machine" according to Poullet (2006) and, following this principle, business systems and services should be built in order to meet certain

technical challenges that stem from the legal and regulatory requirements as outlined above.

The Concept of "Purpose"

A very important requirement derived from the fundamental privacy principles is that of purpose specification and binding; any collection and/or processing of data should take place for a well-specified purpose, explicitly communicated to the data subject, while personal data collected for some specific and legitimate purposes should not be used for other purposes, incompatible with those for which they have been originally collected. The concept of purpose is present in approaches for privacy policies specification, such as the Platform for Privacy Preferences (P3P) (World Wide Web Consortium, 2006), and it constitutes the baseline common denominator of all privacy-aware access control models. In fact, the incorporation of purpose in the access control decision making processes in Hippocratic Databases (Agrawal et al., 2002; LeFevre et al., 2004) has spotlighted the emergence of privacy-aware access control technologies.

Obligations

In several cases, access to the data must be complemented by the execution of certain actions, which are often referred to in the literature as "obligations" (Hilty, Basin & Pretschner, 2005). For instance, the legislation specifies interactions with the data subject (e.g., information or provision of consent) and the Privacy Authorities, etc. Therefore, access control systems are often empowered with functionalities that enable the execution of obligations; especially as far as privacy is concerned, the term "privacy obligations" (Casassa Mont, 2004) has emerged and characterizes a variety of models.

Some obligations must be fulfilled in a specific time interval. In this context, they are divided in two categories: the *pre-obligations* that concern actions that should be fulfilled before access permission and the *post-obligations* that refer to complementary actions that should be accomplished after a permitted access in order for the request to be fulfilled. In addition, there are cases where an obligation is conditional, depending on constraints, or on the execution of other obligations. In fact, something that should not be neglected is that obligations are actions and, therefore, to fulfill an obligation some privileges are required as well. If the privileges needed are not available, such an obligation is not fulfillable. The problem can become more complex because policies related to these privileges may further require execution of other obligations. Therefore, techniques used for analyzing the interactions between obligations and policies should be devised in order to detect invalid policies due to unfulfillable obligations.

Separation of Duty

Separation of duty (SoD) is an important security principle used for prevention of fraud and errors. It is used to describe and enforce conflict of interest policies, requiring that two or more different users be responsible for the completion of a task or set of related tasks. The purpose of SoD in RBAC is "to ensure that failures of omission or commission within an organization are caused only as a result of collusion among individuals".

The simplest form of the SoD principle states that, if a sensitive task consists of two steps, then different users should perform different steps. Generally, when a sensitive task consists of j steps, a SoD policy requires the cooperation of at least i (for some $i \leq j$) different users to complete the task. A SoD policy may be enforced either statically or dynamically. In static enforcement, Static SoD (SSoD) policies are specified. SSoD enforces constraints on the assignment of users to roles. Each SSoD policy states that no $k - 1$ users together have all permissions to complete a sensitive task. It seems that if an SSoD policy is satisfied, then the corresponding SoD policy is also satisfied. Dynamic SoD (DSoD) allows a user to be authorized for two or more roles that do not create a conflict of interest when acted independently, but produce policy concerns when activated simultaneously. DSoD relations, like SSoD relations, are intended to limit the permissions that are available to a user.

Conflict Resolution

A crucial aspect of policy specification in access control is to ensure that a policy is not conflicted with other existing policies. A validation approach should be used to detect the conflicts between security policies (Charalambides et al., 2006). Possible conflict situations in an access control model are caused for example due to inclusion of a specific policy entity set (subject, action, object) in more than one entity sets or in situations that there are conflicting sub-interval relations between authorization rules as well as inconsistencies between purposes, contextual conditions and/or obligations. For example, one rule may *"allow a subject (s) access to an object (o), while a second rule may deny group (g), of which s is a member, access to o"*. Since it is not possible to generate all system states, there is no guarantee to detect all conflicts of policies. Therefore, a conflict resolution mechanism is required for resolving the identified conflicts systematically. In general, the conflict resolution method is the algorithm that an access control system uses for determining which rule, of a set of rules in conflict, will take precedence over others.

Hierarchies

Hierarchies have been employed for propagation of authorization decision in the majority of access control models and constitute an important concern in privacy-preserving models. In that respect, role, data, purpose and conditions hierarchies are usually specified. Role hierarchies are used to reflect the structure of roles in an organization's lines of authority and responsibility. They enable the assignment of roles to individual organizations, which allows the roles to be customized to fit the needs of each organization. To ensure the highest levels of security, delegated administrators can grant access to only those privileges that they themselves have been granted. The top-down hierarchy creates a secure, efficient model for organizations to modify roles to meet their needs without circumventing the limitations of their access.

On the other hand, purposes mentioned in privacy policies constitute often high-level business services, e.g. "network measuring". This poses the requirement that more specific privacy permissions may deal with more specific purposes that fall under the domain of a high-level purpose. In that respect, in common business environments, purposes naturally should have some hierarchi-

cal relationships among them, i.e., generalization and specialization relationships in order for their management to be simplified. Usually they are represented as trees. A parent node represents a more general purpose than those represented by its children nodes grouping of more particular purposes into more general ones.

On the other side, data objects referred to in privacy permissions are often high-level classifications of data, such as customer contact information. These data objects are used to distinguish classifications of collected data that need to be treated differently from a privacy point of view. Organizing the high level data according to a hierarchy, usually in a tree structure, not only directly models common data organizations, but also improves the expressiveness of permissions. For example, a permission referring to a high-level data applies to all its parts, thus reducing the total number of permissions.

Finally, for the same reasons hierarchies are also important in the field of contextual information. In that respect, many access control models adopt this approach and all the different conditional constraints related with time, location as well as history may be organized in hierarchies in order for complex access control policies to be enforced and managed in an effective and flexible way.

CONTEXT-AWARENESS

Context is an elusive concept, referring to all kind of information describing a specific situation. Context includes static environmental characteristics like a person's position to an organization, as well as dynamic attributes like time of a data request, location from where a request takes place, etc. Contextual parameters, concerning the subject, object or action of an access control request, usually affect the activation of a role, or the enforcement of a rule. The most important parameters regarding context-awareness in access control are the temporal, spatial and history-based ones as well as their combination.

With temporal contexts, it should be possible to express that an action made by a user on a specific object is authorized only at a given time or during a given time interval. Temporal context is expressed by means of temporal constraints, which are statements of access control policies that involve time-based restrictions on access to resources. Temporal constraints may also be required to limit resource use or for controlling time-sensitive activities. These constraints must be dynamically evaluated in order to conclude in an authorization decision. Temporal constraints may also be required in static environments as well. For example it is possible that there are temporal constraints that limit role enabling and activation only to specific time intervals. Using the basic temporal contexts, more complex temporal contexts can be defined. On the other hand, the history-based context depends on previous actions the subject has performed in the system. In that respect, some access control policies related to temporal constraints constitute the history-based access control policies. In these policies, previous access events are used as one of the decision factors for the next access authorization. This poses the requirement that a historical system state control for tracking and maintaining of past access events is necessary.

Furthermore, the location from where the user makes the request can be useful in order to specify the access control policy. For example a CEO may be granted the right to read all employees' salaries only if he is located in his own office inside the organization. Spatial context is used to express these conditions and it could be distinguished in two different types: the physical and the logical. The first one corresponds to the physical location of the user, namely his office or a specific building, etc. The latter corresponds to the "logical location" referring for example to the computer machine or the network, etc. In some cases, physical and logical spatial contexts are highly correlated. The user's network IP address probably is related with a specific physical place such as a department inside an organization.

A Spatially Aware RBAC (GEO-RBAC)

GEO-RBAC model (Bertino et al., 2005) extends the RBAC model with a complete specification of spatial constraints. A geometric model for the representation of objects, user positions and roles assignment is used. Geometries in the model are related with different types of topological relations which can be binary and mutually exclusive. The notions of spatial objects, roles and permissions are extended by inheritance features represented by partial order relationships. Regarding the location it incorporates specification for both real and logical positions. Logical positions are modeled as constants and are computed by real positions through specific mapping functions. With respect to privacy, the coarse location is introduced in order to hide the actual position of a user.

Generalized Temporal Role Based Access Control (GTRBAC)

The GTRBAC (Joshi et al., 2005) model contains significant characteristics that are related to privacy aspects. The model constitutes an extension of RBAC that supports temporal authorizations in an efficient and completed way. It also includes the concepts of DSoD and SSoD as well as constraints related with spatial context. The main feature of the model is the distinction between the notions of role enabling and role activation specifying the state of a role. Temporal constraints are divided in six categories in order for the model to take into consideration all the relevant possible situations and dynamic context-aware access control requirements of an enterprise. In particular, the model allows expressing periodic, as well as duration, constraints on role enabling, user-role assignments, and role-permission assignments.

In an interval, activation of a role can further be restricted as a result of numerous activation constraints including cardinality constraints and maximum active duration constraints. It also supports run-time events, trigger expressions and role hierarchies. Furthermore, the model provides a conflict resolution mechanism regarding all the possible detected types of conflicts.

An XML-Based Policy Specification Framework and Architecture for Enterprise-Wide Access Control (X-GTRBAC)

The X-GTRBAC system (Bhatti et al., 2005) is based on the GTRBAC model and incorporates all its characteristics enriched by an XML-based ((World Wide Web Consortium, 2006) policy specification language. It constitutes a complete Java implemented framework. The framework supports all the context-aware dynamic access control requirements of a modern business environment and its development is motivated by the heterogeneity of the collaborative entities in a distributed enterprise environment. In that respect, the use of XML provides the necessary flexibility and interoperability features regarding the access control enforcement mechanism in such kind of environments due to the ease of its syntax and semantics' extension. Therefore, it provides all the implementation aspects regarding the temporal constraints of the GTRBAC model enriched by an attribute-based credential and constraint specification framework. The term attribute-based credential refers to the users grouping based on their credentials and the enforcement of a common set of attribute-value pairs for each group. The information related with the credentials concerns the role assignment for each user group.

An Extended RBAC Profile of XACML (RBAC FOR XACML)

This extended profile (Haidar et al., 2006) is based on RBAC and can be easily integrated with other access control models due to the fact that it incorporates all the XACML's expressive power with additional characteristics related to context-aware aspects. Unlike the common approach of the correlation of the context with the roles that the majority of the proposed access control models adopt, this model relates all context information with the security rules. With respect to context information specification, the framework adopts the OrBAC model's approach, presented in the following section, and is able to express all kind of context (temporal, spatial and historical). In that respect, the profile extends the XACML engine with the Enablement Authorities notion which refers to assignment policy sets concerning role, view, activity and context assignment policies. Each Enablement Authority evaluates the query to determine the value of the entity it has in charge (role, activity, view and context value) that matches the query entities (subject, action and object). The response of the evaluation can be "Permit", "Deny", "NotApplicable" or "Indeterminate" for each request. The response Permit means that the corresponding value is assigned. After receiving the assignment values (those for which the XACML response is "Permit"), the Enablement Authorities will reiterate the evaluation for each value found, to be sure that there are no additional junior values assigned. Finally, the framework provides the means for permission inheritance concerning roles, views, activities and context through hierarchies' specification between these concepts. Obligations are also supported with the same mechanism as XACML engine does.

Integrating GSTRBAC Spatial Constraints in X-GTRBAC (GSTRBAC+X-GTRBAC)

The GSTRBAC + X-GTRBAC framework (Haseeb et al., 2009; Samuel, Ghafoor & Bertino, 2008) extends the X-GTRBAC model adopting all its specific features concerning context constraints specification, integrating the detail spatial constraints specification of the GSTRBAC model which constitutes a crucial aspect concerning the effective information security. In more detail, the system introduces the notions of role enabling, spatial role activation, spatial user role assignment and spatial role permission assignment, in accumulation with the temporal constraints specification of the GTRBAC model. The model could be extended in order to support spatial SoD characteristics as well as spatial role hierarchies.

SEMANTICS IN ACCESS CONTROL

Evidently, the particular type characterizing each data item constitutes a parameter of significant importance for the determination of the procedures of which the data subject will be and, consequently, of the adaptation of a business process or service behavior, as also is made clear by the privacy principles. The semantics of the business process or service itself, the underlying collection and processing purposes, as well as the entities involved, are of equal importance and altogether are part of what we could characterize as the "privacy context".

Discovery and interoperability among different organizations' information sources, as well as their representation in dynamic, open and heterogeneous environments can be improved by the technologies of the Semantic Web and ontologies expressed in the Web Ontology Language (OWL) (World Wide Web Consortium, 2004). OWL ontologies provide rich expressiveness, as well as advanced reasoning capabilities and

constitute an interesting tool for the semantics representation in access control systems, which has been leveraged by some models.

Role Based Access Control in OWL (R*OWL*BAC)

R*OWL*BAC model (Finin et al., 2008) constitutes an extension of RBAC model representing all its characteristics in OWL. The advantage of using OWL is related with the high expressive power that the language provides concerning the complex policy specification. Individuals, classes of individuals, properties and axioms as well as specific constraints over them can be easily expressed in OWL. This feature could be very effective and useful in distributed environments involving cooperation between different entities. R*OWL*BAC can model all the versions of RBAC model including the flat, hierarchical, constraint and symmetric ones enriched with a more complex representation and specification of context constraints. In that respect, all the important characteristics concerning context such as the temporal, spatial and historical ones can be incorporated and expressed by the model, despite the fact that it focuses on the SSoD/DSoD constraints, obligations and role hierarchies' aspects.

A Temporal Semantic-Based Access Control Model (TSBAC)

TSBAC model (Ravari et al., 2008) incorporates the same characteristics with the GTHBAC model through the exploitation of the semantic web advantages representing all the basic entities in OWL ontologies. The model introduces the following set of ontologies: the Subjects-Ontology, the Objects-Ontology and the Actions-Ontology. The representation of the basic access control domains using ontologies aims at considering semantic relationships in different levels of ontology to perform inferences to make decisions about an access request. The model attempts to reduce semantic relations into the subsumption relations and use them in the access control process. In that respect the specification and manipulation of complex policies and expressions in an easily way is possible.

Supporting RBAC with XACML+OWL (XACML + OWL)

RBAC with XACML+OWL constitutes a framework (Ferrini & Bertino, 2009) that integrates OWL ontologies and XACML policies in order to support RBAC model. XACML is a widely used language for access control policies expression and specification. Furthermore, due to the fact that it is an easily extended and flexible policy language, it can be adopted by many access control models. In this model the extended XACML provides the capability of many important RBAC characteristics expression such as the SSoD/DSoD, role hierarchies with respect to the propagation of authorizations along with role inheritance hierarchies. The flexibility of the framework relies on the fact that the representation of the constraints as well as the relevant RBAC hierarchies is decoupled from the XACML policies' specification and enforcement. The cooperation between the XACML policies and OWL ontology is accomplished through specific semantic functions which are specified in the model. In more detail, the relevant OWL properties that represent role hierarchies along with the appropriate semantic functions are integrated inside the XACML policy rules in order for the relevant information to be retrieved and combined for the evaluation of the rule. After the evaluation procedure, the necessary interactions with the ontology take place in order for the obligations and other constraints specified in the policy to be fulfilled. The model does not provide a specific representation of context-aware information related with time, location or history of accesses but all the relevant XACML engine's features could be probably deployed.

A Generalized Temporal History Based Access Control Model (GTHBAC)

GTHBAC (Ravari et al., 2010) constitutes an access control model which is not a role-centric model despite the fact that roles can be expressed as attributes inside the authorization rules. Therefore, the model uses the general terms of subject, action and object as central entities of the access control policy rules. However, it provides a comprehensive mechanism of historical context constraints expression and enforcement. Generally, the authorization decision is taken after the evaluation of the relevant authorization rules along with the temporal constraints related with the history of accesses. The temporal constraints use both the notions of real and logical time related each other through logical operators. Temporal authorization rules are represented by triples that contain the authorization valid time interval along with the reference set of subject, action, object and the definition formula of temporal constraint. The evaluation procedure can be accomplished by checking of the relevant credentials disposed by the subject in the form of X.509 Attribute Certificates (International Telecommunication Union, 2005) along with relevant information stored in a History Base. In addition, the model provides mechanisms for several kinds of conflicts resolution that concern the following four different strategies: negative authorization rule takes precedence (NTP) strategy, positive authorization rule takes precedence (PTP) strategy, most specific rule takes precedence, and newer rule overrides older. Finally, the model is considered as a very applicable model due to the fact that integrates the temporal constraints over history of accesses in a generic access control model that can be easily replaced by other access control models.

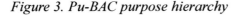

Figure 3. Pu-BAC purpose hierarchy

PRIVACY–AWARE ACCESS CONTROL

As aforementioned, privacy-aware access control has become during the last decade an important research area of growing interest while the first influential approach has been the so-called the Hippocratic Databases, that leveraged purpose as a core parameter for providing access to information, resulting in purpose-aware transformations of queries requesting data from relational databases. Since then, a variety of models have emerged, introducing a plethora of interesting concepts. This section reviews some of the most important and representative of them. These models incorporate privacy-context features derived from the privacy principles, context-aware constraints specification and some of them exploit the aforementioned technologies of the Semantic Web for access control information representation.

Purpose Based Access Control (Pu-BAC)

As it is already mentioned purpose constitutes one of the basic concepts on which privacy-aware access decisions are made. In Pu-BAC model (Byun, Bertino & Li, 2005) purposes are organized in a hierarchical structure based on is-a relationships denoting the concepts of specialization/ generalization which are widely used in business environments.

Privacy policies allow the access to specific data item only if the purpose allows the access to the data. In that respect, purposes are associated with data and are referred to as intended purposes stating for which purposes data can be accessed. The term access purpose is also introduced which is checked against the intended purpose for the data when access to data is requested. Purposes in this model support both positive and negative privacy policies to provide greater flexibility. In case of conflicting purposes the prohibited intended purposes override the allowed intended purposes. The authorization for each user is granted for a set of access purposes and the relevant authorization permits users to access data relevant with a particular purpose. The authorizations are granted through the users' roles. The concept of role in this model is based on attributes relevant with the roles and is organized in an hierarchical structure allowing the inheritance of attributes. In this context, the Conditional Role concept is introduced which is based on Role and System attributes in order to limit the access to individuals. The role attributes can be viewed as a cached user information that is relevant to the specific roles, and the role attribute values of a user are updated if the user information changes. The system attributes concerns conditions related with the states of the system where the authorizations should become effective (or ineffective). These conditions refer to temporal as well as spatial context information. For the access control enforcement every data is tagged

Figure 4. PuRBAC

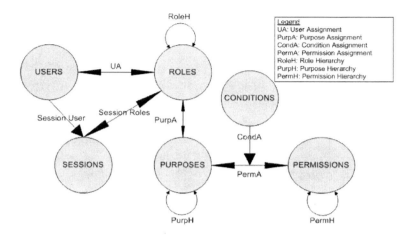

with indented purpose labels. Data are also hierarchically organized with the "instance-of", "sub element-of" and "reference-of" relations. In order to provide more efficiency the model exploits the hierarchies and introduces the concept of implicit intended purpose ensuring that all the instances of the data object (and all its sub elements) will be governed by the intended purpose. For conflicts resolution between the intended purposes the model defines the concepts of strong and weak indented purposes. The strong intended purposes cannot be overridden by intended purposes associated with the instances of the type (or sub elements of the object) while a weak intended purpose can be overridden. Consequently the Pu-BAC model proposes a method for determining access purposes, in an efficient way but it does not deal with significant characteristics such as obligations and complex conditions definition.

Purpose-Aware Role-Based Access Control (PuRBAC)

The extended RBAC model referred as PuRBAC (Masoumzadeh & Joshi, 2008) defines the concept of purpose as an intermediate entity between role and permission in order to perform privacy-aware

access control decisions. This privacy-aware model includes also constraints and obligations on assignment of permission. With the term assignment it refers to entities' relationships. In this context, a purpose is assigned to proper roles and as a consequence a subject should specifically assert the purpose of accessing data in its request to access a piece of data.

Furthermore the model specifies conditions for the assignment validation process. Assignment is valid in a situation if and only if its condition is satisfied. Conditions are Boolean predicates and in case there are multiple applicable conditional assignments all of them should be aggregated to be enforced. Hierarchies constitute also a significant contribution of the PuRBAC model. Hierarchies of roles, purposes and permissions (through the data hierarchy specification) are defined as partial order hierarchies. Conditions are completed with the specification of concepts such as temporal context, pre and post obligations as well as constraints related with the user consent, data retention, data use and logging actions. As conditions include obligations in addition to constraints, the unified set of conditions can result in inconsistencies or conflicts between obligations for enforcement. Moreover, enforcement of individual obligations may have inconsistencies or conflicts with the ongoing obligations in the system. In the case of two inconsistent obligations, the inconsistency can be resolved by overriding the one that can subsume the other. But in the case of conflict, where none of the obligations can subsume the other, the system needs a meta-policy according to which it can determine which obligation should override, or possibly the access is being denied if no resolution is possible.

Organization Based Access Control (OrBAC)

The Organization Based Access Control (OrBAC) framework (Cuppens & Cuppens-Boulahia, 2008) provides the means for the specification of dynamic, flexible and privacy-aware access control policies. OrBAC is centered around the concept of the Organization, i.e., the entity responsible for managing a security policy. OrBAC policies are modeled at the organizational level, following an implementation-independent way; instead of modeling the policy by using the concrete and implementation-related concepts of subject, action and object, OrBAC suggests reasoning with the roles that subjects, actions or objects play in the organization. The role of a subject is simply called as a role as in the RBAC model, the role of an action is called an activity whereas the role of an object is called a view.

OrBAC policies define permissions, prohibitions, obligations and dispensations that apply within an organization to control the activities performed by roles on views. The defined rules are dynamic and incorporate the notion of context, meaning all the additional conditions that should be satisfied for the rule activation. Roles, Views, Activities, Contexts and Organizations are structured to hierarchies and rules are inherited through these hierarchies, providing a flexible way for policies' specification. As conflicts might occur between positive and negative authorizations, OrBAC provides conflict management strategies to detect and resolve such potential conflicts (Cuppens et al., 2007). In addition, SoD provisions between roles within the same or in different organizations can be expressed.

Context constitutes a very important and well-studied concept in OrBAC. The conditions include several context types, such as temporal, spatial, prerequisite, user-declared, consent and provisional ones. They can be combined in order to form composite conditions with conjunctive, disjunctive and negative relationships. The model also defines global constraints, i.e., conditions associated with the security policy. If a global constraint is not satisfied, then this means that this security policy is not consistent. Historical aspects related with the access control policies can also be expressed by means of the provisional context, as well as the post and pre obligation characteristics.

The provisions specifically targeting privacy protection are mostly implemented leveraging context (Ajam et al., 2010). The concept of purpose is modeled as a user-declared context, which is claimed by the data requestors prior to any data disclosure, while there exist predefined mappings between purposes and the roles that can claim them. The specification of the consent context permits the notification of the data subject when his personal information is accessed. Consistently with the collection limitation principle, OrBAC enables fine-grained access to data, depending on the purpose and the subject; in other words, OrBAC exploits the concept of different levels of data accuracy when making access control decisions, whereas the accuracy attribute is introduced through the hierarchy of Views. Finally, the provisional context enables the realization of usage control over the collected data during their lifetime.

Privacy-Aware Role Based Access Control (P-RBAC)

P-RBAC model (Ni et al., 2010) deals with the most significant characteristics related with the privacy-aware access control such as purposes,

Figure 5. OrBAC

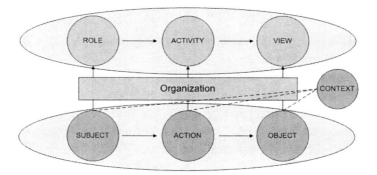

obligations and conditions which are expressed in a comprehensive way. These characteristics are defined through the combination of four advanced models which have different modeling capabilities; the Core P-RBAC, the Hierarchical P-RBAC, the Conditional P-RBAC and the Universal P-RBAC. P-RBAC encapsulates data, action, purpose, condition, and obligation as privacy data permission. Core P-RBAC is based on RBAC model and is used to express privacy policies. Hierarchical P-RBAC introduces the notions of Role, Object and Purpose hierarchy supporting partial order relations between objects and purposes. Roles hierarchy is based on the RBAC model's related specification. Conditional P-RBAC introduces the concepts of Permission Assignments Sets and complex Boolean expression in order to express complex conditions and

specify both conjunction and disjunction relations between different permission assignments. Universal P-RBAC provides in addition to the aforementioned models features such as negative permissions, flow control of obligation execution and permission combination principles to address possible inconsistencies.

Furthermore the P-RBAC family model uses a simple custom language referred as LC_0 in order to express conditions using context variables. It also specifies the notion of temporal constraint that represents sequence of time intervals. In that respect, the model supports the concepts of SoD, pre and post obligations including characteristics such as data use and disclosure as well as user's consent. Finally, the model incorporates conflict resolution mechanism between two conflicting permission assignments.

Figure 6. P-RBAC family

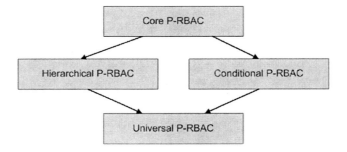

PRISM Access Control Model (PRISM)

The PRISM access control model (Gogoulos et al., 2010) proposes a novel approach for privacy-preserving traffic monitoring, able to serve the needs of both real-time and non-real-time applications. It provides a generalized RBAC-based, privacy and context aware access control framework. The approach is based on policies that are evaluated and enforced by the system in order to take access decisions. The authorization procedures are accomplished by credentials exchange between the relevant entities in the form of X.509 Attribute Certificates.

The fundamental components that comprise the policy framework are the sets of personal data types, purposes, roles, actors, rules, conditions and obligations. The latter three represent, respectively, the actual access control rules, i.e., permissions and prohibitions, and real-time constraints to the applicability of the rules. The set of personal data types is characterized by three relationships, reflecting respectively the inheritance of characteristics, the detail level of the same concept and the inclusion of a data type to another one; similar relationships (AND and OR trees) are also defined for the purposes and the roles.

The access control rules, from which also the authorization provisions are derived, are always associated with a {personal data types, purpose, role} triad. The access control rules can be either positive or negative; resulting to positive or negative authorizations, respectively, as far as the underlying action is concerned. The actors of the system are assigned with roles; this creates the Role Assignments set. Additionally, purposes are assigned to roles as permissions, since, intuitively, not all types of roles are permitted to act (i.e., execute a monitoring function offered by an application) with respect to serving all possible purposes. This creates a Purpose-to-role associa-tion set. The association of personal data types with {purpose, role} associations creates the concept of the permitted data types reflecting positive read authorizations on data. In addition, the model defines sets of Mutually Excluded Data Types. These sets are queried regarding the existence of "forbidden" data combinations.

In order for the access control framework to be enforced, the approach adopted (Lioudakis et al., 2009) is to express all types of information described by means of an ontology, implemented using OWL. This concerns not only the personal data, purposes and roles, but also the rules, contextual conditions and other provisions. Each condition is related with one or more rules, either by being directly connected, or as part of a structure of conditions. Structures of conditions are defined creating AND-OR trees concerning temporal, spatial and historical context constraints. An additional characteristic offered by the semantic model is the support for privacy pro-active and post-active obligations that should be executed along with the enforcement of a rule. Each obligation follows a pattern characterized by attributes and implemented as annotation properties concerning the information of the data subjects or even the request for an explicit consent in real-time, the notification of some Privacy Authority upon the application of a rule, and the specification of the retention of the data.

ANALYSIS AND DISCUSSION

The following table summarizes the specific privacy related features of the studied models. All the aforementioned approaches deal with the majority of the aspects described in previous sections, in a different way, exploiting several technologies and means, providing significant contribution to the domain of privacy protection and access control in business environments.

Figure 7. PRISM ontology

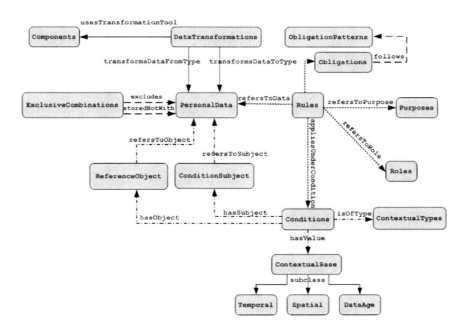

Table 1. Comparative overview of the access control models

Privacy- preserving Models	Context -awareness			Obligations	SoD		Hierarchies				Conflicts Resolution	Ontology Based	Certificates Based
	Temporal	Spatial	Historical		SSoD	DSoD	Role	Purpose	Data	Context			
Context-based access control models (with privacy-context characteristics)													
GEO-RBAC	×	✓	×	×	✓	×	✓	×	✓	×	×	×	×
GTRBAC	✓	×	×	×	✓	✓	×	×	×	×	✓	×	×
X-GTRBAC	✓	×	×	×	✓	✓	×	×	×	✓	✓	×	×
RBAC for XACML	✓	✓	✓	✓	✓	✓	✓	×	✓	×	×	×	×
GSTRBAC+ X-GTRBAC	✓	✓	×	×	✓	✓	×	×	×	✓	✓	×	×
Semantic-based access control models (with privacy-context characteristics)													
R*OWL*BAC	✓	✓	✓	×	✓	✓	✓	×	×	✓	×	✓	×
TSBAC	✓	×	✓	×	✓	×	×	×	✓	✓	✓	✓	×
XACML+ OWL	✓	×	×	✓	✓	✓	✓	×	×	✓	✓	✓	×
GTHBAC	✓	×	✓	×	✓	×	×	×	×	✓	✓	✓	✓
Privacy-aware access control models (context-awareness and/or ontologies use)													
Pu-BAC	✓	✓	×	×	✓	×	✓	✓	✓	✓	✓	×	×
PuRBAC	✓	×	×	✓	✓	×	✓	✓	✓	×	✓	×	×
OrBAC	✓	✓	✓	✓	✓	×	✓	✓	✓	✓	✓	×	×
P-RBAC	✓	×	×	✓	✓	✓	✓	✓	✓	✓	✓	×	×
PRISM	✓	✓	✓	✓	×	×	✓	✓	✓	✓	✓	✓	✓

"Privacy-Context" Features Incorporation

The notion of "purpose" is introduced in five of the aforementioned models. P-RBAC, Pu-BAC, PuRBAC, OrBAC and PRISM define purpose as a core part of the privacy policies that indicates the reason and the circumstances under which the data should be collected and used. Purposes in these models are structured in hierarchies supporting inheritance relationships.

The obligations feature also constitutes a very important aspect of privacy-aware access control. Therefore, several of the models incorporate this characteristic. In P-RBAC, PuRBAC and OrBAC, pre and post obligations, including privacy features such as data use and disclosure, as well as user's consent are defined. In the RBAC profile for XACML, obligations are supported with the same mechanism as XACML engine. The same approach is adopted by the XACML+ OWL framework with the main difference that upon the obligations fulfillment the necessary interactions with the ontology are taken place, in order for the relevant information to be updated on the ontology. PRISM introduces the notion of pro-active and post-active obligations implemented by an OWL class as complementary actions that should be executed along with the enforcement of a rule. Each obligation follows a pattern which is characterized by attributes such as disclosure of data or user's consent etc.

Concerning the SoD characteristic it is observed that the majority of the models support the SSoD feature except the PuRBAC and PRISM approaches. On the other hand, the notion of the DSoD is not so widely introduced in the models. More precisely, the frameworks that support the DSoD characteristic are mainly the GTRBAC family model, the P-RBAC as well as the approaches that exploit the XACML'S and OWL's expressive power. From the hierarchies feature perspective, it is worth mentioning that four of the models; P-RBAC, Pu-BAC, OrBAC and PRISM, support inheritance of characteristics in all the basic entities of their access control model specification. It should be also noted that the PuRBAC and TSBAC models specify hierarchical relationships concerning roles, purposes and data in one case and roles, data and context in the other.

Several conflicts resolution mechanisms and algorithms are also presented from the models regarding conflicting situations in permission assignments. The P-RBAC approach provides a detail specification of possible conflicting situations regarding conflicts between conditions as well as due to hierarchies. Regarding the Pu-BAC model, conflicts detection and resolution mechanisms are defined preventing conflicts between prohibited and allowed purposes. On the other hand, the GTRBAC models as well as the PuRBAC model present such kind of mechanisms regarding conflicts caused by the different constraints enforcement. In the first case, the model defines for this purpose lower and higher priority rules. Concerning PuRBAC, in the case of two inconsistent obligations, the inconsistency can be resolved by overriding the one that can subsume the other. The GTHBAC and TSBAC models define strategies for conflicts resolution in the cases that there is inclusion of a specific entity set in more than one entity sets as well as in situations that there are conflicting sub-interval relations between authorization rules. As regards XACML+OWL model, conflict detection concerning constraints and obligations is supported through ontology inconsistencies checking. In such case, the authorizations are denied and the ontology is automatically updated with the relevant information. Finally, the PRISM approach anticipates and prevents conflicting situations through the definition of specific annotation ontology properties relevant with each authorization rule that concern hierarchical relationships, mutually excluded combinations of data types etc.

Advantages and Limitations

The studied models attempt to extend the RBAC model to deal with the majority of the aforementioned "privacy-context" features. Nevertheless, some of the models present certain advantages as well as limitations over the others, in terms of applicability, usability and comprehensiveness. More precisely, some of these approaches, such as GEO-RBAC, GTRBAC, X-GTRBAC, GSTRBAC+X-GTRBAC and Pu-BAC, suggest combining the concept of role with spatial or/and temporal contextual conditions to obtain "contextual" roles. We argue that a context should not be attached to the role but to the security rules due to the fact that the notion of "contextual" role generally corresponds to artificial roles and sometimes to ambiguous roles. For instance, if manager is a role and O1 is an organization, a "combined" role such as O1 physician is ambiguous since it may be interpreted as a "contextual" role (corresponding to manager located in organization O1) or an "organizational" role (corresponding to manager empowered in organization O1).

Regarding the context-awareness several of the models incorporate characteristics concerning the three significant contextual features (temporal, spatial and history-based). However, only the temporal context information is investigated by the majority of the models. In more detail, all the aforementioned models, except the location centric GEO-RBAC, deal with temporal constraints. On the other hand, the combined impact of location and time in access decision is considered only in the Pu-BAC, OrBAC, GSTRBAC+X-GTRBAC and PRISM approaches. This information can also be easily introduced in the more generic and standards-based models such as XACML for RBAC and R*OWL*BAC due to the fact that these models are easily extended. On the other hand, the historical context feature is introduced and defined in the minority of the aforementioned models such as OrBAC, GTHBAC, TSBAC, PRISM and possibly the XACML for RBAC

and R*OWL*BAC frameworks. In this respect, it should be noted that according to GSTRBAC, all permissions available to a role can be executed whenever and wherever this role is enabled. However the model ignores the spatiotemporal nature of the RBAC permission. For example, the basic employee role can be invoked by a person working in an organization in the morning session as well as in the afternoon session, although in the model, the online attendance is permitted through employee role only in the morning session. With respect to the capability of complex constraints expression, it is worth mentioning that OrBAC, GSTRBAC+X-GTRBAC, RBAC profile for XACML, R*OWL*BAC, XACML+OWL and PRISM models are able to express all kind of conditions in an efficient and complete way.

Furthermore, a high level of abstraction concerning the semantic representation of the model's entities constitutes an important advantage due to the fact that in this context the model can express other access control models and makes the update and manipulation of access rules easier. The RBAC profile of XACML, R*OWL*BAC, XACML+OWL, TSBAC, GTHBAC and PRISM are generic and adaptable enough to express, additionally to RBAC, the needs of any model based on the idea of views, classes or activities.

Finally, considering the purpose-based access control models, it should be noted that P-RBAC although quite powerful, we argue that it is moving away from the simplicity of policy administration spirit of RBAC. P-RBAC encapsulates data, action, purpose, condition, and obligation as privacy data permission. However, with the use of roles as the intermediary entities between users and permissions, RBAC shifts from simply-represented but hard-to-manage paradigm that only consists of authorization rules, to a more manageable user-role and permission-role assignment approach. However, privacy data permissions in P-RBAC do not consider that characteristic, and in presence of data and purpose hierarchies, the policy administration is complex. On the other hand,

PuRBAC, Pu-BAC and PRISM model considers purpose as an intermediary entity between role and permission entities.

Implementation Issues

Another worth mentioning feature is the representation and the secure exchange of the relevant access control information in order for efficient and comprehensive authorization mechanisms to be provided, as well as implementation issues regarding the access control models.

Regarding the specification of privacy policies, the majority of the models exploit powerful and widely adopted languages such as XACML, OWL and XML-based solutions. Related worth mentioning work in this field, constitutes the Enterprise Privacy Authorization Language (EPAL) specification (Ashley et al., 2003) that describes a language to represent privacy policies. This work makes advancements but it only provides general guidelines. Furthermore, SecPAL4P (Becker et al., 2009) approach constitutes a satisfactory solution for specifying and matching users' privacy preferences and services' data-handling policies. It is easily human-readable, provides formal specification of when a policy satisfies a preference and can express useful in practice statements, such as obligations and restrictions on third-party information disclosure.

On the other hand, it is obvious that the minority of the models define mechanisms for the exchange of information (e.g., SAML or certificate-based solutions that are one of the widely adopted mechanisms for the exchange of access control information). More precisely, only the GTHBAC and PRISM frameworks enhance such kind of solution adopting the X.509 Attribute Certificates use.

From an implementation point of view, that constitutes a significant aspect for an access control model to be complete, it is observed that the majority of the studied models provide prototype system architectures based on well-established and specified standards such as ISO/IEC 10181-3 specification for access control (International Telecommunication Union, 1996) and technologies such as Java and MySQL. The use of such kind of technologies and standards provides many advantages concerning issues of scalability, interoperability, adaptability and performance.

Summary

Summarizing it is worth mentioning that none of the described models incorporates all the relevant aspects regarding privacy-preserving access control procedure. In more detail, the majority of the purpose-centric access control models lack the ability of providing complex context constraints specification and focus mainly in the privacy-preserving characteristics such as "privacy obligations", as well as other features such as hierarchies and SoD. In that respect, significant contextual aspects including spatial and history-based ones, required for an efficient access control procedure which provides the capability of the limited exchange of information in business environments according to time, location and history of accesses, are missing. On the other hand, context focused models support a detail specification of these parameters but have the disadvantage of not providing the basic means for privacy protection, because of the fact that they are not based on basic privacy-preserving characteristics such as "purpose of access" definition and "privacy obligations". Furthermore, regarding the semantic-based models it is obvious that the exploitation of the semantic technologies such as ontologies, that offer effectual representation and management of information, enriches them with great efficiency and flexibility of complex context parameters specification and definition. In that respect, the aforementioned semantic-based models incorporate the majority of contextual characteristics along with the basic privacy-preserving features.

CONCLUSION AND FUTURE RESEARCH DIRECTIONS

This chapter presented and analyzed the legal and technical requirements of privacy-aware access control in business environments, along with an extended study of the proposed solutions in the literature. The use of semantic web technologies, such as ontologies, constituted also a significant domain of interest for the chapter, because of their great expressive power concerning the representation and management of every kind of information. In this context, the most important privacy, context and semantic aware access control models have been studied, providing a detailed description and comparative study of their privacy related characteristics, as a starting point for an extended research, as well as efficient and comprehensive solutions to be specified and provided in the future.

Future research directions covering the privacy protection issue through access control mechanisms involve several aspects. Most research to date, concerning access control, has been based on a single organization's point of view. However a natural consequence in modern business environments deals with managing access rights in large-scale and collaborating systems that participate in a single business process (virtual organization). In particular, enterprises might need to "decompose" a service into more specific ones since they are not able to entirely provide it by themselves, and so they may outsource the provisioning of sub-parts to third parties. These issues mainly affect the definition of the access control policy governing the business process since the privacy policy cannot be directly mapped to it without introducing unnecessary authorizations. Therefore in the future, greater interest should be shown in Business-to-Business and Business-to-Consumer access control applications, exploiting role based access control technology for separating responsibilities in cross-organization systems.

Another consequence of the organizational emphasis in past research approaches is that assigning a role or/and a permission to a user is generally considered an administrative task of some other user or administrator. Developing a comprehensive and efficient administrative model to cover this scope constitutes a challenging research task.

More recently, the Web has morphed into a social space where privacy becomes a more fundamental concern. The exploitation of Web 2.0 on social networking, sharing, collaboration, blogs, and user-generated content, makes nowadays Web more significantly a two-way medium than it was before. As people increasingly use the Web for social networking, the need for control over privacy becomes an essential concern of using the Web. Hence, privacy-aware access control mechanisms for such kind of environments constitute an important future research direction.

Finally, a significant and promising future research topic is the privacy-preserving workflow-based access control. A workflow separates the different activities of a given process inside an organization into a set of tasks. These tasks are executed according to the organization's specified policies to achieve certain objectives. Among these policies, security and privacy policies are crucial for ensuring that the organization is adhering to its hard security objectives. However, many workflows deal with different types of data that originate from various sources. Once the data are retrieved for a particular workflow case, the organization is responsible for maintaining data confidentiality as per the organization's privacy policy. In this context, well defined workflow privacy-preserving access control mechanisms, such as Thomas et al., (1997), would help the organization to attain its security objectives by assigning tasks' execution to authorized resources only.

ACKNOWLEDGMENT

This work has been supported in part by the European Commission, under the 7th Framework Programme, specifically the projects PRISM

(Privacy-Aware Secure Monitoring) and DE-MONS (Decentralized, Cooperative and Privacy-Preserving Monitoring for Trustworthiness). The authors would like to express their gratitude to the PRISM and DEMONS consortia for the fruitful discussions.

REFERENCES

Acquisti, A. (2010). *The economics of personal data and the economics of privacy*. OECD Conference Centre. WPISP-WPIE Roundtable. Retrieved on November 29, 2010, from http://www.oecd.org/dataoecd/8/51/46968784.pdf

Agrawal, R., Kiernan, J., Srikant, R., & Xu, Y. (2002). Hippocratic databases. In *Proceedings of the 28th International Conference on Very Large Data Bases (VLDB '02)* (pp. 143-154). USA: VLDB Endowment.

Ajam, N., Cuppens-Boulahia, N., & Cuppens, F. (2010). Contextual privacy management in extended role based access control model. In Garcia-Alfaro, J., Navarro-Arribas, G., Cuppens-Boulahia, N., & Roudier, Y. (Eds.), *Data privacy management and autonomous spontaneous security* (pp. 121–135). Berlin, Germany: Springer. doi:10.1007/978-3-642-11207-2_10

Ashley, P., Hada, S., Karjoth, G., Powers, C., & Schunter, M. (2003). *Enterprise privacy authorization language (EPAL 1.2)*. Retrieved November 29, 2010, from http://www.zurich.ibm.com / security/ enterprise-privacy/epal/Specification/index.html

Becker, M. Y., Malkis, A., & Bussard, L. (2009). *A framework for privacy preferences and data-handling policies*. Technical Report MSR-TR-2009-128. Microsoft Research.

Bertino, E., Catania, B., Damiani, M. L., & Perlasca, P. (2005). GEO-RBAC: A spatially aware RBAC. In *Proceedings of the 11th ACM Symposium on Access Control Models and Technologies (SACMAT '06)* (pp. 29-37). New York, NY: ACM.

Bhatti, R., Ghafoor, A., Bertino, E., & Joshi, J. B. D. (2005). X-GTRBAC: An XML-based policy specification framework and architecture for enterprise-wide access control. *Journal of ACM Transactions of Information and System Security*, *8*(2), 187–227. doi:10.1145/1065545.1065547

Birnhack, M. D. (2008). The EU data protection directive: An engine of a global regime. *Computer Law & Security Report*, *24*(6), 508–520. doi:10.1016/j.clsr.2008.09.001

Byun, J.-W., Bertino, E., & Li, N. (2005). Purpose based access control for privacy protection in relational database systems. In *Proceedings of the 10th ACM symposium on Access control models and technologies*. New York, NY: ACM.

Byun, J.-W., Bertino, E., & Li, N. (2005). Purpose based access control of complex data for privacy protection. In *Proceedings of the 10th ACM Symposium on Access Control Models and Technologies (SACMAT 'O5)* (pp. 102-110). New York, NY: ACM.

Casassa Mont, M. (2004). Dealing with privacy obligations: Important aspects and technical approaches. In *Proceedings of the International Workshop on Trust and Privacy in Digital Business (TrustBus 2004)* (LNCS 3184, pp. 120-131). Berlin, Germany: Springer.

Casassa Mont, M. (2005). *A system to handle privacy obligations in enterprises. Technical Report, HPL-2005-180*. Hewlett-Packard Labs.

Casassa Mont, M., & Thyne, R. (2006). A systemic approach to automate privacy policy enforcement in enterprises. In *Proceedings of the 6th Workshop on Privacy Enhancing-Technologies (PET 2006)* (LNCS 4258). Berlin, Germany: Springer-Verlag.

Charalambides, M., Flegkas, P., Pavlou, G., Rubio-Loyola, J., Bandara, A. K., & Lupu, E. C. … Dulay, N. (2006). Dynamic policy analysis and conflict resolution for DiffServ quality of service management. In *Proceedings of Network Operations and Management Symposium (NOMS 06)* (pp.294-304).

Cuppens, F., & Cuppens-Boulahia, N. (2008). Modeling contextual security policies. *International Journal of Information Security, 7*(4), 285–305. doi:10.1007/s10207-007-0051-9

Cuppens, F., Cuppens-Boulahia, N., & Ben Ghorbel, M. (2007). High level conflict management strategies in advanced access control models. *Journal of Electronic Notes in Theoretical Computer Science, 8*, 3–26. doi:10.1016/j.entcs.2007.01.064

European Commission. (2000). Commission decision of 26 July 2000 pursuant to Directive 95/46/EC of the European Parliament and of the Council on the adequacy of the protection provided by the safe harbour privacy principles and related frequently asked questions issued by the US Department of Commerce. *Official Journal of the European Communities, L 215*, 7-47.

European Parliament and Council. (1995). Directive 95/46/EC of the European Parliament and of the Council on the protection of individuals with regard to the processing of personal data and on the free movement of such data. *Official Journal of the European Communities, L 281*, 31-50.

European Parliament and Council. (2002). Directive 2002/58/EC of the European Parliament and of the Council concerning the processing of personal data and the protection of privacy in the electronic communications sector (Directive on privacy and electronic communications). *Official Journal of the European Communities, L 201*, 37-47.

European Parliament and Council. (2006). Directive 2006/24/EC of the European Parliament and of the Council of 15 March 2006 on the retention of data generated or processed in connection with the provision of publicly available electronic communications services or of public communications networks and amending Directive 2002/58/EC. *Official Journal of the European Communities, L 105*, 54-63.

Ferraiolo, D. F., Sandhu, R. S., Gavrila, S., Kuhn, R. D., & Chandramouli, R. (2001). Proposed NIST standard for role-based access control. *ACM Transactions on Information and System Security, 4*(3), 224–274. doi:10.1145/501978.501980

Ferrini, R., & Bertino, E. (2009). Supporting RBAC with XACML+OWL. In *Proceedings of the 14th ACM Symposium on Access Control Models and Technologies (SACMAT '09)* (pp. 145-154). New York, NY: ACM.

Finin, T., Joshi, A., Kagal, L., Niu, J., Sandhu, R. S., Winsborough, W., & Thuraisingham, B. (2008). R*OWL*BAC: Representing role based access control in OWL. In *Proceedings of the 13th ACM Symposium on Access Control Models and Technologies* (pp. 73-82). New York, NY: ACM.

Gallup Organization. (2008). *Data protection in the European Union: Citizens' perceptions – Analytical report (Flash Eurobarometer 225)*. Retrieved November 29, 2010, from http://ec.europa.eu/public_opinion/flash/fl_225_en.pdf

Gogoulos, F., Antonakopoulou, A., Lioudakis, G. V., Mousas, A. S., Kaklamani, D. I., & Venieris, I. S. (2010). Privacy-aware access control and authorization in passive network monitoring infrastructures. In *Proceedings of the 3rd IEEE International Symposium on Trust, Security and Privacy for Emerging Applications (IEEE TSP-2010)* (pp. 1114-1121). Los Alamitos, CA: IEEE Computer Society.

Haidar, D. A., Cuppens-Boulahia, N., Cuppens, F., & Debar, H. (2006). An extended RBAC profile of XACML. In *Proceedings of the 3rd ACM Workshop on Secure Web Services (SWS '06)* (pp. 13-22). New York, NY: ACM.

Haseeb, H., Masood, A., Ahmed, M., & Ghafoor, A. (2009). Integrating GSTRBAC spatial constraints in X-GTRBAC. In *Proceedings of the 6th International Conference on Frontiers of Information Technology (FIT '09)*. New York, NY: ACM.

Hilty, M., Basin, D. A., & Pretschner, A. (2005). On obligations. In *Proceedings of the 10th European Symposium on Research in Computer Security (ES-ORICS '05)*. Berlin, Germany: Springer-Verlag.

International Telecommunication Union. (1996). *Information technology – Open systems interconnection – Security frameworks for open systems: Access control framework, ITU-T Recommendation ISO/IEC 10181-3*. Retrieved November 29, 2010, from http://webstore.iec.ch/preview/info_isoiec10181-3%7Bed1.0%7Den.pdf

International Telecommunication Union. (2005). *Information technology – Open systems interconnection – The directory: Public-key and attribute certificate frameworks: ITU-T recommendation X.509*. Retrieved November 29, 2010, from http://www.itu.int/rec/T-REC-X.509-200508-I

Joshi, J. B. D., Bertino, E., Latif, U., & Ghafoo, A. (2005). A generalized temporal role-based access control model. *Journal of IEEE Transactions on Knowledge and Data Engineering, 15,* 4–23. doi:10.1109/TKDE.2005.1

LeFevre, K., Agrawal, R., Ercegovac, V., Ramakrishnan, R., Xu, Y., & DeWitt, D. J. (2004). Limiting disclosure in Hippocratic databases. In *Proceedings of the 30th International Conference on Very Large Databases (VLDB 2004)*. Toronto, Canada.

Lioudakis, G. V., Gaudino, F., Boschi, E., Bianchi, G., Kaklamani, D. I., & Venieris, I. S. (2010). Legislation-aware privacy protection in passive network monitoring. In Portela, I. M., & Cruz-Cunha, M. M. (Eds.), *Information communication technology law, protection and access rights: Global approaches and issues*. New York, NY: IGI Global. doi:10.4018/978-1-61520-975-0.ch022

Lioudakis, G. V., Gogoulos, F., Antonakopoulou, A., Kaklamani, D. I., & Venieris, I. S. (2009). Privacy protection in passive network monitoring: an access control approach. In *Proceedings of the IEEE 23rd International Conference on Advanced Information Networking and Applications (AINA-09)* (pp. 109-116). Washington, DC: IEEE Computer Society.

Masoumzadeh, A., & Joshi, J. B. D. (2008). PuRBAC: Purpose-aware role-based access control. In *Proceedings of the On the Move to Meaningful Internet Systems: OTM 2008* (LNCS 5332). Berlin, Germany: Springer.

Massacci, F., Mylopoulos, J., & Zannone, N. (2005). Minimal disclosure in hierarchical Hippocratic databases with delegation. In *Proceedings of the 10th European Symposium on Research in Computer Security (ESORICS 2005)*. Milan, Italy.

Massacci, F., Mylopoulos, J., & Zannone, N. (2006). Hierarchical Hippocratic databases with minimal disclosure for virtual organizations. [New York, NY: Springer-Verlag.]. *The International Journal on Very Large Data Bases, 15*(4), 370–387. doi:10.1007/s00778-006-0009-y

National Computer Security Center – NCSC. (1987). *A guide to understanding discretionary access control in trusted system*. Report NSCD-TG-003 Version1.

Ni, Q., Bertino, E., Lobo, J., Brodie, C., Karat, C. M., Karat, J., & Trombetta, A. (2010). Privacy-aware role-based access control. [New York, NY: ACM.]. *Journal of ACM Transactions Information System Security, 13*(3), 1–31. doi:10.1145/1805974.1805980

Organization for Economic Co-operation and Development – OECD. (1980). *Guidelines on the protection of privacy and transborder flows of personal data.* Retrieved November 29, 2010, from http://www.oecd.org/document/18/0,3343, en_2649_34255_1815186_1_1_1_1,00.html

Organization for the Advancement of Structured Information Standards – OASIS. (2004). *OASIS eXtensible access control markup language (XACML) TC.* Retrieved November 29, 2010, from http://www.oasis-open.org/committees/xacml/

Organization for the Advancement of Structured Information Standards – OASIS. (2004). *OASIS privacy policy profile of XACML v2.0.* Retrieved November 29, 2010, from www.oasis-open.org/committees/access-control

Pfleeger, C. P. (1997). *Security in computing.* New Jersey, USA: Prentice-Hall PTR.

Poullet, Y. (2006). EU data protection policy. The directive 95/46/EC: Ten years after. *Journal of Computer Law & Security Report, 22*(3), 206–217. doi:10.1016/j.clsr.2006.03.004

Ravari, A. N., Amini, M., Jalili, R., & Jafarian, J. H. (2008). A history based semantic aware access control model using logical time. In *Proceedings of the 11th International Conference on Computer and Information Technology (ICCIT 2008)* (pp. 43-50). Khulna, Bangladesh.

Ravari, A. N., Jafarian, J. H., Amini, M., & Jalili, R. (2010). GTHBAC: A generalized temporal history based access control model. *Journal of Telecommunication Systems, 45*(2), 111–125. doi:10.1007/s11235-009-9239-9

Samuel, A., Ghafoor, A., & Bertino, E. (2008). A framework for specification and verification of generalized spatio-temporal role based access control model. *CERIAS Technical Report 2007-08.* Purdue University.

Sandhu, R. S., Coyee, E. J., Ferinstein, H. L., & Youman, C. E. (1996). Role-based access control model. *IEEE Computer, 29*(2), 38–47.

Schunter, M., & Ashley, P. (2002). The platform for enterprise privacy practices. In *Proceedings of the Information Security Solutions Europe (ISSE 2002).* Paris, France.

Solove, D. J. (2006). A brief history of information privacy law. In Wolf, C. (Ed.), *Proskauer on privacy: A guide to privacy and data security law in the information age* (pp. 1–46). New York, NY: Practising Law Institute.

Thomas, R. K., & Sandhu, R. S. (1997). Task-based authorization controls (TBAC): A family of models for active and enterprise-oriented authorization management. In *Proceedings of the IFIP WG11.3 Workshop on Database Security* (pp. 166-181).

United Nations. (1948). *Universal declaration of human rights.* Retrieved November 29, 2010, from http://www.ohchr.org/EN/UDHR/Documents/60UDHR/bookleten.pdf

Warren, S. D., & Brandeis, L. D. (1890). The right to privacy. *Harvard Law Review, 4*(5), 193–220. doi:10.2307/1321160

Westin, A. F. (1967). *Privacy and freedom.* New York, NY: Atheneum.

World Wide Web Consortium. (2004). *Web ontology language (OWL).* Retrieved November 29, 2010, from http://www.w3.org/2004/OWL/

World Wide Web Consortium. (2006). *Extensible markup language (XML) XML 1.1* (2nd edition). Retrieved November 29, 2010, from http://www.w3.org/TR/2006/REC-xml11-20060816

ADDITIONAL READING

Acquisti, A. (2010). The Economics of Personal Data and the Economics of Privacy. *OECD Conference Centre. WPISP-WPIE Roundtable.* Retrieved on November 29, 2010, from http://www.oecd.org/dataoecd/8/51/ 46968784.pdf.

Agrawal, R., Kiernan, J., Srikant, R., & Xu, Y. (2002). Hippocratic Databases. In *Proceedings of the 28th International Conference on Very Large Data Bases (VLDB '02)* (pp. 143-154). USA: VLDB Endowment.

Ardagna, C. A., Cremonini, M., De Capitani di Vimercati, S., & Samarati, P. (2008). A Privacy-Aware Access Control System. *Journal of Computer Security*, *16*(4), 369–397.

Article 29 Data Protection Working Party (2007). *Opinion 4/2007 on the Concept of Personal Data.* Retrieved June 25, 2009, from http://ec.europa.eu/justice_home/fsj/privacy /docs/wpdocs/2007/wp136_en.pdf.

Bertino, E., Carminati, B., & Ferrari, E. (2004). Access Control for XML Documents and Data. *Journal of Information Security Technical Report*, *9*(3), 19–34. doi:10.1016/S1363-4127(04)00029-9

Birnhack, M. D. (2008). The EU Data Protection Directive: An Engine of a Global Regime. *Computer Law & Security Report*, *24*(6), 508–520. doi:10.1016/j.clsr.2008.09.001

Biskup, J. (2009). *Security in Computing Systems. Challenges, Approaches and Solutions.* New York: Springer.

Botha, R. A., & Eloff, J. H. P. (2001). Separation of Duties for Access Control Enforcement in Workflow Environments. *Journal of IBM Systems*, *40*(3), 666–682. doi:10.1147/sj.403.0666

Carminati, B., & Ferrari, E. (2008). Privacy-Aware Collaborative Access Control in Web-Based Social Networks. In *Proceedings of the 22nd Annual IFIP WG 11.3 Working Conference on Data and Applications Security* (LNCS 5094). New York: Springer.

Casassa Mont, M. (2004). Dealing with Privacy Obligations: Important Aspects and Technical Approaches. In *Proceedings of the International Workshop on Trust and Privacy in Digital Business (TrustBus 2004)* (LNCS 3184, pp. 120-131). Berlin, Germany: Springer Berlin/Heidelberg.

Coma, C., Cuppens-Boulahia, N., Cuppens, F., & Cavalli, A.-R. (2008). Context Ontology for Secure Interoperability. In *Proceedings of the 2008 Third International Conference on Availability, Reliability and Security* (pp. 821-827). Washington: IEEE Computer Society.

Cuppens, F., & Cuppens-Boulahia, N. (2008). Modeling Contextual Security Policies. *International Journal of Information Security*, *7*(4), 285–305. doi:10.1007/s10207-007-0051-9

Cuppens, F., Cuppens-Boulahia, N., & Ghorbel, M. B. (2007). High Level Conflict Management Strategies in Advanced Access Control Models. *Journal of Electronic Notes in Theoretical Computer Science*, *186*, 3–26. doi:10.1016/j.entcs.2007.01.064

Damiani, M. L., Bertino, E., & Perlasca, P. (2007). Data security in Location Aware Applications; an Approach Based on RBAC. [Switzerland: Inderscience Publishers.]. *International Journal of Information and Computer Security*, *1*(1/2), 5–38. doi:10.1504/IJICS.2007.012243

Damiani, M. L., & Perri, P. (2010). Privacy Issues in Location-Aware Browsing. In *Proceedings of the 3rd ACM SIGSPATIAL International Workshop on Security and Privacy in GIS and LBS (SPRINGL '10)* (pp. 60-64). New York: ACM.

European Commission (2000). Commission Decision of 26 July 2000 pursuant to Directive 95/46/EC of the European Parliament and of the Council on the adequacy of the protection provided by the safe harbour privacy principles and related frequently asked questions issued by the US Department of Commerce. *Official Journal of the European Communities, L* 215, 7-47.

Ferraiolo, D. F., Sandhu, R. S., Gavrila, S., Kuhn, R. D., & Chandramouli, R. (2001). Proposed NIST Standard for Role-Based Access Control. *ACM Transactions on Information and System Security, 4*(3), 224–274. doi:10.1145/501978.501980

Foresti, S. (2011). *Preserving Privacy in Data Outsourcing (First Edition)*. New York: Springer.

Joshi, J. B. D., Bertino, E., & Ghaffor, A. (2005). An Analysis of Expressiveness and Design Issues for the Generalized Temporal Role-Based Access Control Model. *Journal of IEEE Transactions on Dependable and Secure Computing, 2*(2), 157–175. doi:10.1109/TDSC.2005.18

Joshi, J. B. D., Bertino, E., & Ghafoor, A. (2002). Temporal Hhierarchies and Iinheritance Ssemantics for GTRBAC. In *Proceedings of the seventh ACM symposium on Access control models and technologies (SACMAT '02)* (pp. 74-83). New York: ACM.

Joshi, J. B. D., Shafiq, B., Ghafoor, A., & Bertino, E. (2003). Dependencies and Separation of Duty Constraints in GTRBAC. In *Proceedings of the eighth ACM symposium on Access control models and technologies (SACMAT '03)* (pp. 51-64). New York: ACM.

Kabir, E. Md., Wang, H., & Bertino, E. (2011). A Conditional Purpose-Based Access Control Model with Dynamic Roles. *Journal of Experts Systems and Applications, 38*(3), 1482–1489. doi:10.1016/j.eswa.2010.07.057

Kapitsaki, G. M., Lioudakis, G. V., Kaklamani, D. I., & Venieris, I. S. (2010). Privacy Protection in Context-Aware Web Services: Challenges and Solutions. In Sheng, M., Yu, J., & Dustdar, S. (Eds.), *Enabling Context-Aware Web Services: Methods, Architectures, and Technologies*. Chapman and Hall/CRC. doi:10.1201/EBK1439809853-c14

Lioudakis, G. V., Gaudino, F., Boschi, E., Bianchi, G., Kaklamani, D. I., & Venieris, I. S. (2010). Legislation-Aware Privacy Protection in Passive Network Monitoring. In Portela, I. M., & Cruz-Cunha, M. M. (Eds.), *Information Communication Technology Law, Protection and Access Rights: Global Approaches and Issues*. New York: IGI Global Pubs. doi:10.4018/978-1-61520-975-0.ch022

Ni, Q., Bertino, E., Lobo, J., Brodie, C., Karat, C. M., Karat, J., & Trombetta, A. (2010). Privacy-Aware Role-Based Access Control. *Journal of ACM Transactions Information System Security, 13*(3), 1–31. doi:10.1145/1805974.1805980

Organization for Economic Co-operation and Development – OECD. (1980). *Guidelines on the Protection of Privacy and Transborder Flows of Personal Data*. Retrieved November 29, 2010, from http://www.oecd.org/document/18/0,3343,en_2649_34255_1815186_1_1_1_1,00.html.

Portela, I. M., & Cruz-Cunha, M. M. (Eds.). (2010). *Information Communication Technology Law, Protection and Access Rights: Global Approaches and Issues*. New York: IGI Global Pubs. doi:10.4018/978-1-61520-975-0

Smari, W. W., Zhu, J., & Clemente, P. (2009). Trust and Privacy in Attribute Based Access Control for Collaboration Environments. In *Proceedings of the 11th International Conference on Information Integration and Web-based Applications & Services (iiWAS '09)* (pp. 49-55). New York: ACM.

Solove, D. J. (2006). A Brief History of Information Privacy Law. In Wolf, C. (Ed.), *Proskauer on Privacy: A Guide to Privacy and Data Security Law in the Information Age* (pp. 1–46). New York, NY, USA: Practising Law Institute.

Toahchoodee, M., Ray, I., Anastasakis, K., Georg, G., & Bordbar, B. (2009). Ensuring Spatio-Temporal Access Control for Real-World Applications. In *Proceedings of the 14th ACM symposium on Access control models and technologies (SACMAT '09)* (pp. 13-22). New York: ACM.

Youssef, M., Atluri, V., & Adam, N. R. (2005). Preserving Mobile Customer Privacy: an Access Control System for Moving Objects and Customer Profiles. In *Proceedings of the 6th international conference on Mobile data management (MDM '05)* (pp. 67-76). New York: ACM.

KEY TERMS AND DEFINITIONS

Access control: The mechanisms for allowing access to resources, systems or services to authorized persons or other valid subjects and denying unauthorized access.

Context: Set of facts, information or conditions that surround a situation or event.

Ontology: A formal representation of knowledge as a set of concepts within a domain, and the relationships between those concepts.

Personal data: Any information relating to an identified or identifiable natural person ('data subject'); an identifiable person is one who can be identified, directly or indirectly, in particular by reference to an identification number or to one or more factors specific to his physical, physiological, mental, economic, cultural or social identity.

Policy: Well-defined and specified rules governing the operation of a system.

Privacy: The claim of individuals, groups, or institutions to determine for themselves when, how, and to what extent information about them is communicated to others.

Security: The protection, in terms of integrity, confidentiality, authenticity and availability, of information and systems from malicious parties and situations.

Semantics: Branch of linguistics concerned with nature, structure, and development of meaning in language as well as branch of semiotics concerned with relationship between signs or symbols and what they denote.

Chapter 4

Self–Protecting Access Control:
On Mitigating Privacy Violations with Fault Tolerance

Anne V. D. M. Kayem
University of Cape Town, South Africa

Patrick Martin
Queen's University, Canada

Selim G. Akl
Queen's University, Canada

ABSTRACT

Self-protecting access control mechanisms can be described as an approach to enforcing security in a manner that automatically protects against violations of access control rules. In this chapter, we present a comparative analysis of standard Cryptographic Access Control (CAC) schemes in relation to privacy enforcement on the Web. We postulate that to mitigate privacy violations, self-protecting CAC mechanisms need to be supported by fault-tolerance. As an example of how one might to do this, we present two solutions that are inspired by the autonomic computing paradigm[1]. Our solutions are centered on how CAC schemes can be extended to protect against privacy violations that might arise from key updates and collusion attacks.

INTRODUCTION

The ability to execute multiple transactions across a myriad of applications has made the Internet a prime platform for building Web applications. Applications like Facebook (Facebook, 2010) and MySpace (MySpace, 2010), attest to this

popularity and have been rated as being the most popular social networking applications in the English speaking world. Increasingly, business organizations are taking advantage of these social networking applications and other web applications to collect personal information about consumers and likewise consumers have shown a keenness for the web as a medium of communication because of the interactivity and fast

DOI: 10.4018/978-1-61350-501-4.ch004

response time it offers. Yet, the same qualities of flexibility and interactivity that the web is famous for have become an impediment in the face of the growing incidences of data privacy violations. For example, in October 2010 a Wall Street Journal Investigation revealed that many popular Facebook applications were transmitting consumer personal information to advertising and Internet tracking companies (Slattery, 2010), (Foremski, 2010). Cases like this have fueled growing concerns, on the part of consumers, that their data can be leaked without their consent to third parties. In this section, we discuss the context in which data privacy violations occur and why this happens in spite of the fact that access control mechanisms can be implemented to protect the information.

Context and Motivation

The Internet is built on the assumption that the users of the network can be trusted to behave honestly and so do not use the system or behave in ways that could compromise the performance and/or credibility of the system. Yet, this quality of open access makes web-applications inherently vulnerable to violations of information privacy rules (accidental or intentional) that can compromise the levels of data protection that these applications promise users (Harrison, February 2007), (Sandhu, 2005), (Tanenbaum & Steen, 2007). In many cases, privacy violations occur because consumers assume that they have "correctly" applied some access control mechanism that will prevent illegal access to their information. For instance, in social networking applications, it often is the case that a user will post "confidential" information and forget to set the parameter to prevent transitive disclosures to friends of the user's friends.

As well, consumers have a tendency to naively assume that business organizations will do what they promise, while business organizations are sometimes unaware of the far-reaching consequences of certain management decisions. In the

case of Facebook, one could imagine that a third-party made contact by indicating that they would like to test the popularity of a new application. Facebook probably agreed because usage of the application might attract new members. However, the acceptance agreement might not have indicated clearly that the application could not collect information about the users who choose to use the application and/or people whom the users know might be interested in using the application (Fung, Wang, Chen, & Yu, 2010). Data privacy leaks like the one we describe are a growing concern for organizations because they result in a loss of revue (Foremski, 2010).

Until recently, organizations simply focused on defining a security domain and security policies were used to control access to information. The assumption was that if correctly specified, failure (either deliberate or not), on the part of users, to adhere to data privacy policies would be unlikely. However, the emergence of concepts like service-oriented architectures and cloud computing have dissolved inter-organization boundaries. Consequently, web applications and/or services can interact flexibly across multiple security domains and in ways that are not easy to predict at runtime. Therefore, security policies and access control schemes need to be modeled or extended to cope with situations in which changes in security requirements result in privacy violations.

In this chapter, we discuss the growing need to extend access control models to enforce privacy in scenarios involving changing security requirements like the Web. More specifically, we consider the literature on the more popular access control models like mandatory, discretionary, and role-based access control, and discuss some of the ways in which these models have been extended to enforce data privacy requirements. In recent years, cryptographic access control (CAC) is has received increased attention as a method of enforcing data privacy on the Web. CAC schemes have the advantage of providing protection for data in untrustworthy environments like the Web.

However, CAC schemes have been criticized for being impractical in terms of performance and so have not gained wide spread popularity. We postulate that data privacy is intertwined with dependability and so, self-protecting CAC schemes can efficiently protect against data privacy violations if the CAC schemes are supported with fault tolerance solutions.

In order to extend CAC schemes to incorporate fault tolerance, we use the autonomic computing paradigm. The autonomic computing paradigm was proposed in 2001 by IBM (Corbi, 2003), (Chess, 2005) and suggests that computing systems can be modeled to be self-managing and self-configuring. Self-management implies a reduced need manual management which is time consuming and self-configuration, the ability to adapt to new scenarios (Hart, Davoudani, & McEwan, 2007), (Huebscher & McCann, 2008).

Organization

The rest of the chapter is structured as follows. In Section 2, we discuss privacy and access control in the business context and consider how access control models have been extended in recent years to enforce data privacy on the Web. Section 3 presents cryptographic access control (CAC) models in order to highlight the advantages of using these CAC schemes over standard access control schemes in privacy enforcement. Changing and conflicting security requirements on the Web make adaptability in an access control scheme a desirable quality in data privacy enforcement. In Section 4 we present two examples to show how the autonomic computing paradigm can be used as an inspiration for designing self-protecting CAC schemes. Future research directions and challenges are discussed in Section 5 and we offer concluding remarks in Section 6.

PRIVACY VIA ACCESS CONTROL IN THE WEB CONTEXT

The popularity of service oriented architectures (SOAs) and more recently, cloud computing, indicate that Mark Weiser's vision of ubiquitous computing has become a reality in the business context (Weiser, 1999). More and more, business organizations are using the Web to collect personal information from consumers in order to find adequate responses to queries and/or provide the services that a consumer requests. Inter-service interactions often result in compositions that are not easy to predict and so there is growing concern about the potential violation of consumer data privacy (Byun & Li, 2008), (Ren and Lou, 2007).

Inter-domain information exchanges are handled, in general, within a trusted security framework. In SOAs and cloud computing environments it is difficult to predict how security policies belonging to different domains will be combined to enforce access control. Additionally, verifying that the combination of security policies actually enforces the minimum access control requirements of the services and/or applications involved in accessing portions of data on the system is a challenging problem for manual security mechanisms.

In general, security models for access control on the Internet can be classified into one of three categories: discretionary, mandatory, or role-based (Tanenbaum & Steen, 2007), (Osborn, 2002), (Rjaibi, 2004). The discretionary access control approach allows a user to decide to whom they choose to authorize access and is a good access control approach for data sharing applications that users can join or leave spontaneously. In mandatory access control, access to data is regulated by a lattice that is used to monitor the flow of information among communicating users by assigning labels to files to restrict accessibility to authorized users. This is a good approach for government and military organizations with stricter requirements of access to data. Finally, role-based access control is popular in business organizations mainly because of its flexibility. Role-based access control combines the concepts of discretionary and mandatory access control, by allowing organizations to assign roles to users according to the permissions of access that a security administrator wishes to grant the user. A user can have one or more roles and these roles can be temporary or for the long term.

We use the example of a hypothetical e-business application that relies on a data sharing environment to serve as a backbone for business operations. In this example, users can join or leave the social networking environment spontaneously and use the e-business application to purchase goods. Users are categorized into groups according to interest and a user's group determines the privileges of access (read, write, modify, and/or delete) that he/she is allowed. The advantage of using a social networking environment as a backbone is that it serves platform on which the e-business application can attract a clientele without the cost of advertising on regular channels like radio and television. Examples of real world data sharing applications include Chat Systems, Shared White boards, and "social networking" environments like Facebook, (Facebook, 2010), (Nazir, 2008), and MySpace (MySpace, 2010), (Besmer, 2009). In the following, we review the three models of access control, highlighting their pros and cons in relation to enforcing self-protection against data privacy violations.

Discretionary Access Control

The concept of discretionary access control (DAC) is probably as old as the concept of network-based or distributed computing. It basically rests on the principle that each user of a system should be able to decide on the privileges that are assigned to users wishing to view files that he/she created. The DAC principle is used in many data sharing web applications like Facebook, MySpace, and Flickr because it is simple and straight-forward to

implement in a distributed environment like the Internet. Using a DAC mechanism gives users control over the access rights to their files without the need to comply with a set of pre-specified rules. When these rights are managed correctly, only those users specified by the file owner may have some combination of access permissions on the file (Pfleeger & Pfleeger, 2003), (Tanenbaum & Steen, 2007) and consequently privacy violations are not possible unless the access rules are violated.

Consider the case in which a DAC model is used to enforce access control in a social networking environment that serves as a backbone for an e-business application. As shown in Figure 1, Jane can choose to create a folder containing files with photographs that she wishes to sell and make access available only to members who fulfill a certain number of criteria. For instance, Jane could decide that only the members of her photography club can have access to the files. So, as Figure 1 shows, John who belongs in Jane's class can access the photographs that Jane makes available whereas Sam, who does not belong in her class, has no access rights.

An access control matrix is a simple but effective model for expressing and enforcing simple security policies in situations like the one depicted in Figure 1 (Gollmann, 2006). With an access control matrix, access rights can be defined individually for each combination of users and files/folders. The rules of access depicted in Figure 1, can be expressed using an access control matrix like the one given in Figure 2.

Although the DAC approach is a good way of providing a standard framework for enforcing access control in a social networking environment it has certain disadvantages that limit its ability to enforce privacy. An example of such a problem is the confinement problem that Lampson (Lampson, 1973) cited, which is to determine whether there is a mechanism by which a user authorized to access a file may leak information contained in that file to users that are not authorized to ac-

Figure 1. Discretionary access control

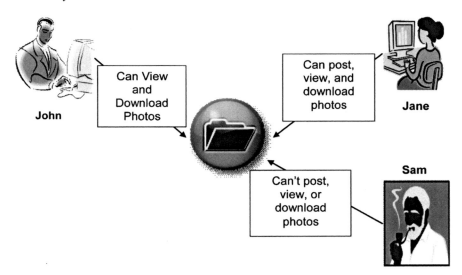

Figure 2. An example of an access control matrix

	Photographs Folder
Sam	-
Jane	{View, Download, Upload}
John	{View, Download}

cess that file. Harrison et al. (Harrison, Munro, & Spiller, 2007) formally showed that the confinement problem is undecidable due to the characteristic of discretionary transfer of access rights between users in the DAC model. An added consideration is that although the DAC model is effective for specifying security requirements and is also easier to implement in practice, its inability to control information flow implies it is not well-suited to the context of Web-based collaborative applications where central control in some form is desirable (Jeong & Kim, 2004). Moreover, since users applying a DAC model do not have a global picture of the data on the system, it is difficult to take the semantics of the data into consideration in assigning access rights so, information might unknowingly be revealed to unauthorized users leading to privacy violations.

Mandatory Access Control

Apart from the confinement and information semantics problems inherent in the DAC model, a key problem that the DAC model faces is vulnerability to Trojan Horse attacks (Bell & Lapadula, 1973), (Biba, 1977), (Sandhu, R., 1993). In order to violate confidentiality and privacy, Trojan Horse attacks exploit two possibilities of access rights management:

- Changes in access rights to a file are handled by the file owner and are not centrally controlled so a malicious user can masquerade as the file owner and grant read-access to a file against the owner's desire.
- Users authorized to access a file are typically allowed to create copies of the file, so a malicious user can create a copy of the file or part of it and grant read-access to users to whom the owner has not authorized access.

For instance, as shown in Figure 3, John can download information from Jane's photographs folder and then proceed to make these pictures

Figure 3. A case of transitive disclosures in the DAC model

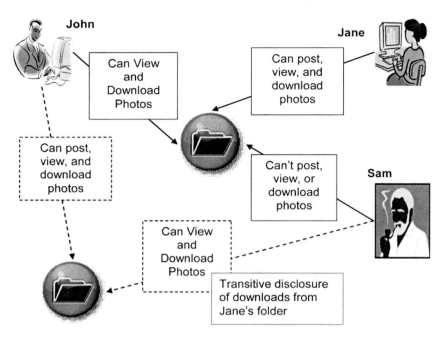

available to Sam. Sam can then proceed to sell the photographs to an unscrupulous e-business owner or modify the photographs and post false/ damaging information about Jane.

The mandatory access control (MAC) model counters these threats by controlling access centrally. An ordinary user (i.e., not the central authority) cannot change the access rights a user has with respect to a file, and once a user logs on to the system the rights he/she has are always assigned to all the files he/she creates. This procedure allows the system to use the concept of information flow control to provide additional security (Gollman, 2005).

Information flow control allows the access control system to monitor the ways and types of information that are propagated from one user to another which is an advantage for privacy enforcement. A security system that implements information flow control typically classifies users into security classes and all the valid channels along which information can flow between the classes are regulated by a central authority or se-

curity administrator (Denning, 1976). Therefore, privacy violations are more difficult to perpetuate than in the DAC model because information can only be shared in ways that are authorized by the security administrator.

In the MAC model, each user is categorized into a security class and the files are tagged with security labels that are used to restrict access to authorized users (Rjaibi, 2004). The example shown in Figure 3 can be extended to handle a security scenario in which a security administrator prevents transitive disclosures, by the users accessing Jane's Photographs Folder, by using data labels to monitor information flow. Each data object is tagged with the security clearance labels of each of the users in the system. As shown in Figure 3, by extending the discretionary access example we gave in Figures 1 and 2, a transitive disclosure could occur if a user, in this case Sam, gains access to Jane's photographs folder because he belongs in John's list of "friends". The MAC model prevents such disclosures by defining a hierarchy, such as the one depicted in Figure 4,

Figure 4. MAC model – Information flow control to prevent privacy violations

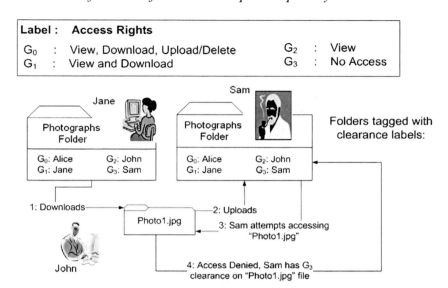

to monitor information flow centrally. The users are assigned labels according to their security clearance and information flow is regulated by authenticating a user and then granting access to the file based on their privileges. Since each file is labeled with a security clearance tag, so Sam can no longer access files that John downloads from Jane's Photographs Folder because Sam does not have a security clearance that allows him access. When the access control policy of a system is based on the MAC model, the security of the system ceases to rely on voluntary user compliance but rather is centrally controlled, making it easier to monitor usage patterns and prevent privacy violations.

Multilevel Access Control

The multilevel security (MLS) model is essentially a special case of how the MAC model is implemented for different contexts or scenarios. In the MLS model, a security goal is set and information flow is regulated in a way that enforces the objectives determined by the security policy (Rjaibi, 2004). Practical implementations of ac-

cess control schemes based on the MLS concept include the Bell-Lapadula (BLP), Biba Integrity Model, Chinese wall, and Clark-Wilson models (Rjaibi, 2004), (Bell & Lapadula, 1973), (Clark & Wilson, 1987), (Brewer & Nash, 1988), (Huang & Shen, 2004), (Liu & Chen, 2004). In the following, we briefly discuss each of these four MLS models but for a detailed exposition of the field one should see the works of McLean (McLean, 1990), Sandhu (Sandhu, R., 1993), Nie et al. (Mie, Feng, Che, & Wang, 2006), and Gollmann (Gollman, 2005).

- **The BLP and BIBA models:** In the BLP model (Bell & Lapadula, 1973), high level users are prevented from transmitting sensitive information to users at lower levels, by imposing conditions that allow users at higher levels to only read data at lower levels but not write to it. On the other hand, users at lower levels can modify information at higher levels but cannot read it. This method of information flow control circumvents privacy violations but allows users at lower levels to write information to files at higher levels that they cannot read. This can result in a situation where violations of data integrity are difficult to trace (Liu & Chen, 2004). So, a malicious use can modify data to provoke violations of the data privacy policy that the access control scheme is meant to enforce. Violations to data integrity are a serious problem for privacy schemes because the corrupted data not only misinforms the user but can lead to inference of unauthorized information. The Biba integrity model (Biba, 1977) addresses the problem of data integrity by checking the correctness of all write operations on a file. However, this approach opens up the possibility of privacy violations by inference of high level information from low level information.

- **The Chinese wall model:** In 1989, Brewer and Nash proposed a commercial access control model called the Chinese wall model (Brewer & Nash, 1988). The basic idea is to build a family of impenetrable walls, called Chinese walls, amongst the datasets of competing companies. So, for instance, the Chinese wall model could be used to specify access rules in consultancy businesses where analysts need to ensure that no conflicts of interest arise when they are dealing with different clients. Conflicts can arise when clients are in direct competition in the same market or because of ownerships of companies. Therefore, analysts need to adhere to an access control policy that enforces a strict privacy policy. Such a privacy policy needs to prohibit information flows that cause a conflict of interest. The access rights in this model are designed along the lines of the BLP model but with the difference that access rights are re-assigned and re-evaluated at every state transition whereas they remain static in the BLP model. Unfortunately, their mathematical model was faulty and

the improvements proposed have failed to completely capture the intuitive characteristics of the Chinese wall security policy (Lin, 2000), (Lin T., 2006).

- **The Clark-Wilson (CLW) Model:** Like the BIBA model, the CLW model addresses the access control requirements of commercial applications in where data integrity is more important than data privacy and confidentiality (Clark & Wilson, 1987). The CLW model uses programs as an intermediate control level between users and data (files). Users are authorized to execute certain programs that can in turn access pre-specified files. Security policies that are modeled using the CLW model are based on five rules:

  1. All data items must be in a valid state at the time when a verification procedure is run on it.
  2. All data transformation procedures need to be set a priori and certified to be valid.
  3. All access rules must satisfy the separation of duty requirements.
  4. All transformation procedures must be stored in an append-only log.
  5. Any file that has no access control constraints must be transformed into one with one or more access control constraints before a transformation procedure is applied to it.

The CLW model is more of a security policy specification framework that extends the concepts in the BIBA model to the general case. Therefore, like the Biba model, the CLW model is vulnerable to privacy violations that are due to inference of high level information from low level information.

Role Based Access Control

Role-based access control (RBAC) is a combination of mandatory and discretionary access control.

In the role-based access control model, a role is typically a job function or authorization level that gives a user certain privileges with respect to a file and these privileges can be formulated at a high level (e.g. in simple English) or at a low level (e.g. formally specified and hard coded into an application). RBAC models are more flexible than their discretionary and mandatory counterparts because a user can be assigned several roles and a role can be associated with several users. Unlike the traditional DAC approach to access control; RBAC assigns permissions to specific operations with a specific meaning within an organization, rather than to low level files. For example, a DAC mechanism could be used to grant or deny a user modification access to a particular file, but it does not specify the ways in which the file could be modified. By contrast, with the RBAC approach, access privileges are handled by assigning permissions in a way that is meaningful, because every operation has a specific pre-defined meaning within the application.

Dynamic role based access control (DRBAC) aims to extend the standard RBAC model to cope with situations that require adapting to changing security requirements. For instance, in context-aware environments, a security policy might need to adapt its settings to cope with a change in context (Zhang & Parashar, 2004). Moreover, the DRBAC approach to access control is more flexible than the one in the DAC and MAC models in the sense that roles can have overlapping responsibilities and privileges, so users belonging to different roles may need to perform common operations.

RBAC assumes that all permission needed to perform a job can be neatly encapsulated so that the role in which a user gained membership is not mutually exclusive of others roles that the user already has. The operations and roles can be subject to organizational policies or constraints and, when operations overlap, hierarchies of roles are established. Instead of instituting costly auditing to monitor access, organizations can put constraints on access through DRBAC. For example, it may

seem sufficient to allow all the users on the system (Jane, John and Sam) to have 'view' and 'download' access to the Photographs Folder, if their accesses are monitored carefully to prevent violations of privacy. By using DRBAC, constraints can be placed on user access and context so that they do not tamper with contents of the Photographs Folder. However, role engineering is a challenging problem because guaranteeing data privacy requires a model that ensures data security and makes security administration less cumbersome than it currently is (Gollman, 2005). On the one hand, for stronger security, it is better for roles to be more granular, thus having multiple roles per user. On the other hand, for easier administration, it is better to have fewer roles to manage. Organizations need to comply with privacy and other regulatory mandates and to improve enforcement of security policies while lowering overall risk and administrative costs. Meanwhile, web-based and other types of new applications are proliferating, and the Web services application model promises to add to the complexity by weaving separate components together over the Internet to deliver application services.

An added drawback RBAC faces in privacy enforcement is that roles can be assigned such that conflicts are created which can open up loopholes in the access control policy. For example in the scenario in Figure 5, we can assume that Jane is the security administrator for the pay-per-view Movies Folder, and that she chooses to assign roles to users in a way that allows the users to either download or upload movies but not both. Now suppose that at a future date Jane decides to assign a third role that grants a user, say Sam, the right to veto an existing user's (e.g. Alice's) uploads. In order to veto Alice's uploads, Sam needs to be able to download as well as temporarily delete questionable uploads, verify the movies and, if satisfied, reload the movies to the site. So, essentially Sam has the right to both download and upload movies to Movies Folder, a role assignment that conflicts with the initial security

Figure 5. A case of conflicting access assignments

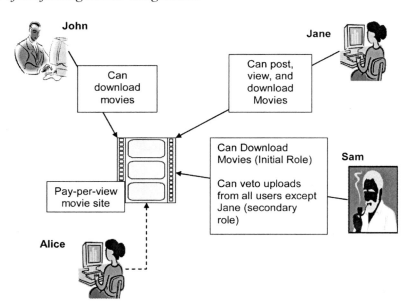

policy specification that Jane made. Security policy combinations or extensions like the one have just described need to be handled with care to prevent violations of privacy. Therefore extensions RBAC model to enforce privacy and incorporate adaptability to cope with scenarios of changing security requirements, need to be evaluated and/or implemented with care.

Extensible Access Control Markup Language: A Privacy Discussion

In the previous sections, we presented and discussed some of the standard access control models highlighting the challenges that they face in handling scenarios of privacy violations on the Web. Although RBAC schemes offer a number of advantages over the DAC and MAC models in terms of security management, they too are not designed to prevent violations of privacy. The objective of this section therefore, is to explore extensions to the RBAC model as well as other access control paradigms for privacy enforcement on the Web.

The principal paradigm in distributed systems before the emergence of the World Wide Web had been the client-server architecture (Tanenbaum & Steen, 2007), (Gollman, 2005). The latter, in its simplest form, allows the server to protect information by authenticating a client requesting access. Kerberos is an example of an authentication service designed for such an environment (Tanenbaum & Steen, 2007). This client-server architecture has however changed in many aspects. For instance, when a client looks at a web page, the client's browser will run programs embedded in the page. So, instead of handling simple accesses either to an operating system or a database, programs are being sent from the server to be executed at the client side. Clients receive programs from servers and can store the session states in "cookies". The Internet has also created a new avenue for software distribution via downloads that can sometimes result in privacy violations and so organizations have learnt, sometimes through the hard way, to restrict the kinds of programs that they allow their employees to download. As well, while the Internet has not created fundamentally new problems data privacy violations, it has changed the context in which privacy needs to be enforced. Consequently, the design of access control paradigms is currently going through a transitory phase in which standard paradigms are being re-thought and evolved to cope with the scenarios that arise on the Internet.

Inherent in the current paradigm shift in designing access control schemes, is the desire to allow users more control over how their personal information is managed (Ardanga et al., 2010). The main focus in terms of extending access control schemes for privacy enforcement has been on the Extensible Access Control Markup Language (XACML) and IBMs XML Access Control Language (XACL). XACML is based on the eXtensible Markup Language (XML) (Chadramouli, 2003). The Extensible Access Control Markup Language (XACML) is a general-purpose language for specifying access control policies (Hu, Martin, Hwang, & Xie, 2007). In XML terms, it defines a core schema with a namespace that can be used to express access control and authorization policies for XML objects. Since it is based on XML, it is, as its name suggests, easily extensible. XACML supports a broad range of security policies (Chadramouli, 2003), (Hu, Martin, Hwang, & Xie, 2007), and uses a standardized syntax for formatting requests so that any one of the following responses to an access request will be valid:

- Permit: action allowed
- Deny: action disallowed
- Indeterminate: error or incorrect/missing value prevents a decision
- Not Applicable: request cannot be processed

As shown in Figure 6, XACML's standardized architecture for this decision-making uses two primary components: the Policy Enforcement Point (PEP) and the Policy Decision Point (PDP). The PEP constructs the request based on the user's attributes or credentials, the resource requested, the action specified, and other situation-dependent information provided through a Policy Information Point (PIP). The PDP receives the constructed request, compares it with the applicable policy and system state through the Policy Access Point (PAP), and then returns one of the four replies specified above to the PEP. The PEP then allows or denies access to the resource. The PEP and PDP components may be embedded within a single application or may be distributed across a network. This is an advantage for incorporating extensions for privacy enforcement because privacy enforcing security policies can be verified at the PEP. While user credentials can be checked at the PDP. The combination of both mechanisms makes privacy enforcement easier than in standard DAC, MAC, or RBAC mechanisms and also allows for the establishment of a trust infrastructure where users can manage their identities and personal information.

In order to make the PEP and PDP work, XACML provides a policy set, which is a container that holds either a policy or other policy sets, plus links to other policies. Each individual policy is stated using a set of rules. Conflicts are resolved through policy-combining algorithms which are good for handling cases of potential privacy violations that could result from combining security policies belonging to different domains. XACML also includes methods of combining these policies and policy sets, allowing some to override others. This is necessary because the policies may overlap or conflict. For example, a simple policy-combining algorithm is "Deny Overwrites", which causes the final decision to be "Deny" if any policy results in an "Overwrite". Conversely, other rules could be established to allow an action if any of a set of policies results in "Allow".

Determining what policy or policy set to apply is accomplished using the "Target" component. A target is a set of rules or conditions applied to each subject, object, and operation. When a rule's conditions are met for a user (subject), object, operation combination, its associated policy or policy set is applied using the process described

Figure 6. XACML access control model (Verma, 2004)

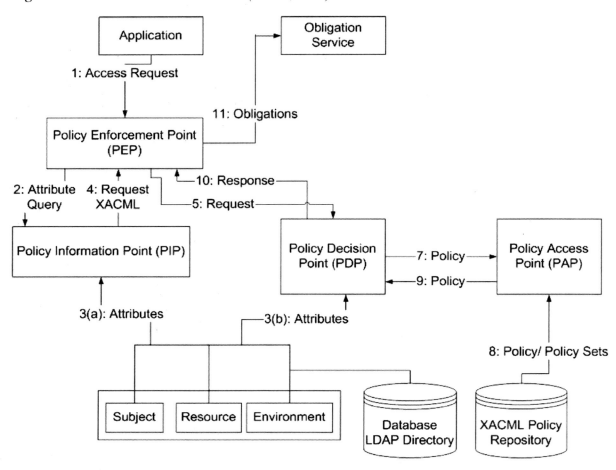

above. The associated access control data for a given enterprise domain can then be encoded in an XML document, and the conformance of data to the enterprise access control model can be obtained by validating the XML document against the XML schema that represents the enterprise access control model using XML parsers. These XML parsers are based on standard application programming interfaces such as the Document Object Model (DOM) (Wikipedia DOM, 2010), and the parser libraries are implemented in various procedural languages to enable an application program to create, maintain, and retrieve XML-encoded data.

XML-based, and other, access control languages provide capabilities for composing policies

from scratch, by allowing users to specify access control policies, together with the authorizations through the programming of the language. They however lack a formal specification language for access control constraints (like historical-based and domain constraints) that prevent assigning overlapping privileges. As an example, consider the case of constraints that require the manipulation and recording of access states (such as granted privileges). This is to avoid creating situations that result in users who were previously denied access to certain files being unknowingly granted access in a future state. Like most access control languages, XACML does not provide tools for the expression of historical constraints for historical-based access control policies, thus leaving the completeness of the constraint logics to the policy writer. This case is similar to the one that was evoked in Section 2.2 where Sam unintentionally gets a combination of "view" and "download" rights with respect to photographs belonging to Jane that John downloads to his *Photographs Folder*.

Domain constraints are based on the semantic information pertaining to an enterprise context. Therefore a grammar-based language cannot deal with content-based constraints. Consequently, an XML schema is insufficient for a complete specification of the RBAC model for an enterprise since the latter contains content-based domain constraints. An example is not allowing more than one user to be assigned to the role of security administrator (role cardinality constraint) and not allowing the roles "viewer" and "uploader" to be assigned to the same user (separation-of-duty constraint).

XML schema provides a very extensible means for specifying document structures through a comprehensive type definition language. So, advocates for XML access control hold that XML is a good candidate for a linguistic framework that is needed to express an access control model that embodies multiple policy requirements.

Considerable effort has gone into extending XML-based security frameworks to express privacy policies based on the credentials users provide (Ardanga et al., 2010). For instance, recent extensions to XACML incorporate RBAC support for privacy enforcement (Ardagna, De Capitani di Vimercati, Paraboschi, Pedrini, & Samarati, 2009). Other extensions include credential-based access control extensions to XACML to ensure that there is a framework to correctly authenticate user access to data, but also enforce privacy (Ardanga et al., 2010).

Examples of proposals on extending XACML for privacy include the XACML-based privacy centered access control system that provides credential based management and privacy support as well as credential-based access control

extensions to XACML (Ardanga, De Capitani di Vimercati, Paraboschi, Pedrini, & Samarati, 2009) (Ardanga et al., 2010). The Ardanga et al. proposal combines XACML with PRIME (Privacy and Identity Management for Europe) to produce an infrastructure that handles access control in a way the enforces privacy policies flexibly. The PRIME system handles five aspects, namely, resource representation, subject identity, secondary use, context representation, and ontology integration. All of these aspects are used to specify the access control requirements and conditions that are used to release data to a user based on their role, or context. The ontology integration aspect allows the system to apply access control rules by using concepts defined in the ontology. This approach provides a first step in integrating privacy constraints into access control mechanisms while taking into account the context and role of the user requesting the access. In credential-based access control, the idea is to build a trust framework in which service providers use a user's credentials to detremine what data to release to the user. Ardangaet al. suggest that the specification of how these credentials are authenticated be based on some formalisation that determines which attributes of the information have to be disclosed and to whom. Therefore, a key advantage of credential-based mechanisms is that they allow the user more control over their data and consequently gives the users more privacy.

However, it is worth noting that both credential and privacy based systems need some form of record of a user in order to decide whether or not to grant access to that data. This implies that a user needs to provide some information about themselves in order to access the data which in certain cases may expose them. For instance, in the pay-per-view movies scenario that we described in Section 2.2 (see Figure 5), a user may not be comfortable with allowing Jane to know that they like watching "Horror" movies. So, if Jane bases access to the movies on a credentials system she may not attract as many clients as

Table 1. Comparison: DAC, MAC, RBAC, and XACML

	DAC	MAC	RBAC	XACML
Control Point	User	Server	Server	Server/User
Authentication (Control Point)	User	Server	Server	Server/User
Review of Access Rights	User	Server	Server	Server/User
Access Right Propagation	User	Server	Server	Server/User
Access Right Revocation	User	Server	Server	Server/User
Information Flow Control	None	Yes	Yes	None unless security policy specified
User-reliant Security Policy	Yes	No	No	No unless authorized in security policy
Extension for Privacy	No	To some extent via information flow control	Possible through specialized role definition	Yes – Privacy policy specification and enforcement via the policy enforcement point and the policy decision point

she would have if she required less information to grant access to the movies. It is also worth noting that, as with the previous approaches that we discussed, the specification languages and/or frameworks assume a static environment where changes in access control policies are generally effected manually by a security administrator. When security policy combinations involve different domains handling the conflicts that arise might require dynamic adjustments to the combined security policy. Resolving these conflicts to establish a global security policy that satisfies the minimum requirements of the security domains involved, requires an access control scheme that is able to redefine the constraint rules adaptively. While XACML provides features to specify a broad range of policies, a formal specification is still needed to define constraint rules adaptively in order to enforce privacy on the Web.

The common pattern inherent in all the approaches discussed above is the inability to predict privacy violation scenarios mainly because these approaches need to be extended to handle situations of changing security requirements adaptively. For instance, Norton's Symantec Anti-virus software is taking steps towards building pre-emptive anti-virus software that incorporates

adaptability by using machine learning and data mining techniques. This is an indication that professional organizations also recognize the need for an evolution towards adaptive security mechanisms (Harrison, Munro, & Spiller, 2007), (Chess, 2005). Adaptive intrusion detection algorithms are also still at a budding stage but the idea of moving towards schemes that can adjust to changing security requirements and enforce privacy is inherent in all these approaches.

Table 1 summarizes our discussion of the DAC, MAC, RBAC, and XACML approaches to access control in relation to privacy enforcement. From the table below, it can be noted that one of the key reasons that these models fail to enforce privacy effectively is that access control is typically handled from the server's end. Therefore, users are not rights to allow them to manage their identities and privacy. The DAC model offers users some autonomy but as discussed earlier (see Figure 1, Section 2.1), poses a problem of information flow control.

This discussion illustrates that although no single access control scheme can be designed to handle every possible security scenario, web-based security scenarios are increasingly difficult to predict and control manually. Privacy violations typically arise because of mismanaged access control constraints and so the dynamic nature of the Web adds a further complication to the problem. In these cases, therefore, the needs for good security and consequently privacy enforcement are strongly intertwined with performance. This is because the delays created in trying to address new situations manually can be exploited maliciously and so a lead to privacy violations. In the next section we consider cryptographic access control schemes as a method of enforcing privacy and consider some extensions to allow for adaptability in situations of changing security requirements. Cryptographic access control schemes offer the advantage of being simpler to model mathematically and so lessen the security administrator's burden of security policy specification. In the next section we briefly explain how hierarchical cryptographic access control schemes are designed to work and proceed in Section 4 to discuss extensions for privacy enforcement and adaptability.

CRYPTOGRAPHIC ACCESS CONTROL FOR PRIVACY ENFORCEMENT

Hierarchical cryptographic access control (CAC) schemes emerged as an attempt to design MLS models that are more general and capable of providing security in different contexts without requiring extensive changes to the fundamental architecture (Akl & Taylor, 1983), (Mackinnon, Taylor, Meijer, & Akl, 1985), (De Capitani Di Vimercati, Foresti, Jajodia, Paraboschi, & Samarati, 2007). For instance, in situations that require data outsourcing, CAC schemes are useful because the data can be double encrypted to prevent a service provider from viewing the information yet be able to run queries or other operations on the data and return a result to a user who can decrypt the data using the keys in their possession (De Capitani Di Vimercati, Foresti, Jajodia, Paraboschi, &

Samarati, 2007). In this case, CAC schemes are a good way of enforcing privacy and improving the performance of the access control scheme. The performance improvements come from the fact the encryption ensures data privacy and saves the data owner from having to dedicate management resources to looking after the data.

CAC schemes are typically modeled in the form of a partially ordered set (poset) of security classes that each represents a group of users requesting access to a portion of the data on the system. Cryptographic keys for the various user groups requiring access to part of the shared data in the system are defined by classifying users into n disjoint security classes U_i, represented by a poset $(S, \prec=)$, where $S=\{U_0, U_1, \ldots, U_{n-1}\}$ (Akl & Taylor, 1983). By definition, in the poset, $U_i \prec= U_j$ implies that users in class U_j can have access to information destined for users in U_i but not the reverse. In the following paragraphs we present the two models on which CAC schemes are designed and discuss some approaches for performance improvements.

Hierarchical Cryptographic Access Control Models

Hierarchical Cryptographic Access Control (CAC) models are typically designed on the basis of the concept of posets and are generally divided into two main categories: independent and dependent CAC schemes. Independent CAC schemes originate from the multicast community where the concern is securing intra-group communications efficiently. In these protocols, the focus is on how to manage keys within a group in a way that minimizes the cost of key distribution when the membership of the group changes (Yu, Sun, & Liu, 2007). The reason for updating the keys is to prevent users who have left the group from continuing to access information available to group members. This aligns itself with our theme of privacy enforcement because in essence, we

Figure 7. An example of an independent CAC model

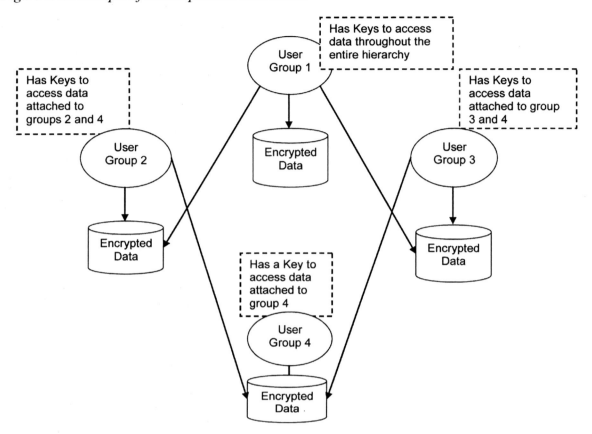

want CAC schemes to control access to the data by preventing all users who are not authorized to view information from accessing it.

Independent CAC schemes approach hierarchical access control by assigning each security class all the keys they need to access information both at their level and below. Accesses are granted only if the user requesting access holds the correct key (Akl & Taylor, 1983), (Atallah & Frikken, 2006). While this method of CAC is easier to implement in practical systems because of its flexibility, the cost of key distribution as well as the possibility of violations, both security and privacy, due to mismanaged or intercepted keys, is higher than that in dependent CAC schemes (Hassen, Bouabaallah, Bettahar, & Challal, 2007). In fact, in the worst case scenario where all the

keys in the hierarchy are updated, $2n+1$ keys are redistributed (where n represents the maximum number of security classes in the hierarchy), making key re-distribution more costly than in dependent CAC schemes where only n keys are redistributed (Hassen, Bouabaallah, Bettahar, & Challal, 2007), (Yu, Sun, & Liu, 2007).

As shown in Figure 7 the data is encrypted to ensure that only the users in possession of the correct keys are allowed access. In order to access the encrypted data a user belonging say to Group 1 will have to use the required key to download and decrypt the data to which access is sought. Since these keys might be available to several users at a time, each time the group membership changes, the keys affected by the change are replaced and the data reencrypted. This is to prevent the departed

Table 2. Key management models: Comparison (Kayem, 2008)

	Dependent Model	**Independent Model**
Security	Fewer keys distributed	More keys distributed
Encryption Cost	More re-encryption	Less re-encryption
Effect of Rekeying	Changing one key implies updating the whole hierarchy	Change only affected keys, and distribute to users requiring the keys
Key Distribution Cost (Number of keys transmitted)	n keys	$2n + 1$ keys

user from continuing to access the date. When a user who holds many of the keys departs this is a problem because it requires replacing and encrypting several portions of the data which is time-consuming. As well, as mentioned before, delays in encrypting the data can be exploited maliciously to provoke privacy violations.

A good way to alleviate these problems is to design the CAC scheme in a way that minimizes the number of keys distributed to any security class in the hierarchy. This model, typically referred to as the dependent key management (DKM) scheme, defines a precedence relationship between the keys assigned to the security classes in the hierarchy whereby keys belonging to security classes situated at higher levels in the hierarchy can be used to mathematically derive lower level keys. Access is not possible if the derivation function fails to yield a valid key. So for instance, in Figure 7, the data associated with Group 2 would be inaccessible to users in Group 1 if the assigned key does not allow them to mathematically derive the key with which the data at Group 2 was encrypted. This minimizes the cost of key assignment and distribution because a user only needs to hold one key from which all the other required keys can be derived. However, the problem of costly encryptions to cope with key updates remains (Hassen, Bouabaallah, Bettahar, & Challal, 2007), (Yu, Sun, & Liu, 2007), (Yu, Sun, & Liu, 2007). In Table 2 we summarize the differences between the independent and dependent CAC models in relation to the implications to privacy enforcement.

From Table 2, we note that the independent CAC model's main drawback lies in the cost of key distribution while the dependent CAC model's main drawback lies in the cost of encryption to cope with key updates. We also note, that either drawback does not help the case for privacy enforcement because encrypting large volumes of data can be quite time consuming and so create a wide window of vulnerability during which the data is unprotected. A solution would be to withdraw the data and handle encryption offline but this creates a problem of data availability that might affect the system's ability to meet its service level agreements (Meziane & Benbornou, 2010).. On the other hand with the independent CAC model, key distribution and the potential for interception also poses a privacy risk. When highly sensitive data is concerned this can become a serious problem because tracing illegal key usage is a challenging problem. For instance, if our hypothetical scenario of an e-business application is extended to include a health insurance service, it would be unwise to implement a CAC scheme that increases the risk of exposure of patient data. In Section 3.2 we discuss some approaches that have been proposed to alleviate both the problems of key distribution and costly encryptions to handle updates in group membership to ensure data privacy.

Other CKM Schemes

In order to minimize the amount of information distributed during key replacements variants of independent CAC model that appear in the literature (Shen & Chen, 2002), (Kuo, Shen, Chen, & Lai, 1999) propose ways of making key updates (distributions) easier and more secure by encrypting the keys that are to be distributed with a public key. The encrypted keys are then placed in some public location and a secret key is transmitted to each group. Access to a particular set of keys is only allowed if a user is in possession of the correct secret key. This makes it easier to exclude users that are compromised and reduces the number of keys distributed but the advantage comes at the cost of added public key information that increases the chances of an adversary correctly guessing at the secret keys being used (Crampton, Martin, & Wild, 2006).

Other approaches in the area of secure group communications have proposed batching key update requests to minimize the long term cost of rekeying (Li, Yang, Gouda, & Lam, 1999). Batching operates by accumulating requests for key updates during a preset interval at the end of which the keys are then replaced. Although this improves on the cost of rekeying, it widens the vulnerability window of the key management scheme.

Still along this line of batching key update requests, Crampton has suggested using lazy re-encryption to minimize the cost of data re-encryption (Crampton, 2007). Lazy re-encryption operates by using correlations in data updates to decide whether or not to update a key and re-encrypt the old data when group membership changes. In this way, since data re-encryption accounts for the larger part of the cost of key replacement, re-encryption is only performed when the data changes significantly, after a user's departure, or if the data is highly sensitive and requires immediate re-encryption to prevent the user from accessing it. The problem of having to re-encrypt the data after a user's departure still remains. Moreover, if the file is a sensitive file that does not change frequently, lazy re-encryption can allow a malicious user time to copy off information from the

file into another file and leave the system without ever being detected.

More recently, Ateniese et al. (Ateniese, Fu, Green, & Hohenberger, 2006) have proposed an improvement on the variant of IKM schemes that Blaze et al. (Blaze, Bleumer, & Strauss, 1998) proposed in 1998 whereby proxy-reencryption is used to assign users access to particular files associated with another user or group. Basically, each group or user in the hierarchy is assigned two keys (a master key and a secondary key). The secondary key is used to encrypt files and load them into a block store where they are made accessible to users outside of the group. In order to access encrypted data from the block store a user must retrieve the encrypted data and present both the encrypted data and their public key to an access control server. The access control server re-encrypts the data in a format that is decryptable with the user's secret key, only if the presented secondary public key authorizes them access. The problem of having to re-encrypt, update and distribute new keys when group membership changes remains.

Therefore irrespective of how a CAC scheme is designed, rekeying is handled by replacing the affected key and re-encrypting the associated data. Rekeying ensures that data privacy is always enforced but the rekeying process is time consuming which increases the vulnerability window. As mentioned before, an increased vulnerability window size makes a CAC scheme susceptible to two issues: delayed response time in handling key updates and an increased possibility of privacy. In Section 4, we present two approaches to ensuring privacy under changing security conditions without impeding performance. The first approach alleviates the cost of encryption by using data replication as a fault tolerance mechanism. Data replication is handled by predicting encryption and key update requirement. This indicates that by extending a CAC scheme to allow adaptability to a situation of changing security requirements, an access control scheme can meet its goals of

Figure 8. The autonomic computing feedback control loop (Kayem, 2008)

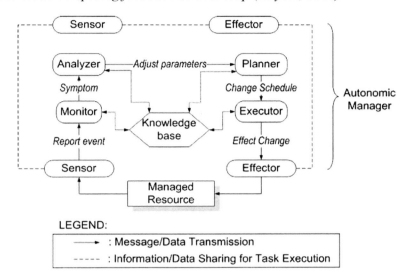

privacy. The second approach evokes the problem of collusion which basically occurs when two or more users gain access to unauthorized data by performing illegal key combinations. Our second proposition shows how one might prevent such violations of privacy by monitoring key assignments to prevent collusion susceptible keys from being assigned to users.

SELF-PROTECTING CRYPTOGRAPHIC ACCESS CONTROL

Our self-protecting cryptographic access control scheme is based on the paradigm of autonomic computing. This paradigm emerged in a bid to design applications with the ability to adaptively handle scenarios of varying complexity (Kephart & Chess, 2005). From our discussions in the previous sections, it is safe to say that there is a growing need for access control mechanisms with the ability to adjust to new scenarios adaptively.

Autonomic Computing and Privacy

Security via the autonomic computing paradigm was first proposed by Chess et al. in 2003 (Chess, 2005). In order to address the challenge of handling complex situations for which security needs to be ensured, they suggest using the paradigm of autonomic computing that IBM proposed in 2001 (Kephart & Chess, 2003), (Kephart & Chess, 2005). The paradigm of autonomic computing supposes that a system can be designed to self-regulate by using automatic reactions to defend, optimize and heal. The functions of an autonomic system are modeled using a feedback control loop that has two major components: the autonomic manager and the managed resource. The autonomic manager adjusts the behavior of the managed resource on the basis of recorded observations.

The autonomic model shown in Figure 8 is comprised of six basic functions: the sensor, monitor, analyzer, planner, executor, and effector. The sensor captures information relating to the behavior of the managed component and transmits this information to the monitor.

The monitor determines whether or not an event is abnormal by comparing observed values to threshold values in the knowledge base. The analyzer, on reception of a message from the monitor, performs a detailed analysis to decide what parameters need to be adjusted and by how much, and transmits this information to the planner where a decision is made on the action to be taken. The executor inserts the task into a scheduling queue and calls the effector to enforce the changes on the managed resource in the order indicated by the planner.

Autonomic computing aims to provide survivability and fault-tolerance for security schemes by allowing access control schemes to self-manage and self-configure to minimize security violations (Chess, 2005), (Johnson, Sterritt, Hanna, & O'Hagan, 2007). Johnston et al. (Johnson, Sterritt, Hanna, & O'Hagan, 2007) propose a preliminary approach that uses reflex autonomic computing in the development of a multi-agent security system. This is an interesting approach to self-protecting security, but the authors indicate that real-world implementations of their prototype system would require additional security controls and the prototype do not allow a security class to operate independently. As Moreno et al. (Moreno, Sanchez, & Isern, 2003) have pointed out, the connection to the rest of the system is lost. We note also that this work on autonomic access control focuses mainly on security policy definitions and restrictions on the messages sent and received by entities (users and/or agents) in the system as opposed to handling cases requiring some form of adaptability in the access control policy. Other approaches include trust and access control negotiation frameworks that are aimed at enforcing privacy in conflict situations in collaboration environments (Ryutov, Zhou, Neuman, Leithead, & Seamons, 2005), (Smari, Zhu, & Clemente, 2009), (Kuang & Ibrahim, 2009). The problem of designing adaptive access control schemes to support security policy definitions in ways that allow an access control mechanism to cope with changing scenarios still needs to be addressed.

Data Replication for Self-Protecting Cryptographic Access Control

We use an example of a simple read-intensive scenario to explain how data replication enhances the performance of CAC schemes in scenarios requiring key updates (Kayem, Martin, Akl, & Powley, 2008). Our CAC scheme is supported by a feedback control loop that is inspired by the autonomic computing paradigm (Chess, 2005). As shown in Figure 9, the CAC scheme can be supported by a framework that is structured in the form of an autonomic computing feedback control loop (see Figure 8). We note that this framework is formed simply by restructuring the model given in Figure 8 to suit the specific case of key updates.

The monitor module observes the behavior of the users on the system via a sensor that captures requests for key updates that are emitted either by a user or the security administrator. The monitor studies the rate at which key update request arrive over a given period and then transmits the information to the Analyzer module. At the Analyzer module, a computation to predict future the rate of future key update requests is made and this prediction information is transmitted to the Planner module. The Planner module computes the optimal number of resources (keys and encrypted replicas) that the security system needs to generate in order to cope with future key update requests. Once this is done a message is sent to the Executor module to generate the keys and replicas in anticipation of the key update requests. The Effector takes care of distributing new keys, making available new encrypted replicas, and deleting the old keys as well as the associated data.

An example of how this works is given in Figure 10 where we have a situation in which the feedback control loop is embedded in the key server and the Monitor module observes user behavior during a

Figure 9. An autonomic computing framework for handling key update requests

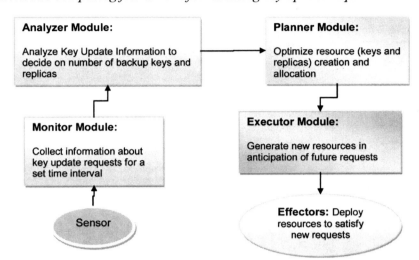

period W_1. The information is transmitted to the Analyzer module after the observation period is over and it is determined that one rekey request is likely to arrive from User Group 1 during a future monitoring period W_x. This information is transmitted to the Planner module where it is determined that in order to handle the rekey request one backup key and replica need to be generated in anticipation of this request. As depicted in Figure 10 the key server, via the Executor module, creates a new backup key, for the User Group 1, and transmits this key to the Effector where it is kept in a secret registry. The Effector then generates a new copy of the data and encrypts it with the new key. When a request for a key update arrives from User Group 1, the Effector will proceed to destroy the old data and replace it with the new encrypted version. The users remaining in the group will then be sent a copy of the key needed to decrypt the new data. Copy consistency is not a real concern in this case because our example is one of a read-intensive scenario. Updates are only authorized by the security administrator. So by anticipating key update requests we can alleviate the delays caused by key update requests and consequently avoid privacy violations that occur because of malicious exploitations of a wide vulnerability window.

Collusion Resolution in an Access Control Hierarchy

A common problem that leads to privacy violations in CAC schemes is the one that occurs when two or more users illegally compute a key to access information that they are not authorized to access. This problem also known as the collusion attack is one that all key management algorithms supporting CAC schemes seek to avoid. Checking assigned key to ensure that collusion is avoided, is a challenging problem and particularly so under changing security conditions. For instance, it is difficult to check if a new key that is assigned in response to a key update request cannot be used to provoke a collusion attack. Therefore, guaranteeing privacy under these conditions is also a challenging problem. We propose solving this problem with a self-protecting scheme that is inspired by the autonomic computing paradigm.

Basically, as in the framework we described earlier to handle replication, we will create a framework that is structured in the form of the autonomic computing feedback control loop. In the

Figure 10. Data replication and rekeying to handle update requests (an example)

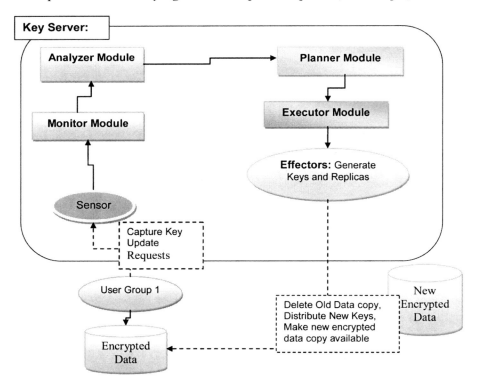

framework key updates are handled preemptively by monitoring, via a sensor, the rate at which key update requests occur. This information is then used by the Analyzer module to determine which parts of the CAC hierarchy need new keys and new keys are selected in a way that prevents collusions from occurring. The Analyzer module then calls the Planner module to generate a rule set that represents the new hierarchy for the new keys. This information is shared with the Executor module that keeps track of the old hierarchy and the new hierarchy. When a key update request needs to be handled the Effector assigns the affected user group a new key that is provided by the Executor module.

An example of how this can be done occurs when a hierarchy of keys is created using the key generation function that Akl and Taylor proposed (i.e. $K_i = K_0^{t_i} \mod M$, where t_i is an integer value that is assigned to a security class and M the

product of two large primes). In this case, the exponent set is $V = \{1, 2, 3, 4, 6, 9\}$. According to the Akl and Taylor scheme (Akl & Taylor, 1983), the greatest common divisor (GCD) at level 1 is 1, level 2, 1 and level 3, 1; and since the GCDs at all three levels are the same, it implies that the keys at levels 1 and 2 will be collusion liable. We note also that in each of the cases collusion is possible either because the combined GCD at a given level yields a value that is a divisor of some or all of the exponents at the higher levels (here levels 0 and/or 1) or is a divisor of the combined GCD of the exponents at levels 0 and/or 1. As shown in Figure 11 the monitor maintains a graph of the current key assignments and notes in this case that the potential assignment of keys K_2 and K_9 are likely to provoke collusions. This is indicated by the table (see Figure 11 – Monitor Module) that shows that collusions be-

Figure 11. A feedback control loop framework for collusion resolution

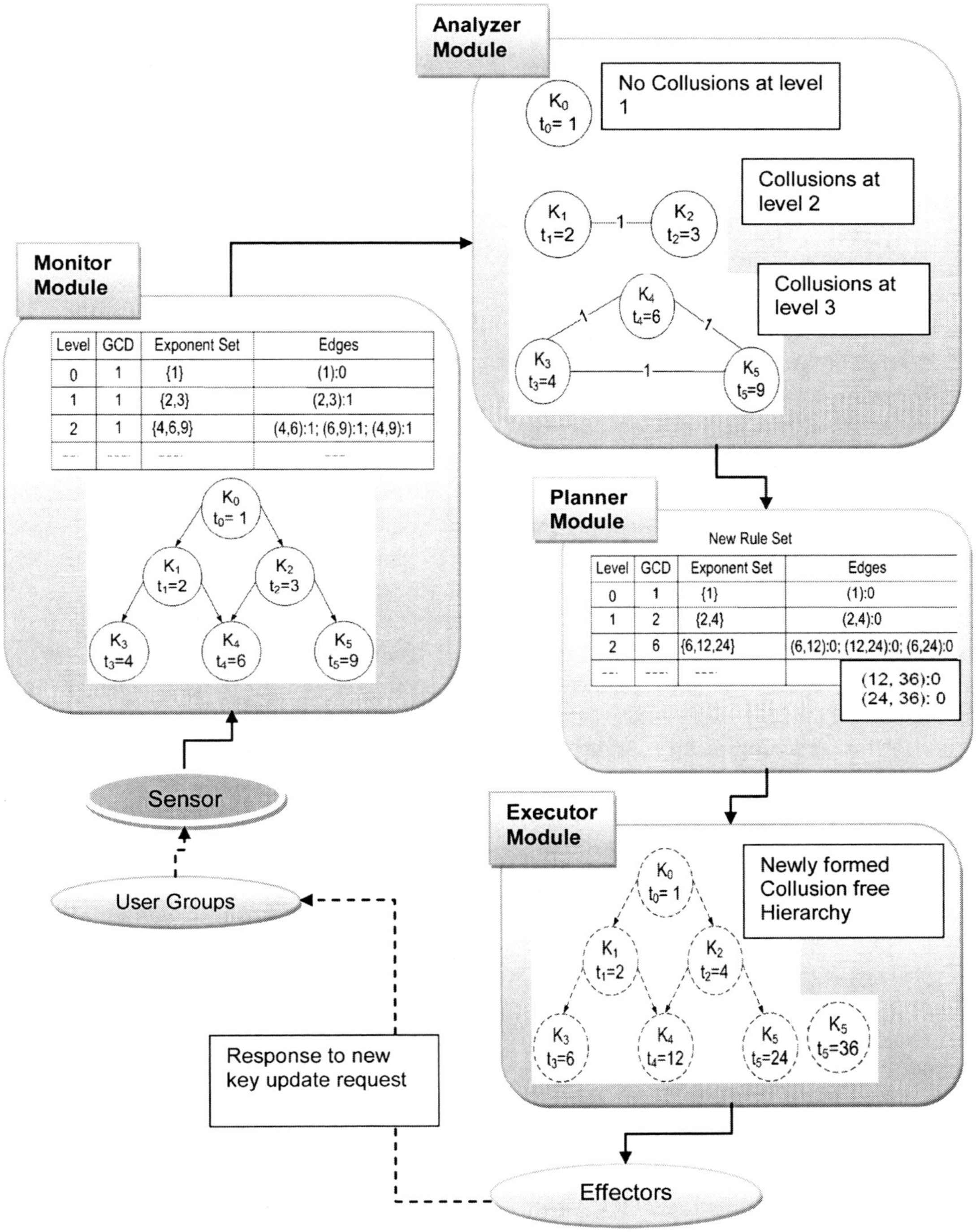

tween keys K_3, K_4, and K_9 are possible because of the exponent choice.

In order to remove the collusion-liable keys, the collusion resolution algorithm, that is located in the Analyzer module, operates as follows. In the first step, the algorithm is executed for level 0.

There is nothing higher than t_0, t_0 retains the value of 1. At level 1, as shown in Figure 11 (see Analyzer Module), the GCD $\{2, 3\} = 1$ which is equal to t_0, this indicates that there is a possibility that the keys K_1 and K_2 that are formed from $t_1 = 2$ and $t_2 = 3$ can be used to provoke a collusion attack. The collusion prevention algorithm, at the Planner Module, prevents this occurrence, by selecting a random value for t_2 such that GCD $\{t_1, t_2\}$ 6= 1 and both t_1 and t_2 remain multiples of t_0. A randomly chosen value of 4 is selected and since GCD$\{2, 4\} = 2$ which is not a divisor of the GCD at level 0, and both are multiples of t_0, t_2 retains the randomly assigned value of 4.

Likewise at level 2, as shown in Figure 11(see Analyzer Module), first $t_3 = 4$ which has been assigned to t_2, and GCD$\{4, 9\} = 1 = t_0$, GCD$\{4, 6\} = 2 = t_1$ and $t_5 = 9$ is not a multiple of t_2. Hence, the collusion prevention algorithm needs to re-assign integer values to t_3, t_4, and t_5 such that GCDs of the pairs of t_i at level 2 are not a factor of any GCDs at levels 0 and 1 and that additionally, the divisibility condition continues to hold. The random assignments in Figure 11(see Analyzer Module) present two possibilities of assignments, $t_3 = 12$, $t_4 = 24$, $t_5 = 36$ and $t_3 = 6$, $t_4 = 12$, $t_5 = 24$. So one of the sets is chosen and finally in the new assignment of exponents is such that collusion is prevented (see Planner Module – Figure 11). The Executor module is then called to construct the key graph (see Figure 11 – Executor Module) and make the new keys available to the Effector when the need arises.

It is obvious from this illustration that several different combinations would generate correct and valid independent sets. We could use a heuristic to control the size of the GCD of the exponent pairs

at all of the levels in the hierarchy. However, we do not consider having different exponent sets to be a disadvantage but rather an advantage because different sets could be generated off line and attributed when there is a demand for a new set of keys. This would be the case when a user joins or leaves the system and the original structure is maintained. In this way the method can in the best case contribute to an improvement in the efficiency of the key generation scheme (Mackinnon, Taylor, Meijer, & Akl, 1985).

The approach we adopt for identifying collusion liable keys is to map the keys on to a graph where the vertices represent the keys and the edges the probability of their being combined to provoke collusions. Adjacent keys indicate a higher likelihood of attack than non-adjacent keys. A collusion removal algorithm that is based on the principle of computing an independent set from the vertices in a graph is used to remove collusion liable keys from a key set.

Using the independent set approach to resolve this problem shows that the problem of removing the collusion liabilities in a key set is similar to the classic graph theory problem of computing a largest independent set. As the problem is NP-hard (Levitin, 2003), a heuristic was used to achieve an efficient (but perhaps suboptimal) solution in polynomial time. Nevertheless, as illustrated, the solution is feasible. It should be noted also that it is a good idea to have this work with the data replication approach that we described in Section 4.2.

FUTURE RESEARCH DIRECTIONS

The open problems that emerge from our discussions in the preceding sections include the prevention of inference and covert channels and so we discuss each in a little more detail below.

Inference and Covert Channels: Inference and covert channels can be categorized as problems of internal and privacy violations. These problems

Figure 12. Indirect information access via covert channels (Kayem, 2008)

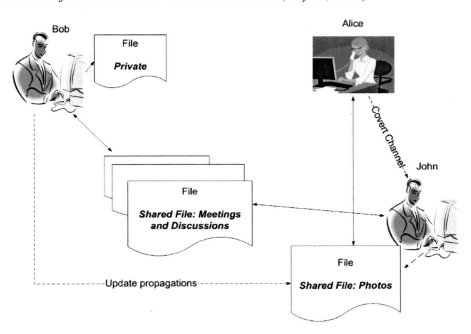

occur when a valid (authentic) user abuses his/her privileges either to transfer information to a user that is not authorized to view the information or to illegally gain access to data. Basically inference occurs when users are able to piece together information through legal access channels, in order to deduce information at another security level (Brodsky, Farkas, & Jajodia, 2000), (Farkas & Jajodia, 2002). Covert channels represent another manifestation of indirect violations of security policies in the context of hierarchical access control (Rjaibi, 2004). A covert channel refers to a transfer of information, from one level in the hierarchy to another, which violates the partial order between the security classes. This occurs when, for example, a higher level user employs their legal key to access information at their level and then deposits this information in a memory or storage location that can be accessed by the user with the lower security clearance.

Figure 12 depicts a scenario based on our hypothetical example of an e-business application that uses a social networking environment (e.g. Facebook) as a backbone. In this case, we consider two examples where indirect access to information is achieved via inference channels and covert channels. A user, say, Alice, happens to be on the "friends" profile of several users. Imagine for instance that she seeks to obtain information on another user, say Bob, whose "friends" profile she does not belong to. She however is on John's "friends" profile and John in turn is on Bob's "friends" profile, so when Bob posts information to his "wall" (environment accessible by all his friends), John, can read the information. Now suppose that John comments on a message Bob has posted, Alice can, from reading information on John's public space, infer information related to Bob. For instance, she may infer that if Bob is watching certain movies that he purchased from Jane's pay-per-view service (see Figure 5) then Bob will probably be going out to watch a certain other similar movie at a certain time. Furthermore with a little cooperation from John, a covert channel can be opened between herself and John that allows her to directly receive all the updates that Bob propagates. These weaknesses are not easy to handle with standard CAC schemes and also usually occur because of weakness in functional, multivalued and join dependencies in the databases that support these systems (Brodsky, Farkas, & Jajodia, 2000), (Pfleeger & Pfleeger, 2003). Moreover, these weaknesses result in very subtle privacy violations that are difficult to detect. Handling problems like these manually is also challenging and time-consuming because it is hard to determine what kinds of inferences can be made from the information that is available publicly. We however, believe that embedding functions that allow access control schemes to adjust to new scenarios adaptively is a good starting point for addressing these problems.

CONCLUSION

The discussion in this chapter has been centered on the extensions that need to be made to standard access control schemes in order to enforce privacy on the Web. We highlighted the pros and cons of each one discussing also some of the extensions that have been made to some to cater to privacy needs on the Web. The most extensive work has been on the Extensible Access Control Markup Language (XACML) with proposals to incorporate privacy checking mechanisms. We noted that one of the challenges in enforcing privacy is the fact that the Web environment is inherently dynamic and so security requirements can change on-the-fly. This can affect privacy enforcing schemes negatively leading to vulnerabilities that can be exploited maliciously. We noted also that some of the key problems that result in privacy violations include: inefficiencies in management of access control schemes and a lack of inbuilt mechanism to handle dynamic scenarios adaptively. Moreover, until recently, the assumption was that a well specified security solution will implicitly enforce privacy.

In this chapter we have shown, using two examples from cryptographic access control (CAC) schemes that the assumption that a good security scheme is privacy enforcing, is not always true. We proposed extending CAC schemes with an autonomic computing framework that is structured in the form of a feedback control loop to ensure self-protection, in a system, against privacy violations. Specifically we considered the problem of efficient key updates and looked at how to assign keys in a way that prevents collusion and also makes for less expensive data encryptions.

In order to address these concerns, we proposed embedding in the autonomic framework fault tolerance mechanisms like data replication and backup keys to anticipate key update requests. Replication is used to overcome the cost of encryption and consequently overcome the associated risk of privacy violations due to delays in re-encryptions of the data with the newly generated keys. Backup keys are created and checked preemptively to prevent assignments that can lead to privacy violations through collusions between assigned keys. The collusion resolution strategy is to map the keys onto a key graph and then compute and independent set of the graph using a heuristic. The autonomic computing framework allows the CAC scheme to enforce self-protection by simply monitoring the rate at which key updates are required and generating keys as well as encrypted replicas to respond to the requests preemptively as opposed to on demand. The advantage of this approach is that it allows the access control scheme to adjust its behavior based on the scenario with which it is faced making privacy enforcement somewhat simpler.

REFERENCES

Ahmed, Q., & Vrbsky, S. V. (2002). Maintaining security and timeliness in real-time database system. *Journal of Systems and Software, 61,* 15–29. doi:10.1016/S0164-1212(01)00111-X

Akl, S. G., & Taylor, P. D. (1983). Cryptographic solution to a problem of access control in a hierarchy. *ACM Transactions on Computer Systems, 1*(3), 239–248. doi:10.1145/357369.357372

Ardagna, C. A., De Capitani di Vimercati, S., Paraboschi, S., Pedrini, E., & Samarati, P. (2009). An XACML-based privacy-centered access control system. In *Proceedings of the First ACM Workshop on information Security Governance* (pp. 49-58). Chicago, IL: ACM.

Ardanga, C. A., De Capitani di Vimercati, S., Paraboschi, S., Pedrini, E., & Samarati, P. (2010). Enabling privacy preserving credential-based access control with XACML and SAML. *Proceedings of the 10th IEEE International Conference on Computer and Information Technology, CIT 2010,* (pp. 1090-1095). Bradford, West Yorkshire, UK.

Atallah, M., Frikken, K. B., & Blanton, M. (2009). Dynamic and efficient key management for access hierarchies. *ACM Transactions on Information and System Security, 12*(3), 190–202. doi:10.1145/1455526.1455531

Atallah, M. J., & Frikken, K. (2006). Key management for non-tree hierarchies. *ACM Symposium on Access Control Models and Technologies* (pp. 11-18). Lake Tahoe, CA: ACM.

Ateniese, G., De Santis, A., Ferrara, A. L., & Masucci, B. (2006). Provably-secure time-bound hierarchical key assignment schemes. In *Proceedings of the 13th ACM Conference on Computer and Communications Security* (pp. 288-297). Alexandria, Virginia, USA, October 30 - November 03, 2006: CCS '06. New York, NY: ACM.

Ateniese, G., Fu, K., Green, M., & Hohenberger, S. (2006). Improved proxy re-encryption schemes with applications to secure distributed storage. *ACM Transactions on Information and System Security, 9*(1), 1–30. doi:10.1145/1127345.1127346

Bell, D., & Lapadula, L. (1973). *Secure computer systems: Mathematical foundtaions and model,* (p. 2). MITRE report, MTR2547.

Bertino, E., & Sandhu, R. (2005). Database security - Concepts, approaches, and challenges. *IEEE Transactions on Dependable and Secure Computing, 2*(1), 2–19. doi:10.1109/TDSC.2005.9

Biba, K. (1977). *Integrity considerations for secure computer systems.* Bedford, MA, April 1977: Technical Report ESD-TR-76-372 ESD/AFSC, Hanscom AFB.

Blaze, M., Bleumer, G., & Strauss, M. (1998). Divertible protocols and atomic proxy cryptography. *In Proceedings of EUROCRYPT'98,* (pp. 1403:127-144).

Brewer, D. D., & Nash, M. (1988). The Chinese wall security policy. *IEEE Symposium on Security and Privacy* (pp. 206-214). Oakland, CA: IEEE.

Brodsky, A., Farkas, C., & Jajodia, S. (2000). Secure databases: Constraints, inference channels and monitoring disclosures. *IEEE Transactions on Knowledge and Data Engineering, 12*(6), 900–919. doi:10.1109/69.895801

Byun, J.-W., & Ninghui, L. (2008). Purpose based access control for privacy protection in relational database systems. *The VLDB Journal, 17,* 603–619. doi:10.1007/s00778-006-0023-0

Chadramouli, R. (2003). A policy validation framework for enterprise authorization specification. *ACSAC: In Proceedings of the 19th Annual Computer Security Applications Conference* (pp. 319-328). Washington, DC: IEEE Computer Society.

Chess, D. M. (2005). Security in autonomic computing. *SIGARCH Comput. Archit. News, 33*(1), 2–5. doi:10.1145/1055626.1055628

Chien, H.-Y. (2004). Efficient time-bound hierarchical key assignment scheme. *IEEE Transactions on Knowledge and Data Engineering, 16*(10), 1301–1304. doi:10.1109/TKDE.2004.59

Clark, D. R., & Wilson, D. (1987). A comparison of commercial and militrary computer security policies. In *Proceedings 1987 IEEE Symposium on Security and Privacy* (pp. 184-194). Oakland, CA: IEEE.

Corbi, A. G. (2003). The dawning of the autonomic computing era. *IBM Systems Journal, 42*(1), 5–18. doi:10.1147/sj.421.0005

Crampton, J. (2007). Cryptographically-enforced hierarchical access control with multiple keys. *In Proceedings 12th Nordic Workshop on Secure IT Systems (NordSec 2007)*, (pp. 49-60).

Crampton, J., Martin, K., & Wild, P. (2006). On key assignment for hierarchical access control. *In Proceedings 19th IEEE Workshop on Computer Security Foundations* (pp. 98-111). S. Servolo Island, Italy: IEEE.

Dai, Y.-S. (2005). Autonomic computing and reliability improvement. *In Proceedings 8th IEEE Symposium on Object-Oriented Real-Time Distributed Computing (ISORC'05)*, (pp. 204-206).

Das, M. L., Saxena, A., Gulati, V. P., & Phutak, D. B. (2005). Hierarchical key management scheme using polynomial interpolation. *SIGOPS Oper. Syst. Rev., 39*(1), 40–47. doi:10.1145/1044552.1044556

De Capitani Di Vimercati, S., Foresti, S., Jajodia, S., Paraboschi, S., & Samarati, P. (2007). Over-encryption: Management of access control evolution on outsourced data. *VLDB'07: Proceedings of the 33rd International Conference on Very Large Databases* (pp. 123-134). Vienna, Austria: VLDB Endowment.

De Santis, A., Ferrara, A. L., & Masucci, B. (2008). New constructions for provably-secure time-bound hierarchical key assignment schemes. *Theoretical Computer Science, 407*(1-3), 213–230. doi:10.1016/j.tcs.2008.05.021

Denning, D. E. (1976). A lattice model of secure information flow. *Communications of the ACM, 19*(5), 236–243. doi:10.1145/360051.360056

Du, S., & Joshi, J. (2006). Supporting authorization query and inter-domain role mapping in presence of hybrid role hierarchy. *In Proceedings of the 11th ACM Symposium on Access Control Models and Technologies* (pp. 228-236). ACM.

Farkas, C., & Jajodia, S. (2002). The inference problem: A survey. *ACM SUGKDD Explorations Newsletter, 42*(1), 5–18.

Fernandez-Medina, E., & Piattini, M. (2005). Designing secure databases. *Information and Software Technology, 4*, 6–11.

Foremski, T. (2010, October 18). *TRUSTe responds to Facebook privacy leaks*. Retrieved October 28, 2010, from http://www.siliconvalleywatcher.com/mt/archives/2010/10/truste_responds.php

Fujii, K., & Suda, T. (2009). Semantics-based context-aware dynamic service composition. *ACM Trans. Auton. Adapt. Syst., 4*(2), 1–31. doi:10.1145/1516533.1516536

Fung, B. C., Wang, K., Chen, R., & Yu, P. S. (2010). Privacy-preserving data publishing: A survey of recent developments. *ACM Computing Surveys, 42*(4), 1–53. doi:10.1145/1749603.1749605

Ganek, A., & Corbi, T. (2003). The dawning of the autonomic computing era. *IBM Systems Journal, 42*(1), 5–18. doi:10.1147/sj.421.0005

Gollman, D. (2005). *Computer security*. John Wiley and Sons, Ltd.

Harn, L., & Lin, H. (1990). A cryptographic keys generation scheme for multilevel data security. *Computers & Security*, *9*, 539–546. doi:10.1016/0167-4048(90)90132-D

Harrison, K., Munro, B., & Spiller, T. (2007). Security through uncertainty. *Elsevier -. Network Security*, 4–7. doi:10.1016/S1353-4858(07)70016-8

Hart, E., Davoudani, D., & McEwan, C. (2007). Immunological inspiration for building a new generation of autonomic systems. In *Proceedings of the 1st International Conference on Autonomic Computing and Communication Systems (Autonomics '07). ICST (Institute for Computer Sciences, Social-Informatics and Telecommunications Engineering), ICST*, (pp. 1-9). Brussels, Belgium.

Hassen, R. H., Bouabaallah, A., Bettahar, H., & Challal, Y. (2007). Key management for content acess control in a hierarchy. *Computer Networks*, *51*, 3197–3219. doi:10.1016/j.comnet.2006.12.011

Hengartner, U. (2008). Location privacy based on trusted computing and secure logging. In *Proceedings of the 4th International Conference on Security and Privacy in Communication Netowrks* (pp. 1-8). Istanbul, Turkey, September 22 - 25, 2008: SecureComm '08. New York, NY: ACM.

Hsu, C. L., & Wu, T. S. (2003). Cryptanalyses and improvements of two cryptographic key assignment schemes for dynamic access control in a user hierarchy. *Computers & Security*, *22*(5), 453–456. doi:10.1016/S0167-4048(03)00514-5

Hu, V. C., Martin, E., Hwang, J., & Xie, T. (2007). Conformance checking of access control policies specified in XACML. In *Proceedings 31st Annual International Computer Software and Applications Conference, COMPSAC 2007*, (pp. 275-280).

Huang, Q., & Shen, C. (2004). A new MLS mandatory policy combining secrecy and integrity implemented in highly classified secure OS. In *Proceedings 7th International Conference on Signal Processing (ICSP '04)*, (pp. 2409-2412).

Huebscher, M. C., & McCann, J. A. (2008). A survey of autonomic computing - Degrees, models, and applications. *ACM Computing Surveys*, Article 7 (August 2008), 28 pages. http://doi.acm.org/10.1145/1380584.1380585

J-W., B., & Li, N. (2008). Purpose based access control for privacy protection in relational database systems. *The VLDB Journal*, *17*, 603–619. doi:10.1007/s00778-006-0023-0

Jeong, M., & Kim, J. a. (2004). A flexible database security system using multiple access control policies. *IEEE International Conference on Systsem, Man, and Cybernetics* (pp. 5013-5018). IEEE.

Johnson, S. E., Sterritt, R., Hanna, E., & O'Hagan, P. (2007). Reflex autonomicity in an agent-based security system: The autonomic access control system. *4th IEEE International Workshop on Engineering Autonomic and Autonomous Systems (EASe '07)*, (pp. 68-78).

Jonker, C. M., Robu, V., & Treur, J. (2007). An agent architecture for multi-attribute negotiation using incomplete preference information. *Autonomous Agents and Multi-Agent Systems*, 221–252. doi:10.1007/s10458-006-9009-y

Kayem, A. (2008). *Adaptive cryptographic access control for dynamic data sharing environments*. Kingston, Canada: Queen's University.

Kayem, A., Martin, P., & Akl, S. (2010). Enhancing identity trust in cryptographic key management systems for dynamic environments. *Security and Communication Networks, 4*. Retrieved from http://onlinelibrary.wiley.com/doi/10.1002/sec.164/abstract

Kayem, A., Martin, P., Akl, S., & Powley, W. (2008). A framework for self-protecting cryptographic key management. In *Proceedings of the 2nd IEEE International Conference on Self-Adaptive and Self-Organizing Systems*, (pp. 191-200). Venice, Italy.

Kephart, J. O., & Chess, D. M. (2003). The vision of autonomic computing. *IEEE Computer, 36*(1), 41–50. doi:10.1109/MC.2003.1160055

Kephart, J. O., & Chess, D. M. (2005). Research challenges of autonomic computing. In *Proceedings 27th International Conference on Software Engineering*, (pp. 15-22). St. Louis, MO, USA.

Knuth, D. E. (1981). *The art of computer programming* (seminumerical algorithms, 2nd ed., vol. 2). Reading, MA: Addison Wesley.

Kuang, T. P., & Ibrahim, H. (2009). Security privacy access control policy integration and conflict reconciliation in health care organizations collaborations. *International Conference on Information Integration and Web-based Applications & Services* (pp. 750-754). Kuala Lumpur, Malaysia: ACM.

Kuo, F., Shen, V., Chen, T., & Lai, F. (1999). Cryptographic key assignment scheme for dynamic access control in a user hierarchy. *IEEE Proceedings. Computers and Digital Techniques, 146*(5), 235–240. doi:10.1049/ip-cdt:19990311

Lampson, B. W. (1973). A not on the confinement problem. *Communications of the ACM, 16*(10), 613–615. doi:10.1145/362375.362389

Lecue, F., Delteil, A., & Leger, A. (2008). Towards the composition of stateful and independent Semantic Web services. *SAC '08: In Proceedings of the 2008 ACM Symposium on Applied Computing* (pp. 2279-2285). Fortaleza, Brazil: ACM.

Levitin, A. (2003). *Introduction to the design and analysis of algorithms. Pearson.* Addison-Wesley.

Li, H., Ahn, D., & Hung, P. C. (2004). Algorithms for automated negotiations and their applications in information privacy. *In Proceedings IEEE International Conference* (pp. 255-262). e-Commerce Technology, 2004. CEC 2004.

Li, X., Yang, Y., Gouda, M., & Lam, S. (1999). Batch rekeying for secure group communications. *WWW10, 99*(7), 525-534.

Lin, T. (2006). Managing information flows on discretionary access control models. *2006 IEEE International Conference on Systems, Man., and Cybernetics*, (pp. 4759-4762).

Lin, T. Y. (2000). Chinese Wall security model and conflict analysis. *24th IEEE Computer Society International Computer Software and Applications Conference (COMPSAC 2000)*, (pp. 122-127). Taipei, Taiwan.

Liu, Y., & Chen, X. (2004). A new information security model based on BLP Model and BiBA Model. *In Proceedings 7th International Conference on Signal Processing (ICSP '04)*, (pp. 2643-2646).

Mackinnon, S. J., Taylor, P. D., Meijer, H., & Akl, S. G. (1985). An optimal algorithm for assigning cryptographic keys to control access in a hierarchy. *IEEE Transactions on Computers, 34*(9), 797–802. doi:10.1109/TC.1985.1676635

McLean, J. (1990). The specification and modeling of computer security. *IEEE Computer, 23*(1), 9–16. doi:10.1109/2.48795

Meziane, H., & Benbernou, S. (2010). A dynamic privacy model for Web Services. *Computer Standards & Interfaces, 32*, 288–304. doi:10.1016/j.csi.2010.02.001

Mie, X.-W., Feng, D.-G., Che, J.-J., & Wang, X.-P. (2006). Design and implementation of security operating system based on trusted computing. *International Conference on Machine Learning and Cybernetics*, (pp. 2776-2781).

Moreno, A., Sanchez, D., & Isern, D. (2003). Security measures in a medical multi-agent system. *Frontiers in Artificial Intelligence and Applications, 100*, 244–255.

Nazir, A., Raza, S., & Chuah, C.-N. (2008). Unveiling Facebook: A measurement study of social network based applications. *IMC '08: Proceedings of the 8th ACM SIGCOMM conference on Internet measurement* (pp. 43-56). Vouliagmeni, Greece: ACM.

Osborn, S. (2002). Integrating role graphs: A tool for security integration. *Data & Knowledge Engineering, 43*, 317–333. doi:10.1016/S0169-023X(02)00130-1

Pauley, W. A. (2010). Cloud provider transparency – An empirical evaluation. *IEEE Security and Privacy*, November-December 2010, 32-38.

Pfleeger, C. P., & Pfleeger, S. L. (2003). *Security in computing*. New Jersey: Pearson Education, Prentice Hall.

Ren, K., & Lou, W. (2007). Privacy-enchanced, attack-resilient access control in pervasive computing environments with optional context authentication capability. *Mobile Networks and Applications, 12*, 79–92. doi:10.1007/s11036-006-0008-7

Rjaibi, W. (2004). A multi-purpose implementation of mandatory access control in relational database management systems. *In Proceedings 30th VLDB Conference,* (pp. 1010-1020). Toronto, Canada.

Ryutov, T., Zhou, L., Neuman, C., Leithead, T., & Seamons, K. E. (2005). Adaptive trust negotiation and access control. *2005 Symposium on Access Control Models and Technologies* (pp. 139-146). Stockkholm, Sweden: ACM.

Sandhu, R. (1988). Cryptographic implementation of a tree hierarchy for access control. *Information Processing Letters, 27*, 95–98. doi:10.1016/0020-0190(88)90099-3

Sandhu, R. (1993). Lattice-based access control models. *IEEE Computer, 26*(11), 9–19. doi:10.1109/2.241422

Shen, V., & Chen, T. (2002). A novel key management scheme based on discrete logarithms and polynomial interpolations. *Computers & Security, 21*(2), 164–171. doi:10.1016/S0167-4048(02)00211-0

Slattery, B. (2010, March 31). *Facebook flub leaks private e-mail addresses*. Retrieved October 28, 2010, from http://www.pcworld.com/article/193009/ facebook_flub_leaks_private_email_addresses.html

Smari, W. W., Zhu, J., & Clemente, P. (2009). Trust and privacy in attribute based access control for collaboration environments. *International Conference on Information Integration and Web-based Applications & Services* (pp. 49-55). Kuala Lumpur, Malaysia: ACM.

Tanenbaum, A. S., & Steen, V. (2007). *Distributed systems: Principles and paradigms*. Upper Saddle River, NJ: Prentice Hall.

Tzeng, W.-G. (2002). A time-bound cryptographic key assignment scheme for access control in a hierarchy. *IEEE Transactions on Knowledge and Data Engineering, 14*(1), 182–188. doi:10.1109/69.979981

Verma, M. (2004, October). *XML security: Control information access with XACML*. Retrieved from http://www.ibm.com/developerworks/xml/library/x-xacml/

Wang, S.-Y., & Laih, C.-S. (2006). Merging: An efficient solution for time-bound hierarchical key assignment scheme. *IEEE Transactions on Dependable and Secure Computing, 3*(1), 91–100. doi:10.1109/TDSC.2006.15

Weiser, M. (1998). The future of ubiquitous computing on campus. *Communications of the ACM, 41*(1), 41–42. doi:10.1145/268092.268108

Weiser, M. (1999). The computer for the 21st century. *SIGMOBILE Mob. Comput. Commun. Rev.*, *3*(1), 3–11. doi:10.1145/329124.329126

Wikipedia. (2010, October 27). *Facebook*. Retrieved October 28, 2010, from http://en.wikipedia.org/wiki/Facebook

Wikipedia. (2010, October 28). *MySpace*. Retrieved October 28, 2010, from http://en.wikipedia.org/wiki/MySpace

Wikipedia. (2010, November 20). *Domain model*. Retrieved November 25, 2010, from http://en.wikipedia.org/wiki/Domain_model

Yang, C., & Li, C. (2004). Access control in a hierarchy using one-way functions. *Elsevier: Computers and Security*, *23*, 659–664.

Yao, D., Frikken, K., Atallah, M., & Tamassia, R. (2008). Private information: To reveal or not to reveal. *ACM Transactions on Information and System Security*, *12*(1), 1–27. doi:10.1145/1410234.1410240

Yi, X. (2005). Security of Chien's efficient time-bound hierarchical key assignment scheme. *IEEE Transactions on Knowledge and Data Engineering*, *17*(9), 1298–1299. doi:10.1109/TKDE.2005.152

Yi, X., & Ye, Y. (2003). Security of Tzeng's time-bound key assignment scheme for access control in a hierarchy. *IEEE Transactions on Knowledge and Data Engineering*, *15*(4), 1054–1055. doi:10.1109/TKDE.2003.1209023

Yu, W., Sun, Y., & Liu, R. (2007). Optimizing the rekeying cost for contributory group key agreement schemes. *IEEE Transactions on Dependable and Secure Computing*, *4*(3), 228–242. doi:10.1109/TDSC.2007.1006

Zhang, G., & Parashar, M. (2004). Context-aware dynamic access control for pervasive application. *In Proceedings of the Communication Networks and Distributed Systems Modeling and Simulation Conference* (pp. 21-30). Society for Modeling and Simulation International.

Zou, X., & Ramamurthy, B. (2004). A GCD attack resistant CRTHACS for secure group communications. *In Proceedings International Conference on Information Technology: Coding and Computing (ITCC'04)*, (pp. 153-154).

ADDITIONAL READING

Besmer, A., Watson, J., & Lipford, H. R. (2010). The impact of social navigation on privacy policy configuration. In *Proceedings of the Sixth Symposium on Usable Privacy and Security* (Redmond, Washington, July 14 - 16, 2010). SOUPS '10, vol. 485. ACM, New York, NY, 1-10. DOI=http://doi.acm.org/10.1145/1837110.1837120

Bishop, M. (2008). *Computer Security: Art and Science*. Addison-Wesley.

Carminati, B., Ferrari, E., & Perego, A. (2009, Oct.). Enforcing access control in Web-based social networks. *ACM Transactions on Information and System Security*, *13*(1), 1–38. doi:10.1145/1609956.1609962

Dandalis, A., & Prasanna, V. K. 2004. An adaptive cryptographic engine for internet protocol security architectures. *ACM Trans. Des. Autom. Electron. Syst.* 9, 3 (Jul. 2004), 333-353. http://doi.acm.org/10.1145/1013948.1013952

Fayssal, S., Alnashif, Y., Kim, B., & Hariri, S. 2008. A proactive wireless self-protection system. In *Proceedings of the 5th international Conference on Pervasive Services* (Sorrento, Italy, July 06 - 10, 2008). ICPS '08. ACM, New York, NY, 11-20. DOI= http://doi.acm.org/10.1145/1387269.1387272

Ferraiolo, D. F., Kuhn, D. R., & Chandramouli, R. (2003). *Role-Based Access Control, Computer Security Series*. Boston, London: Artech House.

Ganek, A., & Corbi, T. (2003). The Dawning of the Autonomic Computing Era. *IBM Systems Journal, 42*(1), 5–18. doi:10.1147/sj.421.0005

Gollman, D. (2005). *Computer Security*. John Wiley and Sons, Ltd.

Hafner, M., & Breu, R. (2009). *Security Engineering for service Oriented Architectures*. Berlin, Heidelberg: Springer-Verlag.

Hart, E., Davoudani, D., & McEwan, C. 2007. Immunological inspiration for building a new generation of autonomic systems. In *Proceedings of the 1st international Conference on Autonomic Computing and Communication Systems* (Rome, Italy, October 28 - 30, 2007). Autonomics, vol. 302. ICST (Institute for Computer Sciences Social-Informatics and Telecommunications Engineering), ICST, Brussels, Belgium, 1-10.

Hellerstein, J. L. 2009. Engineering autonomic systems. In *Proceedings of the 6th international Conference on Autonomic Computing* (Barcelona, Spain, June 15 - 19, 2009). ICAC '09. ACM, New York, NY, 75-76. DOI= http://doi.acm.org/10.1145/1555228.1555254

Kayem, A., Akl, S., & Martin, P. (2010). *Adaptive Cryptographic Access Control. Advances in Information Security, 48*. Springer.

Kayem, A., Martin, P., & Akl, S. (2010). Enhancing Identity Trust In Cryptographic Key Management Systems for Dynamic Environments. *Security and Communication Networks*, http://onlinelibrary.wiley.com/doi/10.1002 /sec.164/abstract.

Kayem, A., Martin, P., Akl, S., & Powley, W. (2008). A framework for self-protecting cryptographic key management. *In Proceedings, 2nd IEEE International Conference on Self-Adaptive and Self-Organizing Systems*, (pp. 191--200). Venice, Italy.

Kephart, J. O., & Chess, D. M. (2003). The Vision of Autonomic Computing. *IEEE Computer, 36*(1), 41–50. doi:10.1109/MC.2003.1160055

Kephart, J. O., & Chess, D. M. (2005). Research Challenges of Autonomic Computing. *In Proceedings. 27th International Conference on Software Engineering*, (pp. 15-22). St. Louis, MO, USA.

Lee, J., Jeong, K., & Lee, H. 2010. Detecting metamorphic malwares using code graphs. In *Proceedings of the 2010 ACM Symposium on Applied Computing* (Sierre, Switzerland, March 22 - 26, 2010). SAC '10. ACM, New York, NY, 1970-1977. DOI= http://doi.acm.org/10.1145/1774088.1774505

Osborn, S. (2002). Integrating Role Graps: A tool for Security Integration. *Data & Knowledge Engineering, 43*, 317–333. doi:10.1016/S0169-023X(02)00130-1

Pfleeger, C. P., & Pfleeger, S. L. (2003). *Security in Computing*. New Jersey: Pearson Education, Prentice Hall.

Rosen, K. (2003). *Discrete mathematics and Its Applications* (5th ed.). McGraw Hill.

Ryutov, T., Zhou, L., Neuman, C., Leithead, T., & Seamons, K. E. 2005. Adaptive trust negotiation and access control. In *Proceedings of the Tenth ACM Symposium on Access Control Models and Technologies* (Stockholm, Sweden, June 01 - 03, 2005). SACMAT '05. ACM, New York, NY, 139-146. DOI= http://doi.acm.org/10.1145/1063979.1064004

Squicciarini, A. C., Shehab, M., & Paci, F. 2009. Collective privacy management in social networks. In *Proceedings of the 18th international Conference on World Wide Web* (Madrid, Spain, April 20 - 24, 2009). WWW '09. ACM, New York, NY, 521-530. DOI= http://doi.acm.org/10.1145/1526709.1526780

Tanenbaum, A. S., & Steen, V. (2007). *Distributed Systems: Principles and Paradigms.* Upper Saddle River, NJ 07458: Prentice Hall.

Vincenzo Taddeo, A., Marcon, P., & Ferrante, A. 2009. Negotiation of security services: a multi-criteria decision approach. In *Proceedings of the 4th Workshop on Embedded Systems Security* (Grenoble, France, October 15 - 15, 2009). WESS '09. ACM, New York, NY, 1-9. DOI= http://doi.acm.org/10.1145/1631716.1631720

Watson, J., Whitney, M., & Lipford, H. R. 2009. Configuring audience-oriented privacy policies. In *Proceedings of the 2nd ACM Workshop on Assurable and Usable Security Configuration* (Chicago, Illinois, USA, November 09 - 09, 2009). Safe-Config '09. ACM, New York, NY, 71-78. DOI= http://doi.acm.org/10.1145/1655062.1655076

KEY TERMS AND DEFINITIONS

Access Control: Method of protecting data from access by unauthorized users usually done by classifying users into groups according to privilege of access.

Autonomic Management: This a method of system management whereby a system is designed and/or implemented to be self-managing and self-configuring to reduce the delays and risks of failure that are inherent in manually managed systems.

Cloud Computing: This is an Internet-based concept that is an extension of the service oriented architecture concept whereby resources like memory, software and information are made available to users on demand.

Cryptographic Key Management: Access control model based on the assignment of cryptographic keys that users can use to encrypt or decrypt data.

Data Privacy Protection: This is the concept of designing access control mechanisms to ensure that the mechanisms protect data from being accessed by unauthorized users and also from being used in ways that violate the rules of access to the data.

Fault Tolerance: Ability of a system to cope with failure usually with some form of backup solution that ensures that the system is available to perform the tasks required of it on-demand.

Keywords: Data Privacy Protection, Access Control, Cryptographic Key Management, Fault Tolerance, Autonomic Management, Self-Protection, Cloud Computing.

Self-Protection: This is the ability of any system, and in particular an access control mechanism, to protect itself from failure by using autonomic management to reduce human error and to provide efficient management.

ENDNOTES

[1]   The autonomic computing paradigm aims at creating systems that are self managing and self-configuring to reduce human error and make systems more efficient time wise.

Chapter 5
Privacy Hash Table

Xiaoxun Sun
Australian Council for Educational Research, Australia

Min Li
University of Southern Queensland, Australia

ABSTRACT

A number of organizations publish microdata for purposes such as public health and demographic research. Although attributes of microdata that clearly identify individuals, such as name, are generally removed, these databases can sometimes be joined with other public databases on attributes such as Zip code, Gender, and Age to re-identify individuals who were supposed to remain anonymous. These linking attacks are made easier by the availability of other complementary databases over the Internet. K-anonymity is a technique that prevents linking attacks by generalizing or suppressing portions of the released microdata so that no individual can be uniquely distinguished from a group of size k. In this chapter, we investigate a practical full-domain generalization model of k-anonymity and examine the issue of computing minimal k-anonymous solution. We introduce the hash-based technique previously used in mining associate rules and present an efficient and effective privacy hash table structure to derive the minimal solution. The experimental results show the proposed hash-based technique is highly efficient compared with the binary search method.

INTRODUCTION

Several microdata disclosure protection techniques have been developed in the context of statistical database, such as scrambling and swapping values and adding noise to the data while maintaining an overall statistical integrity of the

DOI: 10.4018/978-1-61350-501-4.ch005

result (Adam et al. 1989). However, many applications require release and explicit management of microdata while maintaining truthful information within each tuple. This data quality requirement makes inappropriate those techniques that disturb data and therefore, although preserving statistical properties, compromise the correctness of the single pieces of information. Among the techniques proposed for providing anonymity in the release of microdata, we focus on two techniques in particular: generalization and suppression (in the Statistics literature, this approach is often called recoding), which unlike other existing techniques, such as scrambling or swapping, preserve the truthfulness of the information.

K-anonymity is a technique that prevents joining attacks by generalizing and/or suppressing portions of the released microdata so that no individual can be uniquely distinguished from a group of size k. There are a number of models for producing an anonymous table. One class of models, called global-recoding (Adam et al. 1989) map the values in the domains of quasi-identifier attributes to other values. This chapter is primarily concerned with a specific global-recoding model, called full-domain generalization. Full-domain generalization was proposed by Samarati and Sweeney (Samarati, 2001; Sweeney, 2002) and maps the entire domain of each quasi-identifier attribute in a table to a more general domain in its domain generalization hierarchy. This scheme guarantees all values of a particular attribute in the anonymous table belong to the same domain.

For any anonymity mechanism, it is desirable to define some notions of minimality. Intuitively, a k-anonymous table should not generalize, suppress, or distort the data more than is necessary to achieve such k-anonymity. Indeed, there are a number of ways to define minimality. One notion of minimality is defined so as to generalize or suppress the minimum number of attribute values in order to satisfy a given k-anonymity requirement. Such a problem is shown to be NP-hard (Meyerson et al. 2004). As to our model, the notion of minimal full-domain generalization was defined in (Samarati, 2001; Sweeney, 2002) using the distance vector of the domain generalization. Informally, this definition says that a full-domain generalized private table PT is minimal if PT is k-anonymous, and the height of the resulting generalization is less than or equal to that of any other k-anonymous full-domain generalization.

In this chapter, we focus on this specific global-recoding model of k-anonymity. Our objective is to find the minimal k-anonymous generalization (table) under the definition of minimality defined by Samarati (Samarati, 2001). By introducing the hash-based technique, we provide with a new privacy hash table structure to generate minimal k-anonymous tables that not only improves the search algorithm proposed by Samarati (Samarati, 2001) but is also useful for computing other optimal criteria solution for k-anonymity. Further, we also extend our algorithm to cope with l-diversity.

RELATED WORK

Protecting anonymity when publishing microdata has long been recognized as a problem, and there has been much recent work on computing k-anonymity for this purpose. The u-Argus system (Willenborg, 1996) was implemented to anonymize microdata but considered attribute combinations of only a limited size, so the results were not always guaranteed to be k-anonymous.

In recent years, numerous algorithms have been proposed for implementing k-anonymity via generalization and suppression. The framework was originally defined by Samarati and Sweeney (Samarati, 2001; Sweeney, 2002). Sweeney proposed a greedy heuristic algorithm for full-domain generalization ("Datafly") (Sweeney, 2002). Although the resulting generalization is guaranteed to be k anonymous, there are no minimality guarantees. Samarati proposed the binary search algorithm for discovering a single minimal full-domain generalization. LeFevre et al. described an efficient search algorithm called Incognito, for anonymous full-domain generalization (LeFevre et al. 2005). The concept of l-diversity is introduced by Machanavajjhala et al. in (Machanavajjhala, et al. 2006) to prevent attackers with background knowledge. In (Li, et al. 2007), distribution of sensitive attributes is first considered. Based on this, a more robust privacy measure (which we refer to as t-closeness) is proposed. Their work guarantees that the distribution of any sensitive attribute within each group (equivalence class) is close to its global distribution in the table. In (Xiao et al. 2006), Xiao et al. proposed to let individuals specify privacy policies about their own attributes. The method developed in this chapter effectively improves the results obtained by Samarati.

Cost metrics intended to quantify loss of information due to generalization were described in (Iyengar, 2002). Given such a cost metric, Iyengar (Iyengar, 2002) developed a genetic algorithm and Winkler (Winkler, 2002) described a stochastic algorithm based on simulated annealing to find locally minimal anonymous table. Top-down (Fung et al. 2005) and bottom-up (Wang et al. 2004) greedy heuristic algorithms were proposed to produce anonymous data. Bayardo and Agrawal (Bayardo et al, 2005) described a set enumeration approach to find an optimal anonymous table according to a given cost metric. Subsequent work shows that optimal anonymity under this model may not be as good as anonymity produced with a multi-dimension variation (LeFevre et al. 2006). Finally, Meyerson and Williams (Meyerson et al. 2004) and Aggarwal et al. (Aggarwal et al. 2005) proved the optimal k-anonymity is NP-hard (based on the number of cells and number of attributes that are generalized and suppressed) and describe approximation algorithms for optimal k-anonymity. Sun et al. (Sun et al. 2008a) recently showed that the k-anonymity problem is still NP-hard when restricting the size of the alphabet. Apart from the theoretical results, several approximation algorithms have been proposed to find the near optimal solution of k-anonymity problem (Meyerson et al. 2004, Aggarwal et al. 2005, Sun et al. 2008a). There are other works investigate the characteristics of k-anonymity as well. For example, Aggarwal discusses the curse of dimensionality related to k-anonymity (Aggarwal, 2005). In particular, he shows that it is not possible to create even a 2-anonymous table in high dimensional space without considerable

information loss. In (Yao et al, 2005), Yao et al. show that, when several microdata tables are disclosed, even if each of them satisfies k-anonymity, by pooling them together, k-anonymity may be violated. They further design algorithms to detect such violations. Zhong et al. (Zhong et al. 2005) devise a protocol for obtaining k-anonymous tables in distributed environments.

PRELIMINARIES

In this section, we introduce some background knowledge that is used in this chapter.

Definition 1. [K-anonymous requirement] Each release of data must be such that every combination of values of quasi-identifiers can be indistinctly matched to at least k respondents.

The concept of k-anonymity (Samarati, et al. 1998, Samarati, 2001, Sweeney, 2002) tries to capture one of the main requirements that have been followed by the statistical community and by agencies releasing data on the private table (PT). According to the requirement, the released data should be indistinguishably related to no less than a certain number of respondents. The set of attributes included in the private table, also externally available and therefore exploitable for linking, is called quasi-identifier (QI).

Since it seems highly impractical to make assumptions on the datasets available for linking to external attackers or curious data recipients, essentially k-anonymity takes a safe approach requiring that the respondents should be indistinguishable (within a given set) with respect to the set of attributes in the released table. To guarantee the k-anonymity requirement, k-anonymity requires each value of a quasi-identifier in the released table to have at least k occurrences. Formally, we have the following definition.

Definition 2. [K-anonymity] Let $PT(A_1,...,A_m)$ be a private table and QI be a quasi-identifier, associated with it. PT is said to satisfy k-anonymity with respect to QI if and only if each sequence of

Table 1. An example of microdata

Gender	Age	Zip	Disease
Male	25	4370	Cancer
Male	25	4370	Cancer
Male	22	4352	Cancer
Female	28	4373	Chest Pain
Female	28	4373	Obesity
Female	34	4350	Flu

values in PT[QI] appears at least with k occurrences in PT[QI].

A QI-group in the modified microdata T' is the set of all records in the table containing identical values for the QI attributes. There is no consensus in the literature over the term used to denote a QI-group. This term was not defined when k-anonymity was introduced (Samarati, et al. 1998, Samarati, 2001, Sweeney, 2002). More recent papers use different terminologies such as equivalence class (Li, et al. 2007, Machanavajjhala, et al. 2006, Xiao et al, 2006) and QI-cluster (Traian et al, 2006, Sun et al. 2008b).

If a set of attributes of external tables appears in the quasi-identifier associated with the private table (PT) and the table satisfies k-anonymity, then the combination of the released data with the external data will never allow the recipient to associate each released tuple with less than k respondents. For instance, consider the released microdata in Table 1 with quasi-identifier QI={Gender, Age, Zip}, we see that the table satisfies k-anonymous

with k=1 only since there exists single occurrence of values over the considered QI (e.g., the single occurrence of "Male, 22 and 4352" and "Female, 34 and 4350").

GENERALIZATION RELATIONSHIP

Among the techniques proposed for providing anonymity in the release of microdata, the k-anonymity proposal focuses on two techniques in particular: generalization and suppression, which unlike other existing techniques, such as scrambling or swapping, preserve the truthfulness of the information. Generalization consists in substituting the values of a given attribute with more general values. We use * to denote the more general value. For instance, we could generalize two different Zip codes 4370 and 4373 to 437*. The other technique, referred to as data suppression, removes the part or entire value of attributes from the table. Since suppressing an attribute (i.e., not

Table 2. A 3-anonymous microdata

Gender	Age	Zip	Disease
Male	[22-25]	43**	Cancer
Male	[22-25]	43**	Cancer
Male	[22-25]	43**	Cancer
Female	[28-34]	43**	Chest Pain
Female	[28-34]	43**	Obesity
Female	[28-34]	43**	Flu

releasing any of its values) to reach k-anonymity can equivalently be modeled via a generalization of all the attribute values to the most generalized data *. Note that this observation holds assuming that attribute suppression removes only the values and not the attribute (column) itself. This assumption is reasonable since removal of the attribute (column) is not needed for k-anonymity. In this chapter, we consider only data generalization.

The notion of *domain* (i.e., the set of values that an attribute can assume) is extended to capture the generalization process by assuming the existence of a set of *generalized domains*. The set of original domains together with their generalizations is referred to as *Dom*. Each generalized domain contains generalized values and there exists a mapping between each domain and its generalizations. (For example, Zip codes can be generalized by dropping the least significant digit at each generalization step; Ages can be generalized to an interval, and so on). This mapping is described by means of a *generalization relationship* $\leq_D$. Given two domains D_i and $D_j \in Dom$, $D_i \leq_D D_j$ states that values in domain D_j are generalizations of values in D_i. The *generalization relationship* $\leq_D$ defines a partial order on the set *Dom* of domains, and is required to satisfy the following two conditions:

$$C_1 : \forall D_i, D_j, D_z \in \text{Dom} :$$
$$D_i \leq_D D_j, D_i \leq_D D_z \Rightarrow D_j \leq_D D_z \vee D_z \leq_D D_j$$
$$C_2 : all \max imal\ element\ of\ \text{Dom}\ are\ singletons$$

Condition C_1 states that for each domain D_i, the set of domains generalization of D_i is totally ordered and we can think of the whole generalization domain as a chain of nodes, and if there is an edge from D_i to D_j, we call D_j the *direct generalization* of D_i. Note that the *generalization relationship* $\leq_D$ is transitive, and thus, if $D_i \leq_D D_j$ and $D_j \leq_D k$, then $D_i \leq_D D_k$. In this case, we call D_k the *implied generalization* of D_i. Condition C_1 implies that each D_i has at most one *direct generalization* domain D_j.

thus ensuring determinism in the generalization process. Condition C_2 ensures that all values in each domain can be generalized to a single value. For each domain $D \in Dom$, the definition of a generalization relationship implies the existence of a totally ordered hierarchy, called the *domain generalization hierarchy*, denoted DGH_D. Pathes in the *domain generalization hierarchy* correspond to *implied generalizations* and edges correspond to *direct generalizations*. For example, consider DGH_{Z0} in Figure 1. Z_1 is the direct generalization of Z_0 and Z_2 is the implied generalization of DGH_{Z0}.

A *value generalization relationship* denoted $\leq_V$ can also be defined, which associates with each value in domain D_i a unique value in domain D_j. For each domain $D \in Dom$, the value generalization relationship implies the existence of a *value generalization hierarchy*, denoted VGH_D. It is easy to see that the value generalization hierarchy VGH_D is a tree, where the leaves are the minimal values in D and the root (i.e., the most general value) is the value of the maximum element in VGH_D.

Example 1. Figure 1 illustrates an example of domain and value generalization hierarchies for domains: Z_0, A_0 and G_0. Z_0 represents a subset of the Zip codes in Table 1; A_0 represents Age; and G_0 represents Gender. The generalization relationship specified for Zip codes generalizes a 4-digit Zip code, first to a 3-digit Zip code, and then to a 2-digit Zip code. The attribute Age is first generalized to the interval (22-25) and (28-34), then to the interval (22-34). The Gender hierarchy in the figure is of immediate interpretation.

Since the approach in \cite{sam2001} works on sets of attributes, the generalization relationship and hierarchies are extended to refer to tuples composed of elements of Dom or of their values. Given a domain tuple DGH_{D_z} such that $D_i \in Dom$, $i=1,...,n$, the domain generalization hierarchy of DT is DGH_{D_z} where the Cartesian product is ordered by imposing coordinate-wise order. Since each DGH_{Di} is totally ordered, DGH_{DT} defines a

Figure 1. Domain and value generalization hierarchies for zip code, age, and gender

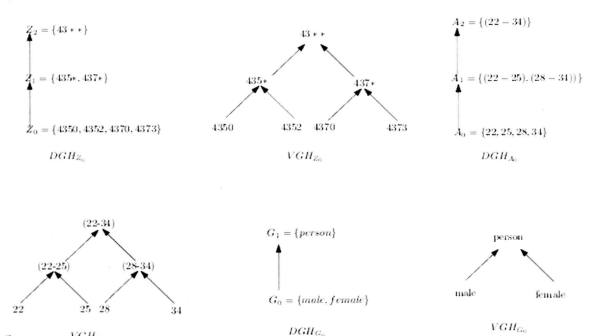

lattice with DT as its minimal element and the tuple composed of the top of each DGH_{Di}, $i=1,\ldots,n$ as its maximal element. Each path from DT to the unique maximal element of DGH_{DT} defines a possible alternative path, called generalization strategy for DGH_{DT}, which can be followed when generalizing a quasi-identifier of attributes on domains $D_1,\ldots,D_n$. In correspondence with each generalization strategy of a domain tuple, there is a value generalization strategy describing the generalization at the value level. Such a generalization strategy hierarchy is actually a tree structure. The top unique maximal element can be regarded as the root of the tree and the minimal element on the bottom is the leaf of the tree. Let $L[i,j]$ denote the jth data at height i (The bottom data is at the height 0) and $L[i]$ denote the number of data at the height i.

Example 2. Consider domains G_0 (Gender) and Z_0 (Zip code) whose generalization hierarchies are illustrated in Figure 1. Figure 2 illustrates the domain generalization hierarchy of the domain tuple $<G_0,Z_0>$ together with the corresponding domain and value generalization strategies. There are three different generalization strategies corresponding to the three paths from the bottom to the top element of lattice DGH_{D_z} shown in Figure 3. In the generalization strategy 1, $L[0,2]$ is (male, 4370), $L[0]=6$ and $L[2,2]$ is (person, 435*), $L[2]=2$.

Figure 2. The hierarchy of $DGH_{<G0, Z0>}$

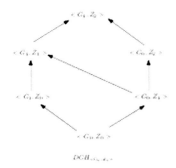

Figure 3. Domain and value generalization strategies

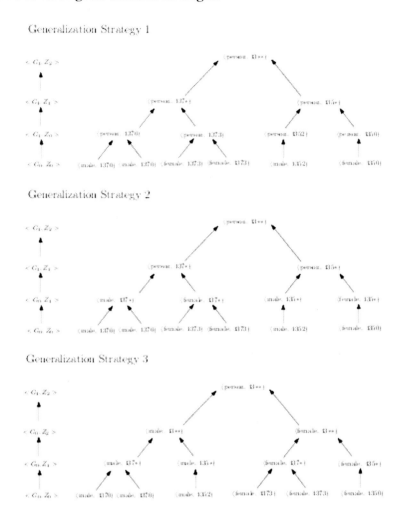

MINIMAL GENERALIZATION

Given a private table (PT), our approach to provide k-anonymity is to generalize the values stored in the table. Intuitively, attribute values stored in the private table (PT) can be substituted with generalized values upon release. Since multiple values can be mapped to a single generalized value, generalization may decrease the number of distinct tuples, thereby possibly increasing the size of the clusters containing tuples with the same values. We perform generalization at the attribute level. Generalizing an attribute means substituting its values with corresponding values from a more general domain. Generalization at the attribute level ensures that all values of an attribute belong to the same domain. In the following, $dom(A_i, PT)$ denotes the domain of attribute A_i in private table PT.

Definition 3. [Generalized table] Let $PT_i(A_1, \ldots A_n)$ and $PT_j(A_1, \ldots A_n)$ be two tables defined in the same set of attributes. PT_j is said to be a generalization of PT_i, written $PT_i \preceq PT_j$, if and only if: (1) $PT_i = PT_j$; (2) for all $A_z \in \{A_1, \ldots A_n\}$: $dom(A_z, PT_i) \leq_D dom(A_z, PT_j)$; and (3) It is pos-

Figure 4. Generalized table for PT - a) PT; b) $GT_{[0,2]}$; c) $GT_{[1,1]}$; d) $GT_{[1,2]}$

G_0	Z_0
Male	4370
Male	4370
Male	4352
Female	4373
Female	4373
Female	4350

Fig 4. 1: *PT*

G_0	Z_2
Male	43**
Male	43**
Male	43**
Female	43**
Female	43**
Female	43**

Fig 4. 2: $GT_{[0,2]}$

G_1	Z_1
person	437*
person	437*
person	435*
person	437*
person	437*
person	435*

Fig 4. 3: $GT_{[1,1]}$

G_1	Z_2
person	43**
person	43**
person	43**
person	43**
person	43**
person	43**

Fig 4. 4: $GT_{[1,2]}$

sible to define a bijective mapping between PT_i and PT_j that associates each tuple $pt_i \in PT_i$ with a tuple $pt_j \in PT_j$ such that $pt_i[A_z] \leq_V pt_j[A_z]$ for all $A_z \in \{A_1, \ldots A_n\}$.

Example 3. Consider the private table PT illustrated in Figure 4.1 and the domain and value generalization hierarchies for G_0(Gender) and Z_0 (Zip) illustrated in Figure 2. Assume QI={Gender, Zip} to be a quasi-identifier. The following three tables in Figure 4 are all possible generalized tables for PT. For the clarity, each table reports the domain for each attribute in the table. With respect to k-anonymity, $GT_{[1,1]}$ satisfies k-anonymity for k=1, 2; $GT_{[0,2]}$ satisfies k-anonymity for k=1, 2, 3 and $GT_{[1,2]}$ satisfies k-anonymity for k=1, 2, 3, 4, 5, 6.

Given a private table PT, different possible generalizations exist. However, not all generalizations can be considered equally satisfactory. For instance, the trivial generalization bringing each attribute to the highest possible level of generalization provides k-anonymity at the price of a strong generalization of the data. Such extreme generalization is not needed if a table containing more specific values exists which satisfies k-anonymity as well. This concept is captured by the definition of minimal k-anonymity (generalization). To introduce it we first introduce the notion of distance vector.

Definition 4. [Distance vector] Let $PT_i(A_1, \ldots A_n)$ and $PT_j(A_1, \ldots A_n)$ be two tables such that

$PT_i \lesssim PT_j$. The distance vector of PT_j from PT_i is the vector $DV_{\{i,j\}} = [d_1, \ldots d_n]$ where each d_z, $z=1,\ldots,n$, is the length of the unique path between $D_z = dom(A_z, PT_i)$ and $dom(A_z, PT_j)$ in the domain generalization hierarchy DGH_{D_z}.

Example 4. Consider the private table PT and its generalizations illustrated in Figure 4. The distance vectors between PT and each of its generalized tables is the vector appearing as a subscript of the table. A generalization hierarchy for a domain tuple can be seen as a hierarchy (lattice) on the corresponding distance vectors. Figure 5 illustrates the lattice representing the dominance relationship between the distance vectors corresponding to the possible generalizations of $<G_0, Z_0>$.

We extend the dominance relationship $\leq_D$ on integers to distance vectors by requiring coordinate-wise ordering as follows. Given two distance vectors $DV=[d_1, \ldots d_n]$ and $DV'=[d'_1, \ldots d'_n]$, $DV \in DV'$ if and only if $d_i \leq d'_i$ for all $i=1,\ldots,n$. Moreover, $DV<DV'$ if and only if $DV \leq DV'$ and $DV \neq DV'$.

Intuitively, a generalization $PT_i(A_1, \ldots A_n)$ is minimal k-anonymity (generalization) if and only if there does not exist another generalization $PT_z(A_1, \ldots A_n)$ satisfying k-anonymity and whose domain tuple is dominated by PT_j in the corre-

Figure 5. Hierarchy DGH$_{<G0, Z0>}$ and corresponding lattice on distance vectors

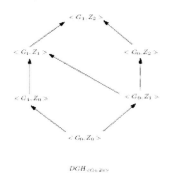 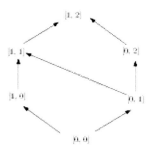

sponding lattice of distance vectors). Formally, we can define it as follows:

Definition 5. [Minimal k-anonymity] Let $PT_i(A_1,\ldots A_n)$ and $PT_j(A_1,\ldots A_n)$ be two tables such that $PT_i \lesssim PT_j$. PT_j is said to be a minimal k-anonymity (generalization) of PT_i if and only if: (1) PT_j satisfies k-anonymity; and (2) $PT_z : PT_z \lesssim PT_j, PT_z$ satisfies k-anonymity $\Rightarrow DV_{i,z} <= DV_{i,j}$.

Example 5. Consider table PT and its generalized tables illustrated in Figure 3. For k=2 two minimal k-anonymous table exist, namely $GT_{[0,2]}$ and $GT_{[1,1]}$. $GT_{[1,2]}$ is not minimal because it is a generation of $GT_{[1,1]}$ and $GT_{[0,2]}$. Also, there is only one minimal k-generalized tables with k=3, which is $GT_{[0,2]}$.

Privacy Hash Table

A hash table is a data structure that will increase the search efficiency from O(log(n)) (binary search) to O(1) (constant time) (Cormen, et al. 2002).

A hash table is made up of two parts: an array (the actual table where the data to be searched is stored) and a mapping function, known as a hash function. The hash function is a mapping from the input data space to the integer space that defines the indices of the array (bucket). In other words, the hash function provides a way for assigning numbers to the input data such that the data can then be stored at the array (bucket) with the index corresponding to the assigned number. For example, the data in Table 1 are mapped into buckets labeled 0, 1, 2, 3 in Table 3. The data in the bucket with the same assigned number is called a hash equivalence class. Depending on the different problems, we could choose different hash functions to classify our input data as we need. For instance, consider quasi-identifier QI={Age, Zip} in Table 1. We hash them into different buckets with the function ((Age-20)+(Zip-4350)) mod 4 (see Table 3).

From Table 3, we see that two identical data (25, 4350) and (28, 4353) in the quasi-identifier fall into two different hash equivalence classes.

Table 3. An example of hashed table

Bucket	0	1	2	3
Content	(22, 4352)	(25, 4370) (25, 4370)	(34, 450)	(28, 4373) (28, 4373)

Table 4. Hashed table with COUNT

Bucket	0	1	2	3
COUNT	1	2	1	2
Content	(22, 4352)	(25, 4370) (25, 4370)	(34, 450)	(28, 4373) (28, 4373)

Further, if we add a row (labeled COUNT) to record the number of contents in the corresponding buckets (see Table 4), we can easily determine whether or not the table satisfies the k-anonymity requirement. For instance, according to the row COUNT in Table 4, Table 1 only satisfies k-anonymity with k=1.

This hash-based technique is not new in data mining. In (Park et al, 1995), the authors used this technique to present an efficient hash-based algorithm for mining association rules which improves previous well-known A priori algorithm. In this chapter, we integrate this technique into computation of minimal k-anonymous table. By using such a technique, we can reduce the number of potential sets that need to be checked whether they are k-anonymous during binary search and thus improve the time complexity in (Samarati, 2001).

Concerning the efficiency of hash table and binary search, we note the following. (1) Hash table has a faster average lookup time O(1) (Cormen, et al. 2002) than the binary search algorithm O(log(n)). Note that the worst case in hash tables happens when every data element is hashed to the same value due to some bad luck in choosing the hash function and bad programming. In that case, to do a lookup, we would really be doing a straight linear search on a linked list, which means that our search operation is back to being O(n). The worst case search time for a hash table is O(n). However, the probability of that happening is so small that, while the worst case search time is O(n), both the best and average cases are O(1). Hash table shines in very large arrays, where O(1) performance is important. (2) Building a hash table requires a reasonable hash function, which sometimes can be difficult to write well, while binary search requires a total ordering on the input data. On the other hand, with hash tables the data may be only partially ordered.

The Hash-based Algorithm

A number of convincing parallels exist between Samarati and Sweeney's generalization framework (Samarati, 2001; Sweeney, 2002) and ideas used in mining association rules (Agrawal, et al. 1994; Srikant, et al. 1995) and the hash-based technique used in (Park et al. 1995). By bringing these techniques to bear on our model of full-domain generalization problem, we develop an efficient hash-based algorithm for computing k-minimal anonymity.

In (Samarati, et al. 2001), Samarati describes an algorithm for finding a single minimal k-anonymous full-domain generalization based on the specific definition of minimality outlined in the previous section. The algorithm uses the observation that if no generalization of height h satisfies k-anonymity, then no generalization of height h'<h will satisfy k-anonymity. For this reason, the algorithm performs a binary search on the height value. If the maximum height in the generalization lattice is h, the algorithm begins by checking each generalization at height h/2. If a generalization exists at this height that satisfies k-anonymity, the search proceeds to look at the generalizations of height h/4. Otherwise, generalizations of height 3h/4 are searched, and so forth. This algorithm is proven to find a single minimal k-anonymous table.

Algorithm 1. Finding minimal k-anonymity in k-anonymous class

```
Input: the k-anonymous class
1.  Sort the data in k-anonymous class.
2.  Computer the number n(i) of L[i,j] at each height i,
3.  If n(i) ≠ L[i], discard all of the L[i,j] at the height i.
4.  Otherwise, keep them.
Output: The height at which the first data is in the remaining k-anonymous
class, and generalize the data to this height could obtain the minimal k-anon-
ymous table.
```

We integrate the hash technique into the algorithm and develop a more efficient algorithm based on our definition of minimality (Definition 5). A drawback of Samarati's algorithm is that for arbitrary definitions of minimality this binary search algorithm is not always guaranteed to find the minimal k-anonymity table. We conjecture that the hash technique used in this chapter might be suitable for the further improvement of algorithms based on other optimal criteria for k-anonymity.

Let the domain generalization hierarchy be DGH_{DT}, where DT is the tuples of the domains of the quasi-identifier. Assume that the top generalization data with the highest height in DGH_{DT} satisfies the required k-anonymity. The idea of the algorithm is to hash the data in DGH_{DT} to a different hash equivalence class. Under our definition of the minimality, the hash function that we choose should hash all generalizations with height h>0 in DGH_{DT} that satisfies k-anonymity to the same hash equivalence class, which is called the k-anonymous class. (The bucket labeled 2 in Table 4). The hash-based algorithm consists of two main steps. At the first stage, the data

that satisfies k-anonymity are hashed into the k-anonymous class. The second step is to use Algorithm 1 to find the minimal k-anonymous table in the k-anonymous class.

Algorithm 1 illustrates how to find the minimal k-anonymous table in k-anonymous class. Consider Table 1 and its generalization strategy 1 in Figure 3. Generalized data L[1,1], L[1,2], L[2,1], L[2,2] and L[3,1] are hashed into the k-anonymous class. We sort the data in k-anonymous class as L[1,1], L[1,2], L[2,1], L[2,2], L[3,1]. Since L[1]=4 and the number of data at the height 1 in k-anonymous class is 2. According to Step 3 in Algorithm 1, we delete L[1,1] and L[1,2] from k-anonymous class. At last, the output height is 2, and we could generalize the table to this height so that it satisfies 2-anonymity with quasi-identifier QI={Gender, Zip}.

Next, we illustrate how to hash the generalization data in DGH_{DT} to the k-anonymous class. Denote Children[i,j] the number of children that the jth data at the height i have. For example, in generalization strategy 1 in Figure 3, Children[1,3]=1 and Children[2,1]=4. Suppose we have the requirement of k-anonymity. The desired

Table 5. Hash table of generalization strategy 1 in Figure 3

Bucket	0	1	2
Children[i,j]	0	1	≥2
Content	L[0,1], L[0,2], L[0,3] L[0,4], L[0,5], L[0,6]	L[0,1] L[1,4]	L[1,1], L[1,2] L[2,1], L[2,2], L[3,1]

Algorithm 2. Hash-based algorithm for minimal k-anonymity

```
Input: Generalization hierarchy DGH_DT; anonymous requirement k;
Output: A minimal k-anonymous table.
1. Create a table with k+1 column labeling 0,1, …, k-1, k.
2. For l=0,1 …, k-1
If Children[i,j]=l, put Children[i,j] to the bucket labeled l. Else put
Children[i,j] to the bucket labeled k.
3. Apply Algorithm 1 to compute the minimal k-anonymous table.
```

hash table contains k+1 buckets, labeled as 0, 1, 2,..., k-1, k, the labeled number 0, 1, …, k-1 denotes the value of Children[i,j] in DGH_{DT} and the kth bucket has the data whose Children[i,j] <= k. Note that the bucket labeled k is actually the k-anonymous class. We could see the following Table 4 as an example (where k=2). All the potential generalization data satisfying 2-anonymity are classified into the third bucket, which consists of the k-anonymous class.

Algorithm 2 is our hash-based algorithm. Compared to Samarati's binary search algorithm, Algorithm 2 finds the minimal k-anonymous table in the k-anonymous class}, which is smaller than the potential sets that need to be checked in Samarati's algorithm. Because of the hash technique we used in Algorithm 2, the search complexity is reduced from O(log(n)) (binary search) to O(1) (Cormen, et al. 2002).

PROOF-OF-CONCEPT EXPERIMENTS

Experiments were made to compare the performance of the binary search algorithm (Samarati, 2001) and the hash-based algorithm for finding minimal k-anonymous solutions.

Data Sets

We deploy two real world data sets, Adult database and Census database. The Adult database can be downloaded at the UC Irvine Machine Learning Repository (http://www.ics.uci.edu/-mlearn/ML-Repository.htm), which has become the benchmark of this field and was adopted by (Fung et al. 2005, LeFevre et al. 2005, Machanavajjhala et al. 2006). We used a configuration similar to (LeFevre et al. 2005, Machanavajjhala et al. 2006). We eliminated the records with unknown values. The resulting data set contains 45222 tuples. Seven of the attributes were chosen as the quasi-identifier. We add a column with sensitive values called "Health Condition" consisting of {HIV, Cancer, Phthisis, Hepatitis, Obesity, Asthma, Flu, Indigestion} to the extracted data and randomly assign one sensitive value to each record of the extracted data by. The random technique works in the following way. First, assign a number to each sensitive attribute, i.e., {1:HIV, 2:Cancer, 3:Phthisis, 4:Hepatitis, 5:Obesity, 6:Asthma, 7:Flu, 8:Indigestion}. Second, for each tuple (record), generate a random number from 1-8. Then, assign the corresponding sensitive attribute value to the tuple. For example, for the first tuple in the data set, if the random number is 5, then this record has the sensitive value "Obesity". Table 6 briefly describes the data we used including the name of the attribute, the type of the data, the number of different values in each attribute and the height of the domain (value) generalization hierarchy of each attribute. The Census database (downloadable at http://ipums.org) is commonly used in the literature (Xiao et al. 2006), which contains the personal information of 500K American

Table 6. Features of adult database

Attribute	Type	Distinct values
Age	Numerical	74
Work class	Categorical	8
Education	Categorical	16
Country	Categorical	4
Marital Status	Categorical	7
Race	Categorical	5
Gender	Categorical	2
Health Condition	Sensitive	8

Table 7. Summary of census database

Attribute	Type	Distinct values
Age	Numerical	78
Gender	Categorical	2
Education	Categorical	17
Marital	Categorical	6
Race	Categorical	9
Work-class	Categorical	8
Country	Categorical	83
Salary-class	Sensitive	50

adults. The data set has 9 discrete attributes, and we select 7 attributes as the non-sensitive ones, and the salary class as the sensitive attributes. We summarize them in Table 7.

Results

Data used for Figure 6(a) is generated by re-sampling the Adult and Census data sets while varying the percentage of data from 10% to 100%. For both data sets, we evaluate the running time of the hash-based algorithm for the k-anonymity with default setting k=10. For both data sets, the execution time is increasing with the increased data percentage. This is because as the percentage of data increases, the computation cost increases too. The result is expected since the overhead is increased with the more dimensions.

Next, we evaluate how the parameters affect the cost of computing. We use the whole sets of Adult and Census data for these sets of experiments and we evaluate by varying the value of k. Figure 6(b) displays the results of running time by varying k from 10 to 35 for both data sets. The cost drops when k grows. This is expected, because the larger the k is, the more the number of records included in each QI-group, which reduces the computation of hash-based algorithm.

Figure 6. Running time comparison on adult and census data sets vs (a) data percentage varies; (b) k varies

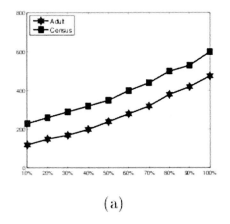

(a)

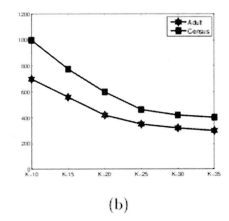

(b)

Figure 7. Running time comparison of hash and binary methods vs (a) data percentage varies (adult); (b) k varies (census)

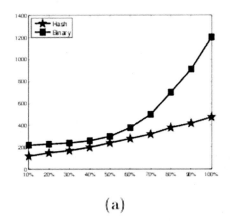

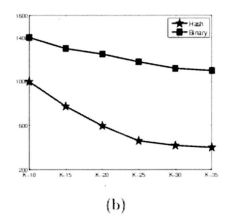

(a)

(b)

In addition to show the scalability and efficiency of the hash-based algorithm itself, we also experimented the comparison between the hash-based algorithm (Hash) and the binary search algorithm (Binary) (Samarati, 2001). We implemented both algorithms and studied the impact of the execution time on the data percentage and the value of K. Figure 7(a) plots the running time of both hash-based and binary algorithms on the Adult data set. It describes the trend of the algorithms by varying the percentage of the data set. From the graph, the hash-based algorithm is far more efficient than the binary algorithm especially when the volume of the data becomes larger. The running time comparisons of both algorithms in Census data set by varying the value of k is shown in Figures 7(b). Even on a larger data set, the hash-based algorithm outperformed the binary algorithm, and the running time of Hash is quick enough to be applied in practical.

CONCLUSION AND FUTURE WORK

In this chapter, we focus on a specific global-recoding model of k-anonymity. Our objective is to find the minimal k-anonymous generalization

(table). By introducing the structure of privacy hash table, we provide a new approach to generate minimal k-anonymous table, which improves previous search algorithm proposed by Samarati (Samarati, 2001).

In future work, we conjecture this hash-based technique might be suitable for further improvement of the Incognito (LeFevre et al. 2005) for full-domain generalization, since it might significantly reduce the number of 2-attribute candidate sets. The technique might also apply in multilevel generalization. For many applications, it is difficult to find required k-anonymity tables at low or primitive levels of the generalization hierarchy due to the sparsity of data in multidimensional space. K-anonymous table generated at very high levels in the generalization hierarchy might be suitable for some attributes, however, to some extent, it may be too generalized in some attributes. Therefore, data mining system should provide capability to generate k-anonymous tables at multiple levels of the generalization hierarchy and traverse easily among different generalization levels. The privacy hash table may provide a new point of view and a more efficient way to make multilevel k-anonymous tables.

REFERENCES

Adam, N. R., & Wortman, J. C. (1989). Security-control methods for statistical databases: A Comparative study. *ACM Computing Surveys, 21*(4), 515–556. doi:10.1145/76894.76895

Aggarwal, C. C. (2005). On k-anonymity and the curse of dimensionality. In *Proceedings of VLDB*, (pp. 901-909).

Aggarwal, G., Feder, T., Kenthapadi, K., Motwani, R., Panigrahy, R., Thomas, D., & Zhu, A. (2005). Anonymizing tables. In *Proc. of the 10th International Conference on Database Theory* (ICDT '05), (pp. 246-258). Edinburgh, Scotland.

Agrawal, R., & Srikant, R. (1994). Fast algorithms for mining association rules. In *Proc. of the 20th Int'l Conference on Very Large Databases*, August 1994.

Bayardo, R., & Agrawal, R. (2005). Data privacy through optimal k-anonymity. In *Proceedings of the 21st International Conference on Data Engineering* (ICDE), 2005.

Cormen, T. H., Leiserson, C. E., Rivest, R. L., & Stein, C. (2001). *Introduction to algorithms* (2nd ed.). MIT Press and McGraw-Hill.

Fung, B. C. M., Wang, K., & Yu, P. S. (2005) Top-down specialization for information and privacy preservation. In *Proceedings of ICDE* (pp. 205-216).

Iyengar, V. (2002). Transforming data to satisfy privacy constraints. In *Proceedings of the 8th ACM SIGKDD International Conference on Knowledge Discovery and Data Mining*, 2002.

LeFevre, K., DeWitt, D., & Ramakrishnan, R. (2005). Incognito: Efficient full-domain k-anonymity. In *ACM SIGMOD International Conference on Management of Data*, June 2005.

LeFevre, K., DeWitt, D. J., & Ramakrishnan, R. (2006). Mondrian multidimensional k-anonymity. In *Proceedings of ICDE* (pp. 21-28).

Li, N., Li, T., & Venkatasubramanian, S. (2007). t-Closeness: Privacy beyond k-anonymity and l-diversity. *ICDE, 2007*, 106–115.

Machanavajjhala, A., Gehrke, J., Kifer, D., & Venkitasubramaniam, M. (2006). l-diversity: Privacy beyond k-anonymity. In *Proc. 22nd Intnl. Conf. Data Engg.* (ICDE), (p. 24).

Meyerson, A., & Williams, R. (2004). On the complexity of optimal k-anonymity. In *Proc. of the 23rd ACM-SIGMOD-SIGACT-SIGART Symposium on the Principles of Database Systems*, (pp. 223-228). Paris, France, 2004.

Park, J. S., Chen, M. S., & Yu, P. S. (1995). An effective hash-based algorithm for mining association rules. *Proceedings of the 1995 ACM SIGMOD International Conference on Management of Data* (pp. 175-186).

Samarati, P. (2001). Protecting respondents' identities in microdata release. In *Proceedings of IEEE Trans. Knowl. Data Eng.* (pp. 1010-1027).

Samarati, P., & Sweeney, L. (1998). Generalizing data to provide anonymity when disclosing information (Abstract). In *Proc. of the 17th ACM-SIGMODSIGACT- SIGART Symposium on the Principles of Database Systems*, (p. 188). Seattle, WA, USA.

Srikant, R., & Agrawal, R. (1995). Mining generalized association rules. In *Proc. of the 21st Int'l Conference on Very Large Databases*, August 1995.

Sun, X., Wang, H., & Li, J. (2008). On the complexity of restricted k-anonymity problem. *APWeb, 2008*, 287–296.

Sun, X., Wang, H., Li, J., & Truta, T. M. (2008). Enhanced p-sensitive k-anonymity models for privacy preserving data publishing. *Transactions on Data Privacy, 1*(2), 53–66.

Sweeney, L. (2002). k-anonymity: A model for protecting privacy. In *Proceedings of International Journal of Uncertainty, Fuzziness and Knowledge-Based Systems* (pp. 557-570).

Traian, T. M., & Bindu, V. (2006). *Privacy protection: p-sensitive k-anonymity property.* International Workshop of Privacy Data Management (PDM2006), In Conjunction with 22th International Conference of Data Engineering (ICDE), Atlanta, 2006.

Wang, K., Yu, P. S., & Chakraborty, S. (2004). Bottom-up generalization: A data mining solution to privacy protection. In *Proceedings of ICDM* (pp. 249-256).

Willenborg, L., & DeWaal, T. (1996). Statistical disclosure control in practice. Springer-Verlag, 1996.

Winkler, W. (2002). *Using simulated annealing for k-anonymity.* Research Report 2002-07, US Census Bureau Statistical Research Division, 2002.

Xiao, X., & Tao, Y. (2006). Personalized privacy preservation. In *SIGMOD '06: Proceedings of the 2006 ACM SIGMOD International Conference on Management of Data,* 2006.

Yao, C., Wang, S., & Jajodia, S. (2005). Checking for k-anonymity violation by views. In *International Conference on Very Large Data Bases,* Trondheim, Norway, August 2005.

Zhong, S., Yang, Z., & Wright, R. N. (2005). Privacy-enhancing k-anonymization of customer data. In *ACM Conference on Principles of Database Systems*(PODS), 2005.

ADDITIONAL READING

Aggarwal, G., Panigrahy, R., Feder, T., Thomas, D., Kenthapadi, K., Khuller, S., & Zhu, A. (2010) Achieving anonymity via clustering. In *Proceedings of ACM Transactions on Algorithms.* (21-58).

Agrawal, R., & Srikant, R. Privacy-Preserving Data Mining. (2000) In *Proceedings of SIGMOD Conference.* 2000, 439-450.

Campan, A., & Truta, T. M. (2008) Data and Structural k-Anonymity in Social Networks. In *Proceedings of PinKDD.* 2008, 33-54.

Dinur, I., & Nissim, K. (2003). Revealing information while preserving privacy. In *Proceedings of PODS.* 2003, 202-210.

Fung, B. C. M., Wang, K., & Yu, P. S. (2007) Anonymizing Classification Data for Privacy Preservation. In *Proceedings of IEEE Trans. Knowl. Data Eng.* 711-725.

LeFevre, K., DeWitt, D. J., & Ramakrishnan, R. (2006) Mondrian Multidimensional K-Anonymity. In *Proceedings of ICDE.* 114-120.

Meyerson, A., & Williams, R. (2004) On the Complexity of Optimal K-Anonymity. In *Proceedings of PODS,* 223-228.

Samarati, P., & Sweeney, L. (1998). Generalizing Data to Provide Anonymity when Disclosing Information (Abstract). In *Proceedings of PODS.* 1998.

Sun, X., Wang, H., & Li, J. (2008) L-Diversity Based Dynamic Update for Large Time-Evolving Microdata. In *Proceedings of Australasian Conference on Artificial Intelligence.* 2008, 461-469.

Sun, X., Wang, H., Li, J., & Truta, T. M. (2008) Enhanced P-Sensitive K-Anonymity Models for Privacy Preserving Data Publishing. In *Proceedings of Transactions on Data Privacy.* 2008, 53-66.

Terrovitis, M., Mamoulis, N., & Kalnis, P. (2008) Privacy-preserving anonymization of set-valued data. In *Proceedings of PVLDB.* 115-125.

Wang, H., & Lakshmanan, L. V. S. (2006) Probabilistic privacy analysis of published views. In *Proceedings of WPES*.81-84.

KEY TERMS AND DEFINITIONS

Algorithm: an algorithm is an effective method expressed as a finite list of well-defined instructions for calculating a function.

Anonymity: anonymity typically refers to the state of an individual's personal identity.

Experiment: experimentation is the step in the scientific method that helps people decide between two competing explanations – or hypotheses.

Hash Table: A hash table or hash map is a data structure that uses a hash function to map identifying values, known as keys (e.g., a person's name), to their associated values (e.g., their telephone number).

NP-Hard: NP-hard (non-deterministic polynomial-time hard), in computational complexity theory, is a class of problems that are, informally, "at least as hard as the hardest problems in NP".

Privacy: is the ability of an individual or group to seclude themselves or information about themselves and thereby reveal themselves selectively.

Statistical Disclosure Control: Statistical disclosure control (SDC) concerns safeguarding the confidentiality of the information about people and businesses.

Chapter 6
Developing Secure Business Processes:
A Model Driven Approach

Alfonso Rodríguez
University of Bio-Bio, Chile

Eduardo Fernández-Medina
University of Castilla-La Mancha, Spain

Mario Piattini
University of Castilla-La Mancha, Spain

ABSTRACT

Business processes are valuable resources for enterprises to maintain their competitiveness. They are characterized by describing the set of activities that enterprises perform to reach their objectives. On the other hand, security is also an essential element in current competitiveness. Enterprises invest resources in keeping their assets protected and worry about maintaining their customers' trust. In this way, aspects such as confidentiality, integrity, and availability are important in relation to enterprise activities. In this work, we will define business processes that incorporate the viewpoint of the business analyst regarding security. The result is a secure business process model that is used for software creation under a model-driven approach. In this work, we will show the main aspects of this proposal, taking into consideration a case study that allows us to show its applicability.

INTRODUCTION

Current globalized enterprises must constantly evolve to maintain their competitiveness. The enterprise performance has been linked to the capability that each enterprise has to adapt itself to the changes that arise in the market. In this context, Business Processes (BP) have become valuable resources that have been used to maintain competitiveness. Business processes, defined as a set of procedures or activities which collectively pursue a business objective or policy goal (WfMC, 1999), are a good answer to the complexity of this environment, represented by the speed required by

DOI: 10.4018/978-1-61350-501-4.ch006

new products and the growing number of actors involved in the organization's activities.

Another characteristic of the current competitive environment is the intensive use of communication and information technologies. This has let enterprises expand their businesses but it has increased their vulnerability. As a consequence of this, and with the increase in the list of vulnerabilities and sophisticated threats as well as in the number of attacks on systems, it is highly probable that sooner or later an intrusion may be successful (Quirchmayr, 2004).

Although the importance of business process security is widely accepted, until now the business analyst perspective in relation to security has hardly been dealt with. In the majority of cases, the identification of security requirements has been somewhat confused owing to the fact that, in general, there has been a tendency to identify functional security requirements. These types of requirements vary according to the type of application. On the other hand, security requirements do not vary at a high level of abstraction. The reason for this is that at this level the assessment and vulnerability of the assets is the same (Firesmith, 2004). Moreover, if we consider that empirical studies show that it is common at the business process level for customers and end users to be able to express their security needs (Lopez, Montenegro, Vivas, Okamoto, & Dawson, 2005), then it will be possible to obtain a high level of security requirements which are easily identifiable to those who model business processes. In addition, requirements specification usually results in a specification of the software system which should be as exact as possible (Artelsmair & Wagner, 2003), since effective business process models facilitate discussion among the different stakeholders in the business, allowing them to agree on the key fundamentals as well as to work towards common goals (Eriksson & Penker, 2001).

Concerning software engineering, at present, it is greatly influenced by the Model Driven Architecture (MDA) (Object Management Group, 2003), a new paradigm which claims to work at the model and metamodel level. Among the objectives pursued, we can find the separation between business-neutral descriptions and platform dependent implementations, the expression of specific aspects of a system under development with specialized domain-specific languages, the establishment of precise relations between these different languages within a global framework and, in particular, the capability to express operational transformations between them (Bézivin, 2004). The MDA approach is composed of the following perspectives: (i) the computation independent viewpoint (represented by the Computation Independent Model or CIM) which focuses on the environment of the system, (ii) the platform independent viewpoint (represented by the Platform Independent Model or PIM) which focuses on the operation of a system while hiding the details necessary for a particular platform, and (iii) the platform specific viewpoint (represented by the Platform Specific Model or PSM) which combines the platform independent viewpoint with an additional focus on the detail of the use of a specific platform by a system (Object Management Group, 2003). Because these models represent a different abstraction from the same system, an integration/transformation mechanism is required to establish how to go from one level (e.g. CIM) to another (e.g. PIM). Thus, transformations are a core element in the MDA. According to MDA, a transformation is the process of converting one model into another model belonging to the same system.

In short, in this work we have addressed security in business processes with the purpose of making it possible: (i) to take into account the business analyst's viewpoint in relation to security, thereby enriching the business process specification, and (ii) to provide a starting point for the software development process, since a Secure Business Process specification can be transformed into models closer to implementation following an MDA approach.

The structure of the remainder of the paper is as follows: in Section 2, we will present how security has been dealt with in the early stage of software construction, in Section 3 we will present our proposal based on the Secure Business Process definition, in Section 4 we will show a case study oriented to demonstrate the applicability of our proposal. Finally, in Section 5, our conclusions will be drawn.

SECURITY IN EARLY STAGES OF SOFTWARE DEVELOPMENT

In the last years, security has become more and more important for many organizations. That's why, at present, it is considered a permanent challenge. There are two factors especially influencing this scenario. The first factor is the complexity of the environment in which enterprises interact while the second factor is the growing technological dependency of enterprises to drive and automate their processes. In this context, security cannot be considered as a stand-alone discipline. Given that security is a business problem, the organization must activate, coordinate, deploy, and direct many of its existing core competencies to work together to provide effective solutions. Consequently, the organization must move toward a security management process that is strategic, systematic, and repeatable, in other words, efficient at using security resources and effective at meeting security goals on a consistent basis (Caralli, 2004).

The early definition of security requirements constitutes a challenge due to the level of abstraction at which such specification is made. Moreover, there is a need and an opportunity to improve software products because security requirements can be transformed from high levels of abstraction to products closer to implementation. Nowadays, high levels of abstraction are identified as business process models that are often a starting point for the development and definition of requirements for software design and construction (List & Ko-

rherr, 2005; Störrle, 2005). In the same way, the description of a business process with security is a source of requirements that must be incorporated into a software development process

In general, software is obtained from these specifications by applying a model-driven software development framework. This approach has the purpose of solving cost, time and resource problems in relation to the implementation of technological solution. The development of this approach has been important in the last years and has implied the appearance of languages and tools that allow us to carry out the transition from more abstract models to more concrete ones. Particularly, the OMG proposal called MDA (Model Driven Architecture) (Object Management Group, 2003) considers QVT language (Query/View/Transformation) (QVT, 2005) that lets us specify transformations.

In the following sections, we will deal with both subjects, security and model driven, considering the need to include security in the design and specification of business processes. This will allow us to understand the way in which we propose to incorporate the business analyst's perspective in relation to security.

Security Requirements in Business Processes

A security requirement is defined as a limitation or restriction expressed over a system's behavior. Traditionally, three security objectives have been identified: confidentiality, integrity and availability. More recently, authentication has gained in importance (Haley, Laney, & Nuseibeh, 2004). If we consider security from the viewpoint of the people and organizations that use computers, they can be expressed as secret, integrity, availability and responsibility (Lampson, 2004). From the point of view of work flows, aspects such as authorization, audit, anonymity and separation of duties can be added (Atluri, 2001). Nonetheless, although security requirements are widely

Figure 1. Combination of sources for security requirements

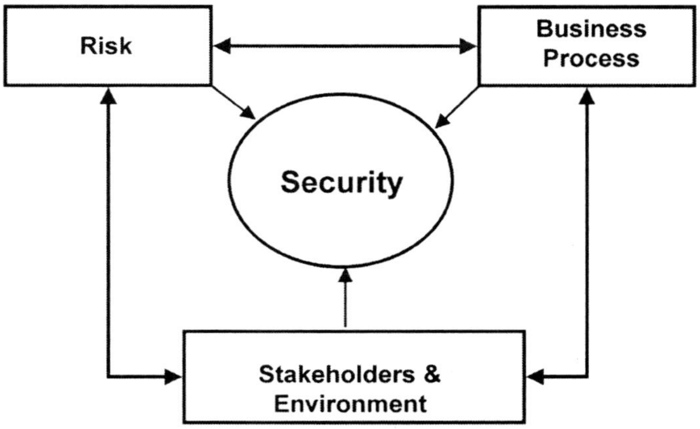

dealt with in the literature, it is difficult to find a definition that is wide enough to describe all their properties and the range that they cover (Zuccato, 2004).

Additionally, there are several sources that can be used for the identification and classification of security requirements. For instance, ISO27000 (that replaces BS7799/ISO17799), CobiT (Control OBjectives for Information and related Technology), ISF (Information Security Forum), NIST (National Institute of Standard and Technology 800-14) (Caralli, 2004), Common Criteria (Common Criteria, 2005) and Magerit 2.0 (Ministerio de Administraciones Públicas, 2005) among others, can be used.

In spite of the fact that security requirements are widely dealt with in the literature, it is difficult to find a holistic definition in which their properties and the range they cover are described (Zuccato, 2004). Consequently, security requirements must be defined according to three elements (see Figure 1) in a way that the combination of the different sources and interactions existing between them allows us to obtain a holistic set of security requirements (Zuccato, 2004)

Nonetheless, we are interested in security requirements definitions which are comprehensible for business area specialists, and clear and unambiguous enough for security experts. It is

obvious that the availability of a much more technical and detailed description which allows us to specify security requirements at lower levels of abstraction such as PSM (Platform Specific Model) or code is necessary. However, definitions at higher levels of abstraction (CIM-PIM; Computation Independent Model - Platform Independent Model) that can be used as a reference for the later implementation of solutions that satisfy the defined security requirements are also necessary. In this work, we have taken as a reference the taxonomy proposed in (Firesmith, 2004) for obtaining security requirements.

A secure Business Process will contain security requirements which take into account the business analyst's perspective. This perspective had not previously been captured together with the definition of the business process. Our proposal solves this problem by incorporating certain security requirements which are clearly understood by business analysts and whose specification is independent of their implementation.

According to (Firesmith, 2004), a security requirement at a high level of abstraction does not vary from one application to another because at that level, the valuation and vulnerability of the assets is the same. The author defines security as the degree to which the valuable assets are protected against significant threats from malicious

Figure 2. Taxonomy of security requirements (Firesmith, 2004)

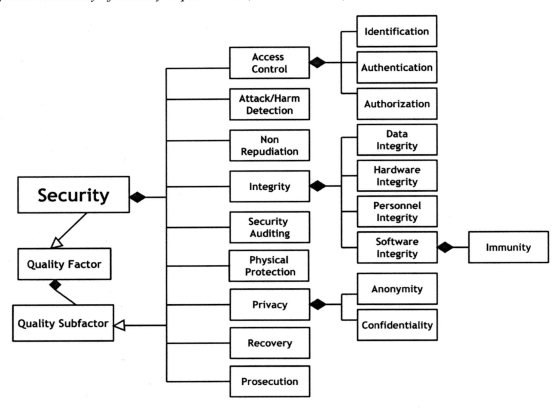

attackers. Thus, security is a quality factor that is decomposed into a hierarchical taxonomy such as that shown in Figure 2.

Although security is important for business processes performance, security modeling in these processes presents two fundamental problems. The first one has to do with modeling itself since it has been inadequate because generally those who specify security requirements are requirements engineers that have accidentally tended to replace security requirements by architecture specific restrictions(Firesmith, 2003). The second problem, that has been the most common one in practice, is that security has been integrated late, often during the actual implementation of the process (Backes, Pfitzmann, & Waider, 2003) in an ad-hoc manner, during the system administration stage (Lodderstedt, Basin, & Doser, 2002) or simply it has been considered as an external

service that will be provided by a third party (Maña, Ray, Sánchez, & Yagüe, 2004). This is partly explained by the fact that although security is a cross-cutting aspect that affects the components of an application early, it is not correctly understood and there is a lack of tools that support security engineering (Lodderstedt, Basin, & Doser, 2002).

The incorporation of security into business processes constitutes a challenge that must be dealt with taking into consideration that: (i) there is a growing need to incorporate security as part of the way in which organizations perform their daily, (ii) there is a greater knowledge and consciousness of the importance of security and finally, (iii) languages and notations have experienced important improvements that allow us to describe the different perspectives composing the business in a more precise way.

Figure 3. MDA development sequence (Harmon, 2004)

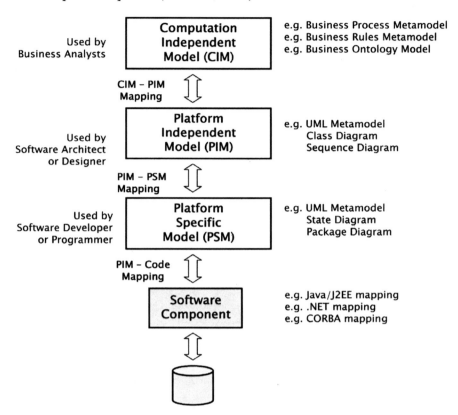

Model-Driven Approach

In the last years, software engineering is being influenced by model transformation with the aim of solving time, cost and quality problems associated with software creation. The way of solving this problem is within the scope of the general denomination of Model-Driven Engineering (MDE). Model-Driven Engineering is the software engineering discipline that considers models as first class entities whose purpose is their development, maintenance and evolution through the performance of model transformations (Mens & Van Gorp, 2006). The key idea of this approach is that of replacing the principle stating that *everything is an object* by the new principle establishing that *everything is a model* (Bézivin, 2004).

The Model Driven Architecture (see Figure 3) is a framework oriented to software development; it is within the MDE scope and its main objective is to allow the creation of models totally independent of technological implementation. MDA provides an approach for, and enables tools to be provided for (Object Management Group, 2003):

- Specifying a system independently of the platform that supports it.
- Specifying platforms.
- Choosing a particular platform for the system.
- Transforming the system specification into one for a particular platform.

MDA is concerned with models and talks about them in two different ways (Harmon, 2004):

- Model Standardization. Firstly, MDA is concerned with techniques that assure that all models used in software development can be aligned with each other. This focus emphasizes the use of MOF (Meta Object Facility) and metamodels.
- Models for Software Development. Secondly, MDA is concerned with organizing models used in the software development process so that developers can move from abstract models to more concrete models. This focus emphasizes the use of Computation Independent Models (CIM), Platform Independent Models (PIMs), Platform Specific Models (PSM) and mappings that allow a developer to transform one model into another.

Business process models created by business analysts are considered as computation-independent models (CIM) that can be converted into platform-independent models (PIM) through model transformations. At this level, the main users are software architects or software engineers. Platform-independent specifications can be transformed into specifications for a specific platform and finally into a software component.

The relationship between a business model and the software development process is clearly established mainly because it is possible to extract from business process models the essential requirements for software construction (List & Korherr, 2005; Lopez, Montenegro, Vivas, Okamoto, & Dawson, 2005).

For a model specified through the MDA approach to be able to relate to others, it must be based on MOF. In other words, each MDA model has its own correspondence toward MOF so that it can communicate with any other model of the MOF-subordinated type (Harmon, 2004).

In this context, languages for model transformation constitute a fundamental aspect. Transformations must be clearly and precisely expressed so, it is advisable to use a language defined for that purpose. Among the most widespread ones, we can find VIATRA (VIsual Automated TRAnsformations) (Csertan, Huszerl, Majzik, Pap, Pataricza, & Varro, 2002), ATL (Atlas Trasformation Language) (Bézivin, Breton, Dupé, & Valduriez, 2003) and QVT (Query-View-Transformation) (QVT, 2005), among others.

QVT is compatible with the MDA standard since its abstract syntax is defined as a MOF 2.0. metamodel. Basically, it offers the possibility to manipulate models considering:

- Queries: Taking a model as input and selecting specific elements of it according to a search pattern.
- Views: Corresponding to models derived from other models.
- Transformations: Taking as a reference one or more input models to obtain an output model or result.

In the model-driven approach, business processes are used in software modeling because they allow us to (i) identify the system information that better supports the business operation, (ii) find functional requirements, (iii) find non-functional requirements, (iv) act as a basis for the analysis and design of systems, (v) and finally, because they let us identify appropriate software components (Eriksson & Penker, 2001).

SECURE BUSINESS PROCESS DEFINITION: OUR PROPOSAL

The basic aspects of our proposal are shown in Figure 4. The first column (on the left) shows two types of models which conform to the MDA. The central part shows our proposal and the artifacts which are derived from its application. The business process specification is made by using UML 2.0-AD (Activity Diagram) or BPMN-BPD (Business Process Diagram). It is possible to define a Secure Business Process (SBP) model

Figure 4. Our proposal overview

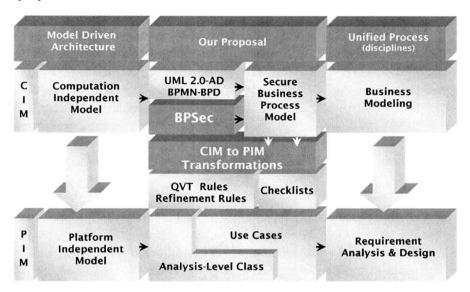

by applying the BPSec extension (in dark grey). The model transformations, from CIM to PIM (in dark grey) which we propose take the SBP model as its starting point and use QVT rules, refinement rules and checklists to obtain a set of analysis level classes and use cases. In the last column (on the right), we have incorporated the workflows of the Unified Process (Jacobson, Booch, & Rumbaugh, 1999). Our purpose is to show that not only SBP specification but also analysis-level classes and use cases can be used in a complementary way in a consolidated and successful software development process such as the UP (Fuggetta, 2000). In this way, taking into consideration a certain parallelism between our proposal and the unified process, the SBP model will be built at the "Business Model" stage and the analysis level classes and use cases will be defined and refined at the "Requirements" and "Analysis & Design" stages.

In the following sections, we will present a general overview of the extension that allows us to specify security requirements in business processes and the method through which such extension can be applied in an ordered way.

BPSec: Extension for Secure Business Process Definition

In this section, we will show a language extension for UML 2.0-AD (Rodríguez, Fernández-Medina, & Piattini, 2006) and BPMN-BPD (Rodríguez, Fernández-Medina, & Piattini, 2007b) through which a business analyst will be able to specify a business process including security requirements. This extension, called BPSec (Business Process Security), allows us to adapt UML 2.0-AD and BPMN-BPD to make the specification of security requirements in the business process dominion possible. These security requirements, which are specified at a high level of abstraction, will be translated into more concrete models and security mechanisms at the same time as the software development process advances.

From the security taxonomy proposed by Firesmith (2004), we have selected a subset of security requirements, taking into account the clarity of their definition, their ease of use by business analysts and finally, whether or not the definition is independent of security specific solutions. This subset of security requirements can be widened if necessary, and is composed of the following elements:

- Access Control: This signifies the degree to which the system limits the access to its resources only to authorized external people.
- Attack harm detection: This is considered as the degree to which an attack attempt or a successful attack is registered and notified.
- Non-repudiation: This is the degree to which a party to an interaction (e.g., message, transaction, transmission of data) is prevented from successfully repudiating (i.e., denying) any aspect of the interaction.
- Integrity: This is the degree to which components are protected from intentional and unauthorized corruption. Integrity with regard to data refers to the degree to which data components (including communications) are protected from intentional corruption (e.g., via unauthorized creation, modification, deletion, or replay)
- Privacy: This is the degree to which unauthorized parties are prevented from obtaining sensitive information. With regard to privacy, we can distinguish between anonymity, which is the degree to which the identity of users is prevented from unauthorized storage or disclosure, and confidentiality, which is the degree to which sensitive information is not disclosed to unauthorized parties (e.g., individuals, programs, processes, devices, or other systems), and finally
- Security Audit: This corresponds to the possibility of the security staff to collect, analyze and give information about the state and use of security mechanisms.

These requirements are the basis of the BPSec extension. Each requirement or set of requirements could be explicitly indicated in a business process. A special case is that of the Audit Security requirement, which, being basically a register of information that will be used in a security audit process must be specified as an additional characteristic of other security requirements.

For the definition of the BPSec extension, we have specialized UML and BPMN by using the extensibility mechanism proposed by UML. This mechanism is called *profile* and is used for providing a: (i) terminology adapted for a specific platform or dominion, (ii) additional syntax for developers that a determined notation does not have, (iii) notation different from the already existing one, created by aggregating symbols or semantics, that is not specified in the metamodel (Object Management Group, 2005b).

A *profile* is composed of stereotypes, restrictions and labeled values. A stereotype is an element of the model defined by its name and the base class from which it is inherited. Restrictions are applied to stereotypes with the purpose of indicating limitations (for example, pre-conditions, post-conditions or invariants). These restrictions can be expressed in natural language, programming language or a specialized language such as OCL (Object Constraint Language) (Object Management Group, 2005a). Labeled values are additional meta-attributes that are specified as name/value pairs.

In our proposal, we have considered the following stereotypes:

- AccessControl: This corresponds to the limitation of access to resources to authorized users only.
- AttackHarmDetection: This is defined as the detection, registration and notification of an attempted attack or threat, whether it is successful or not.
- AuditRegister: This contains audit register specifications related to a security requirement specification. Each audit register type must be indicated in some of its subclasses.

- G-AuditRegister: This is made up of the audit specifications related to those security requirements which coincide with the information that is necessary to store.
- Integrity: This is related to the protection of components from intentional and non-authorized alteration. The integrity specification is valued as low, medium, and high.
- NonRepudiation: This establishes the need to avoid the denial of any aspect of the interaction (e.g. message, transaction, transmission of data).
- NR-AuditRegister: This contains the audit specifications related to the NonRepudiation security requirement.
- Privacy: This is related to conditions of information protection concerning a determined individual or entity, limiting access to sensitive information by non-authorized parties.
- SecureActivity: A secure activity contains security specifications related to requirements, role identifications, and permissions
- SecurityPermission: This contains permission specifications related to an AccessControl specification. A permission specification must contain details about the objects and operations involved.
- SecurityRequirement: An abstract class containing security requirement specifications. Each security requirement type must be indicated in some of its subclasses.
- SecurityRole: This contains a role specification. These roles must be obtained from Access Control and/or Privacy specifications
- SP-AuditRegister: This contains the audit specifications related to the access control security requirement which gives rise to SecurityPermission

The stereotypes forming the proposed extension have been grouped into two packages; BPSec and Types BPSec (see Figure 5). Firstly, in the BPSec package, the most important stereotype is «SecureActivity» in UML 2.0-AD and «SecureBusinessProcessDiagramy» in BPMN-BPD which, as already stated, specialize the Activity and BusinessProcessDiagram classes respectively. The relationship between «SecureActivity»/«SecureBusinessProcessDiagramy» and the «SecurityRequirement» stereotype establishes that there will be a secure activity only if at least one security requirement is specified.

In the second place, the Types BPsec package contains the definition of new data types which are necessary for BPSec definition. Conceptually, «import», is equivalent to importing an element to each individual member of the imported namespace. In this case, the «import», relationship established between the packages implies that the importing namespace (Types BPSec) adds the names of the members of the package to the BPSec namespace, thus allowing us to use the new labeled values in the definition of stereotypes.

All the stereotypes composing Types BPSec are inherited from the Enumeration metaclass. The types of data allow us to define:

- RequirementType which contains the values accepted in the individual or combined specifications of security requirements
- PermissionOperation which allows us to specify the permitted values for the operation permissions defined for all the objects that are within the scope of an Access Control Specification.
- ProtectionDegree which contains a classification of the defined protection together with an Integrity specification
- PrivacyType which describes the values associated with a Privacy specification

Due to the fact that in our proposal the specification of security requirements is performed by a business analyst, we have paid special attention to the graphical representation of these requirements. To do so, we have chosen a padlock considered

Figure 5. High level view of BPSec extension and types BPSec

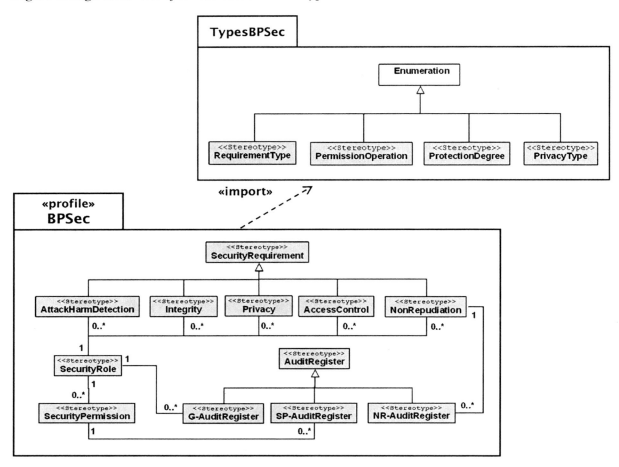

a de facto standard associated with security. In Figure 6, part a, we will show the basic symbol over which a determined security requirement is specified. In Figure 6, part b, the same symbol but with one of the edges folded, associated with the symbol used to represent a comment, annotation or register will be used to represent a security requirement which also requires the audit register.

As the chosen symbol allows us to perform a generic representation of security, it is necessary to indicate precisely which requirement we aim to specify. To do so, each security requirement has been associated with an abbreviation, as detailed below:

Figure 6. Icons used to represent security requirements in BPSec

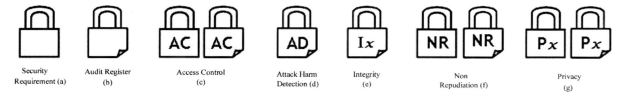

- AC: associated with Access Control. In this case, it is possible to specify either Access Control or Access Control with audit register (see Figure 6, part c).

- AD: associated with Attack Harm Detection requirement. This requirement is specified with compulsory audit register (see Figure 6, part d).

- Ix: for Integrity security requirement. This requirement must be specified with compulsory audit register. Furthermore, it is necessary to indicate the desired degree of integrity. To do so, x is replaced by the letter w when we wish to specify low integrity, by the letter m to specify medium integrity and by the letter h to indicate high integrity (see Figure 6, part e).

- NR: for Non Repudiation requirement. This requirement is alternatively specified with or without audit register (sees Figure 6, part f).

- Px for Privacy requirement. This requirement can be specified with or without audit register. We must additionally indicate the type of privacy required. To do so, the letter x is replaced by a letter a to indicate anonymity or a letter c to indicate confidentiality (see Figure 6, part g).

M-BPSEc: Method for Security Requirement Elicitation

For the adequate utilization of the extension presented in the previous section, we have created a method which allows the specification of secure business processes in an unambiguous manner. The purpose of the M-BPSec method (Rodríguez, Fernández-Medina, & Piattini, 2007d) is to allow the incorporation of security requirements into the business process specification. This method is a guide which lets us apply the BPSec extension in an ordered and effective way.

M-BPSec, which will be shown in its entirety in Figure 7, is composed of a set of stages, roles, tools and artifacts which, in an engineering and systematic approach, allow us to create secure business processes and obtain useful artifacts for software development.

The three first stages of M-BPSec are related to the definition of a secure business process. Through them, it is possible to design a business process, add security requirements to it and refine such specifications. The fourth and last stage is a complement through which analysis classes and use cases that can be used as a complement in a software construction process are automatically generated. Thus, through the use of M-BPSec, we will be able to capture requirements early, with special emphasis on security requirements. The resulting model (SBP) will be transformed into a set of artifacts which are useful for software construction under a model driven approach.

Each of the stages of M-BPSec is technologically supported by the BPSec-Tool. This tool is used to design the Secure Business Process, to automatically transform models and to update the data contained in the secure business process repository. The BPSec-Tool was built by using a 3-tiered architecture to separate the presentation, application, and storage components, using MS-Visio, C#, and MS-Access technology respectively.

Model Transformation: From Secure Business Process Specification to Analysis Level Classes and Use Cases

Business process transformations can be performed in two directions: *horizontal* and *vertical*. In a *horizontal* transformation, we obtain a computation-independent model from another computation-independent model (from CIM to CIM) while in a *vertical* transformation, we obtain a platform-independent model from a computation-independent model (from CIM to PIM).

Both types of transformations have been scarcely dealt with in the related literature and are

Figure 7. M-BPSec: A method for security requirement elicitation

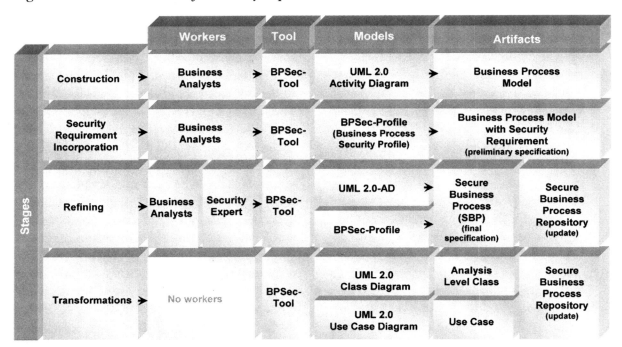

Stages	Workers		Tool	Models	Artifacts
Construction	Business Analysts		BPSec-Tool	UML 2.0 Activity Diagram	Business Process Model
Security Requirement Incorporation	Business Analysts		BPSec-Tool	BPSec-Profile (Business Process Security Profile)	Business Process Model with Security Requirement (preliminary specification)
Refining	Business Analysts	Security Expert	BPSec-Tool	UML 2.0-AD / BPSec-Profile	Secure Business Process (SBP) (final specification) / Secure Business Process Repository (update)
Transformations	No workers		BPSec-Tool	UML 2.0 Class Diagram / UML 2.0 Use Case Diagram	Analysis Level Class / Use Case / Secure Business Process Repository (update)

not described in detail in the MDA specification (Object Management Group, 2003) either. In this type of specification, attention has been paid preferentially to transformations from PIM to PSM.

In the particular case of business process specifications, *horizontal* transformations, in other words, transformations between computation-independent models (abbreviated as C2C) will be feasible if we establish a correspondence between specifications made with different languages. In this work, we have paid attention to transformations between UML and BPMN. In the review of the literature related to this type of transformations, we have found the proposal of (White, 2004) in which the author makes a comparison between UML 2.0-AD and BPMN-BPD, considering the technical capacity of each notation to represent patterns and its readability. However, in this work, the way in which elements from one notation can be mapped to the other is not considered.

The *vertical t*ransformations correspond to the mapping between models situated at a differ-

ent level of abstraction. In the case of business processes, the vertical transformation is carried out from a computation-independent model (the business process) to platform-independent models (abbreviated as C2P). In the review of the related works, we have paid special attention to those describing transformations of business process specifications to analysis classes and the use cases of UML.

In our review of the related literature, ranging from business processes to analysis-level class transformations, we have found two works that deal directly with this type of transformations. In the first one, (Barros & Gomes, 2000) activity diagrams are transformed into analysis classes. This transformation is not automatically performed, and a previous version of UML 2.0 is used. In the second work, (Wararat Rungworawut & Senivongse, 2006), the software designer studies the business process model described with BPMN by extracting the UML classes which are later refined. The differences between these proposals and ours are that, firstly we use QVT for transformation specifications, secondly we pay special attention to security requirements, and finally we connect the result of transformations to a software development process.

In the works related to the obtention of use cases from business process specifications, we have found that in (Wararat Rungworawut & Senivongse, 2005), the authors suggest the possibility of obtaining use cases from a business process specification made with BPMN, and in (Liew, Kontogiannis, & Tong, 2004), it is proposed the automatic obtention of UML artifacts from a BP description that was made using BPMN. The authors extend BPMN (Extension Level-1) to add information about the sequence and the input and output flows. This allows them to apply rules from which use cases, state diagrams, sequence and collaboration are achieved. In (Štolfa & Vondrák, 2004), it is stated a transformation performed from a business process described with UML 2.0 activity diagrams to use cases and finally, in (Dijkman & Joosten, 2002), use cases are obtained from business process models that are not represented by activity diagrams. The differences with our proposal are basically the following: (i) even in works where there are automatic transformations, previous manual intervention is required, ii) transformations are not described by using languages specially designed for this purpose, iii) the result of transformations does not appear to be linked to a business process development and finally, iv) none of them is related to security aspects.

In previous works, we have dealt with both transformations; from secure business processes to analysis classes (Rodríguez, Fernández-Medina, & Piattini, 2007a) and use cases (Rodríguez, Fernández-Medina, & Piattini, 2007e) of UML.

CASE STUDY

The case study (Rodríguez, Fernández-Medina, & Piattini, 2007c) has been developed in a co-operative which is dedicated to the distribution of electricity in rural areas. The Coopelan Ltda. (www.coopelan.cl) cooperative came into being in 1957, and currently maintains 2,200 kms of electrical lines which are used to supply more than 12,000 customers. In recent years, we have seen the commercialization of goods and services, both for their customers for electrical energy (who are associates of the cooperative) and for the public in general. From an organizational point of view, the cooperative is made up of a technical area which is related to the distribution of electricity, a commercial area which is in charge of goods and services, and an administrative area. The cooperative has a total of 70 employees.

Because the cooperative's main customers live in rural areas, the way in which payment for the consumption of electricity is received presents two problems: (i) delivery of the invoice detailing the consumption of electrical energy and (ii) receipt of payment of said debt. Business analysts have used a traditional method to modify the business process associated with the recovery of energy consumption debts, and have incorporated an electronic debt advisor and electronic payment. This complementary method has increased the index of debt recovery. The cooperative has neither the technical nor the operative capacity through which to receive electronic payments (via the Internet) and for this reason it has decided to employ an external collector to carry out this task.

The business process which we shall describe as a part of our case study is about payment for consumption of electrical energy. The case study was carried out with the assistance of the cooperative's business analysts. M-BPSec was used in the development of this case study. The result of the first three stages is a Secure Business Process called "Payment for consumption of Electrical Energy", shown in Figure 8.

In the following sections, we will present the stages of M-BPSec and we will show the result of its application to this case study.

Figure 8. Secure business process: Payment for consumption of electrical energy

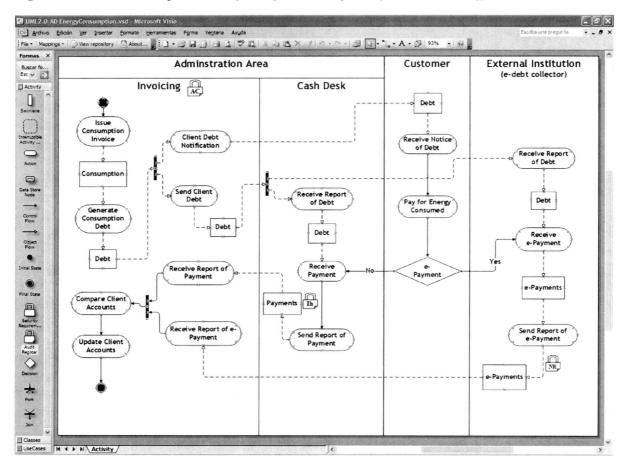

Construction Stage

At this stage the objective is to build the business process model. To attain this objective, UML 2.0-AD must be used. The Construction stage is carried out by the business analyst, who sets the time and place of the work activities, ensures that they have a beginning and an end, and clearly explains the business viewpoint. The BPSec-Tool is used to make a business process design with UML 2.0-AD. The final result of this stage is a Business Process Model.

In this case, the business process was described by using UML 2.0-AD. The areas which were identified were the following Activity Partitions: "External Institution", "Customer", and "Admin-istration Area", which was divided into two central Activity Partitions called "Invoicing" and "Cash Desk". This business process is initiated when the "Issue Consumption Invoice" activity is carried out, and terminates with receipt of payments and an updating of customers' debts.

Security Requirement Incorporation Stage

At this stage security requirements can be added to the business process description from the business analyst's viewpoint. The business analyst must be able to identify the potential threats in the business process model. Security requirements must subsequently be incorporated, using BPSec

Table 1. Security requirements priorities

Requirement	Specified in	Priority
AccessControl	Invoicing	must be
Nonrepudiation	e-Payment	must be
Integrity (high)	Payment	must be

Table 2. Permissions associated with the access control specification in invoicing

Name	UML 2.0-AD element	Permission
Issue Consumption Invoice	Action	CheckExecution
Consumption	DataStore	Update
Generate Consumption Debt	Action	CheckExecution
Debt	DataStore	Update
Client Debt Notification	Action	Execution
Send Client Debt	Action	Execution
Receive Report of Payment	Action	Execution
Receive Report of e-Payment	Action	Execution
Compare Client Accounts	Action	Execution
Update Client Account	Action	CheckExecution

extension (supported by the BPSec-Tool). The output artifact at this stage is a Business Process Model with Security Requirement.

The business analyst identifies vulnerable areas in: (i) the information which is sent from "External collector" to "Invoicing", for which Non-repudiation is specified, (ii) the information related to the payments received by the "Cash Desk", for which a high level of Integrity is specified, and (iii) the activities and information related to the Invoicing Activity Partition for which Access Control is specified.

Refinement Stage

At the Refining stage the security requirements specified in the business process description must be reviewed and complemented. The employees, the business analyst and the security expert, work together and the specifications that will finally be incorporated into the business process are agreed. The BPSec-Tool must be used to achieve a Secure Business Process (final specification). The repository which contains information about the secure business process specification is also automatically generated.

The priority specification of each security requirement (see Table 1) and the security permissions associated with the access control specification (see Table 2) are also refined at this stage.

In Table 1, the first column describes the security requirement that was specified in the secure business process definition, the second column shows the element of the secure business process where the security requirement was indicated and

the last column represents the priority assigned to each security requirement.

In Table 2, the first column shows the name of the element of UML 2.0-AD within the access control scope, the second column corresponds to the kind of element of UML 2.0-AD and the last column indicates the permission associated with the element of the secure business process description.

Transformation Stage

Finally, at the Transformation stage, the analysis-level classes and use cases are obtained and stored in the repository. This stage does not require workers because the artifacts and the repository are automatically generated.

Transformations to analysis-level classes, from CIM to PIM (C2P), require a set of rules which have been specified in QVT language and also a set of refinement rules (Rodríguez, Fernández-Medina, & Piattini, 2007a). For transformations to use cases (C2P) it is necessary to specify a set of

Figure 9. Class diagram from "payment for consumption of electrical energy"

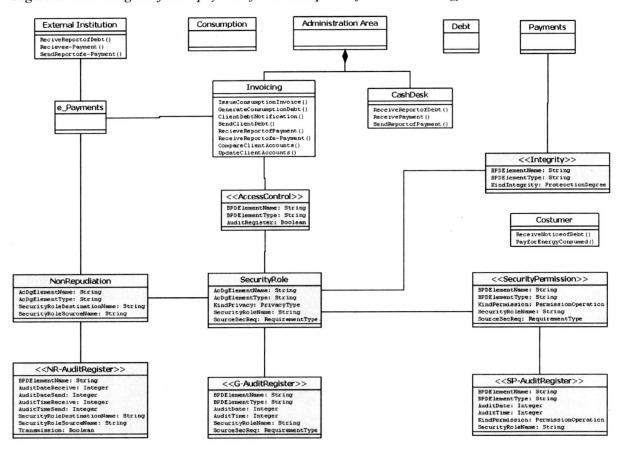

QVT rules, refinement rules and a checklist (Rodríguez & García-Rodríguez de Guzmán, 2007).

The result of the application of the QVT rules and the refinement rules in relation to the attainment of analysis-level classes can be seen in Figure 9.

The application of the transformations associated with the obtention of use cases allows us to achieve a general use case (see Figure 10).

Finally, the checklists applied to the security requirement specifications in the business process let us identify the following subjects:

- *Access Control* over the *Invoicing* partition with Invoicing and Security Team as actors. The associated use cases will be aimed at carrying out tasks such as roles validation,

verification of revelation permissions and storage permissions (see Figure 11).

- *Non repudiation* over the *e-Payment* message flow that goes from external institution to Invoicing with External Institution, Invoicing and Security Team as actors. These actors must perform tasks related to the assignment and validation of security roles (see Figure 12).

- *Integrity* over *Payment*, with Cash Desk and Security Team as actors, related to the use cases oriented to determine to check special permissions to update the data, make security backups and audit registers (see Figure 12).

Figure 10. General use cases specification

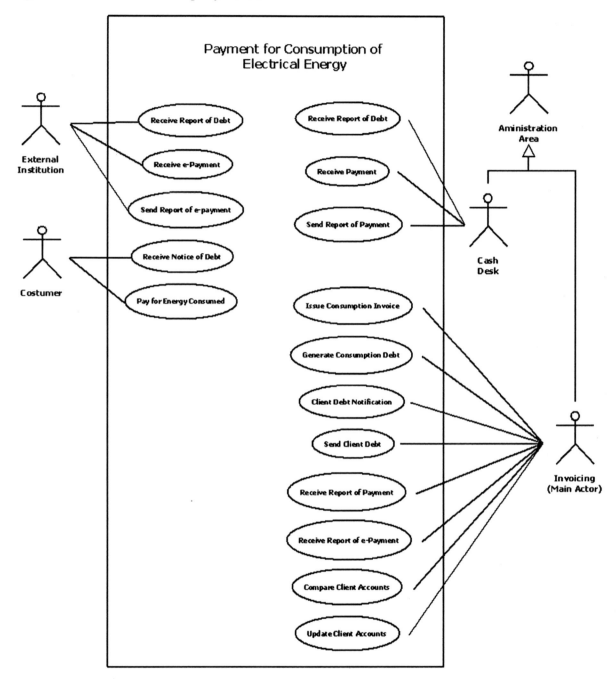

Figure 11. Access control security use cases specification

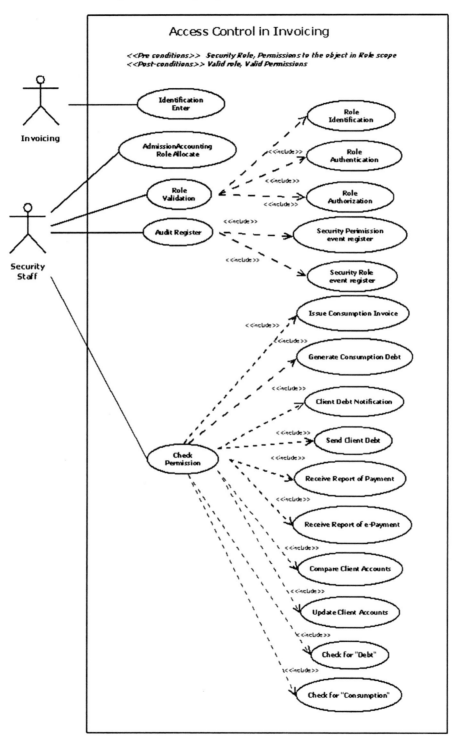

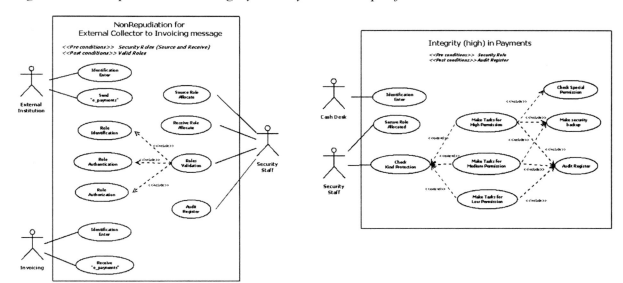

Figure 12. Non-repudiation and integrity security use cases specification

Both the secure business process and the analysis classes and use cases have been used as input in the software development process which Coopelan Ltda. used to carry out its software creation.

Study Case Conclusions

The development of the case study has let us apply M-BPSec in a real environment as well as verify in practice that the method allows us to specify and design secure business processes. Additionally, not only the analysis classes but also the use cases automatically obtained have been included as an additional input at the first stages of software creation.

The lessons learned through the application of this method to the above described case study are as follows:

- The organization has valued very positively the possibility to express requirements through a standard language for business process design in which its viewpoint in relation to security is reflected.

- The learning curve associated with the application of the method has been acceptable, considering that the business analysts did not have any experience in business process security modeling and they only had a scarce experience in business process modeling in general.

- The use of a prototype (BPSec-Tool) to support the application of the M-BPSec method has favoured the development of the case study because it has facilitated the work not only of business analysts but also of those who have driven the case study application.

- We could detect aspects to be improved in the prototype. The main improvements were made at the presentation layer in relation to the attainment of security requirements. In the same sense, we made some changes that allowed the improvement of the readability of the artifacts derived from the transformation stage. In spite of the fact that the technological environment where the case study was developed allowed an adequate use of BPSec-Tool, we think that the prototype must be more flexible to adapt itself to the characteristics specific to each organization.

CONCLUSION AND FUTURE WORK

In this work, we have shown the main elements of the proposal that allows the development of secure business processes under a Model-Driven approach. We have considered the incorporation of security requirements into business processes, thus allowing business analysts to improve the models they design. The business analyst's point of view in relation to security (i.e., access control, attack harm detection, non-repudiation, integrity, privacy and security audit) allows us to enrich the most technical perspectives existing so far. In addition, the secure business process has been used for the obtention of artifacts including security. Such artifacts are useful in a software creation process. The proposal, as a whole, has been proved in a case study, allowing us to verify its pertinence and validity. Our future work will let us incorporate new security requirements as well as improve the prototype created to support the application of our proposal.

ACKNOWLEDGMENT

This research is part of the following projects: QUASIMODO (PAC08-0157-0668), and MIS-TICO (PBC06-0082) both partially supported by the FEDER and the "Consejería de Ciencia y Tecnología de la Junta de Comunidades de Castilla-La Mancha", Spain, COMPETISOFT (506AC087), granted by CYTED and ESFINGE (TIN2006-15175-C05-05/) granted by the "Dirección General de Investigación del Ministerio de Ciencia y Tecnología", Spain.

REFERENCES

Artelsmair, C., & Wagner, R. (2003, July 27-30). *Towards a security engineering process.* Paper presented at the The 7th World Multiconference on Systemics, Cybernetics and Informatics, Orlando, Florida, USA.

Atluri, V. (2001). Security for workflow systems. *Information Security Technical Report, 6*(2), 59–68. doi:10.1016/S1363-4127(01)00207-2

Backes, M., Pfitzmann, B., & Waider, M. (2003, June 26-27). *Security in business process engineering.* Paper presented at the International Conference on Business Process Management (BPM), Eindhoven, Netherlands.

Barros, J. P., & Gomes, L. (2000, 2-6 October). *From activity diagrams to class diagrams.* Paper presented at the Workshop Dynamic Behaviour in UML Models: Semantic Questions In conjunction with Third International Conference on UML, York, UK.

Bézivin, J. (2004). In search of a basic principle for model driven engineering. *UPGRADE. European Journal for the Informatics Professional, 5*(2), 21–24.

Bézivin, J., Breton, E., Dupé, G., & Valduriez, P. (2003). *The ATL transformation-based model management framework. (No. Nº 03.08).* IRIN-Université de Nantes.

Caralli, R. (2004). *Managing for enterprise security.* Software Engineering Institute, Carnegie Mellon University.

Common Criteria. (2005). *Introduction and general model,* version 3.0, revision 2. (No. CCMB-2005-07-001): Common Criteria for Information Technology Security Evaluation. Retrieved from http://www.commoncriteriaportal.org/

Csertan, G., Huszerl, G., Majzik, I., Pap, Z., Pataricza, A., & Varro, D. (2002). *VIATRA-Visual automated transformations for formal verification and validation of UML models.* Paper presented at the 17th IEEE International Conference on Automated Software Engineering (ASE).

Dijkman, R. M., & Joosten, S. M. M. (2002). *An algorithm to derive use cases from business processes.* Paper presented at the 6th International Conference on Software Engineering and Applications (SEA), Boston, USA.

Eriksson, H.-E., & Penker, M. (2001). *Business modeling with UML.* OMG Press.

Firesmith, D. (2003). Engineering security requirements. *Journal of Object Technology, 2*(1), 53–68. doi:10.5381/jot.2003.2.1.c6

Firesmith, D. (2004). Specifying reusable security requirements. *Journal of Object Technology, 3*(1), 61–75. doi:10.5381/jot.2004.3.1.c6

Fuggetta, A. (2000, June 4-11, 2000.). *Software process: A roadmap.* Paper presented at the ICSE 2000, 22nd International Conference on Software Engineering, Future of Software Engineering, Limerick Ireland.

Haley, C. B., Laney, R. C., & Nuseibeh, B. (2004, March 22-24, 2004). *Deriving security requirements from crosscutting threat descriptions.* Paper presented at the 3rd International Conference on Aspect-Oriented Software Development (AOSD), Lancaster, UK.

Harmon, P. (2004). *The OMG's model driven architecture and BPM.* Retrieved May, 2005, from http://www.bptrends.com/publication-files/ 05%2D04%20NL%20MDA%20and%20 BPM%2Epdf

Jacobson, I., Booch, G., & Rumbaugh, J. (1999). *The unified software development process.*

Lampson, B. W. (2004). Computer security in the real world. *IEEE Computer, 37*(6), 37–46. doi:10.1109/MC.2004.17

Liew, P., Kontogiannis, P., & Tong, T. (2004). *A framework for business model driven development.* Paper presented at the 12 International Workshop on Software Technology and Engineering Practice (STEP).

List, B., & Korherr, B. (2005). *A UML 2 profile for business process modelling.* Paper presented at the 1st International Workshop on Best Practices of UML (BP-UML) at ER-Conference, Klagenfurt, Austria.

Lodderstedt, T., Basin, D., & Doser, J. (2002). *SecureUML: A UML-based modeling language for model-driven security.* Paper presented at the UML, 5th International Conference, Dresden, Germany.

Lopez, J., Montenegro, J. A., Vivas, J. L., Okamoto, E., & Dawson, E. (2005). Specification and design of advanced authentication and authorization services. *Computer Standards & Interfaces, 27*(5), 467–478. doi:10.1016/j.csi.2005.01.005

Maña, A., Ray, D., Sánchez, F., & Yagüe, M. I. (2004, Septiembre 2004). *Integrando la ingeniería de seguridad en un proceso de ingeniería software.* Paper presented at the VIII Reunión Española de Criptología y Seguridad de la Información, RECSI, Madrid. España.

Mens, T., & Van Gorp, P. (2006). A taxonomy of model transformation. *Electronic Notes in Theoretical Computer Science, 152*, 125–142. doi:10.1016/j.entcs.2005.10.021

Ministerio de Administraciones Públicas. (2005). *MAGERIT – versión 2. Metodología de análisis y gestión de riesgos de los sistemas de información.* Retrieved June 15, 2005, from http://www.csi.map.es/csi/pg5m20.htm

Object Management Group. (2003). *MDA guide version 1.0.1*. Retrieved from http://www.omg.org/docs/omg/03-06-01.pdf

Object Management Group. (2005a). *OCL 2.0 Specification, Version 2.0*. Retrieved from http://www.omg.org/docs/ptc/05-06-06.pdf

Object Management Group. (2005b). *Unified modeling language: Superstructure*. Retrieved from http://www.omg.org/docs/formal/05-07-04.pdf

Quirchmayr, G. (2004, January 2004). *Survivability and business continuity management*. Paper presented at the ACSW Frontiers 2004 Workshops, Dunedin, New Zealand.

QVT. (2005). *Meta object facility (MOF) 2.0 query/view/transformation specification*.

Rodríguez, A., Fernández-Medina, E., & Piattini, M. (2006, September 4-8). *Towards a UML 2.0 extension for the modeling of security requirements in business processes*. Paper presented at the 3rd International Conference on Trust, Privacy and Security in Digital Business (TrustBus), Krakow-Poland.

Rodríguez, A., Fernández-Medina, E., & Piattini, M. (2007a, September 3–7). *Analysis-level classes from secure business processes through models transformations*. Paper presented at the 4th International Conference on Trust, Privacy and Security in Digital Business (TrustBus), Regensburg, Germany.

Rodríguez, A., Fernández-Medina, E., & Piattini, M. (2007b). A BPMN extension for the modeling of security requirements in business processes. *IEICE Transactions on Information and Systems. E (Norwalk, Conn.), 90-D*(4), 745–752.

Rodríguez, A., Fernández-Medina, E., & Piattini, M. (2007c, October 14-16). *CIM to PIM transformation: A reality*. Paper presented at the IFIP International Conference on Research and Practical Issues of Enterprise Information Systems (CONFENIS), Beijing, China.

Rodríguez, A., Fernández-Medina, E., & Piattini, M. (2007d). *M-BPSec: A method for security requirement elicitation from a UML 2.0 business process specification*. Paper presented at the 3rd International Workshop on Foundations and Practices of UML, Auckland, New Zealand.

Rodríguez, A., Fernández-Medina, E., & Piattini, M. (2007e, 24-28 September). *Towards CIM to PIM transformation: From secure business processes defined by BPMN to use cases*. Paper presented at the 5th International Conference on Business Process Management (BPM), Brisbane, Australia.

Rodríguez, A., & García-Rodríguez de Guzmán, I. (2007). *Obtaining use cases and security use cases from secure business process through the MDA approach*. Paper presented at the Workshop on Security in Information Systems (WOSIS), Funchal, Madeira - Portugal.

Rungworawut, W., & Senivongse, T. (2005). A guideline to mapping business processes to UML class diagrams. *WSEAS Trans. on Computers, 4*(11), 1526–1533.

Rungworawut, W., & Senivongse, T. (2006). Using ontology search in the design of class diagram from business process model. *Enformatika, Transactions on Engineering. Computing and Technology, 12*, 165–170.

Štolfa, S., & Vondrák, I. (2004, June 2004). *A description of business process modeling as a tool for definition of requirements specification*. Paper presented at the Systems Integration 12th Annual International Conference, Prague, Czech Republic.

Störrle, H. (2005). Semantics and verification of data flow in UML 2.0 Activities. *Electronic Notes in Theoretical Computer Science, 127*(4), 35–52. doi:10.1016/j.entcs.2004.08.046

WfMC. (1999). *Workflow management coalition: Terminology & glossary*.

White, S. A. (2004). *Process modeling notations and workflow patterns*. Retrieved from http://www.ebpml.org/bpmn.htm

Zuccato, A. (2004). Holistic security requirement engineering for electronic commerce. *Computers & Security, 23*(1), 63–76. doi:10.1016/S0167-4048(04)00065-3

KEY TERMS AND DEFINITIONS

Access Control: This signifies the degree to which the system limits the access to its resources only to authorized external people.

Attack Harm Detection: This is considered as the degree to which an attack attempt or a successful attack is registered and notified.

Business Process: A business process is defined as a combination of a set of activities within an enterprise with a structure which describes their logical order and dependence whose objective is to produce a desired result.

Integrity: This is the degree to which components are protected from intentional and unauthorized corruption. Integrity with regard to data refers to the degree to which data components (including communications) are protected from intentional corruption (e.g., via unauthorized creation, modification, deletion, or replay).

MDA: Model Driven Architecture, a paradigm which claims to work at model and metamodel levels. Among the objectives pursued, we can find the separation of business-neutral descriptions and platform dependent implementations, the expression of specific aspects of a system under development with specialized domain-specific languages, the establishment of precise relations between these different languages within a global framework and, in particular, the capability to express operational transformations between them.

Model Transformation: According to the MDA standard, a model transformation is the process of converting one model into another model from the same system. Model transformations are composed of fine-grained rules that transform elements defined in a specific source metamodel into other elements of the target metamodel.

Non-Repudiation: This is the degree to which a party to an interaction (e.g., message, transaction, transmission of data) is prevented from successfully repudiating (i.e., denying) any aspect of the interaction.

Privacy: This is the degree to which unauthorized parties are prevented from obtaining sensitive information. With regard to privacy, we can distinguish between anonymity, which is the degree to which the identity of users is prevented from unauthorized storage or disclosure, and confidentiality, which is the degree to which sensitive information is not disclosed to unauthorized parties (e.g., individuals, programs, processes, devices, or other systems).

Security Audit: This corresponds to the possibility of the security staff to collect, analyze and give information about the state and use of security mechanisms.

Security Requirement: A security requirement is defined as a limitation or restriction expressed over a system's behavior. Traditionally, three security objectives have been identified: confidentiality, integrity and availability. More recently, authentication has gained in importance. If we consider security from the viewpoint of the people and organizations that use computers, they can be expressed as secret, integrity, availability and responsibility. From the point of view of work flows, aspects such as authorization, audit, anonymity and separation of duties can be added. Nonetheless, although security requirements are widely dealt with in the literature, it is difficult to find a definition that is wide enough to describe all their properties and the range that they cover.

Chapter 7

Privacy by Design:
Origins, Meaning, and Prospects for Assuring Privacy and Trust in the Information Era

Ann Cavoukian
Information and Privacy Commissioner, Canada[1]

ABSTRACT

This chapter traces the origins of the Privacy by Design (PbD) concept and leadership by the Office of the Information and Privacy Commissioner (IPC) of Ontario, Canada, from the mid-1990s to the current day (2011), with specific attention to three major themes: The evolution of PbD from its early emphasis on information technologies, which also apply to organizational practices and processes, and to broader information eco-systems and architectures; The evolution of the need to articulate and promote a set of universal principles to help guide the design of privacy, from Fair Information Practices to PbD's 7 Foundational Principles; An account of the evolving work of the IPC in support of the new or "enhanced" FIPs that were codified in the PbD Foundational Principles. The chapter will outline recognition for PbD received, and the challenges ahead.

INTRODUCTION

"Privacy is good for business" has been a long-standing mantra of the Office of the Information and Privacy Commissioner of Ontario, Canada (IPC) that has, within 15 years, become a legal,

market and functional requirement, not only for businesses but for ALL organizations—public and private sector—that handle personal information. The edict is straightforward: build privacy in early and thoroughly into your data management systems, and reap the many rewards that will result from enhanced trust.

DOI: 10.4018/978-1-61350-501-4.ch007

In his March 2010 Opinion issued on the eve of a major European undertaking to review and revise European Data Protection Laws, the European Data Protection Supervisor, Peter Hustinx, observed that:

"Trust, or rather its absence, has been identified as a core issue in the emergence and successful deployment of information and communications technologies. If people do not trust ICT, these technologies are likely to fail. ... Such trust will only be secured if ICTs are reliable, secure, under individuals' control and if the protection of their personal data and privacy is guaranteed. To significantly minimise the risks and to secure users' willingness to rely on ICTs, it is crucial to integrate, at practical level, data protection and privacy from the very inception of new ICTs. This need for a "Privacy by Design" approach should be reflected in the EU data protection legal framework at different levels of laws and policy making" (European Data Protection Supervisor [EDPS], 2010).

His call for a more comprehensive, proactive approach to privacy is being echoed by Data Protection authorities around the world. In October 2010, a landmark resolution was approved by International Privacy and Data Protection Commissioners at their annual conference recognizing *Privacy by Design* (*PbD*) as an "essential component of fundamental privacy protection." The resolution, which was co-sponsored by Canadian Privacy Commissioner Jennifer Stoddart and Commissioners from Berlin, New Zealand, the Czech Republic, and Estonia, also:

• Encourages the adoption of the principles of *Privacy by Design* as part of an organization's default mode of operation; and
• Invites Data Protection and Privacy Commissioners to promote *Privacy by Design*, foster the incorporation of its Foundational Principles in privacy policy and legislation in their respective jurisdictions, and encourage research into *Privacy by Design* (International Conference of Privacy and Data Protection Commissioners [ICPDPC], 2010).

Since then, public officials and regulators in the United States and Europe have issued formal proposals and recommendations for *Privacy by Design* principles to be embedded in reformed oversight and governance regimes for the management of personal information by organizations. More than a concept, *Privacy by Design* is becoming a legal and regulatory requirement in major jurisdictions around the world.

This paper traces the origins of the *Privacy by Design* concept from the mid-1990s to the current day (2011), and the leadership of the Office of the Information and Privacy Commissioner of Ontario, with specific attention to three major themes:

1. The evolution of *Privacy by Design,* from its early emphasis on information technologies, to also apply to organizational practices and processes, and to broader information eco-systems and architectures;
2. The evolution of the need to articulate and promote a set of universal principles to help guide the design of privacy, from Fair Information Practices to the 7 Foundational Principles of *PbD*.
3. An account of the evolving work of the IPC in support of the new or "enhanced" FIPs introduced by the *PbD's* 7 Foundational principles, notably:
   a. **Proactive not Reactive** means establishing clear leadership priorities to set and enforce the highest privacy standards, at the beginning of any data usage.
   b. **Privacy Embedded into Design** means verifiable commitment to these priorities in all design and operational

processes. A systemic program or methodology in place to ensure that privacy commitments are thoroughly integrated into the technology, process or architecture in question.

c. ***Positive-Sum not Zero-Sum*** means demonstrating practical, measurable and proven results that reflect the positive presence of multiple objectives. All legitimate non-privacy objectives and functionalities should be accommodated (taking an innovative win-win approach).

The paper will show how — and why — the IPC promoted each of these *PbD* principles in the area of technology, organizational practices, and information eco-systems, outlining the recognition received to date, and the challenges that lie ahead.

BACKGROUND

The Internet and Information Privacy

The advent of the Internet and information and communication technologies has, in one generation, radically changed the ground rules for managing data. These trends carry profound implications for privacy in the Information Age. The global creation of information is accelerating, and this data is being replicated and stored everywhere. We can no longer speak meaningfully of information destruction, as we once did with paper records, because digital bits and bytes have now attained near immortality on the Internet, thwarting efforts to successfully remove it from the "public" domain. At the same time, the practical obscurity of personal information —the default privacy protection of yesteryear— is also fast disappearing as data becomes digitized and connected to the grid. We've all but given up trying to inventory and classify information, and now rely more on advanced searching, rather than

sorting, techniques to manage it. The combined effect is that while information has become cheap to distribute, copy, and recombine —too cheap to meter— personal information has also become far more available and consequential, yet also far more difficult to control or protect. The information privacy solution requires a combination of data minimization techniques, credible safeguards, individual involvement in managing this data, and accountability measures informed by an enhanced set of universal privacy principles that are better suited to modern realities.

The Decline of Accountability?

The proposition that "privacy is good for business" is one that is enshrined in all principles of Fair Information Practices (FIPs) around the world and, through them, in the many laws and organizational practices upon which they are based. By setting out universal principles for handling personal data, FIPs seek to ensure the privacy of individuals and to promote the free flow of personal data and, through them the growth of commerce.

The enduring confidence of individuals, business partners and regulators in organizations' data-handling practices is a function of their ability to express the FIPs' core requirements. These are: to limit collection, use and disclosure of personal data; to involve individuals in the data life-cycle, and to apply appropriate safeguards in a thoroughgoing manner. These requirements, in turn, are premised upon organizational openness and accountability. The ultimate results include enhanced trust, improved efficiencies, greater innovation, and heightened competitive advantages. Privacy *is* good for business.

But the early FIPs drafters and adopters had in mind large mainframe computers and centralized databases. They could never have imagined how leapfrogging revolutions in sensors, bandwidth, storage, and processing power would converge into our current hyper-connected "Web 2.0" networked world of ubiquitous data availability.

It has become trite to observe that data is the lifeblood of the new economy, but who today can truly grasp how large the arteries are becoming, how they are multiplying, where they may lead, and to what end? Everywhere we see near-exponential growth of data creation, transmission, use and storage, by an ever-expanding universe of actors, somewhere out there in the opaque "cloud." Most of this data is personally-identifiable. And most of it is now controlled by someone other than the individual data subject. Thanks to new information flows, today we enjoy unprecedented and nearly unimaginable new services and benefits, but these have been accompanied by unprecedented and once unimaginable privacy threats and harms. Some say that privacy is effectively dead or dying in the Information Age. Whether it is or is not, the privacy landscape is rapidly changing shape.

The need for organizational accountability remains constant – indeed, it has become more urgent today than ever before. What is changing are the means by which accountability may be demonstrated, whether to individuals, regulators or to business partners. Beyond policy statements, what is needed now are more innovative and more robust methods for assuring that personal data is, in fact, being managed responsibly.

There are many paths to enhanced account-ability and assurance, typically involving a mix of technology, policies and practices, and of regulation. More than ever before, a comprehensive *Privacy by Design* approach to information management is called for – one which assures end-to-end chain of custody and responsibility, right from the very start.

All organizations today face growing complex information management challenges. Not only has personally identifiable information (PII) become more ubiquitous, it is also accessible by more and more entities, for more and more purposes, across ever-expanding (and increasingly complex) networks. A further complicating factor is the need to comply with legal and regulatory requirements across multiple jurisdictions while, at the same

time, business organization models and strategies are being radically transformed by the many effects of information and communication technologies.

In brief, the scale and complexity of current data systems, networks and practices require a new and updated set of universally-accepted privacy design and practice principles that are robust, comprehensive, and capable of assuring privacy and trust amid the new global realities.

History provides a useful precedent: in 1973 —at the dawn of the mainframe, computerization and digital network eras— a report by the U.S. Department of Health, Education and Welfare (HEW) articulated a set of comprehensive information management principles that effectively established the global benchmark for protecting privacy in the ensuing digital era. Within twenty-five years of the seminal HEW report, a veritable canon of fair information practice principles was developed by a variety of governmental and inter-governmental agencies around the world, extending privacy protections more deeply and pervasively into society's fabric of law, regulation, organizational practices, and individual rights.

Enter *Privacy by Design*, a concept developed in the mid-nineties by Ann Cavoukian, the Information and Privacy Commissioner of Ontario, Canada, that seeks to raise the bar for privacy protection, and which is now being advanced around the world by data protection authorities, regulators, privacy advocates, technologists and leading organizations.

PbD ORIGINS (1996~2001)

Origins and Birth of PbD Concepts

In brief, *Privacy by Design* refers to the philosophy and approach of embedding privacy directly into the design and operating specifications of information technologies and systems. This may be achieved by building on the principles of Fair Information Practices at the earliest stages of information system design and deployment. This approach originally had technology as its primary area of application, but has since expanded its scope to embrace organizational practices, physical spaces, and even to overarching information architectures and networked eco-systems. There is even speculation today that *Privacy by Design* concepts may be applied to legislation and systems of regulatory oversight and governance.

As a broad overarching concept, *Privacy by Design* originated from many emerging practices and trends in the 1990s, notably:

1. Recognition that privacy interests and concerns must be addressed;
2. Application of basic principles expressing universal spheres of privacy protection;
3. Early mitigation of privacy concerns when developing information technologies and systems, across the entire information life-cycle;
4. Need for dedicated and qualified privacy leadership and/or professional input; and
5. Adoption and integration of Privacy-Enhancing Technologies (PETs).

Recognizing the Benefits of Addressing Privacy Interests and Concerns

Privacy by Design begins with the understanding of both the value and benefits of adopting good privacy practices. By the mid-'90s, there was considerable public discussions in the European Union, Canada and the United States about the merits of good privacy practices with the anticipated coming into force of the *European Data Protection Directive* which sought to strike a balance between a high level of protection for the privacy of individuals and the free movement of personal data. Significantly, the *EU Directive* (when transposed to EU Member national law) required foreign jurisdictions and businesses to meet "adequacy" requirements as a necessary condition for transfers of any personal informa-

tion of EU citizens. In Canada, broad coalitions of business and consumer interests were meeting to establish a national, voluntary privacy code to guide the legitimate information requirements of business, industry and institutions operating in the information age. In the United States, negotiations began with the EU on a "Safe Harbor" framework agreement to establish similar ground rules for the processing of personal information by U.S. businesses.

Against this background, there was a growing expectation that all organizations that collect, use and disclose personal information should accommodate the informational privacy interests and rights of individuals in their operations. More than a moral imperative, respecting privacy was becoming a business and market requirement. As the IPC argued, good privacy offered positive-sum dividends to all concerned. The "payoff" to organizations included: improved customer satisfaction and trust; enhanced reputations; reduced legal liabilities; more efficient operations; commercial gains and enhanced ROI; and, ultimately, enduring competitive advantage.

Applying Universal Principles of Fair Information Practices

Privacy by Design is characterized by a *principled* approach. In order to be effective and credible, building privacy into technologies and operations had to be done in a systematic way, with reference to time-honoured privacy principles, standards and other relevant guidance. The principles of Fair Information Practices give practical expression to individual privacy rights and the obligations of organizations to observe them.

Voluntary international FIPs such as the 1980 *OECD Guidelines on the Protection of Privacy and Transborder Flows of Personal Data*, have served as the blueprint for the development of similar privacy codes, statutes and regulations in national and European arenas, but in the mid-90s the IPC recognized that they could also inform the design of information systems (Wright, 1995).

Identifying and Mitigating Privacy Concerns Early and Comprehensively

If adhering to privacy norms was the cost of doing business in the emerging information era, then going further to build them in early and deeply into ICTs could realize important efficiencies, serve as a market differentiator, and also confer competitive advantages. "Build in privacy from the outset and avoid making costly mistakes later on, requiring expensive retrofits." The IPC has long advocated for the earliest and most iterative identification of privacy issues —preferably at the design stage, but also at the development and implementation stages (Registratiekamer and IPC, 1995).

The need to address privacy systematically, at the policy and organizational levels requires a framework and methodology for building privacy into applications "right from the start." (Advanced Card Technology Association of Canada [ACTA], 1997). Privacy Impact Assessment (PIA) tools and similar methodologies have become central to the *Privacy by Design* approach, and both of the Ontario and Canadian governments have emerged as leaders in the development and adoption of PIAs for ICT projects involving personal information. A PbD-PIA is now being developed.

Involving Dedicated, Qualified Leadership and Professional Input

Privacy doesn't build itself into information technologies and systems: dedicated, qualified leadership is needed. Applying privacy design practices, features and standards requires increasingly specialized expertise from architects and engineers, as information technologies and systems become more complex and more essential to an organization's operations. If the expertise does not reside in-house, then an ability to set clear

specifications and requirements for contracted parties to meet and adhere to is needed.

At the same time, knowledge of the organization and of the related privacy sub-domains (legal compliance, technology, business operations, customer relations) are also critical for successful *Privacy by Design* efforts. The IPC was a pioneer in advocating dedicated and well-resourced Chief Privacy Officers (CPOs) or similar positions to be established in order to ensure strong privacy leadership, accountability, and results.

Adopting and Integrating Privacy-Enhancing Technologies (PETs)

The growth of computer applications, digitized data and networks in every aspect of our lives has brought novel and profound privacy concerns. Fortunately, we can enlist technology to support rather than invade privacy. In the 1990s, the emergence of encryption technologies to secure private or confidential communications and files from unwanted tampering and access provided a clear example of a privacy-enhancing technology.

From a privacy perspective, information and communication technologies (ICTs) are essentially neutral. What matters are the choices we make when designing and using them — ICTs may be privacy-invasive or privacy-enhancing, depending on their design and use. "Privacy enhancing technologies" express fundamental privacy principles by minimizing unnecessary collection, disclosure and use of personal data, by maximizing data security, and by empowering individuals. As mentioned earlier, PETs can be engineered directly into the design of information technologies, architectures and systems.[2]

As we shall see further below, the *PbD* approach has since expanded beyond a narrow focus on ICTs to apply more broadly to organizational processes, to overarching information architectures and even to entire governance eco-systems. Yet even today many still associate *Privacy by Design* closely with PETs, so it is worthwhile to review the basis for this early association, and its evolution.

Privacy-Enhancing Technologies (PETs)

Traditional PETs

Privacy-Enhancing Technologies refer to information technologies that strengthen the protection of personal privacy in an information system by preventing the unnecessary or unlawful collection, use and disclosure of personal data, or by offering tools to enhance an individual's control over his/her personal data.

PETs were conceived and developed in the 1990s with the goal of enlisting the support of technology to enhance privacy, rather than encroach upon it. Western government efforts to restrict the use and export of encryption products, and to engineer surveillance "backdoors" into the emerging digital telecommunications infrastructures met with fierce resistance from cryptographers, privacy advocates, rights groups, and business interests, who saw threats to privacy, freedoms and civil liberties. [3]

By 2000, organizers of the 10th annual Conference on Computer, Freedom and Privacy (CFP) in Toronto set aside their traditionally strong focus on legal remedies as essential instruments in the fight to ensure freedom and privacy, recognizing that "the law is often very slow to catch up to technology" and "has limited reach when considering the global scope of modern communication and information technologies." In their exploratory full-day *Workshop on Freedom and Privacy by Design*, participants explored the use of technology to bring about strong protections of civil liberties which are guaranteed by the technology itself (Computer, Freedom and Privacy [CFP], 2000).

The workshop reached out to programmers, cryptographers, and systems architects (but also lawyers, social scientists, writers and users/experts) in an effort to identify real-world solutions and to develop principles for designing and implementing information architectures, strategies and evaluation criteria that could be inherently protective of privacy. If Lawrence Lessig's famous proposition that "Code is Law" was correct, as I believe it is, then could this adage also be reversed, to wit, that Law (or policy) be embedded in Code?

Since popularizing the term "PETs" in 1995 with the Dutch Data Protection Authority, the IPC has emphasized the need to incorporate universal principles of Fair Information Practices directly into the design and operation of information processing technologies and systems.

First codified internationally by the OECD in 1980, FIPs come in a variety of flavours, including the E.U. Directive on Data Protection, Canada's CSA Privacy Code, the Asia-Pacific Economic Cooperation (APEC) Privacy Framework, the U.S. Safe Harbor Principles, and, most recently, the harmonized Global Privacy Standard, which the IPC led with international Privacy and Data Protection Commissioners, in 2006 (Cavoukian, 2006).

Despite minor differences in language and emphases, these FIPs all share the following fundamental common denominators:

- **Limiting processing:** the collection, use, disclosure and retention of personally identifiable information should be limited wherever, and to the fullest extent, possible;
- **User participation:** individuals should be empowered to play a participatory role and to exercise effective controls throughout the life cycle of their own personal data; and
- **Enhanced security:** the confidentiality, integrity and availability of personal data should be safeguarded, as appropriate to its sensitivity.

Engineering privacy principles early and comprehensively into information technologies and systems is a core requirement of good PETs and of *Privacy by Design.* By enhancing privacy, applied *Privacy by Design* principles can also enhance users' confidence, trust and further uses of the technologies and systems.

Traditional PETs Promote User Participation and Empowerment

PETs should ideally promote *all* three meta-principles. For example, an organization's use of encryption to secure customer records against unauthorized access, while valuable in and of itself, speaks little to data minimization, and almost nothing to user participation.

Traditional PETs contribute to the privacy ideals of informational self-determination, that is, to an *individual's* ability to exercise control over the collection, use and disclosure of their personal information. Given the history of PETs development in the 1990s around concerns with communications interception and online surveillance, this is not surprising. As a result, online PETs are often defined as performing the following privacy-enhancing functions:

- preventing unauthorized access to personal communications and stored files;
- automating the retrieval of information about data collectors' privacy practices and automating users' decision-making on the basis of these practices;
- preventing automated data capture through cookies, HTTP headers, web bugs, spyware;
- preventing communications from being linked to a specific individual;
- facilitating transactions that reveal minimal personal information; and
- filtering unwanted messages.

These are *user-centric* tools and functions. The list has not significantly lengthened in over a decade, and strongly suggests that PETs are understood as discrete technologies that put individuals in direct or greater control of their own personally identifiable information.

But have unnecessary boundaries been placed upon PETs? Can they be, variously, cryptographic primitives, software or hardware applications, components embedded in larger systems, or entire information systems? Should PETs be understood to include only technologies under the exclusive control of the individual, or is there room for a more expansive definition that includes critical and complementary infrastructure components beyond the control of the individual and which must be trusted? As we shall see below, the door to a more expansive understanding had to be opened.

Measuring and Evaluating PETs

At the dawn of the millennium, the IPC was engaging a global community of privacy and data protection authorities, technology developers, business and standards development organizations, and privacy advocates in a broad-based effort to formalize and evaluate PETs under a common standard, recognized internationally. Similar efforts were underway in Europe (European Committee for Standardization [CEN], 2002; EU Privacy Incorporated Software Agent [EU PISA], 2003; Borking et al., 2003).

In March 2001, the IPC partnered with other Privacy and Data Protection Commissioners to form an international group to develop testing criteria for PETs. Called the *Privacy Enhancing Technologies Testing and Evaluation Project*, PETTEP members also included privacy and standards experts from the government, industry, academic and legal communities.

PETTEP members sought to design privacy protections for PETs by mapping the Fair Information Practices to an existing international ISO standard, the *Common Criteria for Information Technology Security Evaluation*[4] (which already had a placeholder developed for privacy technologies that dealt with observability, linkability, traceability and anonymity). PETTEP members sought to translate privacy claims into technology functionalities, and to provide a universal method for assuring that the process of privacy specification, implementation and evaluation of a computer security product had been conducted in a rigorous and standard manner. Independent testing labs around the world, already accredited *Common Criteria* certifiers, could certify to the new the privacy protection profiles (Gurski:2003). Pilot projects involving intelligent software agents, smart cards, and anonymous "onion routing" networks, among others, were considered (Anderson, 2003).

PETTEP members worked through 2001–2005, convening international workshops to develop the necessary requirements and system design documents, but progress was slow. PETTEP participation was voluntary, and the subject area was a highly complex one which needed to take into account standardization work in and across many other domains. One of the biggest challenges was simply agreeing upon a single harmonized set of common Fair Information Practices that would serve as the basis of a *Common Criteria* Privacy Protection Profile.

The Wroclaw Resolution (2004)

In early 2004, ISO's Joint Technical Committee (JTC) established a Privacy Technology Study Group (PTSG) to examine the need for developing a privacy technology standard and, if so, how to proceed. Lacking official standing in ISO, international Privacy and Data Protection Commissioners issued a joint resolution in September 2004 to strongly "support the development of an effective and universally accepted international privacy technology standard" based on the Fair Information Practices (ICPDPC, 2004). The Commissioners insisted that the standard "provide evaluation and testing criteria regarding the privacy functionality of any system or technology" as well as "a level of assurance regarding

the privacy claims of technologies and systems used to manage personal information."

Wishing to make available to ISO its expertise, the resolution also called upon ISO to recognize PETTEP as an official liaison organization through which Privacy and Data Protection Commissioners could work directly within the ISO PTSG to present, discuss and contribute to the development of an ISO privacy technology standard.

The resolution at Wroclaw would be the first of many in the coming years by international Privacy and Data Protection Commissioners intended to promote greater cooperation, collaboration and concerted action in articulating and promoting international privacy standards.

Work in PETTEP was set aside pending ISO JTC discussions and decisions about creating a new subcommittee and standards development process. In the end, ISO JTC decided against creating the new privacy work item. But by then, PETTEP's work had lost much of its urgency and feasibility, and work in the project ceased altogether, a consequence of a number of factors, including:

- Growing realization of the enormity of the challenges of developing and applying a universal standard to test and evaluate privacy technologies, and the consequent need to unpack these challenge into more manageable steps or discrete projects;
- General lack of preparedness or ability on the part of Commissioners to engage in on-going technical discussions and standards processes that lie outside of their formal oversight mandates;
- Lack of a single clear ISO forum or body for consultation or input by commissioners, who must work within their respective national standardization hierarchies and processes;
- Growing understanding of the naivety of focusing too narrowly upon information technologies and PETs as the solution for

privacy, to the exclusion of larger operating contexts and non-technological factors;

- Changing privacy threat model and regulatory landscape after 2001; and
- A shift in emphasis towards more immediate, practical privacy results and outcomes.

The last three bullets are discussed in the next section.

Work on PETs was important, but it was no longer enough. A more holistic, integrative approach, complemented by a robust application of responsible information practices by organizations, and supported by enhanced oversight and accountability structures, was needed. (Cavoukian, 2005) User-centric technologies *alone* wouldn't – couldn't – solve the emerging privacy challenges and problems in the new Millennium.

Beyond PETs

Recognizing the Importance of Infrastructure

The concept of PETs had to be expanded. The starting point was to recognize that virtually all PETs possess an infrastructure component in order to perform to optimal levels. For example, a standalone file and email encryption program isn't truly user-empowering unless it is developed and made available by others in a secure, trusted manner, and integrates well with computing devices, public networks, remote servers, and other parties..

The same reliance upon infrastructure and other parties is also true for another quintessential PET, the Platform for Privacy Preferences (P3P), in which users can establish their machine-readable privacy preferences, which are then automatically matched against the privacy policies of participating websites visited. In order to have any privacy relevance or utility for individuals, P3P protocols must be supported "by the infrastructure."

Finally, it should be noted that anonymizing proxy servers or networks, which allow individuals to surf or communicate anonymously, pseudonymously, or in an otherwise untraceable manner, depend critically upon a trusted, enabling infrastructure and actors. There may be some linked component that resides on a user's computer that is under that person's control, but the network is itself the PET, and the user interface is just that – an interface (Thomson and Naraine, 2007).

Recognizing the Importance of Architecture and Design

Do traditional stand-alone PETs, when built into the "infrastructure" suddenly stop functioning as a PET? In a word: No. For example, password managers, "cookie cutters" and spam filters are often held up as examples of PETs, because they are discrete tools that empower users and minimize the unwanted processing of sensitive data. But when these PETs are integrated into operating systems and browsers, do they necessarily lose their privacy-enhancing qualities? Is there a difference between a stand-alone password manager and the one integrated into one's browser or operating system? Are spam filters that are installed and configured exclusively on one's home computer or client application any more of a PET than those installed and operating at the internet service provider infrastructure level?

PETs can be one or the other, or both. Either way, it is vitally important to recognize that the infrastructure is often an essential component of PETs, and can sometimes even become the *entire* PET, in which case architecture design becomes critical. The advent of Secure Socket Layers (SSL) to authenticate websites and encrypt all online communications with them — and for which capability is built into every browser by default — has advanced online privacy, security and trust immeasurably, is a process that is effectively "baked into the architecture."

Acknowledging the Need to Foster User Confidence and Trust

The importance of information architectures, design and infrastructure has implications for user empowerment and control. Because the behaviour of infrastructure components is often beyond the direct access and control of individuals, a certain degree of reliance and trust is essential.[5] In the context of networked cloud computing and the exponential creation, use and disclosure of personally identifiable information by more and more actors, this reliance and trust must in turn become extensible and scale. It does not mean that PETs are becoming less relevant. Rather, PETs must evolve in tandem, and make possible a new era of privacy confidence and trust.

Take, for example, so-called "enterprise" or "corporate" PETs, meeting both the needs of the organization *and* protecting individual privacy. These are privacy-enhancing technologies that are deployed entirely within information architectures and systems owned, operated or otherwise controlled by organizations, not by individuals. "Enterprise" PETs can facilitate better organizational controls and privacy compliance for all uses of personal data. The privacy-enhancing requirements of data minimization and strong safeguards may be fully operationalized but, in place of direct individual participation, the focus is on ensuring system transparency, performance, and accountability. One example would be an enterprise privacy technology that attaches privacy policies directly to personal data and automatically tracks usage, enforcing those policies across the entire enterprise, and beyond (IBM, 2005).

At this point, while the degree of direct individual participation may diminish, privacy does not. It only takes a short step to recognize that PETs can be built directly into organizational infrastructures in such a way that privacy benefits are achieved with minimal or no user participation.

Summary

Engineering universal privacy principles into the design and operation of information and communications technologies remains an essential core element of *Privacy by Design*. The evolution of PETs beyond a narrow focus on user-controlled ICTs reflects the growing complexity in computing devices and their interactions with networked environments, with the corresponding need for enhanced *trust* and user confidence as the essential glue holding together the component parts. The international PET Award, given to the most outstanding peer-reviewed research paper on PET research each year, illustrates this trend: from an early focus on anonymizing technologies, the award has since been granted to decidedly non-technological research on the psychology of user activities in e-commerce transactions and to a taxonomic review of U.S. privacy statutes.[6] By 2005, it was becoming evident that a broader, more holistic yet flexible approach to designing, implementing and assuring privacy was needed in the age of Google and anti-terrorism efforts.

DEVELOPMENT OF PRIVACY BY DESIGN CONCEPTS (2001–2009)

The Shift to Positive-Sum Thinking

The events and consequences of September 11, 2001 challenged assumptions among many privacy advocates, freedom fighters and technologists that individual privacy was necessarily paramount to other interests in society. Historically, privacy has been a socio-culturally determined value, waxing and waning in response to various determinants. Privacy advocates found it increasingly difficult to defend privacy interests in an atmosphere characterized by visceral public fears, desires for collective security and a right "not to be blown to pieces."

Almost overnight, the privacy threat model changed. Governments enacted legislation and put in place initiatives that trumped privacy legislation and information rights, enlisting public- and private-sector organizations to collect, use and disclose more and more granular personal information for public safety purposes. How could privacy be assured when the collection, disclosure, and use of personal information might not even involve the individual?

This was a classic zero-sum paradigm: more of one good (public security) necessitates less of another (individual privacy). But this win/lose approach, using the "balance" metaphor posed a major threat to privacy, since the public appetite for safety was very high, and continuing the post 9/11 debate within this framework threatened the very foundation of privacy.

The IPC was the first to challenge the underlying premise that privacy necessarily had to be ceded in order to gain security benefits, arguing that both could be achieved at the same time. Many security technologies could be redesigned to remain effective, while minimizing or eliminating their privacy-invasive features. By substituting a new premise — that privacy and security were two complementary sides of an indivisible whole (not opposites) — technologies could be designed to protect public safety *without* sacrificing privacy, *positive*-sum, not zero-sum.

The IPC asserted that security technologies could *enable* both security and privacy, and promoted this message with a three-pronged advocacy strategy:

1. Challenging the privacy community to question the paradigm assumptions and to raise the level of debate on security and privacy above traditional, simplistic, either/or viewpoints.
2. Challenging "specification writers" to be more mindful of how privacy interests could be accommodated in their work. By "specification writers" the IPC targeted

two distinct groups: 1) legislators, policy analysts and legal counsel that draft legislation focused on security and public safety, and 2) directors, managers, individuals, who develop Requests for Proposals (RFPs) and set the procurement 'specs' for security technologies.

3. Challenging 'solution providers' - developers of technology and their industry associations - to introduce privacy concepts into the policy statements of their organizations and associations, and to incorporate privacy into the concept, design and implementation of their technology solutions (Cavoukian, 2002).

As alluded to above, the broadening context for evaluating and applying *Privacy by Design* went well beyond a narrow fixation on ICTs to include the "soft" legal, policy, procedural and other organisational controls and operating contexts in which PETs might be embedded. A holistic, integrative approach to embedding privacy required taking into account developments in other areas:

Evolving Legal and Regulatory Requirements

Legal, contractual and regulatory requirements that apply to an organization's processing of PII are often starting points for designing, operating and evaluating information management systems in a holistic, accountable manner. But data privacy, security, accountability and law enforcement requirements were multiplying across sectors and jurisdictions during the first decade of the new Millennium – challenging straightforward data privacy and compliance requirements (Bennett, 2009).

Evolving Organizations

Firms were undergoing radical changes in response to evolving business environments, and their information management needs were changing along with their business models and organizational structures. In response to market imperatives, organizations were becoming technology- and data-intensive, decentralized, service-oriented, hierarchically-flat, flexible, innovative —and global. Managing a database would never be the same again.

Evolving Computing and Networked Contexts

Ongoing revolutions in computing, data storage, sensorware, and networks were fuelling innovation at light speed. Personal data multiplied, became ubiquitous, semi-public and instantly retrievable. Like the Internet itself, networks of all kinds were becoming increasingly complex, sophisticated and decentralized. The emergence of Cloud computing and new Web 2.0 and mobile device platforms were altering traditional information flows in dramatic new ways, posing daunting challenges for data privacy.

Evolving Consumer Expectations and Tastes

Complicating matters further, it was becoming evident that individuals and consumers weren't always opposed to new "privacy-invasive" innovations and services. While they wanted privacy and control, they also wanted the many conveniences, efficiencies and benefits of "free" services by being connected in exchange for their personal information. Consumers didn't always understand, or want, complete and granular control over their personal information, opting instead to trust the reputations and the behaviour of data custodians. No one predicted the phenomenal growth of social networks in which hundreds of millions of people would voluntarily place detailed personal information about their selves and their online activities into the public domain, making user-generated content a formidable challenge.

In these contexts, the faith in privacy-enhancing technology or "code" alone to ensure privacy seemed, at best, naïve. The failure of most consumer privacy-enhancing tools and services to attract sufficient market success only reinforced the idea that a more holistic approach to protecting and promoting privacy was necessary. The limits to traditional or "pure" PETs were becoming understood, in tandem with a growing recognition of the need to accommodate other information system participants and legitimate non-privacy objectives in any calculation of privacy-enhancing designs and operations. *Privacy by Design* would also have to evolve.

Emphasis on Practical Results and Outcomes

Privacy remains a human right in many quarters, but abstract principles and rights-based arguments for privacy have not had an easy time winning the day against the many competing interests (Privacy International *et al*, 1998, 2003, 2007, 2011; Ford, 2004). The seminal 1980 OECD Privacy Guidelines – the model for so many national laws and policies – was also intended to enable the free flow of information and the emergence of online commerce. But it has been unclear at times how privacy rights should be given effective expression, especially in a fast-changing global environment. A more preventative and practical, evidence-based approach was becoming necessary in the first decade of the new Millennium.

When it comes to privacy, individuals generally want clear and enforceable privacy promises. They want organizational transparency, accountability, and timely notification of breaches. They expect fair dealings, default protections against foreseeable and preventable harms, and quick restitution for any negative effects on them resulting from the behaviour of others. They want understandable privacy interfaces and controls, and effective mechanisms to address their concerns, problems and grievances. They want to *trust* organizations with their personal data, and the governance, risk and compliance mechanisms that are in place to ensure effective oversight.

Organizations that process personal information generally want clearer global rules and guidelines to operate. They want a minimum certainty and consistency in these rules, but also freedom to innovate, develop, and manage their information management systems and practices without undue restriction. Generally, they want to be free from complex, opaque, variable and burdensome regulations, and to let market forces sort out the issues and solutions to the extent possible. Privacy tends to be understood from the perspective of the bottom line, and efforts to assure privacy must be justified on the basis of quantifiable risks and business cases.

Privacy regulators have three typical functions: promoting good practices, abjudicating complaints, and securing compliance (Bennett and Raab, 2006). They generally want proactive accountability, credible assurances and evidence of compliance from the organizations that they oversee. They prefer heightened awareness and understanding of the privacy risks and benefits among all stakeholders, the adoption of best practices, and early resolution of problems whenever possible. Regulatory agencies on both sides of the Atlantic have tended to prioritize resources and priorities by focussing on specific issue areas and activities that offer the best prospects for minimizing harms and achieving measurable privacy results (Federal Trade Commission [FTC], 2001, 2010; UK Information Commissioner's Office [ICO], 2009).

Trust is becoming the new currency of business. This meant making and keeping privacy and security promises. There has been a growing emphasis on practical, measurable and immediate privacy results, and on defining new universal privacy values and common benchmarks for the Information Age. This requires specialized leadership that can integrate the diverse interests at stake in personal information, including knowledge of law, information technologies, marketing and communications, organizational design, sociology and human psychology.

As the IPC defined it, "privacy pragmatism is both optimistic and realistic, principled and passionate, yet calculating, inclusive and utilitarian, infused throughout with the resolve and energy needed to ensure that privacy values continue to endure and flourish in coming generations. Privacy pragmatism explicitly recognizes that privacy is not an absolute right or value but, rather, a social value that is continually defined, determined and enforced by society, through informed discourse and dialogue and, yes, at times, by 'balance'. Privacy values and its benefits are best achieved through open public discourse and social dialogue, by a thorough airing of all interests and views" (Cavoukian, 2008).

Privacy pragmatism involves a strategic focus of efforts on areas of high-risk and early opportunity. It involves a return to the very basis and essence of privacy and data protection principles, namely, to reconcile overlapping and, at times, competing interests over the use of personal data, whether for public or commercial use.

APPLIED PRIVACY BY DESIGN

The *PbD* concept has evolved, broadening its scope and extending beyond traditional FIPs to emphasize proactive leadership and the setting of high privacy priorities, creating methods to express and realize those privacy priorities, and achieving practical, win-win solutions. As noted earlier, *PbD* may be applied to specific technologies, organizational practices, and entire information architectures and ecosystems.

Information Technologies

Leadership

As discussed earlier, *PbD* originated from the concept of PETs, and so a focus on specific information and communications technologies remains a source of inspiration for building in privacy from the outset. The IPC has taken advance positions on new and emerging information technologies with privacy implications, flagging potential risks, remediating approaches and solutions in areas as diverse as biometrics (Cavoukian, 1999) radio-frequency identification devices (RFID) (Cavoukian, 2004, 2008) "smart" cards (ACTA, 1997), electronic toll systems (Cavoukian, 1998), government Public Key Infrastructure (PKI), digital rights management (Cavoukian, 2002), video surveillance (Cavoukian, 2007), intelligent transport systems (Wright, 1995), and intelligent software agents (Dutch Data Protection Agency, 1999).

Methods

Given the IPC's oversight of provincial and municipal government operations, and its forward-looking presence on technology issues, we have been widely consulted by both public and private sector organizations for advice and guidance on building in privacy at the early design stages of new technologies and technology-enabled systems. Building upon earlier efforts to develop privacy and technology design principles (US Department of Justice, 2000) in May 2002 the IPC developed more formalized schemas for doing that (IPC, 2002) as part of the larger ongoing international project described earlier to define, evaluate and independently certify PETs (Cavoukian, 2004).

By 2004, the IPC was advocating that privacy principles be integrated into security technologies of surveillance, identification, threat prevention, tracking and monitoring, and intelligence systems to achieve multiple goals, and to overcome zero-sum thinking, by identifying opportunities early in the design stages.

The IPC partnered with standards developers, privacy advocates and technology developers to encourage the development and adoption of privacy-modeling and expression languages that could, for example, negotiate machine-to-machine privacy preferences (Centre for Democracy and Technology [CDT], 2000) or express the statutory requirements of privacy and access to information law in a way that might be applied automatically by computers and organizations (IBM, 2005).

Results

Certain kinds of privacy and security technologies, such as encryption, access control and auditing tools, are easy to promote because the benefits of using them are self-evident and tend to outweigh the costs. Legal requirements such as mandatory breach notification also provide additional incentives to proactively adopt *Privacy by Design* technologies.

Extending PETs to become positive-sum in practice leads to the designation of "PETs Plus" (Cavoukian, 2009) and transformative technologies (Cavoukian, 2009) because these technologies incorporate *Privacy by Design* principles that actually transform privacy-invasive technologies into privacy-protective ones, in an innovative ways. Examples include solutions capable of real-time obscuring of identities of individuals in CCTV footage (Martin and Plataniotis, 2008). Biometric Encryption techniques that put individuals in control of their own biometric identifiers, with no universal template that can be matched to templates stored in other databases (Cavoukian and Stoianov, 2007–2009), Other positive-sum solutions include a tear-away "clipped tags" for use on consumer items[7].and user-controlled on-off switch for embedded RFID tags in identity and payment cards (Cavoukian, 2009).

Privacy by Design IT products and services are being certified in Europe by EuroPriSe, a consortium led by the Independent Centre for Privacy Protection Schleswig-Holstein. In 2007, EuroPriSe introduced a European Privacy Seal for IT-products and IT-based services that have proven privacy compliance under European law in a two-step independent certification procedure. The project offers pilot certification according to the European Privacy Seal procedure in Germany, Austria, United Kingdom, Slovakia, Spain, Sweden and in further EU countries on request. The privacy certificate aims to facilitate an increase of market transparency for privacy relevant products and an enlargement of the market for Privacy-Enhancing Technologies and finally an increase of trust in IT. The EuroPriSe certificate has been awarded to nearly 20 IT products and services to date.[8]

The creation, recognition and adoption of PETs as a means to achieve *Privacy by Design* goals is being actively promoted by the European Commission not only as a major ongoing research funding initiative under the Framework Programme[9] but notably in the context of the current EU review of, and possible amendments to, the *Data Protection Directive* (European Commission, 2007, 2010, 2011).

Organization Practices

While *Privacy by Design* approaches and concepts are often best illustrated by specific technologies (the more user-centric the better), it was the *organization* that became a more central and effective focus of *PbD* efforts, especially to comply with privacy laws.

Leadership: Problem Definition and General Guidance

The business case for privacy focuses, in essence, on gaining and keeping customer trust, loyalty, repeat and higher-value business, and avoiding "churn." The value proposition typically breaks down as follows:

1. Consumer trust drives successful customer relations management and lifetime value... in other words, revenues;
2. Broken trust will result in a loss of market share, loss of revenue, and lower stock value;
3. Consumer trust hinges critically on the strength and credibility of an organization's data privacy policies and practices. (Cavoukian, 2002; ICO, 2010)

The 'privacy payoff' also worked in reverse, that is, poor privacy resulted in additional costs and foregone opportunities and revenues. A lack of attention to data privacy could have many negative consequences, including:

- harm to clients or customers whose personal data is used or disclosed inappropriately;
- damage to an organization's reputation and brand;
- financial losses associated with deterioration in the quality or integrity of personal data;
- financial losses due to a loss of business or delay in the implementation of a new product or service due to privacy concerns;
- loss of market share or a drop in stock prices following negative publicity;
- violations of privacy laws; and
- diminished confidence and trust in the industry (Ponemon, 2009–2010).

A series of IPC joint papers with business consultancies, schools, research institutes and consortia clarified the risks, rewards and challenges ahead and case for applying privacy throughout an organization in a thoroughgoing manner (Deloitte & Touche, 2004).

An IPC-commissioned study by the Ponemon Institute on corporate privacy practices. provided insights on what Canadian and U.S. companies were doing to achieve privacy programs that protect sensitive personal information about customers, target customers and employees (Ponemon,

2004). According to the study, the areas of greatest weakness and vulnerability were the objective measurement of program effectiveness and the monitoring of sensitive personal data collected about customers, target customers and employees. Rather presciently, the study also concluded that as the outsourcing of data management functions to third parties (within and outside North America) becomes the prevalent business practice, there would be an increased need for greater data privacy controls, due diligence and verification methods.

In 2005, the IPC partnered with an international business research syndicate led by Don Tapscott that was investigating the changing shape of businesses and ways to achieve new competitive advantages by adopting strategic information technologies into and business practices. It was clear that the lifeblood of the 21st century economy is personally-identifiable information (PII), which must be viewed as both an asset and a liability that requires responsible management practices. A new model of the corporation was emerging, and any organization embracing the "Enterprise 2.0" models is confronted with fundamental questions relating to its treatment of information:

1. With whom will it share its PII?
2. How will it manage that data internally?
3. How should it involve customers in managing their own PII?
4. What personal data will and should it receive from other sources?
5. Where should it set the limits of PII collection by new technologies?

These are the five major information privacy challenges facing organizations *for the next generation* and which they must learn to successfully master by adopting a comprehensive *Privacy by Design* approach. The paper describes these challenges in more detail and offers the outlines of the likely solutions (Tapscott, 2005).

In 2005, the IPC argued that a significant part of the modern identity fraud and theft problem was attributable to *organizations*, rather than individuals (Cavoukian, 2005). As first identified by noted security expert Ross Anderson, the root of the problem was a *misalignment of incentives* that caused firms to under-invest in information security, since the negative consequences of data breaches fell mainly upon individuals. Breaches were not typically reported publicly prior to 2005, until mandatory breach notification requirements swept across North America, including Ontario. Fortunately, adopting good privacy proactively, by applying *Privacy by Design* principles, was essential to ensuring a credible information security program.

Methods

Without knowledge action is useless, and knowledge without action is futile. Informed leadership is a prerequisite for action and success: the IPC and the Schulich School of Business (York University) argued that privacy protection starts at the top and must be have a C-suite level presence to provide real and effective organizational accountability. The paper outlined specific steps businesses should take, including self-assessments, educating staff regarding privacy, appointing a Chief Privacy Officer, making privacy an integral part of performance evaluations and compensation packages, executing regular privacy audits, and asking senior management the right questions about privacy (Schulich, 2003). As if in response, there has been a significant emergence, growth and professionalization of chief privacy officers in the first decade of the new Millennium.

Privacy Diagnostic and Self-Assessment Tools

In August 2001 the IPC released, with Guardent and PricewaterhouseCoopers, the *Privacy Diagnostic Tool (PDT) Workbook* (IPC, 2001), a practical tool, based on fair information practices questions and answers to help organizations determine what their state of privacy readiness was, and also what steps they needed to take to identify and address what is missing by systematically applying *Privacy by Design* across their entire enterprise. The IPC followed up with high-level procedural guidance on how to design privacy into technology-enabled systems (IPC, 2002). Organizational privacy self-assessment checklists have since become available from many sources (Office of the Privacy Commissioner of Canada [OPCC], 2004; American Institute for Chartered Public Accountants/Canadian Institute for Chartered Accountants [AICPA/CICA], 2010).

Privacy Impact Assessments

Canada is a world leader in developing and adopting Privacy Impact Assessment (PIAs) which are mandatory in the Ontario and federal public sectors to receive program funding. And in June 2005, following the coming into force of Ontario's Health Information Privacy law, the IPC issued *Privacy Impact Assessment Guidelines for the Ontario Personal Health Information Protection Act* (Cavoukian, 2005), a comprehensive tool for health information custodians to ensure privacy protections are built into all their operations and processes. Privacy Impact Assessments are central to the *Privacy by Design* approach and for demonstrating proactive due diligence. Not surprisingly, they have caught on in public sectors around the world as a best practice, and are being adapted for use throughout the private sector. Working with diverse industry associations over the years, the IPC has advanced *Privacy by Design* best practices in numerous joint guidance publications (Canadian Marketing Association [CMA], 2004; ACTA, 2007; Hewlett-Packard [HP], 2008). Again, Privacy impact assessment methodologies and guidance documents have multiplied around the world (Office of the Privacy Commissioner of Canada [OPCC], 2007; ICO, 2007, 2009; Office of the Privacy Commissioner of Australia [OPCA], 2010).

Risk Management

Support for formal risk management disciplines, such as recent joint exploration and guidance on privacy risk management (Ontario Lottery and Gaming [OLG] & YMCA, 2010) is another notable development for *Privacy by Design*, especially for a privacy regulator. It evidences an evolutionary and pragmatic approach to privacy by shifting oversight methods towards emphasizing the responsibility of organizations to demonstrate proactive, verifiable due diligence in its own privacy enforcement programs. A follow-up guidance paper in partnership with Nymity on risk optimization (McQuay, 2010) introduces a Privacy Risk Optimization Process (PROP), a process that enables the implementation of privacy into operational policies and procedures, which results in *Privacy by Design* for business practices. The PROP is based on the International Organization for Standardization (ISO) concept that risk can be both positive and negative. Based on this concept, ISO also defines Risk Optimization as a process whereby organizations strive to maximize positive risks and mitigate negative ones. The PROP uses these concepts to implement privacy into operational policies and procedures.

Accountability-Enhancing Measures

In 2009 the IPC partnered with leading U.S. firms to describe and illustrate how *Privacy by Design* could be applied to enhance organizational accountability to, and compliance with, international privacy laws and other requirements (Abrams et al, 2010). This paper was part of a larger international initiative and efforts by international data protection authorities and business associations to expand upon accountability requirements which are specified in all privacy laws (Centre for Information Policy Leadership [CIPL], 2009, 2010; European Commission [EC], 2010).

Results

The 2004 IPC-Ponemon study sought to determine what companies were doing to move beyond compliance with regulations to build trusted relationships with stakeholders and to increase revenue and strengthen reputation and brand. The report showed that leading companies were more likely to execute the following business practices as an integral part of their enterprise privacy program:

- Integrate information security and privacy into one virtual team;
- Incorporate perspectives of legal, marketing, human resources and IT into privacy strategy;
- Centralize privacy program responsibility under one senior executive sponsor;
- Whenever feasible, consider using privacy enabling technologies;
- Empower local managers to get involved, especially in communications, training and outreach;
- Obtain real budget authority to implement enterprise programs;
- Build process standards that resemble six sigma or ISO programs;
- Establish upstream communication and fair redress;
- Conduct privacy impact assessments to objectively determine issues, problems and mistakes;
- Provide good reporting and disclosure tools to all stakeholders;
- Listen to customers about their privacy preferences, concerns and issues;
- Balance privacy goals against practical business objectives;
- Obtain trust seals to signal good privacy practices, especially in web and e-mail outreach to customers.

Current work on defining accountability by data protection authorities is also establishing best practices in the area of organizational *Privacy by Design* practices. In addition to the joint paper with the Center for Policy leadership and Hewlett-Packard, mentioned above, the IPC is making available an ongoing suite of other joint papers and case studies demonstrating how *Privacy by Design* principles are being implemented in various organizational contexts and scenarios, such as remote health care and the emerging "smart grid".[10]

Perhaps the most exciting chapters on achieving *Privacy by Design* results have yet to be written. In December 2010 the U.S. Federal Trade Commission released a major consultation paper setting out a framework for privacy enforcement that places considerable emphasis on applied *Privacy by Design* as one of three central planks. FTC is actively seeking best practices in this area (FTC, 2010). In Europe, the Commission and Council are also advocating inserting a *Privacy by Design* "principle" in a revised and updated Data Protection Directive (EC, 2010, 2011).

Information Architectures, Ecosystems and Governance Regimes

In recent years, it has become clear that *Privacy by Design* approach can and should be applied to the broader information ecosystems in which both technologies and organizations are embedded and must function. Privacy benefits from taking a holistic, integrative approach that considers as many contextual factors as possible – even (or especially) when these factors lie outside of the direct control of any particular actor, organization or component in the system. For example: a privacy-enhancing browser feature or plug-in that defeats online tracking via cookies cannot prevent tracking via alternate means, such as by IP addresses, locally-stored objects, deep packet inspection, or browser fingerprinting. An RFID tag or other globally unique identifier embedded in enhanced drivers' licences intended for secure border management and control purposes, or online security, can introduce profound privacy threats in other use-case scenarios. In each situation, the privacy benefits of a particular technology or process could be defeated by larger systemic considerations over which the individual -or any single organization- has little control or influence.

A broader, architectural view is required. It makes sense to start asking how *Privacy by Design* approach could be proactively applied to overarching information architectures and interoperable networks, such as federated or interoperable identity systems (Cameron, 2005; Cavoukian, 2006, 2009; Posch *et al.*, 2008; European Network and Information Security Agency [ENISA], 2009; U.S. White House, 2010) online social networks (International Working Group on Data Protection in Telecommunications [IWGDPT], 2008) and other "Web 2.0" phenomena (Cavoukian, 2008), e-Government (Cavoukian, 2009), behavioral advertising networks and systems, cloud computing (NEC, 2010), location-based services, an "internet of things," Internet protocols, and even "smart" systems of regulation (Cavoukian, 2009; Schwartz *et al*, 2007; CIPPIC, 2007; Romanosky et al, 2008).

Globalized privacy challenges require taking a global approach, global cooperation and global solutions. Leadership is essential to articulate and pursue the highest possible privacy ideals and standards possible. In addition, design methods and systems must be created for ensuring these ideals are driven through the entire information architecture and eco-systems in a coordinated manner, and to demonstrate innovative, concrete, real-world, practical, measurable "win-win" results for the modern era.

PRIVACY BY DESIGN CURRENT AND FUTURE PROSPECTS (2009 –)

Common understandings, ideals, reference points, commitments and standards are needed. The efforts since 2005 of the International Privacy and Data Protection Commissioners to articulate common privacy norms, in the form of resolutions on rights and enforcement actions, is illustrative (ICPDPC, 2009). Equally important have been their efforts to harmonize the various privacy codes and practices currently in use around the world. These coordinated actions are inspired by the growing recognition that personal data flows are global in nature, and the approach to ensuring privacy must evolve in a similar manner.

Establishing the 7 Foundational Principles of Privacy by Design

While attempting to develop a single global law on data protection was beyond reach, the IPC was confident that we could develop a single privacy instrument, globally. To this end, the Commissioner chaired a working group of international privacy and data protection commissioners in 2005–2006 to create a single harmonized instrument, the *Global Privacy Standard* (GPS) (Cavoukian, 2006), which for the first time explicitly identified *data minimization* as a universal privacy principle, and also required that the purposes for collection, use and disclosure not only be identified early but that they be clear, limited and relevant to the circumstances. The final version of the GPS was formally tabled and accepted in the United Kingdom, on November 3, 2006, at the 28th International Data Protection Commissioners Conference.

The *Privacy by Design* concept continues to evolve and mature, in tandem with the need to address the ever-growing and systemic effects of information and communication technologies, and of large-scale networked data systems.

In 2009 the *Privacy by Design* concept was codified in the form of the *7 Foundational Principles*, with brief commentary (Cavoukian, 2009). To provide continuity with traditional principles of fair information practices, as well as to serve as a framework for understanding, implementation and verification, these principles were mapped to FIPs, with the three "new" principles flagged, with additional commentary and guidance (Cavoukian, 2010).

The intent of the IPC mapping exercise was to serve as a reference framework for developing detailed criteria for application and audit/verification purposes in specific domains.

The framework guidance begins by mapping four of the seven *PbD* Foundational principles to "traditional" FIPs representing data minimization, user participation, safeguards, and accountability. The three remaining *PbD* principles represent new enhancements that correspond to:

1. **Proactive not Reactive:** means establishing clear privacy leadership priorities;
2. **Privacy Embedded into Design:** means verifiable commitment to these priorities in all design and operational processes; and
3. **Positive-Sum not Zero-Sum:** means measurable and proven privacy results that reflect the positive presence of multiple objectives.

These *PbD* principles go beyond traditional Fair Information Practices and seek to establish a universal framework for the strongest protection of privacy in the Information Age

Proactive not Reactive; Preventative not Remedial

The Privacy by Design approach is characterized by proactive rather than reactive measures. It anticipates and prevents privacy invasive events before they happen. PbD does not wait for privacy risks to materialize, nor does it offer remedies for resolving privacy infractions once they have occurred — it aims to prevent them from occurring. In short, Privacy by Design comes before-the-fact, not after.

Implementation Guidance

Whether applied to information technologies, organizational practices, physical designs, or networked information ecosystems, *Privacy by Design* begins with an explicit recognition of the value and benefits of proactively adopting strong privacy practices, early and consistently (for example, preventing (internal) data breaches from happening in the first place). This implies:

- A clear commitment, at the highest levels, to set and enforce high standards of privacy —higher than the minimal standards set out by global laws and regulation.
- A privacy commitment that is demonstrably shared throughout by user communities and other stakeholders, in a culture of continuous improvement.
- Established methods to recognize poor privacy designs, anticipate poor privacy practices and outcomes, and to correct the negative impacts before they occur in proactive, systematic, and innovative ways.

Privacy as the Default Setting

We can all be certain of one thing — the default rules! Privacy by Design seeks to deliver the maximum degree of privacy by ensuring that personal data are automatically protected in any given IT system or business practice. If an individual does nothing, their privacy still remains intact. No action is required on the part of the individual to protect their privacy — it is built into the system, by default.

Implementation Guidance

This *PbD* principle is particularly informed by the following FIPs:

- **Purpose Specification:** the purposes for which personal information is collected, used, retained and disclosed shall be communicated to the individual at or before the time the information is collected. Specified purposes should be clear, limited and relevant to the circumstances.
- **Collection Limitation:** the collection of personal information must be fair, lawful and limited to that which is necessary for the specified purposes.
- **Data Minimization:** the collection of personal information should be kept to a strict minimum. The design of programs, information technologies, and systems should begin with non-identifiable interactions and transactions, as the default. Wherever possible, identifiability, observability, and linkability of personal information should be minimized.
- **Use, Retention, and Disclosure Limitation:**– the use, retention, and disclosure of personal information shall be limited to the relevant purposes identified to the individual, for which he or she has consented, except where otherwise required by law. Personal information shall be retained only as long as necessary to fulfill the stated purposes, and then securely destroyed.

Where the need or use of personal information is not clear, there shall be a presumption of privacy and the precautionary principle shall apply: the default settings shall be the most privacy protective.

Privacy Embedded into Design

Privacy by Design is embedded into the design and architecture of IT systems and business practices. It is not bolted on as an add-on, after the fact. The result is that privacy becomes an essential component of the core functionality being delivered. Privacy is integral to the system, without diminishing functionality.

Implementation Guidance

Privacy must be embedded into technologies, operations, and information architectures in a holistic, integrative and creative way. Holistic, because additional, broader contexts must always be considered. Integrative, because all stakeholders and interests should be consulted. Creative, because embedding privacy sometimes means reinventing choices because existing alternatives are unacceptable.

- A systemic, principled approach to embedding privacy should be adopted – one that relies upon accepted standards and frameworks, which are amenable to external reviews and audits. All fair information practices should be applied with equal rigour, at every step in the design and operation.
- Wherever possible, detailed risk and impact assessments should be carried out and published that clearly document the privacy risks and all measures taken to mitigate those risks, including consideration of alternatives and selection of metrics.
- The privacy impacts of the resulting technology, operation or information architecture and their uses should be demonstrably minimized, and not easily degraded through use, misconfiguration or error.

Full Functionality – Positive-Sum, not Zero-Sum

Privacy by Design seeks to accommodate all legitimate interests and objectives in a positive-sum "win-win" manner, not through a dated, zero-sum approach, where unnecessary trade-offs are made. Privacy by Design avoids the pretense of false dichotomies, such as privacy vs. security, demonstrating that it is possible to have both.

Implementation Guidance

Privacy by Design is not just about declarations and commitments – it is about satisfying all of an organization's legitimate objectives – not just its privacy goals. It is about achieving real, practical results and beneficial outcomes for everyone concerned.

- When embedding privacy into a given technology, process, or system, it should be done in such a way that full functionality is not impaired, or, to the greatest extent possible, that all requirements are optimized.
- Privacy is often positioned as having to compete with other legitimate human values, design objectives, and technical capabilities in a given domain. *Privacy by Design* rejects taking such an approach - it embraces legitimate non-privacy objectives and accommodates them all in an innovative positive-sum manner.
- All interests and objectives must be clearly documented, desired functions articulated, metrics agreed upon and applied, and trade-offs rejected as often being unnecessary, in favour of finding a solution that enables multi-functionality.

Extra credit is always given for creativity and innovation in achieving all objectives and functionalities in an optimal integrative, positive-sum way! Entities that succeed in overcoming outmoded zero-sum choices in the design and operation of technologies, systems and spaces are demonstrating world-class global privacy leadership.

End-to-End Security: Full Lifecycle Protection

Privacy by Design, having been embedded into the system prior to the first element of information being collected, extends securely throughout the entire lifecycle of the data involved — strong security measures are essential to privacy, from start to finish. This ensures that all data are securely retained, and then securely destroyed at the end of the process, in a timely fashion. Thus, Privacy by Design ensures cradle to grave, secure lifecycle management of information, end-to-end.

Implementation Guidance

Privacy must be continuously protected across the entire domain and throughout the life-cycle of the personal data in question. There should be no gaps in either protection or accountability. While all FIPs apply, the "Security" principle has special relevance simply because without strong security, there can be no privacy.

- **Security:** Entities must assume responsibility for the security of personal information (commensurate with its degree of sensitivity) throughout its entire lifecycle, consistent with standards that have been developed by recognized standards development bodies.
- **Applied security:** standards must assure the confidentiality, integrity and availability of personal data throughout its lifecycle and include, *inter alia*, methods of secure destruction, appropriate encryption, and strong access control and logging methods.

Visibility and Transparency

Privacy by Design seeks to assure all stakeholders that whatever the business practice or technology involved, it is in fact, operating according to the stated promises and objectives, subject to independent verification. Its component parts and operations remain visible and transparent, to users and providers alike. Remember, trust but verify.

Implementation Guidance

Visibility and transparency are essential to establishing accountability and trust. This *PbD* principle tracks well to the Fair Information Practices in their entirety, but for auditing purposes, special emphasis may be placed upon the following FIPs:

- **Accountability:** Collection of personal information entails a duty of care for its protection. Responsibility for all privacy-related policies and procedures shall be documented and communicated as appropriate, and assigned to a specified individual. When transferring personal information to third parties, equivalent privacy protection through contractual or other means shall be secured.
- **Openness:** Openness and transparency are key to accountability. Information about the policies and practices relating to the management of personal information shall be made readily available to individuals.
- **Compliance:** Complaint and redress mechanisms should be established, and information communicated about them to individuals, including how to access the next level of appeal. Necessary steps to monitor, evaluate, and verify compliance with privacy policies and procedures should be taken.

Respect for User Privacy: Keep it User-Centric

Above all, Privacy by Design requires architects and operators to keep the interests of the individual uppermost by offering such measures as strong

privacy defaults, appropriate notice, and empowering user-friendly options. Keep it user-centric.

Implementation Guidance

The best *Privacy by Design* results are usually those that are consciously designed around the interests and needs of individual users or data subjects, who have the greatest vested interest in the management of their personal data.

Empowering data subjects to play an active role in the management of their own data may be the single most effective check against abuses and misuses of privacy and personal data. Respect for User Privacy is supported by the following FIPs:

- **Consent:** The individual's free and specific consent is required for the collection, use or disclosure of personal information, except where otherwise permitted by law. The greater the sensitivity of the data, the clearer and more specific the quality of the consent required. Consent may be withdrawn at a later date.
- **Accuracy:** personal information shall be as accurate, complete, and up-to-date as is necessary to fulfill the specified purposes.
- **Access:** Individuals shall be provided access to their personal information and informed of its uses and disclosures. Individuals shall be able to challenge the accuracy and completeness of the information and have it amended as appropriate.
- **Compliance:** Organizations must establish complaint and redress mechanisms, and communicate information about them to the public, including how to access the next level of appeal.

Respect for User Privacy goes further than these FIPs, and extends to the need for human-machine interfaces to be human-centered, user-centric and person-friendly so that informed privacy decisions may be reliably exercised. Similarly, business operations and physical architectures should also demonstrate the same degree of consideration for the individual.

Global Recognition

Privacy by Design has indeed gone viral! The concept of *Privacy by Design* has attracted the attention of officials on a number of continents. Both Viviane Reding (Vice-President, Justice, Fundamental Rights and Citizenship, European Commission) and Peter Hustinx (European Data Protection Supervisor) have spoken of how *PbD* will increase consumer trust in information and communication technologies, thereby accelerating their adoption (Reding, 2011).

Peter Hustinx has also noted that *PbD* is an approach which should be incorporated in the framework of revisions to EU data protection legislation (EDPS, 2010). He is recommending that the European Commission embed *Privacy by Design* into EU Laws and policies, in four ways:

a. Propose to include a general provision on *PbD* in the legal framework for data protection.
b. Elaborate this general provision in specific provisions, when specific legal instruments in different sectors are proposed. These specific provisions could already now be included in legal instruments; on the basis of Article 17 of the Data Protection Directive (and other existing law).
c. Include *PbD* as a guiding principle in Europe's Digital Agenda.
d. Introduce *PbD* as a principle in other EU-initiatives (mainly non legislative).

European Privacy Commissioners have supported *PbD* as a promising approach to be recognized and included in reforms of EU privacy laws. The EU Article 29 Working Party, comprised of all European Privacy and Data Protection Commissioners, issued an Opinion on the "Future of

Privacy" in December 2009 as contribution to the Consultation of the European Commission on the legal framework for the fundamental right to protection of personal data (EC, 2009).

In October 2010, a landmark resolution proposed by Ontario's Information and Privacy Commissioner, Dr. Ann Cavoukian, was unanimously approved and adopted by international Data Protection and Privacy Commissioners in Jerusalem at their annual conference, making it a global standard. (ICPDPC, 2010)

The resolution recognized the concept of *Privacy by Design* as an "essential component of fundamental privacy protection." The resolution, which was co-sponsored by Canadian Privacy Commissioner, Jennifer Stoddart and Commissioners from Berlin, New Zealand, the Czech Republic, and Estonia, also:

*   Encourages the adoption of the principles of *Privacy by Design* as part of an organization's default mode of operation; and
*   Invites Data Protection and Privacy Commissioners to promote *Privacy by Design*, foster the incorporation of its Foundational Principles in privacy policy and legislation in their respective jurisdictions, and encourage research into *Privacy by Design*.

On November 4, 2010, the European Commission released a draft version of its Communication proposing "a comprehensive approach on personal data protection in the European Union" with a view to modernizing the EU legal system for the protection of personal data (EC, 2010). The Communication is the result of the Commission's review of, and public consultations on, the current legal framework, and explicitly supports greater use of PETs and the "*Privacy by Design*" principle in support of ways of ensure that data controllers put in place effective policies and mechanisms to ensure compliance with data protection rules. On March 1, 2011, the Council of the European

Union released its conclusions in support of the Commission (EC, 2011).

In the U.K., the Information Commissioner's office has been engaged since 2007 in holding *PbD* workshops and conferences, commissioning studies, and charting a strategic plan for *PbD* implementation (ICO, 2008–2010).

In Washington, DC, *Privacy by Design* has been heard in the context of congressional testimony dealing with behavioural advertising and workshops on privacy and innovation.[11] A series of FTC-sponsored privacy roundtables identified what FTC Chairman Jon Liebowitz described as the three key principles of online privacy. The first one on his list was *Privacy by Design* (FTC, 2010).

Five months later, on December 1, 2010, the Federal Trade Commission released its long-awaited report on online privacy entitled "Protecting Consumer Privacy in an Era of Rapid Change: A Proposed Framework for Businesses and Policymakers." The FTC report introduces a privacy framework to "establish certain common assumptions and bedrock protections on which both consumers and businesses can rely as they engage in commerce," including "*Privacy by Design* – Companies should "incorporate substantive privacy and security protections into their everyday business practices and consider privacy issues systemically, at all stages of the design and development of their products and services" by employing reasonable safeguards, collecting information to fulfill a specific need, implementing reasonable data retention periods, taking reasonable steps to ensure the accuracy of data they collect, and developing comprehensive, company-wide privacy programs." (FTC, 2010)

Similarly, *Privacy by Design* is being actively considered in the development of the U.S. Smart Grid (National Institute of Standards and Technology [NIST], 2010; CDT, 2009; Rowland, 2010).

PbD is now being advocated by leading public figures in Canada (OPCC, 2010), the US (CDT, 2009–2010) and Europe (London Economics, 2010) in discussions about how best to stimulate innovation in the digital economy. Malcolm Crompton, former Privacy Commissioner of Australia, has brought *PbD* to Australian government projects and to IT industry associations. (Crompton, 2010)

In Arizona, a new *Privacy by Design* Research Lab was launched in 2009, focused on exploring and developing methods for businesses to protect customer information online. The *Privacy by Design* Research Lab, a part of the W. P. Carey School of Business, will bring together representatives from organizations around the world to develop privacy standards for businesses to follow and perform research for how they can be implemented. (Arizona State University [ASU], 2009)

International researchers, practitioners and academics are examining *PbD* more closely now in prestigious research publications (Springer, 2010). In 2010, the IPC launched the *Privacy by Design* Ambassador Program to publicly acknowledge the efforts that individuals and organizations in various parts of the world have made to implement privacy protection through *Privacy by Design*. Those named as Individual *PbD* Ambassadors are "notable for their consistent efforts to educate organizations about the need to build privacy into their technology and business practices." Organizational *PbD* Ambassadors are businesses or public sector organizations that have embedded the principles into their day-to-day operations.[12] At least one major consultancy has developed a "*Privacy by Design* Assessment Methodology" which is based on the Principles of *PbD*. Others have expressed interest in similar undertakings.

On January 28, 2009 — International Data Privacy Day — the IPC inaugurated and hosted the *Privacy by Design* Challenge with the Toronto Board of Trade. Among the speakers each year are executives from the world's major companies, as well as emerging companies and researchers, each showcasing their innovative privacy technologies. The *Privacy by Design* Challenge event is now held every year on Data Privacy Day, and features a competition and award for best privacy design. Three *PbD* Challenge events have now been held.[13]

A reference framework for developing detailed criteria to apply and audit/verify adherence to *Privacy by Design* principles has been sketched out, showing how the *PbD* principles map to the fair information practices, and go well beyond them. Now, global collaboration and leadership are needed to firmly establish a universal framework for the strongest protection of privacy in the Information Age.

SUMMARY AND CONCLUSION

In the past two decades profound changes have occurred around the world, requiring a continual adaptation and refinement of informational privacy approaches and methods.

There is a growing understanding that innovation and competitiveness must be approached from a "design-thinking" perspective — namely, a way of viewing the world and overcoming constraints that is at once holistic, interdisciplinary, integrative, creative, innovative, and inspiring.

Privacy, too, must be approached from the same design-thinking perspective. Privacy must be incorporated into networked data systems and technologies, by default. Privacy must become integral to organizational priorities, project objectives, design processes, and planning operations. Privacy must be embedded into every standard, protocol, and practice that touches our lives.

This chapter has documented the origins and evolution of *Privacy by Design* from the mid-90s to the current day (2011). We have seen how a narrow focus on information and communications technologies has evolved to apply more broadly to information systems of all types, be they technological, procedural, meta-systemic or even physical. This evolution has been in response to events, developments, and changing circumstances in society that require taking a more holistic and practical approach to preserving privacy.

We have also seen how, along the way, the *PbD* foundational principles represent the successor to traditional principles of Fair Information Practices, incorporating FIPs but going beyond them to encompass the requirements for proactive leadership, verifiable methods, and measurable positive-sum results.

Privacy by Design is on the cusp of becoming a regulatory requirement in two major jurisdictions, but there remains much work ahead in defining its requirements more precisely, according to each domain of application. *PbD* will continue to evolve as it is adopted around the world and adapted to myriad circumstances and needs, giving us cause to be both hopeful and confident that a strong basis has been established for ensuring the survival of privacy in the 21st century. Our freedom and privacy may be at stake – what could be more important?

REFERENCES

American Institute for Chartered Public Accountants (AICPA) and Canadian Institute for Charted Accountants. (CICA). (2010). *Generally accepted privacy principles (GAPP) and criteria and the AICPA/CICA Privacy Maturity Model based on generally accepted privacy principles.* Retrieved April 8, 2011, from http://bit.ly/ePrxwg

Anderson, K. (2003). *Bringing PETs to the mainstream by using evaluation.* Presentation to the 24th International Conference of Privacy and Data Protection Commissioners, Australia, Office of the Information and Privacy Commissioner of Ontario, Canada. Retrieved April 8, 2011, from http://bit.ly/ezrgOB

Arizona State University (ASU). (2009, November). *Announcement of the Privacy by Design Research Lab.* Retrieved April 8, 2011, from http://bit.ly/gIbLCs

Bennett, C. J. (2009). International privacy standards: A continuing convergence. Retrieved April 8, 2011, from http://bit.ly/hBk3oX

Bennett, C. J., & Raab, C. D. (2006). *The governance of privacy: Policy instruments in global perspective.* MIT Press. Retrieved April 8, 2011, from http://bit.ly/icWiUh

Borking, J. (2003) The PET story: Privacy enhancing technologies - Online and offline. Paper presented to 25th International Conference of Privacy and Data Protection Commissioners, Sydney Australia. Retrieved April 8, 2011, from http://bit.ly/hQQ6tj

Cameron, K. (2005). *The laws of identity.* Identity Blog. Retrieved April 8, 2011, from http://bit.ly/eAHmWu

Cameron, K., Posch, R., & Rannenberg, K. (2008). *Proposal for a common identity framework: A user-centric identity metasystem.* Retrieved April 8, 2011, from http://bit.ly/i6lAfE

Canadian Internet Policy and Public Interest Clinic (CIPPIC). (2007). Approaches to security breach notification: A White Paper. Retrieved April 8, 2011, from http://bit.ly/fqzEQ6

Cavoukian, A. (1998). 407 express toll route: How you can travel the 407 anonymously. Office of the Information and Privacy Commissioner of Ontario, Canada. Retrieved April 8, 2011, from http://bit.ly/gJ3h74

Cavoukian, A. (1999). *Privacy and biometrics, consumer biometric applications: A discussion paper, and Biometrics and policing: Comments from a privacy perspective.* Office of the Information and Privacy Commissioner of Ontario, Canada. Retrieved April 8, 2011, from http://bit.ly/gqpJZU

Cavoukian, A. (2002). *Security technologies enabling privacy (STEPs): Time for a paradigm shift.* Office of the Information and Privacy Commissioner of Ontario, Canada. Retrieved April 8, 2011, from http://bit.ly/fjpfrt

Cavoukian, A. (2002). *Privacy and digital rights management (DRM): An oxymoron?* Office of the Information and Privacy Commissioner of Ontario, Canada. Retrieved April 8, 2011, from http://bit.ly/gfeQ99

Cavoukian, A. (2002). *Concerns and recommendations regarding government public key infrastructures for citizens.* Office of the Information and Privacy Commissioner of Ontario, Canada. Retrieved April 8, 2011, from http://bit.ly/fzNlbs

Cavoukian, A. (2004). *Building in privacy from the bottom up: How to preserve privacy in a security-centric world.* Presentation to Carnegie-Mellon University, Office of the Information and Privacy Commissioner of Ontario, Canada. Retrieved April 8, 2011, from http://bit.ly/e8YERK

Cavoukian, A. (2004). *Tag, you're it: Privacy implications of radio frequency identification (RFID) technology.* Office of the Information and Privacy Commissioner of Ontario, Canada. Retrieved April 8, 2011, from http://bit.ly/egro18

Cavoukian, A. (2005). *Privacy impact assessment guidelines for the Ontario Personal Health Office of the Information Protection Act.* Office of the Information and Privacy Commissioner of Ontario, Canada. Retrieved April 8, 2011, from http://bit.ly/hheuQh

Cavoukian, A. (2005). *Identity theft revisited: Security is not enough.* Office of the Information and Privacy Commissioner of Ontario, Canada. Retrieved April 8, 2011, from http://bit.ly/hRq4Fn

Cavoukian, A. (2005). *The new breed of practical privacy: An evolution.* Speech to the 26th International Conference of Privacy and Data Protection Commissioners, Montreux, Switzerland, Office of the Information and Privacy Commissioner of Ontario, Canada. Retrieved April 8, 2011, from http://bit.ly/gyOimo

Cavoukian, A. (2006). *The 7 laws of identity: The case for privacy-embedded laws of identity in the digital age.* Office of the Information and Privacy Commissioner of Ontario, Canada. Retrieved April 8, 2011, from http://bit.ly/g9nmJK

Cavoukian, A. (2006). *Video: A word about RFIDs and your privacy in the retail sector.* Office of the Office of the Information and Privacy Commissioner of Ontario, Canada. Retrieved April 8, 2011, from http://bit.ly/idq5vd

Cavoukian, A. (2006). *Creation of a global privacy standard.* Office of the Information and Privacy Commissioner of Ontario, Canada. Retrieved April 8, 2011, from http://bit.ly/hU0OaU

Cavoukian, A. (2007). *Guidelines for the use of video surveillance cameras in public places.* Office of the Information and Privacy Commissioner of Ontario, Canada. Retrieved April 8, 2011, from http://bit.ly/eQKOPz

Cavoukian, A. (2008). Privacy in the clouds. *Identity in the Information Society, 1,* 89–108. doi:10.1007/s12394-008-0005-z

Cavoukian, A. (2008). *Privacy in the clouds: A white paper on privacy and digital identity: Implications for the Internet.* Office of the Information and Privacy Commissioner of Ontario, Canada. Retrieved April 8, 2011, from http://bit.ly/Gwud7v

Cavoukian, A. (2008). *Privacy & radical pragmatism: Change the paradigm.* Office of the Information and Privacy Commissioner of Ontario, Canada. Retrieved April 8, 2011, from http://bit.ly/h1MT9W

Cavoukian, A. (2008). *RFID and privacy: Guidance for health-care providers.* Office of the Information and Privacy Commissioner of Ontario, Canada. Retrieved April 8, 2011, from http://bit.ly/hN6KY3

Cavoukian, A. (2009). *Moving forward from PETs to PETs plus: The time for change is now.* Office of the Information and Privacy Commissioner of Ontario, Canada. Retrieved April 8, 2011, from http://bit.ly/fkeHt8

Cavoukian, A. (2009). *Transformative technologies deliver both security and privacy: Think positive-sum not zero-sum.* Office of the Information and Privacy Commissioner of Ontario, Canada. Retrieved April 8, 2011, from http://bit.ly/dTi0jh

Cavoukian, A. (2009). *Privacy and government 2.0: The implications of an open world.* Office of the Information and Privacy Commissioner of Ontario, Canada. Retrieved April 8, 2011, from http://bit.ly/f7kHAn

Cavoukian, A. (2009). *A discussion paper on privacy externalities, security breach notification and the role of independent oversight.* Office of the Information and Privacy Commissioner of Ontario, Canada. Retrieved April 8, 2011, from http://bit.ly/gdtufG

Cavoukian, A. (2009). *Adding an on/off device to activate the RFID in enhanced driver's licences: Pioneering a made-in-Ontario transformative technology that delivers both privacy and security.* Office of the Information and Privacy Commissioner of Ontario, Canada. Retrieved April 8, 2011, from http://bit.ly/fbSbpl

Cavoukian, A. (2009 rev 2011). *Privacy by design: The 7 foundational principles.* Office of the Information and Privacy Commissioner of Ontario, Canada. Retrieved April 8, 2011, from http://bit.ly/gwzJgw

Cavoukian, A. (2010). Privacy by design: The next generation in the evolution of privacy. *Special issue of Identity in the Information Society, 3*(2). Retrieved April 8, 2011, from http://bit.ly/fo6l1q

Cavoukian, A. (2010 rev. 2011). *Privacy by design - The 7 foundational principles: Implementation and mapping of fair office of the information practices.* Office of the Information and Privacy Commissioner of Ontario, Canada. Retrieved April 8, 2011, from http://bit.ly/hXwZp5

Cavoukian, A., & Hamilton, T. (2002). *The privacy payoff: How successful businesses build customer trust.* McGraw-Hill Ryerson.

Cavoukian, A., & McQuay, T. (2010). A pragmatic approach to privacy risk optimization: Privacy by design for business practices. *Identity in the Information Society, 3*, 405-413. Retrieved April 8, 2011, from http://bit.ly/hC7hED

Cavoukian, A., & Stoianov, A. (2007). *Biometric encryption: A Positive-sum technology that achieves strong authentication, security and privacy.* Office of the Information and Privacy Commissioner of Ontario, Canada. Retrieved April 8, 2011, from http://bit.ly/gr5VyY

Cavoukian, A., & Stoianov, A. (2009). *Biometric encryption chapter from the Springer Encyclopaedia of Biometrics.* Office of the Information and Privacy Commissioner of Ontario, Canada. Retrieved April 8, 2011, from http://bit.ly/eay2DO

Cavoukian, A., Stoianov, A., & Carter, F. (2008). Biometric encryption: Technology for strong authentication, security and privacy. In *Policies and Research in Identity Management, IFIP Advances in Information and Communication Technology, 261*, 57-77. Springer. Retrieved April 8, 2011, from http://bit.ly/eBK5I9

Cavoukian, A., & Tapscott, D. (2005). *Privacy and the open-networked enterprise.* Office of the Information and Privacy Commissioner of Ontario, Canada. Retrieved April 8, 2011, from http://bit.ly/eTdiya

Cavoukian, A., Taylor, S., & Abrams, M. (2010). Privacy by design: Essential for organizational accountability and strong business practices. *Identity in the Information Society, 3*, 405-413. Retrieved April 8, 2011, from http://bit.ly/dOJYOc

Cavoukian, A., & Center for Democracy & Technology. (2000). *P3P and privacy: An update for the privacy community.* Office of the Information and Privacy Commissioner of Ontario, Canada. Retrieved April 8, 2011, from http://bit.ly/giSK04

Cavoukian, A., & Deloitte & Touche. (2004). *The security-privacy paradox: Issues, misconceptions and strategies.* Office of the Information and Privacy Commissioner of Ontario, Canada. Retrieved April 8, 2011, from http://bit.ly/fdzn1B

Cavoukian, A., & Schulich School of Business. (2007). *Privacy and boards of directors: What you don't know can hurt you.* Office of the Information and Privacy Commissioner of Ontario, Canada. 2003, rev. Retrieved April 8, 2011, from http://bit.ly/eTknsz

Cavoukian, A., & U.S. Department of Justice, Office of Justice. (2000). *Privacy impact assessment for justice information systems.* Office of the Information and Privacy Commissioner of Ontario, Canada. Retrieved April 8, 2011, from http://bit.ly/eIuyOZ

Cavoukian, A., & U.S. Department of Justice, Office of Justice. (2000). *Programs, privacy design principles for an integrated justice system – A working paper.* Office of the Information and Privacy Commissioner of Ontario, Canada. Retrieved April 8, 2011, from http://bit.ly/hKW8ow

Center for Democracy and Technology (CDT). (2009). *Perspective on PbD*. Retrieved April 8, 2011, from http://bit.ly/fuxn0t

Center for Democracy and Technology (CDT). (2009). *Privacy by design in the Smart Grid*. Retrieved April 8, 2011, from http://bit.ly/f6pZDO

Center for Democracy and Technology (CDT). (2009). The role of privacy by design in protecting consumer privacy. Comments submitted to the FTC Consumer Privacy Roundtable. Retrieved April 8, 2011, from http://1.usa.gov/eMH4jv

Center for Democracy and Technology (CDT). (2010). Comments on a national broadband plan for our future. NBP Public Notice #29, GN Docket Nos. 09-47, 09-51, 09-137. Retrieved April 8, 2011, from http://bit.ly/fC5nCo

Centre for Information Policy Leadership (CIPL). (2009). *Data protection accountability: The essential elements: A document for discussion*. Retrieved April 8, 2011, from http://1.usa.gov/hvlZcD

Centre for Information Policy Leadership (CIPL). (2010). *Demonstrating and measuring accountability: A discussion document accountability phase II - The Paris project*. Retrieved April 8, 2011, from http://bit.ly/gRFrob

Computers, Privacy and Freedom (CFP). (2000, April). *Privacy by Design Workshop Proceedings*. Toronto, Ontario, Canada. Retrieved April 8, 2011, from http://bit.ly/e5UegE

Crompton, M. (2010). *Privacy by design: An oxymoron, an impossibility or the way to go?* Presentation to the National ICT Australia Seminar. Retrieved April 8, 2011, from http://bit.ly/eaA2L5

Dutch Data Protection Agency. (2004). *Privacy-enhancing technologies*. White Paper for Decision-Makers. Retrieved April 8, 2011, from http://bit.ly/dFRV8q

European Commission (EC). (2007). *European Commission supports PETs: Promoting data protection by privacy enhancing technologies - Press release*. Retrieved April 8, 2011, from http://bit.ly/epnO5w

European Commission (EC). (2007). *Communication from the Commission to the European Parliament and the Council on Promoting Data Protection by Privacy Enhancing Technologies (PETs), COM (2007) 228 final*. Brussels, 2.5.2007 and Background Memo. Retrieved April 8, 2011, from http://bit.ly/hRdu8n

European Commission (EC). (2009). *The future of privacy: Joint contribution to the consultation of the European Commission on the legal framework for the fundamental right to protection of personal data - Article 29: Data protection working party, WP 168*. Retrieved April 8, 2011, from http://bit.ly/gWJ56l

European Commission (EC). (2010). *Communication from the commission to the European parliament, the council, the economic and social committee and the committee of the regions: A comprehensive approach on personal data protection in the European Union*. Technical report. Retrieved April 8, 2011, from http://bit.ly/grpr4w

European Commission (EC). (2010). *Study on the economic benefits of privacy-enhancing technologies*. Final Report to The European Commission, DG Justice, Freedom and Security. Retrieved April 8, 2011, from http://bit.ly/heQNQT

European Commission (EC). (2010). *Opinion 3/2010 on the principle of accountability - Article 29: Data protection working party, WP 173*. Retrieved April 8, 2011, from http://bit.ly/eEFeaq

European Council. (2011, February). *Council conclusions on the Communication from the Commission to the European Parliament and the Council - A comprehensive approach on personal data protection in the European Union*. 3071st Justice and Home Affairs Council meeting, Brussels. Retrieved April 8, 2011, from http://bit.ly/gx4wS0

European Network and Information Security Agency (ENISA). (2009). *Privacy and e-ID: Press release and position paper*. Retrieved April 8, 2011, from http://bit.ly/dNNRD6

European Parliament & Council. (1995). *Directive 95/46/EC of 24 October 1995 on the protection of individuals with regard to the processing of personal data and on the free movement of such data* [Official Journal L 281 of 23.11.1995]. Retrieved April 8, 2011, from http://bit.ly/gcF0Uq

European Union. (2003). *Privacy incorporated software agent: Building a privacy guardian for the electronic age* (PISA Project). 2001–2003.

Ford, R. (2004). Beware rise of Big Brother state, warns data watchdog. *The Sunday Times*. Retrieved April 8, 2011, from http://thetim.es/hw1abr

Gurski, M. (2003). *PETTEP history and future: Making the ISO connection*. Office of the Information and Privacy Commissioner of Ontario, Canada. Retrieved April 8, 2011, from http://bit.ly/i7Ytu7

Hustinx, P. (2008, April). *EDPS issues policy paper on his role in EU research and technological development*. Press Release. Retrieved April 8, 2011, from http://bit.ly/hKCs5x

Hustinx, P. (2010, March). *Opinion of the European Data Protection Supervisor on promoting trust in the information society by fostering data protection and privacy*. EDPS. Retrieved April 8, 2011, from http://bit.ly/h9qzmP

Hustinx, P. (2010, March). *Press release: EDPS opinion on privacy in the digital age: Privacy by design as a key tool to ensure citizens' trust in ICTs*. EDPS/10/6. Retrieved April 8, 2011, from http://bit.ly/hNJDZy

IBM. (2005). *Research on SPARCLE (Server Privacy ARrchitecture and CapabiLity Enablement) policy workbench*. Retrieved April 8, 2011, from http://bit.ly/hgddlJ

Initiative for Privacy Standardization in Europe (IPSE), European Committee for Standardization (CEN). (2002). *Final report of the EU CEN/ISSS initiative on privacy standardization in Europe*. Retrieved April 8, 2011, from http://bit.ly/hZX7io

International Conference of Privacy and Data Protection Commissioners (ICPDPC). (2004). *Resolution on a draft ISO privacy framework standard*. Adopted at Wroclaw, Poland, September 2004. Retrieved April 8, 2011, from http://bit.ly/eGMJtB

International Conference of Privacy and Data Protection Commissioners (ICPDPC). (2009). *International standards on the protection of personal data and privacy: The Madrid Resolution*. Adopted at Madrid, Spain, October 2009. Retrieved April 8, 2011, from http://bit.ly/hqKTVA

International Conference of Privacy and Data Protection Commissioners (ICPDPC). (2010). *Adopted resolutions*. Retrieved from http://bit.ly/i1Oo4r.

International Conference of Privacy and Data Protection Commissioners (ICPDPC). (2010). *Privacy by design resolution*. Adopted at Jerusalem, Israel, October 27–29, 2010. Retrieved April 8, 2011, from http://bit.ly/fffv0l

International Working Group on Data Protection in Telecommunications (IWGDPT). (2008). *Report and guidance on privacy in social network services "Rome Memorandum"*, 675.36.5. Retrieved April 8, 2011, from http://bit.ly/er5SjW

London Economics. (2010). *Study on the economic benefits of privacy-enhancing technologies.* Final Report to The European Commission, DG Justice, Freedom and Security. Retrieved April 8, 2011, from http://bit.ly/heQNQT

Martin, K., & Plataniotis, K. N. (2008, August). Privacy protected surveillance using secure visual object coding. *IEEE Transactions on Circuits & Systems for Video Technology: Special Issue on Video Surveillance, 18*(8), 1152–1162. doi:10.1109/TCSVT.2008.927110

Naraine, R. (2007). Sensitive government e-mails leak through Tor exit nodes. *ZDNet.* Retrieved April 8, 2011, from http://zd.net/f68r72

NIST Smart Grid Interoperability Panel – Cyber Security Working Group. (2010). *NIST guidelines for smart grid cyber security.* NISTIR 7628. Retrieved April 8, 2011, from http://1.usa.gov/dIAJhx

Office of the Information and Privacy Commissioner of Ontario. Canada & The Netherlands Data Protection Authority. (1995). *Privacy-enhancing technologies: The path to anonymity* (volume I). Office of the Information and Privacy Commissioner of Ontario, Canada. Retrieved April 8, 2011, from http://bit.ly/fw55Dj

Office of the Information and Privacy Commissioner of Ontario. Canada & The Netherlands Data Protection Authority. (1995). *Privacy-enhancing technologies: The path to anonymity,* (volume II). Office of the Information and Privacy Commissioner of Ontario, Canada. Retrieved April 8, 2011, from http://bit.ly/ihllwd

Office of the Information and Privacy Commissioner of Ontario. Canada & Advanced Card Technology Association of Canada (ACTA). (1997). *Smart, optical and other advanced cards: How to do a privacy assessment.* Office of the Information and Privacy Commissioner of Ontario, Canada. Retrieved April 8, 2011, from http://bit.ly/hoxPKL

Office of the Information and Privacy Commissioner of Ontario. Canada & The Netherlands Data Protection Authority. (1999). *Intelligent software agents, turning a privacy threat into a privacy protector.* Office of the Information and Privacy Commissioner of Ontario, Canada. Retrieved April 8, 2011, from http://bit.ly/hNrINH

Office of the Information and Privacy Commissioner of Ontario. Canada, Guardent, & PriceWaterHouseCoopers. (2001). *Privacy diagnostic tool workbook and FAQ.* Office of the Information and Privacy Commissioner of Ontario, Canada. Retrieved April 8, 2011, from http://bit.ly/gAhbsN

Office of the Information and Privacy Commissioner of Ontario. Canada. (2002). *Seven essential steps for designing privacy into technology.* Office of the Information and Privacy Commissioner of Ontario, Canada. Retrieved April 8, 2011, from http://bit.ly/fxt4oF

Office of the Information and Privacy Commissioner of Ontario. Canada & Canadian Marketing Association (CMA). (2004). *Incorporating privacy into marketing and customer relationship management.* Office of the Information and Privacy Commissioner of Ontario, Canada. Retrieved April 8, 2011, from http://bit.ly/gqELYD

Office of the Information and Privacy Commissioner of Ontario. Canada & The Ponemon Institute. (2004). *Cross-national study of Canadian and U.S. corporate privacy practices.* Office of the Information and Privacy Commissioner of Ontario, Canada. Retrieved April 8, 2011, from http://bit.ly/hZQxxs

Office of the Information and Privacy Commissioner of Ontario. Canada & IBM/Tivoli. (2005). *EPAL translation of the Freedom of Information and Protection of Privacy Act.* Office of the Information and Privacy Commissioner of Ontario, Canada. Retrieved April 8, 2011, from http://bit.ly/dGw5P9

Office of the Information and Privacy Commissioner of Ontario. Canada & Advanced Card Technology Association of Canada (ACTA). (2007). *Contactless smart card applications: Design tool and privacy impact assessment.* Office of the Information and Privacy Commissioner of Ontario, Canada. Retrieved April 8, 2011, from http://bit.ly/fy3k5b

Office of the Information and Privacy Commissioner of Ontario. Canada & Hewlett-Packard. (2008). *RFID and privacy: Guidance for healthcare providers.* Office of the Information and Privacy Commissioner of Ontario, Canada. Retrieved April 8, 2011, from http://bit.ly/hN6KY3

Office of the Information and Privacy Commissioner of Ontario. Canada & Liberty Alliance. (2009). *The new federated privacy impact assessment (F-PIA) building privacy and trust-enabled federation.* Office of the Information and Privacy Commissioner of Ontario, Canada. Retrieved April 8, 2011, from http://bit.ly/f89UMs

Office of the Information and Privacy Commissioner of Ontario. Canada & Ontario Lottery Gaming Corporation & YMCA Canada. (2009). *Privacy risk management: Building privacy protection into a risk management framework to ensure that privacy risks are managed by default.* Office of the Information and Privacy Commissioner of Ontario, Canada. Retrieved April 8, 2011, from http://bit.ly/gGMA4r

Office of the Information and Privacy Commissioner of Ontario. Canada & NEC Computing. (2010), *Modelling cloud computing architecture without compromising privacy: A privacy by design approach.* Office of the Information and Privacy Commissioner of Ontario, Canada. Retrieved April 8, 2011, from http://bit.ly/fqnA8v

Office of the Information and Privacy Commissioner of Ontario. Canada & Nymity. (2010). *A pragmatic approach to privacy risk optimization: Privacy by design for business practices.* Office of the Privacy Commissioner of Ontario, Canada. Retrieved April 8, 2011, from http://bit.ly/hl0ws8

Office of the Privacy Commissioner of Australia (OPCA). (2010). *Privacy impact assessments (PIA) guide.* Retrieved April 8, 2011, from http://bit.ly/hRQu0a

Office of the Privacy Commissioner of Canada (OPCC). (2004). *A guide for businesses and organizations: Your privacy responsibilities.* Office of the Privacy Commissioner of Canada. Retrieved April 8, 2011, from http://bit.ly/fRKncL

Office of the Privacy Commissioner of Canada (OPCC). (2007). *Fact sheet on PIAs.* Office of the Privacy Commissioner of Canada. Retrieved April 8, 2011, from http://bit.ly/dTZ8Aj

Office of the Privacy Commissioner of Canada (OPCC). (2010). *Privacy, trust and innovation – Building Canada's digital advantage.* Submission to the Digital Economy Consultation, Office of the Privacy Commissioner of Canada. Retrieved April 8, 2011, from http://bit.ly/gJPihD

Organization for Economic Co-operation and Development (OECD). (1980). *Guidelines on the protection of privacy and transborder flows of personal data.* Retrieved April 8, 2011, from http://bit.ly/gdim0T

Privacy and Innovation Symposium. (2010, May). Washington, D.C. Retrieved April 8, 2011, from http://1.usa.gov/hBdIrt

Privacy International. (1998–2003). *Privacy and human rights, annual reports.* Retrieved April 8, 2011, from http://bit.ly/hjKLSe

Privacy International and Electronic Privacy Information Center (EPIC). (2007). *Privacy and human rights 2006: An international survey of privacy laws and developments.* Retrieved April 8, 2011, from http://bit.ly/g9wOAh

Privacy International, the Electronic Privacy Information Center (EPIC) and the Center for Media and Communications Studies (CMCS). (2011). *European privacy and human rights 2010.* Retrieved April 8, 2011, from http://bit.ly/gnFZoC

Reding, V. (2010, January). *Privacy: The challenges ahead for the European Union.* Keynote Speech at the Data Protection Day, European Parliament, Brussels. Retrieved April 8, 2011, from http://bit.ly/fCRTK9

Romanosky, S., Telang, R., & Acquisti, A. (2011). Do data breach disclosure laws reduce identity theft? *Journal of Policy Analysis and Management, 30*(2). Retrieved April 8, 2011, from http://bit.ly/heVW6q

Rowland, K. (2010, September). Privacy by design, or privacy by disaster? *Intelligent Utility.* Retrieved April 8, 2011, from http://bit.ly/gS2Fz1

Schwartz, P. M., & Janger, E. J. (2007). Notification of data security breaches. *Michigan Law Review, 105*, 913. Brooklyn Law School, Legal Studies Paper No. 58. Retrieved April 8, 2011, from http://bit.ly/hQjHT0

The Ponemon Institute. (2010). *2009 annual study: Cost of a privacy breach sponsored by PGP Corp.* Retrieved April 8, 2011, from http://bit.ly/eRxyMK

The Ponemon Institute. (2011). *The true costs of compliance: A benchmark study of multinational organizations.* Independent Research Report. Retrieved April 8, 2011, from http://bit.ly/e13LZT

Thomson, I. (2007). Hushmail turns out to be anything but. *ITNews.* Retrieved April 8, 2011, from http://bit.ly/gePNsZ

U.K. Information Commissioner's Office (ICO). (2006). *Data protection technical guidance note: Privacy enhancing technologies.* ICO. Retrieved April 8, 2011, from http://bit.ly/e36Upn

U.K. Information Commissioner's Office (ICO). (2007). *An international study of PIA law, policies and practices.* ICO. Retrieved April 8, 2011, from http://bit.ly/hB381i

U.K. Information Commissioner's Office (ICO). (2008). *Privacy by design report.* ICO. Retrieved April 8, 2011, from http://bit.ly/gZ4CYm

U.K. Information Commissioner's Office (ICO). (2008). *Privacy by design – An overview of privacy enhancing technologies.* Enterprise Privacy Group. Retrieved April 8, 2011, from http://bit.ly/hquBBQ

U.K. Information Commissioner's Office (ICO). (2008). *Privacy by design report recommendations: ICO implementation plan.* ICO. Retrieved April 8, 2011, from http://bit.ly/hpjWhw

U.K. Information Commissioner's Office (ICO). (2008). *Privacy by Design Conference (website).* Manchester. Retrieved April 8, 2011, from http://bit.ly/f6MbGq

U.K. Information Commissioner's Office (ICO). (2009). Protecting people: A data protection strategy for the Information Commissioner's Office. ICO. Retrieved April 8, 2011, from http://bit.ly/gi5vW1

U.K. Information Commissioner's Office (ICO). (2009). *PIA handbook,* ICO. Retrieved April 8, 2011, from http://bit.ly/eEKU06

U.K. Information Commissioner's Office (ICO). (2010). *The privacy dividend: The business case for investing in proactive privacy protection.* ICO. Retrieved April 8, 2011, from http://bit.ly/eF2fM1

U.S. Federal Trade Commission (FTC). (2001). *Remarks by Tim Muris, FTC Chairman at the Privacy 2001 Conference.* Retrieved from http://1.usa.gov/eupYzF.

U.S. Federal Trade Commission (FTC). (2010, December). *Protecting consumer privacy in an era of rapid change: A proposed framework for businesses and policymakers.* Technical report. Retrieved April 8, 2011, from http://1.usa.gov/eupYzF

U.S. Federal Trade Commission (FTC). (2010). *Testimony regarding consumer online privacy by John Liebowitz, FTC Chairman before the Committee on Commerce, Science, and Transportation, U.S. Senate.* Washington, D.C. Retrieved April 8, 2011, from http://1.usa.gov/gFLtDw

U.S. Secretary's Advisory Committee on Automated Personal Data Systems. (1973). *Records, computers and the rights of citizens.* HEW Report. Retrieved April 8, 2011, from http://bit.ly/e63jZ6

U.S. White House. (2010). *Draft national strategy for trusted identities in cyberspace: Creating options for enhanced online security and privacy.* Retrieved April 8, 2011, from http://1.usa.gov/hNs1jw

Wright, T. (1995). *Privacy protection models for the private sector.* Office of the Information and Privacy Commissioner of Ontario, Canada. Retrieved April 8, 2011, from http://bit.ly/hXnEmV

Wright, T. (1995). *Eyes on the road: Intelligent transportation systems and your privacy.* Office of the Information and Privacy Commissioner of Ontario, Canada. Retrieved April 8, 2011, from http://bit.ly/fxaVpv

ADDITIONAL READING

Borking, J. J. (2001). Privacy Incorporated Software Agent (PISA): Proposal for Building a Privacy Guardian for the Electronic Age. In Federrath, H. (Ed.), *Designing Privacy Enhancing Technologies* (pp. 130-140). Springer Berlin / Heidelberg. Doi: 10.1007/3-540-44702-4_8

Borking, J. J. (2005). "Privacy Standards for Trust" presentation to the London conference of Data Protection Authorities. Retrieved April 8, 2011, from http://bit.ly/gTjOVq

Borking, J. J., & Raab, C. (2001). Laws, PETS and other technologies for privacy protection, in *Journal of Information, Law and Technology*, no. 1.

FIDIS Project. (2007), Identity and impact of privacy enhancing technologies. Retrieved April 8, 2011, from http://bit.ly/e8A0aG

International Security, Trust and Privacy Alliance (ISTPA). (2007). Analysis of Privacy Principles: Making Privacy Operational. Retrieved April 8, 2011, from http://bit.ly/gZu2pm

International Security, Trust and Privacy Alliance (ISTPA). (2009). Privacy Management Reference Model 2.0 v.2.0: A framework for resolving privacy policy requirements into operational privacy services and functions. Retrieved April 8, 2011, from http://bit.ly/dUMaiD

Kenny, S., & Borking, J. (2002). 'The Value of Privacy Engineering', Refereed Article, *The Journal of Information, Law and Technology* (JILT) 2002 (1). Retrieved April 8, 2011, from http://bit.ly/gk9P3E

Microsoft Corp. (2006). Privacy Guidelines for Developing Software Products and Services. Retrieved April 8, 2011, from http://bit.ly/ijIMVk

Organisation for Economic Co-operation and Development (OECD). (2003). Directorate for Science, Technology and Industry, Committee for Information, Computer and Communications Policy, Inventory of Privacy-Enhancing Technologies (PETs). Retrieved April 8, 2011, from http://bit.ly/hrFQIs

Organisation for Economic Co-operation and Development (OECD). (2008). At a Crossroads: "Personhood" and the Digital Identity in the Information Society (STI Working Paper 2007/7). Retrieved April 8, 2011, from http://bit.ly/gFBhlQ

PISA Consortium. (2001–2003). Privacy Incorporated Software Agent (PISA): Building a privacy guardian for the electronic age (PISA Project). International Security, Trust and Privacy Alliance (ISTPA).

PISA Project. (2003). Handbook of Privacy-Enhancing Technologies – The Case of Intelligent Software Agents, The Hague. Retrieved April 8, 2011, from http://bit.ly/f32fns

PRIME Project. (2007). PRIME White paper v2. Retrieved April 8, 2011, from http://bit.ly/hry9Og

Spiekermann, S., & Cranor, L. F. Engineering Privacy (2008, September). IEEE Transactions on Software Engineering, Forthcoming. Available at SSRN: http://ssrn.com/abstract=1085333

U.K. Royal Academy of Engineering Society. (2007). Report: Dilemmas of Privacy and Surveillance: Challenges of Technological Change. Retrieved April 8, 2011, from http://bit.ly/gJUmJm

U.K. Royal Academy of Engineering Society. (2007). Press release: http://bit.ly/hSo1O0. Retrieved April 8, 2011.

U.K. Royal Academy of Engineering Society.

KEY TERMS AND DEFINITIONS

Accountability: the governance model that is based on organizations taking responsibility for protecting privacy and information security appropriately and protecting individuals from the negative outcomes associated with privacy-protection failures. Accountability goes beyond responsibility by obligating an organization to be answerable for its actions. Accountability was first framed as a privacy principle in the *OECD Guidelines on the Protection of Privacy and Transborder Flows of Personal Data.*

Fair Information Practices (FIPs): widely agreed principles that serve as the ground rules for the collection, use and disclosure of personal information, whether in statute, policy or technology. These overlapping and cumulative principles vary slightly between jurisdictions, but generally include concepts of: Consent; Accountability; Purposes; Collection Limitation; Use, Retention, and Disclosure Limitation; Accuracy; Security; Openness; Access; and Compliance.

Global Privacy Standard (GPS): A set of universal privacy principles, harmonizing those found in various sets of fair information practices currently in existence and enhancing them with the explicit addition of data minimization under the Collection Limitation principle. The Global Privacy Standard was developed by an international Working Group of Data Protection Commissioners, and approved in 2006 at the 28th International Data Protection Commissioners Conference.

Information Privacy: Also referred to as informational self-determination, information privacy relates to an individual's ability to exercise control over the collection, use, disclosure and retention of his or her personal information.

Information Security: the management of information to assure its confidentiality, integrity and availability. In the context of Fair Information Practices, security refers to an organization's responsibility to protect personal information in its custody throughout its lifecycle using reasonable physical, technical, and administrative safeguards that are appropriate to the sensitivity of the information. Security is a necessary but insufficient condition for privacy. It is possible to have security without privacy, but not privacy without security.

Personal Information (aka Personally Identifiable Information): includes any information about an identifiable individual. This includes information such as name, address, telephone number, sex, race, religion, ethnic origin, sexual orientation, medical records, psychiatric history, fingerprints, criminal record, credit rating, marital status, education, and employment history. An individual's name need not be attached to the information in order for it to qualify as personal information.

Positive-sum: A term originating in Game Theory that refers to the outcome of a dispute or negotiation among parties. Positive-sum is similar to win-win, in which both parties enjoy a beneficial result, and is contrasted with zero-sum, in which one party's wins are offset by another's losses.

Privacy by Design: a concept developed by Ontario Information and Privacy Commissioner, Dr. Ann Cavoukian, in the 1990's. *Privacy by Design* refers to the act of embedding privacy into the design specifications of technologies, organizational processes, and networked infrastructures as a core functionality. *Privacy by Design* is articulated in seven Foundational Principles that go beyond the Principles of Fair Information Practices.

Privacy Impact Assessment (PIA): a formal risk management tool used to identify the actual or potential effects that a proposed or existing information system, technology, or program may have on an individual's privacy. A PIA also identifies the ways in which privacy risks can be mitigated.

Privacy: famously described in 1890 by American Justices Warren and Brandeis as the "right to be let alone." Practically, privacy is the ability of an individual or group to seclude themselves or information about themselves and thereby reveal themselves selectively.

Privacy-Enhancing Technologies: information technologies that strengthen the protection of personal privacy in an information system by preventing the unnecessary or unlawful collection, use and disclosure of personal data, or by offering tools to enhance an individual's control over his/her personal data.

Standard: a benchmark or reference against which to measure and/or evaluate a product, process or claim.

Transparency: in the context of Fair Information Practices, generally refers to an organization's openness about its policies and practices relating to the management of personal information. The principle of transparency can also be applied to the design and operation of information technologies and networked systems, in order to empower users and to foster confidence and trust in the processing of personal information.

User-Centric: In the context of privacy, and in particular of *Privacy by Design*, refers to keeping the interests of the individual uppermost in the design and architecture of systems and processes by offering such measures as strong privacy defaults, appropriate notice, and empowering user-friendly options.

ENDNOTES

[1]   I gratefully acknowledge the work of Fred Carter, Senior Policy & Technology Advisor, Office of the Information and Privacy Commissioner of Ontario, Canada, in the preparation of this paper.

[2]   August 1995. Registratiekamer and IPC:1995, Vol II. see pp.13 and 34

[3]   See Wikipedia entries for, *inter alia*, "crypto wars," "CALEA," "clipper chip," "PGP," and "Phil Zimmerman."

4   More at www.commoncriteriaportal.org and at http://en.wikipedia.org/wiki/Common_Criteria,

5   How that trust is secured can vary enormously, e.g., open-source code, open competition and availability of alternatives, third-party testing and certification, warranties and guarantees, reputation, direct audit tools, etc. Indeed, one emerging class of PETs identified is transparency and audit tools that allow individuals to make better informed privacy decisions in their online and offline interactions.

6   See Privacy-Enhancing Technologies ("PETs") Award for Outstanding Research in Privacy Enhancing Technologies: PETS Symposium, Past Winners at http://petsymposium.org/2010/award/winners.php

7   2003. Cavoukian. *Wall Street Journal* Innovation Award nomination at www.zurich.ibm.com/news/06/rfid.html or discussion and references at Wikipedia entry on Clipped tags at http://en.wikipedia.org/wiki/Clipped_Tag

8   EuroPriSe European Privacy Seal awards at www.european-privacy-seal.eu/awarded-seals

9   See list of European Commission-funded projects, ICT Research in FP7, Research activities in trust, privacy and identity in the digital economy at: http://cordis.europa.eu/fp7/ict/security/projects_en.html

10   All available at www.privacybydesign.ca

11   May 2010. Privacy and Innovation Symposium, Washington, D.C at www.commerce.gov/news/secretary-speeches/2010/05/07/remarks-privacy-and-innovation-symposium

12   For details see www.privacybydesign.ca/ambassadors/individuals/ and www.privacybydesign.ca/ambassadors/organizations/

13   Details at www.privacybydesign.ca/events/past/

Section 2
Privacy Protection in Specific Business Domains

Chapter 8
Privacy Considerations for Electronic Health Records

Mary Kuehler
University of Tulsa, USA

Nakeisha Schimke
University of Tulsa, USA

John Hale
University of Tulsa, USA

ABSTRACT

Electronic Health Record (EHR) systems are a powerful tool for healthcare providers and patients. Both groups benefit from unified, easily accessible record management; however, EHR systems also bring new threats to patient privacy. The reach of electronic patient data extends far beyond the healthcare realm. Patients are managing their own health records through personal health record (PHR) service providers, and businesses outside of the healthcare industry are finding themselves increasingly linked to medical data. The Health Insurance Portability and Accountability Act (HIPAA) Privacy Rule and other regulatory measures establish baseline standards for protecting patient privacy, but the inclusion of medical images in patient records presents unique challenges. Medical images often require specialized management tools, and some medical images may reveal a patient's identity or medical condition through re-linkage or inherent identifiability. After exploring EHR systems in-depth and reviewing health information policy, the chapter explores how privacy challenges associated with EHR systems and medical images can be mitigated through the combined efforts of technology, policy, and legislation designed to reduce the risk of re-identification.

DOI: 10.4018/978-1-61350-501-4.ch008

INTRODUCTION

Electronic Health Record (EHR) systems promise to reduce the cost of healthcare while improving patient care. Through the American Recovery and Reinvestment Act of 2009, the U.S. government allocated $19.2 billion to improve health information technology, primarily by encouraging widespread adoption of EHR systems (HITECH Answers, 2010). Eliminating administrative overhead and improving medical record workflow help reduce human error and improve the quality of service. Moreover, the transition to EHR systems offers great potential for collaboration and data sharing, enabling medical research and knowledge discovery on a global scale. This is especially true for efforts where large-scale collection is limited by cost and subject enrollment. For example, the Alzheimer's Disease Neuroimaging Initiative (ADNI), a multisite collaborative research effort, has collected images from over 40 sites and distributed data to more than 1,300 investigators to date (Kolata, 2010; Mueller, et al., 2005). The success of ADNI has led to the establishment of similar efforts for Parkinson's disease.

Along with the push for medical entities to utilize EHR systems comes a heightened threat to the privacy of patient medical data. In the U.S., regulation of patient privacy in EHR systems falls under the Health Insurance Portability and Accountability Act (HIPAA), which defines protected health information (PHI) and how it can be used. Improvements in technology have enabled EHR systems to incorporate medical images alongside data found in traditional paper charts. As the capabilities of capturing medical images progress, privacy measures and regulations regarding electronic medical data must also advance to encompass these images.

Discussions of patient privacy are often confined to the realm of healthcare and insurance providers, but the subtleties of the prevailing industry environment concerning medical data extend far beyond entities that are legally required to protect patient privacy. Businesses that are not subject to healthcare privacy laws also handle medical data, often unknowingly, when employees manage and disseminate health information using company resources. This may expose the company to potential liability. Beyond EHR systems, other sources may disclose PHI, such as Internet search terms or calendar appointments. These incidental exposures, along with the inherent privacy risks posed by certain classes of medical images, should be considered as much a threat to privacy as an EHR system data breach within the healthcare industry. It is essential that businesses and consumers be made aware of these issues.

This chapter gives an overview of EHR systems and explores health information privacy in the context of two emerging themes — the expanding reach of PHI, and the proliferation of medical images. Policy, technology and organizational solutions are considered to help enterprises within healthcare and beyond meet the challenges they present.

BACKGROUND

EHR Systems

EHR systems store a wide range of patient data and information types — patient demographics, progress notes, problems, medications, vital signs, past medical history, immunizations, laboratory data and radiology reports (HIMSS, 2010). The information in an EHR is stored as either structured or semi-structured data. Structured data refers to information in pre-determined data fields with a finite set of acceptable input. Semi-structured data allows for the input of free-text responses by the medical professional.

Fields with a predetermined list of acceptable input are advantageous within an EHR system because there is no ambiguity concerning the data collected. The pervasiveness of medical coding is a great example of how structured data is used to increase efficiency and accuracy in medical billing by linking numerical codes to specific medical conditions. In particular, the ICD-9 coding system is used internationally and was designed to "promote comparability in the collection, processing, classification, and presentation of mortality statistics" (CDC, 2009). A specific example of an ICD-9 code is 944.08, which denotes a "burn of unspecified degree of multiple sites of wrist(s) and hand(s)" (ICD9Data.com, 2009). Pre-defined values limit flexibility but offer uniformity and reduce the risk of input errors.

Semi-structured data can offer a more accurate picture of a patient's health because the physician is not constrained by selecting from a list of predetermined values. Some examples of semi-structured data include physician notes, medication lists, pathology reports, and patient histories. Semi-structured data is usually managed by creating predefined sections or fields that accept free-text input. In this way the physician can include as much descriptive information as necessary while still allowing for data processing to be performed by keyword searching within the semi-structured fields.

Medical images are also considered semi-structured data. The most prevalent standard for storing and handling medical images is Digital Imaging and Communications in Medicine (DICOM) (NEMA, 2009). DICOM is used across many imaging modalities and equipment manufacturers. A DICOM image consists of *name:value* pairs of attributes to store both metadata and pixel data (the image itself). For example, attributes may describe the imaging equipment (manufacturer, device serial number), imaging session (institution name, operator name), or patient (patient id, patient telephone). At first glance, the pre-defined attributes seem to be structured data; however, attribute values can sometimes be semi-structured in the case of free-form text and pixel data.

Several kinds of entities store, process, or transmit patient data. *Healthcare providers,* which are involved in the initial collection and storage of the data, include physicians, EHR system providers, billing departments, and insurance companies. Some *third-party companies* that process medical data are not subject to laws protecting medical data. These companies house public health databases, research organizations, health registries, and patient initiated health records such as Google Health and Microsoft HealthVault. Another classification encompasses third-party businesses that have incidental contact with or exposure to health information. Incidental contact happens when employees use work resources to access health information, an employer provides access to a patient-managed health information system or sponsors a group health plan, or an email or calendar application contains medical data or details about doctor appointments. An emerging category is that of patients who use a third-party company to store their medical information. This category is patient initiated and gives the patient more control over who can access their data.

Depending on a healthcare provider's implementation strategy for their EHR system, patient data may either reside with the provider or remotely with an application service provider (ASP) that provides EHR services to healthcare organizations as an external function accessed via the Internet. This methodology shifts most of the infrastructure burden from the medical entity to the ASP and reduces the initial cost of implementing an EHR system. In-house data storage requires that the medical provider own and maintain a server, which can be costly, but provides more control over the data. Since an ASP houses the EHR system offsite, the data is also stored remotely, and the medical provider is reliant on Internet connectivity and a third-party to securely store their data and prevent unauthorized access. Additionally, this limits the liability of the healthcare provider by transferring the risk inherent in maintaining secure data storage to the ASP.

Some EHR systems provide functionality to selectively and automatically upload anonymized

Figure 1. Health information flow, originating from the patient

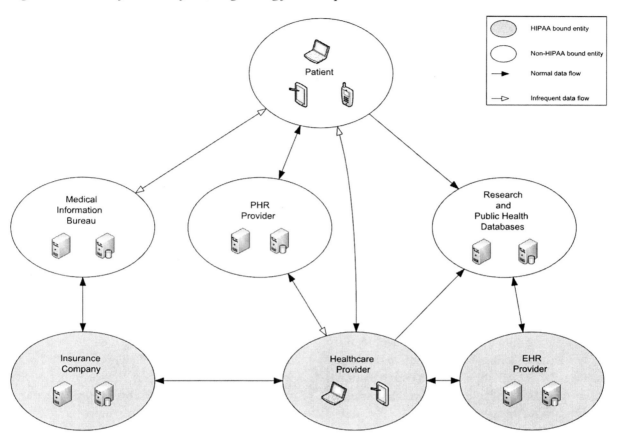

data to a central repository for large research studies. This collection of data can then be used by research organizations to study conditions across large patient populations. Providing this data to researchers can be immensely helpful when studying diseases and developing new treatment plans, but can cause major privacy concerns if the anonymized data can somehow be re-linked to an individual patient.

The benefits of EHR systems are many. Immediate and simultaneous access of a patient's record by multiple constituents in a healthcare environment is chief among them. Ideally, all medical professionals providing care to a patient would have access to all patient notes, treatment plans and test results. The net effect of this pervasive and instantaneous access to medical data is end-to-end transparency about a patient and ultimately superior healthcare. The accuracy and quality of information is improved by eliminating hand-written notes in a paper chart and providing the means to verify information in real time. Quality of care is also enhanced where EHR systems provide point-of-care decision support by integrating evidence-based clinical guidelines. A canonical example of these benefits is an EHR application that alerts a physician to potentially dangerous drug interactions as they are prescribing a new medication to a patient.

However, the move to EHR systems poses heightened challenges in maintaining patient privacy as compared to traditional paper systems. Greater access to digital medical records increases the threat to patient privacy. Patient records can be copied from remote locations and distributed at the speed of light. Moreover, EHR systems facilitate sharing a much richer collection of information about a patient, including medical images. Data entry in EHR systems is performed by medical clerical staff, lab technicians, nurses, physician assistants, and physicians. This means that a wider set of medical personnel could have access to stored medical images in an EHR, and not just the physician that initially requested them.

Because of this, EHR systems must track who accesses the patient record and what changes they make. The US Department of Health and Human Services mandates that change tracking criteria, termed *access control*, must be utilized and requires that the EHR "assign a unique name and/or number for identifying and tracking user identity and establish controls that permit only authorized users to access electronic health information" (2010). Being able to track changes and identify the individual making these changes in electronic health records is an improvement over traditional paper records because it removes the burden of logging from employees.

HIPAA

Health information in the United States is subject to regulation under the Health Insurance Portability and Accountability Act (HIPAA) of 1996 as determined by the Department of Health and Human Services (2009). In 2003, the HIPAA Privacy Rule and HIPAA Security Rule were enacted to supplement HIPAA and establish national standards for the protection and security of specified health information. The Privacy Rule is focused on formalizing national security standards to protect what has been identified by HIPAA as PHI. The Security Rule focuses on national security standards to protect all electronic PHI that is created, maintained, and transmitted in digital form.

HIPAA requires that a single person assume responsibility for a covered entity's electronic PHI. A thorough risk assessment must be conducted by each medical entity. Regular review and revision of security policies, procedures, and decisions are also required (Scholl, et al., 2008). In addition to these regularly scheduled reviews, a new risk assessment should also be performed when a medical entity implements large-scale changes, such as the transition to an EHR system. It is recommended that these policies are updated to address the changing landscape of medical data storage, especially considering that medical images are now digitized and included in the patient's EHR.

From a patient's perspective, HIPAA compliance consists of acknowledging, by signing a waiver, that they have received the privacy practices of the medical entity treating them. In some cases this waiver can also ask the patient to waive certain rights concerning the privacy of their medical information. In practice, to stress the importance of HIPAA compliance, most health care providers require medical employee training that highlights the importance of abiding by HIPAA in such areas as not sharing information with persons not directly associated with caring for a patient or by having medical professionals logout of any programs containing patient information before leaving their workstation.

An interesting wrinkle within the legal realm of health information is that third-party companies storing medical information on behalf of patients are not held accountable under HIPAA legislation. Third-party services including Microsoft HealthVault and Google Health are able to bypass HIPAA regulations via a contract with the patient to store their medical data (Office of Civil Rights, 2008). Many of these online health storage sites can directly interact with medical entities to share patient data, but only at the request of the patient.

Figure 2. Re-linkage. Adapted from (Ohm, 2010; Sweeney, 2002).

DICOM Image Database (DICOM Tag)			
Occupation (0010,2180)	Birth Date (0010,0030)	Gender (0010,0040)	Address (zip code) (0010,1040)
Nurse	1959	M	75287
Welder	1966	F	75335
Entrepreneur	1966	F	75074
Firefighter	1955	M	75261
Auditor	1978	M	75261

Name	Birth Date	Gender	Zip Code	Diagnosis
Andrew	01/06/1953	M	75038	Concussion
Alice	08/29/1978	F	75240	Bronchitis
Katie	04/18/1966	F	75074	Sprained ankle
Ben	06/04/1982	M	75038	Asthma

Patient Name	Occupation	Birth Date	Gender	Zip Code	Diagnosis
Katie	Entrepreneur	04/18/1966	F	75074	Sprained ankle

HEALTH INFORMATION PRIVACY

De-Identified and Anonymous Data

Preserving patient privacy relies on processes to sanitize or hide elements of medical and personal data. This process of anonymization is intended to produce a dataset that meets the de-identification requirements of HIPAA. Even tightly controlled de-identified data can be used to link and re-identify the patient.

Re-linkage can occur when multiple versions of the same data are distributed with different elements of PHI. This is made possible by connecting entries from one table to those in another by matching shared information in multiple tables. Consider the simple example in Figure 2, where the two tables on the left represent distinct image data sets, each containing minimal patient information. The top-left table is derived from an image database and includes occupation and the medical images but does not include medical diagnoses, while the bottom-left table contains names and diagnoses. The overlapping identifiers (birth year, gender, and zip code) are used to construct a new table that reveals more information than either table by itself, as demonstrated by the single record on the right that links Katie to a more specific birth date, occupation, and diagnosis, as well as revealing her image. Constructing multiple tables for data sharing may seem advantageous because of the ability to include only relevant data, but this can have the opposite effect by hiding potential privacy breaches.

A *de-identified* dataset under the HIPAA Privacy Rule can be distributed and used without any restrictions. Data is considered de-identified when:

1. A formal determination is made by a qualified statistician, or
2. The removal of specified identifiers of the individual and of the individual's relatives, household members, and employers is required, and is adequate only if the covered entity has no actual knowledge that the remaining information could be used to identify the individual (Office of Civil Rights, 2008).

The eighteen identifiers designated by HIPAA as PHI are listed in Table 1 (Office of Civil Rights, 2008). The removal of these identifiers qualifies a data set as de-identified, but this list is open to interpretation, particularly with the addition of (R), a catch-all identifier.

The notion of *anonymization* is not as well defined. Truly anonymous data should be com-

Table 1. HIPAA-defined PHI

A. Names
B. All geographic subdivisions smaller than a state…except for the three digits of a zip code
C. All elements of dates (except year) for dates directly related to the individual
D. Telephone numbers
E. Fax numbers
F. Email addresses
G. Social security numbers
H. Medical record numbers
I. Health plan beneficiary numbers
J. Account numbers
K. Certificate/license numbers
L. Vehicle identifiers and serial numbers, including license plate numbers
M. Device identifiers and serial numbers
N. URLs
O. IP addresses
P. Biometric identifiers, including finger and voice prints
Q. Full face photographic images and any comparable images
R. Any other unique identifying number, characteristic or code

pletely unable to be re-identified; however, in practice, it is often the case that what passes for anonymity lies somewhere in between true anonymity and some acceptable potential for re-identification. This creates an environment in which patients are misled to believe their data is protected while circumventing the underlying issue: PHI often contains relevant and necessary information. The de-identification and anonymization problems ostensibly only apply to publicly available or shared datasets; perhaps a more likely scenario is information leakage by insiders who have access to the full datasets. Still, the process of de-identification is useful and when applied correctly can protect a patient's identity.

It has been stated that "data can either be useful or perfectly anonymous but never both" (Ohm, 2010). The delicate balance between usefulness and anonymity demands that the healthcare industry strive for anonymity through de-identification. Quantifying an acceptable level is a difficult challenge. HIPAA offers little guidance on the subject,

other than requiring the removal of zip codes with fewer than 20,000 people and ages over 89. It does not, however, establish restrictions on small populations, such as those whose rare conditions may increase the risk of re-identification.

The inclusion of medical images and their metadata poses new threats to privacy that compel re-evaluation of the terms de-identified and anonymization. Medical images can be exploited in several ways: (1) they may reveal something private about the patient's condition, (2) they may be used to link the patient to other private data, (3) their existence may be used to infer something about the patient, and (4) they may be used to identify a patient. Due to their size, medical images are often stored in a manner different from other patient data, requiring separate access control and audit mechanisms. Many of the solutions that have been implemented to protect privacy in structured records also extend to medical images; however, the distinct nature of medical images requires careful consideration beyond traditional privacy practices, particularly because they are semi-structured attributes. Metadata can be anonymized by simply removing the attribute or replacing it with dummy data, but the images themselves cannot be easily anonymized in this manner.

Retaining the usefulness of the dataset is a more difficult problem in de-identifying medical images. The relevant data can be an inherent threat to privacy, as in neuroimages or those with a distinct feature. It is unlikely that a single x-ray of the hand can uniquely identify a patient without the presence of metadata, yet high resolution neuroimages are comparable to a full face photographic image (item Q in HIPAA's eighteen identifiers). For neuroimages to meet de-identification requirements, it is therefore necessary to remove enough of the facial features so that facial reconstruction cannot be sufficiently performed.

The Expanding Reach of PHI

Traditional healthcare providers, health systems, health plans, and healthcare clearinghouses are expected to strictly adhere to HIPAA to ensure that patient privacy is always preserved. This becomes especially important with regard to medical images because they are often stored in a different format and attached to the electronic health record.

There also exist companies storing medical data that are not bound by HIPAA. These companies enter into an agreement with the patient to store data on their behalf. Eliminating the healthcare provider from this agreement means that the third-party company does not have to adhere to HIPAA regulations. The main problem with this scenario is that patients are often not aware of this distinction and assume that any company storing medical data is regulated by HIPAA. Privacy issues can arise if the third-party company does not clearly state how the data is stored or who has access to this data.

An emerging trend in electronic health records is patients assuming an active role as participants in tracking their medical information. Patient involvement can take several forms. The first and most basic form consists of the patient accessing a healthcare provider's system to review their medical history. In some systems the patient can make additions to their records. Another way for patients to take charge of their medical information is by using a third-party personal health record (PHR). A PHR differs from traditional EHR in that PHRs are initiated by the patient and not a medical professional. By using a PHR, the patient can choose what information will be stored and permit healthcare providers or even friends to view or upload data.

One of the primary benefits of PHRs is the ability to perform large-scale analyses. While the need to remove traditional identifiers such as the patient's name may be obvious, other metadata could potentially be utilized to re-identify the patient. Fields such as the healthcare provider's name or date of service can contribute to re-identification. Furthermore, the issue becomes even more clouded when dealing with medical images. With neuroimages that contain a likeness of the patient, de-identification becomes a much more difficult task than simply omitting accompanying data because the identifying attributes are embedded in the image itself.

Most PHR systems allow healthcare providers to view the patient's records if the patient has given permission for them to do so. They may even be able to download information directly into their EHR system. In most cases, providers are also allowed to upload data to the personal health record with the patient's permission. This enables the patient to view their records and make it available to other medical professionals.

These advances have empowered the patient to maintain a more thorough health record for themselves. With patient consent, this enables authorized physicians to utilize knowledge of concurrent treatment plans, so as not to suggest a contraindicative treatment. A downside to this approach is that the patient could alter the records uploaded by a healthcare provider, thus compromising the integrity of the data. Any modification, omission, or deletion, accidental or otherwise, could contribute to an inaccurate picture of the patient's health.

Online health registries also fall into the category of third-party, non-HIPAA compliant businesses that handle medical data. These companies traditionally elicit the subject's participation by having them fill out a survey about their medical history. This data is then reviewed by researchers to determine if a subject matches the criteria to be involved in an upcoming study, at which point they would be contacted and asked to participate. Often these registries apply for a Certificate of Confidentiality from the National Institute of Health as is the case with the Kentucky Women's Health Registry (Center for the Advancement of Women's Health, 2009) and the Illinois Women's Health Registry at Northwestern University (Institute for Women's Health Research, 2008).

Public health registries are not bound by HIPAA. Interestingly, HIPAA-bound medical entities may give protected patient information to a health registry without the patient's explicit consent. In the particular case of immunization registries, this is due to the fact that "public health authorities operate most registries in the country, and state laws mandate or allow the sharing of immunization data" (Minnesota Department of Health, 2010). Since the registries themselves are not bound by HIPAA they can then disseminate this information as they choose. While these registries may be bound by data use agreements that prohibit re-identification, voluntarily adherence to HIPAA regulations is encouraged. This serves as a baseline for privacy standards and may provide clarity on how patient data is handled.

Businesses that do not specifically handle medical data need to be aware of the possibility that their network could be transmitting or storing medical data, and they could potentially be held liable for breaches or misuse of the data. This incidental access to patient data can occur when an employee uses company email to communicate with their doctor's office about appointments or even discuss treatment plans. While the company may have a 'no personal use' email policy, this does not ensure compliance. In this instance, the very mention of a doctor's name could imply what kind of treatment the employee is seeking. Consider the example where an email mentions a well-known oncologist for treating tumors of the female reproductive system. The mere existence of this knowledge within a company's network could compromise the privacy of the individual if a coworker were to infer that they have cancer.

An employer may also be privy to protected health information when they provide a group health plan or membership in a personal health record service. The employer may provide incentives or rebates in exchange for voluntary enrollment and participation in employer-sponsored programs such as smoking-cessation, preventative maintenance, or personal fitness plans. Enrollment and utilization information could reveal medical conditions or general health information about which the employer would not have otherwise known. Also, it is possible for a company offering a group insurance policy to receive "'summary' information to use to obtain premium bids or changes in coverage" (Privacy Rights Clearinghouse, 2010). This may give the employer a general idea of the collective health status of their employees. If this summary contains a medical anomaly, it could be possible to narrow down the employee that may have this condition, breaching the privacy of the employee.

Medical Images

As the ability to store and process medical image data increases and the cost of implementation decreases, the need to consider the privacy implications of doing so becomes more pressing. Medical images face many of the same privacy challenges that plague EHR, but the semi-structured nature of image data introduces new problems. While metadata can provide a wealth of information about the patient, the images themselves can also pose a direct threat to patient privacy and cannot be as easily de-identified.

Medical images are generated by a wide range of modalities, including magnetic resonance imaging (MRI), computed tomography (CT), and x-rays for structural images, and positron emission tomography (PET) and functional MRI (fMRI) for functional images. Others like electroencephalography (EEG) may not result in an image in the traditional sense but still produce structural or functional data that can be considered an image. The anatomical scope of medical images can also vary widely, ranging from highly localized at the cellular level to full body scans, each encumbering its own set of privacy risks, such as the potential to reveal a condition or to be used to re-identify the patient. Images are often accompanied by metadata, such as acquisition parameters or patient name, address, birthdate, and other identifying information.

Most imaging modalities require specialized equipment and thus enjoy mature standards for handling, storing, and transmitting images. However, medical images can also include photographs. The ubiquity of digital cameras and camera-enabled cell phones makes creating and sharing medical images a nearly effortless task but also introduces new privacy risks. Policies and workflows for obtaining, storing, and transmitting photographs may not be as tightly controlled as those for medical images requiring specialized equipment. For example, digital photographs are commonly stored on flash memory in cameras and transmitted via email.

Most medical images cannot be easily linked to a specific individual if accompanying patient data is removed. However, not all channels over which medical images are transmitted require patient data to be removed, and removing patient data will not ensure anonymization for some images, such as structural neuroimages, that are inherently identifiable.

A direct threat to privacy is the data gleaned from the medical image itself. An anomaly or feature in an image could be used to re-identify the patient, or the image may simply reveal a condition or diagnosis. This case applies to all entities that store medical images.

Perhaps the most common scenario is the linkage problem in which anonymized medical data can be used in conjunction with other data to re-identify a patient. A specific example of re-linkage occurred when anonymized data from the Massachusetts Group Insurance Commission (GIC) were linked to voter registration lists (Sweeney, 2002). Using the overlapping fields (birth date, zip code, and sex), the medical records of the Massachusetts governor were identified.

Another incident exploited the rarity of a medical diagnosis to dispute a patient's claim (Najera, 2009; Novella, 2009). The patient had announced their case to the media, disclosing gender, age range, geographic region, and a general timeline. Members of the scientific community doubted the diagnosis and used these details to find the particular entry in the Vaccine Adverse Event Report System, a publicly available sanitized data set maintained by the Centers for Disease Control and Prevention. In this case, fields designated as non-personally identifiable information (non-PII) were used to identify the entry from a list already shortened to those mentioning the rare disorder. The overlapping data used in both of these cases is commonly found as attributes in medical images.

A third exploit of medical images may also disclose a condition or diagnosis through the very existence of an image. This occurs frequently in professional sports. In 2010, Mike Shanahan, head coach for the Washington Redskins announced that player Albert Haynesworth would undergo an MRI on his knee, kicking off a flurry of speculation by fans and media of injuries (Associated Press, 2010; Reid, 2010). Ultimately, the MRI showed no structural damage, but the mere existence of the image erroneously implied that Haynesworth had been injured, an assumption that could have serious consequences on his NFL career.

In some cases, medical images can be inherently identifying. For example, high resolution neuroimages such as MRI contain detailed facial features that can be rendered into an approximation of the patient's likeness. The approximation could then be used to identify or confirm the identity of a patient by visual or automated recognition. Figure 3 is a facial approximation generated using 3D Slicer (2010), a freely available software tool for visualization and analysis of medical images. The result is a 3D image that is clearly recognizable as a human face.

The HIPAA Privacy Rule specifies that "full face photographic and any comparable images" are protected health information (PHI). Approximations like the one shown above should be considered comparable to full face images. The argument has been made that facial recognition technology is unreliable, especially when lighting conditions and viewing angles are inconsistent (Zhao, Chellappa, Phillips, & Rosenfeld, 2003), and these challenges extend to recognition of the MRI approximation as well. However, because MRI scans can produce an image that is instantly recognizable as a face, they are comparable to full face photographs and should arguably be treated as such. The potential for re-identification should be a significant concern to healthcare providers that share data with centralized repositories and to institutions that share data for research purposes.

It has been stated that the images alone are not PII. This is based on the notion that the technology is not sophisticated enough to recognize a patient with absolute certainty. This argument is founded on two shaky assumptions: (1) the current technology will never improve, and (2) only correct identifications pose a risk to patient privacy.

As facial reconstruction and facial recognition techniques improve, so do the means for re-identification. Likewise, as storage capacity

Figure 3. Facial approximation from MRI using 3D Slicer

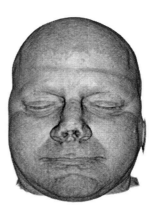

expands, it will be possible to maintain databases of faces for a larger number of patients, with higher resolution, resulting in more comprehensive and accurate matching. Furthermore, digital reconstruction offers the ability to alter lighting conditions and viewing angle of the patient, two factors that play an important role in the performance of facial recognition techniques. As processing power and storage grow, a virtually endless number and variety of approximations can be generated and used to match an image to a patient.

The second assumption relies on the ability to correctly identify a patient. However, identification from medical images does not need to be completely accurate to breach the patient's privacy. The perception that facial reconstruction and recognition are reliable and proven technologies gives more weight to identification from medical images than metadata alone. If a patient is incorrectly re-identified, a condition or diagnosis may be falsely assumed.

Healthcare providers and research organizations alike must carefully consider privacy concerns regarding medical images. Research organizations that may not be subject to HIPAA must also take into account the implications of re-identification, particularly when dealing with a small subset of the population. This is a concern when handling studies with few subjects or those that focus on rare disorders. Furthermore, an individual's participation in a study may suggest a certain condition, even if they are a member of the control group.

SOLUTIONS AND RECOMMENDATIONS

The rapidly changing landscape of health information technology has the potential to transform healthcare for both the patient and the provider. However, the ability to easily upload, access, and share one's medical data demands consideration of the privacy risk of doing so. As the healthcare industry embraces EHR systems, technology, policies, and practices must evolve to ensure patient privacy.

Third-party storage sites for medical and image data should comply with regulations similar to those followed by institutions that manage medical data. Therefore, complementary legislation could be enacted to cover entities that deal with medical data but are exempt from HIPAA, namely PHR providers. In addition, all businesses should create an internal policy to handle incidental or unintended exposure to medical information that outlines proper steps for reporting, containing, and correcting the incident.

These policy solutions will not positively impact businesses unless standards exist to bridge the gap between policies and their implementation. Standards to enforce and supplement policy must evolve with technology to address changing privacy needs and the increasing ability to exploit medical data. Also, the development and implementation of proper workflow management will allow researchers, scientists, and medical professionals to easily interact with data in a structured manner.

Businesses should develop an information security baseline that includes security controls to mitigate the threat of a data breach and accompanying legal consequences. Risk assessments should be performed regularly with thorough documentation of all updates and changes. Every company should have employee training regarding the hazards of storing and transmitting personal medical information on company resources. A written company policy regarding resources and personal use should be signed by every employee to illustrate the importance of keeping this information out of the workplace.

Healthcare providers must protect patient privacy by properly de-identifying data before releasing it to any group for research purposes. This may require enlisting the help of an outside party that is well-versed in privacy legislation. It would be prudent to develop one anonymized version of each data set that is available for requesting researchers. This prevents aggregation by re-linking multiple de-identified data sets to recreate the original data.

Businesses not subject to HIPAA that regularly handle medical data are encouraged to voluntarily adhere to HIPAA. This will help protect and maintain the privacy of customers and could protect the company against any threats of legal action regarding the use and storage of private information.

An important component in maintaining the privacy of electronic medical data is patient education. At the most basic level, for example, medical entities should encourage patients not to share passwords used to access healthcare-provided health records. PHR providers should educate users about the differences between an EHR and PHR and any inherent risks associated with using a PHR. All individuals should be knowledgeable about where and how their medical information is being used and stored and the privacy policies covering their data. The patient must also be aware of what networks their information is traversing.

Policy and legislation must complement technology initiatives in protecting the privacy of medical images. Two major contributions would include a step-by-step process for de-identifying unstructured data, including each major category

Figure 4. Reconstruction after skull stripping (left) and defacing (right)

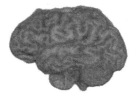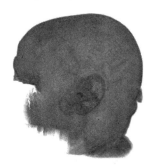

of images, and a new policy that addresses privacy in all of the existing technologies and the images produced. Such a policy would be updated regularly to adapt to privacy needs as the context of medical images evolves. In accordance with HIPAA, individual organizations should develop an internal, standardized policy to ensure that unstructured data and medical images are managed in a consistent manner.

Neuroimages are a special case in which the pixel data itself is inherently identifiable and should be removed prior to data sharing. Two approaches most commonly used for neuroimage de-identification are skull stripping and defacing, shown in Figure 4. *Skull stripping* refers to the process of removing all non-brain tissue, leaving only the brain volume behind. The second approach, *defacing*, is a more conservative alternative that identifies facial features, removing only the voxels (three-dimensional pixels) that are labeled as face and have zero probability of being brain tissue (Bischoff-Grethe, et al., 2007). These two techniques satisfy the removal of item Q (comparable full face photographic images) according to HIPAA.

After de-identification, the remaining brain volume is still not guaranteed to be anonymous. Removing metadata from image headers is a fairly straightforward process that can help mitigate this issue. By identifying the offending fields, the data can be removed or replaced with dummy values. Tools such as the LONI De-identification

Debabelet (LONI De-identification Debabelet, 2005) and DICOMBrowser (DICOM Browser, 2010) can guide the metadata de-identification process. However, such tools should be considered a first pass at de-identification and should be verified before data sharing to ensure that other fields do not contain PHI.

When coupled with skull stripping or defacing for neuroimages, metadata removal can provide a sufficient layer of privacy when sharing data for research purposes. It does not, however, address privacy in EHRs where identifiability is inherent (personal use) or necessary (clinical use). In these cases, educating both the patient and healthcare personnel as to the privacy threats and how to avoid data breaches is critical to retaining both the usefulness of the data and the privacy of the patient.

CONCLUSION

The use of electronic health records is ushering in dramatic changes to healthcare. Along with opportunities for improved quality of care and better economies of scale come heightened threats to patient privacy. This is supremely evident in the medical imaging arena, where the data itself is inherently identifiable information.

As governments and the healthcare industry try to keep pace with these changes, technological innovations and phenomena such as cloud computing and mobile networking introduce confounding elements to the equation. Many of these developments place the responsibility and power of medical record management in the hands of the patient. Thus, personal health record (PHR) service providers and even businesses with no apparent connection to healthcare can now find themselves inextricably connected to medical records.

The potential for re-identification, identity linkage through inference, or even diagnostic association represents a unique challenge for handling medical images. Solutions must be developed that combine technology, policy, practice and education to effectively deal with these challenges in an ever-evolving landscape.

REFERENCES

Answers, H. I. T. E. C. H. (2010). *About the HI-TECH Act*. Retrieved September 10, 2010, from http://www.hitechanswers.net/about/about-the-hitech-act-of-2009/

Associated Press. (2010, August 5). *Albert Haynesworth to have MRI*. Retrieved October 22, 2010, from http://sports.espn.go.com/nfl/trainingcamp10 /news/story?id=5439254

Bischoff-Grethe, A., Ozyurt, I. B., Busa, E., Quinn, B. T., Fennema-Notestine, C., & Clark, C. P. (2007, September). A technique for the deidentification of structural brain MR images. *Human Brain Mapping, 28*(9), 892–903. doi:10.1002/hbm.20312

CDC. (2009, September 1). *Classification of diseases, functioning, and disability*. Retrieved October 14, 2010, from http://www.cdc.gov/nchs/icd/icd9.htm

Center for the Advancement of Women's Health. (2009, December 9). *Kentucky women's health registry*. Retrieved October 16, 2010, from https://www.mc.uky.edu/kyhealthregistry/ default.asp

Department of Health and Human Services. (2010, July 28). Health information technology: Initial set of standards, implementation specifications, and certification criteria for electronic health record technology; Final Rule. *45 CFR Part 170* [US Department Of Health And Human Services, Centers for Medicare & Medicaid Services.]. *Federal Register, 75*(144), 44590–44654.

Fennema-Notestine, C., Ozyurt, I. B., Clark, C. P., Morris, S., Bischoff-Grethe, A., & Bondi, M. W. (2006, February). Quantitative evaluation of automated skull-stripping methods applied to contemporary and legacy images: Effects of diagnosis, bias correction, and slice location. *Human Brain Mapping, 27*(2), 99–113. doi:10.1002/hbm.20161

Group, M. I. B. Inc. (2010). *About MIB Group*. Retrieved November 3, 2010, from http://www.mib.com/html/about_mib_group.html

Group, M. I. B. Inc. (2010). *Consumer guide*. Retrieved November 3, 2010, from http://www.mib.com/html/consumer_guide.html

HIMSS. (2010). *Electronic health record*. Retrieved October 1, 2010, from http://www.himss.org/ASP/topics_ehr.asp

ICD9Data.com. (2009). *Free searchable ICD-9-CM diagnosis codes*. Retrieved October 14, 2010, from http://www.icd9data.com/2009/Volume1/800-999/940-949/944/944.08.htm

Institute for Women's Health Research. (2008). *Illinois women's health registry*. Retrieved October 16, 2010, from https://whr.northwestern.edu/

Kolata, G. (2010, August 12). Rare sharing of data leads to progress on Alzheimer's. *New York Times*.

Minnesota Department of Health. (2010, July 22). *Disclosure to public health under the HIPAA privacy rule*. Retrieved October 16, 2010, from http://www.health.state.mn.us/divs/idepc/ immunize/registry/hipaa.html

Mueller, S. G., Weiner, M. W., Thal, L. J., Petersen, R. C., Jack, C., & Jagust, W. (2005, November). The Alzheimer's disease neuroimaging initiative. *Neuroimaging Clinics of North America, 15*(4), 869–877. doi:10.1016/j.nic.2005.09.008

Najera, R. (2009, November 4). *Records show case of dystonia is psychogenic and not related to flu vaccine.* Retrieved October 13, 2010, from http://www.examiner.com/disease-prevention-in-baltimore/records-show-case-of-dystonia-is-psychogenic-and-not-related-to-flu-vaccine

National Health Statistics Group. (2010, October 28). *National health expenditure data.* Retrieved November 6, 2010, from http://www.cms.gov/NationalHealthExpendData/02_NationalHealthAccountsHistorical.asp

NEMA. (2009). *The DICOM standard.* Retrieved October 14, 2010, from ftp://medical.nema.org/medical/dicom/2009/

Novella, S. (2009, October 30). *The dystonia flu shot case.* Retrieved October 12, 2010, from http://theness.com/neurologicablog/?p=1152

Office of Civil Rights. (2008, December 15). *Personal health records and the HIPAA privacy rule.* Retrieved September 6, 2010, from http://www.hhs.gov/ocr/privacy/hipaa/ understanding/special/healthit/phrs.pdf

Office of Civil Rights. (2008, May 7). *Summary of the HIPAA privacy rule.* Retrieved October 18, 2010, from http://www.hhs.gov/ocr/privacy/hipaa/ understanding/summary/index.html

Ohm, P. (2010). Broken promises of privacy: Responding to the surprising failure of anonymization. *UCLA Law Review. University of California, Los Angeles. School of Law, 57,* 1701–1776.

Privacy Rights Clearinghouse. (2010, September). *Fact sheet 8a: HIPAA basics: Medical privacy in the electronic age.* Retrieved October 17, 2010, from http://www.privacyrights.org/fs/fs8a-hipaa.htm

Reid, J. (2010, August 5). *Redskins insider.* Retrieved October 22, 2010, from http://voices.washingtonpost.com/ redskinsinsider/3-4-defense/shanahan-albert-haynesworth-to.html

Scholl, M., Stine, K., Hash, J., Bowen, P., Johnson, A., Smith, C. D., et al. (2008, October). An introductory resource guide for implementing the health insurance portability and accountability act (HIPAA) security rule. *NIST Special Publication 800-66 Revision 1.* National Institute of Standards and Technology. US Department of Commerce.

3D Slicer. (2010). Retrieved October 13, 2010, from http://slicer.org/

Sweeney, L. (2002). k-anonymity: A model for protecting privacy. *International Journal on Uncertainty, Fuzziness and Knowledge-based Systems, 10*(5), 557–570. doi:10.1142/S0218488502001648

US Department of Health & Human Services. (2009). *Health information privacy.* Retrieved October 14, 2010, from HHS.gov: http://www.hhs.gov/ocr/privacy/

Zhao, W., Chellappa, R., Phillips, P. J., & Rosenfeld, A. (2003). Face recognition: A literature survey. *ACM Computing Surveys, 35*(4), 399–458. doi:10.1145/954339.954342

ADDITIONAL READING

Aalseth. (2006). Medical Coding: What It Is and How It Works. Sudbury: Jones and Bartlett.

American Medical Association. (2009, February 20). H.R. 1, the "American Recovery and Reinvestment Act of 2009". Retrieved October 22, 2010, from http://www.ama-assn.org/ama1/pub/upload/mm/399/arra-hit-provisions.pdf

An, J., Ranji, U., & Salganicoff, A. (2008). Health Information Technology. Retrieved November 8, 2010, from KaiserEDU.org: http://www.kaiseredu.org/Issue-Modules/Health-Information-Technology/Background-Brief.aspx

Cannon, J. (2005). *Privacy: What Developers and IT Professionals Should Know*. Boston: Addison-Wesley.

Centers for Medicare & Medicaid Services. (2010). Personal Health Records (PHR). Retrieved November 9, 2010, from Medicare.gov: http://www.medicare.gov/navigation/manage-your-health/personal-health-records/personal-health-records-overview.aspx

Commission on Systemic Interoperability. (2005). Ending the Document Game: Connecting and Transforming Your Healthcare Through Information Technology. Retrieved November 5, 2010, from http://endingthedocumentgame.gov/PDFs/entireReport.pdf

Dolan, P. L. (2008, October 13). Is your EMR legal? A document can look like a medical record, but not meet the legal definition. Retrieved October 18, 2010, from American Medical Association: http://www.ama-assn.org/amednews/2008/10/13/bisa1013.htm

eCast: Metrics in Medicine. (2008, November 18). A White Paper on EHR Data Supporting Pharmacovigilance Studies. Retrieved November 8, 2010, from http://www.ecastcorp.com/Downloads/WhitePaper-EHRDatawithPharmacovigilanceStudies.pdf

Federal Trade Commission. (1995, June 21). Nation's Largest Insurance Reporting Agency Agrees To Expand Consumer Rights. Retrieved November 9, 2010, from Federal Trade Commission: http://www.ftc.gov/opa/1995/06/mib.shtm

Garfinkel, S. (2000). *Database Nation: The Death of Privacy in the 21st Century*. Sebastopol: O'Reilly & Associates, Inc.

Hogan, W., & Wagner, M. (1996). Free-Text Fields Change the Meaning of Coded Data. American Medical Informatics Association, 517-521.

Howell, C. (2009, February 19). Stimulus package contains $19 billion for health care technology spending and adoption of electronic health records. Retrieved November 1, 2010, from http://wistechnology.com/articles/5523/

Johnson, M. E. (2009). Data Hemorrhages in the Health-Care Sector. In R. Dingledine, & P. Golle (Eds.), Financial Cryptography and Data Security (Vol. 5628, pp. 71-89). Springer Berlin / Heidelberg.

Johnson, S. B., Bakken, S., Dine, D., Hyun, S., Mendonca, E., Morrison, F., et al. (2008). An Electronic Health Record Based on Structured Narrative. Retrieved October 1, 2010, from Journal of the American Medical Informatics Association: http://www.ncbi.nlm.nih.gov/pmc/articles/PMC2274868/

Liu, J., Erdal, S., Silvey, S., Ding, J., Riedel, J., Marsh, C., et al. (2009). Toward a Fully De-identified Biomedical Information Warehouse. AMIA Annual Symposium (pp. 370-374). San Francisco: PubMed Central.

Medical Information Reporting Standards Trust (MIRST). (2009, July 22). Who is the Medical Information Bureau? Retrieved November 9, 2010, from mirst.org: http://www.mirst.org/howto-request-medical-report/whois-mib-inc/

Meystre, S., Friedlin, J., South, B., Shen, S., & Samore, M. (2010). Automatic de-identification of textual documents in the electronic health record: a review of recent research. Retrieved October 2, 2010, from BMC Medical Research Methodology: http://www.ncbi.nlm.nih.gov/pmc/articles/PMC2923159/

MITRE Corporation. (2006). Electronic Health Records Overview. Retrieved November 5, 2010, from National Institutes of Health National Center for Research Resources: http://www.ncrr.nih.gov/publications/informatics/ehr.pdf

Newton, E. M., Sweeney, L., & Malin, B. (2005). Preserving privacy by de-identifying face images. *IEEE Transactions on Knowledge and Data Engineering*, 232–243. doi:10.1109/TKDE.2005.32

Ohm, P. (2010). Broken Promises of Privacy: Responding to the Surprising Failure of Anonymization. *UCLA Law Review. University of California, Los Angeles. School of Law, 57*, 1701–1776.

Rowley, M. D. R. (2009, September 25). Medical Data in the Internet "Cloud" - Data Privacy. Retrieved November 9, 2010, from Healthcare IT News: http://www.healthcareitnews.com/blog/medical-data-internet-"cloud"-data-privacy

Sarathy, S., & Muralidhar, K. (2002). The Security of Confidential Numerical Data in Databases. *Information Systems Research, 13*(4), 389–403. doi:10.1287/isre.13.4.389.74

U.S. Department of Health & Human Services. (2010). Health Information Privacy: Summary of the HIPAA Security Rule. Retrieved from U.S. Department of Health & Human Services: http://www.hhs.gov/ocr/privacy/hipaa/understanding/srsummary.html

Van Horn, J. D., & Toga, A. W. (2009). Is it time to re-prioritize neuroimaging databases and digital repositories? *NeuroImage, 47*(4), 1720–1734. doi:10.1016/j.neuroimage.2009.03.086

Zetter, K. (2009, October 19). Medical Records: Stored in the Cloud, Sold on the Open Market. Retrieved November 3, 2010, from Wired: http://www.wired.com/threatlevel/2009/10/medical-records/

KEY TERMS AND DEFINITIONS

Anonymized Dataset: Data that contains no PHI and is unable to be re-linked to a patient.

De-Identified Dataset: Data with most PHI removed and that cannot be re-linked to a patient without outside information.

Defacing: An anonymization technique for neuroimages that removes facial features but leaves brain volume intact to prevent re-identification.

DICOM (Digital Imaging and Communications in Medicine): A standard for transmitting, storing, and processing medical images.

EHR (Electronic Health Record): Medical chart in electronic format.

HIPAA (Health Insurance Portability and Accountability Act): United States law that regulates the use of health information.

Medical Images: Images gathered in a clinical or research environment that relate to the health and well-being of the subject, including traditional medical imaging (such as x-ray, CT, MRI, ultrasound) and photography.

PHI (Protected Health Information): Information contained in a medical record that can be used to identify an individual patient as defined by HIPAA.

PII (Personally Identifiable Information): Information that can be used to identify a single individual.

Chapter 9
Privacy Protection Issues for Healthcare Wellness Clouds

Tyrone Grandison
IBM Thomas J. Watson Research Center, USA

Pei-yun S Hsueh
IBM Thomas J. Watson Research Center, USA

Liangzhao Zeng
IBM Thomas J. Watson Research Center, USA

Henry Chang
IBM Taiwan Corporation, Taiwan

Yi-Hui Chen
Asia University, Taiwan

Ci-Wei Lan
IBM Taiwan Corporation, Taiwan

Hao-Ting (Howard) Pai
National Chung Cheng University, Taiwan

Li-Feng Tseng
IBM Taiwan Corporation, Taiwan

ABSTRACT

Healthcare is ubiquitous in every business organization. Whether as the primary focus of the business or as a function of the well-being of a firm's employees, health issues play a dominant role in commerce. This recognition and the demonstrated benefits of a healthy contributor or worker have promoted a rejuvenated emphasis on wellness. In order to garner the benefits of cloud computing and foster improved employee health, the Taiwan Collaboratory is developing a first instance of a Wellness Cloud, which is an integrated, interconnected, and intelligent well-being platform. As the data held in this cloud is potentially very sensitive, the protection of this data is of utmost importance. In this chapter, we present issues and solutions for protecting user data while enabling the data to be usefully processed and for value to be derived, by using advanced technology and by harnessing the cumulative knowledge or wisdom of the collective of users.

DOI: 10.4018/978-1-61350-501-4.ch009

INTRODUCTION

Though there is no universally accepted definition of wellness (Baranowski, 1981; Savolaine & Granello, 2002), it is generally acknowledged that the abstract concept of wellness centers around *the active process of becoming aware of and making choices toward a more successful existence* (Mackey, 2000; Corbin & Pangrazi, 2001). Physical wellness involves the collection, analysis and presentation of actionable personal information over time in order to help patients prevent illness, positively manage current conditions, and make healthier choices.

There is a rich history of forwarding-thinking governments and enterprises that offer wellness incentive programs (Goetzel et.al., 1994; Maes, 1998; Ozminkowski et.al., 2002; Loong, 2009; Nakamura, 2010), such as smoking cessation rebates, weight management and fitness goal rewards. Unfortunately, the current set of wellness initiatives and tools are generally siloed solutions that are refreshed annually and are not integrated with other wellness and health management systems.

BACKGROUND

In late December 2009, the Taiwanese government embarked on a project to leverage novel technologies in addressing the wellness needs and desires of the people of Taiwan (Zane, 2009). Partnering with IBM, they established a collaboratory, which is a (virtual) laboratory where IBM researchers worldwide co-locate with local universities, government, or commercial partners to share skills, assets, and resources to achieve a common research goal (Nystedt, 2009).

The Taiwan Collaboratory utilizes cloud computing systems, remote monitoring technologies and advanced user interface techniques and methodologies to ingest and integrate large volumes of data on multiple aspects of the (current) condition of a citizen. This data is combined with the citizen's historical data to provide invaluable feedback to them on their continued progress towards their pre-specified goal or to help them recognize when they are on a path to unfavorable outcomes. The data is also securely leveraged with the data of others to perform advanced analytics in order to detect trends and insight that would have otherwise been undiscoverable.

As wellness is a sub-discipline of the broader healthcare domain that has only been examined and implemented as manual, human-intensive efforts, there are no comparable wellness software solutions with similar goals to the collaboratory. However, the closest Personal Health Record (PHR) systems that may be thought of as offering similar functionality are Microsoft HealthVault (http://www.healthvault.com), Google Health (http://www.google.com/health/) and Personal Care Connect (Blount et.al., 2007). Both Google Health and Microsoft HealthVault are healthcare information portals that allow patients to 1) consolidate their information from disparate data sources, 2) set personal health goals, 3) track their progress, 4) share their health information, and 5) enable the companies' partners to access patient data and provide services. Both systems do not support real-time monitoring of a patient's wellness state and the internal analysis and processing of incoming data for positive and negative trends. Additionally, the security and privacy safeguards utilized throughout their ecosystems are steeped in obscurity and supported by a trust model that is rooted in relying on the "goodness" of each company's brand. Personal Care Connect (PCC) is a standards-based, open solution that was developed by IBM to facilitate the remote monitoring of patients in order to provide timely access to a patient's health status. Though, PCC addresses the real-time monitoring deficiency of the previous two solutions, it still suffers from the lack of native advanced analytics and the opacity in privacy and security.

It should also be noted that all these systems must comply with legislative policy rules that stipulate privacy and security mandates. The Health Insurance Portability and Accountability Act (HIPAA, 1996) is the regulatory foundation in the United States. It establishes safeguards to protect the privacy of individually identifiable protected personal health information (PHI), sets limits and conditions on the uses and disclosures that may be made on PHI with and without patient authorization, and gives patients rights over their PHI. The Health Information Technology for Economic and Clinical Health Act (HITECH, 2009) and the healthcare-specific amendments in the American Reinvestment and Recovery Act (ARRA) has enhanced HIPAA over the last few years.

The construction of a Wellness Cloud is a bold instance of the building an integrated, interconnected and intelligent wellness care system that is focused on helping people with their personal wellness goals, the discourse in this chapter is meant to be instructive (not exhaustive or definitive) in the development and or use of similarly purposed systems. More specifically, the general focus of this work is to provide a blueprint for others on the privacy issues involved and the protection mechanisms that can be used to address these concerns.

WELLNESS CLOUD ISSUES

This undertaking requires an ecosystem of many stakeholders, from different backgrounds, with varying motivations, but with the same common purpose – to collaborate and use wellness information to make people better informed, and to improve and expand the services that can be offered by the system (or its constituent stakeholders). Some of the stakeholders in the Wellness Cloud include medical device manufacturers, fitness outlets, healthcare providers and government administrators. The insight harnessed from the amalgamation of the data acquired or generated by each partner is the most important value delivered

to the cloud's end-users. It is this value and the power of data compounding that is the driving force behind partners' decision to participate in this cloud.

However, as Personally Identifiable Information (PII) will be generated from each party, mechanisms are utilized to ensure the security and privacy of the information as it is communicated from the partner to the cloud and vice versa. Once, PHI is ingested into the Wellness Cloud, the information is transformed in order to be compliant with international standards for representing and storing healthcare data. Then, techniques are employed to ensure that data integration, data processing and analytics are performed in a privacy-preserving manner. When information is requested by a citizen or other stakeholders, policy-driven techniques for protecting the rendered information are used to ensure that there is a low probability of inadvertent information leakage.

In the chapter, we discuss all the areas of concern with regards to the privacy of information in the Wellness Cloud, and we provide an analysis of the best practices for protecting against these concerns; stating the approach employed by the Taiwan Collaboratory. As this effort is, at the core, a dynamic, virtual business organization constructed from multiple businesses, we envision that the issues and techniques presented will be applicable not only to this scenario, but to many other virtual business collaborations. As with all other systems, we start with a description of the core architectural components.

THE WELNESS CLOUD ARCHITECTURE

Enabling wellness management on a cloud system requires that particular (user) expectations must be axioms of the computing platform. Some of the more interesting expectations or requirements include mechanisms for personalization, native handling and management of events, support

Figure 1. GreenOlive cloud platform for wellness management

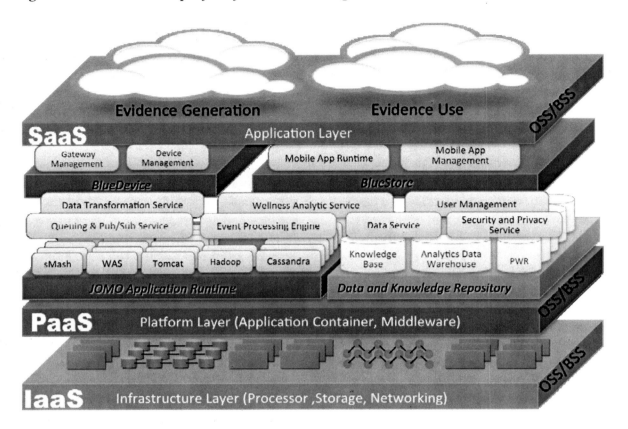

for dynamicity, and the ability to be scalable in a number of dimensions. These imperatives preclude the use of the current set of publicly available cloud platforms, such as the Amazon Web Service (Lerner, 2006), Eucalyptus (Nurmi, 2008) and Force.com (Tibken, 2010) for wellness management.

In order to tackle these challenges, the team developed the *GreenOlive* cloud platform (Figure 1), which consists of three layers:

1. Infrastructure Layer: this layer provides Infrastructure-as-a-Service (IaaS) for platform services. The infrastructure resource includes processing, storage and networking that are required by provisioning the platform services.

2. Platform Layer: this layer consists of an application runtime platform (codenamed JOMO), a collection of data & knowledge repositories, a collection of services that run on top of JOMO, and data & knowledge repositories. The services include queuing and publish-subscribe (hereafter referred to as pub-sub) services that provide communication channels among services; security and privacy services that ensure that user privacy is protected; data transformation services that transfer different data/event sources to a standard format; event processing services that manage events in real-time; data services that provide access to Application Programming Interfaces (APIs) for data and knowledge repository; user services that manage user information; and wellness analytic services

Figure 2. Standard data collection in a cloud

that generate new guidelines or new insights of existing guidelines for wellness management. It should be noted that each of the above services provide a set of open APIs that allow partners to develop new services or applications. On top of these services, two management services (i.e. BlueDevice and BlueStore) are created, wherein BlueDevice provides gateway and device management and BlueStore provides mobile application runtime and management services.

3. Application Layer: this layer adopts and implements the Software-as-a-Service (SaaS) paradigm to provision applications. These applications are developed using the open APIs on the platform layer. Further, the platform provides application composition or mashup mechanisms that enable multiple applications to form an ecosystem. This then enables the development of the novel offering of an Ecosystem-as-a-Service (EaaS). In particular, our solution focuses on two categories of application, i.e. evidence generation and evidence use. Evidence generation aims to generate new clinical evidence, guidelines and insights based on collected data in the cloud, while evidence use is concerned with the delivery of clinical knowledge to users, based on clinical context information.

The interested reader can peruse Hsueh, et.al. (2010) and Zeng et.al. (2010) for a more detailed description of the current and future states of the platform. Using our architectural discussion as a base, we proceed with a discussion of the protection issues involved in data collection, as data is transported and distributed within the cloud and when it is used.

PRIVACY PROTECTION IN DATA COLLECTION

Figure 2 shows the typical ingestion model for cloud computing systems. In the contemporary ingestion model, it is assumed that the information being sent to the cloud only needs to be safe-

Figure 3. Wellness cloud ingestion model

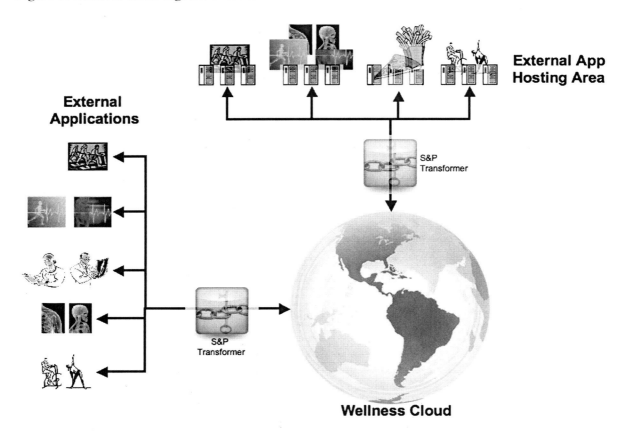

guarded once it enters the cloud. This assumption cannot be made for wellness management clouds, because wellness data typically have higher levels of sensitivity and significantly higher risk profiles.

There are a number of other privacy factors that highlight that the conventional cloud data collection paradigm is insufficient. These factors include: 1) the users' privacy expectations, 2) the legislative mandates to protect PII and, 3) the latent objective to foster and ensure openness, accountability and trust in the user population in order to ensure future system use. The compromise of any of the factors has the potential to negatively impact platform sustainability. With these issues in mind, design decisions must be made to ensure that the data is protected from the point of collection to the point of insertion into the cloud (Figure 3).

Security controls must be in place when data is captured at the human-machine interaction point (whether it is a medical device, custom-made web portal, mobile platform or conventional computer), when data travels from the interaction point to the cloud ingestion point via the communication channel, and when it is about to be ingested into the cloud. The data falls into one of the following categories: demographic, body measurement, past history, current activity and social & psychological; and the decision to protect each piece of data is dependent on its sensitivity, which is determined a priori and periodically re-evaluated. As shown in Figure 3, the Security and Privacy (S&P) Transformer is the secure gateway for all data to be ingested into the Wellness Cloud.

Generally, for end-to-end preservation of privacy in a networked environment (Beresford

& Stajano, 2003; Chan & Perrig, 2003; Mokbel, 2007; Langheinrich, 2009), controls may be required on the identity (i.e., of the sender or recipient), content (i.e. the message being sent) or the context (i.e. details, such as message or identity metadata, that can reveal or lead to inference on private information).

In order to safeguard identity, protection techniques, such as Mixes (Chaum, 1981) and Onion Routing (Goldschlag, 1999), have been proposed. A Mix is a mediator between service consumers and service providers that performs cryptographic transformations on incoming messages, and then forwards the messages to the relevant party. Onion routing refers to the idea of using a set of onion routers, where each router unwraps a layer of encryption around a message that was repeatedly encoded to reveal routing instructions. This prevents intermediary nodes from knowing the source, destination or message. In the context of a Wellness Cloud, identity is needed for internal processing and routing of updates to the appropriate agents. For example, it is often useful to have the results of your cardio-vascular session sent to your personal wellness record or to your doctor. Thus, these techniques are not ideally suited for this environment.

For content protection, using public key cryptography with strong encryption keys is regarded as the best practice. Current mechanisms used in this space are SSL (Secure Socket Layer) and HTTPS (Hypertext Transfer Protocol Secure). However, Bissias et.al. (2005) have demonstrated that it is possible to successfully perform traffic analysis attacks on encrypted HTTP streams. Thus, there is further research to be done on this topic.

In terms of context protection, location data is the contextual attribute that has been the most extensively studied. Gruteser et.al. (2003) promote the application of a distributed anonymity algorithm before access is granted to a service provider. Ozturk et.al. (2004) propose augmented routing protocols to protect the location of the source during sensor transmissions. Gedik and

Ling (2005) propose an information sharing framework that allows individual nodes to specify how large a group they wish to hide in and then generalizes location based on the group size. In practice, contextual attributes other than location still require investigation. For the Wellness Cloud effort, location may be relevant for analytic services. Thus, that specific contextual attribute is included as is.

For the Taiwan Collaboratory, each device manufacturer employs their own techniques to secure the sensitive data, i.e. identifiers and quasi-identifiers, on the device. The partner then engages a secure channel to the gateway of the Wellness Cloud (WC) – this is the S&P Transformer (SPT) or the Security and Privacy Transformation Unit previously mentioned. Currently, this secure channel is a SSL (Secure Sockets Layer) session and the SPT transforms incoming data into its anonymized form, using a set of rules gathered from analysis of legal requirements and customer requests.

It should be noted that the physical location of the SPT is a design decision that impacts the overall security and privacy of the system. A SPT host that is a trusted authority with a dedicated and direct line to the WC would be the optimal configuration for risk and liability reduction. A SPT host that is co-located with the WC would be the most system-efficient and would reduce the likelihood of data exposure or disclosure.

In order to ensure that each device manufacturer is identifiable within the cloud and that only de-identified information is held and processed by the WC, the SPT utilizes an algorithm that randomly selects a transformation algorithm (TA) for the data stream based on a set of identifier modification options. The system maintains a pool of TAs that perform tasks that range from simple transpositions (e.g. switching male to female for gender) to more complex functionality (e.g. converting diagnosis and condition information into their abstract form via ICD10 – International Classification of Diseases, 10th Edition). Based on the device

Figure 4. Data transportation and distribution

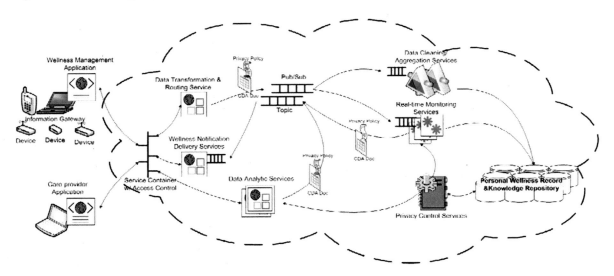

id, the patient identifier and the incoming data, TAs are chosen and applied to both identifiable information and possibly sensitive information. A hash function is selected to create pseudonyms for identifiable information and TAs are chosen to transform possible sensitive information. The metadata for the mappings are stored by the SPT and are utilized when information needs to be sent from the cloud to service consumers in its raw form. Though the pseudonym life cycle management is simpler than contemporary approaches (Lysyanskaya, 2000), its simplicity is well suited for a system with a large number of users and demanding response time requirements. The trust model behind the pseudonymisation approach is beyond the scope of this chapter.

After ingestion, there are further controls in place within the cloud to further reduce the security and privacy risk.

PRIVACY PROTECTION WITHIN THE CLOUD

There are two key issues to be addressed within the cloud. The first issue occurs when data is being transported and distributed to the different services inside the cloud. As these data may contain residual private information (i.e. groups of seemingly innocuous data items that can be collated and used to uniquely identify people), they should only be distributed to those services that provide services for the user. The second issue occurs when there is information that needs to be sent to users, where this information may also contain (residual) private information that should only be delivered to a specific person and related family members. Both of these concerns are addressed in the literature by using rule-based enforcement mechanisms either at the database layer (Agrawal et.al., 2002), at the application layer (Pearson et.al., 2009; Pearson, 2009; Wang, 2009) or the network layer (del Alamo et.al, 2010). The Wellness Cloud currently utilizes the filtering and transformation rule approach to policy enforcement at the database level.

Figure 4 illustrates some data transportation and distribution scenarios within the cloud. The scenarios include two kinds of applications: (i) Wellness Management Applications, and (ii) Care Provider Applications. Wellness Management Applications collect information and tend to be interfaces developed by device manufacturers or wellness program developers. Care Provider Applications enable medical practitioners to help patients achieve their wellness goals and manage their general health.

When the data are collected and sent to the cloud infrastructure, we assume all data will be translated to the Clinical Document Architecture (CDA) format via the *Data Transformation and Routing Services* component. In the WC, multiple CDA documents, when combined, may unlock different levels of private information at a more complete or aggregate level. For example, one CDA document may contain care data and clinical environment data (in various transformed states) that may be innocuous in their own streams, but may become more sensitive as each person's wellness record grows over time; due to the input of system partners. Another document may only contain de-identified information.

When the system distributes these CDA documents inside the cloud infrastructure, privacy polices are adopted to describe who can receive CDA documents. For example, if a CDA document contains all the private information of a user, it should only be delivered to her or his own primary care physician or applications and services operated by her or his primary care physician. While a CDA document that only contains completely anonymous information may be distributed to any care providers who are interested in clinical data encoded in CDA documents and who agree to comply with the cloud's data use agreements.

When notification or feedback information (encoded as CDA documents) is created by wellness services (e.g., real-time monitoring services), these CDA documents may also contain private information. Therefore, privacy control in distributing these CDA documents is also required. For the Wellness Cloud, fine-grained, data-level protection technologies (Bird et.al., 2005; Grandison et.al., 2007) are used in privacy policy management in order to ensure disclosure compliance. For example, if the CDA documents contain users' personal information, the documents should be delivered only to users, their family member and their primary care physicians. The policy management tools allow the patient to state the exact set of people they want to have access rights to their data.

Now we discuss the privacy policy enforcement in information distribution. In our solution, we adopt a pub-sub mechanism to distribute the CDA document. In a typical pub-sub system, the information providers publish messages that information consumers subscribe to by registering subscriptions. There are three kinds of pub-sub systems, namely topic-based, attribute-based and content-based. In topic-based pub-sub, all the messages published to a topic are delivered to message consumers who subscribe the topic. In attribute-based pub-sub systems, each message is associated with a collection of attributes, while a subscription is a Boolean predicate on attributes. When a message is published, if the consumer's Boolean predicate is evaluated to true, the message is delivered to the subscriber. Different from attribute-based pub-sub, in content-based systems, the Boolean predicate covers the entire content of the whole message. In our system, the above three pub-sub systems are adopted for different kinds of information distribution among users, services and service providers. However, existing pub-sub systems do not support privacy policy enforcement. In our system, when the pub-sub system is matching the message and subscriptions, it will first use privacy policy filters on the subscriptions. For example, a CDA document is associated with a policy that states that only user's primary care physician can access it. Therefore, when matching the CDA document with a subscription, the system retrieves the user's primary care physician list and uses the list to filter the subscription before evaluating the subscription predicates.

PRIVACY PRESERVATION IN WELLNESS ANALYTICS

One important motivation of the Wellness Cloud design in the Taiwan Collaboratory is to support the dynamic formation of wellness ecosystems. The expectation is that this will facilitate the provisioning of personalized services and satisfy the long tail of wellness care needs in an economically viable way. Typically, wellness ecosystems are composed of multiple service providers, each responsible for one part of the collaborative care solution. The Wellness Cloud architecture is therefore designed to enable streams of patient data to be transported and distributed to different service providers in a secure way. Nevertheless, the data obtained from various providers proves to be challenging for the stakeholders to comprehend. Consequently, wellness analytics services have been proposed to help transform the collected patient data into actionable knowledge for stakeholders.

Three common wellness analytic services have been identified and are supported. The first helps determine who is in need and what major risk factors should be attended for further intervention. For example, a case manager needs to be alerted if any of the residents in a long-term care institute are developing an increased risk for chronic conditions. The second enables providers to learn from a user's personal wellness history so as to provide the user with personal recommendations of intervention plans. For example, registered dietitians in an out-patient nutrition service center, when given information about their patients' nutrition compliance history, could better select education materials and adjust meal plans for the patients. The third leverages wellness status determination analysis services in an online fashion to monitor the change in a user's wellness status and to introduce the selected intervention plan at the point of change. For example, the recognition of a significantly lowered heart rate and low blood sugar levels by the WC may trigger a call to the closest ambulatory unit, if the patient has a history of strokes.

Even though all these services use only datasets that conform to legislation, such as the Health Insurance Portability and Accountability Act (HIPAA), there still exist risks of privacy intrusion (Liu & Terzi, 2009; Maximilien et.al., 2009; Becker & Chen, 2010). Many prior cases have shown that important personal information can still be recovered with carefully crafted queries from de-identified records during analysis. For one, Samarati (2001) and Sweeney (2002) have identified the medical records of the former governor of Massachusetts by cross-referencing the voter registration lists and the anonymous National Association of Health Data Organizations (NAHDO) hospital records. To protect dangerous information leakage, previous research has proposed various auditing and data perturbation methods. Some propose auditing tools to restrict queries and avoid malicious attacks. Others mask or introduce noise to randomize the input dataset (Kim and Winkler, 1997; Lindell and Pinkas, 2002; Wilson and Rosen, 2003; Loukides and Shao, 2006), or return a noisy version of output analysis (Dinur and Nissim, 2003; Chen et al., 2007). While these methods all have their merits, they are designed with the assumptions that service providers own the data they ingest and protection mechanisms are skewed in the favor of providers (Grandison, 2010). In the context of cloud-based wellness ecosystems, usually more than one data source is used for analysis. It is therefore impractical to put any single service provider in charge of overseeing the privacy issue.

The challenges and opportunities incurred by the multi-provider environment on the privacy protection mechanism in a Wellness Cloud are two-fold. On the one hand, although it is difficult for single service providers to measure the level of privacy risk associated with a particular individual, the auditing mechanism can be extended to operate in the cloud and actively avoid choosing the records belonging to those who are already at a high privacy risk, i.e. easily identifiable individuals, for analysis. On the other hand, beyond legislative regulations, the data owners, i.e. patients, may all have different privacy requirements for their own personal information. There is currently no easy way for the data owners to specify their requirements. In the remainder of this section, we will continue the discussion of extending the cloud-based auditing mechanism to actively monitor the privacy risk and select the right mitigation strategy according to patient's specifications.

Privacy-Preserving Active Sampling for Risk Modeling

Most wellness analytic services originate from the need to infer incoming users' wellness status, i.e., the propensity to various conditions. Our prior work has focused on designing a large-scale distributed infrastructure that can monitor the wellness information data streams of a large population and learn how to discriminate the status of incoming data streams from previous records (Zeng at al., 2010). To satisfy the long tail of demand with personalized services, feature selection and sampling approaches are needed to scan across the available databases and select subsets of data to develop models for characterizing wellness status of the target individual (Hsueh et al., 2010). The developed models based on risk grouping are then used to single out the major risk factors associated with a target individual and provide personalized recommendations of suitable follow-up intervention plans.

Because the personalized wellness analytics services are designed to use as little data as possible for economic reasons, we propose the utilization of an active sampling framework, which aims to find the smallest subset of data that is sufficiently representative of the risk group without degrading the performance on wellness status estimation. Previous proposals include using a filter approach to identify a subset of data that exhibit the strongest

global utility for describing the target wellness status. However, without considering privacy issues, many of the personal wellness attributes of data owners in a risk group can be automatically inferred, e.g., by majority voting. With the privacy issue in consideration, the active sampling framework is then recast as follows:

- **Input:** Data records in the same risk group $R(f1,...fn, S)$; the privacy requirement θ (which is represented as the maximum allowed number of inferable attributes);
- **Output:** the subset of records that maximize the wellness status association without compromising the privacy requirement.

The development of such an active sampling framework requires the auditing mechanism in the back end (usually run by the cloud operator) to record the personal wellness attributes associated with a particular data owner. The privacy risk is estimated by the number of inferable attributes with the selected data records of the same risk group.

For the online version of wellness analytic services, the auditing mechanism is extended to monitor the changes in privacy risks, using a sliding window approach. The privacy risk at time *t-1* and *t* are profiled as y_{t-1} and y_t. The wellness attributes (which, in combination, may represent different levels of privacy risks) are represented as F_{t-1} and F_t, and the risk factors of privacy level change (which describe events associated with changes in privacy risk levels) as $P_c(F_{t-1})$ and $P_c(F_t)$. As shown in Formula (1), the goal is to search for a privacy risk level pair that simultaneously maximizes $P_A(F_{t-1},y_{t-1})$ and $P_A(F_t,y_t)$, i.e., the likelihood of the estimated privacy risk level at the two time points, and minimizes the penalty of risk level change from time *t-1* to *t*, i.e., the likelihood of risk change at the two time points $(w_2P_c(F_{t-1})+w_3P_c(F_t))$ and the imposed penalty on risk change, φ. The weightings of the terms in the scoring function are learned from privacy intrusion history. If there is a privacy risk level change, the system will raise alerts to the service provider for mitigation.

$$g(<y_{t-1}, y_t>) = w_1 P_A(F_{t-1}, y_{t-1}) + w_1 P_A(F_t, y_t) + \quad (1)$$
$$\varphi(y_{t-1} \neq y_t)(w_2 P_c(F_{t-1}) + w_3 P_c(F_t))$$

Having measured the amount of information leakage associated with a particular person, it then comes down to the question of how to identify the right risk mitigation strategy for the active sampling framework. This is a problem that is difficult for any single data provider to handle on their own, but can be rendered more easily on Wellness Clouds with the aid of a personal privacy requirement handler.

Decision Support Framework for Personal Privacy Requirement Handler

Selecting the right privacy risk mitigation strategy for an individual data owner requires understanding what composes a privacy threat to the individual. Different countries have different regulations concerning individual privacy rights. Moreover, data owners under similar circumstances may perceive privacy threats differently; even for the same wellness attribute, sometimes they would weigh the importance of information leakage differently. For example, a recently diagnosed diabetes patient may prefer more protection against the leakage of related information than long-time patients. Therefore, a personal privacy requirement handler should allow data owners to specify their privacy requirements. Default country-specific or institute-specific requirement templates can be provided by the privacy-responsible authorities.

The selection of risk mitigation strategy can then be characterized as an inference problem. Given the alternative action plans (*AP*) following

different strategies, each represented as a set of plan features f_i, the goal is to rank the action plans according to how well a plan serves to address the specified privacy threat of the data owner at risk. The importance of ap_t (*t*th action plan in consideration) on u_a (*a*th user) is measured with the multiple-attribute value function:

$$imp(u_a, ap_t) = \sum_{f_i \in ap_t} w_{f_i}' imp(u_a, f_i)$$
$$w_{f_i}' = w_{f_i} \bigg/ \sum_{i=1}^{n} w_{f_i} \quad (2)$$

where f_i is the *i*th privacy risk factor considered in ap_t, and w_{f_i}' is the owner-specified weight on f_i.

If the privacy threat is not specified by the data owner, the system then applies a collaborative filtering approach to rank action plans, using the requirements of data owners in the same risk group, *N*. The importance of a factor is determined by the weighted average of importance ratings, adjusted by the similarity between the owners.

$$imp(u_a, f_i) = \frac{\sum_{n \in N} sim(u_a, u_n) imp(u_n, f_i)}{\sum_{n \in N} sim(u_a, u_n)}$$

$$(3)$$

The analytics services can start offering privacy handling with the auditing mechanism, privacy-preserving active sampling framework, and personal privacy requirement handler in development. However, there are still questions remaining. For one, we only implement two threat models: owner-specified and collaborative filtering-based attribute weighting. Taking a step back, we need to understand how to model the privacy threats. Different scenarios inherit different tradeoffs between privacy and analysis requirements. Yet the sampling approach may come with different granularity: e.g., spatial, temporal, and identity. How do we estimate temporal changes effectively and efficiently without having to compromise the privacy threshold set by each individual in the sample set? Also, recent research shows that unsupervised clustering approaches can effectively group utility functions of individuals into a prototypical function according to how close they are to each other in a multi-dimensional space. The unsupervised approach can further assist the development of the online version of the privacy protection mechanism. In addition, owing to the nature of wellness services invoked by vital sign monitoring devices (e.g., for analyzing abnormal glucose patterns after meals), the system needs to support flexible and scalable service provisioning. This includes the support of high-throughput privacy-preserving risk grouping and risk mitigation through the cloud-based load balancing mechanism.

The privacy risk mitigation mechanism proposed here has a significant impact on wellness education and monitoring. With the better privacy control mechanism in place, the wellness analytics service sets the stage for a new generation of personal wellness decision support systems, which aim to reinstate individuals' self-assessment capabilities and a better sense of control over their own wellness management process.

IMPLICATIONS AND FUTURE WORK

For the average business organization that is deploying a cloud, care must be taken in the design and implementation of the privacy and security controls at data collection, during transit and while it is being held in the cloud. Often, this may require a collaboration with the partners that produce the devices or the platform from which data is to be ingested and an agreement with the affiliate service consumers that build services on top of the cloud.

The strategic research initiatives involve 1) infusing specialized cryptographic schemes in the cloud data ingestion and transformation processes, 2) building more intuitive and friendly interfaces for policy acquisition and management, 3) innovating sophisticated risk management algorithms and technologies, and 4) moving toward a software-hardware hybrid system where specialized hardware components are included to handle (computationally intense) CDA processing and execute cryptographic methods.

Tactically, it is expected that there will be lessons learned from the current deployments as the system continues to be used and users make requests to improve their experience and interaction.

CONCLUSION

In this chapter, we introduced the Wellness Cloud – an integrated, interconnected and intelligent healthcare well-being system – that is developed to help citizens achieve their wellness goals. We presented the issues around privacy protection on wellness devices, while data is being transmitted from device to cloud, when it is being processed within the cloud and while it is being used by analytic services. We also presented the approaches taken and highlight the future direction of the effort.

It is our hope that this articulation will serve as 1) a spark for discussion, and 2) a template for entities who either want to develop ecosystem components or similarly purposed systems.

REFERENCES

Agrawal, R., Kiernan, J., Srikant, R., & Xu, Y. (2002). Hippocratic databases. *Proceedings of the 28th Int'l Conf. on Very Large Databases*, Hong Kong, China.

Agrawal, R., & Srikant, R. (2000). Privacy-preserving data mining. *Proceedings of the ACM SIGMOD Conference on Management of Data*, Dallas, Texas, USA.

Baranowski, T. (1981). Toward the definition of concepts of health and disease, wellness and illness. *Journal of Health Values, 5*(6), 246–256.

Becker, J., & Chen, H. (2010). Measuring privacy risk in online social networks. *Proceedings of the Web 2.0 Security and Privacy* (W2SP).

Beresford, A. R., & Stajano, F. (2003). Location privacy in pervasive computing. *IEEE Pervasive Computing / IEEE Computer Society [and] IEEE Communications Society, 2*(1), 46–55. doi:10.1109/MPRV.2003.1186725

Bird, P., Grandison, T., Kiernan, J., Logan, S., & Rjaibi, W. (2005). Extending relational database systems to automatically enforce privacy policies. *Proceedings of the 21st International Conference on Data Engineering* (ICDE), Tokyo, Japan.

Bissias, G. D., Liberatore, M., & Levine, N. B. (2005). Privacy vulnerabilities in encrypted HTTP streams. *Proceedings of the Privacy Enhancing Technologies Workshop*, Dubrovnik, Croatia.

Blount, M., Batra, V. M., Capella, A. N., Ebling, M. R., Jerome, W. F., & Martin, S. M. (2007). Remote health-care monitoring using Personal Care Connect. *IBM Systems Journal, 46*(1), 95–113. doi:10.1147/sj.461.0095

Chan, H., & Perrig, A. (2003). Security and privacy in sensor networks. *IEEE Computer, 36*(10), 103–105. doi:10.1109/MC.2003.1236475

Chaum, D. (1981). Untraceable electronic mail, return addresses and digital pseudonyms. *Communications of the ACM, 24*(2), 84–88. doi:10.1145/358549.358563

Chen, B., Lefevre, K., & Ramakrishnan, R. (2007). Privacy skyline: Privacy with multidimensional adversarial knowledge. *Proceedings of the 33rd International Conference on Very Large Data Bases* (VLDB), University of Vienna, Austria.

Corbin, C. B., & Pangrazi, R. P. (2001). *Towards a uniform definition of wellness: A commentary*. President's Council on Physical Fitness and Sports. Series 3, No. 15. Retrieved April 4, 2011 from http://eric.ed.gov/PDFS/ED470691.pdf

Dasu, T., Krishnan, S., Venkatasubramanian, S., & Yi, K. (2006). *An information-theoretic approach to detecting changes in multi-dimensional data streams.*

del Alamo, J. M., Monjas, M. A., Yelmo, J. C., San Miguel, B., Trapero, R., & Fernandez, A. M. (2010). Self-service privacy: User-centric privacy for network-centric identity. *Proceedings of the IFIP Advances in Information and Communication Technology, 321*, 17–31. doi:10.1007/978-3-642-13446-3_2

Dinur, I., & Nissim, K. (2003). Revealing information while preserving privacy. *Proceedings of the Twenty-Second ACM SIGACT-SIGMOD-SIGART Symposium on Principles of Database Systems* (PODS), San Diego, California.

Gedik, B., & Ling, L. (2005). Location privacy in mobile systems: A personalized anonymization model. *Proceedings of the 25th IEEE International Conference on Distributed Computing Systems* (pp. 620-629).

Goetzel, R., Sepulveda, M., Knight, K., Eisen, M., Wade, S., Wong, J., & Fielding, J. (1994). Association of IBM's "A Plan for Life" health promotion program with changes in employees' health risk status. *Journal of Occupational Medicine., 36*(9), 1005–1009.

Goldschlag, D., Reed, M., & Syverson, P. (1999). Onion routing. *Communications of the ACM, 42*(2), 39–41. doi:10.1145/293411.293443

Grandison, T. (2010). Patient-centric privacy: Envisioning collaboration between payers, providers & patients with the patient at the core. *Proceedings of the 6th IEEE International Conference of Collaborative Computing: Networking, Applications, and Worksharing* (CollaborateCom), Chicago, Illinois.

Grandison, T., Johnson, C., & Kiernan, J. (2007). Hippocratic databases: Current capabilities and future trends. In Jajodia, S., & Gertz, M. (Eds.), *Handbook of database security: Applications and trends.* doi:10.1007/978-0-387-48533-1_17

Gruteser, M., Schelle, G., Jain, A., Han, R., & Grunwald, D. (2003). Privacy-aware location sensor networks. *Proceedings of The 9th Conference on Hot Topics in Operating Systems* (HOTOS), Berkeley, CA, USA.

Health Information Technology for Economic and Clinical Health Act (HITECH). (2009). *Enforcement rule.* Retrieved April 4, 2011 from http://www.hhs.gov/ocr/privacy/hipaa/ administrative/enforcementrule/ hitechenforcementifr.html.

Health Insurance Portability and Accountability Act (HIPAA). (1996). *Privacy and security.* Retrieved April 4, 2011, from http://www.intelli-mark-it.com/privacysecurity/hipaa.asp

Hsueh, P., Lin, R., Hsiao, J., Zeng, L., Ramakrishnan, S., & Chang, H. (2010). Cloud-based platform for personalization in a wellness management ecosystem: Why, what, and how. *Proceedings of the 6th IEEE International Conference of Collaborative Computing: Networking, Applications, and Worksharing* (CollaborateCom), Chicago, Illinois.

Kim, J., & Winkler, W. (1997). *Masking microdata files.* Technical Report of Bureau of the Census. Retrieved April 4, 2011, from http://www.census.gov/srd/papers/pdf/rr97-3.pdf

Langheinrich, M. (2009). A survey of RFID privacy approaches. *Journal of Personal Ubiquitous Computing, 13*(6), 413–421. doi:10.1007/s00779-008-0213-4

Lerner, R. M. (2006). Amazon Web services. *Linux Journal, 143*, 20–24.

Lindell, Y., & Pinkas, B. (2000). Privacy preserving data mining. *Proceedings of the Advances in Cryptology* (pp. 20-24), *LNCS 1880.* Springer-Verlag.

Liu, K., & Terzi, E. (2009). A framework for computing the privacy scores of users in online social networks. *Proceedings of the IEEE International Conference on Data Mining* (ICDM). Miami, Florida. USA.

Loong, L. H. (2009). Preparing for an aging population - The Singapore *experience. The Journal: AARP International*, (Winter), 12-17. Retrieved April 4, 2011, from http://www.nus.edu.sg/nec/InnoAge/ documents/AARPjournal-winter09_PMLee.pdf

Loukides, G., & Shao, J. (2008). Data utility and privacy protection trade-off in k-anonymisation. *Proceedings of the First International EDBT Workshop on Privacy and Anonymity in the Information Society* (PAIS), Nantes, France.

Lysyanskaya, A., Rivest, R. L., Sahai, A., & Wolf, S. (2000). Pseudonym systems. *Selected Areas in Cryptography -. Lecture Notes in Computer Science, 1758*, 184–199. doi:10.1007/3-540-46513-8_14

Mackey, S. (2000). Towards a definition of wellness. *Journal of Holistic Nursing Practice, 7*(2), 34–38.

Maes, S., Verhoeven, C., Kittel, F., & Scholten, H. (1998). Effects of a Dutch work-site wellness-health program: The Brabantia Project. *American Journal of Public Health, 88*(7), 1037–1041. doi:10.2105/AJPH.88.7.1037

Maximilien, E. M., Grandison, T., Sun, T., Richardson, D., Guo, S., & Liu, K. (2009). Enabling privacy as a fundamental construct for social networks. *Proceedings of the Workshop on Security and Privacy in Online Social Networking* (SPOSN), Vancouver, Canada.

Mokbel, M. F. (2007). Privacy in location-based services: State-of-the-art and research directions. *Proceedings of The International Conference On Mobile Data Management*, Mannheim, Germany.

Nakamura, D. (2010). *Fat in Japan? You're breaking the law.* Retrieved April 4, 2011, from http://www.globalpost.com/dispatch/japan/091109/fat-japan-youre-breaking-the-law

Nurmi, D., Wolski, R., Grzegorczyk, C., Obertelli, G., Soman, S., Youseff, L., & Zagorodnov, D. (2008). The eucalyptus open-source cloud-computing system. *Proceedings of Cloud Computing and Applications* (CCA), Chicago, Illinois, USA. Retrieved April 4, 2011, from http://www.cca08.org/papers/Paper32-Daniel-Nurmi.pdf

Nystedt, D. (2009). Taiwan to host IBM's first joint healthcare IT research unit. *PC World*. Retrieved April 4, 2011, from http://www.pcworld.com/article/185193/taiwan_to_host_ibms_first_joint_healthcare_it_research_unit.html

Ozminkowski, R. J., Ling, D., Goetzel, R. Z., Bruno, J. A., Rutter, K. R., Isaac, F., & Wang, S. (2002). Long-term impact of Johnson & Johnson's health & wellness program on health care utilization and expenditures. *Journal of Occupational and Environmental Medicine, 44*(1), 21–29. doi:10.1097/00043764-200201000-00005

Ozturk, C., Zhang, Y., & Trappe, W. (2004). Source-location privacy in energy-constrained sensor network routing. *Proceedings of The 2nd ACM Workshop on Security of Ad Hoc and Sensor Networks* (pp. 88-93). New York, NY, USA.

Pearson, S. (2009). Taking account of privacy when designing cloud computing services. *Proceedings of the ICSE Workshop on Software Engineering Challenges of Cloud Computing* (pp. 44-52).

Pearson, S., Shen, Y., & Mowbray, M. (2009). A privacy manager for cloud computing. *Lecture Notes in Computer Science, 5931*, 90–106. doi:10.1007/978-3-642-10665-1_9

Samarati, P. (2001). Protecting Respondents' Identities in Microdata Release. *IEEE Transactions on Knowledge and Data Engineering, 13*(6), 1010–1027. doi:10.1109/69.971193

Savolaine, J., & Granello, P. F. (2002). The function of meaning and purpose for individual wellness. *The Journal of Humanistic Counseling, Education and Development, 41*, 178–189.

Sweeney, L. (2001). K-anonymity: A model for protecting privacy. *International Journal on Uncertainty, Fuzziness and Knowledge-based Systems, 10*(5), 557–570. doi:10.1142/S0218488502001648

Tibken, S. (2010). Salesforce CEO touts mobility, social networking. *Dow Jones Newswires*. Retrieved April 4, 2011, from http://www.totaltele.com/view.aspx?C=4&ID=459551

Wang, J., Zhao, Y., Jiang, S., & Le, J. (2009). Providing privacy preserving in cloud computing. *Proceedings of the International Conference on Test and Measurement* (pp. 213-216).

Wilson, R. L., & Rosen, P. A. (2003). Protecting data through perturbation techniques: Impact on the knowledge discovery process. *Journal of Database Management, 14*(2), 14–26. doi:10.4018/jdm.2003040102

Zane, R. (2009). *IBM research collaborates with leading Taiwanese institutions to deliver wellness-centric healthcare via cloud computing.* Press Release. Retrieved April 4, 2011, from http://www-03.ibm.com/press/us/en/pressrelease/29086.wss

Zeng, L., Hsueh, P., Chang, H., Chung, C., & Huang, R. (2010). GreenOlive: An open platform for wellness management ecosystem. *Proceedings of the IEEE/INFORMS International Conference on Service Operations and Logistics, and Informatics* (SOLI), Beijing, China.

ADDITIONAL READING

Adam, N. R., & Wortmann, J. C. (1989). Security-Control Methods for Statistical Databases: A Comparative Study. *ACM Computing Surveys, 21.*

Applebaum, P. S. (2000). Threats to the Confidentiality of Medical Records—No Place to Hide. *Journal of the American Medical Association, 283*(6), 795–796. doi:10.1001/jama.283.6.795

Bayardo, R. J., & Agrawal, R. (2005). Data Privacy Through Optimal k-Anonymization. Proceedings of the 21st Int'l Conf. on Data Engineering (ICDE), Tokyo, Japan.

Department of Health and Human Services. (1999). Standards for Privacy of Individually Identifiable Health Information. *Federal Register, 64*(212).

Etzioni, A. (1999). Medical Records: Enhancing Privacy, Preserving the Common Good. Hastings Center Report (pp. 14–23), Mar–Apr 30.

Grandison, T., & Davis, J. (2007). The Impact of Industry Constraints on Model-Driven Data Disclosure Controls. Proceedings of the 1st International Workshop on Model-Based Trustworthy Health Information Systems, Nashville, Tennessee.

Lefevre, K., Agrawal, R., Ercegovac, V., Ramakrishnan, R., Xu, Y., & DeWitt, D. (2004) Limiting Disclosure in Hippocratic Databases. Proceedings of the 30th Int'l Conf. on Very Large Databases, Toronto, Canada.

Sweeney, L. (1997). Weaving Technology and Policy Together to Maintain Confidentiality. *The Journal of Law, Medicine & Ethics, 25,* 98–110. doi:10.1111/j.1748-720X.1997.tb01885.x

KEY TERMS AND DEFINITIONS

Application Programming Interfaces (API): A pre-determined set of functions that specify how programmers utilize the features of a software program (which can be a library, an application, an operating system, or a network device driver).

Ecosystem-as-a-Service (EaaS): An economic community formation model which produces goods and services of value to customers, who are themselves members of the ecosystem.

Data Perturbation: Techniques that are used to insert minor biases into databases, either directly on the data or on the output of query result.

Health Insurance Portability and Accountability Act (HIPAA): The HIPAA Privacy Rule provides federal protection for the confidentiality, integrity, and availability of Personal Health Information (PHI) held by covered entities. It gives patients an array of administrative, physical, and technical protections with respect to PHI and specifies rules for the disclosure of PHI needed for patient care or research purposes.

Health Information Technology for Economic and Clinical Health Act (HITECH): Integrated as part of the economic stimulus bill, American Recovery and Reinvestment Act of 2009, to encourage healthcare providers to use electronic record-keeping and ordering system.

Hypertext Transfer Protocol Secure (HTTPS): Is a combination of the Hypertext Transfer Protocol with the SSL/TLS (Secure

Sockets Layer/Transport Layer Security) protocol to provide encrypted communication and secure identification of a network web server.

Infrastructure-as-a-Service (IaaS): A provisioning model utilized by a platform operator to outsource its equipment to support third-party operations, including processes, storage, and networking components. It is typically operated on a pay-as-you-go basis.

Personal Health Information (PHI): PHI includes demographic information, medical history, test and laboratory results, insurance information and other data that is collected by a healthcare professional to identify an individual and determine appropriate care.

Personally Identifiable Information (PII): Data about an individual that could distinguish and trace an individual, such as name, age, email address, mailing address, telephone number, social security number, fingerprints, other biometric data, medical or financial information.

Publish-Subscribe Service (Pub-Sub): Pub-sub service provides communication chan-

nels among services to allow one service send a message on a particular topic, and all the other services that have subscribed to this topic to receive the message.

Secure Sockets Layer: a cryptographic protocol developed by Netscape for transmitting private documents via the Internet.

Software-as-a-Service (SaaS): An on-demand software distribution model that made available the applications hosted by a service provider to end users through web services in a service-oriented architecture. It is typically operated on a pay-as-you-go basis.

Wellness: the active process of becoming aware of and making choices toward a more successful existence.

Wellness Cloud (WC): A Wellness Cloud is an integrated, interconnected and intelligent platform for the ingestion, processing and management of wellness data that delivers services to multiple independent software vendors (ISVs), service providers, and other stakeholders.

Chapter 10
Ensuring Privacy and Confidentiality in Digital Video Surveillance Systems

Aniello Castiglione
Università degli Studi di Salerno, Italy

Alfredo De Santis
Università degli Studi di Salerno, Italy

Francesco Palmieri
Seconda Università degli Studi di Napoli, Italy

ABSTRACT

Both private and public organizations are considering the implementation of video surveillance technology for the purposes of general Law Enforcement and Public Safety programs. In several situations, such solutions, often characterized by high-speed network connections, plenty of storage capacity, and a high computational power, may be suitable in protecting public safety, detection or deterring, as well as assisting in the investigating of criminal activity. In this scenario, privacy protection, lawful evidence enforcement (through incontrovertible documentary proof), and content confidentiality are the most challenging security topics relating to several information society sectors (Finance, Homeland Security, Healthcare, etc.) that require interdisciplinary input from legal experts, technicians, privacy advocates, as well as security consultants.

Starting from these ideas and concepts, this chapter aims at presenting an innovative network-based digital video surveillance solution that meets all the aforementioned security and privacy requirements ensuring that the recorded data will be only accessible to a subset of authorities, trusting each other under precisely defined policies, agreements, and circumstances. This would aid the surveillance activities, when needed, without disrupting the privacy of individuals.

DOI: 10.4018/978-1-61350-501-4.ch010

INTRODUCTION

With the increasing demand for greater security, following the 9/11 terrorist attacks on the United States, video surveillance technologies are starting to be used in most of the critical locations in every country, such as airports, banks, public transport as well as busy city centers. These systems are being used for different tasks, ranging from object detection, vehicle tracking, analysis of human behavior, to people searching and counting, thus assuming a fundamental role for personal safety, traffic control, resources planning and Law Enforcement. The success of these tasks relies on the existence of specific hardware and software infrastructures that can guarantee the efficient capture and storage of visual data, while providing means that not only improve individual privacy protection but also secure the data against illegitimate activities. Visual data may be illegally intercepted for a use that is different to the originally intended one. It may also be maliciously manipulated in order to either hide and/or introduce fake evidence. For example, within a health-care context, the interception/use of images by anyone outside of the environment infringes patient privacy rights. While, in a banking, industrial or military context where either the replacement of a camera with a fake one or the falsification of its video output can be used to hide hostile activity.

In order to avoid the aforementioned problems, electronic means should be used in conjunction with robust ad hoc architectural features, introducing a reliable way to protect, possibly with lawful enforcement, the produced images and video streams originating from the source capture devices. Specifically, modern digital video surveillance systems need to use effective data authentication procedures to confirm the origin of the surveillance data and their credibility as investigation material in order to prevent and trace any illegal manipulation or falsification of the data as well as ensure their validity as legal proof with law-enforcement authorities (Welsh

& Farrington, 2002). Furthermore, since video surveillance systems can be operated to collect personal information about identifiable individuals, to be processed only for specific, explicit and legitimate purposes, all the organizations accessing such data must have the authority to collect, view or use them fairly according to all the existing laws and rules. The European Union is one of the first places in the world that has adopted a specific set of rules and laws explicitly protecting privacy rights and regulating the handling of personal data (EU Parliament, 1995; Becker et al., 2008). In order to cope with all these issues, the primary security measure that can be employed by video surveillance systems is encryption, which can both provide the required degree of confidentiality as well as deny any third party access to their content. On the other hand, the application of robust asymmetric cryptosystems on visual data for real-time applications not only further aggravates the processing requirements but also introduces several impairment factors such as expansion of the packet size, ciphering latency and jitter, which adversely condition the overall video quality.

One possible solution to avoid these problems is the use of hybrid encryption technologies, providing asymmetrical key agreement schemes based on X.509 digital certificates, for initial end-to-end strong authentication between the involved entities, and high-performance symmetric stream encryption, in order to efficiently handle the ciphering of video streams. This hybrid approach relies on using an effective combination of both symmetric and asymmetric encryption schemes, exploiting their specific features and strengths in order to achieve an acceptable security level. In fact, there currently seems to be no systematic method capable of breaking this security scheme in realistic time. Some privileged entities, such as Government or police/law-enforcement agencies, also need to be able to access the data stored in the video surveillance archival systems. Nevertheless, it is not desirable that a single subject or organization be granted full access rights to the video surveillance data since there is a significant risk of misuse by a malicious party, using its privileges to break the privacy of the involved contents, and/or compromising the overall system security. In order to safely distribute the random symmetric keys used for video encryption among the different trusted parties, a key-sharing solution that relies on the Shamir threshold-based secret sharing scheme has been used. It guarantees that only the correct combination of authorized entities can be granted access to secured contents.

Consequently, this chapter presents a novel video surveillance system architecture, ensuring robust privacy protection and content confidentiality within a distributed trust scenario. This architecture leverages on an effective hybrid cryptosystem that is modeled on a multi-party threshold-based key-sharing scheme. Because of the great flexibility of this scheme, the proposed approach can handle the problem of losing private-key shares that are required for reconstructing video material as well as ensure the cooperation of several mutually trusting authorities that manage content reconstruction under precisely defined policies, agreements and circumstances. The proposed architecture can be considered as satisfactorily secure since there seems to currently be no systematic method capable of breaking its security in realistic times, with it also being fast enough to be efficiently run on low-cost special purpose devices.

BACKGROUND

This section briefly introduces some of the basic concepts that will be useful in explaining the proposed architectural framework, by presenting the current technological scenario as well as the fundamental architectural elements behind it.

The Evolution of Video Surveillance Systems

Video surveillance systems are part of the Physical Security category, whose major goals are deterrence, detection, and verification (Smith & Robinson, 1999). Current video surveillance systems are currently undergoing a transition from traditional analog solutions (e.g., Closed Circuit Television or CCTV) to more advanced digital ones, often based on IP technologies and networked architectures. In several cases, digital video and digital video storage are merely a replacement for existing Video Cassette recorders (VCRs) and Video Home System (VHS) tapes. Specifically, the conventional use of analog cameras still provides an effective and economical way of recording events, after analog-to-digital conversion, to tapes or hard disks for storage and instant playback.

However, newer digital implementations present substantial benefits over analog ones. When compared to traditional analog video surveillance systems, a digital video surveillance offers greater flexibility in video content processing and transmission. In order to be considered a complete security management package, a "digital surveillance system" should provide several facilities: from storage and retrieval, to surveillance and network capabilities. These systems can alleviate a lot of time and effort, as well as drastically improve the performance of existing or new surveillance infrastructures. At the same time, it can also easily implement advanced features such as motion detection, facial recognition and object tracking. When operating in a large distributed environment, each digital camera can be wired up to an Ethernet or Wide Area Network (WAN) – such as ATM or Frame Relay – with an IP address being assigned to each of them. In this way, the system can leverage on existing IP-based networks regardless of the specific technology used to transport the video flows. In addition, the use of such packet switching based networks makes it possible for several streams to be simultaneously delivered on the same transport media by sharing the available transmission capacity through statistical multi-plexing, while optimizing the infrastructure costs by mixing video surveillance data with other data, video and voice flows.

The latest step of the evolution aims at further increasing the scalability through the migration to wireless interconnections by exploiting ubiquitous cameras powered by low-cost wireless technolo-gies (Sedky *et al.*, 2005; Cisco, 2006; Norris *et al.*, 2004). Thus, depending on design requirements and site environment, seamlessly placing cameras of different types and functions in strategic loca-tions can allow for the real-time monitoring and recording of areas under scrutiny. Such a flexible networked surveillance environment allows for an easier implementation of fully automated or remotely managed applications. Several examples include the detection of lost luggage in railway sta-tions or airports, as well as the remote monitoring of vehicle queues on high traffic roads (Wolf et al., 2002; Bramberger et al., 2006). In particular, when IP-based cameras are connected through large-bandwidth networks, with the problems introduced by the transport infrastructure being considered as negligible, remote video analysis might be similar to local processing.

Furthermore, due to the presence of large WAN infrastructures and ubiquitous Internet connec-tions, the online monitoring of remote cameras located tens or hundreds of kilometers away is possible without the aid of any form of specific infrastructure. Authorized users can access the view from a computer located anywhere in the world in order to see either live or recorded stills from any camera, independently from its location. In the long run, it becomes more cost-effective, as networks can be configured to manage hours of video, with very little personnel or support necessary. This can be considered increasingly strategic in recent times where finding available human resources to sit and watch these images is becoming more and more expensive, while

hardware technologies used to capture and store video imagery has become significantly cheaper.

The Architecture of Modern Digital Video Surveillance Systems

A state-of-the-art digital video surveillance solu-tion classically consists of several video camera sources deployed over a wide area that broadcast live video information to a central site for collec-tion, processing and monitoring. Typical sources are digital mega-pixel network cameras, widely available on the market, which can record at a considerably higher resolution than the previous ones, with the compromise of considerably higher costs and network bandwidth requirements. These cameras, usually powered by high performance Digital Signal Processing (DSP)-based Charged Couple Device (CCD) sensors, may also be remotely controlled by using different kinds of operation, such as "pan-tilt-zoom" (PTZ) or "fixed" movements, depending on the distance and angle coverage desired. As both resolution and frame rate are the factors that ultimately affect the quality and file size of the recordings, in-depth analysis of the security profile for each of the respective areas are needed in order to obtain the optimal balance between the two. The output of each video can be considered as a sequence of independent Joint Photographic Experts Group (JPEG) pictures/images, in order to realize what is informally known as Motion JPEG (M-JPEG), or a continuous video stream generated with various video encoding and compression options such as H.261 or Moving Pictures Expert Group (MPEG). Motion JPEG is generally used when the main reason for video recording is trial evidence, since each recorded stream can be divided into separate image frames that can be examined in a totally independent way from the previous and subsequent ones. Since JPEG frames can adopt different levels of compression, M-JPEG can also achieve signifi-cant bandwidth savings. H.261, with a commonly used bandwidth of 64 Kbps, is mainly used for teleconference meetings. Its resolution is very low compared to that of regular TV monitors, which therefore is not suitable for supervision. To-date most of the available surveillance solutions run MPEG-4 or analogous differential video encoding schemes (H.264). However, all the MPEG-based encoding options need a larger bandwidth. Each camera directly generating MPEG-encoded video typically requires between 1 and 10 Mbps for an high quality stream with a resolution of 640×480 pixels and a 25 fps frame rate (Koutsakis et al., 2005).

The increasing success of modern IP cameras, fully integrating hardware-based video capturing and encoding mechanisms within the same device, has drastically reduced the need for separate components with the functions of video-encoders, converters, etc. (Cai et al., 2003). The video streams coming from the live surveillance cameras can be transmitted via dedicated end-to-end transport connections on the underlying IP network, to a data collection and archival server or digital video recording system (DVR) which permanently saves them on its own storage equipment. Typical DVR systems consist of either a generic cluster server providing a huge hard disk capacity or connected to various kinds of storage arrays, such as NAS or SAN equipments (Gemmell et al., 1995). Transmissions from each camera to the DVR must be accomplished through secure communication channels and protected against interception. Protection against interception is particularly important if a wireless transmission system is used or if any footage is transferred via the Internet. In these cases, the data must be encrypted while in transit. The digital information records may then be conveniently stored, searched and indexed online for infinite replay and analysis.

Videos recorded today might still be needed for many years to come. Since surveillance cameras are mainly used in commercial contexts or security and safety-sensitive public or private environments (i.e. banks, parking places, office

buildings, transport areas, etc.), camera output has to be recorded, according to appropriate security and privacy enforcement policies, on dedicated storage hierarchies, which typically consist of disks and tapes or optical storage means that are either rewritten periodically or stored in video archives. The organizations involved must store all the data and retain the storage devices required for evidentiary purposes in accordance with their own policies until Law Enforcement authorities request them. After a crime occurs – a store is robbed, a car stolen or people physically injured – investigators can go back after the fact has occurred, by examining the stored video records to see what happened. In order to guarantee lawful evidence as well as the reliability of all the captured data, it is important to prove that each stored video stream has not been altered, before or during transmission, and that its capturing source, date and time can be proven with absolute certainty.

Considering that an IP network is a fully distributed infrastructure, recording and retrieving the surveillance data can be also carried out in a distributed manner. In detail, it is possible to have a large number of video monitoring stations located in different physical places, each one with its own access privileges and private view. Consequently, the DVR is connected locally or through the Internet, to one or more Monitoring/Surveillance Stations (MS). MS systems are in most cases software-based. They typically run on generic COTS workstation hardware. The ultimate bottleneck of large video surveillance systems is often the processing power required by the MS workstation to decode or decrypt the obtained video streams. Due to the heavy hardware requirements, there are many custom solutions on a hybrid hardware-plus-software level capable of reducing the problems associated to unsuitable or inadequate general-purpose hardware and/or software. Figure 1 shows the reference architecture for a state-of-the-art surveillance system.

Figure 1. The reference architecture

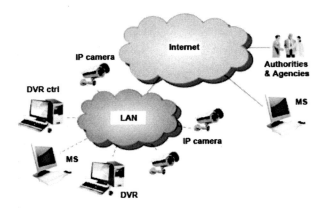

PROVIDING SECURITY AND PRIVACY IN DIGITAL VIDEO SURVEILLANCE

While video surveillance represents a paradigm shift in the security industry, it has produced unique legal considerations. As video surveillance equipment and technologies become smarter and compact, it is easier and easier to violate the privacy and property rights of others. Cases of misuse or unauthorized video disclosure are regularly reported. Ubiquitous access through wireless technologies and the Internet have made things worse. Video recordings might give information about some private activities that may not be under the lawful scope of the organization or individual doing the recording. In the public sphere, several complicated issues are emerging about the adoption of video surveillance technologies by governments. In fact, governments and Law Enforcement authorities can use surveillance technologies in several circumstances, running from crime prevention, traffic supervision, urban environments and buildings safety enforcement, to the context of specific criminal investigations. However, when such sensitive information is directly put into the hands of a single government agency, it is not sure how these agencies will manage it. For example, in some countries, video surveillance together with

face recognition technologies can be used to track attendance at political rallies, which could have an enormous chilling effect on the rights of free speech and free assembly. The main question is who watches the watchers, making sure our data is not used against us? Furthermore, in recent times, data sharing between the government agencies of several countries has also increased. As a consequence, the uncontrolled sharing of data between agencies may introduce a purpose-creep in which the data collected for a specific purpose are used for another one, which also causes the duplication of highly sensitive data in some government agencies that cannot be expected to adequately protect these data.

On the other hand, regarding the use in private areas, the universal free speech and expression rights would guarantee the permission of recording and using "visual" information collected on a private property. Such data inherently helps to guarantee the individual's property rights. In fact, video surveillance is being increasingly used by private entities for their own private and property protection purposes: to monitor their assets, business and commercial areas; to watch out for thieves and pickpockets in shopping malls and casinos; to observe private gated communities and travelers on airplanes, trains and buses; to keep an eye on children and nannies ("nanny cams");

to exchange pictures by using mobile phone or detect drug dealing activities at schools as well as frauds in offices and banking organizations. In countries where there are no specific laws and policies regulating video surveillance, it becomes fundamental to assess whether the monitoring activities of these private entities should be controlled, or at least fall under the same constraints as government agencies. These developments, also raise several question about *where* and *how* the involved surveillance data should be stored and *who* has the rights to access and analyze them as well as *when*.

Whereas these considerations should not condition the technology development, they will continue to be origin of debates concerning the best method for protecting the aforementioned rights in an increasingly advanced society. What is actually necessary is a solution allowing the disclosure/recovery of secret data only after the combined consensus of several subjects (agencies, authorities or private companies) mutually trusting and controlling each other, according to appropriately crafted policies. This implies the definitions of various access levels and procedures for authenticating individuals in each organization involved and their associated privileges and responsibilities. Another fundamental concern is to store the surveillance information in a safe fashion, so that breaking into a storage server or eavesdropping on the network does not weaken the privacy of the data. Namely, the plain video streams should not be available in any component party of the surveillance system other than the source cameras (for a few milliseconds).

The main security technology that can be used to cope with all the aforementioned challenges and requirements is the strong encryption of surveillance data, which can provide the required degree of confidentiality and deny unauthorized third party access to video content. Clearly, for security sake, encryption keys have to be updated periodically and stored in a secure way into a specific separate repository to be associated with the

video data streams. However, meeting the needs of the law/privacy enforcement personnel and authorities also implies that a means of revealing the hidden video data should be provided only under specific circumstances. Specifically, rights and privileges to access surveillance data have to be managed through well-designed corporate/government security policies.

For example, some sections (i.e. specific day/times) in a video cannot be decrypted unless explicitly authorized by two government agencies and a Court order. This implies the necessity of a key management solution to safely distribute encryption keys, and therefore access rights, between the co-operating authorities (that only combined together, according to specific policies can be granted access) and periodically check the integrity of the camera devices so that the video sources cannot be maliciously substituted or tampered with to generate fake video data.

Accordingly, to provide the required security and privacy guarantees in a modern video surveillance system, a simple reference architectural scheme is proposed, structured according to the aforementioned principles, composed of several surveillance cameras connected through an IP-based infrastructure to a Surveillance Server, whose main task is to control the access to the contents originated by the cameras together with their security-related attributes (mainly the encryption keys) as well as a data collection and archival server (the DVR, previously defined) physically recording the video streams (see Figure 2).

The Surveillance Server also interfaces the available MSs in order to grant access to the encrypted data stored on the DVR and dispatch the key shares needed for decryption. Once these keys have been acquired, and after the completion of the authorization procedure, the MSs can request specific video data to the DVR and decrypt them on the fly. The data can be accessed offline, at any time, or almost synchronously, immediately after they have been stored on the DVR, for online monitoring. The individual cameras are capable

Figure 2. The operating scenario

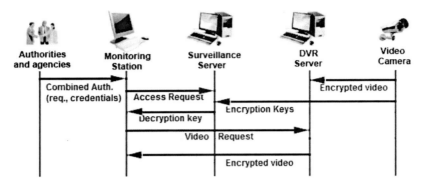

of capturing either single photos or entire video streams and transmit them to the DVR in real-time using common IP-based transport protocols. Clearly, video streams are encrypted directly on the respective source cameras and decrypted only on the end monitoring systems obtaining an authorized access to them, so that they never travel through the network or are stored on any intermediate system (i.e. the DVR) in clear form. In order to guarantee lawful evidence as well as the trustworthiness of all the surveillance data stored on the DVR, it is essential to prove the integrity of each involved video stream, both before and during the transmission, as well as that the video capturing sources have been correctly trusted by the system before transmitting or generating any encrypted data. Thus, the system needs to apply, in advance, end-to-end mutual authentication between any camera or monitoring station and the corresponding servers, in order to guarantee strong identity trust in each transmission. This, therefore, certifies the origin of any transaction between the communicating parties. Moreover, in order to ensure timing consistency, all the components of the Surveillance system should be synchronized on a common time reference, e.g. by using the Network Time Protocol (D. Mills, J. Martin, Ed. and W. Kasch (2010). In a non-authenticated environment, external hostile elements can (often transparently) insert themselves into the data path between cameras and servers, sub-

sequently collecting and disrupting the information through Man-in-The-Middle (MiTM) or eavesdropping attacks, by impersonating each endpoint to the satisfaction of the other. Since these are essentially attacks on mutual authentication, the choice of providing strong end-to-end authentication and data confidentiality between all the system components through asymmetric encryption techniques such as X.509 certificates and SSL/TLS, makes the proposed scheme robust against these threats, by preventing their occurrence at all.

However, this kind of encryption introduces a significant computational burden. In harsher environments such as real-time video monitoring, the encryption activity can be considered as the system bottleneck; with it being common knowledge that carrying out full stream encryption may not be a good choice (Liu and Eskicioglu, 2003). Therefore, a hybrid solution, based on using asymmetric encryption for end-to-end authentication and key exchange, as well as faster symmetric streamline encryption only for the transmission of the encoded video streams, has been adopted.

The order according to which the video encoding and streamline encryption activities are combined needs specific attention for the overall effectiveness of the security framework. In fact, the adoption of encryption techniques over compressed video channels is not straightforward. Specifically, encryption destroys any redundancy

Figure 3. The video-processing scheme

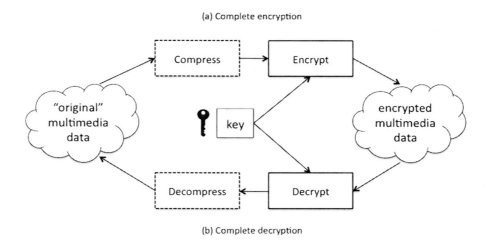

structure existing in the video data, thus invalidating the capability to carry out any meaningful video-processing task. In fact, typical encoders implement a compression/decompression scheme that is strongly based on the assumption that any input signal consists in an ordered sequence of individual image frames. Excluding a few atypical situations, the difference between two consecutive frames is very small (since in most cases the background is almost totally unchanging). For instance, all the widely used standards for compressed encoding take advantage of this evidence by generating in their output streams only the difference between consecutive frames. Due to such inter-frame difference being typically very small, these encoders are highly effective in compressing the amount of involved video data, making it very close to the information entropy value. Evidently, if the video stream is encrypted before encoding, it looses the above characteristics ensuring an optimal compression performance in the encoding phase, since it is completely randomized by the ciphering process. Encryption, therefore, has to take place only after the encoding/compression phase and consequently each video track stored on the DVR needs to be decrypted before any decoding/visualization operation. Figure 3 shows a typical video-processing scheme.

Following the encryption, the video must be sent to the DVR where it is archived to be accessed, when needed, by the requiring cooperating agencies. The keys that have been used for the encryption of the videos must be periodically changed (by regenerating interval-wise a new random master key on the source camera) in order to minimize the risk of access to the video through cryptanalysis techniques. In addition, due to all the keys used for the encryption being generated independently by each camera, they must be sent (by using strongly encrypted end-to-end connections) to the Surveillance Server on each change, to be reliably saved in a specific data repository, allowing for an easy and effective association with the related encrypted video information stored on the DVR server. The separation between encrypted data and encryption/decryption keys on separate servers further improves the security of the proposed architecture. In fact, the overall system security is compromised only if both these systems are compromised.

The Video-Encoding Framework

The video streams generated by the video camera sources are encoded according to the MPEG video standards (ISO-IEC, 1992-1, ISO-IEC, 1992-2). In the MPEG encoding standard, each frame, corresponding to a single picture in a video sequence, is encoded according to one of three possible encoding modes: intra frames (I), predictive frames (P), and interpolative frames (B). Such frames usually appear within a periodic sequence, parameterized by its number of component frames N, and by the spacing between the P-frames, M. Each periodic frame sequence is known as a Group of Pictures (GOP). The first frame belonging to each GOP is an I-frame, which is only statically compressed. Its former task is to effectively estimate and correct the motion errors "accumulated" throughout each GOP. Any other frame within a GOP is then encoded by difference, either indirectly or directly, starting from the initial I-frame. Therefore, I-frames are the highest quality frames in a video sequence since they are encoded independently from any other frame appearing in the sequence. They present the minimum level of compression.

A color frame (in RGB format) is at first converted into a luminance/chrominance representation space (YUV), then the U and V chrominance values are sub-sampled in relation to the luminance channel Y and each channel is subsequently partitioned into 8 x 8 pixel blocks. Grouping together some of these luminance and chrominance blocks (specifically one U-block, one V-block and four Y-blocks) generates a macro-block. After applying a discrete cosine transform to each of these blocks, the resulting coefficients are then quantized through run-length and variable-length encoding. While, in the encoding process, I-frame compression is accomplished by reducing the spatial redundancies within the individual video frame itself, the P-frame encoding mechanism has the sake of reducing the temporal redundancies across multiple consecutive frames, thus achieving better compression rates. Hence, compression

is implemented by fully encoding the first frame in the sequence and only the amount of motion between consecutive frames (consisting in a single vector) for each other frame in the GOP.

The original video frame sequence may be easily re-generated by using the motion vectors through step-by-step motion-correction starting from the first I-frame. The decoding of each P-frame is thus accomplished by warping the previous frame on the motion vector basis, and, finally, adding the motion errors to the result. By removing any temporal redundancies, the P-frames give better compression than the I-frames, but with a certain loss in quality. Similarly, each B-frame is encoded by using a motion compensation technique. Differently from P-frames, motion estimation in B-frame encoding can be based on future, past or both of its neighboring frames.

Enforcing Security through Hybrid Encryption

The two main security requirements of the digital surveillance architecture presented in this work, specifically video content privacy/confidentiality and trust on video capturing devices seem to be in contrast with each other. Really, all the methods relying on digital signatures, certificates and PKI infrastructures, necessary to guarantee strong authentication between the communicating parties, are completely unusable when trying to ensure confidentiality, because of their impact on the overall quality and performance of the encoding mechanism.

As a result, the entire framework adopts a feasible solution to fulfill real-time video encryption and lawful identity enforcement, by using a hybrid cryptography system which employs asymmetrical key-agreement mechanisms derived from X.509 digital certificates for the initial point-to-point authentication between each camera and the Servers (both the DVR and the Surveillance), together with an efficient symmetric encryption algorithm required for satisfactory performances.

For the purpose of imposing the collaboration of various independent entities during the decryption phase, the related decryption tokens are split among several Agencies/users. During the decryption phase, each user needs its own share of the entire decryption key, that is present in encrypted format only on the Surveillance Server. It is important to highlight that the whole decryption/encryption key is never kept in clear form in the system or exposed during the information exchange steps needed in the decryption phase. Furthermore, the keys used for the encryption of video data must be chosen interval-wise and periodically changed in order to minimize risks of access to stored video contents through cryptanalysis techniques. Since each camera periodically re-generates the random keys to be used for encryption, all the shares computed by starting from such keys must be sent to the Surveillance Server on every key change.

The most straightforward solution is to merely encrypt the whole data stream by using a general-purpose algorithm that uses symmetric keys such as AES. This solution is normally known as the *naïve* solution. The benefit of this approach is not only an easy implementation, but that it also gives the opportunity to use code modularity, allowing simple changes in key-distribution mechanisms, encryption algorithms and even in the video encoding algorithm to be used. Nevertheless, the computation overhead introduced by cryptographic operations is an unambiguous drawback. In a system where the hardware is used for the decoding of some data, it is clear that a software decryption module could result in a bottleneck. A reasonable choice could be the use of lightweight selective encryption in which only some pieces of video content are encrypted, with the consequence of reducing the computational effort at the expense of weakening some security constraints.

This technique is generally appropriate for video surveillance solutions because the full encryption of the video is not essential. Selective methods do not handle the video stream as regular IP packets. They make use of the specific features of the compression and encoding algorithms of video streams to follow up their distinctive features. When considering the MPEG encoding format, the *B* and *P* frames convey less information than the *I*-frames. Consequently, the application of cryptographic operations only to a subset of *I*-frames could result in a satisfactory performance with various degrees of video security.

An interesting example can be observed in the proposal of the Video Encryption Algorithm (VEA) by (Qiao and Nahrstedt, 1997), in which they apply a symmetric encryption algorithm to the whole encoded video data stream. The idea relies on the intrinsic properties of the MPEG format by lowering the quantity of data that is encrypted as well as the Shannon's "confusion and diffusion" concept (Shannon, 1949) in order to preserve the overall security to a reasonable level. In the VEA algorithm, a piece of the *I*-frame is split in two halves. The two halves are XORed each other and then combined in one half. Using a symmetric encryption algorithm such as DES or AES the remaining half is encrypted. This can result in an almost 50% improvement in terms of execution time when compared to the naïve solution.

The encryption scheme adopted in the proposed framework is based on the VEA basic scheme with some additional features aimed at avoiding byte modifications in the video ciphertext.

The following steps can describe the overall scheme:

- Each *I*-frame lump, $a_1, a_2, a_3 \ldots a_{2n-1}, a_{2n}$ is partitioned into two byte streams $a_2, a_4 \ldots a_{2n}$ and $a_1, a_3 \ldots a_{2n-1}$ respectively associated to the even and odd byte.
- On these byte streams a bitwise XOR is performed with the result of a new byte stream $c_1, c_2, \ldots c_{n-1}, c_n = a_2, a_4 \ldots a_{2n} \oplus a_1, a_3 \ldots a_{2n-1}$
- An appropriate ciphering function $E(.)$ is selected for the encryption of the "even"

•

Figure 4. PCBC encryption mode

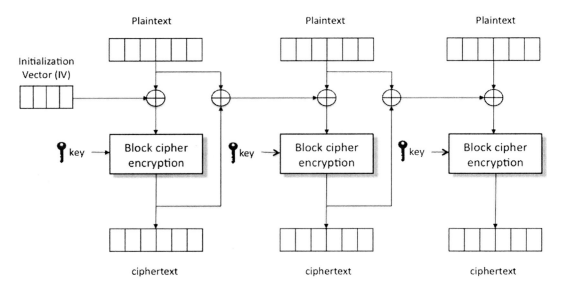

stream $a_2, a_4 \ldots a_{2n}$ resulting in a cipher-text stream that has the form $c_1, c_2, \ldots c_n$ $E(a_2, a_4 \ldots a_{2n})$. Clearly, if $a_2, a_4 \ldots a_{2n}$ do not have patterns that are repeated, then the entire cipher-text confidentiality relies on function E since $a_2, a_4 \ldots a_{2n}$ is a one-time pad that is known (Simmons, 1992) to be secure.

- As the last step, considered that it is required to work with an always-equal transformation on groups of bits (the two halves blocks) that have fixed-length, the entire encryption framework is organized in accordance with a block-ciphering reference model. In order to be more specific, a Propagating Cipher Block Chaining (PCBC) scheme is adopted. This leads to small changes in the ciphertext to be spread when decrypting along the entire cipher-text, and thus assures that any unauthorized operation on the cipher-text would result in the damage of all the following cipher-texts (see Figure 4). A block-wise HMAC (Menezes, 1997) may be added to further strengthen the integrity of the entire cipher-text.

The encryption function $E(.)$ is based on the AES symmetric encryption paradigm with an m-bits secret calculated according to a key-sharing algorithm.

Alternatively, the key management and media encryption methods could be based on several Conditional Access (CA) systems, as in the schemes commonly adopted by the modern digital broadcasting televisions. The various CAs, by way of summary, scramble the video data by using very small keys known as "Control Words" (CWs) periodically generated and sent to the customers (e.g. every few seconds in the latest versions of Videoguard and Nagravision). These CWs are decrypted by using a different key, regenerated less frequently, typically on a monthly basis, and kept on the customer's smartcard. Only the customers who own an official PayTV smartcard can use the dCWs to decrypt the stream.

However, the PayTV scenario is significantly different from the video surveillance one because the above CWs are employed only during real-time decryption activities and destroyed after each use. On the other hand, in any really secure video surveillance system, all the keys used for encryption must be carefully saved in order to decode the video data when needed. Furthermore, in a PayTV scenario, the scrambling mechanism is effective if and only if the CWs are updated frequently (i.e. at least about every 10 seconds). For this reason, a secure video surveillance system must be based on a strong cryptosystem (AES or DES), that is known to be much more secure than the scrambling system used for PayTVs.

Sharing the Secrets

Secret sharing schemes form a particular group of multi-party key establishment protocols (Menezes, 1997). Such schemes provide reliable mechanisms for protecting cryptographic keys without an increased risk of disclosure. They also enable the distribution of control or trust in many critical activities, such as most strategic, military or banking operations. The idea behind a secret sharing scheme is to divide a key S into n pieces $S_1, S_2, ... S_n$, called shadows or shares, such that any group of k elements, combined together, can be used to reconstruct the whole original key. Using any number of shares less than k will not help to reconstruct the original message. Furthermore, on their own, the individual shares give no information about the secret. This scheme is referred to as a (k, n) threshold scheme. In a (k, n) prepositioned secret sharing scheme, the n secret shares are distributed to the participants before the activation of the scheme itself (Simmons, 1990-1; Simmons, 1990-2). If $k=n$ then all the participants are required together to reconstruct the secret.

The polynomial approach (Shamir, 1979) will be used to show this concept, while there are other approaches such as the Vector Scheme (Blakley, 1979) and Asmuth-Bloom (Asmuth, 1983) that could be used. The Shamir threshold key-sharing scheme has several desirable properties that make it an optimal choice for the proposed framework:

- First of all, it is a perfect threshold scheme. Namely, the secret S can be reconstructed from knowledge of any k or more shares,

whereas the knowledge of fewer that k shares provides no information about S.
- The size of each share does not exceed the size of the secret S.
- Assigning different number of shares to users can create different levels of control.
- Its security does not rely on unproven mathematical assumptions.

The Shamir (k, n) threshold scheme is based on the Lagrange interpolation for random degree polynomials over the finite Galois Field $GF(p)$. Suppose that a (k, n) threshold scheme has to be used to share a secret S where $k \leq n$. At first, k-1 coefficients $a_1, a_2, a_3 ... a_{k-1}$ must be chosen in a random way, so that the secret S must be the a_0 of the generating polynomial function. Let p be a prime number, then a generating polynomial with intermediate x values over the finite field Z_p has the following expression form:

$$f(x) = \left(\sum_{i=0}^{k-1} a_i x^i \right) \bmod p$$

where the coefficients $a_0, ..., a_{k-1}$ are unknown elements of Z_p.

The n key shares $S_1, S_2 .... S_n$ can be constructed as pair of values $S_i = (x_i, f(x_i))$ where $1 \leq i \leq n$.

The polynomial function $f(x)$ is destroyed after each shareholder possesses a pair of values S_i so that no single share holder knows the secret value a_0. Given any subset of k of these pairs, the coefficients of the polynomial by Lagrange interpolation can be found:

$$S = a_0 = f(0), \quad f(x) = \sum_{i=1}^{n} S_i \lambda(x, i), \quad \lambda(x, i) = \prod_{\substack{k=1 \\ k \neq i}}^{n} \frac{x - k}{i - k}$$

that is, k linear equations in the k unknowns a_0, ..., a_{k-1} can be obtained, where all the arithmetic is done in Z_p. If the equations are linearly independent, there will be a unique solution, and a_0, which is the secret, will be revealed.

Putting it all Together: The Proposed Scheme at Work

The entire procedure is made up of three main steps: in the first one, the cameras acquire the frames in YUV format. Subsequently, these frames are processed, by creating several video frames organized according to the MPEG-1 structure. Finally, the above video frames are encrypted while being processed by making use of the previously introduced encryption algorithm. The keys K_{C_i} (from now on, the "encryption keys") used by the ciphering are derived on each camera by using a pseudo-random algorithm. Such keys are never stored in the cameras and starting from them the session keys are generated for each camera (and by each camera) by making use of a secret sharing scheme. That is to say that the "session keys" are blocks of the "encryption keys" K_{C_i} that have been divided among the various authorities involved. Each authority holds a pair of private/public keys, and the public part of such keys is used on each camera, to encrypt the session keys derived from the encryption keys K_{C_i}.

The DVR and the Surveillance Servers, as a basis for supporting mutual end-to-end authentication, have a pair of private/public keys. As for the authorities, such public keys are employed on the cameras and monitoring stations to create a mutually authenticated communication channel with the (DVR and Surveillance) Servers over an encrypted TLS/SSL session. The chunks of the session keys are never stored on every camera and are dispatched in encrypted form, over the properly created secure channel, to the Surveillance Server in order to be saved for later use. Only the authorities that own the matching private key associated to the public key which has been used in the encryption process, would be allowed

to decrypt that piece of the encryption key. The various shares are essential for the decryption of the video data. The duty of the Surveillance Server, apart of being in charge of the storage of the encrypted shares, is also responsible, at the camera start-up time or when a new camera joins the framework, for the authentication tasks.

One more important task that is attributable to the Surveillance Server is to give out the right shares to the various authorities when the decryption of a video part is required. Following the aforementioned steps, in which the setup of the whole system is principally performed, each camera would be able to deliver the encrypted video material to the DVR Server. Consequently, the video chunks cannot be viewed unless the correct (according to the Shamir secret sharing scheme) number of cooperating authorities will take part in the decryption process.

Considering the security of the private information involved, the authentication of the Surveillance Server with the cameras can be achieved in at least two ways:

1. Secret information used in the authentication process with the Surveillance and DVR Servers as well as the public keys involved (of the authorities and of both servers) can be stored on a PIN-protected smartcard that is held by each camera. Consequently, no secret information will be saved on the memory of the cameras avoiding, de facto, the possibility of a third party accessing them in case of abuse or theft. The main benefit of this approach is the strong level of security at the cost of usability. In fact, when the whole architecture is switched on, or just a single camera join the architecture, it is required that someone will provide the smartcard with the correct PIN in order to let the secret information needed for the authentication be released to the system;

2. Secret information which is handy when starting an authentication protocol based

on Challenge-Response paradigm may also be obtained starting for a specific exclusive item/code which is usually on the camera, like for example the camera serial number or a common string embedded in its firmware implementation. As a result, no human interaction will be required, resulting in a completely automatic setup operation. The advantage of this method is the ease of use, while the main drawback is that the firmware of the cameras can be reverse-engineered or, simply, someone could guess the "secret" used for the authentication, resulting in compromising the entire security of the system. A malicious user could try to pass itself off as a rightful camera and attempt to weaken the entire system. It is worth noting that, even when considering such more vulnerable scenario, normally the cameras are installed in a place that is almost inaccessible, and at the same time, with each camera monitoring other cameras. In such a case, any strive to perform camera manipulation will be recognized and prosecuted without difficulty.

When considering Trusted Computing technology, the approach that makes use of the secret information embedded on the camera can also be rated as nearly secure as the first one because, in such a case, the secret information on the camera (the serial number or a specific string in the firmware) will be guaranteed by the architecture provided by the trusted device.

The authors, in order to implement a proof-of-concept prototype, have chosen the straightforward case, that is the one where the secret data is located on the camera. To be more precise, the choice has been to make use of the serial number of the camera. Such a choice find the basis only on the fact that the authors were not interested in producing a real trusted camera device but can be effortlessly substituted by a more secure choice such as a Trusted Computing device or a smartcard. This simplification does not threaten the entire security of the architecture.

Following the initial setup stage, the entire system is ready to be put in service. All the cryptographic procedures are supervised by several keys:

1. the master key K_{C_i} randomly and independently generated by each camera C_i (being different from camera to camera);

2. the n shares $S_{C_i}^{1}, \cdots, S_{C_i}^{n}$ generated by using the secret sharing scheme for each K_{C_i} key;

3. a private/public key pairs relative to each of the involved authorities;

4. the encryption keys $P(S_{C_i})$, which are "protected" by using the public key of the authorities. Such keys are encrypted before being sent to the Surveillance Server, and are used for real-time encryption during the normal operations.

The cameras generate individually and randomly each master key that is later used for the encryption of the video data. Each camera can be considered to be a trusted object if the entities involved in the activities are performed by trust enforcement technologies, like, for example, Trusted Computing (TPM) devices or smartcards. At the same time, similar hardening security policies and technologies should be used to secure all the associated operational resources (the Surveillance and DVR Servers).

Regarding the keys at step 3, it is assumed that such keys are already held by each authority. Thanks to the adoption of certificates adhering to the X.509 standard, each authority can store their keys wherever their policies require (e.g. by using a smartcard protected by a PIN). Cameras will change the master key K_{C_i} which is used for the normal encryption activities, on a time basis (for example every 5 minutes), destroying and regenerating it after its expiration.

Figure 5. Data allocation taxonomy

Surveillance Server			
Key LifeTime Interval	t_0	...	t_M
Camera ID	Key Shares		Key Shares
C_1	$P(S_{C_1}^{1,0}),\dots,P(S_{C_1}^{n,0})$	...	$P(S_{C_1}^{1,M}),\dots,P(S_{C_1}^{n,M})$
...	...	...	...
C_N	$P(S_{C_N}^{1,0}),\dots,P(S_{C_N}^{n,0})$	...	$P(S_{C_N}^{1,M}),\dots,P(S_{C_N}^{n,M})$

DVR Server			
Key LifeTime Interval	t_0	...	t_M
Camera ID	Encryped Video Chunk		Encryped Video Chunk
C_1	$V_{C_1}^0$	...	$V_{C_1}^M$
...	...	...	...
C_N	$V_{C_N}^0$	...	$V_{C_N}^M$

The shares $S_{C_i}^1, \cdots, S_{C_i}^n$ each one related to the n involved authorities, are protected by encrypting them with the public key of the matching authority and are dispatched to the Surveillance Server by mean of a secure TLS/SSL channel. These shares are then stored on the Surveillance Server, in encrypted format, in order to be fetched later on by the authorities involved in a decryption process. The entire data taxonomy allocation used in the proposed framework is presented in Figure 5.

In a certain interval of time t_j $(0 \leq j \leq M)$, for each camera C_i $(1 \leq i \leq N)$, there exist p shares $S_{C_i}^{1,j}, \cdots, S_{C_i}^{n,j}$ $(1 \leq k \leq n)$ related to the encryption keys K_{C_i} which are stored encrypted on the Surveillance Server.

Similarly, for each time frame t_j, and for each camera, the DVR Server will store the corresponding video data chunk $V_{C_i}^j$ encrypted with the secret K_{C_i}.

Performance Analysis

The fundamental parameter characterizing the discernible performance of the proposed encryption framework is the coding efficiency. Clearly, it is of great significance that the coding performance is not influenced too much during the encryption phase.

For these reasons, three cases have been analyzed, with the average encoding time of the frame having been compared: the case where the encryption is not applied at all (i.e. when only the "original" MPEG-1 encoding is performed), the case in which the naïve AES approach has been adopted (i.e. when a 128 bit key has been used to encrypt all the packets) and the encryption scheme proposed in this chapter (which makes use of selective lightweight encryption). For this purpose, the case in which no data is encrypted (i.e., corresponding to the original MPEG-1 encoding), in conjunction with the cases where encryption is performed using the naive AES approach (all the stream packets are encrypted by using a 128 bits key) and the presented selective encryption scheme, have been analyzed by comparing their average frame encoding time.

More in depth, looking at Table 1 it can be seen that the proposed approach introduces only a slight influence on the coding efficiency. The data in Table 1 refers to a 10-minute video excerpt recorded on a PC equipped with an Intel Centrino

Table 1. Coding performance

Format	Framing	Avg Frame Size	Time for frame		
			No Encryption	Naïve Encryption	Selective scheme
320 x 200	30 fps	3000 bytes	0.11	0.433	0.304
640 x 480	30 fps	12000 bytes	0.28	1.3	0.9

1.6GHz Dual-Core CPU at different resolutions (320x240 and 640x480 at 30 fps).

Security and Resiliency Analysis

A confidentiality enforcement scheme based on encryption provides an acceptable level of security when the cost of breaking the underlying encryption method requires an investment greater than the one necessary for obtaining the key. In this case, the time needed to break the ciphering scheme exceeds the useful lifetime of the encrypted data. Furthermore, an encryption scheme can be considered satisfactorily secure, when the encryption method on which it is based can resist ciphertext-only and known-plaintext attacks. In the ciphertext-only attack, the attacker has to reconstruct the original plaintext data from the encrypted values through cryptanalysis techniques or brute force attacks. As explained in previous sections, the overall ciphertext secrecy depends on the symmetric encryption mechanism used on the sequence (AES in this case). The security strength of this algorithm firstly depends on the length of the symmetric encryption key. Since the minimum length of the AES cipher key is 128 bits, which provides 2^{128} possible keys, performing exhaustive searches in this huge key-space is considered infeasible (Al Hasib and Haque, 2008), with the presented framework thus being immune to brute force attacks.

The encryption scheme introduced is based on one-time-pads as well as the AES algorithm, and consequently is not threatened by *replacement* attacks (Podesser et. al., 2002). However, some studies have shown that the AES scheme is exposed to *side channel ciphertext-only* attacks, like for example the timing attack (Bernstein, 2005; Bonneau and Mironov, 2006). This attack can occur with implementations that do not run in a fixed time but is dependant from the length of the input. There are several solutions which ensure that AES continues to be provably immune to ciphertext-only attacks at the cost of making it a bit slower than usual.

In the *known-plaintext* attack, an attacker owns some samples of both the original plaintext data and the corresponding encrypted values and starting from them tries to break the used encryption scheme.

As previously stated, the encryption keys are renewed on a time-basis when the video chunks are transferred to the DVR Server. For this reason, when choosing short enough key lifetimes, the proposed scheme can be ensured to be also secure against known-plaintext attacks. This is also guaranteed by enforcing the encrypted transmission of each newly generated key within the MPEG video stream through a TLS/SSL connection, using the public key of the receiver (i.e., the DVR). The adopted secret sharing scheme also improves error resiliency in the case of key loss or corruption.

In the proposed scheme k shares of the secret, used for the encryption of the data stream, will be dished out among p (with $p \geq k$) available ones. Thanks to the versatility of the (k, p) threshold scheme, the framework is able to manage both the situation when a key share is lost or stolen, as well as provide the inclusion of new authorities to the entire process of video material decryption. That is possible due to the fact that a change or loss of a key can be overlooked. Nevertheless, it is normal that significant, but tolerable, computational costs are introduced by adopting such advanced features. If more than k keys have been assigned to the corresponding authorities and, if a key share is lost, the residual k keys can be employed for the reconstruction of the desired video data, thanks to the secret sharing scheme by Shamir. If any content, which has been previously encrypted, is modified for some reasons, the introduced PCBC concatenation and (eventually) the HMAC can be used to discern whether an error has occurred or if there is a possible violation of the integrity of the video content.

PROOF OF CONCEPT IMPLEMENTATION

A prototype system has been realized, just as a proof-of-concept, in order to verify the usefulness of the entire security framework introduced in this work. The emphasis has been put on the adoption of today-available COTS (Commercial Off-The-Shelf) devices as well as open source components in order to keep away from legalities and licensing costs. The adoption of COTS component during the construction phase of the prototype allows the system to be effortlessly deployed on an industrial large scale, allowing it to improve in terms of performance as well as to reduce the overall costs, and finally to take advantage of the progressive improvement of the COTS devices.

The prototype implementation is based on Linux machines (running the 2.6.19 kernel), together with wired and wireless IP cameras realizing the basic authentication scheme, that is the one providing the initial automatic setup by using the serial number of the camera. The code has been written in pure ANSI C. Due to the generic implementation, any client (running different OSes can be used to access the Servers for the decryption of the recorded material. In a real scenario, for example, Security Officers or policemen who

have the right combination of key shares needed for the specific policy implemented therein, can interact using their laptops or PDAs (eventually equipped with smart-card readers if their private keys are stored on a smart-card) with the Surveillance Server, and be able to access the video data recorded by the involved secure cameras.

The system uses several open-source solutions to implement the modules taking part in the process. The Video for Linux (de Goede, 2010) library is used to interface the devices for the video input, in other words to deal with the cameras. This library is very handy when a Linux box is required to deal with video devices and offers a powerful tool to the developers thanks to the great level of abstraction when dealing with non hardware-specific resources. The V4L library allows programmers to focus on particular programming task without being confused by hardware-related issues. The graphical user interface has been realized by using the GTK+ library, which provides programmers with different languages such as Python, C/C++, etc., enabling them to work on a common graphical framework that offers many interesting features. The module that handles the structural elements of the video compression has been chosen to be the DALI library (by the Cornell University). This library has been used for the preparation of the MPEG-1 container starting from a set of acquired YUV format images. The OpenSSL library has been used for all the encryption and key generation steps.

Figure 6 presents the interface of the module that is responsible for the generation of the encryption keys. This module, called "Key Generation", requires the value of the parameters (k, n) of the Shamir scheme together with the size (in byte) of the initial random key, which will be used as a seed for the generation of the shares for each authority. In the above example, the system makes use of 128 bit keys, there are 5 authorities involved and, in order to decrypt a protected video, the collaboration of (at least) 2 authorities is required. After preparing the shares, they must be encrypted

Figure 6. Key generation interface

 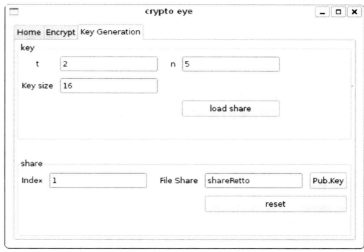

with the public keys of each authority. In order to carry out this operation, the authority (by means of its "Index") and the file name ("File Share") that will contain the public-key-protected share of the ith authority must be specified. This operation must be carried out for each authority involved (in the example shown in Figure 6 for 5 times).

After the key encryption operation, the file containing the shares protected with the public-keys are transferred to the Surveillance Server by using a TLS/SSL protected channel. For the generation of the master key K_{C_i}, the authors make use of the PRNG function present in the OpenSSL library. This library also offers all the functions required for the operations related to the X.509 certificates, such as the encryption of the shares with the public key and the decryption of the shares with the corresponding private key. OpenSSL is adopted even for the symmetric algorithm responsible for the real-time video data (DES and AES).

For the generation of the shares, the authors make use of the SSSS library (Shamir Secret Sharing Scheme), which is slightly modified in order to be adapted to the authors' needs. The prototypal application allows an operator to download each share in encrypted format from the Surveillance Server in order to decrypt them by using the appropriate keys (i.e. the private keys). Following the decryption process of the required shares, the decryption key K_{C_i} is reconstructed and the video decryption process for the camera C_i can be performed.

FUTURE RESEARCH DIRECTIONS

Future research work will focus on managing keys in distributed public-key cryptosystems, while keeping the number of local shares contained to a reasonable number. New anti-tampering solutions (other than TPM) and protocols to ensure the absolute trust of camera sources will also be explored. Furthermore, the security properties of the proposed approach will be further investigated as well as the compatibility of this scheme with existing COTS video surveillance solutions. In particular, cryptanalysis techniques will be exploited to assess the security of the proposed scheme, by making use of a detailed analysis of video stream encoding and compression. How to implement the presented framework into a practical embedded device/commercial camera, which can be used in industrial production, will be also investigated.

CONCLUSION

The presented privacy and security enforcing architecture has been proposed as a flexible and standard-based solution for a modern video surveillance system, supporting the trustworthiness and dependability requirements of today mission-critical and business-oriented applications. A media-aware hybrid encryption scheme based on key distribution and secret sharing scheme has been designed and implemented to effectively guarantee lawful evidence as well as full confidentiality of the video data in an exposed and insecure networked context. It should be highly useful in easing the diffusion and deployment of video surveillance infrastructures, thus leading to the overcome of most of the privacy worries which many times negatively influence all the steps involved in the management of sensible data.

Great efforts have been invested in trying to improve processing efficiency, ensuring an optimal interaction among the various modules, resulting in the enhancement of the security of the whole system. Further work will focus on improving the performance in terms of better execution time, in order to achieve real-time requirements. The authors believe that this cross-domain application could shed new light onto existing problems, as well as discover new threats that can emerge with the interaction of several technologic solutions that can be adopted in interdisciplinary areas.

REFERENCES

Al Hasib, A., & Haque, A. A. (2008). A comparative study of the performance and security issues of AES and RSA cryptography. *ICCIT '08: Proceedings of the 2008 Third International Conference on Convergence and Hybrid Information Technology*, (pp. 505-510).

Asmuth, C. (1983). A modular approach to key safeguarding. *IEEE Transactions on Information Theory, IT-29*(2).

Becker, A., Arnab, A., & Serra, M. (2008). Assessing privacy criteria for DRM using EU privacy legislation. In *Proceedings of the 8th ACM workshop on Digital Rights Management*, (pp. 77–86). Alexandria, Virginia, USA.

Bernstein, D. J. (2005). *Cache-timing attacks on AES.* Retrieved March 15, 2011, from http://cr.yp.to/antiforgery/cachetiming-20050414.pdf

Blakley, G. R. (1979). Safeguarding cryptographic keys. *Proceedings of the National Computer Conference 1979*, vol. 48. American Federation of Information Processing Societies.

Bonneau, J., & Mironov, I. (2006). Cache-collision timing attacks against AES. *Cryptographic Hardware and Embedded Systems, CHES 2006*, (pp. 201–215). Retrieved March 15, 2011, from http://research.microsoft.com/users/mironov/aes-timing.pdf

Bramberger, M., Doblander, A., Maier, A., Rinner, B., & Schwabach, H. (2006). Distributed embedded smart cameras for surveillance applications. *IEEE Computer, 39*(2), 68–75. doi:10.1109/MC.2006.55

Cai, X., Ali, F. H., & Stipidis, E. (2003). MPEG-4 over local area mobile surveillance system. In *Proceedings of the IEE Symposium on Intelligence Distributed Surveillance Systems*, (15/1-15/3).

Cisco. (2006). *Cisco Systems IP network-centric video surveillance*. White paper.

de Goede, H. (2010). *Video4Linux v4l-utils and libv4l*. Retrieved March 15, 2011, from http://freshmeat.net/projects/libv4l/

EU Parliament. (1995). Directive 95/46/EC of the European Parliament and of the Council. *Official Journal L 281*, 23/11/1995, 31-50.

Gemmell, D. J., Vin, H. M., Kandlur, D. D., Venkat Rangan, P., & Rowe, L. A. (1995). Multimedia storage servers: A tutorial. *IEEE Computer, 28*(5), 40–49. doi:10.1109/2.384117

ISO-IEC. (1992). Coded representation of picture and audio information. *International Standard ISO-IEC/JTC1/SC29/WG11*, MPEG Test Model 2.

ISO-IEC. (1992). Coding of moving pictures and associated audio for digital storage media up to 1.5 Mbit/s Part 2, video. *International Standard ISO-IEC/JTC1/SC29/WG11*, DIS11172-1.

Koutsakis, P., Psychis, S., & Paterakis, M. (2005). Integrated wireless access for videoconference from MPEG-4 and H.263 video coders with voice, E-mail, and web traffic. *IEEE Transactions on Vehicular Technology, 54*(5), 1863–1874. doi:10.1109/TVT.2005.853460

Liu, X., & Eskicioglu, A. (2003). *Selective encryption of multimedia content in distributed networks: Challenges and new directions. IASTED Communications, Internet & Information Technology*. CIIT.

Menezes, J., van Oorschot, P. C., & Vanstone, S. A. (1997). *Handbook of applied cryptography*. CRC Press.

Mills, D., & Martin, J. (Eds.). & Kasch, W. (2010). *Network time protocol version 4: Protocol and algorithms specification*. RFC5905, Internet Engineering Task Force (IETF). Retrieved March 15, 2011, from http://datatracker.ietf.org/doc/rfc5905/

Norris, C., McCahill, M., & Wood, D. (2004). The growth of CCTV: A global perspective on the inter-national diffusion of video surveillance in publicly accessible space. *Surveillance & Society. CCTV Special Issue, 2*(2/3), 376–395.

Podesser, M., Schmidt, H., & Uhl, A. (2002). Selective bitplane encryption for secure transmission of image data in mobile environments. In CD-ROM *Proceedings of the 5th IEEE Nordic Signal Processing Symposium (NORSIG 2002)*, Tromso-Trondheim, Norway.

Qiao, L., & Nahrstedt, K. (1997). A new algorithm for MPEG video encryption. In *Proceedings of The First International Conference on Imaging Science, Systems, and Technology (CISST'97)*, Las Vegas, Nevada, July 1997, (pp. 21–29).

Sedky, M. H., Moniri, M., & Chibelushi, C. C. (2005). Classification of smart video surveillance systems for commercial applications. In *Proceedings of the IEEE Conference on Advanced Video and Signal Based Surveillance (AVSS)*, (pp. 638-643).

Shamir, A. (1979). How to share a secret. *Communications of the ACM, 22*, 612–613. doi:10.1145/359168.359176

Shannon, C. E. (1949). Communication theory of secrecy systems. *Bell System Technical Journal, 28*(4), 656-715. Retrieved March 15, 2011, from http://netlab.cs.ucla.edu/wiki/files/shannon1949.pdf

Simmons, G. J. (1990). *How to (really) share a secret. Advances in Cryptology, Crypto '88 Proceedings* (pp. 390–448). Springer-Verlag.

Simmons, G. J. (1990). *Prepositioned shared secret and/or shared control schemes. Advances in Cryptology, Eurocrypt '89 Proceedings* (pp. 436–467). Springer-Verlag.

Simmons, G. J. (1992). *Contemporary cryptology: The science of information integrity*. IEEE Press.

Smith, C. L., & Robinson, M. (1999). The understanding of security technology and its applications. In *Proceedings of the IEEE International Carnahan Conference on Security Technology*, (pp. 26-37).

Welsh, B., & Farrington, D. (2002). *Crime prevention effects of closed circuit television: A systematic review*. London, UK: Home Office Research, Development and Statistics Directorate.

Wolf, W., Ozer, B., & Lv, T. (2002). Smart cameras as embedded systems. *IEEE Computer*, *35*(9), 48–53. doi:10.1109/MC.2002.1033027

ADDITIONAL READING

Agi, I., & Gong, L. (1996). An Empirical Study of Secure MPEG Video Transmissions, *Symposium on Network and Distributed System Security*, 137-144.

Akkuş, I. E., Özkasap, Ö., & Civanlar, M. R. (2006), Secure Transmission of Video on an End System Multicast Using Public Key Cryptography, *Lecture Notes in Computer Science, Springer Verlag, 4105*, 603-610.

Alattar, A. M., & Al-Regib, G. I. (1999). Evaluation of Selective Encryption Techniques for Secure Transmission of MPEG Compressed Bit-streams, *IEEE International Symposium on Circuits and Systems*, 340-343.

Baaziz, N., Lolo, N., Padilla, O., & Petngang, F. (2007). Security and privacy protection for automated video surveillance. *Signal Processing and Information Technology, 2007 IEEE International Symposium on*, 15(18) 17-22.

But, J., & Armitage, G. J. (2005). Implementing encrypted streaming video in a distributed server environment. In *Proceedings of Advances in Computer Entertainment Technology*, 322-325.

Freeman, J. P. (2001). 2001 report on the closed circuit TV & video surveillance market. In *A. Laurin, Impressive CCTV growth but analog technology lags behind, Axis Company Leaflet*. Retrieved Online March 15, 2011 from http://www.axis.com/documentation/whitepaper/video/2460_article.pdf

Halsall, F. (2001). *Multimedia Communications: Applications, Networks, Protocols, and Standards*. Reading, MA: Addison-Wesley.

In-Stat (2006). *In-Sights: Video Surveillance Systems on the Move to IP*. Industry Report.

Kraus, K.; Martikainen, O.; Reda, R. (2008). Security management process or video surveillance systems in heterogeneous communication networks. *Wireless Days, 2008. WD '08. 1st IFIP*, vol., no., 1-5

Liu, Z., Peng, D., Zheng, Y., & Liu, J. (2005). Communication protection in IP-based video surveillance systems. In *Multimedia, International Symposium on, Seventh IEEE International Symposium on Multimedia (ISM'05)*, 69-78.

Raju, C. N., Umadevi, G., Srinathan, K., & Jawahar, C. V. (2008). A novel video encryption technique based on secret sharing. *Image Processing, ICIP 2008. 15th IEEE International Conference*, (12)15, 3136-3139

Schaffer, M., & Schartner, P. (2005). Video Surveillance: A Distributed Approach to Protect Privacy. *Communications and Multimedia Security, 2005*, 140–149. doi:10.1007/11552055_14

Spanos, G. A., & Maples, T. B. (1995). Performance Study of a Selective Encryption Scheme for the Security of Networked Real-time Video. *Computer Communications and Networks, International Conference on, Fourth International Conference on Computer Communications and Networks (ICCCN '95)*, 2-10.

Tang, L. (1999). Methods for Encrypting and Decrypting MPEG Video Data Efficiently, *ACM International Conference on Multimedia*, Boston, MA, USA, 219-229.

The Royal Academy of Engineering. (2007). *Dilemmas of Privacy and Surveillance Challenges of Technological Change*. Technical Report. Retrieved Online March 15, 2011 from http://www.raeng.org.uk/news/publications/list/reports/dilemmas_of_privacy_and_surveillance_report.pdf

Tosun, A. S., & Feng, W.-C. (2000). Efficient Multi-layer Coding and Encryption of MPEG Video Streams, *International Conference on Multimedia and Expo, 2000*, 119-122.

Zhang, W. Cheung, S. and Chen M. (2005). Hiding privacy information in video surveillance systems. *IEEE International Conference on Image Processing*, Genova, Italy.

Ziliani, F. (2005). The importance of 'scalability' in video surveillance architectures. In *Proceedings of the IEE International Symposium on Imaging for Crime Detection and Prevention (ICDP)*, 29-32.

KEY TERMS AND DEFINITIONS

Encryption: the process of transforming information (referred to as plaintext) using an algorithm (called cipher) to make it unreadable to anyone except those possessing special knowledge, usually referred to as a key. It also implicitly refers to the reverse process, decryption, to make the encrypted information readable again.

Homeland Security: an umbrella term for security efforts to protect a nation against perceived internal and external threats, extending and recombining responsibilities and cooperation issues of several government agencies and security-related entities.

Privacy: the ability of an individual or group to seclude personal information about themselves and thereby reveal themselves selectively only under specific authorization.

Secret Sharing: method for distributing a secret amongst a group of participants, each of who is allocated a share of the secret. The secret can be reconstructed only when a sufficient number of shares are combined together; individual shares are of no use on their own.

Strong Authentication: the act of establishing or confirming the identity or trustworthiness of some entity, through a cryptographic process, often based on asymmetric cryptography and/or a challenge response protocol.

Transport Layer Security (TLS), Secure Sockets Layer (SSL): cryptographic protocols that provide communications security over the Internet. They encrypt the segments of network connections above the Transport Layer, using symmetric cryptography for privacy and a keyed message authentication code for message reliability.

Video Encoding: the technique used for codifying the bits of data that make up a digital video recording by preparing it for delivery in a digital format, according to a set of specific standards and parameters.

Video Streaming: a continuous exchange of data over a communication network. In particular, video surveillance pictures require an efficient streaming in order to actuate crime prevention and realize the basic functions of deterrence, detection and verification.

Video Surveillance: the use of video cameras for monitoring and crime prevention in sensitive areas such as banks, casinos, airports, seaports, military installations and convenience stores.

X.509 Certificate or Digital Certificate: also known as a digital identity certificate, is an electronic document that uses a digital signature to bind a public key with an identity — information such as the name of a person or an organization, their address, and so forth. The certificate can be used to verify that a public key belongs to an individual.

Chapter 11

Protecting Privacy by Secure Computation:
Privacy in Social Network Analysis

Florian Kerschbaum
SAP Research Karlsruhe, Germany

Daniel Funke
SAP Research Karlsruhe, Germany

ABSTRACT

We consider collaborative social network analysis without revealing private inputs of the participants. This problem arises in criminal investigations of federal police organization where single organizations may not reveal their data without probable cause, but the aggregation of all data entails new information, such as the entire social network structure. We present algorithms for securely computing either the entire, anonymized graph or only specific metrics for individuals. We use secure computation protocols to disclose nothing, but the output of the analysis, i.e. anything that cannot be derived from one's input and output – including other parties' input – remains private. We have implemented a prototype for SAP's investigative case management system – a derivate of its customer relationship management.

INTRODUCTION

In federated states or organization of states, such as the European Union or the United States, a mutual approach to organized crime is necessary. For this purpose, federal law enforcement

agencies, such as Europol or the FBI, have been established. Nevertheless, data privacy laws or simply data governance concerns restrict institutions from sharing their data, unless there is hard corroborating evidence on a case and subject under investigation. In particular, in the European Union (EU, 1995) data privacy is regarded as a high social and political value and the dilemma

DOI: 10.4018/978-1-61350-501-4.ch011

on how to generate evidence without violating privacy laws is evident.

A common tool for the criminal investigator is social network analysis. It graphically depicts the suspects and their connections to other people or artifacts, such as telephone numbers or bank accounts, and allows the computation of certain metrics. Not all the facts composing the entire picture of a case may be known to one investigator. In particular, in pan-European organized crime, local police forces may only be aware of a partial view of the picture.

This necessitates data exchange between the institutions, but European data privacy laws prohibit data exchange without probable cause and in excessive amounts. Therefore we propose a solution where the local investigator or an investigator at the superordinate institution has access to all information, but without revealing sensitive or private details. This allows the investigator to still use SNA and profit from its achievements without breaking individual privacy rights or guidelines of other institutions.

Privacy-Preserving SNA has been suggested in the literature before, but we have found the solutions to be insufficient for the requirements of our scenario. In (Frikken and Golle, 2006) a fully anonymized version of the social network is computed. This does not allow the investigator to track his suspect anymore and he cannot gain additional information or collect evidence about him. In (Canny, 2002) a recommendation value metric is proposed, suitable for privacy-preserving calculation. However, investigators are used to centrality metrics they are trained on, such as betweeness and closeness (Xu and Chen, 2005).

In this chapter we will present

- an algorithm that computes the entire social network from distributed sources without revealing personally identifying information while keeping track of the local view of each party.

- an algorithm to compute the important centrality metrics of betweeness and closeness without revealing personally identifying information and without revealing the entire social network.

The first algorithm, called "Compute Entire Network", allows the investigator to gain an overview of the entire social network. He can compute metrics on his subject as possible with the second algorithm, but he also gains additional information about the entire structure of the criminal organization. The second algorithm, called "Compute Metrics", provides higher privacy guarantees, as it does not even reveal the entire social network (except its size), but still allows important metrics to be computed about the subject. These metrics allow the identification of the role the subject is playing within the criminal organization (Xu and Chen, 2005).

RELATED WORK

SNA has been used for criminal investigations for a long time (Harper and Harris, 1975; Sparrow, 1991; Xu and Chen, 2005). Recent research suggests using graphical tools and investigates the impact of SNA (Xu and Chen, 2005). We can conclude that SNA is a widely accepted tool in criminal investigations.

Privacy-Preserving SNA has been first proposed by Frikken and Golle (2006). They compute an anonymized graph of the social network, such that no one should be able to track their position in the graph. They allow for certain modifications of the correctness of the anonymized graph in order to prevent tracking of one's position, e.g. they may bound the number of incoming connections or apply similar restrictions.

While this provides strong privacy guarantees it does not match the requirements of our scenario. An investigator intends to gather additional information to his present view of the social network. It is therefore unacceptable to anonymize his view, but the goal is to augment it with additional information about the entire network.

Collaborative filtering is the process of collaboratively identifying "*outstanding*" information items. It is particularly useful for recommender systems in e-commerce where outstanding items correspond to products likely to be bought. It is related to SNA, since both compute metrics for vertices in the network. Special collaborative filtering algorithms for graphs have been proposed in (Canny, 2002; Canny, 2002; Polat and Du, 2003), but the research on SNA for criminal investigations suggests that well-known metrics, such as betweeness and closeness, are more useful to investigators (Xu and Chen, 2005).

Similarly a new algorithm for link analysis is proposed in (Duan et al., 2005). Link analysis is a special collaborative filtering technique for a network or a graph of vertices. As a criticism, it applies here as well that practitioners prefer established metrics. It is important to note here, that different metrics require different protocols for computing them. In particular one can often optimize the performance of a privacy-preserving protocol by picking a metric that easy to compute in a privacy-preserving manner, but that might be less useful to the user. Our focus is clearly on maximizing the added value to the investigator as an end-user of the system.

Privacy-Preserving SNA can be seen as a special case of secure multi-party computation (SMC) which can solve any distributed function privately. SMC has been suggested by Yao (1982) for the two-party case. The first multi-party solution have been suggested in (Goldreich et al., 1987) for the computational setting and in (Ben-Or et al., 1988) for the information-theoretic setting. Efficient constructions have been identified for different secret sharing schemes (Cramer et al., 2000; Cramer et al., 2001). Nevertheless, as in (Frikken and Golle, 2006) stated, a straight-forward

application of these techniques would result in an unpractical protocol.

BACKGROUND

Social Network Analysis

A social network is a structure made up of individuals, which are linked by specific types of connections. In criminal investigations types of connections can be observations, e.g. at a crime scene, like identification of a weapon, phone calls or places of common observation.

This social structure can be represented by a graph. The individuals are the nodes s, t, u, v, ... and the connections are the edges. Social network analysis (SNA) is the analysis of this graph structure using graph or network theory. Since the underlying graph structures can be very large and complex, SNA can unearth a wealth of new information. Xu and Chen (2005) have shown this for criminal investigations.

A common form of analysis is for a single node in the network is a centrality metric. A centrality metric measures how well an individual is connected within the network. Usually a more central role is associated with more power in the represented society. In this chapter we consider two important centrality metrics: betweeness and closeness.

The betweeness centrality metric ranks vertices by the number of shortest paths that run through them and identifies vertices which connect strongly connected components. Vertices with a high betweeness metric indicate gatekeeper functionality between two criminal organizations (Xu and Chen, 2005). Let $\sigma_v(s,t) \in \{0,1\}$ be the number of shortest paths from s to t running through v. Betweeness is defined as

$$C_B(v) = \sum_{\substack{s,t \in V \\ s \neq t, s \neq v, t \neq v}} \frac{\sigma_v(s,t)}{(|V|-1)(|V|-2)}$$

The closeness centrality metric ranks vertices by their distance to all other nodes. Vertices with a high closeness metric indicate leadership in criminal organizations (Xu and Chen, 2005). Let $\delta(v,t)$ be the length of the shortest path from v to t in G. Closeness is defined as

$$C_C(v) = \sum_{\substack{t \in V \\ v \neq t}} \frac{|V|-1}{\delta(v,t)}$$

COMPUTING THE ENTIRE SOCIAL NETWORK

Building Blocks

In the first algorithm we use a *commutative* encryption scheme. In a commutative encryption scheme the order of encryption (with different keys) does not matter. We denote the encryption with Alice's key as $E_A()$ and with Bob's key as $E_B()$. Then, in a commutative encryption scheme, it holds that

$$E_A(E_B(x)) = E_B(E_A(x))$$

As we compare ciphertext, the encryption system cannot be semantically secure, but may be secret key. A candidate encryption system with all these properties is Pohlig-Hellman encryption (Pohlig and Hellman, 1978).

Protocol

A social network can be represented as a graph $G = (V, E)$ consisting of a set V of (connected) vertices and a set E of edges between the vertices. Each vertex v represents a person or other

artifact, such as a telephone number or company, and is associated with some personally identifying, unique information (such as the name or the telephone number). An edge e connects a pair of vertices v_1 and v_2 and is in correspondence with our application undirected.

The graph G may be distributed among n data sources, such that each party X_i holds a part of the graph $G_i = (V_i, E_i)$. The combination of the data sources result in the entire graph

$$V = \bigcup_{i=1}^{n} V_i \qquad\qquad E = \bigcup_{i=1}^{n} E_i$$

The parts may be overlapping, such that the intersection may not be the empty set.

$$\bigcap_{i=1}^{n} V_i \neq \varnothing \qquad\qquad \bigcap_{i=1}^{n} E_i \neq \varnothing$$

The goal of the algorithm is to compute the entire graph G, but without revealing the identifiers of the vertices. The algorithm must maintain the partial view of the graph, such that each participant can track its information in the assembled graph. The algorithm may reveal the source of each vertex or edge, the size of each part of the graph and the overlapping sets, such as the vertices or edges already known to the local participant.

The source information can be used by the investigator to selectively request additional information from other institutions that can enhance the case. Therefore this tool can be used to combine data sources selectively, such that personally identifying information is only revealed when there is probable cause.

Before the protocol begins, each participant X_i holds a key for encryption $E_i()$ in the commutative, secret key encryption scheme and another key $E'_i()$. $E'_i()$ should be in the same (commutative) encryption scheme.

The "Compute Entire Network" protocol proceeds as follows:

Each participant X_i prepares for each of his edges $e_j = (v, v') \in E_i$ a tuple

$$\langle i, E'_i(v), E'_i(v'), E_i(v), E_i(v') \rangle$$

2. Each participant X_i sends his tuples to the next participant X_{i+1}. Participant X_n sends to participant X_1.
3. Each participant X_{i+1} encrypts the last two fields of each received tuple.

$$\langle i, E'_i(v), E'_i(v'), E_{i+1}(v), E_{i+1}(v') \rangle$$

4. All participants repeat steps 2 and 3 n times.
5. Each participant X_i keeps a copy of the received tuples and forwards them to participant X_{i+1}. They repeat this step $n-1$ times.

After the "Compute Entire Network" protocol, each participant X_i holds a set T of tuples representing all edges E plus some potential duplicates. Let $E^n(v)$ denote the encryption with all keys $E_i()$ $i = 1,...,n$. Note that due to the commutative encryption the order of encryption does not matter. A tuple after the protocol therefore looks like this:

$$\langle i, E'_i(v), E'_i(v'), E^n(v), E^n(v') \rangle$$

The local investigator can now

• remove duplicates, since duplicates have the same two last fields, resulting in the set E.
• build an anonymized graph G from E with the pseudonyms $E^n(v)$ for v and e.g. visualize it.
• track his input by identifying the tuples with (his) i in the first field and deanony-

mizing those pseudonyms by decrypting the second and third field.

The investigator ends up with an anonymous view of the entire social network with a partial non-anonymous view of his present knowledge. He can then perform SNA (e.g. metrics computation) on his suspects without having learnt personally identifiable information from his collaborators. He may request additional information from some collaborators, since he now can target individual collaborators that are likely to have useful information. This protects the privacy of suspects, since it reduces the overall data exchange to reasonable amounts that are likely to contribute positively to the case. The information about likely innocent people remains protected.

Analysis

The protocol operates in the semi-honest model (Goldreich, 2002). We strongly argue that this is appropriate for our application, since we are concerned with cooperating police organizations and officers whose main concern is protecting the privacy of the suspects and keeping practical data governance. That is, the organizations are inclined to follow the protocol, since their objective is not only the outcome of the collaborations, but also the process of data privacy protection. Since interest in collaboration can be assumed, the organizations could simply exchange data by bypassing the protocol, if they were not interested in data protection.

The main security goal of the protocol is to not leak identifiable information as in the labels of the vertices. We state the following theorem:

Theorem 1: The identifier of any vertex **v** *known only to participants* $\mathbf{X}_i \in \mathbf{X}$ *is inaccessible to any participant* $\mathbf{X}_j \notin \mathbf{X}$.

Proof Sketch

The identifier of v only leaves the systems of a participant X_i encrypted under $E_i()$.

Therefore the security of the identifier is based on the security of the encryption.

Comparison to Privacy Model of Frikken and Golle

The paper from Frikken and Golle (2006) presents a privacy definition for SNA. Our paper takes a different stance on privacy. Their main concern is that an attacker is able to track his position in the network and thereby possibly identify some other vertices in the network. They assume that one may have partial information about the network and exploit this knowledge to gain additional information.

On the contrary we assume that one completely divulges one's partial information. The threat is that an attacker might learn additional identifying information accidentally revealed during the protocol. In contrast to Frikken and Golle (2006) where no quantification of the previous knowledge was given, we prove that absolutely no private (i.e. identifying) information is being leaked. This implies that the attack with previous knowledge does not apply in our framework, since the attacker would simply reveal that information and then the revealed information would be part of the result of the computation. Obviously the result is not protected by our (or for that matter any) protocol.

COMPUTING SNA METRICS

The previous protocol reveals the entire social network before it can be analyzed. Although no personally identifiable information is revealed, the network itself can be considered sensitive in a very strict interpretation of the European data privacy law. In any case, the utmost protection of privacy is a high social and political value, especially if similar results can be achieved while still protecting it. This protocol therefore computes the important SNA centrality metrics of betweeness and closeness without revealing the network.

The "Compute Metrics" algorithm computes betweeness and closeness without revealing the network structure.

Building Blocks

In the "Compute Metrics" protocol we use a homomorphic, threshold encryption system. Let $E^*()$ denote encryption in this homomorphic, threshold encryption system. We require the homomorphic property to allow (modular) addition of the plaintexts. It then holds that

$$E^*(x)E^*(y) = E^*(x+y)$$

From which by simple arithmetic it follows that

$$E^*(x)^y = E^*(xy)$$

In a threshold encryption system the decryption key is replaced by a distributed protocol. Only if t or more parties collaborate they can perform a decryption. No coalition of less than t parties can decrypt a ciphertext. We require a collaboration of all parties, i.e. $t = n$ (since we operate in the semi-honest model and do not consider faults). Then a ciphertext can only be decrypted if all parties collaborate.

The homomorphic, threshold encryption system is furthermore public-key, i.e. any party can perform the encryption operation $E^*()$ (by itself). The ciphertexts are semantically secure, i.e. their ciphertext reveals nothing about the plaintext. More precisely, the ciphertexts are indistinguishable under chosen plaintext attack (IND-CPA). This implies an important property of re-randomization

Algorithm 1. Floyd-Warshall algorithm

```
for k:= 1 to n
  for i:= 1 to n
    for j:= 1 to n
      M[i][j] = min(M[i][j], M[i][k] + M[k][j])
```

where an input ciphertext is modified, such that it cannot be linked to its original anymore without modifying the plaintext. In our encryption system this is best performed by "adding 0": $E^*(x)E^*(0) = \hat{E}^*(x)$, but $E^*(x)$ and $\hat{E}^*(x)$ are unlinkable without the decryption key.

An encryption system satisfying all our requirements has been described in (Damgard and Jurik, 2001), a variation of (Paillier, 1999).

Protocol

In order to compute the two centrality metrics we need to compute the shortest path between all pairs of vertices. Shortest paths have been privately computed in (Brickell and Shmatikov, 2005), but they assume that the graph is public and only the weights are private. We need to keep the graph private as well.

We use the Floyd-Warshall algorithm (Floyd, 1962) as basis for our computation. The Floyd-Warshall algorithm computes the all-pairs shortest path and is an example of dynamic programming. Privacy-preserving dynamic programming was introduced by (Atallah et al., 2003) for two party cases, while we consider the multi-party setting.

The Floyd-Warshall algorithm is shown in Algorithm 1.

Initially the matrix M contains the edges E, i.e. $M[i][j] = 1$ if $(v_i, v_j) \in E$ and $M[i][j] = \infty$ otherwise ($M[i][j] = 0$). Intuitively the algorithm checks whether a shorter path from v_i to v_j exists via v_k. At the end of the algorithm the matrix M contains the length of the shortest path from v_i to v_j at its i,j-th position.

We keep the elements of the matrix M encrypted under $E^*(x)$, such that no party individually has access to it. Every participant X_i keeps a record of the current state of the matrix, i.e. the encryptions of each element. They then need to collaboratively engage in a "Minimum" protocol to compute the new element of the matrix. All participants engage in $|V|^3$ of these "Minimum" protocols following the Floyd-Warshall algorithm.

Minimum-Protocol

The input to the "Minimum" protocol are ciphertexts (values encrypted under $E^*(x)$). In our case this is one value from the matrix M and a second value computed by homomorphically adding two ciphertexts from the matrix M. The output of the "Minimum" protocol is a ciphertext of the element with the minimum plaintext value of the two inputs. It is important that no participant can infer which of the inputs is the minimum element, as this would reveal information about the graph G in the "Compute Metrics" protocol.

Let x_1, x_2 be the two input values. At the beginning of the protocol, each of the n participants holds ciphertexts of the two values: $E^*(x_1), E^*(x_2)$. We assume that the modulus of the homomorphic operation is much larger than the domain of our arithmetic operations, such that we can map negative numbers in our arithmetic domain to upper numbers in the modulus domain. The protocol proceeds as follows:

1. Participant X_1 computes the following value c. He randomly chooses a very large value r that can multiplicatively hide an

input value and a smaller random value r' $(0 \leq r' < r)$. He then computes $E^*(c) = (E^*(x_1) E^*(-x_2))^r E^*(-r') = E^*(r(x_1-x_2)-r')$. Note that X_1 can compute the negation of the plaintext of $E^*(x_2)$ by computing the muplicative inverse of the ciphertext, i.e. he can compute it without knowing the modulus of the homomorphic operation.

2. Participant X_1 sends $E^*(x_1)$, $E^*(x_2)$, $E^*(c)$ to X_2.

3. Each participant X_k $(k = 2 ... n)$ re-randomizes the ciphertexts $E^*(x_1)$, $E^*(x_2)$ of the input values. He then chooses two very large random values r and r' $(0 \leq r' < r)$ and flips a coin $\in \{0, 1\}$. If the coin is 0, he sends $E^*(x_1)$, $E^*(x_2)$, $E^*(rc-r')$ to X_{k+1} (X_n sends to X_1). If the coin is 1, he (randomizes and) negates the random value $E^*(c)$, switches the ciphertexts of the input values and sends $E^*(x_2)$, $E^*(x_1)$, $E^*(-rc+r')$ to X_{k+1}.

4. Each participant X_k $(k = 1 ... n-2)$ keeps a record of the result and forwards it to X_{k+1}.

5. All participants X_k $(k = 1 ... n)$ collaboratively engage in the decryption protocol and decrypt c. If c is negative, then the first ciphertext is the ciphertext of the minimum plain-text value. If c is non-negative, then the second ciphertext is the ciphertext of the minimum. Note, that a plaintext value can be considered negative, if it exceeds the maximum of the arithmetic domain.

The algorithm is correct, since $c < 0$ if and only if $x_1 \leq x_2$. Rerandomization of c does not change its sign, unless the ciphertexts are switched as well. Therefore the minimum element x_m is always at position $(c > 0) + 1$ of the ciphertexts forwarded between the participants. For the security of the algorithm we assume that a value x_i can be effectively hidden by multiplying it with a much larger value r. In order to prevent factoring of the result we additionally subtract a smaller value r', since otherwise the hidden value must consist of the factors of the result. Due to the re-randomization no one can infer which side of the coin showed up at any participant X_k $(k = 2 ... n)$.

There is a straight-forward generalization to m input values $x_1 ... x_m$. The parties compute pair-wise minimums of $\lfloor m/2 \rfloor$ pairs x_{2i-1}, x_{2i}. The resulting ciphertexts of the minimums are iteratively used as input for another round of the protocol until only 1 minimum remains. The protocol requires $\lceil log_2 m \rceil$ rounds.

Computing the Initial Matrix

The parties can now compute the iteration step of the dynamic program, but the matrix M must be initialized with the values from the set E of edges.

First, the participants must agree on a common set V of vertices. The vertex labels must not reveal identifiable information, just as in the "Compute Entire Network" protocol. Therefore, the participants must agree on an anonymized version of V. The anonymization for v is as before $E^n(v)$, but care must be taken that the overlapping sets of V_i are not being revealed. The participants compute the set union of their anonymized local sets V_i. A set-union protocol does not reveal the overlaps in the input sets. Set-union protocols can be found in the literature in (Brickell and Shmatikov, 2005; Frikken, 2007; Kissner and Song, 2005). We propose a multi-party version of (Brickell and Shmatikov, 2005), since it uses a "Minimum" protocol and we can use the protocol just described above. The overall protocol proceeds as follows:

1. First compute the pseudonyms without revealing the anonymized sets V_i. Note that the size of V_i is revealed. This can be prevented by padding with random values.

    a. Each participant X_i encrypts his vertices $v_j \in V_i$ by $E_i()$ and $E'_i()$: $E_i(E'_i(v_j))$. He sends them to participant X_{i+1}.

    b. Each participant X_{i+1} doubly encrypts the received and already encrypted vertices with $E_{i+1}()$: $E_{i+1}(E_i(E'_i(v_j)))$. He sends the result to participant X_{i+2}.

c. All participants X_i repeat step 1b $n-2$ more times, such that each participant X_i receives his initial values as $E^n(E'_i(v_j))$.

d. Each participant decrypts the received vertices with $D'_i()$ resulting in $E^n(v_j)$. Note that due to the commutative encryption the order of encryption does not matter.

2. Second compute the set-union of the anonymized vertices.

a. Each participant X_i sorts his list of anonymized vertices $E^n(v_j)$ in ascending order of the ciphertext.

b. Each participant X_i encrypts his minimum element $E^n(v_j)$ with $E^*()$ and sends $E^*(E^n(v_j))$ to X_i. He indicates the special element ■, if he has no more pseudonyms.

c. All participants X_i engage in the "Minimum" protocol for the inputs as described above.

d. All participants X_i commonly decrypt the result $E^n(v_m)$. Each participant that has the pseudonym $E^n(v_m)$ in his list, removes it.

e. They repeat steps 2b. through 2d. until all participants' lists are empty. Participants whose lists are empty use a top element $E^n(■)$ outside of the domain of anonymized vertices as input. If this element ■ is computed as the minimum element the protocol ends, as now all lists are empty.

Each participant now holds the set V of anonymized vertices $E^n(v)$ and knows the pseudonyms for his vertices v. He can then compute the anonymized set E_i of his edges $(E^n(v), E^n(v'))$. The participants must now compute the matrix M. The rows and columns of M each correspond to an anonymized vertex $E^n(v)$. Each participants sorts the set V in lexicographically ascending order of the ciphertexts. All elements of M can then be initialized with ∞ ($M[i][j] = 0$). Now each participant must set the values of M corresponding to his edges $(E^n(v), E^n(v'))$ to 1. To achieve this they can run this protocol:

1. Participant X_l prepares the initial matrix M with: $M[i][j] = E^*(\infty)$ $\forall$ $i,j \in \{1 \ldots |V|\}$; $M[i][i] = E^*(0)$ $\forall$ $i \in \{1 \ldots |V|\}$

2. Participant X_k ($k = 1$) replaces the entries for edges in M with $E^*(1)$: $M[i][j] = E^*(1)$ $\forall$ $i,j \in E_k$
He rerandomizes all ciphertexts and sends the result to X_{k+1}.

3. Each participant X_k ($k = 2 \ldots n$) performs step 2.

4. Each participant X_k ($k = 1 \ldots n-2$) keeps a record of the matrix M and forwards it to X_{k+1}.

The algorithm is correct, since all edges in E will be set and duplicates are not noticed, since no participant knows whether he replaces an encryption of 1 or a ∞ with his encryption of 1.

The participants have then successfully initialized the matrix M and can run the dynamic program of the Floyd-Warshall algorithm. They compute the minimum for each iteration by choosing the corresponding matrix element and homomorphically computing the sum of the other two elements. In the end, they will end up with an encrypted version of the matrix M that has plaintexts of the length of the shortest paths between all pairs of vertices.

Computing the Metrics

So far we have computed the shortest-path matrix in the Floyd-Warshall algorithm, but our goal is to compute the centrality metrics of closeness and betweeness for one vertex, a suspect. Let X_l

be the investigator who has a suspect he wants query in the matrix. The other participants X_2 ... X_n should not learn which the queried vertex is. They can do so using the following protocols.

Closeness

Let v_s be the vertex for which intelligence is gathered. The investigator X_1 selects the row s for vertex v_s in M and computes

$$c_c = \prod_{i=1}^{m} M[s][i] = E^* \left(\sum_{i=1}^{m} \delta_{s,i} \right)$$

X_1 rerandomizes c_c to c'_c and distributes it to all participants. All participants jointly decrypt c'_c and X_1 can compute

$$C_C(v_s) = \frac{|V| - 1}{D^*(c'_c)}$$

Betweeness

Betweeness is more complicated to compute. X_1 needs to calculate the number of shortest paths through V_s. He keeps a second matrix T of size $|V|_2$. All entries of T are encrypted with $E^*()$, just as those of M. He initializes the matrix T at the beginning of the "Compute SNA Metrics" protocol as follows

T[s][j] = E*(1) ∀ j ≠ s

T[s][j] = E*(0) otherwise

In each "Minimum" protocol for *M[i][j]* in the Floyd-Warshall algorithm he augments the messages with the corresponding elements of T, i.e. in the message field for *M[i][j]* he adds another field *T[i][j]* and in the message field for *M[i][k] + M[k][j]* he adds a field *T[i][k] + T[k]*

[j]. He computes the addition of the plaintexts by the multiplication of the ciphertexts due to their homomorphic property and the ciphertexts are re-randomized by all other parties, such that X_1 cannot track the entries. After each "Minimum" protocol he updates *T[i][j]* with the value from the field in the minimum index *m*.

At the end of the Floyd-Warshall algorithm *T[i] [j]* ∈ *{0,1}* indicates with a 1 if the path from v_i to v_j is via v_s. From the computation of *T[i][j]* during the iteration it follows that it is an invariant of the algorithm that *T[i][j]* equals the number of times the path from v_i to v_j crosses v_s as an intermediary (i.e. all except the destination) vertex. Since the Floyd-Warshall algorithm computes the shortest path at its completion, no path can cross v_s more than one time in the final matrix T.

After the completion of the Floyd-Warshall algorithm X_1 computes

$$c_b = \prod_{i=1\ldots s-1,s+1\ldots m} \prod_{j=1\ldots s-1,s+1\ldots m} T[i][j] = $$
$$E^* \left(\sum_{i=1\ldots s-1,s+1\ldots m} \sum_{j=1\ldots s-1,s+1\ldots m} \sigma_{i,j} \right)$$

Participant X_1 rerandomizes c_b to c'_b and distributes it to all participants. All participants jointly decrypt c'_b and X_1 can compute

$$C_B(v_s) = \frac{D^*(c'_b)}{(|V| - 1)(|V| - 2)}$$

Analysis

The "Compute SNA Metrics" protocol operates in the semi-honest setting. The same arguments apply for the appropriateness of the model as in the "Compute Entire Network" protocol.

The proof of security is standard and follows the methodology of (Goldreich, 2002) by giving a simulator for the views of the participants.

Important is the distinction from the "Compute Entire Network" protocol: No information about the graph G except the centrality metrics is leaked. This follows from the correct implementation of the functionality, i.e. the function implemented by the "Compute SNA Metrics" protocol is to just compute the two metrics, closeness and betweeness, for one vertex in question. The "Compute SNA Metrics" protocol therefore offers a higher degree of privacy compared to the "Compute Entire Network" protocol, but it limits the result of the computation.

Performance

Let n be the number of vertices, i.e. $n = |V|$ and m be the number of participants. For notational issues we let $k = \lceil log_2 n \rceil$ be the number of bits to represent an index into the vertices.

Our protocol has the same complexity as a protocol using circuit construction, i.e. n^3 minimum operations for two elements are required during the main loops of the Floyd-Warshall type algorithm. To compute the initial matrix n minimum operations for m elements are required which following our tree-like algorithm corresponds to $n(m-1)$ minimum operations for two elements. Since the loops can be completely unrolled into operations with static indices no special array operations are required for array indexing (Malkhi et al., 2004). Therefore we can conclude that the performance of the minimum operation (for two elements) is the decisive factor for performance.

Generally it is difficult to compare the performance of different secure multi-party computations schemes. We focus on the general model of (Cramer et al., 2000) which has been successfully implemented in (Bogetoft et al., 2006; Bogetoft et al., 2009). For our precise analysis we use the threshold homomorphic scheme of (Cramer, 2001) which corresponds to our use of threshold homomorphic encryption.

It is an accepted fact in the community that general circuit construction protocols are too slow despite recent advancements in reduction in circuit complexity (Kolesnikov and Schneider, 2008). Therefore special protocols have been developed for important problems, such as minimum. Note that our protocol requires a minimum protocol for the multi-party case using encrypted inputs which excludes many special protocols for two-party Yao's millionaires' problem (Yao, 1982). E.g. the most efficient protocol for Yao's millionaires' problem requires bit-wise (potentially encrypted) input values (Damgard et al., 2008). The conversion from an integer ciphertext to bit-wise encryption is more complex than comparison itself (Damgard et al., 2006; Toft, 2007). In the framework of (Cramer et al, 2001) a special constant-round protocol for comparison has been developed (Damgard et al., 2006; Toft, 2007).

As a point reference we use the further optimized version (Toft, 2007) for the case where k is smaller than the number of bits in the plaintext domain. This protocol requires *14k* multiplication protocols from (Cramer et al., 2001), 2 decryption operations according to Damgard and Jurik (2001) and *4k+2* additional modular exponentiations. This results in *46k+6* modular exponentiations altogether. Note, that one additional multiplication protocol for computing the ciphertext of the minimum element would need to be performed.

The running time of secure multi-party computation protocols is still dominated by computational effort, especially for complex problems. Modular exponentiations are difficult operations to perform and dominate the running time of many cryptographic protocols.

Our minimum protocol operates differently than Toft's (2007). Not every participant is active at the same time and performs the same operations. Instead we have constructed a ring protocol.

We therefore need to analyze the performance slightly differently.

First each participant chooses two random numbers and encrypts one of them: 2 modular exponentiations. Then each participant encrypts two 0s for re-randomization: another 2 modular exponentiations. Then, in sequential turn, each participant multiplies (using homomorphic encryption) the comparison value with the other random number: m modular exponentiations. Re-randomizations and the (homomorphic) additions can be performed as much less critical modular multiplications. In the end one decryption is necessary: 2 additional modular exponentiations in the semi-honest case (performed by each participant). In summary our minimum protocol requires $m+6$ modular exponentiations. A draw-back of our protocol is that the ciphertext size is linear in the number of participants.

Information Leakage

The "Compute Metrics" algorithm claims to improve over the "Compute Entire Network" algorithm by not revealing the entire network. The question remains what can be inferred from the metrics about the entire network. This is a common question in secure multi-party computations, since their security definition does not capture what can be inferred from the output.

We establish a theoretical upper limit on the information leakage about the entire graph. Note, that the size of the graph $|V|$ (number of vertices) is publicly known. Then there are $e = \frac{1}{2}(|V|(|V|-1))$ possible edges and 2^e possible graphs. On the other hand betweeness can take one of $(|V|-1)(|V|-2)+1$ different values and closeness one of $\frac{1}{2}|V|(|V|-3)$ different values. Extreme values, such as a betweeness of $(|V|-1)(|V|-2)$, reveal the entire graph, but the average information leakage bound is much more favorable. We assume the worst case and the attacker computes the metrics for all c (out of $|V|$) vertices he knows. The upper bound θ of

the fraction of the average information entropy revealed can be written as

$$\theta = \frac{\log\left(\left(\left(|V|-1\right)\left(|V|-2\right)+1\right)^c \left(\frac{|V|\left(|V|-3\right)}{2}\right)^c\right)}{\log 2^{\frac{|V|\left(|V|-1\right)}{2}}}$$

Figure 1 plots the graph (as percentages) of the formula for small graphs ($|V| \in \{50, 100, 150, 200, 250\}$) and known number of vertices ($c \in [0, 50]$). The bigger the graph size the less is revealed about its entire structure. Even when a large percentage of the graph is known ($|V| = 250$, $c = 50$), very little is revealed about the entire graph (1.4%). Even when the entire graph is known ($|V| = c = 50$) there is still significant uncertainty on average about the entire graph.

IMPLEMENTATION ISSUES

Synonyms

Encryption is sensitive to spelling and capitalization mistakes. Therefore a person with two almost identical synonyms results in two very different ciphertexts and therefore vertices. This is a known problem and can be solved existing software solutions. Such solutions provide unique identifiers by expanding names into all possible synonyms. Note that, there exist privacy-preserving extensions to these technologies using cryptographic hashing, but they do not extend to SNA as required in our case.

Prototype

The following section describes the prototype built on top of the SAP the Investigative Case Management (ICM) system, a derivative of the

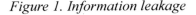

Figure 1. Information leakage

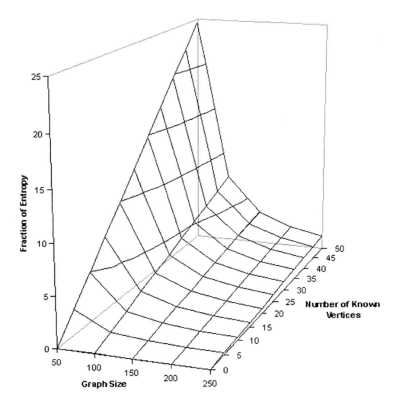

SAP Customer Relationship Management (CRM) system. Firstly, a high level architectural overview is given; secondly, the prototype is explained in greater detail. The high level architecture of the prototype is depicted in Figure 2.

The main protocol execution is within the ABAP stack of ICM system. A supplementary Java server is used for all encryption purposes, as ABAP lacks the comprehensive Big Integer functionalities of Java.

Two use cases are supported by the prototype:

1. In a regularly scheduled batch job, all participants execute the protocol for their entire dataset. This job should be run e.g. once a week to build a comprehensive encrypted view on all data owned by the participating institutions.

2. In an ad-hoc investigation, the protocol is executed for a specific entity of the initiating party.

The general processing can be structured as follows and corresponds to the steps of the "Compute Entire Network" protocol:

- **Initialization:** Setup of communication and encryption environment.
- **Acquisition:** Acquisition of the data from the ICM system and preparation of the tuples as described in step 1 of the protocol.
- **Encryption:** All parties execute step 2 through 4 of the protocol, obtaining $E^n()$ encryptions of their edges.

Figure 2. High level architecture of PPSNA prototype

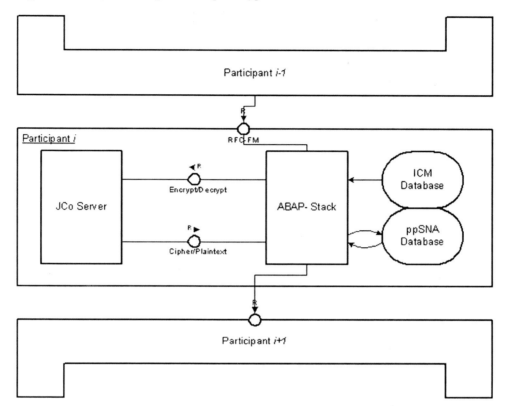

- **Gathering:** All parties gather the $E^n()$ encrypted edges of all other parties; step 5 of the protocol.
- **Evaluation:** Each party cleanses the data and visualizes the received edges. It may decrypt its own vertices and identify the source of foreign ones. The Social Network is visualized using specialized technology.

The ring property of the theoretical protocol is lost in the implementation due to synchronization issues. Therefore the structure of all collaborating police institutions must be known to each participant. Due to the wish to identify the source of the anonymized vertices to possibly obtain plaintext information, we do not consider this a shortcoming in privacy-preservation but rather additional administrative effort.

CONCLUSION

Social Network Analysis is becoming an important tool for investigators, but all the necessary information is often distributed over a number of sites. Privacy legislation and data governance concerns prohibit freely sharing the information. We have presented two protocols that allow the selective disclosure of information for Social Network Analysis.

In the first protocol the entire network is computed in an anonymized view except the local information is preserved. This allows the investigator to perform many analyses and can also direct the successive disclosure of information. It thereby preserves the privacy of personally identifiable information of suspects and limits the data exchange.

The second protocol is even more restrictive. It only discloses the results of Social Network Analysis: two important centrality metrics. It thereby allows an investigator to gather intelligence on a suspect by querying remote data sources without disclosing even anonymized data.

We have implemented the first protocol in a commercial enterprise system supporting criminal investigations and show first results. This shows that Social Network Analysis can be used in a privacy-preserving manner by investigators.

REFERENCES

Atallah, M. Kerschbaum, F. and Du, W. (2003). Secure and private sequence comparisons. In *Proceedings of the 2nd ACM Workshop on Privacy in the Electronic Society*, (pp. 39-44).

Ben-Or, M., & Wigderson, A. (1988). Completeness theorems for non-cryptographic fault-tolerant distributed computation. In *Proceedings of the 20th Annual ACM Symposium on Theory of Computing*, (pp. 1-10).

Bogetoft, P. Christensen, D., Damgard, I., Geisler, M., Jakobsen, T., Kroigaard, M.,... Toft, T. (2009). Multiparty computation goes live. In *Proceedings of the 13th International Conference on Financial Cryptography and Data Security*, (pp. 325-343).

Bogetoft, P., Damgard, I., Jakobsen, T., & Nielsen, K. Pagter, J., & Toft, T. (2006). A practical implementation of secure auctions based on multiparty integer computation. In *Proceedings of the 10th International Conference on Financial Cryptography and Data Security*, (pp. 142-147).

Brickell, J., & Shmatikov, V. (2005). Privacy-preserving graph algorithms in the semi-honest model. In *Proceedings of AsiaCrypt*, (pp. 236-252).

Canny, J. (2002). Collaborative filtering with privacy. In *Proceedings of the IEEE Symposium on Security and Privacy*, (pp. 45-57).

Canny, J. (2002). Collaborative filtering with privacy via factor analysis. In *Proceedings of the 25th International ACM Conference on Research and Development in Information Retrieval*, (pp. 238-245).

Cramer, R., Damgard, I., & Maurer, U. (2000). General secure multi-party computation from any linear secret-sharing scheme. In *Proceedings of EuroCrypt*, (pp. 316-334).

Cramer, R., Damgard, I., & Nielsen, J. (2001). Multiparty computation from threshold homomorphic encryption. In *Proceedings of EuroCrypt*, (pp. 280-299).

Damgard, I., Fitzi, M., Kiltz, E., Nielsen, J., & Toft, T. (2006). Unconditionally secure constant-rounds multi-party computation for equality, comparison, bits and exponentiation. In *Proceedings of Theoretical Cryptography Conference*, (pp. 285-304).

Damgard, I., Geisler, M., & Kroigaard, M. (2008). Homomorphic encryption and secure comparison. *International Journal of Applied Cryptography*, *1*(1), 22–31. doi:10.1504/IJACT.2008.017048

Damgard, I., & Jurik, M. (2001). A generalisation, a simplification and some applications of paillier's probabilistic public-key system. In *Proceedings of Public Key Cryptography*, (pp. 119-136).

Duan, Y., Wang, J., Kam, M., & Canny, J. (2005). Privacy preserving link analysis on dynamic weighted graph. *Computational & Mathematical Organization Theory*, *11*(2), 141–159. doi:10.1007/s10588-005-3941-2

EU. (1995). *Directive 95-46-EC on the protection of individuals with regard to the processing of personal data and on the free movement of such data.* Retrieved October 13, 2008, from http://ec.europa.eu/justice_home/fsj/privacy

Floyd, R. (1962). Algorithm 97: Shortest path. *Communications of the ACM, 5*(6), 345. doi:10.1145/367766.368168

Frikken, K. (2007). Privacy-preserving set union. In *Proceedings of Applied Cryptography and Network Security,* (pp. 237-252).

Frikken, K., & Golle, P. (2006). Private social network analysis: How to assemble pieces of a graph privately. In *Proceedings of the 5th ACM Workshop on Privacy in the Electronic Society,* (pp. 89-98).

Goldreich, O. (2002). *Secure multi-party computation.* Retrieved October 13, 2008, from http://www.wisdom.weizmann.ac.il/~oded/pp.html

Goldreich, O., Micali, S., & Wigderson, A. (1987). How to play any mental game. In *Proceedings of the 19th ACM Symposium on Theory of Computing,* (pp. 218-229).

Harper, W., & Harris, D. (1975). The application of link analysis to police intelligence. *Human Factors, 17*(2), 157–164.

Kissner, L., & Song, D. (2005). Privacy-preserving set operations. In *Proceedings of CRYPTO,* (pp. 241-257).

Kolesnikov, V., & Schneider, T. (2008). A practical universal circuit construction and secure evaluation of private functions. In *Proceedings of the 12th International Conference on Financial Cryptography and Data Security,* (pp. 83-97).

Malkhi, D. Nisan, N., Pinkas, B., & Sella, Y. (2004). Fairplay - A secure two-party computation system. In *Proceedings of the 13th USENIX Security Symposium,* (pp. 287-302).

Paillier, P. (1999). Public-key cryptosystems based on composite degree residuosity classes. In *Proceedings of EUROCRYPT,* (pp. 223-238).

Pohlig, S., & Hellman, M. (1978). An improved algorithm for computing logarithms over GF(p) and its cryptographic significance. *IEEE Transactions on Information Theory, 24,* 106–110. doi:10.1109/TIT.1978.1055817

Polat, H., & Du, W. (2003). Privacy-preserving collaborative filtering using randomized perturbation techniques. In *Proceedings of the 3rd IEEE International Conference on Data Mining,* (pp. 625-628).

Sparrow, M. (1991). The application of network analysis to criminal intelligence: An assessment of the prospects. *Social Networks, 13,* 251–274. doi:10.1016/0378-8733(91)90008-H

Toft, T. (2007). *Primitives and applications for multi-party computation.* Unpublished doctoral dissertation, University of Aarhus, Denmark.

Xu, J., & Chen, H. (2005). Criminal network analysis and visualization. *Communications of the ACM, 48*(6), 100–107. doi:10.1145/1064830.1064834

Yao, A. (1982). Protocols for secure computations. In *Proceedings of the 23rd IEEE Symposium on Foundations of Computer Science,* (pp. 160-164).

KEY TERMS AND DEFINITIONS

Betweeness: Number of shortest paths that run through a given vertex.

Closeness: Distance of a vertex to all other nodes.

Information Leakage: Private information revealed by a party by engaging in a secure computation protocol.

Privacy: Keeping a piece of information from being revealed to other parties.

Protocol: Convention that controls the evaluation of a joint function in a secure computation. Parties might deviate from the protocol for personal gain.

Secure Computation: Joint evaluation by several parties of a function on the parties' combined inputs, while preserving the privacy of each party's contribution.

Social Network Analysis: Quantitative or qualitative analysis of social networks, by describing features of the network, either through numerical or visual representation.

Chapter 12
A Dynamic Privacy Manager for Compliance in Pervasive Computing

Riccardo Bonazzi
University of Lausanne, Switzerland

Zhan Liu
University of Lausanne, Switzerland

Simon Ganière
Deloitte SA, Switzerland

Yves Pigneur
University of Lausanne, Switzerland

ABSTRACT

In this chapter we propose a decision support system for privacy management of context-aware technologies, which requires the alignment of four dimensions: business, regulation, technology, and user behavior. We have developed a middleware model able to achieve compliance with privacy policies within a dynamic and context-aware risk management situation. We illustrate our model in more details by means of a small prototype that we developed, and we present the current outcomes of its implementation to derive some pointers for the direction of future investigation.

INTRODUCTION

Privacy is generally referred as "a state in which one is not observed or disturbed by others" (Oxford Dictionary, 2010), and privacy management for pervasive technologies can be treated as an information security issue. Security experts have been advocating that information security should result from the alignment of the technical, business, and regulatory dimensions (Anderson, 2001), suggesting an information risk management approach to let the user achieve the best security level according to the environmental threats (Blakley et al. 2001). Therefore one should also look at how to manage the risk that privacy is not assured,

DOI: 10.4018/978-1-61350-501-4.ch012

before looking at how to achieve privacy from a technical point of view.

Contingency theory is a class of behavioral theory that claims that the optimal course of action is contingent upon both the internal and external situations. Such theory postulates that impacts of environmental factors are systemic, rather than entirely situational. That fits the case of mobile payment services that differ between markets, in ways linked to their particular systems, for instance there are differences in payment technology infrastructure, regulation, laws, or habits. Therefore contingency theory can be used as a reference framework to assess the literature on mobile payment published in information system, electronic commerce, and mobile commerce journals, and conference proceedings (Dahlberg et al. 2007). It appears that a contingency factor (Changes in Technological Environment) has been intensively studied, two contingency factors (Changes in Commerce Environment and Changes in Legal, Regulatory, and Standardization Environment) have been addressed by not more than twenty articles, whereas one contingency factor (Changes in Social/Cultural Environment) was not treated in any article.

Literature on privacy risk management can be assessed using three contingency factors suggested by Anderson (2001): technology, business, and legal. To address the gap underlined by Dahlberg et al. (2007) we add a fourth dimension: the user's perception of its environment.

Awareness of Changes in the Technology Environment

Technology awareness concerns the understanding of the technological options for privacy management that are offered in a particular moment in time to the user. The link between pervasive computing and user's privacy risk has been addressed by many researchers, mostly in the field of location privacy. In his literature review of computational location privacy Krumm (2009) claims that "location data

can be used to infer much about a person, even without a name attached to the data."(p. 4). Most applications focus on controlling access and use of user's data, or they propose security algorithms to protect/obfuscate the communication of data between two users. Krumm (2009) lists a set of solutions for location computational privacy. For example "blurring" is a security algorithm, which ensures a certain degree of location privacy by using inaccurate or at least not so accurate location information, in order to obfuscate the communication of users. Another algorithm is "Access control", which ensures that the sensitive data is only accessed by authorized people, in order to protect user's information privacy.

Middleware development has been adapting to evolving technology, and in this sense we mention a solution that deals with conflicting privacy policies (Capra et al., 2003) and another solution that uses an extended version of a privacy policy language that takes into consideration the time dimension (Hong et al., 2005).

In this paper we present the design of software for decision support regarding privacy risk management for pervasive technologies, with a particular interest in context-aware applications, as described by Schilit et al. (1994) and Chen and Kotz (2000). Thus we aim at increasing the user's acceptance of the privacy management system. The theoretical foundation can be found in the technology adoption model proposed by Davis (1989), which assess that user's behavioral intention to adopt a system depends on the perception of usefulness and ease of use. Thus a context-aware privacy management system should protect the user's data and it should reduce the number of actions requested to the user.

Awareness of Changes in the Commerce Environment

A stream of research called economics of security, which Anderson and Blakely's research belongs to, has contributed in adopting economic concepts like "game theory with incomplete information" and "behavioral economics" into IS risk management (e.g. Acquisti, 2003). Recognizing the importance of privacy management as a business process, and a business support process, the use of a context-awareness application casts privacy management into a business perspective with benefits and costs to either party in a process. This is especially relevant for communications operators as brokers, and for communication channels between content owners (individuals, businesses) and enterprise applications.

Privacy risk management is a situation where actors with diverging goals have a temporary interest in cooperating and sharing information to increase mutual trust (Palen and Dourish, 2003). Nalebuff and Brandenburger (1997) describe this situation of cooperation and competition by means of five elements, which is used here as a general framework to assess the state of the art in academic literatures.

1. **Actors involved in the game:** Location privacy can be modeled as a non-cooperative game among peers (Freudiger et al., 2009). In this case the *phone user* and her *peers* are identified as two selfish actors while the *attacker* is a third actor, whose goal is to obtain information about the phone user. The phone user and the peers have an interest in cooperating only once they get close enough to each other and can change pseudonyms in order to confuse the attacker. Extending the work of Hong et al. (2005) a fourth actor emerges, i.e. the *service provider*, for example a weather forecaster of the zone where the phone user is located, who wishes to establish a trusted relationship with his potential users (i.e. he does not want to be considered as an attacker). Yet few authors seem to have recognized the importance of the *privacy system designer*, even if his actions affect other actors and although his goals are not necessarily aligned with any

of those previously mentioned. One might recall the statement by Palen and Dourish (2003) that privacy is the result of a set of dynamically evolving regulations between actors as their goals and level of trust change. Thus the way the system is designed might constrain the flexibility required by other actors.

2. **Added value of each actor:** Palen and Dourish (2003) clearly identify the need for the *phone user* and her *peers* of a trade-off between the advantages of being visible to the others and the risk of exposure to an *attacker*. In what concerns the *attacker* beside the evident trade-off between the risk of being caught and the advantages of stealing personal data, Anderson (2001) notices how an attacker has fewer resources than the security professionals, but aims at finding only one unknown bug to get an immediate advantage. This issue impacts the *privacy system designer* too, since he might not be the one who pays for the consequences of the theft of private data. This lack of moral hazard could lead to a phenomenon known as "liability dumping". On what concerns the *service provider*, one could expect him to look for the greatest number of potential phone users to reach with the least effort, and this could also be a case where the quest for network externalities (i.e. the search for more users to attract even more users) might be to the detriment of the security of private data. Again there is the possibility that the service provider could decide to act as an infomediary, i.e. an information intermediary (Hagel 3rd and Singer, 1999) that collects data from the *phone users* and the *privacy system designer* and dispatches aggregated data while employing best-practices for privacy management. Such data would be valuable both for the *phone users* and to the *privacy system designer*, and will reduce its value to the *attacker*.

3. **Rules of the game:** On the one hand most authors agree on claiming that regulations concerning privacy management for pervasive technologies are still vague and ambiguous. Citing Massey et al. (2010) "specifying legally compliant requirements is challenging because legal texts are complex and ambiguous by nature" (p.119). This might be due to the hard task that aligning business, technological and legal expertise implies. On the other hand a good example of clear privacy policies that can be understood by humans and machine is the Privacy Preferences Platform as described by Reagle and Cranor (1999) and extended by Hong et al. (2005). On the technological side, many security technological solutions have been proposed and with the increasing computational power of mobile devices the number of offers is expected to grow exponentially. Yet on the business and legal side it is not clear yet how much control should be imposed on the actors involved and how much dynamism should be allowed.

4. **Tactics for the players:** Still to the best of our knowledge no author has dealt with the need of an evolution of the privacy system in the phone of the user, as a response of new ways to sense the environment and to enforce privacy policies. Among the security algorithm proposed for privacy protection Freudiger et al. (2009) have taken into account the problem of user's selfishness in their pseudonym change algorithm, but no attempt to combine different tactics and to select dynamically one that fits best a determined state of the environment has been done yet.

5. **Scope of the game:** Regarding the scope of the interaction between actors, two dimensions come up to our minds. The temporal dimension suggested by Hong et al. (2005) implies that the privacy system needs to evolve. For the data to be retained, while most authors focused on techniques to retain as little data as possible for as little time as needed, a quick consideration on the possible need in the future of data retention for regulatory compliance underlines the need of a middleware to mediate among different requirements. A second dimension to be considered is the geographical analysis, i.e. the size of physical area to be assessed. For sake of simplicity we shall assume it to be a circle, whose radius is 50 meters for the GPS-enabled mobile device and 100 meters for a Wi-Fi enabled mobile device.

Awareness of Changes in the Regulatory Environment

Regulatory awareness concerns the continuous assessment of laws and standards that apply to a determined environment. From the regulatory point of view laws on data privacy are present in different business sectors and in different countries, leading to a complex multitude of overlapping and sometimes conflicting regulations that change over time, as described by Ponemon (2000). This commonly leads to ambiguity and to address that situation a standard privacy policy language, i.e. P3P (Reagle and Cranor, 1999) has been recommended by the World Wide Web Consortium. Although P3P has been criticized for its difficulty of implementation a stream of research has grown around it. Therefore we cite the recent work of Manasdeep et al. (2010), who propose a collaborative model for data privacy and its legal enforcement to support a relationship of confidence between the operating system and the user's data repository. Another approach would be to use the set of metrics derived from privacy regulations, which can be found in Herrmann (2007).

Awareness of Changes in Social Environment

From the social point of view there are two levels of analysis which can be investigated. One could consider users' behavior as an external contingency factor that affects the privacy of a specific user, e.g. different cultures and countries are said to behave differently on what concerns privacy (e.g. Japanese are more likely to share data than Swiss users). Yet at the personal level user awareness is also an internal factor. Researches in human computer interaction have underlined this issue (e.g. Barkhuus, 2004), but little has been done to design a privacy risk management application which takes into consideration those behavioral studies that represent users as opportunistic and rationally bounded.

Most papers on privacy management implicitly assume a rational decision model, with the following characteristics:

- **Sure-thing principle**: This was first introduced by the statistician Leonard Jimmy Savage (1954) and it states that a decision maker can rank all options in order of preference and choose the highest one in the ranking.
- **Independence of tastes and beliefs**: this assumption was proposed by the economists Roy Radner and Jacob Marshak (1954) and it states that the decision maker's tastes concerning the outcome of the different options are independent of the options itself, and that her beliefs about the likelihood about the different outcomes are independent of the corresponding outcomes itself. In other words the decision maker is going to assess the outcomes and the likelihood of each option without any bias.
- **Logical and adequate capacity for computing**: from the first two assumptions a third implicit assumption can be derived,

i.e. that the agent should be logical and have potentially unlimited capacity of formulation.

Simon (1959) revised the rational decision model and relaxed the third assumption in his bounded rationality model. Indeed the logical approach to decision maker risk aversion does not imply risk neutrality. A rational user can be either risk neutral or risk averse. In the latter case the risk-averse user looks at the worst probable outcome (thereinafter indicated as "wpo") for each option and then chooses the option with the greatest "wpo" among the list. Therefore let us assume that someone has to make a bet on one of two options. Option A can let him win €100 or lose €50, whereas option 2 lets him win €75 or lose €25. If he wants to avoid risk he will rationally bet on the option B, since it has the greater wpo (-€25 is greater than -€50).

Simon (1959) also relaxed the assumption concerning the potentially unlimited capacity of formulation. Facing high uncertainty humans can not deal with high degree of complexity and look for simplified models to assist them in making choices. Simon et al. (1987) have combined the concepts of bounded rationality and computational costs to introduce sub-optimal solutions that are called "satisfying". According to this model a decision maker starts creating options and ranks them sequentially. Once a satisfactory result is found the decision maker stops searching for other options. This is a dynamic decision rule strategy that drops the other options, even if they might perform better, because the cost of search is greater than the gain in performance.

Radner (2000) has proposed a "truly bounded rationality model" that acknowledges the cost involved in decision making (observation, computation, memory, and communication) and addresses the challenges in ordering the options (inconsistency, ambiguity, and vagueness of the options, unawareness of other options that might rise in the future) using a Bayesian model. But

Figure 1. From the theoretical model to the practical application of the design guidelines

What are the characteristics of privacy management software that increase the user's intention to adopt the system?	What are the design characteristics of a privacy management system that can be derived from the previous model?	How can these design characteristics be converted into design guidelines?
Our **theoretical framework** has three dimensions (technology – context-regulation), which influence a fourth dimension (user's decision)	Our **solution** decomposes the user's decision dimension into a five-step information flow. It combines the other three dimensions we obtain eight scenarios to assess existing privacy management applications for mobile devices	The **implementation** of our solution shows how to combine the technology-context-regulations dimensions into a five-step information flow.

even such a model fails to determine the long-term outcomes of each option, making it hard to rank them properly.

On what concerns security management, Straub and Welke (1998) used the bounded rationality model to explain why managers take apparently irrational risk management decisions to minimize their perceived risk exposure. On what concerns perception Tversky and Kahneman (1974) have shown that people tend to seek for opportunity and avoid risk in an unbalanced way. Therefore users might have the tendency to underestimate their exposures to privacy risks, which are hard to be perceived in the physical world. Therefore a privacy management application should support the user by decreasing the cost of decision making and by reducing the challenges in ordering the options. Otherwise the risk perceptions will be biased and the user is likely to be exposed involuntarily to risk.

From the literature review it seems that the user dimension has received little attention from the information system community. Hence we investigate the implications of user awareness for privacy management system design in more detail. In doing so we assume that privacy risk management is a set of actions that the user expects his devices to perform dynamically in response to his perceived environment at a determined moment in time. Our research question arises accordingly:

What are the design characteristics of a privacy management system for an opportunistic and rationally bounded user using a context-aware mobile device?

In this study we follow a research design approach using the guidelines of Peffers et al. (2007). Thus the remainder of the paper is structured as follows: we start by briefly summarizing the methodology used in this study. Then we describe the design of our solution and how we came to develop it. After that we present a prototype, which we constructed according to our design and in conclusion we describe and illustrate a first evaluating session we performed with experts in the field.

METHODOLOGY

Based on the relevant literatures, we create an artifact in the form of a model (March and Smith, 1995) to express the relationship between user benefit and the amount of personal data disclosed.

We adopt a design science research methodology and we refer to existing guidelines for design theories (Gregor and Jones, 2007). The theories for design and action "give explicit prescriptions on how to design and develop an artifact, whether it is a technological product or a managerial intervention" (Gregor and Jones 2007, p.233). Therefore we advance in three steps as illustrated in Figure 1.

Figure 2. Our theoretical model

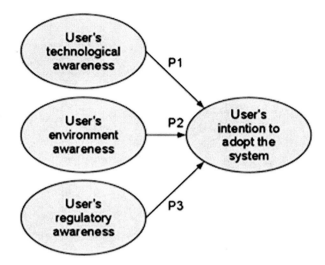

THEORETICAL FRAMEWORK

From the literature review we derive a set of constructs presented in Figure 2.

The first construct is technology awareness, which we define as the possibility for the mobile user to receive updates about the security solutions available on the phone currently used. We suggest measuring this construct using the number of technological updates sent to the user's mobile device.

The second constructs concerns context awareness, which we define as the possibility for the mobile user to receive updates about the privacy risk of the zone where she is currently located. We suggest measuring this construct using the number of sensor updates sent to the user's mobile device.

The third construct is the regulatory awareness, which we define as the possibility for the mobile user to receive updates about the best combination "security solution"-"privacy risk" according to security frameworks and laws. We suggest measuring this construct using the number of rule updates sent to the user's mobile device.

The fourth construct concerns the user's behavioral intention to adopt the system and it is based

on the theory of reasoned action of Fishbein and Ajzen (1975), whose explanatory power has been proved in the past by means of two metanalyses conducted by Sheppard et al. (1988).

The technology adoption model of Davis (1989) and its later extension called Unified Theory of Acceptance and Use of Technology of Venkatesh (2003) stated that a user's perceived usefulness increases the user's intention to use the system. User's awareness of the security technologies available supports the realization of user's identity protection. Therefore we claim that a user's behavioral intention to adopt the system follows the user's technological awareness in a linear way, as illustrated by Figure 3. Our first proposition can be expressed by the following formula:

(P1) User's behavioral intention to adopt the system = a1 + b1*Technological_Updates + n1

Where "a1" is constant that represents the fact that the user would adopt the system even if it does not offer any technological awareness. "a2" is a positive coefficient representing the relationship between the two constructs. "n1" is usually

Figure 3. User's behavioral intention to adopt the system follows the user's technological awareness in a linear way

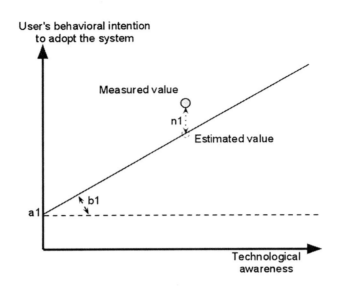

used in linear regression models to represent the difference between our estimated values and the actual values that are measured in reality. This difference is a consequence of variables that are missing in our equation.

The technology adoption model of Davis (1989) and its later extension called Unified Theory of Acceptance and Use of Technology of Venkatesh (2003) also assess that a user's perceived efficiency increases the user's intention to use the system. User's awareness of the surrounding environment allows him/her to clearly decide what security technology to use and how to reduce waste of energy. We base this claim on the previous analysis of a user's bounded rationality and the consequent need of simplification. Therefore we claim that a user's behavioral intention to adopt the system follows the user's context awareness in a linear way.

Our second proposition can be expressed by the following formula:

(P2) User's behavioral intention to adopt the system = a2 + b2*Environment_Updates + n2

Where "a2" is another constant, "b2" is a positive coefficient and "n2" takes into account the estimated noise effect created by the variables missing in our equation.

The theory of trust, control and risk of Das and Teng (2001), which has been applied to information systems by Gallivan and Depledge (2003), describes how controls in place reduce the perceived risk and how that indirectly increases the user's trust in the system. The perceived risk can be decomposed into two parts: (1) the risk that someone steals the user's data, and (2) the risk that the system does not protect the data. The controls can be split into output controls (e.g. a log of all activities done on the mobile to identify intrusions), behavioral controls (e.g. the assessment of how a security algorithm works to protect the user data) or social controls (e.g. observing how surrounding people are behaving and are following the same norm).

User's trust can be towards other people's good intentions or towards the system capacity to protect the user's data. According to this theory a user's awareness of the regulatory environment allows this person to understand the system's controls to reduce the environmental risk, and that increases the user's trust in the system and her intention to adopt it. We ground this claim on the previous analysis of user's co-opting relationship with the surrounding mobile users and the consequent need for mutual trust. Therefore we claim that a user's behavioral intention to adopt the system follows the user's regulatory awareness in a linear way

Our third proposition can be expressed by the following formula:

(P3) User's behavioral intention to adopt the system = a3 + b3*Regulatory_Updates + n3

Where "a3" is another constant, "b3" is a positive coefficient and "n3" takes into account the noise effect created by the variables missing in our equation.

SOLUTIONS AND RECOMMENDATIONS

Before passing to the technical implementations details of the framework, its business implications are worthwhile investigating.

Business Implications of our Model

Previous works regarding middleware for privacy management (Capra et al., 2003; Hong et al., 2005) have positioned their middleware on the server of the service provider. From the business perspective, this approach allows the service provider to obtain compliance in respect to privacy regulations.

To give more data control ownership to users can lead to new value propositions, which in turn can defferentiate a firm from its competitor. A practical example of a firm that is currently gaining money from allowing the users to fine-tune their privacy preferences is the case Allow Ltd described by Angwin and Steel (2011). This London-based company negotiates with marketers on the behalf of users and obtains good deal for the users' data. The business opportunity rises from a proper context-regulation-technology model: in UK (context) the UK's Data Protection Act (regulation) allows user to remove their data from marketers' databases, by means of system (technology) that detects if the data was collected without user's permission.

In addition that we suggest shifting the control of the privacy towards the mobile users, and that enables two additional value propositions:

- **Greater performance for the privacy management system:** in accordance to proposition 1 and 2 of our model the intention to adopt the system of the user is expected to be greater. Therefore one could expect the mobile user to be willing to pay more for this kind of software.
- **Greater trust in the service provider:** in accordance to proposition 3 of our model the trust in the system, and indirectly in the service provider is expected to be greater. Therefore one could expect the service provider to gain from the trusted relationship with the mobile user.

These types of business model considerations for mobile platforms have been already addressed in specific workshops, such as the business models for mobile platform (BMMP) workshop. In this sense Bonazzi et al. (2010) have presented a set of business models that allows different key players in the mobile business sector to gain money from privacy management. But that article misses to explain in details how to technically implement each business model. Therefore we wish to extend their business models by adding a set of design guidelines to our framework.

Figure 4. Information flow to support risk management decisions

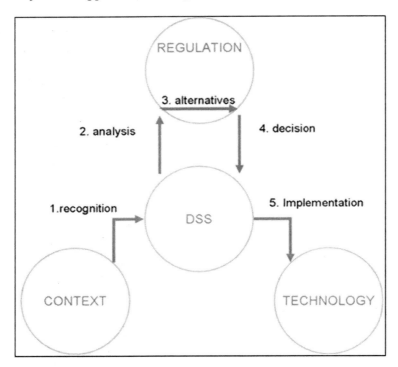

Framework

Figure 4 shows the information flows among the four constructs of our framework illustrated in Figure 2.

We refer to the literature in decision making and use the process proposed by Straub and Welke (1998) to list the five steps of a security risk plan implemented by our system.

The first step is the recognition of security problem, defined by Straub and Welke (1998:450) as "the identification and formulation of problems with respect to the risk of IS security breaches or computer disaster". In our case, the system gets awareness of the context by collecting data from its sensors (e.g. Wi-Fi, GPS, and Bluetooth).

The second step is risk analysis (defined by Straub and Welke, 1998), "the analysis of the security risk inherent in these identified problem areas; threat identification and prioritization of risks". The system gathers the sensor data and

assesses them using the updated roles database to assess the context data.

The third step is the alternatives generation (defined by Straub and Welke, 1998), "the generation of solutions to meet organizational needs specified during risk analysis". A set of regulations might match the context. The profile that has the highest fit is automatically selected.

The fourth step concerns the decisions (defined by Straub and Welke, 1998), "matching threats with appropriate solutions; selection and prioritization of security projects". For a given threat, the profile suggests a set of actions to be enforced.

The fifth step is the implementation (defined by Straub and Welke, 1998), "realizing the plans by incorporating the solutions into the on-going security of the organization". The set of actions is enforced by the information infrastructure and the tuple time-sensor data-risk profile-actions enforced is recorded in a log by the system, for further compliance analyses.

Table 1. Operationalization of variables for the scenarios

Construct	Variable
Context awareness	**Low**: No information about your location **High**: Information about the privacy risks of your current location is constantly updated
Technological awareness	**Low**: No information about the available technological options available is given from the central system **High**: Information about the available optimal technological configuration to protect your privacy are constantly updated from the central system
Regulatory awareness	**Low**: No information about the option is given to you to configure the system **High**: A set of predefined profiles is constantly updated and displayed to help you choose your privacy option. A log of your previous risk exposure levels can be seen to let you enable or disable the privacy functionalities

A set of Scenarios Illustrating Privacy Risk Management on the Client-side

An information risk management approach in the context awareness lets the user achieve the best security level according to environmental threats she currently faces. The design solution envisaged makes use of state of the art technologies and constantly adapts to the environment to take a proactive stance against privacy risk.

We operationalize the construct of our model, as illustrated in Table 1. We obtain 2^n different scenarios, where n is the number of constructs in our model, and 2 is the value that each construct can get (0=Low or 1=High, see Table 2). For the sake of clarity, we briefly describe each scenario, and we link it to existing applications for the Android OS.

As the scenario number one does not concern any construct, we start with the second scenario. The second scenario describes the software that contains a set of profiles that have to be manually changed. Predefined rules are constantly updated from a central system. A log of user's previous risk exposure can be seen to let the user enable/ disable the privacy functionalities. For this scenario, two applications for Android already exist: "Privacy Guard" and "The eye". The third scenario describes the software that contains the information about the available optimal technological configuration to protect user's privacy which is constantly updated from the central system. For this scenario, we have found the following applications for Android: "Mobile Security™", "Lookout Mobile Security", "Antivirus Free", "Norton mobile" and "AVG antivirus Pro". The fourth scenario describes the software that combines the information of technological solu-

Table 2. Eight scenarios obtained by combining the three dimensions of our theoretical model

	Context awareness	Technology awareness	Regulatory awareness
Scenario 1	0 (Low)	0 (Low)	0 (Low)
Scenario 2	0 (Low)	0 (Low)	1 (High)
Scenario 3	0 (Low)	1 (High)	0 (Low)
Scenario 4	0 (Low)	1 (High)	1 (High)
Scenario 5	1 (High)	0 (Low)	0 (Low)
Scenario 6	1 (High)	0 (Low)	1 (High)
Scenario 7	1 (High)	1 (High)	0 (Low)
Scenario 8	1 (High)	1 (High)	1 (High)

Figure 5. The first example (on the left side) and the second example (on the right side)

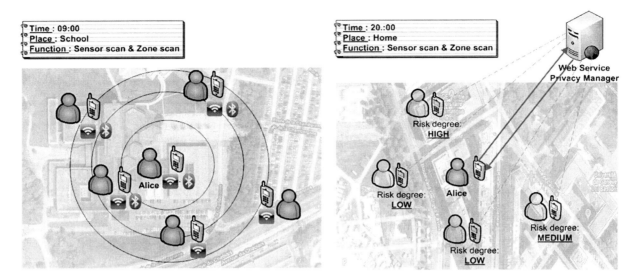

tion and regulation: information about the available optimal technological configuration to protect the user's privacy is constantly updated from the central system. A set of profiles has to be manually changed. Predefined rules are constantly updated from a central system. A log of the user's previous risk exposure can be seen to let you enable /disable the privacy functionalities. For this scenario, we have found the following application for Android: "MyAndroid protection 2.0". The fifth scenario describes the software that contains the information about the privacy risks of the user's current location and where this information is constantly being updated. For this scenario, we have found the following application for Android: "Glympse". The sixth scenario describes the software that combines the information of context and regulation. For this scenario, we have found the following applications for Android: "Locale", "Setting profiles full" and "Toggle settings". The seventh scenario describes the software that combines the information of context and technological solution. For this scenario, we have found no application for android but web services exists: "General crime", "Homicides" and "Victims". The last scenario includes all of the above three

constructs. However, we could not find a corresponding application. Therefore in the rest of the paper we wish to explore the last scenario more in details. We start by illustrating two examples to distinguish the eighth scenario from the other seven, as illustrated by Figure 5.

Example 1: Sensors Analysis for Unknown Environments

Alice is a student at the University of Lausanne. She often uses her mobile phone to buy things online. In order to protect her privacy information from the privacy attacks in her surrounding environment, she installed the software "Privacy Manager" on her mobile phone. This software allows Alice to define and configure her privacy preferences, such as degrees of risk, types of potential attacks and corresponding solutions to protect her private information. After the configuration, the software automatically detects the connection information of mobile devices around her via sensor technologies on the phone. Once it identifies any unknown connections during her purchasing procedure, it responds by taking avoiding action to protect her privacy. For example, one day Alice

Table 3. The five steps of risk management decision making in our two examples

	Exemple 1 – Part 1	Exemple 1 – Part 2	Exemple 2 – Part 1	Exemple 2 – Part 2
Step 1. recognition	Wi-Fi and Bluetooth sensor data.	Wi-Fi and Bluetooth sensor data.	Wi-Fi and Bluetooth sensor data.	Wi-Fi and Bluetooth sensor data. Zone information from infomediary
Step 2. analysis	Many connections	Few connections	Many connections	Many connections. Risky zone.
Step 3. alternatives	"Medium" profile is ranked as first, "Low" profile is ranked as second	"Low" profile is ranked as first, "Medium" profile is ranked as second	"Medium" profile is ranked as first, "Low" profile is ranked as second	"Medium" profile is ranked as first, "Low" profile is ranked as second
Step 4. decision	"Medium" profile is automatically chosen. "Blurring" and "access control" algorithms are chosen to obfuscate the user's position and to protect user's data	"Low" profile is automatically chosen. "Access control" algorithm is chosen.	None profile is imposed by the user. No security algorithm is chosen.	"Medium" profile is automatically chosen. "Blurring" and "access control" algorithms are chosen to obfuscate the user's position and to protect user's data
Step 5. implementation	"Blurring" and "Access control" are executed	"Access control" is executed	No security algorithm is executed	"Blurring" and "Access control" are executed

buys a book when she is in the university. "Privacy Manager" detects that there are many unknown connections around her current position. "Privacy Manager" reports it and adopts two technological solutions (blurring and access control) to protect her online purchasing. After lunch, Alice goes for a walk near the Leman Lake. She wants to book a train ticket with her mobile phone. Again, "Privacy Manager" detects that there is 1 unknown connection. Here reporting a fake location (blurring) is not useful and it should be not implemented to save computational effort and battery energy. Thus "Privacy Manager" implements only "access control" to protect her information.

Example 2: Aggregated Historical Data for Known Environments

After class, Alice goes back home. "Privacy Manager" realizes it is a safe place according to Alice's earlier set configuration and does not implement any protection actions. Now Alice is going to buy a CD online with her mobile phone. "Privacy Manager" allows her phone to connect to the web server and it gets historical data in this zone. This connection has been protected by the security firewall. By combining police database information and private users' devices configuration details, the privacy manager web service can send information to Alice's mobile device about the privacy risk of the zone where she is located. Therefore "Privacy Manager" suggests to Alice to increase her privacy protection level since many mobile users have claimed to have had their mobile phones stolen in that neighborhood. Finally, Alice takes Privacy manager's suggestion and adjusts the risk profile to the "Medium" accordingly.

Table 3 links the two examples to the data flow for decision support presented in figure 4. As previously said the security algorithms have already been implemented with success in mobile applications. Therefore we shall present a prototype that illustrates how to enforce a set of security profile according to contextual privacy risk, which is assessed by means of data sensors collection and zone risk updates sent by a trusted third party.

Figure 6. System architecture

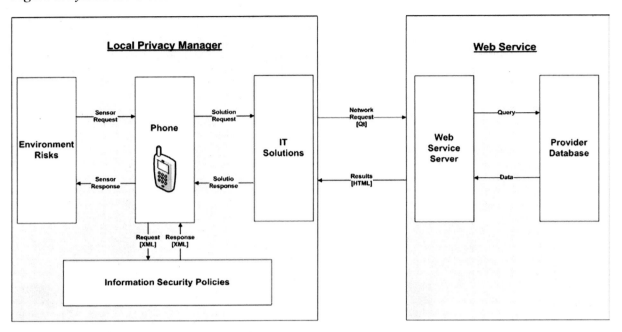

IMPLEMENTATION

We implement a prototype of PRIVACY MANAGER according to the design guidelines discussed earlier. The overall goal in designing PRIVACY MANAGER is to examine the feasibility of our approach and to understand the privacy issues possibly involved. We describe the prototype's system architecture, the frameworks used, as well as the graphical user Interface. In doing so, we give implementation details for Symbian platform (Nokia), even though a prototype for Android platform has been developed as well.

System Architecture

Figure 6 shows the local privacy manager's interaction with the components of the privacy architecture and the web service.

For the configuration of a user's located privacy policies, we use a XML file to store user's preferences on the phone. It allows the user to edit, create and delete their privacy policies at any

time. Detecting the risk of environment is done by using the python socket architecture (Python Software Foundation, 2009); it provides the service of interactive communications between the different sensors of technologies. The local IT privacy solutions can be accessed directly via the information requests of users.

The web service server receives and processes requests vis-à-vis the provider database, before requested data is sent back to the user via QtWeb Network Requests. The resultant information is finally transmitted by the web service to a user-friendly GUI using HTML.

Implementation Details

The application PRIVACY MANAGER for Symbian platform is mostly written in C++, with the toolkit Nokia Qt, which is a cross-platform application and UI framework. It includes a cross-platform class library, integrated development tools and a cross-platform IDE. Using this toolkit,

Figure 7. The Graphic User Interfaces: Configuration interfaces (top left corner); Sensor analysis interfaces (top right corner); Zone risk analysis interfaces (bottom left corner); Risk management interface (bottom right corner)

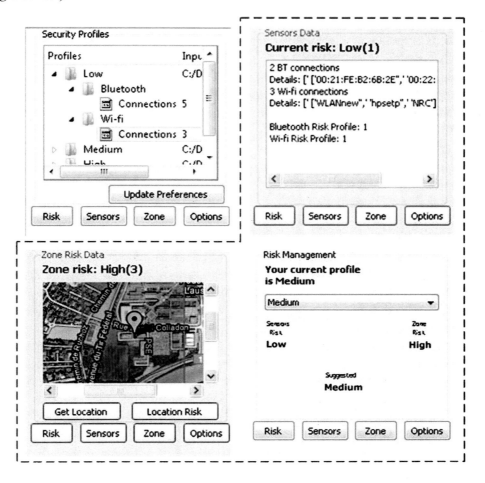

the web-enabled application can be written and deployed across embedded operating systems.

The XML file stores all service provider information, including the risk criteria given by present data, the context of current situation, as well as the corresponding proposed privacy policies.

For the online Web service, we utilized the PHP and a MySQL based framework, which facilitates the development of dynamic Web applications and allows for the exchange of information with web services.

On the client side, the Qt Network Request and Access Manager offers dynamic HTML with

integration of Google Maps technologies, which provides localization and auto-update functions, as well as high performance risk degree parsing.

Graphical User Interface

The designed application aims at a clear layout and a high degree of user friendliness. For a complete review of the graphical user interface, in Figure 7, we focus on the design of the activity, information and interaction. For the user who is a first time user of this application, a welcome page is proposed and used for the configuration of privacy policies, which explains the purpose and the content of the local risk degree, and its proposed privacy policies on related risk. From this starting page, the user has the option to define the degree of attack for each phone's technology, for example the Bluetooth, Wi-Fi, GPRS and so on. Privacy policies are represented by a list that contains a large related security application which could be selected by the user to enforce the rule that fits the current risk degree. All the information about the status change is stored in a file for future use of compliance checking against privacy policies. If a technology or related security application is not listed in the privacy policies list, users can create a new one at any time. Once the local privacy policies are configured by the user, then the 3 main functions of application of the privacy manager are available for use.

Recalling Table 3 we illustrate how to implement the five steps of the decision support for privacy risk management. The first function offers a physical sensor that continuously collects diverse information from the environment. It keeps detecting context information of the technologies of different devices around the user, in order to get an updated context degree of risk in real time, including the technology's name, its MAC address and the specific identification, as well as the number of connections for each technology. In addition, each technology's risk profile is calculated automatically to conform to the user's risk degree configuration. The information of ranking, which represents the average of current risk between all of the technologies detected— is presented at the bottom of the screen.

The second function shows the information about zone risk, which includes 2 tasks: displaying the user's current position and obtaining this position's historical risk.

When clicking the button "Get location", the phone component GPS (Global Positioning System) will be activated and get the user's current position, including the address information of that latitude and longitude. These position values finally are sent to a Web Service Server by PRIVACY MANAGER.

Reverse Geocoding (Google Inc., 2010) is a service of Google Maps available through our Web Server, which can be used to translate latitude and longitude information into an address. This feature is very important for interactions with the user, since positioning technologies provide coordinate information (i.e. "Latitude = 46.5222, Longitude = 6.583555") which is not meaningful to the end user, and users provide location information in the form of an address (i.e. "UNIL Dorigny, 1015 Chavannes-près-Renens, Switzerland") which is not useful to software and positioning technologies. Reverse Geocoding bridges the gap between the end user and the positioning technology and enables user interaction with applications, as well as enabling the other types of services by supplying location information to the software in a usable format. For the sake of simplicity, we did not implement a secure connection between the mobile device and the web server even though we adware of its importance.

In considering the usability aspects and by involving the users, the map user interface service is added in the Web server. This is the ability to display location information in the form of a map, including landmarks and routes, on the mobile phone screen. This service has various levels of control, we can add or remove certain related features on a map, such as add a polygon or showing a significant marker on the map. Users will also be able to select different map views such as regular, satellite, and hybrid that are integrated on phone screen.

Focusing on a zone's risk data sharing, the second button named "location risk" which is set up to allow the phone to contact our online web service to send the information regarding the user's current located risk data to the Web Service Server This web server provides interface to users who authorize to access the application. A database is used to store all information about user's risk. Then the web server will return to the users a risk level which is calculated by the average in a similar area in real time (i.e. each 10 minutes). And here the similar area is defined as a specified area, which is a circumference of a circle with its radius of 500 meters. Finally, the web service will deliver in return the average of the risk degree reported by others users in the same geographic area in an earlier period of time. In order to distinguish the degree of risk in a specific area, an alarm system is integrated, and by using different colors on the map to signify the degree of risk, for example, blue signifies low risk in this area and red signifies high risk.

The last function lists the average degree of risk obtained previously, including the sensors risk (risk value from Wi-Fi and Bluetooth) and the zone risk (risk value from current location). PRIVACY MANAGER calculates the average of sensor risk and zone risk, and provides the final risk value to help user make the decision, which will be used to execute the related security applications in order to deal with the current risk.

DISCUSSION

A first evaluation has been done within experts in Nokia, to whom the prototype has been presented. Although the idea has been accepted as innovative most of the feedback we received regarding future improvements concerned the user interface and the need to include in the prototype an example of a security enforcing policy.

A second evaluation of the prototype has been done within a small sample of mobile users to assess the software usability and the users' intention to use it. We have conducted a pre-test of our prototype using ten volunteers in a controlled environment. Since we cannot perform a benchmark with existing solutions, we opted for a scenario-based test as suggested by Rosson and Carroll (2002). The volunteers were asked to read the two parts of the scenario 8 presented in the previous section. Then they were asked to perform

it using an Android mobile phone, on which the Privacy Manager prototype was installed. Since we did not fully implement the security algorithm we simulated that part. At the end of the experience the volunteers were asked to answer questions concerning technology acceptance taken from Vankestesh et al. (2003). The answers we obtained from the volunteers came as partially unexpected. Most users declared they liked the application and they found it useful but that they did not want to use it in their everyday life. It turned out that most users did not feel their privacy menaced and they did not want to be constrained by this kind of application. Yet the same users agreed they might have been exposed to privacy risks and they declared that if the application informs the user of the consequences of each privacy risk, then they would find it useful. Although the sample size does not allow any statistical interpretation, we are currently investigating more in details the underlying causes behind the test results. If they are due to an effect of adverse selection, as suggested by Anderson (2001), then this impacts the requirements for software development, since the application should protect and inform the user in the proper way. Moreover it could be that for high maintenance information system for security this statement is not always correct. This point is worth a further analysis, since it would have a significant impact on design requirements.

FUTURE RESEARCH DIRECTIONS

In the close future we are going to improve the prototype using the outcome of our preliminary test before testing it on a larger scale using the guidelines illustrated in Table 4. Yet we believe that by now our proposed design makes a contribution since it is a first attempt at empowering the user with a system that allows him to manage the dynamically privacy risk according to his own preference and perceptions. Future research

Table 4. Testing guidelines

Testable Proposition	Testing guideline
P1: User's awareness of the security technologies available supports the achievement of user's identity protection in a linear way.	Measures how the increase of technology updates affects the user's intention to adopt the system
P2: User's awareness of the surrounding environment allows to clearly decide the security technology to use and reduce waste of energy	Measures how the increase of context updates affects the user's intention to adopt the system
P3: user's awareness of the regulatory environment allows to understand the systems controls to reduce the environmental risk, and that increase the user's trust on the system and her intention to adopt it	Measures how the increase of regulatory updates affects the user's intention to adopt the system

directions that we envisage from our work are the following ones:

- **Extending the model, e.g. adding more contingency factors**: in this article we did not take into account other seminal researches, like the five-force model of Porter (1998).
- **Adding more business models for coopetitve users, e.g. for a distributed infomediary:** as previously mentioned the informediary does not have to be a centralized entity. In the extreme case where all the computation is done among mobile users in a distributed fashion the infomediary business model might not work as described here.
- **Technical improvements for the prototype**: a greater amount of effort could be spent analyzing the ways we could improve the human-computer interaction. Security algorithms have to be translated in a common format to be processed by the application, although this has not be done here for technical limitations of the language used. Each protection algorithm has its own limitations. We cite Krumm (2009) for a good review of their strengths and weakness, and we suggest reading Shabtai et al. (2010) for a security assessment of Android OS.

CONCLUSION

In this paper we have presented a model for decision support system regarding privacy risk management associated with pervasive technologies, which we believe is topic with growing importance in these days. Our research question focused on context-aware technologies used by a user that we assume as opportunistic and rationally bounded. Our theoretical model is the first to take into account the four contingency factors (business, technology, regulation and user behavior) that impacts mobile privacy risk management. We illustrated how our theoretical model allows to benchmark all privacy management applications on the market and to extend such market towards a new type of software. The prototype we developed is the first middleware that combines a transparent and reflective approach, as well as a decentralized (sensor analysis) and centralized (zone risk analysis) risk management mechanism. We followed the methodology proposed by Peffers et al. (2007) to structure our design research study, and we used the scenario-based approach of Rosson and Carroll (2002) during the development phase. We presented our results to an audience that was a balanced mix of technology-oriented and management-oriented experts at Nokia and we performed over a set of mobile users to assess their intention to adopt our new system. The guidelines for a new round of tests over a larger sample of users have been illustrated in the previous section.

This study has some limitations. As the development of fully operational prototype is still ongoing we are currently limited in our results by the application that runs on the phone. However, we believe that our work is well aligned with those who believe that a risk management approach is required to assure information security, and that privacy management in pervasive computing is a complex and multidimensional issue that should be addressed taking into consideration time and place. Our contention is that our model is more flexible than previous ones, since it has been conceived to be updated in time and to mitigate and record threats. Some interesting future researches are envisaged, which might involve privacy risk management in the sector of mobile payment, adding more business models for competitive users, and technical improvements for the prototype.

REFERENCES

Acquisti, A., Dingledine, R., & Syverson, P. (2003). On the economics of anonymity. In Wright, R. N. (Ed.), *Financial cryptography, LNCS 2742*. Springer-Verlag. doi:10.1007/978-3-540-45126-6_7

Anderson, R. (2001). Why information security is hard-an economic perspective. In *Proceedings 17th Annual Computer Security Applications Conference, 2001* (pp. 358-365). New Orleans, LA: IEEE.

Angwin, J., & Steel, E. (2011). *Web's hot new commodity: Privacy*. Retrieved March 15, 2011, from http://online.wsj.com/article/SB10001424052748703529004576160764037920274.html

Barkhuus, L. (2004). Privacy in location-based services, concern vs. coolness. In *Proceedings of Workshop paper in Mobile HCI 2004 workshop: Location System Privacy and Control*. Glasgow, UK.

Blakley, B., McDermott, E., & Geer, D. (2001). Information security is information risk management. In *Proceedings of the 2001 Workshop on New Security Paradigms*. Cloudcroft, New Mexico.

Bonazzi, R., Fritscher, B., & Pigneur, Y. (2010, October). Business model considerations for privacy protection in a mobile location based context. *Proceedings of the Second International Workshop on Business Models for Mobile Platforms IEEE*. Retrieved March 15, 2011, from http://people.hec.unil.ch/ypigneur/files/2010/08/10_bmmp.pdf

Capra, L., Emmerich, W., & Mascolo, C. (2003). CARISMA: Context-aware reflective middleware system for mobile applications. *IEEE Transactions on Software Engineering, 29*(10), 929–945. doi:10.1109/TSE.2003.1237173

Chen, G., & Kotz, D. (2000). *A survey of context-aware mobile computing research*. Tech. Rep. TR2000-381, Dartmouth, November 2000.

Dahlberg, T., Mallat, N., Ondrus, J., & Zmijewska, A. (2008). Past, present and future of mobile payments research: A literature review. *Electronic Commerce Research and Applications, 7*(2), 165–181. doi:10.1016/j.elerap.2007.02.001

Das, T. K., & Teng, B. S. (2000). A resource-based theory of strategic alliances. *Journal of Management, 26*(1), 31–61.

Davis, F. D. (1989). Perceived usefulness, perceived ease of use, and user acceptance of information technology. *Management Information Systems Quarterly, 13*(3), 319–340. doi:10.2307/249008

Fishbein, M., & Ajzen, I. (1975). *Belief, attitude, intention, and behavior: An introduction to theory and research*. Reading, MA: Addison-Wesley Pub.

Freudiger, J., Manshaei, M., Hubaux, J. P., & Parkes, D. C. (2009). On non-cooperative location privacy: A game-theoretic analysis. In *Proceedings of ACM Conference on Computer and Communications Security (CCS)*, Chicago, USA.

Gallivan, M. J., & Depledge, G. (2003). Trust, control and the role of interorganizational systems in electronic partnerships. *Information Systems Journal, 13*(2), 159–190. doi:10.1046/j.1365-2575.2003.00146.x

Google Inc. (2010). *Google Maps API - Geocoding*. Retrieved March 15, 2011, from http://code.google.com/apis/maps/documentation/services.html#Geocoding

Gregor, S., & Jones, D. (2007). The anatomy of a design theory. *Journal of the Association for Information Systems, 8*(5), 312–325.

Hagel, J. III, & Singer, M. (1999). *Net worth* (1st ed.). Harvard Business Press.

Herrmann, D. S. (2007). *Complete guide to security and privacy metrics: Measuring regulatory compliance, operational resilience, and ROI* (1st ed.). Auerbach Publications. doi:10.1201/9781420013283

Hong, D., Yuan, M., & Shen, V. Y. (2005). Dynamic privacy management: A plug-in service for the middleware in pervasive computing. In *Proceedings of the 7th International Conference on Human Computer Interaction with Mobile Devices & Services*. Salzburg, Austria.

Krumm, J. (2009). A survey of computational location privacy. *Personal and Ubiquitous Computing, 13*(6), 391–399. doi:10.1007/s00779-008-0212-5

Manasdeep, A. S., Jolly, D. S., Singh, A. K., Srivastava, M. A., & Singh, M. S. (2010). A proposed model for data privacy providing legal protection by e-court. *International Journal of Engineering Science and Technology, 2*(4), 649–657.

March, S. T., & Smith, G. F. (1995). Design and natural science research on information technology. *Decision Support Systems, 15*(4), 251–266. doi:10.1016/0167-9236(94)00041-2

Massey, A. K., Otto, P. N., Hayward, L. J., & Antón, A. I. (2009). Evaluating existing security and privacy requirements for legal compliance. *Requirements Engineering, 15*(1), 119–137. doi:10.1007/s00766-009-0089-5

Moore, G. C., & Benbasat, I. (1991). Development of an instrument to measure the perceptions of adopting an information technology innovation. *Information Systems Research, 2*(3), 192–222. doi:10.1287/isre.2.3.192

Nalebuff, B., & Brandenburger, A. (1997). Co-opetition: Competitive and cooperative business strategies for the digital economy. *Strategy and Leadership, 25*(6), 28–35. doi:10.1108/eb054655

Oxford English Dictionary. (2010.). *Privacy*. Retrieved March 15, 2011, from http://www.askoxford.com

Palen, L., & Dourish, P. (2003). Unpacking privacy for a networked world. In *Proceedings of the ACM Special Interest Group on Computer-Human Interaction (SIGCHI) Conference on Human Factors in Computing Systems*, Florida, USA.

Peffers, K., Tuunanen, T., Rothenberger, M. A., & Chatterjee, S. (2007). A design science research methodology for information systems research. *Journal of Management Information Systems, 24*(3), 45–77. doi:10.2753/MIS0742-1222240302

Ponemon, L. (2000). *Privacy risk management*. Long Beach, CA, USA: Presentation for The National Council of Higher Education Loan Programs.

Porter, M. E. (1998). *Competitive strategy: Techniques for analyzing industries and competitors* (1st ed.). Free Press.

Python Software Foundation. (2010). *Socket — Low-level networking interface — Python v2.6.4 documentation*. Retrieved March 15, 2011, from http://docs.python.org/library/socket.html

Radner, R. (2000). Costly and bounded rationality in individual and team decision-making. *Industrial and Corporate Change, 9*(4), 623–655. doi:10.1093/icc/9.4.623

Radner, R., & Marschak, J. (1954). Note on some proposed decision criteria. In Thrall, R. M. (Eds.), *Decision processes.* John Wiley.

Reagle, J., & Cranor, L. F. (1999). The platform for privacy preferences. *Communications of the ACM, 42*(2), 55. doi:10.1145/293411.293455

Rosson, M. B., & Carroll, J. M. (2002). *Usability engineering: Scenario-based development of human-computer interaction.* Morgan Kaufmann Pub.

Savage, L. J. (1954). *The foundations of statistics* (2nd ed.). New York, NY: Wiley.

Schilit, B., Adams, N., Want, R., et al. (1994). Context-aware computing applications. In *Proceedings of the Workshop on Mobile Computing Systems and Application.* Santa Cruz, CA, (pp. 85–90).

Shabtai, A., Fledel, Y., Kanonov, U., Elovici, Y., Dolev, S., & Glezer, C. (2010). Google Android: A comprehensive security assessment. *IEEE Security & Privacy, 8*(2), 35–44. doi:10.1109/MSP.2010.2

Sheppard, B. H., Hartwick, J., & Warshaw, P. R. (1988). The theory of reasoned action: A meta-analysis of past research with recommendations for modifications and future research. *The Journal of Consumer Research, 15*(3), 325–343. doi:10.1086/209170

Shokri, R., Freudiger, J., Jadliwala, M., & Hubaux, J. P. (2009). A distortion-based metric for location privacy. In *Proceedings of WPES'09, ACM Workshop on Privacy in the Electronic Society* (WPES), Chicago, IL, USA.

Simon, H. A. (1959). Theories of decision-making in economics and behavioral science. *The American Economic Review, 49*(3), 253–283.

Simon, H. A. (1987). Bounded rationality. In Eatwell, J. (Eds.), *The New Palgrave.* London, UK: Maemillan.

Straub, D., & Welke, R. J. (1998). Coping with systems risk: Security planning models for management decision-making. *MIS Quart., 22*(4), 441–469. doi:10.2307/249551

Thompson, J. D. (1967). *Organizations in action: Social science bases of administrative theory.* McGraw-Hill Companies.

Tversky, A., & Kahncman, D. (1974). Judgment under uncertainty: Heuristics and biases. *Science, 28*(5), 1124–1134. doi:10.1126/science.185.4157.1124

Venkatesh, V., Morris, M., Davis, G., & Davis, F. (2003). User acceptance of Information Technology: Toward a unified view. *Management Information Systems Quarterly, 27*(3), 425–478.

Webster, J., & Watson, R. T. (2002). Analyzing the past to prepare for the future: Writing a literature review. *Management Information Systems Quarterly, 26*(2), xiii–xxiii.

ADDITIONAL READING

Abowd, G. D., Atkeson, C. G., Hong, J., Long, S., Kooper, R., & Pinkerton, M. (1997). Cyberguide: a mobile context-aware tour guide. *Wireless Networks, 3*(5), 421–433. doi:10.1023/A:1019194325861

Acquisti, A., Dingledine, R., & Syverson, P. (2003). On the economics of anonymity. In Wright, R. N. (Ed.), *Financial Cryptography. Springer-Verlag, LNCS 2742.*

Anderson, R. (2001). Why information security is hard-an economic perspective. In *Proceedings 17th Annual Computer Security Applications Conference, 2001.* (pp. 358-365). Presented at the ACSAC 2001, New Orleans, Louisiana: IEEE.

Barkhuus, L. (2004). Privacy in Location-Based Services, Concern vs. Coolness. In *Proceedings of Workshop paper in Mobile HCI 2004 workshop: Location System Privacy and Control.* Glasgow.

Biegel, G., & Cahill, V. (2004) 'A framework for developing mobile, context-aware applications', *Proceedings of the 2nd IEEE Conference on Pervasive Computing and Communication*, pp.361–365.

Burrell, J. and Gay, G. (2002) 'E-graffiti: evaluating real-world use of a context-aware system', *Interacting with Computers – Special Issue on Universal Usability*, Vol. 14, No. 4, pp.301–312.

Capra, L., Emmerich, W., & Mascolo, C. (2003). CARISMA: Context-aware reflective middleware system for mobile applications. *IEEE Transactions on Software Engineering*, *29*(10), 929–945. doi:10.1109/TSE.2003.1237173

Chen, G., & Kotz, D. (2000). *A survey of context-aware mobile computing research.*

Chen, H., Finin, T., & Joshi, A. (2003). *'An ontology for context-aware pervasive computing environments'*, *The Knowledge Engineering Review* (*Vol. 18*, pp. 197–207). Cambridge University Press.

Dahlberg, T., Mallat, N., Ondrus, J., & Zmijewska, A. (2008). Past, present and future of mobile payments research: A literature review. *Electronic Commerce Research and Applications*, *7*(2), 165–181. doi:10.1016/j.elerap.2007.02.001

Fahy, P., & Clarke, S. (2004) 'CASS – a middleware for mobile context-aware applications', *Workshop on Context Awareness*, MobiSys 2004.

Freudiger, J., Manshaei, M., Hubaux, J. P., & Parkes, D. C. (2009). On Non-Cooperative Location Privacy: A Game-Theoretic Analysis. In *Proceedings of ACM Conference on Computer and Communications Security (CCS).*

Gu, T., Pung, H. K., & Zhang, D. Q. (2004a) 'A middleware for building context-aware mobile services', *Proceedings of IEEE Vehicular Technology Conference (VTC)*, Milan, Italy.

Harter, A., Hopper, A., Steggles, P., Ward, A., & Webster, P. (2002). The anatomy of a context-aware application. *Wireless Networks*, *8*(2–3), 187–197. doi:10.1023/A:1013767926256

Hofer, T., Schwinger, W., Pichler, M., Leonhartsberger, G., & Altmann, J. (2002) 'Context-awareness on mobile devices – the hydrogen approach', *Proceedings of the 36th Annual Hawaii International Conference on System Sciences*, pp.292–302.

Hong, D., Yuan, M., & Shen, V. Y. (2005). Dynamic privacy management: a plug-in service for the middleware in pervasive computing (p. 8).

Indulska, J., & Sutton, P. (2003) 'Location management in pervasive systems', CRPITS'03: *Proceedings of the Australasian Information Security Workshop*, pp.143–151.

Korpipää, P., & Mäntyjärvi, J. (2003) 'An ontology for mobile device sensor-based context awareness', *Proceedings of CONTEXT*, 2003, Vol. 2680 of Lecture Notes in Computer Science, pp.451–458.

Krumm, J. (2009). A survey of computational location privacy. *Personal and Ubiquitous Computing*, *13*(6), 391–399. doi:10.1007/s00779-008-0212-5

Palen, L., & Dourish, P. (2003). Unpacking privacy for a networked world. In *Proceedings of the ACM Special Interest Group on Computer-Human Interaction (SIGCHI) conference on Human factors in computing systems* (p. 136). Presented at the Conference on Human Factors in Computing Systems, Florida, USA.

Peffers, K., Tuunanen, T., Rothenberger, M. A., & Chatterjee, S. (2007). A Design Science Research Methodology for Information Systems Research. *Journal of Management Information Systems*, *24*(3), 45–77. doi:10.2753/MIS0742-1222240302

Ponemon, L. (2000, June 7). *Privacy Risk Management. Presentation for The National Council of Higher Education Loan Programs*. Presented at the NCHELP Convention, Long Beach, CA, USA.

Rosson, M. B., & Carroll, J. M. (2002). *Usability engineering: scenario-based development of human-computer interaction*. Morgan Kaufmann Pub.

Salber, D., Dey, A. K., & Abowd, G. D. (1999) 'The context toolkit: aiding the development of context-aware applications', *Proceedings of the ACM CHI*, Pittsburgh, PA, pp.434–441.

Schilit, B., Adams, N., Want, R., & Associates. (1994). Context-aware computing applications. In *Proceedings of the workshop on mobile computing systems and applications* (pp. 85–90).

Shokri, R., Freudiger, J., Jadliwala, M., & Hubaux, J. P. (2009). A Distortion-Based Metric for Location Privacy. In *Proceedings of WPES'09*. Presented at the ACM Workshop on Privacy in the Electronic Society (WPES), Chicago, IL; USA.

Straub, D., & Welke, R. J. (1998). Coping with systems risk: Security planning models for management decision-making. *MIS Quart.*, *22*(4), 441–469. doi:10.2307/249551

KEY TERMS AND DEFINITIONS

Bounded Rationality: A rational approach to decision, taking into consideration the player's biases and cognitive limitations.

Context-Aware Technologies: A set of technical solutions that can sense the change in the environment and adapt accordingly.

Contingency Theory: A class of behavioral theory that claims that the optimal course of action is contingent (dependent) upon both the internal and external situations. Such theory postulates that impacts of environmental factors are systemic (=part of the system), rather than entirely situational.

Infomediary: an information intermediary that gathers data and dispatch aggregated analyses.

Middleware: A software layer that situates between the application and the network to provide powerful abstractions and mechanisms that relieve programmers from dealing with low-level details that can change in time.

Opportunism: The agent's act of optimizing the personal payoff, no matter what occurs to other agents.

Privacy: a state in which one is not observed or disturbed by others.

Privacy Risk Management: the identification, assessment, and prioritization of risks caused by the collection and dissemination of user's data.

Risk Aversion: A concept based on human behavior, according to which an agent tries to minimize its loss chance.

Regulatory Awareness: The continuous assessment of laws and standards that apply to a determined/defined environment.

Section 3
Privacy Related Analyses and Evaluations

Chapter 13
Harm Mitigation from the Release of Personal Identity Information

Andrew S. Patrick
Office of the Privacy Commissioner of Canada & Carleton University, Canada

L. Jean Camp
Indiana University, USA

ABSTRACT

In August 2007 approximately 445,000 letters were sent to retirees who belonged to the California Public Employees' Retirement System (CalPERS). This was a routine mailing, but all or a portion of each pensioner's Social Security Number (SSN) was printed on the address panel of the envelopes, making this event all but ordinary. This massive breach of sensitive SSNs, along with names and addresses, exposed these people to potential identity theft and fraud. What are the harms associated with a data breach of this nature? How can those harms be mitigated? What are, or should be, the costs and consequences to the organization releasing the data? While it is very difficult to predict the specific consequences of a data breach of this nature, a statistical model can be used to estimate the likely financial repercussions for individuals and organizations, and the recent settlement in the TJX case provides a good model of harm mitigation that could be applied in this case and similar cases.

INTRODUCTION

In August 2007 approximately 445,000 letters were sent to retirees who belonged to the California Public Employees' Retirement System (CalPERS). This was a routine mailing, but all

or a portion of each pensioner's Social Security Number (SSN) was printed on the address panel of the envelopes, making this event all but ordinary (Bosworth, 2007; Privacy Rights Clearing House, n.d.). This massive breach of sensitive SSNs, along with names and addresses, exposed all of these people to potential identity theft and

DOI: 10.4018/978-1-61350-501-4.ch013

fraud. SSNs are supposed to be kept secret from all but a select few recipients (e.g., employers, tax agencies), and yet this information was plainly printed on the outside of envelopes sent through the regular postal mail.

What are the harms associated with a data breach of this nature? How can those harms be mitigated? What are, or should be, the costs and consequences to the organization releasing the data? This chapter describes the harms caused by the release of personal identity information, and discusses the possible mitigation of financial and non-financial identity theft risks. Different harm mitigation strategies are discussed and the costs of identity protection services are described. The impacts on the releasing organization are also described. Finally, the unique characteristics of vulnerable people, such as pensioners, that might lead to more concerns about the effects of the breach are discussed.

Risk mitigation begins with risk avoidance, so this chapter begins with a discussion of best practices for data governance. Immediately following is a discussion of the consequences of data breaches, and then a classification of the most common consequences, identity theft and account fraud. Near and long-term harm mitigation is then addressed, first for the consumer whose data were exposed and then for the organization that exposed the data. Moving from more generic consequences to specific costs, the next section contains an enumeration of credit monitoring services. We then discuss issues associated with particularly vulnerable populations. We conclude by providing a proposal for harm mitigation that involves moving away from provable damages towards recognizing harm from exposure. Throughout the chapter we return to our motivating case, the large-scale release by CalPERS of personal identity information for a uniquely vulnerable population.

DATA GOVERNANCE BEST PRACTICES

"Data governance" refers to the procedures put in place to mange the collection, storage, and use of information in an organization. With the amount of information being processed by organizations increasing all the time, data governance is crucial not only for maintaining the health and effectiveness of the organization, but also for protecting any sensitive information being held. Good data governance is not optional, and it must be part of a long-term process that ensures that organizations control the data they have been entrusted with (Smith, 2007).

The State of California has recognized the importance of good data governance, and they have also emphasized the special importance of protecting the SSN:

The Social Security Number (SSN) has a unique status as a privacy risk. No other form of personal identification plays such a significant role in linking records that contain sensitive information that individuals generally wish to keep confidential. (California Office of Privacy Protection, 2008)

The public disclosure of the SSN was prohibited starting in 2003 and in 2004 laws were passed banning the use of SSNs on pay stubs. California has even recognized the specific risk involved in the CalPERS case, printing SSNs on the outside of envelopes:

When sending applications, forms or other documents required by law to carry SSNs through the mail, place the SSN where it will not be revealed by an envelope window. Where possible, leave the SSN field on forms and applications blank and ask the individual to fill it in before returning the form or application. (California Office of Privacy Protection, 2008)

The California Civil Code, Sections 1798.85-1798.86 (a) (5), explicitly prohibits the disclosure of SSNs on envelopes:

A social security number that is permitted to be mailed under this section may not be printed, in whole or in part, on a postcard or other mailer not requiring an envelope, or visible on the envelope or without the envelope having been opened.

It is clear, then, that any resident of California would have a reasonable expectation that their SSN would be protected by organizations they have entrusted with its care, especially a state agency such as CalPERS.

The type of inadvertent disclosure that occurred in the CalPERS incident is not the only way that personal identity information can be breached. The Open Security Foundation has described a number of data breach types, including improper disposal of computers, storage media, and documents, lost and stolen laptops, computer viruses, and fraud (see http://datalossdb.org/statistics). A Ponemon Institute (2011) study found that negligence was the most frequent cause of data breaches (41% of breaches). Also, SSNs are not the only type of personal identity information that can be breached. Privacy breaches can include credit card numbers, names, birth dates, employment records, etc. Organizations are collecting and storing a wide range of personal identity information, and often having difficulties keeping it protected.

CONSEQUENCES OF DATA BREACHES

Although it might appear that disclosure of a Social Security Number would be a benign event, in fact there can be serious consequences when personal identity information is exposed. Moreover, disclosure of the SSN, along with a name and address, is often sufficient to enable fraud and identity theft. Unlike account numbers and credit cards, SSNs are very difficult to replace and data breaches involving them are more likely to lead to serious problems (ID Analytics, 2006). For example, a 2005 tracking analysis of the use of personal information following a breach found that a highly sophisticated fraud ring was using the breached data to commit identity theft. Further analysis showed that people whose identity information was exposed in a breach tended to have a higher reported abuse rate of SSNs and higher risk assessment profiles than comparable people not involved with a breach (ID Analytics, 2006).

The main problem with SSNs is that they are used both as an identifier and an authenticator. This means that merely possessing a SSN is often enough to not only claim an identity, but to verify the identity. The FTC has recently described the SSN as the "keys to the kingdom" because of the power it gives an identity thief (Federal Trade Commission, 2008). Even if an institution asks for more authentication than the SSN, the SSN is a necessary component to identity-based fraud and the most important document for preparing a complete false identity. The Government Accounting Office (GAO) has also recognized the central role of the SSN. A 2002 report showed that the SSN is one of the three pieces of information most sought after by identity thieves, with the others being name and birth date (Darrow & Lichtenstein, 2008).

Fraud involving SSNs can be particular hard to prevent and detect. Criminals can pair stolen SSNs with different names to open new accounts without being noticed. It is also extremely difficult to change a SSN once it is assigned, and even if a new number is issued, the old number will usually remain linked to the new account anyway (Bosworth, 2007b). According to the Social Security Administration (SSA), people can only be given a new SSN as a last resort, and only if they have actually been the victim of fraud. Once they are victimized, they must first work with credit bureaus, police agencies, the IRS, and other agencies to resolve their problems. Only if they can demonstrate that all attempts have not worked can they request a new number, and that request may not be granted (Bosworth, 2005).

Even if a new SSN is provided, the SSA admits that it will not resolve all the problems resulting from identity theft:

Keep in mind that a new number probably will not solve all your problems. This is because other governmental agencies (such as the Internal Revenue Service and state motor vehicle agencies) and private businesses (such as banks and credit reporting companies) likely will have records under your old number. Also, because credit-reporting companies use the number, along with other personal information, to identify your credit record, using a new number will not guarantee you a fresh start. This is especially true if your other personal information, such as your name and address, remains the same. (Social Security Administration, 2009)

The value of the SSN as a reliable identifier is very much in question. ID Analytics (2010) recently reported that 40 million SSNs found in commercial records are associated with multiple people. Moreover, 20 million Americans have multiple SSNs associated with their names. Nevertheless, the SSN is the most common form of identification used in the U.S., for both legitimate and fraudulent authentication.

TYPES OF IDENTITY THEFT

Identity theft is the collection and misuse of another person's identity information for the purposes of committing fraud. This can be as simple as using a stolen credit card or as complicated as adopting someone's complete identity, including getting a driver's licence, medical coverage, or even a job in someone else's name. The FTC estimates that as many as 9 million Americans will have their identities stolen each year (Federal Trade Com-

mission, n.d.). It is important to understand the wide range of identity theft that can occur.

Medical Identity Theft

Medical identity theft is the use of personal identity information to commit fraud in the domain of health care. The FTC, an agency that does not handle medical issues, has reported more than 19,000 cases as of 2006 (Dixon, 2006). A GAO report in 2001 found that medical identity theft represented 2% of the fraud cases involving misuse of a SSN (Dixon, 2006). A 2007 report found that more than 250,000 Americans a year were victims of medical identity theft (Konrad, 2009).

The risks of medical identity theft are in two primary categories: (1) financial liabilities resulting from fraudulently obtaining health care services, and (2) contaminated or replaced medical information. At its most extreme, medical data theft can result in serious physical harm because incorrect entries into medical information systems can lead to misinformation about allergies, current prescriptions, or blood type. In one example of financial impact, a Colorado man first learned he was a victim of medical identity theft when a collection agency came seeking $44,000 for a surgery he never had. Someone had stolen his SSN, name, and address and used the false identity when obtaining health care services. Medical identity theft is the most difficult form of identity theft to fix because consumers have limited rights and recourse. The Colorado man had to go through a lengthy procedure to fix his problems, and they were still not resolved after two years (Dixon, 2006).

In an example of medical impact, a Boston-area psychiatrist altered his patients' records, and the records of others, to give them diagnoses of disorders (such as major depression or drug addition) that they did not have in order to inflate his billings to insurance companies. If an identity is falsely associated with particular diagnoses, the fraud could cause someone to fail a background check used for employment or be denied insurance coverage (Dixon, 2006). In some cases, people have been denied health services because their insurance coverage has been "capped" due to someone else obtaining services in their name.

As medical information is handled more and more electronically, it may become more difficult to recover from identity theft because the false information can be disseminated widely. Also, medical identity theft is not usually revealed through normal financial monitoring. People who check their credit reports, for example, often do not find out about medical identity theft (Dixon, 2006). Under the Health Insurance Portability and Accountability Act (HIPAA), patients are entitled to view their medical records, but they may have to pay a large access fee (Konrad, 2009).

A recent Ponemon Institute (2010) study found that medical data breaches are having a large financial impact on the U.S. health care system. Based on interviews with 65 health care organizations, the study found a total cost of data breaches to be $12 billion over two years, or about $1 million per organization per year. This is money that could have been used for health services.

Criminal Identity Theft

Criminal identity theft is the use of a false identity to avoid law enforcement, and this form of theft has resulted in false arrests and detainment of innocent victims. Criminal identity theft has two main types: (1) the use of false financial instruments (such as credit cards) to commit crimes (such as gambling or child pornography), and (2) the use of a false identity to avoid law enforcement or prosecution. An example of the first type is the use of credit cards to make illegal purchases. The investigation of crimes performed by fraudsters may cause the innocent victim to be accused, arrested, detained, or worse. For example, consider the cases of two of the thirty-four people who were charged with downloading child pornography based on credit card records in the United Kingdom. One victim

killed himself within twenty-four hours of the accusation. An extensive investigation (as the victim was a career military officer) found no evidence of any type of files, photos, behaviours, or any other indication of any illicit activity. Another person was fired from his employment in education, divorced, and denied visitation to his children. He killed himself after being cleared by the courts of any wrongdoing, which included the judge regretting from the bench that he could only find him "not guilty," as opposed to "innocent." The other cases are still before the courts (Schlesinger, 2009).

In an example of false criminal records, consider Michael Anderson of Kentucky. Another person, a petty criminal also named Michael Anderson, managed to steal the innocent Michael's SSN and use it when dealing with the courts. Now, whenever the innocent man applies for employment, a routine background check reveals the false criminal record, and the real Michael has lost thousands of dollars due to withdrawn job offers (Davis, 2009).

Financial Identity Theft

Financial identity theft has two primary categories: (1) existing account fraud and (2) new account fraud. Existing account fraud consists of the abuse of extant accounts by placement of unauthorized charges or extraction of wealth. New account fraud refers to the creation of new lines of credit, issuance of mortgages, creation of checking accounts, and any other financial transactions that occur without the action or knowledge of the victim.

Fraud with Existing Accounts

Perhaps the largest case of identity theft involving existing accounts is the case of Heartland Payment Systems. Early in 2009, after being notified by Visa and MasterCard about suspicious activities, Heartland found that it had been a victim of a computer attack. One or more criminals had managed to hack into their networks and install sniffing programs to steal account numbers. It is believed that 130 million credit and debit card numbers had been stolen, sold on underground criminal networks, and used to make fraudulent purchases. It is not clear how many people were victims of the fraud, but at least 200 financial institutions have reported fraudulent transactions resulting from the Heartland data breach.

The Heartland attack was conducted by the same group responsible for the 2007 TJX breach that resulted in the loss of 45 million credit and debit account numbers (Privacy Rights Clearing House, n.d.). In the TJX case, a malicious "sniffer" program was again installed on the corporate computer systems and used to capture credit card data, SSNs, and drivers license numbers. This information was then used to make fraudulent financial transactions, with the stolen money being transferred to offshore accounts before being returned to the United States. The costs to TJX for reacting to the data breach and compensating customers and financial institutions have been estimated at US$200 million.

One method that the credit industry is adopting in an attempt to reduce the use of stolen credit card information is to include an electronic chip in the credit card and require a Personal Identification Number (PIN) when the card is used. The chip contains cryptographic information that makes it, supposedly, very difficult to copy on to fraudulent cards. Since the technology is claimed to be infallible, some financial institutions in the UK (and somewhat in Canada) have attempted to transfer the liability to the consumer for fraudulent transactions where a PIN was used. After several demonstrations of flawed Chip and PIN implementations (e.g., Murdoch, Drimer, Anderson & Bond, 2009), however, the regulations in the UK were changed to return the onus to the financial institutions. Chip and PIN technology is not a foolproof solution, although it may reduce some forms of fraud.

Careful monitoring of account statements can usually uncover fraud with existing accounts. As long as there are reasonable methods for a consumer to report fraudulent transactions on their account and receive reimbursements, these forms of fraud tend to be more of an inconvenience than a serious threat. Usually, large-scale frauds, such as the Heartland and TJX cases, are eventually uncovered through monitoring of transactions.

Fraud with New Accounts

New account fraud occurs when a stolen identity is used to open new accounts, such as credit cards, bank loans, and mortgages, in order to withdraw cash (Lieber, 2008). Although new account fraud represents only 30% of the US identity fraud cases, it is the most difficult to detect and usually results in higher average losses than fraud with existing accounts (IT Facts, n.d.). Moreover, since the authentic person is not involved in any way during the actual fraud event, any resulting thefts come as a shocking surprise and consumers are faced with cleaning up after an incident they had nothing to do with.

New account fraud can only be prevented at the time accounts are created. Financial institutions commonly use a credit bureau to gather background information when an account is created, so these bureaus play an important role in mitigating identity theft risks (discussed below).

HARM MITIGATION

It is clear that a breach of personal identity information, especially a SSN, can lead to profound and serious consequences. What can be done to mitigate the harm? A mitigation strategy must include both a near-term response, as soon as the breach is discovered, and long-term monitoring to prevent lingering problems.

Near-Term Response

Once personal identity information has been leaked, a necessary first step for a consumer to take is to inform any agencies involved with the information. For SSNs, this might include the Social Security Administration, the IRS, banks and other financial institutions, etc. If fraudulent activity is suspected, it is also important to file a police report.

Perhaps most important is to contact the credit bureaus (also called credit reporting agencies). When dealing with the credit bureaus, there are two possible actions that can be taken. A credit file can be "frozen", which means that the credit history cannot be seen by lenders, insurance companies, or employers without an individual's consent. Since many businesses will not open new accounts without being able to view a credit file, a freeze can offer some form of protection. In California, a credit freeze is free to identity theft victims who have filed a police report (otherwise the cost is $10 to freeze each file at the three credit bureaus).

A "fraud alert" can also be placed in a credit file, which should indicate to an institution that fraud might be involved with this account. It is hoped that an institution opening up a new account would seek additional proof of identity when there is a fraud alert, but they are not required to do so (California Office of Privacy Protection, n.d.). Fraud alerts placed on credit records at the credit bureaus normally last for 90 days, although consumers can ask for a special, extended alert that lasts for 7 years.

For each of these responses, it is up to the consumer to act. This can require dealing with large government bureaucracies and negotiating the complex credit reporting agency environment (more on this later). They must also contact all three credit-reporting agencies separately, in writing, if they wish to freeze or unfreeze their credit records. This is different than the one-request method that can be used to get credit reports (Soghoian, 2009).

Long-Term Monitoring

An immediate response to a data breach incident is not enough to mitigate the risks of identity theft. Consumers have to remain vigilant for a long period (measured in years) to make sure that the leaked information is not used for fraud. Once a person receives notification of a data breach, they are four times more likely to suffer identity fraud within the next year (Javelin Strategy and Research, n.d.).

As a result of the increased risk of identity theft following a data breach, affected organizations commonly offer credit-monitoring services to the subjects of the breach. For example, in an incident similar to the CalPERS breach, the US Department of Agriculture (USDA) detected unauthorized access to their stored data in June 2006. The personal data included SSNs, names, photos, and work locations of USDA employees. In response, the USDA offered free credit monitoring services to the affected employees for a period of 12 months (USA.gov, n.d.). In another case, CalOptima, a health services provider, lost and then found unencrypted CDs containing personal data including SSNs, names, addresses, dates of birth, and diagnostic codes. During the time the data was missing, CalOptima was making arrangements with one of the credit bureaus to offer credit-monitoring services to the victims (ComputerWorld, 2009a, 2009b).

Data breach response is becoming so important that specialized services are being offered to organizations that experience a data breach. ID Experts (www.idexpertscorp.com), for example, offers a "Breach Respond" service that helps organizations notify the subjects of the data breach, protect the identities of the breach victims, and recover from any resulting identity thefts. The protection component can involve purchasing credit monitoring and identity theft insurance for the victims, as well as identity theft education programs. The recovery service provides assessments of identity theft claims, and consultations

Figure 1. Time pattern of identity misuse rate following a data breach (from ID Analytics, 2006). The X-axis is time in months, and the Y-axis is the percent of fraud cases.

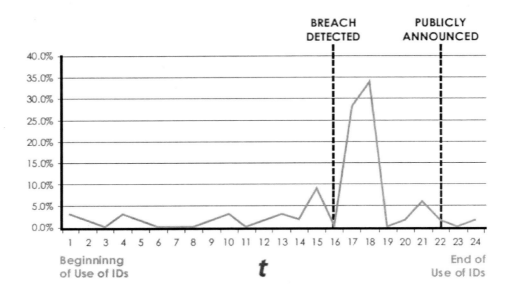

with the victim to dispute any fraudulent activities that have taken place. The recovery service remains active for 3 years following a confirmed case of identity theft. Although recovery packages may appeal to organizations, in a manner that is similar to identity theft insurance, discussed below, these packages may not be as useful as they first appear, and it can be difficult to demonstrate specific losses (Lazzarotti, 2010).

Even when credit monitoring is put in place, it is important to realize that the criminal element is not a passive adversary and criminal behaviours evolve along with the practices implemented to defeat them. One notable change in the past five years has been a tendency to store identity information and only use it after some time has passed. One recent study found that identity thieves had learned to hold data for six months in order to maximize its value (ID Analytics, 2005). Another study (ID Analytics, 2006) found that the use of breach information to open new accounts peaks after a breach is detected, but the fraud actually

takes place over a period of at least 24 months (see Figure 1).

The data shown in Figure 1 comes from a 2005 data breach involving 100,000 consumer identities that included SSN, date of birth, name, and other information. An investigation found that a sophisticated fraud ring was using the leaked information to commit identity theft by opening new accounts. The Y-axis in the figure shows the percentage of fraud cases that occur during each month surrounding the data breach, and the temporal pattern is interesting for a number of reasons. First, a small rate of fraud occurred for many months before the leak was detected. This may have been because the fraudsters used the identity information rarely to avoid detection. Once the breach was discovered, however, there was a large increase in the use of the identity information. This peak occurred many months before the breach was publicly announced.

This temporal pattern means that most of the identity theft occurs before the consumers are even aware that there has been a breach. This is very important because most identity theft insurance plans (see below) do not provide protection for events that occurred prior to the start of the coverage. This graph shows that much of the fraud happens before the breach is discovered, or immediately afterwards. To be useful, identity theft insurance coverage would have to be backdated, but this is not offered in the packages that are available.

COSTS OF BREACHES TO ORGANIZATIONS

Immediate Costs

An organization suffering a data breach will incur a number of immediate costs. There will be costs associated with complying with existing regulations and notifying the appropriate authorities, including legal costs. There will also be costs associated with notifying the subjects of the loss. This notification costs might include mailing costs, but also the publishing of information and the operation of information "hot-lines" or similar services.

There may also be procedural costs associated with restoring data protection. For example, account numbers and identification cards may have to be reissued. There may also be costs associated with an investigation of the data leak and any remedial measures (technical, procedural, administrative) that need to be taken.

The Ponemon Institute (2010) study of health care organizations found a significant lack of resources, trained personnel, policies, and procedures for handling data breaches. This meant that many breaches were undetected until reported by affected patients, and most organizations were left with no confidence in their ability to secure patient records. The agencies reported that it took up to 1 year, or even longer, to resolve data breach incidents. The short-term costs of handling these data breach incidents included time and productivity losses, legal and consulting costs, and lawsuits.

Continuing Costs

The continuing costs to an organization experiencing a data breach depend on the nature of the organization. A commercial company, especially those with a retail relationship with customers, may experience a loss in reputation and a subsequent loss in business, but consistent figures are difficult to find due to different reporting methods and requirements. Schneider (2009) found that 23% of security professionals reported harm to an organization's reputation after the reporting of a data breach. Another study found that 58% of customers reported a decreased sense of trust and confidence in an organization after a breach notification. That data showed that 20% of people reported terminating a business relationship because of a data breach, and another 40% had considered it. Companies themselves reported that from 0 to 7% of the affected customer base closed an account or terminated a relationship (Ponemon, 2005). Greenemeier (2007) reported that 75% of debit cardholders said they would not shop at a retailer after they had reported a data breach, and 84% said they would prefer retailers with better reputations. Another Ponemon (2008) study, involving a survey of over 1,795 consumers, found that 83% had received a data breach notification, and 57% of those affected said they had lost trust and confidence in the organization, while 31% said that they had terminated the relationship.

The Ponemon Institute (2010) study of U.S. health care organizations (who are in the commercial sector) found a number of sources of long-term costs resulting from data breaches. The most common was a loss of brand value and a damaged reputation. Related to this were losses of patient good will and a resulting loss of revenues. The study estimated that each health care institution lost about $9 million in patient "churn" over a two-year period because of data breaches.

Commercial organizations can also experience capitalization losses (a loss in stock value) as a result of a data breach incident. On average, a reported data breach is associated with a loss of 0.6% in the stock market (Acquisti, Telang, & Friedman, 2006). CalPERS and other government organizations are immune from this category of loss, not being publicly listed companies.

Additional costs to private sector organizations take the form of fines and increased merchant fees when credit and debit information is lost. For example, after the famed TJX breach of credit cards, Visa levied an $880,000 fee to the merchants' acquiring bank (McKeay, 2008). (Note this was the fee for the acquiring bank, not the fee assessed against TJX.) Aggregate fines by Visa to merchants and merchant acquiring banks due to breaches and inadequate security increased to $4.6M in 2006 from $3.4M in 2005 but detailed per-firm and per-incident data are not public (Internet Retailer, 2006). These fines are based on the requirements defined by the Payment Card Industry Security Standards Council and levied against those institutions that do not comply with the standards. Public agencies may be immune to this type of cost depending on their relationship with payment processors.

Another data breach cost is the resetting of accounts. In a study of data breaches that occurred in Maine, the majority of affected financial institutions immediately closed the breached accounts. New accounts were opened, and the exposed cards were canceled. Between the time of the delivery of new cards and the cancellation of previous cards, transactions were subjected to increased scrutiny. Of 75 institutions surveyed, only four did not reissue cards unless requested by the customer (Maine Bureau of Financial Institutions, 2008).

Regulatory fines and increased auditing requirements can also result from data breaches. For example, the FTC fined ChoicePoint $15 million in January 2006 for not keeping consumer data confidential (Monahan, 2009). Also, the FTC settlements with ChoicePoint (FTC File No. 052-3069) and B J Wholesale Club (FTC File No. 052-3096) required that twenty years of third party audits be submitted to confirm that the comprehensive

information security programs adopted by these institutions are followed in practice.

For non-commercial organizations, such as a state agency like CalPERS, there is no risk of customers terminating a relationship or moving to another store. CalPERS enjoys a monopoly in providing pension and health care services to California state employees. Thus, the usual commercial motivations for protecting personal information are not present, although there may be political motivations.

There are a number of measures that organizations should take to reduce the chances of a release of personal information. Protective measures should include physical, technical and administrative safeguards. A recent Ponemon Institute (2010) report, although focused on health care, outlines organizational, security, administrative, management, and governance best practices that should be considered by all organizations handling personal information. Other analysts argue that more radical changes are necessary to correct the status quo. For example, Hoofnagle (2009) argues for a risk mitigation approach that focuses on the entities that actually issue credit. His investigation found that criminals were able to obtain credit on clearly limited and partially incorrect data. He argues that risk mitigation requires that the organizations that issue the fraudulent forms of credit be held strictly liable. This approach would place the burden of care on those who offer credit, rather than those who leak data.

Cost Estimates

The costs to an organization that experiences a data breach can be substantial, and the total amount depends on the nature of the breach, the amount and type of fraud that results, and the number of people affected. A recent calculation that included the costs of detection, technical remediation, notification, redress, customer response, and loss of business showed a range from a per-record cost in retail of $131 to a per-record cost in healthcare of $282 -- the average loss was $202 (Ponemon Institute, 2009). In a more recent study of US health care organizations (Ponemon Institute, 2010), the average loss per individual record was $471. Similarly, Microsoft's Adam Shostack estimated a per record cost of $182 (Shostack, 2009). The most recent study from the Ponemon Institute (2011) estimated an average cost per record of $214.

There are also secondary, echo costs from a data breach. Local financial institutions, for example, also pay the costs of identity theft, even when they are not directly involved with a data breach. The Maine study found that costs that could be directly tracked to the TJX breach were about $7.50 per affected customer. Similarly, for a Hannaford breach the cost per customer was $6.50. Overall, the 75 financial institutions included in the study spent over $2.1 million recovering from data breaches in a period of approximately 1.5 years (Maine Bureau of Financial Institutions, 2008).

Negligence Suits and Settlements

One area where organizations have so far avoided costs from data breaches is negligence lawsuits. Although consumers and banks seeking to recover losses resulting from data breaches have filed class action suits, and some out-of-court settlements have been reached, the courts have tended to reject the suits because no actual damages could be proven (Bishop, 2008; Schneider, 2009). The victims have tried to claim *potential* damages because of the exposure of personal identity information, but the courts have rejected this argument:

When an individual's personal information is stolen, there is no guarantee that it will be used fraudulently. In fact, only 2% of stolen credit card information from data breaches is subject to misuse. Of all identity theft reports, only 1.5 to 4% are the result of stolen credit card information....

The consumer suits fail because of the inability to show real damages resulting from the exposure of personal information. Increased likelihood that one's personal information will be used for illicit activity, standing alone, is not sufficient to warrant relief at law. (Schneider, 2009)

Even cases that have only sought credit-monitoring services for the victims have not been successful. In Pisciotta v. Old Nat'l Bancorp, 499 F.3d 629, 639 (7th Cir. 2007), the appeal court, in upholding the initial ruling, found that information loss, alone, could not be considered a type of damage:

Judge Ripple [of the appeal court] also preemptively rejected an argument that tried to analogize personal information exposure to toxic tort cases, where exposure to chemicals may lead to medical problems in the future. Whereas the plaintiffs in this case sought credit monitoring as a preventative measure, those exposed to chemicals in the toxic tort context often seek medical monitoring costs. Finally, Judge Ripple cited several other jurisdictions that have concluded, "[w]ithout more than allegations of increased risk of future identity theft, the plaintiffs have not suffered a harm that the law is prepared to remedy." (Schneider, 2009)

There have been some out-of-court settlements, perhaps motivated by a desire to avoid lengthy civil trials and to restore consumer confidence. In the TJX case, affected consumers received vouchers, cash benefits, credit monitoring, and identification theft insurance. People whose drivers licence information (collected by the stores when they returned goods without a receipt) was compromised were offered credit monitoring services and identity theft insurance for a period of 3 years (an Equifax monitoring product that includes $20,000 in insurance). Victims were also able to seek reimbursement for the cost of replacing a driver's licence. The special nature of the SSN was also confirmed in this settlement

-- people whose drivers licence number was the same as their SSN were offered reimbursement of losses resulting from identity theft.

COSTS OF BREACHES TO INDIVIDUALS

There can be significant costs (economic and personal) for an individual who is the subject of a data breach. These costs can occur even if the individual is in no way responsible for the data loss, as is the case with institutional data breaches. It has been argued that organizations (and governments) are shirking their civic responsibility to protect consumers and are instead forcing them to not only clean up after others' mistakes, but to consume new products in the process, and to feel guilty if they don't:

Instead of the State being responsible for ensuring the safety of people, citizen-consumers are charged with regulating their localized territories through consumption. Additionally, government websites stress that the credit industry is the primary victim of identity theft, so if individuals are irresponsible enough not to protect themselves, by implication they are damaging the national economy upon which everyone depends. (Monahan, 2009)

Even without any identity-related fraud, an individual may feel it necessary to purchase credit monitoring and identity theft insurance products if they are not already offered by the organization that had the data breach. Consumers may also incur legal costs when seeking advice about how to respond to a breach notification. Individuals may also incur accounting costs and lost time as they review all the transactions in their affected accounts.

If identity-related fraud does occur, there can be a host of economic impacts including any direct financial losses that cannot be recovered. There can be indirect costs due to a decrease in financial reputation, and this can include higher interest rates, difficulty getting loans, difficulty renting housing, higher security deposits for utilities, difficulty getting a cell phone contract, and being denied employment due to bad credit. There are also losses related to the time it takes to do all of the tasks necessary to attempt to recover from identity theft, and this often requires time off work (Identity Theft Resource Center, 2010).

It is possible to estimate the cost of recovering from identity theft. A study from the Identity Theft Resource Centre (2010) surveyed identity theft victims and found that they incurred direct expenses (not including fraudulent transactions) that averaged $527 for fraud involving existing accounts, and $2,104 for new account fraud (the most common type). A second study done by the Federal Trade Commission (2007) found a wide range of expenses incurred by identity theft victims. For new account fraud (the kind that is most likely when SSNs are involved), the median loss was $40. However, the distribution of losses was heavily skewed such that 25% of the victims incurred expenses of at least $1,000 and 10% of the victims had expenses of more than $3,000. These expenses did not include any compensation for lost wages. Therefore, when it comes to estimating the cost of identity theft, a reasonable estimate of typical expenses is $1,000 per victim.

There are also personal costs associated with identity theft. Victims often report a sense of personal violation and an increased level of anxiety. If others think that the theft was somehow their fault, people may also experience social consequences due to a loss of personal reputation (Identity Theft Resource Center, 2010).

CREDIT MONITORING SERVICES

One of the most frequent instructions to people who have been the subject of a data breach, or the victim of identity theft, is to monitor their credit reports. This is not an easy task, however. There are three major credit-reporting agencies in the U.S.: TransUnion, Equifax, and Experian, and they each maintain independent credit reports that are used by different lenders and agencies (for a good introduction to how the credit reporting system works, see Soghoian, 2009). This means that an individual must monitor all three reports.

Consumers in the U.S. are entitled by law to receive one free report from each agency each year. However, the procedure for requesting these reports is very confusing. On the Internet, for example, the site FreeCreditReport.com does not, in fact, offer free credit reports. It is instead a commercial service from Experian that will automatically sign-up consumers to a credit monitoring service after 7 days. Truly free reports can only be ordered from AnnualCreditReport.com, although, unlike commercial services, the report is not delivered instantly but is instead mailed after 15 days. Consumers are not able to receive free credit reports from a particular credit bureau more frequently than once per year.

Credit scores, which are numerical summaries of credit worthiness based on the information in a credit report, are offered separately from credit reports. Each of the credit bureaus may use a different credit score methodology, and they charge extra for providing the information to consumers. The FICO score created by the Fair Isaac Corporation is perhaps the best-known credit score, and consumers are often told that it is the main determinant of how they are seen by creditors. It appears that it is impossible for a consumer to learn their FICO score without paying for it.

Perhaps taking advantage of this confusion (Lieber, 2009), a number of credit monitoring services are offered. These services are usually marketed as identity theft prevention services, and they are often targeted to people who have already experienced fraud. They not only provide credit reports, and perhaps credit scores, but they offer to monitor the reports for changes and send alerts to the consumer. It is important to note that these services do not fix any issues that might be

uncovered during the monitoring, they simply inform the consumer, who then has to respond to the issues (perhaps with some help from the service).

The three major credit bureaus, TransUnion, Equifax, and Experian each offer a commercial monitoring service. To some this is considered to be ironic since it is these services that are responsible for maintaining accurate credit information. Consumers are being asked to pay to have the companies provide information so they can then monitor their own credit files (About.com, n.d.). Some third parties also provide credit-monitoring services, and they may provide access to reports from one or more of the credit bureaus. They may also offer different service components, such as address change request monitoring, which is not offered by the credit bureaus.

Service Components

In addition to providing credit reports from the three credit bureaus, credit-monitoring services often provide a number of other service components. Some of these are:

- credit scores based on FICO algorithms or other methods
- daily monitoring of credit reports and immediate alerts if the files change
- monitoring of Internet sites known to be black markets for stolen information
- monitoring for address change requests
- the ability to place a fraud alert on a credit file
- the ability to place a lock or freeze on a credit report
- the services of a private investigator

Table 1 provides a summary of the service components offered by some of the available credit monitoring services. This table also provides monthly and yearly prices that are advertised with these plans. (The table contains data collected dur-

Table 1. Components of identity theft protection services

Component	TransUnion TrueCredit	Equifax ID Patrol	Experian Triple Advantage	Experian ProtectMyID	LifeLock	myFICO Score Watch	Identity Guard Extra Caution	TrustedID CreditLock
$ / Month	$14.95	$14.95	$14.95	$12.95	$10.00	$12.95	$14.99	$14.95
$ / Year					$110.00	$129.95	$149.95	$125.00
Credit Agency Coverage	3	3	3	3	proprietary databases	1	3	3
Daily Monitoring	yes	yes	yes	yes	no	yes	yes	
Internet Monitoring	no	yes	no		yes	no	yes	yes
Address Change Monitoring				yes	yes	no	no	
Lock Credit Report	TransUnion only	Equifax only	no	no	no	no	no	$44.95
Insurance Coverage	$25,000	$1 mil.	$50,000	$1 mil.	$1 mil.		$1 mil.	$1 mil.
Losses	no	unknown	yes	yes	no		yes	no
Legal Fees	yes	unknown	yes	yes	no		yes	yes
Lost Wages	yes	unknown	yes	yes	no		yes	yes
Misc Expenses	yes	unknown	yes	yes	no		yes	yes
Private Detective	no	no	yes	yes	no		yes	no

ing November 2010 from public web sites. Prices and service components are subject to change.)

Many of the credit monitoring plans offer a form of insurance. This insurance will provide funds to a customer if they become a victim of identity theft while they are members of a service plan (excluding any prior incidents). As can be seen in Table 1, the plans differ in the amount of coverage and the kinds of expenses that are included. In many cases direct losses resulting from identity theft are not covered. In the case of Life-Lock, the insurance coverage is only for the assistance services (advice) that will be arranged by the service provider. These insurance plans also require that the individual take whatever steps are necessary to recover from the identity theft (e.g., file police reports, re-file paperwork).

The identity theft protection services vary greatly in terms of how often the consumer receives a credit report. TransUnion TrueCredit provides a report monthly. Equifax ID Patrol provides unlimited reports on request from Equifax only, and annual reports from other credit reporting agencies. Similarly, Experian Triple Advantage similarly provides unlimited reports on request but only from Experian. LifeLock and Trust IDFreeze provide only the annual credit report that is already available to the consumer for free. myFICO Score Watch provides an annual credit report only from Equifax but also includes a credit score. Identity Guard Extra Caution provides unlimited credit reports upon request, and also credit scores, but the reports must be requested and are not automatically generated and distributed by the service.

Weaknesses in Credit Monitoring

The credit monitoring industry is approaching $1 billion in annual sales, and yet the actual value of the service is questionable (Lieber, 2009). Most people do not need the near-real-time monitoring of credit files that the services provide, and even if they do, credit-monitoring services provide only limited protection from identity theft. Only accounts that are included in the reports of the credit bureaus are covered. There are many types of accounts that are not routinely covered by the bureaus, and it is not unusual for reports to be missing important accounts (Soghoian, 2009). The credit bureaus also provide no coverage of non-financial accounts so health care services are not protected. In addition, credit monitoring does nothing to prevent criminal identity theft.

The credit monitoring services that provide guarantees stipulate that the coverage only comes into effect after the plan is purchased—they do not cover any fraud conducted earlier. However, as discussed above, fraud can occur for many months before it is discovered and reported to the consumers. In addition, most of the insurance policies only cover indirect costs resulting from identity theft, such as legal fees and lost wages. Only a few policies cover the direct loss of funds from identity-related fraud.

If victims attempt to pursue a lawsuit related to identity theft, a Supreme Court ruling established that the suit must be filed within 2 years of the harm to their credit rating. It is common, however, for fraud to not become apparent for a long time, perhaps longer than 2 years (Finberg, 2002; Identity Theft Resource Center; 2010). This is especially true if there is a delay in starting a credit monitoring service following a breach of identity information.

Perhaps the largest weakness, however, is the fact that credit monitoring services do not protect customers if other people use their SSNs. Multiple credit files with multiple identities all using the same SSN is one of the biggest problems because of the widespread use of the SSN as an identifier and the difficulty in replacing it. According to a spokesman from Experian, "[we have] no way to establish ownership of a Social Security number, as the Social Security Administration will not provide that type of validation…[t]herefore, we would be unable to determine fraudulent use of one's Social Security number" (Consumer Reports, 2007). The only protection that seems to be available is to scan black markets on the Internet for SSNs that are available for sale, a service offered by ID Secure (see http://www.idsecure.com/).

It is also possible for fraudsters to take advantage of process flaws in the credit reporting system and extract large amounts of money from people who do subscribe to monitoring services. This is because it can often take several days for new accounts to appear in a credit file. By opening a large number of credit accounts very rapidly, identity thieves are able to steal money before the consumer can be alerted (Soghoian, 2009). All of these factors suggest that credit-monitoring services have limited value.

VULNERABLE POPULATIONS

The data subjects involved in the CalPERS breach were pensioners receiving benefits. This means that most of the people were senior citizens (with other people receiving a disability benefit). Seniors are known to be a vulnerable group when it comes to fraud. Previous research has shown that people over 60 account for 26% of the telemarketing fraud victims and 65% of the victims of frauds promising prizes and sweepstakes wins. The same report also found that low-income seniors are the least likely to consult a lawyer. In addition, seniors typically have better credit, more home equity, and more financial resources than younger people, making them an appealing target for fraud (Finberg, 2002).

Seniors are likely unaware of today's fraud risks, so they may be more vulnerable to thieves and scammers who exploit identity information. Also, seniors are often unable to take advantage of the various tools that are available for managing identity, such as Internet-based credit monitoring services.

Many seniors may also be living with cognitive impairments, making it difficult for them to understand subtle issues and learn from their mistakes. They may also experience memory deficits, and this may make them more vulnerable to scams. It has also been found that seniors may be ashamed or frightened to report that they have been victimized (Nerenberg, 2006).

All of these factors mean that the seniors, and other vulnerable people, may be more likely to experience identity-related fraud resulting from a breach, and they may incur more losses and costs than a younger, healthier population. By definition, the older the victim, the shorter the time that person has to recover lost wages and assets. This should be taken into account when determining levels of risk and appropriate mitigation measures.

FROM PROVABLE DAMAGES TO HARM FROM EXPOSURE

As mentioned previously, organizations have so far been immune to successful negligence suits resulting from data breaches. This is because the courts have decided that awarding victims for potential damage that might result from a data breach is not appropriate, and it has been difficult for class actions to prove actual damages. Recently, Jacob Schneider (2009), writing in the *Journal of Science and Technology Law*, has suggested that a different approach may be called for. Instead of attempting to prove real damages resulting from a data breach, litigators could attempt to establish an injury of "personal data exposure." This would be analogous to medical cases where plaintiffs have argued, at least some times successfully, that exposure to toxic substances is enough to justify damage awards.

The legal task then becomes determining the amount of damage that is appropriate. Schneider suggests using a concept of "expected losses", which can be calculated using the formula

$$E = (P \times L) \times N$$

where E is the expected loss, P is the probably of losses happening, L is the average monetary loss that would occur, and N is the number of people involved. So, for example, if 1% of data breach victims experience loss, and the average loss is $1,000 per victim, then the expected level of loss is (0.01 X $1,000) or $10 per person. This figure could then be used to determine payouts to a class of individuals, or it could be used to establish a pool of funds (sized by multiplying the expected loss by the number of victims) to be drawn on by data breach subjects if and when they become victims of identity theft. The CalPERs breach involved 445,000 people, so the pool size in this example would be $4.45 million.

This approach was used in the TJX settlement, where a pool was established for identity theft victims. Instead of trying to determine an expected loss, however, a cap of $1 million was placed on the pool funds and, if claims exceed that amount, victims were to be reimbursed on a prorated basis.

To apply Schneider's approach to new cases we need to come up with reasonable estimates of the probability of losses (P) and the costs of those losses (L). For estimating the probably of an identity theft incident after a data breach we have 3 sources of data. A 2006 study by ID Analytics looked at a data breach where the name, birthdate, SSN and other information of 100,000 people were leaked. That study found a rate of attempted identity theft of 0.098%, which was consistent with other reports from ID Analytics customers that experienced an actual theft rate of 0.07% (ID Analytics, 2006)

A second study conducted by ID Analytics in 2007 examined 12 data breaches involving the personal identity information of over 10 million people. That study found identity theft rates of 0.01 to 0.5%, with larger data breaches having lower identity theft rates. For breaches involving more than 100,000 people, the attempted identification theft rate was 0.01% (ID Analytics, 2007).

The ID Analytic studies, however, did not examine actual subjects of data breaches. Instead, they examined their proprietary database of identification information to look for anomalies in the identification records and compared them to people who were not the subject of data breaches. A more recent study from the Ponemon Institute (2008) actually surveyed people who were subjects of data breaches. That study found that 2% of the data subjects reported experiencing identity theft following a data breach, and 64% were unsure.

Thus, the available identity theft incident rates do vary a great deal, but it does seem reasonable to conclude that the probability of identity theft rate resulting from a data breach is about 1.0%. Further, using the high end of the range of reported incident values can be easily justified when vulnerable individuals are involved.

Earlier, the typical cost to individual victims of identity theft was estimated at $1,000. Using these estimates of probability and loss, a sample calculation can be made to represent the expected loss for the CalPERS population as a result of the data breach:

$$(P \times L) \times N = E$$

$$(0.01 \times \$1{,}000) \times 445{,}000 = \$4.45 \text{million}$$

If new data is available to support different estimates of identity theft probability and loss amounts, then the calculation can be adjusted accordingly.

FUTURE RESEARCH DIRECTIONS

There are a number of areas where more research and investigation are required. Foremost, the harm mitigation model proposed above has not been validated. It is important to know if it provides a good estimate of the risk of identity theft and the resulting personal and organizational costs. There may also be alternative models that do a better job of predicting risks and harms. We also have little information, other than occasional small studies, about the frequency of data breaches and the resulting costs for individuals and organizations. Without detailed data it is not possible to categorize the breach cases effectively, nor to fully explore systematic prevention measures.

We also need more information on the uses and misuses of the SSN and similar identifiers. It is important to know how various institutions treat the SSN when establishing an identity, how frequently SSNs are abused, and it what contexts. Also, we should examine the effectiveness of alternative measures of identification, such as meaningless-but-unique identification numbers?

Privacy violations are often conceived as a problem between particular individuals and the organizations that reveal personal information or the fraudsters who exploit it. This view has led to an approach that emphasizes finding evidence of direct, personal harm when seeking remedies, and an expectation of personal responsibility for the victim to repair any damages. An alternative approach, advocated by Daniel Solove (2003), is to treat privacy violations as an architectural problem -- a problem related to the legal, economic, and social structures in society. In this view, privacy problems cannot be addressed by individual remedies alone, but instead must be addressed by fixing fundamental flaws in the architecture. It is clear that there is are fundamental flaws in the identity architectures we use today, and that much work needs to be done.

CONCLUSION

In August 2007, the Social Security Numbers of 445,000 CalPERS pensioners were exposed because they were visible on letters sent through the regular postal mail. SSNs are used in the U.S. not only for identification, but also for authentication. SSNs are "the keys to the kingdom" for thieves who exploit identity information. Identity theft using names, addresses, and SSNs is common enough to represent a real risk, and people who become victims will likely loose significant amounts of money. Even if funds that are fraudulently taken can be recovered, victims often incur legal expenses, credit monitoring expenses, administrative and accounting expenses, and lost wages due to time off work. This is in addition to the psychological and social impacts of being victimized in such a personal way.

With captive and vulnerable members, the CalPERS case illustrates the importance of offering victims all the protection that is appropriate. Determining what is appropriate requires understanding the harms and the effectiveness of available mitigation methods. Offering credit-monitoring services for some period of time is now common in cases of data breaches of this nature. The protection offered by these services is quite limited, however. Victims still have to bear the burden of recovery once unusual activity is detected, and identity theft insurance has significant limitations in the coverage provided. Lawsuits against the organization for losses resulting from a data breach have strong time limitations, and they will likely be rejected if no direct losses can be proven.

It is very difficult to predict the specific consequences of a data breach of this nature, but a statistical model can be used to estimate the likely financial repercussions for the CalPERS pensioners. Using one set of assumptions, the total harm to the people whose data was leaked could total $4.5 million. Also, the recent settlement in the TJX case provides a good model of harm mitigation that could be applied in this case. Under the TJX model, free credit monitoring services, covering all 3 credit bureaus, should be provided for all the subjects of the data breach for a period of 3 years. Since identity theft insurance has such limited coverage, a pool of funds should also be established for those people who do experience identity theft resulting from the data breach. As was done in the TJX settlement, fraud victims can apply to the fund with proof of the losses and costs they have incurred. Unlike the TJX settlement, however, the pool should arguably remain available for a long period of time, a minimum of 3 years, because it can take a long time for identity information to be exploited, and because the members are required to maintain their association with CalPERS.

Inspired by a particular incident to investigate the harms of a breach of personal identity information and the resulting risks of identity theft, we have found that the financial and personal risks are many and current harm mitigation measures inadequate. However, measures can be taken to reduce the risks of data breaches and protect the affected individuals from undue harm.

REFERENCES

About.com. (n.d.). *Should you buy identity theft insurance or credit monitoring services?* Retrieved from http://financialplan.about.com/od/insurance/a/IDTheftInsure.htm

Acquisti, A., Telang, R., & Friedman, A. (2006). Is there a cost to privacy breaches? An event study analysis. In *Third International Conference on Intelligent Systems (ICIS), Prague, Czech Republic* (pp. 26-33).

Analytics, I. D. (2005). *US national fraud ring analysis 2005.* ID Analytics, Inc. Whitepaper. Retrieved from http://www.idanalytics.com/solutions/white-papers/white-paper-request/index.php?whitepaper=U.S.%20National%20Fraud%20Ring%20Analysis,%202005

Analytics, I. D. (2006). *National data breach analysis.* ID Analytics, Inc. Whitepaper.

Analytics, I. D. (2007). *Data breach harm analysis.* ID Analytics, Inc. Whitepaper.

Analytics, I. D. (2010). *20 million Americans have multiple Social Security numbers associated with their name.* ID Analytics Inc. News Release, August 11, 2010. Retrieved from http://www.idanalytics.rsvp1.com/news-and-events/news-releases/2010/8-11-2010.php

Bishop, D. A. (2008). No harm no foul: Limits on damages awards for individuals subject to a data breach. *Shidler Journal of Law. Commerce and Technology, 4,* 12–13.

Bosworth, M. H. (2005). *Your Social Security number: Vulnerable but inflexible.* ConsumerAffairs.com. Retrieved from http://www.consumeraffairs.com/news04/2005/id_ssn.html

Bosworth, M. H. (2007a). *Data breaches endanger NY, CA retirees: Consultant's bungling, printer's errors put retirees at risk.* ConsumerAffairs.com. Retrieved from http://www.consumeraffairs.com/news04/2007/08/breaches_retirees.html

Bosworth, M. H. (2007b). *Wisconsin mails tax forms with exposed Social Security Numbers.* ConsumerAffairs.com. Retrieved from http://www.consumeraffairs.com/news04/2007/01/wi_ssn.html

California Office of Privacy Protection. (2008). *Recommended practices on protecting the confidentiality of social security numbers.* Retrieved from http://www.privacy.ca.gov/res/docs/pdf/ssnrecommendations.pdf

California Office of Privacy Protection. (n.d.). *How to "freeze" your credit files.* Consumer Information Sheet 10. Retrieved from http://www.oispp.ca.gov/consumer_privacy/consumer/documents/pdf/cis10securityfreeze.pdf

ComputerWorld. (2009a, October 29). CalOptima recovers discs with personal data on 68,000 members. *ComputerWorld.* Retrieved from http://www.computerworld.com/s/article/9140122/CalOptima_recovers_discs_with_personal_data_on_68_000_members?taxonomyId=1

ComputerWorld. (2009b, October 26). CalOptima says data on 68,000 members may be compromised. *ComputerWorld.* Retrieved from http://news.idg.no/cw/art.cfm?id=92D3CA87-1A64-6A71-CEFF3995912328CD

Darrow, J. J., & Lichtenstein, S. D. (2008). Do you really need my social security number? Data collection practices in the digital age. *North Carolina Journal of Law and Technology, 10,* 1–447.

Davis, C. (2009). Identity theft horror story: I'm not a criminal! *FiLife,* Oct. 22. Retrieved from http://www.filife.com/stories/identity-theft-horror-story-im-not-a-criminal

Dixon, P. (2006). Medical identity theft: The information crime that can kill you. *World Privacy Forum,* May 3. Retrieved from http://www.worldprivacyforum.org/pdf/wpf_medicalidtheft2006.pdf

Facts, I. T. (n.d.). *30% of US identity fraud is new account fraud.* Retrieved from http://www.itfacts.biz/30-of-us-identity-fraud-is-new-account-fraud/5729

Federal Trade Commission. (2007). *2006 Identity theft survey report.* Retrieved from www.ftc.gov/os/2007/11/SynovateFinalReportIDTheft2006.pdf

Federal Trade Commission. (2008). *Security in numbers: SSNs and ID theft.* Retrieved from http://www.ftc.gov/os/2008/12/P075414ssnreport.pdf

Federal Trade Commission. (n.d.). *About identity theft.* Retrieved from http://www.ftc.gov/bcp/edu/microsites/idtheft/consumers/about-identity-theft.html

Finberg, J. (2002). Financial abuse of the elderly in California. *Loyola of Los Angeles Law Review, 36*, 667.

Greenemeier, L. (2007, August 1). The TJX effect: Details of the largest breach of customer data are starting to come to light. *InformationWeek.* Retrieved from http://www.informationweek.com/story/ showArticle.jhtml?articleID=201400171

Hoofnagle, C. (2009). Internalizing identity theft. *UCLA Journal of Law and Technology, 13*(2). Retrieved from http://www.lawtechjournal.com/articles/ 2009/02_100406_Hoofnagle.pdf

Identity Theft Resource Center. (2010). *Identity theft: The aftermath 2009.* Retrieved from http://www.idtheftcenter.org/artman2/uploads/1/Aftermath_2009_20100520.pdf

Javelin Strategy and Research. (n.d.). *Data breach notifications: Victims face four times higher risk of fraud.* Retrieved from http://www.javelinstrategy.com/lp/ DataBreachesBrochure.html

Konrad, W. (2009, June 12). Medical problems could include identity theft. *New York Times.* Retrieved from http://www.nytimes.com/2009/06/13/health /13patient.html

Lazzarotti, J. (2010). Does your "cyber" or "data breach" insurance cover what you think it does? *Workplace Privacy, Data Management & Security Report.* Retrieved from http://www.workplaceprivacyreport.com/ 2010/06/articles/information-risk-1/does-your-cyber-or-data-breach-insurance-cover-what-you-think-it-does/

Lieber, R. (2008, May 24). Heading off new account fraud. *New York Times.* Retrieved from http://www.nytimes.com/2008/05/24/business /yourmoney/24moneyside.html

Lieber, R. (2009, November 2). A free credit score followed by a monthly bill. *New York Times.* Retrieved from http://www.nytimes.com/2009/11/03/your-money/credit-scores/03scores.html?_r=1, Maine Bureau of Financial Institutions. (2008). *Main data breach study.* Retrieved from http://www.maine.gov/pfr/financialinstitutions/reports/pdf/DataBreachStudy.pdf

McKeay, M. (2008). *Look to the acquiring banks, not the PCI Security Council.* May 30. Retrieved from http://www.mckeay.net/2008/05/30/look-to-the-acquiring-banks-not-the-pci-security-council/

Monahan, T. (2009). Identity theft vulnerability: Neoliberal governance through crime construction. *Theoretical Criminology, 13*(2), 155. doi:10.1177/1362480609102877

Murdoch, S. J., Drimer, S., Anderson, R., & Bond, M. (2009). Chip and PIN is broken. *Proceedings of the 2010 IEEE Symposium on Security and Privacy,* (pp. 433-446).

Nerenberg, L. (2006). *Preying on elders: A session on financial abuse.* Joint Conference of the National Council on the Aging and the American Society on Aging. March 15. Retrieved from http://www.lisanerenberg.com/media/ preyingOnElders.pdf

Ponemon, L. (2005). *What do data breaches cost companies? Beyond dollars, customers are lost.* Ponemon Institute Report.

Ponemon, L. (2008). *Consumers' report card on data breach notification.* Ponemon Institute, April 15. Retrieved from http://www.ponemon.org/local/upload/fckjail/generalcontent/18/file/Consumer\%20Report\%20Card\%20Data\%20Breach\%20Noti\%20Apr08.pdf

Ponemon Institute. (2009). *Fourth annual US cost of data breach study: Benchmark study of companies.* Retrieved from http://www.ponemon.org/local/upload/fckjail/generalcontent/18/file/2008-2009\%20US\%20Cost\%20of\%20Data\%20Breach\%20Report\%20Final.pdf

Ponemon Institute. (2010). *Benchmark study on patient privacy and data security.* November 9, 2010.

Ponemon Institute. (2011). *2010 annual study: U.S. cost of a data breach.* March.

Reports, C. (2007). Costly credit-monitoring services offer limited fraud protection. *Consumer Reports,* April. Retrieved from http://www.consumerreports.org/cro/money/credit-loan/costly-credit-monitoring-services-offer-limited-fraud-protection-4-07/overview/0704_costly-credit-monitoring-services-offer-limited-fraud-protection_ov.htm

Retailer, I. (2006, December 14). Visa sets new fines, offers incentives to encourage PCI compliance. *Internet Retailer.* Retrieved from http://www.internetretailer.com/internet/ marketing-conference/87667-visa-sets-new-fines-offers-incentives-encourage-pci-compliance.html

Rights, P. (n.d.). [*A chronology of data breaches.* Retrieved from http://www.privacyrights.org/ar/ChronDataBreaches.htm]. *Clearing House (Menasha, Wis.).*

Schlesinger, F. (2009, July 3). Hundreds of men wrongly convicted of being paedophiles after becoming victims of identity theft. *Daily Mail.* Retrieved from http://www.dailymail.co.uk/news/article-1197224/Hundreds-men-wrongly-convicted-paedophiles-victims-identity-theft.html\#ixzz0WDgSXOSg

Schneider, J. W. (2009). Preventing data breaches: Alternative approaches to deter negligent handling of consumer data. *Journal of Science and Technology Law, 15,* 279.

Shostack, A. (2009). *$450 per account? No.* Feb. 10. Retrieved from http://www.emergentchaos.com/archives/2009/02/450_per_account_no.html

Smith, A. M. (2007). *Data governance best practices: The beginning.* Retrieved from http://www.eiminstitute.org/library/eimi-archives/volume-1-issue-1-march-2007-edition/data-governance-best-practices-2013-the-beginning

Social Security Administration. (2009). *Identity theft and your Social Security number.* SSA Publication No. 05-10064, August, ICN 463270. Retrieved from http://www.socialsecurity.gov/pubs/10064.html

Soghoian, C. (2009). Manipulation and abuse of the consumer credit reporting agencies. *First Monday, 14,* 8–3.

Solove, D. J. (2003). Identity theft, privacy, and the architecture of vulnerability. *The Hastings Law Journal, 54,* 1227. Retrieved from http://ssrn.com/abstract=416740.

USA.gov. (n.d.). *USDA possible personal information breach.* Retrieved from http://www.usa.gov/usdainfo.shtml

ADDITIONAL READING

About.com. (n.d.). Should you buy identity theft insurance or credit monitoring services? Retrieved from http://financialplan.about.com/od/insurance/a/IDTheftInsure.htm

Camp, L. J. (2007). *Economics of identity theft: Avoidance, causes and possible cures.* Springer-Verlag.

Cheney, J. S. (2010). Heartland payment systems: Lessons learned from a data breach. FRB of Philadelphia - Payment Cards Center Discussion Paper No. 10-1. Available at SSRN: http://ssrn.com/abstract=1540143

Federal Trade Commission. (2004). Information compromise and the risk of identity theft: Guidance for your business. Retrieved from http://business.ftc.gov/documents/bus59-information-compromise-and-risk-id-theft-guidance-your-business

Identity Theft Resource Center. (2010). Identity theft: The aftermath 2009. Retrieved from http://www.idtheftcenter.org/artman2/uploads/1/Aftermath_2009_20100520.pdf

McCallister, E., Grance, T., & Scarfone, K. (2010). Guide to protecting the confidentiality of personally identifiable information (PII). NIST Special Publication 800-122. Retrieved from http://csrc.nist.gov/publications/nistpubs/800-122/sp800-122.pdf

Privacy Rights Clearing House. Identity theft and data breaches. Retrieved from http://www.privacyrights.org/identity-theft-data-breaches

Schneider, J. W. (2009). Preventing data breaches: Alternative approaches to deter negligent handling of consumer data. *Journal of Science and Technology Law*, *15*, 279.

Sileo, J. (2010). *Privacy means profit: Prevent identity theft and secure you and your bottom line*. Wiley.

Soghoian, C. (2009). Manipulation and abuse of the consumer credit reporting agencies. *First Monday*, *14*, 8–3.

Sproule, S., & Archer, N. (2010). Measuring identity theft and identity fraud. *International Journal of Business Governance and Ethics*, *5*, 51–63. doi:10.1504/IJBGE.2010.029555

KEY TERMS AND DEFINITIONS

CalPERS: California Public Employees' Retirement System, a state agency that manages pension and health benefits for California public employees and retirees.

Credit-Monitoring Service: A service that monitors an individual's credit history to detect unusual activity.

Credit-Reporting Agency: Also known as a credit bureau, an organization that collections information from various sources to provide credit information for various purposes.

Data Breach: An unintentional release of secure information into an untrusted environment.

Data Governance: The procedures put in place to manage the collection, storage, and use of information in an organization.

Fraud: An intentional deception made for personal gain.

Identity Theft: The collection and misuse of another person's identity information for the purposes of committing fraud.

Risk Mitigation: Implementing risk-reducing methods and controls.

SSN: Social Security Number, a 9-digit number issued to individuals in the U.S. for the purpose of tracking income for taxation purposes.

TJX: The TJX Companies, Inc., a large apparel and home fashion store chain in the U.S. and Canada.

Chapter 14
Consumer Privacy Protection in the European Union:
Legislative Reform Driven by Current Technological Challenges

Faye Fangfei Wang
Brunel University, UK

ABSTRACT

With the development of automated information systems, consumers' decisions can be made based on models of individuals' preferences without any personal interaction. This raises serious concerns regarding data-privacy protection. Up-to-date legislation and appropriate technological measures are needed to enhance lawful access, process, and storage of sensitive personal data under automated information systems. This chapter provides the general interpretation of the requirements of security, personal data breach notification systems, and enforcement mechanisms according to the EU data privacy protection legislation. It aims to examine and evaluate whether the EC Data Protection Directive in 1995 and the new EC e-Privacy Directive amended by the Directive 2009/136/EC are sufficient to ensure the security of the future development of automated information systems that automatically capture, process, store, and analyse sensitive personal data across the EU countries. It discusses the impact of the EC directives to business organizations and proposes solutions to enhance the protection of users'/consumers' privacy from a legal perspective.

DOI: 10.4018/978-1-61350-501-4.ch014

INTRODUCTION

With the advent of automated information systems, it is possible for information to be collected from individuals explicitly and implicitly with the requirement of very little human interaction from a technological perspective. That is, information such as personal data can be stored, processed, distributed or transferred automatically by the automated information systems. Such systems have been widely adopted and applied in our daily life - from online shopping platforms to social networking services and from traffic/transportation services to high frequency trading platforms. It has been a common practice for business organisations to use customers' contact details and their preferences such as chosen products and services for targeted marketing purposes since the development of online platforms in the late 1990s.

In recent years, automated information systems have been further developed. Automated information systems can now perform as agents and make decisions for individuals based on models of individuals' preferences. Such preferences have been analysed according to a long history of individuals' activities, behaviours and habits, which may contain personal data of increased sensitivity. For instance, the German Federal Constitutional Court in the Judgment of the First Senate of 27 February 2008 (1 BvR 370, 595/07) expressed that "the use of information technology has taken on a significance for the personality and the development of the individual which could not have been predicted. Modern information technology provides the individual with new possibilities, whilst at the same time entailing new types of endangerment of personality." The new technologies raise serious concerns on personal data and privacy protection for information an individual provides to a system or captured by a computing program as "data provided by individual networked systems can be evaluated and the systems made to react in a certain manner" automatically (1 BvR 370, 595/07, para 109).

The endangerments of users' personability are also noted, that is:

In the context of the data processing process, information technology systems also create by themselves large quantities of further data which can be evaluated as to the user's conduct and characteristics in the same way as data stored by the user. As a consequence, a large amount of data can be accessed in the working memory and on the storage media of such systems relating to the personal circumstances, social contacts and activities of the user. If this data is collected and evaluated by third parties, this can be highly illuminating as to the personality of the user, and may even make it possible to form a profile (1 BvR 370, 595/07, para 112).

With the ever fast-growing technology, legislation is always one step behind the latest invention of computing network services. This leads to a situation where computer scientists and entrepreneurs try to adjust or improve the application of products in order to comply with the existing law, or legislators try to amend the existing law to be compatible with the new technology in order to protect the users' rights and enhance the public safety without jeopardising technological innovation and market development. Currently, there are two main pieces of legislation concerning data and privacy protection in the European Union (EU):

- One is the Directive 95/46/ EC (known as "the EC Data Protection Directive"), which has been under the review of European Commission since 2009. In 2011, the Commission will propose a new general legal framework for the protection of personal data in the EU, covering data processing operations in all sectors and policies of the EU. This framework will then be negotiated and adopted by the European Parliament and the Council.

- The other is the Directive 2009/136/EC which amends Directive 2002/22/EC on universal service and users' rights relating to electronic communications networks and services, Directive 2002/58/EC concerning the processing of personal data and the protection of privacy in the electronic communications sector (known as "the EC e-Privacy Directive") and Regulation (EC) No 2006/2004 on cooperation between national authorities responsible for the enforcement of consumer protection laws. Member states are required to implement the new EC e-Privacy Directive by May 25, 2011.

The EC e-Privacy Directive particularises and complements the EC Data Protection Directive in the electronic communications sector. It is generally required by these two EC Directives that service providers need to ensure that information is appropriately stored and managed; and the access to such information should be restricted to authorised personnel. To comply with those requirements, it may be necessary for business organisations that process personal data to adopt privacy-enhancing technologies (PETs) and/or other appropriate technological and legislative measures. However, the compliance of measures could be costly and complicated. It prompted business organisations to evaluate the pros and cons of the deployment of measures for data privacy protection.

It is argued that data privacy protection is beneficial to business as the "payoff" to organisations can be shown in various aspects such as the improvement of customer satisfaction and trust, enhancement of reputation and reduction of legal liabilities (Cavoukian & Hamilton, 2002). On the other hand, it is notable that the legislative/regulatory and technological measures or initiatives on transfers of personal data and privacy protection in automated information systems may contribute

to a reduction of transaction speed and an increase of transaction costs.

This chapter provides the general interpretation of security, personal data breach notification systems and enforcement mechanisms according to the EU data privacy protection. It aims to examine and evaluate whether the EC Data Protection Directive in 1995 and the new EC e-Privacy Directive amended by the Directive 2009/136/EC are sufficient to ensure the security of the future development of automated information systems that automatically capture, store, analyse and process sensitive personal data across the EU countries. It discusses how the EC directives could impact business organizations and proposes solutions to enhance the protection of users'/consumers' privacy from a legal perspective.

CURRENT EU LEGAL FRAMEWORK FOR DATA PRIVACY PROTECTION

Definition: Data Protection v. Privacy Protection

Data protection and privacy protection have a close relationship which can be understood from a macro perspective that "data protection is to protect the rights of data ownership and balance the benefits between the protection of data ownership and the permission of data free-flow, while privacy protection is to protect fundamental human rights" (Wang & Griffiths, 2010). As stated in Article 8 of the Convention of Human Rights and Fundamental Freedoms (hereafter "the Human Rights Convention") in 1950, private life should be protected that:

(1) Everyone has the right to respect for his private and family life, his home and his correspondence. (2) There shall be no interference by a public authority with the exercise of this right except such as is in accordance with the law and is necessary in a democratic society in the interests of

national security, public safety or the economic well being of the country, for the prevention of disorder or crime, for the protection of health or morals, or for the protection of the rights and freedoms of others.

Article 8 of the Human Rights Convention shows that the right to privacy is a fundamental human right. Mr Rolv Ryssdal, former President of the European Court of Human Rights, also noted that "activities in the field of data protection are firmly rooted in fundamental rights and freedoms" (Ryssdal, 1991).

From a micro perspective, privacy protection is mostly connected with personal data protection in particular sensitive personal data protection. The European Court of Justice explained that:

the right to privacy, set out in Article 1(1) of Directive 95/46 on the protection of individuals with regard to the processing of personal data and on the free movement of such data, means that the data subject may be certain that his personal data are processed in a correct and lawful manner, that is to say, in particular, that the basic data regarding him are accurate and that they are disclosed to authorised recipients. As is stated in recital 41 in the preamble to the directive, in order to carry out the necessary checks, the data subject must have a right of access to the data relating to him which are being processed (C-553/07, 2009).

This explanation highlights the importance of "correct and lawful data processing" and "data disclosure to authorised recipients" in relation to the protection of the right to privacy. The new EC e-Privacy Directive has justified such importance, which can be found in the provisions of "Security" and "Confidentiality" (*see subsections below*).

With regard to the definition of personal data, the EC Data Protection Directive defines "personal data" as "any information relating to an identified or identifiable natural person ('data subject'); and identifiable person is one who can be identified,

directly or indirectly, in particular by reference to an identification number or to one or more factors specific to his physical, physiological, mental, economic, culture or social identity" (Article 2a, Directive 95/46/EC). Member states may have different interpretations of "personal data".

The example of the further interpretation of "personal data" in relation to privacy can be given by a UK leading case *Durant v the Financial Services Authority (FSA)* (2003). The English Court of Appeal held that personal data only refers to information that affects one's personal or family life, business or professional capacity. The UK Information Commissioner also published a discussion of the implications of Durant case (ICO, 2006). The Information Commissioner confirms the court judgments on the measure of the scope of individual information that the individual information in question should be capable of having an adverse impact on the individual's privacy. The two notions of identification are recognised as a biographical sense and an individual focus as the Judge ruled that:

The first is whether the information is biographical in a significant sense, that is, going beyond the recording of [the individual's] involvement in a matter or an event which has no personal connotations; ... The second concerns focus. The information should have the [individual] as its focus rather than some other person with whom he may have been involved or some transaction or event in which he may have figured or have had an interest..." (Durant v the Financial Services Authority, 2003) The above justification provides helpful guidance and greater clarity regarding the complex meaning of "personal data" in relation to privacy.

With regard to "sensitive personal data", the EC Data Protection Directive does not define it in detail although Recital (34) and (70) of the EC Data Protection Directive mention the term "sensitive" data and Article 8 of the EC Data

Protection Directive refers to "the processing of sensitive data" without using the wording of "sensitive" that:

Member States shall prohibit the processing of personal data revealing racial or ethnic origin, political opinions, religious or philosophical beliefs, trade-union membership, and the processing of data concerning health or sex life.

So the above special categories of data are currently prohibited as a general rule, with limited exceptions under certain conditions and safeguards.

On 4 November 2010 the European Commission issued an official recommendation document called "A comprehensive approach on personal data protection in the European Union" (thereafter "the EU Comprehensive Approach 2010") and addressed challengeable legal issues for the communication from the Commission to the European Parliament, the Council, the Economic and Social Committee and the Committee of the Regions. The EU Comprehensive Approach 2010 has identified the importance of understanding the scope of "sensitive personal data" as it proposes that "in the light of technological and other societal developments, there is a need to reconsider the existing provisions on sensitive data, to examine whether other categories of data should be added and to further clarify the conditions for their processing. This concerns, for example, genetic data which is currently not explicitly mentioned as a sensitive category of data" (p. 9). However, the Comprehensive Approach did not mention about giving a definition of "sensitive personal data" under the EC Data Protection Directive.

Principles of Data and Privacy Protection

The Organisation for Economic Co-operation and Development (OECD) in 1980, the Asia-Pacific Economic Co-operation (APEC) in 2004, the United States of America (US), the European Union (EU) as well as the US-EU Safe-Harbor Agreement have specified principles for data privacy protection. Figure 1 outlines those privacy principles comparatively.

As indicated above, there are seven main principles set out in the EU Directives on data-privacy protection. They are: security, confidentiality, data quality, onward transfer, choice, notice and access. There are also five sub-principles with regard to data quality has been set out in Article 6 of the EC Data Protection Directive, whilst there are six sub-principles concerning the transfer of personal data to a third country set out in Article 25 of the EC Data Protection Directive. Are the EU privacy principles laid in the EC Directives on data privacy protection the same as those in international guidelines or the US privacy practices?

As we can see from the above figure, two of the most common principles have not been highlighted in the EU data-privacy legislation: one is accountability and the other is enforceability.

Accountability mechanisms fall into two categories: one is structure and the other is transparency (Wang, 2009). The issue of transparency in data privacy protection has been raised by the EU Comprehensive Approach 2010 and the introduction of "a general principle of transparent processing of personal data in the legal framework" has been proposed accordingly (p. 6).

With regard to enforceability, the principle which has been adopted in the US-EU Safe harbor agreement and the US Federal Trade Commission (FTC) Fair Information Practices is also not strengthened in the EC Data Protection Directive. The amended EC e-Privacy Directive has improved the situation by inserting an article of "implementation and enforcement" (article 15a). Enforcement of privacy protection is not only one of the fundamental principles but also one of the most complicated issues in data privacy protection. The legal certainty of enforcement is vital to build users' trust on automated information

Figure 1. Comparison of data-privacy protection principles

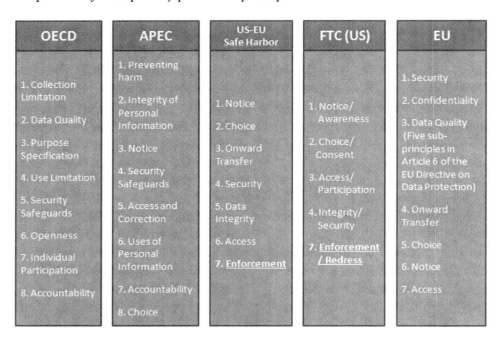

systems and desirable for the smooth transfer of personal information across international boundaries for the development of the global economy. International compatibility of respective domestic or regional privacy regimes is required to achieve that objective. The EU Comprehensive Approach 2010 has proposed to further investigate the issue of enforcement of data protection rules (pp. 9-17).

As to the other EU data-privacy protection principles, there are new sections that are inserted to the exiting articles under the new EC e-Privacy Directive. Principles such as security and confidentiality are particularly enhanced.

Security

"Security" is one of the essential issues for personal data and privacy protection. The provision of "Security" is provided by Article 4 of the EC e-Privacy Directive:

1. The provider of a publicly available electronic communications service must take appropriate technical and organisational measures to safeguard security of its services, if necessary in conjunction with the provider of the public communications network with respect to network security. Having regard to the state of the art and the cost of their implementation, these measures shall ensure a level of security appropriate to the risk presented.

2. In case of a particular risk of a breach of the security of the network, the provider of a publicly available electronic communications service must inform the subscribers concerning such risk and, where the risk lies outside the scope of the measures to be taken by the service provider, of any possible remedies, including an indication of the likely costs involved.

As shown above, the provision of "security" under the EC e-Privacy Directive introduces "taking appropriate technical and organisational measures" and "informing duty" to safeguard security without detailed measures. The new EC e-Privacy Directive makes efforts to increase the legal certainty of security by providing more detailed explanations and procedures. The new EC e-Privacy Directive changes the title/provision heading of Article 4 from "Security" to "Security of Processing" and inserts one subsection in Article 4(1) and three additional sections as Article 4(3)–(5) targeting at mandatory personal data breach notification measures. The new EC e-Privacy Directive further particularises and complements the EC Data Protection Directive by translating the principle of "security" set out in the EC Data Protection Directive into specific rules.

The change of title of Article 4 demonstrates the importance of the "processing" stage for the protection of personal data and privacy. The Article 4 (1a) of the new EC e-Privacy Directive further emphasises the processing part of ensuring security which includes "ensuring that personal data can be accessed only by authorised personnel for legally authorised purposes; protecting personal data stored or transmitted against accidental or unlawful destruction, accidental loss or alteration, and unauthorised or unlawful storage, processing, access or disclosure; and ensuring the implementation of a security policy with respect to the processing of personal data". It is also suggested that "relevant national authorities shall be able to audit the measures taken by providers of publicly available electronic communication services and to issue recommendations about best practices concerning the level of security which those measures should achieve."

The wording of the insertion (Article 4(1a) of the new EC e-Privacy Directive) brings to consistency to the data protection principles outlined in Articles 6, 7 and 17 of the EC Data Protection Directive that personal data must be processed fairly and lawfully.

The other inserted sections from the new EC e-Privacy Directive introduce the new measures of securing the processing of personal data. Those legal measures include "notification obligations

from service providers" (Article 4(3)), "duty from competent national authorities" (Article 4(4)) and "adoption of measures resulting from consultation" (Article 4(5)).

As to the requirement of "notification of personal data breach" from the service provider, the added Article 4(3) from the new EC e-Privacy Directive provides that:

[I]n the case of a personal data breach, the provider of publicly available electronic communications services shall, without undue delay, notify the personal data breach to the competent national authority. When the personal data breach is likely to adversely affect the personal data or privacy of a subscriber or individual, the provider shall also notify the subscriber or individual of the breach without undue delay. Notification of a personal data breach to a subscriber or individual concerned shall not be required if the provider has demonstrated to the satisfaction of the competent authority that it has implemented appropriate technological protection measures, and that those measures were applied to the data concerned by the security breach. Such technological protection measures shall render the data unintelligible to any person who is not authorised to access it. Without prejudice to the provider's obligation to notify subscribers and individuals concerned, if the provider has not already notified the subscriber or individual of the personal data breach, the competent national authority, having considered the likely adverse effects of the breach, may require it to do so.

It further specifies the content requirements of such notification. There are twofold: one is to the subscriber or individual and the other is to the competent national authority. With regard to the notification duty to the subscriber or individual, the service provider is required to describe the nature of the personal data breach and the contact points where more information can be obtained, and shall recommend measures to mitigate the possible adverse effects of the personal data breach. With regard to the notification duty to the competent national authority, the service provider is required to provide additional information describing the consequences of, and the measures proposed or taken by the provider to address, the personal data breach.

The further insertion of "supervision duty from competent national authorities" (Article 4(4) of the EC e-Privacy Directive) includes specific rules of enhancing the supervisory certainty from competent national authorises. That is, the competent national authorities are encouraged to adopt guidelines and issue instructions to the notification of personal data breaches for service providers as well as impose appropriate sanctions in the event of a failure to comply with notification obligations. The EU Comprehensive Approach 2010 has raised discussion on possible solutions to ensure consistency in implementation of such measures, for instance, it suggests the usage of one or more EU standard forms ('privacy information notices') by data controllers (p. 6). In addition, the Article 4(5) of the new EC e-Privacy Directive - "the Commission's adoption of measures resulting from consultation" ensures that the Commission shall serve as a guardian adopting technical implementing measures following consultation with agents, working parties and supervisors.

Confidentiality

The principle of confidentiality has been regulated in Article 5 of EC e-Privacy Directive and Article 16 of EC Data Protection Directive. The revised Article 5(3) of the EC e-Privacy Directive intends to give further explanations to Article 16 of the EC Data Protection Directive that very briefly states:

Any person acting under the authority of the controller or of the processor, including the processor himself, who has access to personal data must not process them except on instructions from the controller, unless he is required to do so by law.

The replacement of Article 5(3) of the EC e-Privacy Directive has introduced the principle of "the consent given by the subscriber or user concerned" for the storing of information, or the gaining of access to information already stored in terminal equipment (e.g mobile phones or laptops). It provides that:

3. Member States shall ensure that the storing of information, or the gaining of access to information already stored, in the terminal equipment of a subscriber or user is only allowed on condition that the subscriber or user concerned has given his or her consent, having been provided with clear and comprehensive information, in accordance with Directive 95/46/EC, inter alia, about the purposes of the processing. This shall not prevent any technical storage or access for the sole purpose of carrying out the transmission of a communication over an electronic communications network, or as strictly necessary in order for the provider of an information society service explicitly requested by the subscriber or user to provide the service.

It clarifies the absolute condition of the subscriber or user's prior consent before processing the stored information or gaining access to it regardless whether the subscriber or user concerned is offered the right to refuse such processing by the data controller or not that was indicated in the old Article 5(3) of the EC e-Privacy Directive.

The enhancement of "prior consent" is also reflected on Recital (66) and Article 6 of the new EC e-Privacy Directive that service providers must inform users before obtaining their consent about the type of data that is collected and the duration and purposes of processing and storage of such data; and service providers shall allow users to give and withdraw their consent freely as users have "the rights to be forgotten". It is debatable what constitutes a meaningful consent and whether "privacy by default" is sufficient. Under the new EC e-Privacy Directive, the use of cookies also requires users' prior consent. Article 29 Working Group on Data Protection addressed that "currently three out of the four most widely used browsers have a default setting to accept all cookies. Not changing a default setting cannot be considered as a meaningful consent" (2010). It is expected that there are various interpretations by member states when the new EC e-Privacy comes into force in May 2011.

In addition, the principle of consent may need to be further considered for situations where the combination of data from different sources are allowed such as key-coded data, location data and 'data mining' technologies, or cases where the confidentiality and integrity in information-technology systems must be ensured (COM 609/3, BvR 370/07).

Implementation and Enforcement

As mentioned earlier, enforceability is one of the fundamental principles of data-privacy protection, which reflects on the insertion of the Article 15a titled - implementation and enforcement - to the EC e-Privacy Directive. It provides that:

1. Member States shall lay down the rules on penalties, including criminal sanctions where appropriate, applicable to infringements of the national provisions adopted pursuant to this Directive and shall take all measures necessary to ensure that they are implemented. The penalties provided for must be effective, proportionate and dissuasive and may be applied to cover the period of any breach, even where the breach has subsequently been rectified. The Member States shall notify those provisions to the Commission by 25 May 2011, and shall notify it without delay of any subsequent amendment affecting them.
2. Without prejudice to any judicial remedy which might be available, Member States shall ensure that the competent national authority

and, where relevant, other national bodies have the power to order the cessation of the infringements referred to in paragraph 1.

3. Member States shall ensure that the competent national authority and, where relevant, other national bodies have the necessary investigative powers and resources, including the power to obtain any relevant information they might need to monitor and enforce national provisions adopted pursuant to this Directive.
4. The relevant national regulatory authorities may adopt measures to ensure effective cross-border cooperation in the enforcement of the national laws adopted pursuant to this Directive and to create harmonised conditions for the provision of services involving cross-border data flows.

The national regulatory authorities shall provide the Commission, in good time before adopting any such measures, with a summary of the grounds for action, the envisaged measures and the proposed course of action. The Commission may, having examined such information and consulted ENISA and the Working Party on the Protection of Individuals with regard to the Processing of Personal Data established by Article 29 of Directive 95/46/EC, make comments or recommendations thereupon, in particular to ensure that the envisaged measures do not adversely affect the functioning of the internal market. National regulatory authorities shall take the utmost account of the Commission's comments or recommendations when deciding on the measures."

As we can see from the subsections - Article 15(a)(2) and (3) of the new EC e-Privacy Directive, there are specifications added to the duty and role of the competent national authorities in data-privacy protection which supplement Article 5 of the EC e-Privacy Directive. The subsection - Article 15(a)(4) of the new EC e-Privacy Directive - has further introduced the responsibility of the national regulatory authorities, especially emphasising the purpose of promoting consistent enforcement measures and creating harmonised conditions for the provision of services involving cross-border data flows. This subsection can be deemed to be an effective complementation to Article 25 of the EC Data Protection Directive that the adequacy of the level of protection on the transfer of personal data to a third country without prejudice to compliance with the national provisions adopted pursuant to the other provisions of the EC Data Protection Directive.

FUTURE LEGISLATIVE REFORM FOR CONSUMER PRIVACY PROTECTION

The new EC e-Privacy Directive has been modernised in response to the current development of technologies. It intends to provide an updated legal framework to protect the users' data-privacy rights and enhance the public safety. However, technologies have been constantly growing which leave legislators with no choice but to re-examine existing rules continually.

For example, drivers who wish to park their cars on the streets of London but have no coins or cash at hand can phone and pay the car parking service by quoting a specific street parking location number, vehicle registration number, parking period, name and credit card number according to the parking instruction post on the side of the streets. Some months later, if he/she wants to use this service again, he/she only needs to call, quoting their name, the specific street parking location number and the last four digits of his/her credit card. The transaction can be done automatically using the stored information/data. With the further development of automated information systems, it is not hard to imagine, in a few years' time, when we park our cars, our credit cards will be automatically charged for the parking fee without any human interaction as the automated system will immediately identify where we are and what

we are doing. Such automated decisions-making systems can also apply to other industries such as travel agencies. The automated travel agent can design and offer a most favourable travel package to an individual based on the information that the individual gives and other data sources that the agent collect such as passenger records, vehicle traffic records, health conditions and annual incomes etc. This is the functional development of automated computing systems. Such systems involve the collection and process of a high volume of personal information for the purposes of statistical analysis and decision making regarding particular individuals. Although consumers could benefit from such system in terms of convenience and efficiency, service providers might face higher risks of infringing personal data and privacy rights if they do not comply with the data privacy legislation with regard to the conditions of collecting, storing, analysing and transferring personal details. Service providers/business organisations must seek users' consent before providing such service.

Apart from the functional development, the growth of the capacity of computing facilities is also astonishing. It is suggested that the capacity of a computer is doubled every 18 months which means that after a period of 15 years, the processing and storage capabilities of our computers are increased by a factor of 1,000 (Wacks, 2010).

In response to rapid technological developments and globalisation, the official recommendation document "the EU Comprehensive Approach 2010" that was issued on 4 November 2010 has specifically addressed challengeable legal issues for the communication from the Commission to the European Parliament, the Council, the Economic and Social Committee and the Committee of the Regions (COM 609/3). The EU Comprehensive Approach 2010 further clarifies the relationship between the EC e-Privacy Directive and EC Data Protection Directive by identifying, examining and analysing specific legal provisions. It confirms a number of key objectives of future assessment and evaluation, which can be summarised as following:

1. To ensure a fair balance and coherent application between data protection and the free circulation of personal data;
2. To introduce a general principle of transparency of personal data processing and the obligations of data controllers including modalities and formalities;
3. To strengthen the principle of data minimisation, the rights of data portability and the rules on consent;
4. To define the categories of sensitive data and harmonise the conditions on the processing of such data;
5. To promote awareness-raising activities on data protection;
6. To enhance remedies including court actions and sanctions and encourage self-regulatory initiatives;
7. To improve and streamline the current procedures for international data transfers, examine the adequacy of such procedures and specify the criteria and requirements for assessing the level of data protection in a third country or an international organisation;
8. To improve the cooperation and coordination between Data Protection Authorities and strengthen the role of Data Protection Supervisors.

In the author's opinion, the EU Comprehensive Approach 2010 reassures the objective of data privacy protection - a fair balance and coherent application between data protection and the free circulation of personal data. This vision has been developed upon the recent case *European Commission v Germany* (C-518/07) on 09 March 2010: the European Court of Justice (Grand Chamber) confirms that the main objective of the Directive was to strike a fair balance between the protection of the right to private life and the free movement of personal data. Although the EU Directives

have the wording of "neither restrict nor prohibit the free flow of personal data" (Article 1(2)) and "ensure the free flow of personal data" (Recital 1) they don't explicitly express the objective of "a fair balance" between data privacy protection and the free flow of personal data. Traditionally, the EU legislation is aimed at protecting individual privacy rights, whilst the US and international guidelines target the promotion of the free flow of cross-border data for the development of global economy (Wang, 2010).

As we can see from the key objectives above, the main methodologies of the legislative reform addressed by the EU Comprehensive Approach 2010 lie in the introduction of new principles and modalities of obligations. The expectation of ultimate outcomes is to create a new coherent general legal framework for consistent and adequate protection on data transfers within EU member states and from EU member states to third countries outside the EU. Due to the rapid development of technologies in terms of functions, speed, processing and storage capabilities, there is a growing need of further considerations on matters such as time limit of rights/obligations and remedies.

Notification/Action and Supervision

The European Data Protection Supervisor (EDPS) welcomes the adoption of a security breach notification system as it will encourage business organizations to improve data security and enhance the accountability of the personal data (O.J. C 128/33). That is, network operators and Internet Service Providers ("ISPs") should notify the National Regulatory Authorities ("NRAs") and also their customers of security breach. This recommendation has been adopted in the amendment of the EC e-Privacy Directive under the Directive 2009/136/EC that in the case of a personal data breach, the provider of publicly available electronic communications services shall, without undue delay, notify the personal data breach to the competent national authority. The provider of publicly available electronic communications services refers to public and private electronic communications sectors and horizontally to all business organizations that process certain types of information.

As discussed in the subsection of "security", the update of Article 4 of the EC e-Privacy Directive introduces the concepts and requirements of "notification of data breach" and "duty from competent national authorities". It well strengthens the principles set out in Article 12(c) and 28 of the EC Data Protection Directive. However, it does not specify a timeframe for the notification of data breach except for the requirement of "without undue delay". Moreover, it does not introduce modalities of the notification of data breach except for the recommendation of guidelines and instructions that may be adopted by competent national authorities. The EU Comprehensive Approach 2010 has identified the necessity of introducing modalities for providing information and drawing up one or more EU standard forms ('privacy information notices') to be used by data controllers, but it is silent on the necessity of interpreting "without undue delay" for the notification of data breach.

In the author's opinion, the interpretation of "without undue delay" is vital as the timing affects the certainty of data-privacy protection. The determination of the appropriation of time limit on notification and remedial action shall be taken into account of the speed, scope and capabilities of spreading personal data under the current and future development of technologies in particular automated information systems. In addition, the consideration of the time-limit issue for notification and remedial action can be learned from the interpretation of the time-limit requirement on the exercise of the right to access in Article 12(a) of the EC Data Protection Directive regarding information storage and disclosure in the case of *College van burgemeester en wethouders van Rotterdam*

v M.E.E. Rijkeboer Netherlands (judgement of 7 May 2009). The judgement provides that:

Article 12(a) of Directive 95/46/EC of the European Parliament and of the Council of 24 October 1995 on the protection of individuals with regard to the processing of personal data and on the free movement of such data requires Member States to ensure a right of access to information on the recipients or categories of recipient of personal data and on the content of the data disclosed not only in respect of the present but also in respect of the past. It is for Member States to fix a time-limit for storage of that information and to provide for access to that information which constitutes a fair balance between, on the one hand, the interest of the data subject in protecting his privacy, in particular by way of his rights to object and to bring legal proceedings and, on the other, the burden which the obligation to store that information represents for the controller.

Rules limiting the storage of information on the recipients or categories of recipient of personal data and on the content of the data disclosed to a period of *one year* and correspondingly limiting access to that information, while basic data is stored for a much longer period, do not constitute a fair balance of the interest and obligation at issue, unless it can be shown that longer storage of that information would constitute an excessive burden on the controller. It is, however, for national courts to make the determinations necessary" (paragraph 71).

Accordingly, it shall be for Member States to fix a time-limit for notification of the personal data breach and remedial action. Where the length of time for which a personal data breach is to be informed to the competent national authority or remedial action is to be taken is very long, the adverse effects of the breach of the personal data or privacy of a subscriber or individual may be higher as the implementation of appropriate technological protection measures may be delayed. The issue of a fixed time limit for notification and remedial action shall be further assessed when the Commission examines the modalities for the introduction in the general legal framework of a general personal data breach notification, including the addressees of such notifications and the criteria for triggering the obligation to notify according to the EU Comprehensive Approach 2010. The obligation of a time-limit for notification of data breach shall also be contained in the future EU standard forms of "privacy information notices".

To avoid the undue delay for notification of data breach, the adoption of regulatory and technological measures of enhancing data controllers' responsibility shall be encouraged. According to the EU Comprehensive Approach 2010, the Commission considers measures of enhancing data controller's responsibility including making the appointment of an independent Data Protection Officer mandatory and harmonising the rules related to their tasks and competences, while reflecting on the appropriate threshold to avoid undue administrative burdens, particularly on small and micro-enterprises; inserting an obligation for data controllers to carry out a data protection impact assessment in specific cases and further promoting the use of Privacy Enhancing Technologies (PETs) and the possibilities for the concrete implementation of the concept of 'Privacy by Design' (p. 12).

With regard to the improvement of the guidance from competent national authorities, as discussed in the subsection of "security", the update of Article 4 of the EC E-Privacy Directive recommends competent national authorities adopting guidelines and issuing instructions on notification for the personal data breach. The EU Comprehensive Approach 2010 proposes that Data Protection Authorities should strengthen their cooperation and better coordinate their activities (p. 12), because the consistent measures rely on the cooperation between competent national data protection authorities especially when data breach issues have a cross-border dimension.

For example, when multinational enterprises are based in several Member States and are carrying out their activities in each of these countries, they might need the guidance from different national authorities and coordinated supervision from the European Data Protection Supervisor (EDPS). An unambiguous procedure for the cooperation between data protection authorities will help dealing with the notification of data breach from multinational business organisations/service providers more efficiently and better encourage the "undue delay notification" duty.

Effective Enforcement Mechanisms

The modernisation of existing legislation is of practical necessity, whilst enforcement is of fundamental importance, because any legislative and technological measures to protect consumers' privacy can only be effective if they are properly implemented and enforced. The mechanisms of enforcement are threefold: the first is by national enforcement authorities; the second is by court litigation and the third is by out-of-court resolutions or self-regulatory enforcement initiatives.

The European Parliament (EP) passed Amendment 133 inserting Article 13.6 of the EC e-Privacy Directive that gives the possibility for Internet access providers and other legal entities such as consumer associations to bring legal action against infringements of any of the provisions of the EC e-Privacy Directive. It was advised that in the area of privacy and data protection the damage inflicted upon a person individually considered, is usually not sufficient in itself for him/her to initiate legal action before a court. Individuals normally do not go to court on their own because they were spammed or because their name was wrongly included in a directory. It would permit consumer associations and trade unions representing the interest of consumers at a collective level to take legal action on their behalf before courts. A greater diversity of enforcement mechanisms is also likely to encourage a better level of compliance and therefore in the interest of an effective application of the provisions of the EC e-Privacy Directive. Unfortunately, neither the Commission nor the Council has accepted it. As a result, any natural or legal person adversely affected by infringements including electronic communications service provider may bring legal proceedings in respect of such infringement according to the revised Article 13.6 of the EC e-Privacy Directive in 2009.

In order to ensure the enforcement of data protection rules, the EU Comprehensive Approach 2010 considers that it is essential to have effective provisions on remedies and sanctions, which include "the possibility of extending the power to bring an action before the national courts to data protection authorities and to civil society associations, as well as to other associations representing data subjects' interests; and assess the need for strengthening the existing provisions on sanctions, for example by explicitly including criminal sanctions in case of serious data protection violations, in order to make them more effective" (p. 9).

However, it is time-consuming and complicated to enforce privacy protection in courts and it is even more complex when the dispute concerns the transfer of data between EU member states or from the EU to a third country outside the EU member states. Self-regulatory enforcement initiatives have been strongly encouraged by the FTC Fair Information Practices Report in 2000, OECD Privacy Online: Policy and Practice Guidance in 2003, and the EU Comprehensive Approach in 2010. Due to the fact that the current provisions on self-regulation (code of conduct) - Article 27 of the EC Data Protection Directive - have rarely been used so far and are not considered satisfactory by private stakeholders, the European Commission continues to encourage self-regulatory initiatives by data controllers, which shall contribute to a better enforcement of data protection rules in its Comprehensive Approach 2010.

It is suggested by the FTC and OECD that a trustmark or privacy seal program would be beneficial for promoting effective enforcement on privacy compliance. Currently, the best known providers for online privacy seals are the American companies such as TRUSTe, BBBOnline and VeriSign which meet the conditions of the international regulations and US-EU Safe Harbor Agreement. Most online privacy seal programs have self-enforcement procedures: users can file a complaint to a seal program provider and the seal program provider will respond to a complaint by imposing sanctions on accredited websites. However, those privacy seal programs cannot require a licensee to pay monetary damages or take further steps to exempt from legal violation. In the EU, the European Commission has proposed to explore the possible creation of EU certification schemes (e.g. 'privacy seals'). Such schemes shall provide the procedure of 'privacy-compliant' processes and the standard of technologies, products and services for both individuals and data controllers (p. 12). The development of EU certification schemes shall take into account of the feasibility of fitting privacy seals with the legal obligation and international technical standards, and ensuring the trustworthiness of such privacy seals. In the author's opinion, a regulation of privacy seals might be necessary to bring consistent conduct of privacy seal providers that opt for certified technologies, products or services in member states. Such regulation shall provide a stronger institutional arrangement for the effective enforcement of data protection rules including the consideration of the role of competent national data protection authorities in implementing an appropriate level of the privacy seal program.

CONCLUSION AND RECOMMENDATION

In the age of the internet and globalisation, it is getting harder to keep personal details private. Shopping online or sharing personal information on social networking sites have become part of daily life (European Commission News, 2010), whilst automated transactions via high-frequency trading platforms have become common in financial industries. Automated decision-making on behalf of consumers is also under way. That is why the EC e-Privacy Directive has been modernised to reflect changes in technology and the way we live. However, the process of modernisation of existing rules has to be ongoing due to continuous development of technologies. New concepts and principles of data privacy protection shall be duly proposed and examined. As proposed in the EU Comprehensive Approach 2010, the review of the EC Directives is expected to ensure the clear vision of keeping a fair balance between the protection of the right to private life and the free movement of personal data C-518/07, paragraphs 24 and 30).

The new EC e-Privacy Directive would bring a significant impact on the security conduct of data processing for both consumers and business organizations. The message shall well reach parties concerned through awareness-raising activities on data protection. As Professor Roymond Wacks suggested, consumers shall be aware of online privacy self-protection by using affordable encryption software, whilst business organizations that process consumers' personal data shall select the most appropriate technology for privacy protection (2010). Moreover, consumers shall be fully aware of their rights of giving and withdrawing consent to the collection and process of their personal data, while business organisations shall make the methods as user-friendly as possible for consumers' giving or withdrawing their consent. With the modernization of the EU legislation in data privacy protection, business organizations that collect and process personal data shall develop technological approaches and tools that are compatible with the requirements of the new legislation. That is, business organisations shall:

1. adopt suitable safeguards by taking appropriate technological and legislative measures;
2. inform users prior to obtaining their consent;
3. enable users to give or withdraw their consent freely;
4. perform the duty of notification of personal data breaches without undue delay; and
5. take possible measures and remedies to reduce or remove the risks according to the guidance of competent national authorities.

The "Study on the economic benefits of privacy-enhancing technologies (PETs): Final Report to The European Commission" in July 2010 indicated that although there may be short-term costs with few tangible benefits, the longer-term impact on the business as a result of reputational gains would be significant (p. 74). Therefore, business organizations that process personal data shall be encouraged to adopt PETs application. That is, business organizations shall have strategic plans to give consumers more control over how personal information is collected and used. This could be done by enhancing the principles of "security", "confidentiality", "transparency", "right to be forgotten" and "data minimisation". However, it was reported some types of PETs appear more widespread than others. For example, data minimisation is a very important aspect of PETs that is realised to varying degrees in the technologies we analysed. In contrast, mechanisms to obtain consumer consent seem to play a relatively minor role (p. viii). Thus, there is a need of modalities on the minimum PETs application.

The procedures of "notification of the personal data breach" system and notify the competent national authorities of data breach without undue delay shall be not neglected by business organisations. Once data breach occurs, business organisations shall maintain a detailed list of personal data breach information, effects and remedial actions taken for the verification of compliance by the competent national authorities. Business organisations can obtain relevant guidelines and instructions from the competent national authorities. In the author's view, there should be standard forms and modalities of notification available and the time-limit of data breach notification for business organisations or service providers should also be confirmed.

The future success of data privacy protection in the EU depends on the consistency in implementing data privacy protection rules within member states. It would be helpful that the current legislative review on EC Data Protection Directive could successfully build a common approach across the EU to remove the obstacle of cross-border legitimate data flow in the near future, so multinational business organisations would only have to deal with one set of rules. As to business organisations that need to send personal information outside the EU (that is so called "international data transfers"), the current schemes are not entirely satisfactory and need to be reviewed and streamlined so as to make transfers simpler and less burdensome (COM 609/3). International agreements on the protection of data transfer and enforcement should be further established between countries to help increasing the legal certainty on data security and privacy protection.

After all, protecting data privacy rights is a challenging and ongoing task for legislators, practitioners and business organisations as existing rules and measures have to be constantly adjusted to be in line with the development of technologies. Nonetheless, consumers' awareness of and education about personal data protection are necessities for the development of a well-balanced information society.

REFERENCES

Case C-518/07. (2010). *European Commission v Germany*. European Court of Justice (Grand Chamber) 09 March 2010 [2010] 3 C.M.L.R. 3, paragraphs 24 and 30.

Case C-553/07. (2009). *College van burgemeester en wethouders van Rotterdam v M.E.E. Rijkeboer*, European Court of Justice (Judgement of 7 May 2009).

Case C-595. 07. (2008). *German Federal Constitutional Court in the Judgment of the First Senate of 27 February 2008*. 1 BvR 370, para 104. Retrieved November 12, 2010, from http://www.bundesverfassungsgericht.de/en/decisions/rs20080227_1bvr037007en.html

Cavoukian, A., & Hamilton, T. (2002). *The Privacy Payoff: How Successful Businesses Build Customer Trust*. Canada: McGraw-Hill.

COM 609/3. (2010). *A comprehensive approach on personal data protection in the European Union* – Communication from the Commission to the European Parliament, the Council, the Economic and Social Committee and the Committee of the Regions, European Commission, Brussels, 04.11.2010 COM(2010) 609/3 - The EU Comprehensive Approach.

Directive 2002/58/EC. (2002). *European Parliament and of the Council of 12 July 2002 concerning the processing of personal data and the protection of privacy in the electronic communications sector* (Directive on privacy and electronic communications). Official Journal of the European Union, L 201, 31 July 2002, P. 0037–0047.

Directive 2009/136/EC. (2009). *European Parliament and of the Council of 25 November 2009 amending Directive 2002/22/EC on universal service and users' rights relating to electronic communications networks and services, Directive 2002/58/EC concerning the processing of personal data and the protection of privacy in the electronic communications sector and Regulation (EC) No 2006/2004 on cooperation between national authorities responsible for the enforcement of consumer protection laws*. Official Journal of the European Union, L 337/11, 18 December 2009, P.0011 – 0036.

Directive 95/46/EC. (1995). *European Parliament and of the Council of 24 October 1995 on the protection of individuals with regard to the processing of personal data and on the free movement of such data.* Official Journal of the European Union, L 281, 23 November 1995, P. 0031–0050.

Durant v the Financial Services Authority (FSA). (2003). EWCA Civ 1746.

London Economics. (20100. *Study on the economic benefits of privacy- technologies (PETs): Final report to The European Commission, DG Justice, Freedom and Security.*

European Commission. (2010). *Opt-out is not sufficient.* European Commission Press Release. 24 June 2010. Retrieved March 15, 2011, from http://ec.europa.eu/justice/policies/privacy/news/docs/pr_26_06_10_en.pdf

European Commission News. (2010). *Safeguarding privacy in the digital age - Justice and citizens rights.* Retrieved November 30, 2010, from http://ec.europa.eu/news/justice/101105_en.htm

ICO. (2006). *Durant Case and its impact on the interpretation of the Data Protection Act 1998.* Information Commissioner's Office, 27 February 2006. Retrieved November 2010 from http://www.ico.gov.uk/upload/documents/ library/data_protection/detailed_specialist_guides/the_durant_case_and_its_impact_on_the_interpretation_of_the_data_protection_act.pdf

O.J. C 128/33. (2009). *Second opinion of the European Data Protection Supervisor on the review of Directive 2002/58/EC concerning the processing of personal data and the protection of privacy in the electronic communications sector (Directive on privacy and electronic communications).*

Ryssdal, R. (1991). *Data protection and the European Convention on Human Rights.* 13th Conf. Data Protection Comm'rs, 39.

Wacks, R. (2010). *Privacy: A very short introduction.* New York, NY: Oxford University Press.

Wang, F. (2009). *Online dispute resolution: Technology, management and legal practice from an international perspective.* Oxford, UK: Chandos Publishing.

Wang, F. (2010). *Law of electronic commercial transactions: Contemporary issues in the EU, US and China.* Oxford, UK: Cavendish-Routledge Publishing.

Wang, F., & Griffiths, N. (2010, July). Protecting privacy in automated transaction systems: A legal and technological perspective in the EU. *International Review of Law Computers & Technology, 24*(2), 153–162. doi:10.1080/13600861003748243

ADDITIONAL READING

Case C-101/01, *Reference for a preliminary ruling from the Göta hovrätt: Bodil Lindqvist*, European Court of Justice (judgment of 6 November 2003).

Case C-518/07, *European Commission v Germany*, European Court of Justice (Grand Chamber), Judgement 09 March 2010, [2010] 3 C.M.L.R. 3.

Case C-553/07, *College van burgemeester en wethouders van Rotterdam v M.E.E. Rijkeboer*, European Court of Justice (Judgement of 7 May 2009).

Case C-595. 07, German Federal Constitutional Court in the Judgment of the First Senate of 27 February 2008, 1 BvR 370, para 104, available at http://www.bundesverfassungsgericht.de/ en/decisions/rs20080227_1bvr037007en.html (last visited on 12 November 2010).

Cavoukian, A. (2009). *Privacy by Design ... Take the Challenge*, Canada: the Office of the Information and Privacy Commissioner of Ontario.

Ferretti, F. (2009). The Credit Scoring Pandemic and the European Vaccine: Making Sense of EU Data Protection Legislation, Issue (1) *Journal of Information, Law & Technology*, available at http://go.warwick.ac.uk/jilt/2009_1/ferretti.

Griffiths, N., & Chao, K. M. (Eds.). (2010). *Agent-Based Service-Oriented Computing*. London: Springer. doi:10.1007/978-1-84996-041-0

Kuner, C. (2010). Data Protection Law and International Jurisdiction on the Internet (Part 1). *Int J Law Info Tech*, *18*(2), 176–193. doi:10.1093/ijlit/eaq002

Kuner, C. (2010). Data Protection Law and International Jurisdiction on the Internet (Part 2). *Int J Law Info Tech*, *18*(3), 227–247. doi:10.1093/ijlit/eaq004

Reding, V. (2010). The Upcoming Data Protection Reform for the European Union, *International Data Privacy Law*, Advance Access 17 November 2010.

Solove, D. J., & Schwartz, P. (2009). *Information Privacy Law: Cases and Materials*. New York: Aspen Publishers.

Study on the economic benefits of privacy- technologies (PETs): Final Report to The European Commission, DG Justice, Freedom and Security, July 2010, by London Economics.

Wacks, R. (2010). *Privacy: A Very Short Introduction*. New York: Oxford University Press.

Wang, F. (2010). *Law of Electronic Commercial Transactions: Contemporary issues in the EU, US and China*. Oxford: Cavendish-Routledge Publishing.

Wang, F., & Griffiths, N. (2010, July). Protecting Privacy in Automated Transaction Systems: A Legal and Technological Perspective in the EU, Vol. 24, No. 2. *International Review of Law Computers & Technology*, ▪▪▪, 153–162. doi:10.1080/13600861003748243

Wong, R. (2009). Social networking: a conceptual analysis of a data controller. *Comms. L.*, *14*(5), 142–149.

Wright, T. (2007). Promoting data protection by privacy enhancing technologies, *C.T.L.R.* 2007, 13(5), 147-149.

KEY TERMS AND DEFINITIONS

Automated Information Systems: To accomplish collection, processing, storage and transfer of data information by using computing technologies and facilities without any human interaction.

Data Controller: The Community institution or body, the Directorate-General, the unit or any other organisational entity which alone or jointly with others determines the purposes and means of the processing of personal data.

Data Protection: To protect the rights of data ownership and balance the benefits between the protection of data ownership and the permission of data free-flow.

European Data Protection Supervisor (EDPS): An independent supervisory authority established in accordance with Regulation (EC) 45/2001. With respect to the processing of personal data, the EDPS is responsible for ensuring that the fundamental rights and freedoms of natural persons, and in particular their right to privacy, are respected by the Community institutions and bodies. The EDPS is also responsible for advising Community institutions and bodies and Data Subjects on all matters concerning the processing of personal data.

Personal Data Breach: A breach of security leading to the accidental or unlawful destruction, loss, alteration, unauthorised disclosure of, or access to, personal data transmitted, stored or otherwise processed in connection with the provision of a publicly available electronic communications service in the Community.

Personal Data: Any information relating to an identified or identifiable natural person ('data subject'); and identifiable person is one who can be identified, directly or indirectly, in particular by reference to an identification number or to one or more factors specific to his physical, physiological, mental, economic, culture or social identity.

Privacy Protection: To protect fundamental human rights for keeping personal data, information, matters and relationships private.

Privacy-Enhancing Technologies (PETs): Coherent systems of information and communication technologies that strengthen the protection of individuals' private life in an information system by preventing unnecessary or unlawful processing of personal data or by offering tools or controls to enhance the individual's control over his/her personal data.

350

Compilation of References

About.com. (n.d.). *Should you buy identity theft insurance or credit monitoring services?* Retrieved from http://financialplan.about.com/od/insurance /a/IDTheftInsure.htm

Ackerman, M. S., Cranor, L. F., & Reagle, J. (1999). *Privacy in e-commerce: Examining user scenarios and privacy preferences.* Paper presented at the 1st ACM Conference on Electronic Commerce.

Acquisti, A., Dingledine, R., & Syverson, P. (2003). On the economics of anonymity. In Wright, R. N. (Ed.), *Financial cryptography, LNCS 2742.* Springer-Verlag. doi:10.1007/978-3-540-45126-6_7

Acquisti, A. (2002). *Protecting privacy with economics: Economic incentives for preventive technologies in ubiquitous computing environments.* Paper presented at the Workshop on Socially-informed Design of Privacy-enhancing Solutions in Ubiquitous Computing.

Acquisti, A. (2010). *The economics of personal data and the economics of privacy.* OECD Conference Centre. WPISP-WPIE Roundtable. Retrieved on November 29, 2010, from http://www.oecd.org/dataoecd/8/51/46968784.pdf

Acquisti, A., Telang, R., & Friedman, A. (2006). Is there a cost to privacy breaches? An event study analysis. In *Third International Conference on Intelligent Systems (ICIS), Prague, Czech Republic* (pp. 26-33).

Adam, N. R., & Wortman, J. C. (1989). Security-control methods for statistical databases: A Comparative study. *ACM Computing Surveys, 21*(4), 515–556. doi:10.1145/76894.76895

Aggarwal, C. C. (2005). On k-anonymity and the curse of dimensionality. In *Proceedings of VLDB,* (pp. 901-909).

Aggarwal, G., Feder, T., Kenthapadi, K., Motwani, R., Panigrahy, R., Thomas, D., & Zhu, A. (2005). Anonymizing tables. In Proc. of the 10th International Conference on Database Theory (ICDT '05), (pp. 246-258). Edinburgh, Scotland.

Agrawal, R., & Srikant, R. (1994). Fast algorithms for mining association rules. In *Proc. of the 20th Int'l Conference on Very Large Databases,* August 1994.

Agrawal, R., & Srikant, R. (2000). Privacy-preserving data mining. *Proceedings of the ACM SIGMOD Conference on Management of Data,* Dallas, Texas, USA.

Agrawal, R., et al. (2003). *An XPath-based preference language for P3P.* Paper presented at the 12th International Conference on World Wide Web.

Agrawal, R., Kiernan, J., Srikant, R., & Xu, Y. (2002). Hippocratic databases. In *Proceedings of the 28th International Conference on Very Large Data Bases (VLDB '02)* (pp. 143-154). USA: VLDB Endowment.

Ahmed, Q., & Vrbsky, S. V. (2002). Maintaining security and timeliness in real-time database system. *Journal of Systems and Software, 61,* 15–29. doi:10.1016/S0164-1212(01)00111-X

Ajam, N., Cuppens-Boulahia, N., & Cuppens, F. (2010). Contextual privacy management in extended role based access control model. In Garcia-Alfaro, J., Navarro-Arribas, G., Cuppens-Boulahia, N., & Roudier, Y. (Eds.), *Data privacy management and autonomous spontaneous security* (pp. 121–135). Berlin, Germany: Springer. doi:10.1007/978-3-642-11207-2_10

Akl, S. G., & Taylor, P. D. (1983). Cryptographic solution to a problem of access control in a hierarchy. *ACM Transactions on Computer Systems, 1*(3), 239–248. doi:10.1145/357369.357372

Al Hasib, A., & Haque, A. A. (2008). A comparative study of the performance and security issues of AES and RSA cryptography. *ICCIT '08: Proceedings of the 2008 Third International Conference on Convergence and Hybrid Information Technology,* (pp. 505-510).

American Institute for Chartered Public Accountants (AICPA) and Canadian Institute for Charted Accountants. (CICA). (2010). *Generally accepted privacy principles (GAPP) and criteria and the AICPA/CICA Privacy Maturity Model based on generally accepted privacy principles.* Retrieved April 8, 2011, from http://bit.ly/ePrxwg

Analytics, I. D. (2006). *National data breach analysis.* ID Analytics, Inc. Whitepaper.

Analytics, I. D. (2007). *Data breach harm analysis.* ID Analytics, Inc. Whitepaper.

Analytics, I. D. (2005). *US national fraud ring analysis 2005.* ID Analytics, Inc. Whitepaper. Retrieved from http://www.idanalytics.com/solutions/white-papers/white-paper-request/index.php?whitepaper=U.S.%20National%20Fraud%20Ring%20Analysis,%202005

Analytics, I. D. (2010). *20 million Americans have multiple Social Security numbers associated with their name.* ID Analytics Inc. News Release, August 11, 2010. Retrieved from http://www.idanalytics.rsvp1.com/news-and-events/news-releases/2010/8-11-2010.php

Anderson, K. (2003). *Bringing PETs to the mainstream by using evaluation.* Presentation to the 24th International Conference of Privacy and Data Protection Commissioners, Australia, Office of the Information and Privacy Commissioner of Ontario, Canada. Retrieved April 8, 2011, from http://bit.ly/ezrgOB

Anderson, R. (2001). Why information security is hard-an economic perspective. In *Proceedings 17th Annual Computer Security Applications Conference, 2001* (pp. 358-365). New Orleans, LA: IEEE.

Andersson, C., et al. (2005). *Trust in PRIME.* Paper presented at the Fifth IEEE International Symposium on Signal Processing and Information Technology.

Angwin, J., & Steel, E. (2011). *Web's hot new commodity: Privacy.* Retrieved March 15, 2011, from http://online.wsj.com/article/SB10001424052748703529004576160764037920274.html

Answers, H. I. T. E. C. H. (2010). *About the HITECH Act.* Retrieved September 10, 2010, from http://www.hitechanswers.net/about/about-the-hitech-act-of-2009/

Ardagna, C. A., De Capitani di Vimercati, S., Paraboschi, S., Pedrini, E., & Samarati, P. (2009). An XACML-based privacy-centered access control system. *In Proceedings of the First ACM Workshop on information Security Governance* (pp. 49-58). Chicago, IL: ACM.

Ardanga, C. A., De Capitani di Vimercati, S., Paraboschi, S., Pedrini, E., & Samarati, P. (2010). Enabling privacy preserving credential-based access control with XACML and SAML. *Proceedings of the 10th IEEE International Conference on Computer and Information Technology, CIT 2010,* (pp. 1090-1095). Bradford, West Yorkshire, UK.

Argyrakis, J., Gritzalis, S., & Kioulafas, C. (2003). Privacy enhancing technologies: A review. In Traunmüller, R. (Ed.), *Electronic government* (*Vol. 2739*, pp. 282–287). Springer. doi:10.1007/10929179_51

Arizona State University (ASU). (2009, November). *Announcement of the Privacy by Design Research Lab.* Retrieved April 8, 2011, from http://bit.ly/gIbLCs

Artelsmair, C., & Wagner, R. (2003, July 27-30). *Towards a security engineering process.* Paper presented at the The 7th World Multiconference on Systemics, Cybernetics and Informatics, Orlando, Florida, USA.

Ashley, P., Hada, S., Karjoth, G., Powers, C., & Schunter, M. (2003). *Enterprise privacy authorization language (EPAL 1.2).* Retrieved November 29, 2010, from http://www.zurich.ibm.com /security/ enterprise-privacy/epal/Specification/index.html

Asmuth, C. (1983). A modular approach to key safeguarding. *IEEE Transactions on Information Theory, IT-29*(2).

Associated Press. (2010, August 5). *Albert Haynesworth to have MRI.* Retrieved October 22, 2010, from http://sports.espn.go.com/nfl/trainingcamp10 /news/story?id=5439254

Atallah, M., Frikken, K. B., & Blanton, M. (2009). Dynamic and efficient key management for access hierarchies. *ACM Transactions on Information and System Security, 12*(3), 190–202. doi:10.1145/1455526.1455531

Atallah, M. J., & Frikken, K. (2006). Key management for non-tree hierarchies. *ACM Symposium on Access Control Models and Technologies* (pp. 11-18). Lake Tahoe, CA: ACM.

Atallah, M. Kerschbaum, F. and Du, W. (2003). Secure and private sequence comparisons. In *Proceedings of the 2nd ACM Workshop on Privacy in the Electronic Society*, (pp. 39-44).

Ateniese, G., Fu, K., Green, M., & Hohenberger, S. (2006). Improved proxy re-encryption schemes with applications to secure distributed storage. [TISSEC]. *ACM Transactions on Information and System Security, 9*(1), 1–30. doi:10.1145/1127345.1127346

Ateniese, G., De Santis, A., Ferrara, A. L., & Masucci, B. (2006). Provably-secure time-bound hierarchical key assignment schemes. *In Proceedings of the 13th ACM Conference on Computer and Communications Security* (pp. 288-297). Alexandria, Virginia, USA, October 30 - November 03, 2006: CCS '06. New York, NY: ACM.

Atluri, V. (2001). Security for workflow systems. *Information Security Technical Report, 6*(2), 59–68. doi:10.1016/S1363-4127(01)00207-2

Backes, M., Pfitzmann, B., & Waider, M. (2003, June 26-27). *Security in business process engineering.* Paper presented at the International Conference on Business Process Management (BPM), Eindhoven, Netherlands.

Bacon, F. (1597). *Meditationes Sacræ.* De Hæresibus.

Baranowski, T. (1981). Toward the definition of concepts of health and disease, wellness and illness. *Journal of Health Values, 5*(6), 246–256.

Barkhuus, L. (2004). Privacy in location-based services, concern vs. coolness. In *Proceedings of Workshop paper in Mobile HCI 2004 workshop: Location System Privacy and Control.* Glasgow, UK.

Barros, J. P., & Gomes, L. (2000, 2-6 October). *From activity diagrams to class diagrams.* Paper presented at the Workshop Dynamic Behaviour in UML Models: Semantic Questions In conjunction with Third International Conference on UML, York, UK.

Bayardo, R., & Agrawal, R. (2005). Data privacy through optimal k-anonymity. In *Proceedings of the 21st International Conference on Data Engineering* (ICDE), 2005.

Becker, A., Arnab, A., & Serra, M. (2008). Assessing privacy criteria for DRM using EU privacy legislation. In *Proceedings of the 8th ACM workshop on Digital Rights Management*, (pp. 77–86). Alexandria, Virginia, USA.

Becker, J., & Chen, H. (2010). Measuring privacy risk in online social networks. *Proceedings of the Web 2.0 Security and Privacy* (W2SP).

Becker, M. Y., Malkis, A., & Bussard, L. (2009). *A framework for privacy preferences and data-handling policies.* Technical Report MSR-TR-2009-128. Microsoft Research.

Bell, D., & Lapadula, L. (1973). *Secure computer systems: Mathematical foundtaions and model*, (p. 2). MITRE report, MTR2547.

Benassi, P. (1999). TRUSTe: An online privacy seal program. *Communications of the ACM, 42*(2), 56–59. doi:10.1145/293411.293461

Bennett, C. J. (2009). International privacy standards: A continuing convergence. Retrieved April 8, 2011, from http://bit.ly/hBk3oX

Bennett, C. J., & Raab, C. D. (2006). *The governance of privacy: Policy instruments in global perspective.* MIT Press. Retrieved April 8, 2011, from http://bit.ly/icWiUh

Ben-Or, M., & Wigderson, A. (1988). Completeness theorems for non-cryptographic fault-tolerant distributed computation. In *Proceedings of the 20th Annual ACM Symposium on Theory of Computing*, (pp. 1-10).

Berendt, B., Günther, O., & Spiekermann, S. (2005). Privacy in e-commerce: Stated preferences vs. actual behavior. *Communications of the ACM, 48*(4), 101–106. doi:10.1145/1053291.1053295

Beresford, A. R., & Stajano, F. (2003). Location privacy in pervasive computing. *IEEE Pervasive Computing / IEEE Computer Society [and] IEEE Communications Society, 2*(1), 46–55. doi:10.1109/MPRV.2003.1186725

Bergmann, M., Rost, M., & Pettersson, J. S. (2006). Exploring the feasibility of a spatial user interface paradigm for privacy-enhancing technology. In A. G. Nilsson, R. Gustas, W. Wojtkowski, W. G. Wojtkowski, S. Wrycza & J. Zupancic (Eds.), *Bridging the gap between academia and industry* (pp. 437--448).

Bernstein, D. J. (2005). *Cache-timing attacks on AES.* Retrieved March 15, 2011, from http://cr.yp.to/antiforgery/cachetiming-20050414.pdf

Bertino, E., & Sandhu, R. (2005). Database security - Concepts, approaches, and challenges. *IEEE Transactions on Dependable and Secure Computing, 2*(1), 2–19. doi:10.1109/TDSC.2005.9

Bertino, E., Catania, B., Damiani, M. L., & Perlasca, P. (2005). GEO-RBAC: A spatially aware RBAC. In *Proceedings of the 11th ACM Symposium on Access Control Models and Technologies (SACMAT '06)* (pp. 29-37). New York, NY: ACM.

Bézivin, J. (2004). In search of a basic principle for model driven engineering. *UPGRADE. European Journal for the Informatics Professional, 5*(2), 21–24.

Bézivin, J., Breton, E., Dupé, G., & Valduriez, P. (2003). *The ATL transformation-based model management framework. (No. N° 03.08).* IRIN-Université de Nantes.

Bhatti, R., Ghafoor, A., Bertino, E., & Joshi, J. B. D. (2005). X-GTRBAC: An XML-based policy specification framework and architecture for enterprise-wide access control. [New York, NY: ACM.]. *Journal of ACM Transactions of Information and System Security, 8*(2), 187–227. doi:10.1145/1065545.1065547

Biba, K. (1977). *Integrity considerations for secure computer systems.* Bedford, MA, April 1977: Technical Report ESD-TR-76-372 ESD/AFSC, Hanscom AFB.

Bird, P., Grandison, T., Kiernan, J., Logan, S., & Rjaibi, W. (2005). Extending relational database systems to automatically enforce privacy policies. *Proceedings of the 21st International Conference on Data Engineering* (ICDE), Tokyo, Japan.

Birnhack, M. D. (2008). The EU data protection directive: An engine of a global regime. *Computer Law & Security Report, 24*(6), 508–520. doi:10.1016/j.clsr.2008.09.001

Bischoff-Grethe, A., Ozyurt, I. B., Busa, E., Quinn, B. T., Fennema-Notestine, C., & Clark, C. P. (2007, September). A technique for the deidentification of structural brain MR images. *Human Brain Mapping, 28*(9), 892–903. doi:10.1002/hbm.20312

Bishop, D. A. (2008). No harm no foul: Limits on damages awards for individuals subject to a data breach. *Shidler Journal of Law. Commerce and Technology, 4*, 12–13.

Bissias, G. D., Liberatore, M., & Levine, N. B. (2005). Privacy vulnerabilities in encrypted HTTP streams. *Proceedings of the Privacy Enhancing Technologies Workshop*, Dubrovnik, Croatia.

Blakley, B., McDermott, E., & Geer, D. (2001). Information security is information risk management. In *Proceedings of the 2001 Workshop on New Security Paradigms*. Cloudcroft, New Mexico.

Blakley, G. R. (1979). Safeguarding cryptographic keys. *Proceedings of the National Computer Conference 1979*, vol. 48. American Federation of Information Processing Societies.

Blaze, M., Bleumer, G., & Strauss, M. (1998). Divertible protocols and atomic proxy cryptography. *In Proceedings of EUROCRYPT '98*, (pp. 1403:127-144).

Blount, M., Batra, V. M., Capella, A. N., Ebling, M. R., Jerome, W. F., & Martin, S. M. (2007). Remote health-care monitoring using Personal Care Connect. *IBM Systems Journal, 46*(1), 95–113. doi:10.1147/sj.461.0095

Bogetoft, P. Christensen, D., Damgard, I., Geisler, M., Jakobsen, T., Kroigaard, M.,... Toft, T. (2009). Multiparty computation goes live. In *Proceedings of the 13th International Conference on Financial Cryptography and Data Security*, (pp. 325-343).

Bogetoft, P., Damgard, I., Jakobsen, T., & Nielsen, K. Pagter, J., & Toft, T. (2006). A practical implementation of secure auctions based on multiparty integer computation. In *Proceedings of the 10th International Conference on Financial Cryptography and Data Security*, (pp. 142-147).

Bonazzi, R., Fritscher, B., & Pigneur, Y. (2010, October). Business model considerations for privacy protection in a mobile location based context. *Proceedings of the Second International Workshop on Business Models for Mobile Platforms IEEE*. Retrieved March 15, 2011, from http://people.hec.unil.ch/ypigneur/files/2010/08/10_bmmp.pdf

Bonneau, J., & Mironov, I. (2006). Cache-collision timing attacks against AES. *Cryptographic Hardware and Embedded Systems, CHES 2006*, (pp. 201–215). Retrieved March 15, 2011, from http://research.microsoft.com/users/mironov/aes-timing.pdf

Borking, J. (2003) The PET story: Privacy enhancing technologies - Online and offline. Paper presented to 25th International Conference of Privacy and Data Protection Commissioners, Sydney Australia. Retrieved April 8, 2011, from http://bit.ly/hQQ6tj

Borking, J. (2009). *Organizational motives for adopting privacy enhancing technologies (PETs)*. Paper presented at the D 7.3 PRISE Conference Proceedings: Towards Privacy Enhancing Security Technologies - The Next Steps.

Bosworth, M. H. (2005). *Your Social Security number: Vulnerable but inflexible*. ConsumerAffairs.com. Retrieved from http://www.consumeraffairs.com/news04/2005/id_ssn.html

Bosworth, M. H. (2007a). *Data breaches endanger NY, CA retirees: Consultant's bungling, printer's errors put retirees at risk*. ConsumerAffairs.com. Retrieved from http://www.consumeraffairs.com/news04/2007/08/breaches_retirees.html

Bosworth, M. H. (2007b). *Wisconsin mails tax forms with exposed Social Security Numbers*. ConsumerAffairs.com. Retrieved from http://www.consumeraffairs.com/news04/2007/01/wi_ssn.html

Bramberger, M., Doblander, A., Maier, A., Rinner, B., & Schwabach, H. (2006). Distributed embedded smart cameras for surveillance applications. *IEEE Computer*, *39*(2), 68–75. doi:10.1109/MC.2006.55

Brewer, D. D., & Nash, M. (1988). The Chinese wall security policy. *IEEE Symposium on Security and Privacy* (pp. 206-214). Oakland, CA: IEEE.

Brickell, J., & Shmatikov, V. (2005). Privacy-preserving graph algorithms in the semi-honest model. In *Proceedings of AsiaCrypt*, (pp. 236-252).

Brodsky, A., Farkas, C., & Jajodia, S. (2000). Secure databases: Constraints, inference channels and monitoring disclosures. *IEEE Transactions on Knowledge and Data Engineering*, *12*(6), 900–919. doi:10.1109/69.895801

Byun, J.-W., & Ninghui, L. (2008). Purpose based access control for privacy protection in relational database systems. *The VLDB Journal*, *17*, 603–619. doi:10.1007/s00778-006-0023-0

Byun, J.-W., Bertino, E., & Li, N. (2005). Purpose based access control of complex data for privacy protection. In *Proceedings of the 10th ACM Symposium on Access Control Models and Technologies (SACMAT '05)* (pp. 102-110). New York, NY: ACM.

Cai, X., Ali, F. H., & Stipidis, E. (2003). MPEG-4 over local area mobile surveillance system. In *Proceedings of the IEE Symposium on Intelligence Distributed Surveillance Systems*, (15/1-15/3).

California Office of Privacy Protection. (2008). *Recommended practices on protecting the confidentiality of social security numbers*. Retrieved from http://www.privacy.ca.gov/res/docs/pdf/ssnrecommendations.pdf

California Office of Privacy Protection. (n.d.). *How to "freeze" your credit files*. Consumer Information Sheet 10. Retrieved from http://www.oispp.ca.gov/consumer_privacy/consumer/documents/pdf/cis10securityfreeze.pdf

Camenisch, J., & Herreweghen, E. V. (2002). Design and implementation of the idemix anonymous credential system. In V. Atluri (Ed.), *9th ACM Conference on Computer and Communications Security (CCS '02)* (pp. 21-30). New York, NY, USA.

Camenisch, J., et al. (2005). *Privacy and identity management for everyone*. Paper presented at the 2005 Workshop on Digital Identity Management.

Cameron, K. (2005). *The laws of identity*. Identity Blog. Retrieved April 8, 2011, from http://bit.ly/eAHmWu

Cameron, K., Posch, R., & Rannenberg, K. (2008). *Proposal for a common identity framework: A user-centric identity metasystem*. Retrieved April 8, 2011, from http://bit.ly/i6lAfE

Canadian Internet Policy and Public Interest Clinic (CIP-PIC). (2007). Approaches to security breach notification: A White Paper. Retrieved April 8, 2011, from http://bit.ly/fqzEQ6

Canny, J. (2002). Collaborative filtering with privacy. In *Proceedings of the IEEE Symposium on Security and Privacy*, (pp. 45-57).

Canny, J. (2002). Collaborative filtering with privacy via factor analysis. In *Proceedings of the 25th International ACM Conference on Research and Development in Information Retrieval*, (pp. 238-245).

Cantor, S., Kemp, J., Philpott, R., & Maler, E. (2005). *Assertions and protocols for the OASIS security assertion markup language (SAML) V2.0*. Retrieved October 26, 2010, from http://docs.oasis-open.org/security/saml/v2.0/saml-core-2.0-os.pdf

Capra, L., Emmerich, W., & Mascolo, C. (2003). CARISMA: Context-aware reflective middleware system for mobile applications. *IEEE Transactions on Software Engineering*, 29(10), 929–945. doi:10.1109/TSE.2003.1237173

Caralli, R. (2004). *Managing for enterprise security*. Software Engineering Institute, Carnegie Mellon University.

Casassa Mont, M. (2005). *A system to handle privacy obligations in enterprises. Technical Report, HPL-2005-180*. Hewlett-Packard Labs.

Casassa Mont, M. (2004). Dealing with privacy obligations: Important aspects and technical approaches. In *Proceedings of the International Workshop on Trust and Privacy in Digital Business (TrustBus 2004)* (LNCS 3184, pp. 120-131). Berlin, Germany: Springer.

Casassa Mont, M., & Thyne, R. (2006). A systemic approach to automate privacy policy enforcement in enterprises. In *Proceedings of the 6th Workshop on Privacy Enhancing-Technologies (PET 2006)* (LNCS 4258). Berlin, Germany: Springer-Verlag.

Case C-518/07. (2010). *European Commission v Germany*. European Court of Justice (Grand Chamber) 09 March 2010 [2010] 3 C.M.L.R. 3, paragraphs 24 and 30.

Case C-553/07. (2009). *College van burgemeester en wethouders van Rotterdam v M.E.E. Rijkeboer*, European Court of Justice (Judgement of 7 May 2009).

Case C-595. 07. (2008). *German Federal Constitutional Court in the Judgment of the First Senate of 27 February 2008*. 1 BvR 370, para 104. Retrieved November 12, 2010, from http://www.bundesverfassungsgericht.de/en/decisions/rs20080227_1bvr037007en.html

CASPIAN. (2006). *Metro future store - Special report overview*. Retrieved March, 2011, from http://www.spychips.com/metro/overview.html

Catlett, J. (2000). *Open letter to P3P developers & replies*. Paper presented at the Tenth Conference on Computers, Freedom and Privacy: Challenging the Assumptions

Cavoukian, A. (2008). Privacy in the clouds. *Identity in the Information Society*, 1, 89–108. doi:10.1007/s12394-008-0005-z

Cavoukian, A., & Hamilton, T. (2002). *The Privacy Payoff: How Successful Businesses Build Customer Trust*. Canada: McGraw-Hill.

Cavoukian, A. (1998). 407 express toll route: How you can travel the 407 anonymously. Office of the Information and Privacy Commissioner of Ontario, Canada. Retrieved April 8, 2011, from http://bit.ly/gJ3h74

Cavoukian, A. (1999). *Privacy and biometrics, consumer biometric applications: A discussion paper, and Biometrics and policing: Comments from a privacy perspective*. Office of the Information and Privacy Commissioner of Ontario, Canada. Retrieved April 8, 2011, from http://bit.ly/gqpJZU

Cavoukian, A. (2002). *Security technologies enabling privacy (STEPs): Time for a paradigm shift*. Office of the Information and Privacy Commissioner of Ontario, Canada. Retrieved April 8, 2011, from http://bit.ly/fjpfrt

Cavoukian, A. (2002). *Privacy and digital rights management (DRM): An oxymoron?* Office of the Information and Privacy Commissioner of Ontario, Canada. Retrieved April 8, 2011, from http://bit.ly/gfeQ99

Cavoukian, A. (2002). *Concerns and recommendations regarding government public key infrastructures for citizens*. Office of the Information and Privacy Commissioner of Ontario, Canada. Retrieved April 8, 2011, from http://bit.ly/fzNlbs

Cavoukian, A. (2004). *Building in privacy from the bottom up: How to preserve privacy in a security-centric world.* Presentation to Carnegie-Mellon University, Office of the Information and Privacy Commissioner of Ontario, Canada. Retrieved April 8, 2011, from http://bit.ly/e8YERK

Cavoukian, A. (2004). *Tag, you're it: Privacy implications of radio frequency identification (RFID) technology.* Office of the Information and Privacy Commissioner of Ontario, Canada. Retrieved April 8, 2011, from http://bit.ly/egro18

Cavoukian, A. (2005). *Privacy impact assessment guidelines for the Ontario Personal Health Office of the Information Protection Act.* Office of the Information and Privacy Commissioner of Ontario, Canada. Retrieved April 8, 2011, from http://bit.ly/hheuQh

Cavoukian, A. (2005). *Identity theft revisited: Security is not enough.* Office of the Information and Privacy Commissioner of Ontario, Canada. Retrieved April 8, 2011, from http://bit.ly/hRq4Fn

Cavoukian, A. (2005). *The new breed of practical privacy: An evolution.* Speech to the 26th International Conference of Privacy and Data Protection Commissioners, Montreux, Switzerland, Office of the Information and Privacy Commissioner of Ontario, Canada. Retrieved April 8, 2011, from http://bit.ly/gyOimo

Cavoukian, A. (2006). *The 7 laws of identity: The case for privacy-embedded laws of identity in the digital age.* Office of the Information and Privacy Commissioner of Ontario, Canada. Retrieved April 8, 2011, from http://bit.ly/g9nmJK

Cavoukian, A. (2006). *Video: A word about RFIDs and your privacy in the retail sector.* Office of the Office of the Information and Privacy Commissioner of Ontario, Canada. Retrieved April 8, 2011, from http://bit.ly/idq5vd

Cavoukian, A. (2006). *Creation of a global privacy standard.* Office of the Information and Privacy Commissioner of Ontario, Canada. Retrieved April 8, 2011, from http://bit.ly/hU0OaU

Cavoukian, A. (2007). *Guidelines for the use of video surveillance cameras in public places.* Office of the Information and Privacy Commissioner of Ontario, Canada. Retrieved April 8, 2011, from http://bit.ly/eQKOPz

Cavoukian, A. (2008). *Privacy in the clouds: A white paper on privacy and digital identity: Implications for the Internet.* Office of the Information and Privacy Commissioner of Ontario, Canada. Retrieved April 8, 2011, from http://bit.ly/Gwud7v

Cavoukian, A. (2008). *Privacy & radical pragmatism: Change the paradigm.* Office of the Information and Privacy Commissioner of Ontario, Canada. Retrieved April 8, 2011, from http://bit.ly/h1MT9W

Cavoukian, A. (2008). *RFID and privacy: Guidance for health-care providers.* Office of the Information and Privacy Commissioner of Ontario, Canada. Retrieved April 8, 2011, from http://bit.ly/hN6KY3

Cavoukian, A. (2009 rev 2011). *Privacy by design: The 7 foundational principles.* Office of the Information and Privacy Commissioner of Ontario, Canada. Retrieved April 8, 2011, from http://bit.ly/gwzJgw

Cavoukian, A. (2009). *Moving forward from PETs to PETs plus: The time for change is now.* Office of the Information and Privacy Commissioner of Ontario, Canada. Retrieved April 8, 2011, from http://bit.ly/fkeHt8

Cavoukian, A. (2009). *Transformative technologies deliver both security and privacy: Think positive-sum not zero-sum.* Office of the Information and Privacy Commissioner of Ontario, Canada. Retrieved April 8, 2011, from http://bit.ly/dTi0jh

Cavoukian, A. (2009). *Privacy and government 2.0: The implications of an open world.* Office of the Information and Privacy Commissioner of Ontario, Canada. Retrieved April 8, 2011, from http://bit.ly/f7kHAn

Cavoukian, A. (2009). *A discussion paper on privacy externalities, security breach notification and the role of independent oversight.* Office of the Information and Privacy Commissioner of Ontario, Canada. Retrieved April 8, 2011, from http://bit.ly/gdtufG

Cavoukian, A. (2009). *Adding an on/off device to activate the RFID in enhanced driver's licences: Pioneering a made-in-Ontario transformative technology that delivers both privacy and security.* Office of the Information and Privacy Commissioner of Ontario, Canada. Retrieved April 8, 2011, from http://bit.ly/fbSbpl

Cavoukian, A. (2010 rev. 2011). *Privacy by design - The 7 foundational principles: Implementation and mapping of fair office of the information practices.* Office of the Information and Privacy Commissioner of Ontario, Canada. Retrieved April 8, 2011, from http://bit.ly/hXwZp5

Cavoukian, A. (2010). Privacy by design: The next generation in the evolution of privacy. *Special issue of Identity in the Information Society, 3*(2). Retrieved April 8, 2011, from http://bit.ly/fo6l1q

Cavoukian, A., & Center for Democracy & Technology. (2000). *P3P and privacy: An update for the privacy community.* Office of the Information and Privacy Commissioner of Ontario, Canada. Retrieved April 8, 2011, from http://bit.ly/giSK04

Cavoukian, A., & Deloitte & Touche. (2004). *The security-privacy paradox: Issues, misconceptions and strategies.* Office of the Information and Privacy Commissioner of Ontario, Canada. Retrieved April 8, 2011, from http://bit.ly/fdzn1B

Cavoukian, A., & McQuay, T. (2010). A pragmatic approach to privacy risk optimization: Privacy by design for business practices. *Identity in the Information Society, 3*, 405-413. Retrieved April 8, 2011, from http://bit.ly/hC7hED

Cavoukian, A., & Schulich School of Business. (2007). *Privacy and boards of directors: What you don't know can hurt you.* Office of the Information and Privacy Commissioner of Ontario, Canada. 2003, rev. Retrieved April 8, 2011, from http://bit.ly/eTknsz

Cavoukian, A., & Stoianov, A. (2007). *Biometric encryption: A Positive-sum technology that achieves strong authentication, security and privacy.* Office of the Information and Privacy Commissioner of Ontario, Canada. Retrieved April 8, 2011, from http://bit.ly/gr5VyY

Cavoukian, A., & Stoianov, A. (2009). *Biometric encryption chapter from the Springer Encyclopaedia of Biometrics.* Office of the Information and Privacy Commissioner of Ontario, Canada. Retrieved April 8, 2011, from http://bit.ly/eay2DO

Cavoukian, A., & Tapscott, D. (2005). *Privacy and the open-networked enterprise.* Office of the Information and Privacy Commissioner of Ontario, Canada. Retrieved April 8, 2011, from http://bit.ly/eTdiya

Cavoukian, A., & U.S. Department of Justice, Office of Justice. (2000). *Privacy impact assessment for justice information systems.* Office of the Information and Privacy Commissioner of Ontario, Canada. Retrieved April 8, 2011, from http://bit.ly/eIuyOZ

Cavoukian, A., & U.S. Department of Justice, Office of Justice. (2000). *Programs, privacy design principles for an integrated justice system – A working paper.* Office of the Information and Privacy Commissioner of Ontario, Canada. Retrieved April 8, 2011, from http://bit.ly/hKW8ow

Cavoukian, A., Stoianov, A., & Carter, F. (2008). Biometric encryption: Technology for strong authentication, security and privacy. In *Policies and Research in Identity Management, IFIP Advances in Information and Communication Technology, 261*, 57-77. Springer. Retrieved April 8, 2011, from http://bit.ly/eBK5l9

Cavoukian, A., Taylor, S., & Abrams, M. (2010). Privacy by design: Essential for organizational accountability and strong business practices. *Identity in the Information Society, 3*, 405-413. Retrieved April 8, 2011, from http://bit.ly/dOJYOc

CDC. (2009, September 1). *Classification of diseases, functioning, and disability.* Retrieved October 14, 2010, from http://www.cdc.gov/nchs/icd/icd9.htm

Center for Democracy and Technology (CDT). (2009). *Perspective on PbD.* Retrieved April 8, 2011, from http://bit.ly/fuxn0t

Center for Democracy and Technology (CDT). (2009). *Privacy by design in the Smart Grid.* Retrieved April 8, 2011, from http://bit.ly/f6pZDO

Center for Democracy and Technology (CDT). (2009). The role of privacy by design in protecting consumer privacy. Comments submitted to the FTC Consumer Privacy Roundtable. Retrieved April 8, 2011, from http://1.usa.gov/eMH4jv

Center for Democracy and Technology (CDT). (2010). Comments on a national broadband plan for our future. NBP Public Notice #29, GN Docket Nos. 09-47, 09-51, 09-137. Retrieved April 8, 2011, from http://bit.ly/fC5nCo

Center for the Advancement of Women's Health. (2009, December 9). *Kentucky women's health registry.* Retrieved October 16, 2010, from https://www.mc.uky.edu/kyhealthregistry/ default.asp

Centre for Information Policy Leadership (CIPL). (2009). *Data protection accountability: The essential elements: A document for discussion.* Retrieved April 8, 2011, from http://1.usa.gov/hvlZcD

Centre for Information Policy Leadership (CIPL). (2010). *Demonstrating and measuring accountability: A discussion document accountability phase II - The Paris project.* Retrieved April 8, 2011, from http://bit.ly/gRFrob

Chadramouli, R. (2003). A policy validation framework for enterprise authorization specification. *ACSAC: In Proceedings of the 19th Annual Computer Security Applications Conference* (pp. 319-328). Washington, DC: IEEE Computer Society.

Chan, H., & Perrig, A. (2003). Security and privacy in sensor networks. *IEEE Computer, 36*(10), 103–105. doi:10.1109/MC.2003.1236475

Charalambides, M., Flegkas, P., Pavlou, G., Rubio-Loyola, J., Bandara, A. K., & Lupu, E. C. … Dulay, N. (2006). Dynamic policy analysis and conflict resolution for DiffServ quality of service management. In *Proceedings of Network Operations and Management Symposium (NOMS 06)* (pp.294-304).

Chaum, D. (1981). Untraceable electronic mail, return addresses and digital pseudonyms. *Communications of the ACM, 24*(2), 84–88. doi:10.1145/358549.358563

Chen, B., Lefevre, K., & Ramakrishnan, R. (2007). Privacy skyline: Privacy with multidimensional adversarial knowledge. *Proceedings of the 33rd International Conference on Very Large Data Bases* (VLDB), University of Vienna, Austria.

Chen, G., & Kotz, D. (2000). *A survey of context-aware mobile computing research.* Tech. Rep. TR2000-381, Dartmouth, November 2000.

Chess, D. M. (2005). Security in autonomic computing. *SIGARCH Comput. Archit. News, 33*(1), 2–5. doi:10.1145/1055626.1055628

Chien, H.-Y. (2004). Efficient time-bound hierarchical key assignment scheme. *IEEE Transactions on Knowledge and Data Engineering, 16*(10), 1301–1304. doi:10.1109/TKDE.2004.59

Cisco. (2006). *Cisco Systems IP network-centric video surveillance.* White paper.

Clark, D. R., & Wilson, D. (1987). A comparison of commercial and militrary computer security policies. *In Proceedings 1987 IEEE Symposium on Security and Privacy* (pp. 184-194). Oakland, CA: IEEE.

Clarke, R. (2008). Business cases for privacy-enhancing technologies. In Subramanian, R. (Ed.), *Computer security, privacy and politics: Current issues, challenges and solutions* (pp. 135–155). Hershey, PA: IGI Global. doi:10.4018/978-1-59904-804-8.ch007

Clement, A., et al. (2008). *The PIPWatch toolbar: Combining PIPEDA, PETs and market forces through social navigation to enhance privacy protection and compliance.* Paper presented at the Technology and Society, 2008. ISTAS 2008. IEEE International Symposium on, http://dx.doi.org/10.1109/68.593394

COM 609/3. (2010). *A comprehensive approach on personal data protection in the European Union* – Communication from the Commission to the European Parliament, the Council, the Economic and Social Committee and the Committee of the Regions, European Commission, Brussels, 04.11.2010 COM(2010) 609/3 - The EU Comprehensive Approach.

Common Criteria. (2005). *Introduction and general model,* version 3.0, revision 2. (No. CCMB-2005-07-001): Common Criteria for Information Technology Security Evaluation. Retrieved from http://www.commoncriteriaportal.org/

Computers, Privacy and Freedom (CFP). (2000, April). *Privacy by Design Workshop Proceedings.* Toronto, Ontario, Canada. Retrieved April 8, 2011, from http://bit.ly/e5UegE

ComputerWorld. (2009a, October 29). CalOptima recovers discs with personal data on 68,000 members. *ComputerWorld.* Retrieved from http://www.computerworld.com/s/article/ 9140122/CalOptima_recovers_discs_with_personal_data_on_68_000_members?taxonomyId=1

ComputerWorld. (2009b, October 26). CalOptima says data on 68,000 members may be compromised. *ComputerWorld.* Retrieved from http://news.idg.no/cw/art.cfm?id=92D3CA87-1A64-6A71-CEFF3995912328CD

Corbi, A. G. (2003). The dawning of the autonomic computing era. *IBM Systems Journal, 42*(1), 5–18. doi:10.1147/sj.421.0005

Corbin, C. B., & Pangrazi, R. P. (2001). *Towards a uniform definition of wellness: A commentary.* President's Council on Physical Fitness and Sports. Series 3, No. 15. Retrieved April 4, 2011 from http://eric.ed.gov/PDFS/ED470691.pdf

Cormen, T. H., Leiserson, C. E., Rivest, R. L., & Stein, C. (2001). *Introduction to algorithms* (2nd ed.). MIT Press and McGraw-Hill.

Coyle, K. (1999). *P3P: Pretty poor privacy? - A social analysis of the platform for privacy preferences (P3P).* Retrieved April, 2011, from http://www.kcoyle.net/p3p.html

Coyle, K. (2000). *A response to "P3P and privacy: An update for the privacy community" by the Center for Democracy and Technology.* Retrieved April 2011 from http://www.kcoyle.net/response.html

Cramer, R., Damgard, I., & Maurer, U. (2000). General secure multi-party computation from any linear secret-sharing scheme. In *Proceedings of EuroCrypt,* (pp. 316-334).

Cramer, R., Damgard, I., & Nielsen, J. (2001). Multiparty computation from threshold homomorphic encryption. In *Proceedings of EuroCrypt,* (pp. 280-299).

Crampton, J. (2007). Cryptographically-enforced hierarchical access control with multiple keys. *In Proceedings 12th Nordic Workshop on Secure IT Systems (NordSec 2007),* (pp. 49-60).

Crampton, J., Martin, K., & Wild, P. (2006). On key assignment for hierarchical access control. *In Proceedings 19th IEEE Workshop on Computer Security Foundations* (pp. 98-111). S. Servolo Island, Italy: IEEE.

Cranor, L. F. (2008). P3P deployment on websites. *Electronic Commerce Research and Applications, 7*(3), 274–293. doi:10.1016/j.elerap.2008.04.003

Cranor, L. F., Guduru, P., & Arjula, M. (2006). User interfaces for privacy agents. *ACM Transactions on Computer-Human Interaction, 13*(2), 135–178. doi:10.1145/1165734.1165735

Cranor, L. F., & Lessig, L. (2002). *Web privacy with* (p. 3P). O'Reilly & Associates, Inc.

Cranor, L. F. (2002). Help! IE6 is blocking my cookies. Retrieved April 2011 from http://www.oreillynet.com/pub/a/javascript /2002/10/04/p3p.html

Cranor, L. F. (2003). *"I didn't buy it for myself" privacy and ecommerce personalization.* Paper presented at the 2003 ACM Workshop on Privacy in the Electronic Society.

Cranor, L. F., Arjula, M., & Guduru, P. (2002). *Use of a P3P user agent by early adopters.* Paper presented at the 2002 ACM Workshop on Privacy in the Electronic Society.

Cranor, L. F., Langheinrich, M., & Marchiori, M. (2002). *A P3P preference exchange language 1.0 (APPEL1.0).* (Working Draft): W3C.

Crompton, M. (2010). *Privacy by design: An oxymoron, an impossibility or the way to go?* Presentation to the National ICT Australia Seminar. Retrieved April 8, 2011, from http://bit.ly/eaA2L5

Csertan, G., Huszerl, G., Majzik, I., Pap, Z., Pataricza, A., & Varro, D. (2002). *VIATRA-Visual automated transformations for formal verification and validation of UML models.* Paper presented at the 17th IEEE International Conference on Automated Software Engineering (ASE).

Cuppens, F., & Cuppens-Boulahia, N. (2008). Modeling contextual security policies. [Berlin, Germany: Springer-Verlag.]. *International Journal of Information Security, 7*(4), 285–305. doi:10.1007/s10207-007-0051-9

Cuppens, F., Cuppens-Boulahia, N., & Ben Ghorbel, M. (2007). High level conflict management strategies in advanced access control models. *Journal of Electronic Notes in Theoretical Computer Science, 8,* 3–26. doi:10.1016/j.entcs.2007.01.064

Dahlberg, T., Mallat, N., Ondrus, J., & Zmijewska, A. (2008). Past, present and future of mobile payments research: A literature review. *Electronic Commerce Research and Applications, 7*(2), 165–181. doi:10.1016/j.elerap.2007.02.001

Dai, Y.-S. (2005). Autonomic computing and reliability improvement. *In Proceedings 8th IEEE Symposium on Object-Oriented Real-Time Distributed Computing (ISORC'05)*, (pp. 204-206).

Damgard, I., Geisler, M., & Kroigaard, M. (2008). Homomorphic encryption and secure comparison. *International Journal of Applied Cryptography*, *1*(1), 22–31. doi:10.1504/IJACT.2008.017048

Damgard, I., & Jurik, M. (2001). A generalisation, a simplification and some applications of paillier's probabilistic public-key system. In *Proceedings of Public Key Cryptography*, (pp. 119-136).

Damgard, I., Fitzi, M., Kiltz, E., Nielsen, J., & Toft, T. (2006). Unconditionally secure constant-rounds multiparty computation for equality, comparison, bits and exponentiation. In *Proceedings of Theoretical Cryptography Conference*, (pp. 285-304).

Darrow, J. J., & Lichtenstein, S. D. (2008). Do you really need my social security number? Data collection practices in the digital age. *North Carolina Journal of Law and Technology*, *10*, 1–447.

Das, M. L., Saxena, A., Gulati, V. P., & Phutak, D. B. (2005). Hierarchical key management scheme using polynomial interpolation. *SIGOPS Oper. Syst. Rev.*, *39*(1), 40–47. doi:10.1145/1044552.1044556

Das, T. K., & Teng, B. S. (2000). A resource-based theory of strategic alliances. *Journal of Management*, *26*(1), 31–61.

Dasu, T., Krishnan, S., Venkatasubramanian, S., & Yi, K. (2006). *An information-theoretic approach to detecting changes in multi-dimensional data streams.*

Davis, F. D. (1989). Perceived usefulness, perceived ease of use, and user acceptance of information technology. *Management Information Systems Quarterly*, *13*(3), 319–340. doi:10.2307/249008

Davis, C. (2009). Identity theft horror story: I'm not a criminal! *FiLife*, Oct. 22. Retrieved from http://www.filife.com/stories/identity-theft-horror-story-im-not-a-criminal

De Capitani Di Vimercati, S., Foresti, S., Jajodia, S., Paraboschi, S., & Samarati, P. (2007). Over-encryption: Management of access control evolution on outsourced data. *VLDB'07: Proceedings of the 33rd International Conference on Very Large Databases* (pp. 123-134). Vienna, Austria: VLDB Endowment.

de Goede, H. (2010). *Video4Linux v4l-utils and libv4l.* Retrieved March 15, 2011, from http://freshmeat.net/projects/libv4l/

De Santis, A., Ferrara, A. L., & Masucci, B. (2008). New constructions for provably-secure time-bound hierarchical key assignment schemes. *Theoretical Computer Science*, *407*(1-3), 213–230. doi:10.1016/j.tcs.2008.05.021

del Alamo, J. M., Monjas, M. A., Yelmo, J. C., San Miguel, B., Trapero, R., & Fernandez, A. M. (2010). Self-service privacy: User-centric privacy for network-centric identity. *Proceedings of the IFIP Advances in Information and Communication Technology*, *321*, 17–31. doi:10.1007/978-3-642-13446-3_2

Denning, D. E. (1976). A lattice model of secure information flow. *Communications of the ACM*, *19*(5), 236–243. doi:10.1145/360051.360056

Department of Health and Human Services. (2010, July 28). Health information technology: Initial set of standards, implementation specifications, and certification criteria for electronic health record technology; Final Rule. *45 CFR Part 170* [US Department Of Health And Human Services, Centers for Medicare & Medicaid Services.]. *Federal Register*, *75*(144), 44590–44654.

Dierks, T., & Rescorla, E. (2008). *The transport layer security (TLS) protocol version 1.2.* The Internet Engineering Task Force (IETF) - Network Working Group. Request For Comments (RFC) 5246. Retrieved October 26, 2010, from http://tools.ietf.org/html/rfc5246

Dijkman, R. M., & Joosten, S. M. M. (2002). *An algorithm to derive use cases from business processes.* Paper presented at the 6th International Conference on Software Engineering and Applications (SEA), Boston, USA.

Dinur, I., & Nissim, K. (2003). Revealing information while preserving privacy. *Proceedings of the Twenty-Second ACM SIGACT-SIGMOD-SIGART Symposium on Principles of Database Systems* (PODS), San Diego, California.

Directive 2002/58/EC. (2002). *European Parliament and of the Council of 12 July 2002 concerning the processing of personal data and the protection of privacy in the electronic communications sector* (Directive on privacy and electronic communications). Official Journal of the European Union, L 201, 31 July 2002, P. 0037–0047.

Directive 2009/136/EC. (2009). *European Parliament and of the Council of 25 November 2009 amending Directive 2002/22/EC on universal service and users' rights relating to electronic communications networks and services, Directive 2002/58/EC concerning the processing of personal data and the protection of privacy in the electronic communications sector and Regulation (EC) No 2006/2004 on cooperation between national authorities responsible for the enforcement of consumer protection laws.* Official Journal of the European Union, L 337/11, 18 December 2009, P.0011 – 0036.

Directive 95/46/EC. (1995). *European Parliament and of the Council of 24 October 1995 on the protection of individuals with regard to the processing of personal data and on the free movement of such data.* Official Journal of the European Union, L 281, 23 November 1995, P. 0031–0050.

Dixon, P. (2006). Medical identity theft: The information crime that can kill you. *World Privacy Forum*, May 3. Retrieved from http://www.worldprivacyforum.org/pdf/wpf_medicalidtheft2006.pdf

Du, S., & Joshi, J. (2006). Supporting authorization query and inter-domain role mapping in presence of hybrid role hierarchy. *In Proceedings of the 11th ACM Symposium on Access Control Models and Technologies* (pp. 228-236). ACM.

Duan, Y., Wang, J., Kam, M., & Canny, J. (2005). Privacy preserving link analysis on dynamic weighted graph. *Computational & Mathematical Organization Theory*, *11*(2), 141–159. doi:10.1007/s10588-005-3941-2

Durant v the Financial Services Authority (FSA). (2003). EWCA Civ 1746.

Dutch Data Protection Agency. (2004). *Privacy-enhancing technologies*. White Paper for Decision-Makers. Retrieved April 8, 2011, from http://bit.ly/dFRV8q

Egelman, S., Cranor, L. F., & Chowdhury, A. (2006). *An analysis of P3P-enabled web sites among top-20 search results.* Paper presented at the 8th International Conference on Electronic Commerce: The New E-commerce: Innovations for Conquering Current Barriers, Obstacles and Limitations to Conducting Successful Business on the Internet.

Eriksson, H.-E., & Penker, M. (2001). *Business modeling with UML*. OMG Press.

EU Parliament. (1995). Directive 95/46/EC of the European Parliament and of the Council. *Official Journal L 281*, 23/11/1995, 31-50.

EU. (1995). *Directive 95-46-EC on the protection of individuals with regard to the processing of personal data and on the free movement of such data.* Retrieved October 13, 2008, from http://ec.europa.eu/justice_home/fsj/privacy

EU. (2002). *Directive on privacy and electronic communications.* 2002/58/EC

European Commission (EC). (2007). *European Commission supports PETs: Promoting data protection by privacy enhancing technologies - Press release.* Retrieved April 8, 2011, from http://bit.ly/epnO5w

European Commission (EC). (2007). *Communication from the Commission to the European Parliament and the Council on Promoting Data Protection by Privacy Enhancing Technologies (PETs), COM (2007) 228 final.* Brussels, 2.5.2007 and Background Memo. Retrieved April 8, 2011, from http://bit.ly/hRdu8n

European Commission (EC). (2009). *The future of privacy: Joint contribution to the consultation of the European Commission on the legal framework for the fundamental right to protection of personal data - Article 29: Data protection working party, WP 168.* Retrieved April 8, 2011, from http://bit.ly/gWJ56l

European Commission (EC). (2010). *Communication from the commission to the European parliament, the council, the economic and social committee and the committee of the regions: A comprehensive approach on personal data protection in the European Union.* Technical report. Retrieved April 8, 2011, from http://bit.ly/grpr4w

European Commission (EC). (2010). *Study on the economic benefits of privacy-enhancing technologies*. Final Report to The European Commission, DG Justice, Freedom and Security. Retrieved April 8, 2011, from http://bit.ly/heQNQT

European Commission (EC). (2010). *Opinion 3/2010 on the principle of accountability - Article 29: Data protection working party, WP 173*. Retrieved April 8, 2011, from http://bit.ly/eEFeaq

European Commission News. (2010). *Safeguarding privacy in the digital age - Justice and citizens rights*. Retrieved November 30, 2010, from http://ec.europa.eu/news/justice/101105_en.htm

European Commission. (2000). Commission decision of 26 July 2000 pursuant to Directive 95/46/EC of the European Parliament and of the Council on the adequacy of the protection provided by the safe harbour privacy principles and related frequently asked questions issued by the US Department of Commerce. *Official Journal of the European Communities, L 215*, 7-47.

European Commission. (2010). *Opt-out is not sufficient*. European Commission Press Release. 24 June 2010. Retrieved March 15, 2011, from http://ec.europa.eu/justice/policies/privacy/ news/docs/pr_26_06_10_en.pdf

European Council. (2011, February). *Council conclusions on the Communication from the Commission to the European Parliament and the Council - A comprehensive approach on personal data protection in the European Union*. 3071st Justice and Home Affairs Council meeting, Brussels. Retrieved April 8, 2011, from http://bit.ly/gx4wS0

European Network and Information Security Agency (ENISA). (2009). *Privacy and e-ID: Press release and position paper*. Retrieved April 8, 2011, from http://bit.ly/dNNRD6

European Parliament & Council. (1995). *Directive 95/46/EC of 24 October 1995 on the protection of individuals with regard to the processing of personal data and on the free movement of such data* [Official Journal L 281 of 23.11.1995]. Retrieved April 8, 2011, from http://bit.ly/gcF0Uq

European Parliament and Council. (1995). Directive 95/46/EC of the European Parliament and of the Council on the protection of individuals with regard to the processing of personal data and on the free movement of such data. *Official Journal of the European Communities, L 281*, 31-50.

European Parliament and Council. (2002). Directive 2002/58/EC of the European Parliament and of the Council concerning the processing of personal data and the protection of privacy in the electronic communications sector (Directive on privacy and electronic communications). *Official Journal of the European Communities, L 201*, 37-47.

European Parliament and Council. (2006). Directive 2006/24/EC of the European Parliament and of the Council of 15 March 2006 on the retention of data generated or processed in connection with the provision of publicly available electronic communications services or of public communications networks and amending Directive 2002/58/EC. *Official Journal of the European Communities, L 105*, 54-63.

European Union. (2003). *Privacy incorporated software agent: Building a privacy guardian for the electronic age* (PISA Project). 2001–2003.

EuroPriSe. (2010). *Welcome! - EuroPriSe - European privacy seal*. Retrieved March, 2011, from https://www.european-privacy-seal.eu/

Facebook. (2011). *Welcome to Facebook - Log in, sign up or learn more*. Retrieved April, 2011, from http://www.facebook.com

Facts, I. T. (n.d.). *30% of US identity fraud is new account fraud*. Retrieved from http://www.itfacts.biz/30-of-us-identity-fraud-is-new-account-fraud/5729

Farkas, C., & Jajodia, S. (2002). The inference problem: A survey. *ACM SUGKDD Explorations Newsletter, 42*(1), 5–18.

Federal Trade Commission. (2007). *2006 Identity theft survey report*. Retrieved from www.ftc.gov/os/2007/11/SynovateFinalReportIDTheft2006.pdf

Federal Trade Commission. (2008). *Security in numbers: SSNs and ID theft*. Retrieved from http://www.ftc.gov/os/2008/12/P075414ssnreport.pdf

Federal Trade Commission. (n.d.). *About identity theft.* Retrieved from http://www.ftc.gov/bcp/edu/microsites/ idtheft/consumers/about-identity-theft.html

Fennema-Notestine, C., Ozyurt, I. B., Clark, C. P., Morris, S., Bischoff-Grethe, A., & Bondi, M. W. (2006, February). Quantitative evaluation of automated skull-stripping methods applied to contemporary and legacy images: Effects of diagnosis, bias correction, and slice location. *Human Brain Mapping, 27*(2), 99–113. doi:10.1002/hbm.20161

Fernandez-Medina, E., & Piattini, M. (2005). Designing secure databases. *Information and Software Technology, 4,* 6–11.

Ferraiolo, D. F., Sandhu, R. S., Gavrila, S., Kuhn, R. D., & Chandramouli, R. (2001). Proposed NIST standard for role-based access control. *ACM Transactions on Information and System Security, 4*(3), 224–274. doi:10.1145/501978.501980

Ferrini, R., & Bertino, E. (2009). Supporting RBAC with XACML+OWL. In *Proceedings of the 14th ACM Symposium on Access Control Models and Technologies (SACMAT '09)* (pp. 145-154). New York, NY: ACM.

Finberg, J. (2002). Financial abuse of the elderly in California. *Loyola of Los Angeles Law Review, 36,* 667.

Finin, T., Joshi, A., Kagal, L., Niu, J., Sandhu, R. S., Winsborough, W., & Thuraisingham, B. (2008). *ROW-LBAC: Representing role based access control in OWL.* In *Proceedings of the 13th ACM Symposium on Access Control Models and Technologies* (pp. 73-82). New York, NY: ACM.

Firesmith, D. (2003). Engineering security requirements. *Journal of Object Technology, 2*(1), 53–68. doi:10.5381/ jot.2003.2.1.c6

Firesmith, D. (2004). Specifying reusable security requirements. *Journal of Object Technology, 3*(1), 61–75. doi:10.5381/jot.2004.3.1.c6

Fishbein, M., & Ajzen, I. (1975). *Belief, attitude, intention, and behavior: An introduction to theory and research.* Reading, MA: Addison-Wesley Pub.

Fitzpatrick, B., Recordon, D., Hardt, D., Bufu, J., & Hoyt, J. (2007). *OpenID authentication 2.0 – Final.* Retrieved October 26, 2010, from http://openid.net/specs/openid-authentication-2_0.html

Flinn, S., & Lumsden, J. (2005). *User perceptions of privacy and security on the Web.* Paper presented at the Third Annual Conference on Privacy, Security and Trust (PST 2005)

Floyd, R. (1962). Algorithm 97: Shortest path. *Communications of the ACM, 5*(6), 345. doi:10.1145/367766.368168

Ford, R. (2004). Beware rise of Big Brother state, warns data watchdog. *The Sunday Times.* Retrieved April 8, 2011, from http://thetim.es/hw1abr

Foremski, T. (2010, October 18). *TRUSTe responds to Facebook privacy leaks.* Retrieved October 28, 2010, from http://www.siliconvalleywatcher.com/mt/ archives/2010/10/truste_responds.php

Freudiger, J., Manshaei, M., Hubaux, J. P., & Parkes, D. C. (2009). On non-cooperative location privacy: A game-theoretic analysis. In *Proceedings of ACM Conference on Computer and Communications Security (CCS),* Chicago, USA.

Frikken, K. (2007). Privacy-preserving set union. In *Proceedings of Applied Cryptography and Network Security,* (pp. 237-252).

Frikken, K., & Golle, P. (2006). Private social network analysis: How to assemble pieces of a graph privately. In *Proceedings of the 5th ACM Workshop on Privacy in the Electronic Society,* (pp. 89-98).

FTC. (2010). *Protecting consumer privacy in an era of rapid change: A proposed framework for businesses and policymakers.* Federal Trade Commission. Retrieved April 2011 from http://www.ftc.gov/os/2010/12/101201 privacyreport.pdf

Fuggetta, A. (2000, June 4-11, 2000.). *Software process: A roadmap.* Paper presented at the ICSE 2000, 22nd International Conference on Software Engineering, Future of Software Engineering, Limerick Ireland.

Fujii, K., & Suda, T. (2009). Semantics-based context-aware dynamic service composition. *ACM Trans. Auton. Adapt. Syst., 4*(2), 1–31. doi:10.1145/1516533.1516536

Fung, B. C., Wang, K., Chen, R., & Yu, P. S. (2010). Privacy-preserving data publishing: A survey of recent developments. *ACM Computing Surveys, 42*(4), 1–53. doi:10.1145/1749603.1749605

Fung, B. C. M., Wang, K., & Yu, P. S. (2005) Top-down specialization for information and privacy preservation. In *Proceedings of ICDE* (pp. 205-216).

Gallivan, M. J., & Depledge, G. (2003). Trust, control and the role of interorganizational systems in electronic partnerships. *Information Systems Journal*, *13*(2), 159–190. doi:10.1046/j.1365-2575.2003.00146.x

Gallup Organization. (2008). *Data protection in the European Union: Citizens' perceptions – Analytical report (Flash Eurobarometer 225)*. Retrieved November 29, 2010, from http://ec.europa.eu /public_opinion/flash/fl_225_en.pdf

Ganek, A., & Corbi, T. (2003). The dawning of the autonomic computing era. *IBM Systems Journal*, *42*(1), 5–18. doi:10.1147/sj.421.0005

Gedik, B., & Ling, L. (2005). Location privacy in mobile systems: A personalized anonymization model. *Proceedings of the 25th IEEE International Conference on Distributed Computing Systems* (pp. 620-629).

Gemmell, D. J., Vin, H. M., Kandlur, D. D., Venkat Rangan, P., & Rowe, L. A. (1995). Multimedia storage servers: A tutorial. *IEEE Computer*, *28*(5), 40–49. doi:10.1109/2.384117

Goetzel, R., Sepulveda, M., Knight, K., Eisen, M., Wade, S., Wong, J., & Fielding, J. (1994). Association of IBM's "A Plan for Life" health promotion program with changes in employees' health risk status. *Journal of Occupational Medicine.*, *36*(9), 1005–1009.

Gogoulos, F., Antonakopoulou, A., Lioudakis, G. V., Mousas, A. S., Kaklamani, D. I., & Venieris, I. S. (2010). Privacy-aware access control and authorization in passive network monitoring infrastructures. In *Proceedings of the 3rd IEEE International Symposium on Trust, Security and Privacy for Emerging Applications (IEEE TSP-2010)* (pp. 1114-1121). Los Alamitos, CA: IEEE Computer Society.

Goldreich, O. (2002). *Secure multi-party computation*. Retrieved October 13, 2008, from http://www.wisdom.weizmann.ac.il/~oded/pp.html

Goldreich, O., Micali, S., & Wigderson, A. (1987). How to play any mental game. In *Proceedings of the 19th ACM Symposium on Theory of Computing*, (pp. 218-229).

Goldschlag, D., Reed, M., & Syverson, P. (1999). Onion routing. *Communications of the ACM*, *42*(2), 39–41. doi:10.1145/293411.293443

Gollman, D. (2005). *Computer security*. John Wiley and Sons, Ltd.

Gomez, J., Pinnick, T., & Soltani, A. (2009). *KnowPrivacy*. Retrieved April 2011 from http://www.knowprivacy.org/report/ KnowPrivacy_Final_Report.pdf

Gomez-Skarmeta, A. F., López, G., Cánovas, O., Pérez, A., Torroglosa, E. M., Gómez, F., et al. (2008). *Identity as a convergence layer*. SWIFT white paper. Retrieved October 26, 2010, from http://www.ist-swift.org/component/option,com_docman/task,doc_download/gid,20/Itemid,37/

Google Inc. (2010). *Google Maps API - Geocoding*. Retrieved March 15, 2011, from http://code.google.com/apis/maps/documentation/services.html#Geocoding

Grandison, T., Johnson, C., & Kiernan, J. (2007). Hippocratic databases: Current capabilities and future trends. In Jajodia, S., & Gertz, M. (Eds.), *Handbook of database security: Applications and trends*. doi:10.1007/978-0-387-48533-1_17

Grandison, T. (2010). Patient-centric privacy: Envisioning collaboration between payers, providers & patients with the patient at the core. *Proceedings of the 6th IEEE International Conference of Collaborative Computing: Networking, Applications, and Worksharing* (CollaborateCom), Chicago, Illinois.

Greenemeier, L. (2007, August 1). The TJX effect: Details of the largest breach of customer data are starting to come to light. *InformationWeek*. Retrieved from http://www.informationweek.com/story/ showArticle.jhtml?articleID=201400171

Greenstadt, R., & Smith, M. D. (2005). *Protecting personal information: Obstacles and directions*. Paper presented at the Fourth Workshop on the Economics of Information Security (WEIS05)

Gregor, S., & Jones, D. (2007). The anatomy of a design theory. *Journal of the Association for Information Systems*, *8*(5), 312–325.

Group, M. I. B. Inc. (2010). *About MIB Group*. Retrieved November 3, 2010, from http://www.mib.com/html/about_mib_group.html

Group, M. I. B. Inc. (2010). *Consumer guide*. Retrieved November 3, 2010, from http://www.mib.com/html/consumer_guide.html

Gruteser, M., Schelle, G., Jain, A., Han, R., & Grunwald, D. (2003). Privacy-aware location sensor networks. *Proceedings of The 9th Conference on Hot Topics in Operating Systems* (HOTOS), Berkeley, CA, USA.

Guarda, P., & Zannone, N. (2009). Towards the development of privacy-aware systems. *Information and Software Technology*, *51*(2), 337–350. doi:10.1016/j.infsof.2008.04.004

Gurski, M. (2003). *PETTEP history and future: Making the ISO connection*. Office of the Information and Privacy Commissioner of Ontario, Canada. Retrieved April 8, 2011, from http://bit.ly/i7Ytu7

Hagel, J. III, & Singer, M. (1999). *Net worth* (1st ed.). Harvard Business Press.

Haidar, D. A., Cuppens-Boulahia, N., Cuppens, F., & Debar, H. (2006). An extended RBAC profile of XACML. In *Proceedings of the 3rd ACM Workshop on Secure Web Services (SWS '06)* (pp. 13-22). New York, NY: ACM.

Haley, C. B., Laney, R. C., & Nuseibeh, B. (2004, March 22-24, 2004). *Deriving security requirements from cross-cutting threat descriptions*. Paper presented at the 3rd International Conference on Aspect-Oriented Software Development (AOSD), Lancaster, UK.

Hansen, M. (2009). *Putting privacy pictograms into practice - A European perspective*. Paper presented at the GI Jahrestagung.

Harmon, P. (2004). *The OMG's model driven architecture and BPM*. Retrieved May, 2005, from http://www.bptrends.com/publicationfiles/ 05%2D04%20NL%20MDA%20and%20 BPM%2Epdf

Harn, L., & Lin, H. (1990). A cryptographic keys generation scheme for multilevel data security. *Computers & Security*, *9*, 539–546. doi:10.1016/0167-4048(90)90132-D

Harper, W., & Harris, D. (1975). The application of link analysis to police intelligence. *Human Factors*, *17*(2), 157–164.

Harrison, K., Munro, B., & Spiller, T. (2007). Security through uncertainty. *Elsevier -*. *Network Security*, 4–7. doi:10.1016/S1353-4858(07)70016-8

Hart, E., Davoudani, D., & McEwan, C. (2007). Immunological inspiration for building a new generation of autonomic systems. *In Proceedings of the 1st International Conference on Autonomic Computing and Communication Systems (Autonomics '07)*. ICST (Institute for Computer Sciences, Social-Informatics and Telecommunications Engineering), ICST, (pp. 1-9). Brussels, Belgium.

Haseeb, H., Masood, A., Ahmed, M., & Ghafoor, A. (2009). Integrating GSTRBAC spatial constraints in X-GTRBAC. In *Proceedings of the 6th International Conference on Frontiers of Information Technology (FIT '09)*. New York, NY: ACM.

Hassen, R. H., Bouabaallah, A., Bettahar, H., & Challal, Y. (2007). Key management for content acess control in a hierarchy. *Computer Networks*, *51*, 3197–3219. doi:10.1016/j.comnet.2006.12.011

Health Information Technology for Economic and Clinical Health Act (HITECH). (2009). *Enforcement rule*. Retrieved April 4, 2011 from http://www.hhs.gov/ocr/privacy/hipaa/ administrative/enforcementrule/ hitechenforcementifr.html.

Health Insurance Portability and Accountability Act (HIPAA). (1996). *Privacy and security*. Retrieved April 4, 2011, from http://www.intellimark-it.com/privacysecurity/hipaa.asp

Hengartner, U. (2008). Location privacy based on trusted computing and secure logging. *In Proceedings of the 4th International Conference on Security and Privacy in Communication Netowrks* (pp. 1-8). Istanbul, Turkey, September 22 - 25, 2008: SecureComm '08. New York, NY: ACM.

Herrmann, D. S. (2007). *Complete guide to security and privacy metrics: Measuring regulatory compliance, operational resilience, and ROI* (1st ed.). Auerbach Publications. doi:10.1201/9781420013283

Hilty, M., Basin, D. A., & Pretschner, A. (2005). On obligations. In *Proceedings of the 10th European Symposium on Research in Computer Security (ESORICS '05)*. Berlin, Germany: Springer-Verlag.

HIMSS. (2010). *Electronic health record*. Retrieved October 1, 2010, from http://www.himss.org/ASP/topics_ehr.asp

Hochheiser, H. (2002). The platform for privacy preference as a social protocol: An examination within the U.S. policy context. *ACM Transactions on Internet Technology, 2*(4), 276–306. doi:10.1145/604596.604598

Hong, D., Yuan, M., & Shen, V. Y. (2005). Dynamic privacy management: A plug-in service for the middleware in pervasive computing. In *Proceedings of the 7th International Conference on Human Computer Interaction with Mobile Devices & Services*. Salzburg, Austria.

Hoofnagle, C. (2009). Internalizing identity theft. *UCLA Journal of Law and Technology, 13*(2). Retrieved from http://www.lawtechjournal.com/articles/2009/02_100406_Hoofnagle.pdf

Hsu, C. L., & Wu, T. S. (2003). Cryptanalyses and improvements of two cryptographic key assignment schemes for dynamic access control in a user hierarchy. *Computers & Security, 22*(5), 453–456. doi:10.1016/S0167-4048(03)00514-5

Hsueh, P., Lin, R., Hsiao, J., Zeng, L., Ramakrishnan, S., & Chang, H. (2010). Cloud-based platform for personalization in a wellness management ecosystem: Why, what, and how. *Proceedings of the 6th IEEE International Conference of Collaborative Computing: Networking, Applications, and Worksharing* (CollaborateCom), Chicago, Illinois.

Hu, V. C., Martin, E., Hwang, J., & Xie, T. (2007). Conformance checking of access control policies specified in XACML. *In Proceedings 31st Annual International Computer Software and Applications Conference, COMPSAC 2007*, (pp. 275-280).

Huang, Q., & Shen, C. (2004). A new MLS mandatory policy combining secrecy and integrity implemented in highly classified secure OS. In *Proceedings 7th International Conference on Signal Processing (ICSP '04)*, (pp. 2409-2412).

Huebscher, M. C., & McCann, J. A. (2008). A survey of autonomic computing - Degrees, models, and applications. *ACM Computing Surveys*, Article 7 (August 2008), 28 pages. DOI=10.1145/1380584.1380585 http://doi.acm.org/10.1145/1380584.1380585

Hustinx, P. (2008, April). *EDPS issues policy paper on his role in EU research and technological development*. Press Release. Retrieved April 8, 2011, from http://bit.ly/hKCs5x

Hustinx, P. (2010, March). *Opinion of the European Data Protection Supervisor on promoting trust in the information society by fostering data protection and privacy*. EDPS. Retrieved April 8, 2011, from http://bit.ly/h9qzmP

Hustinx, P. (2010, March). *Press release: EDPS opinion on privacy in the digital age: Privacy by design as a key tool to ensure citizens' trust in ICTs*. EDPS/10/6. Retrieved April 8, 2011, from http://bit.ly/hNJDZy

IBM. (2005). *Research on SPARCLE (Server Privacy ARrchitecture and CapabiLity Enablement) policy workbench*. Retrieved April 8, 2011, from http://bit.ly/hgddlJ

ICD9Data.com. (2009). *Free searchable ICD-9-CM diagnosis codes*. Retrieved October 14, 2010, from http://www.icd9data.com/2009/Volume1/800-999/940-949/944/944.08.htm

ICO. (2006). *Durant Case and its impact on the interpretation of the Data Protection Act 1998*. Information Commissioner's Office, 27 February 2006. Retrieved November 2010 from http://www.ico.gov.uk/upload/documents/library/data_protection/detailed_specialist_guides/the_durant_case_and_its_impact_on_the_interpretation_of_the_data_protection_act.pdf

Identity Theft Resource Center. (2010). *Identity theft: The aftermath 2009*. Retrieved from http://www.idtheftcenter.org/artman2/uploads/1/Aftermath_2009_20100520.pdf

Initiative for Privacy Standardization in Europe (IPSE), European Committee for Standardization (CEN). (2002). *Final report of the EU CEN/ISSS initiative on privacy standardization in Europe*. Retrieved April 8, 2011, from http://bit.ly/hZX7io

INS. (2010). *Identity and access management for networks and services*. Retrieved October 26, 2010, from http://www.etsi.org/website/document/ technologies/leaflets/identity%20and%20 access%20management%20for%20 networks %20and%20services_2010_02.pdf

Institute for Women's Health Research. (2008). *Illinois women's health registry*. Retrieved October 16, 2010, from https://whr.northwestern.edu/

International Conference of Privacy and Data Protection Commissioners (ICPDPC). (2004). *Resolution on a draft ISO privacy framework standard*. Adopted at Wroclaw, Poland, September 2004. Retrieved April 8, 2011, from http://bit.ly/eGMJtB

International Conference of Privacy and Data Protection Commissioners (ICPDPC). (2009). *International standards on the protection of personal data and privacy: The Madrid Resolution*. Adopted at Madrid, Spain, October 2009. Retrieved April 8, 2011, from http://bit.ly/hqKTVA

International Conference of Privacy and Data Protection Commissioners (ICPDPC). (2010). *Adopted resolutions*. Retrieved from http://bit.ly/i1Oo4r.

International Conference of Privacy and Data Protection Commissioners (ICPDPC). (2010). *Privacy by design resolution*. Adopted at Jerusalem, Israel, October 27–29, 2010. Retrieved April 8, 2011, from http://bit.ly/fffv0l

International Telecommunication Union. (1996). *Information technology – Open systems interconnection – Security frameworks for open systems: Access control framework, ITU-T Recommendation ISO/IEC 10181-3*. Retrieved November 29, 2010, from http://webstore.iec.ch/preview/info_isoiec10181-3%7Bed1.0%7Den.pdf

International Telecommunication Union. (2005). *Information technology – Open systems interconnection – The directory: Public-key and attribute certificate frameworks*: *ITU-T recommendation X.509*. Retrieved November 29, 2010, from http://www.itu.int/rec/T-REC-X.509-200508-I

International Working Group on Data Protection in Telecommunications (IWGDPT). (2008). *Report and guidance on privacy in social network services "Rome Memorandum", 675.36.5*. Retrieved April 8, 2011, from http://bit.ly/er5SjW

IPTF. (2010). *Commercial data privacy and innovation in the internet economy: A dynamic policy framework*: The Department of Commerce, Internet Policy Task Force. Retrieved April 2011 from http://www.ntia.doc.gov/reports/2010/IPTF_Privacy_GreenPaper_12162010.pdf

ISO/IEC 15408-1. (2009). *Information technology -- Security techniques -- Evaluation criteria for IT security -- Part 1: Introduction and general model*. Retrieved April 2011, from http://www.commoncriteriaportal.org/files/ccfiles/CCPART1V3.1R3.pdf, Retrieved

ISO-IEC. (1992). Coded representation of picture and audio information. *International Standard ISO-IEC/JTC1/SC29/WG11*, MPEG Test Model 2.

ISO-IEC. (1992). Coding of moving pictures and associated audio for digital storage media up to 1.5 Mbit/s Part 2, video. *International Standard ISO-IEC/JTC1/SC29/WG11*, DIS11172-1.

Iyengar, V. (2002). Transforming data to satisfy privacy constraints. In *Proceedings of the 8th ACM SIGKDD International Conference on Knowledge Discovery and Data Mining*, 2002.

Jacobson, I., Booch, G., & Rumbaugh, J. (1999). *The unified software development process*.

Javelin Strategy and Research. (n.d.). *Data breach notifications: Victims face four times higher risk of fraud*. Retrieved from http://www.javelinstrategy.com/lp/Data-BreachesBrochure.html

Jensen, C., Potts, C., & Jensen, C. (2005). Privacy practices of internet users: Self-reports versus observed behavior. *International Journal of Human-Computer Studies, 63*(1-2), 203–227. doi:10.1016/j.ijhcs.2005.04.019

Jeong, M., & Kim, J. a. (2004). A flexible database security system using multiple access control policies. *IEEE International Conference on Systsem, Man, and Cybernetics* (pp. 5013-5018). IEEE.

Johnson, S. E., Sterritt, R., Hanna, E., & O'Hagan, P. (2007). Reflex autonomicity in an agent-based security system: The autonomic access control system. *4th IEEE International Workshop on Engineering Autonomic and Autonomous Systems (EASe '07)*, (pp. 68-78).

Jonker, C. M., Robu, V., & Treur, J. (2007). An agent architecture for multi-attribute negotiation using incomplete preference information. *Autonomous Agents and Multi-Agent Systems*, 221–252. doi:10.1007/s10458-006-9009-y

Joshi, J. B. D., Bertino, E., Latif, U., & Ghafoo, A. (2005). A generalized temporal role-based access control model. [Los Alamitos, CA: IEEE Computer Society.]. *Journal of IEEE Transactions on Knowledge and Data Engineering*, *15*, 4–23. doi:10.1109/TKDE.2005.1

J-W., B., & Li, N. (2008). Purpose based access control for privacy protection in relational database systems. *The VLDB Journal*, *17*, 603–619. doi:10.1007/s00778-006-0023-0

Kayem, A. (2008). *Adaptive cryptographic access control for dynamic data sharing environments*. Kingston, Canada: Queen's University.

Kayem, A., Martin, P., & Akl, S. (2010). Enhancing identity trust in cryptographic key management systems for dynamic environments. *Security and Communication Networks*, *4*. Retrieved from http://onlinelibrary.wiley.com/doi/10.1002 /sec.164/abstract

Kayem, A., Martin, P., Akl, S., & Powley, W. (2008). A framework for self-protecting cryptographic key management. In *Proceedings, 2nd IEEE International Conference on Self-Adaptive and Self-Organizing Systems*, (pp. 191-200). Venice, Italy.

Kelley, P. G., et al. (2009). *A nutrition label for privacy*. Paper presented at the 5th Symposium on Usable Privacy and Security.

Kephart, J. O., & Chess, D. M. (2003). The vision of autonomic computing. *IEEE Computer*, *36*(1), 41–50. doi:10.1109/MC.2003.1160055

Kephart, J. O., & Chess, D. M. (2005). Research challenges of autonomic computing. In *Proceedings 27th International Conference on Software Engineering*, (pp. 15-22). St. Louis, MO, USA.

Kim, J., & Winkler, W. (1997). *Masking microdata files*. Technical Report of Bureau of the Census. Retrieved April 4, 2011, from http://www.census.gov/srd/papers/pdf/rr97-3.pdf

Kissner, L., & Song, D. (2005). Privacy-preserving set operations. In *Proceedings of CRYPTO*, (pp. 241-257).

Knuth, D. E. (1981). *The art of computer programming* (seminumerical algorithms, 2nd ed., vol. 2). Reading, MA: Addison Wesley.

Kobsa, A., & Teltzrow, M. (2005). *Contextualized communication of privacy practices and personalization benefits: Impacts on users' data sharing and purchase behavior. Privacy Enhancing Technologies* (Vol. 3424, pp. 329–343). Berlin, Germany: Springer.

Kolata, G. (2010, August 12). Rare sharing of data leads to progress on Alzheimer's. *New York Times*.

Kolesnikov, V., & Schneider, T. (2008). A practical universal circuit construction and secure evaluation of private functions. In *Proceedings of the 12th International Conference on Financial Cryptography and Data Security*, (pp. 83-97).

Kolter, J., Kernchen, T., & Pernul, G. (2010). Collaborative privacy management. *Computers & Security*, *29*(5), 580–591..doi:10.1016/j.cose.2009.12.007

Konrad, W. (2009, June 12). Medical problems could include identity theft. *New York Times*. Retrieved from http://www.nytimes.com/2009/06/13/health /13patient.html

Koutsakis, P., Psychis, S., & Paterakis, M. (2005). Integrated wireless access for videoconference from MPEG-4 and H.263 video coders with voice, E-mail, and web traffic. *IEEE Transactions on Vehicular Technology*, *54*(5), 1863–1874. doi:10.1109/TVT.2005.853460

Krumm, J. (2009). A survey of computational location privacy. *Personal and Ubiquitous Computing*, *13*(6), 391–399. doi:10.1007/s00779-008-0212-5

Kuang, T. P., & Ibrahim, H. (2009). Security privacy access control policy integration and conflict reconciliation in health care organizations collaborations. *International Conference on Information Integration and Web-based Applications & Services* (pp. 750-754). Kuala Lumpur, Malaysia: ACM.

Kuo, F., Shen, V., Chen, T., & Lai, F. (1999). Cryptographic key assignment scheme for dynamic access control in a user hierarchy. *IEE Proceedings. Computers and Digital Techniques*, *146*(5), 235–240. doi:10.1049/ip-cdt:19990311

Lampson, B. W. (1973). A not on the confinement problem. *Communications of the ACM, 16*(10), 613–615. doi:10.1145/362375.362389

Lampson, B. W. (2004). Computer security in the real world. *IEEE Computer, 37*(6), 37–46. doi:10.1109/MC.2004.17

Langheinrich, M. (2009). A survey of RFID privacy approaches. *Journal of Personal Ubiquitous Computing, 13*(6), 413–421. doi:10.1007/s00779-008-0213-4

Lazzarotti, J. (2010). Does your "cyber" or "data breach" insurance cover what you think it does? *Workplace Privacy, Data Management & Security Report*. Retrieved from http://www.workplaceprivacyreport.com/2010/06/articles/information-risk-1/does-your-cyber-or-data-breach-insurance-cover-what-you-think-it-does/

Lecue, F., Delteil, A., & Leger, A. (2008). Towards the composition of stateful and independent Semantic Web services. *SAC '08: In Proceedings of the 2008 ACM Symposium on Applied Computing* (pp. 2279-2285). Fortaleza, Brazil: ACM.

Leenes, R., Schallaböck, J., & Hansen, H. (2008). *PRIME white paper*. Retrieved October 26, 2010, from https://www.prime-project.eu/prime_products/whitepaper/PRIME-Whitepaper-V3.pdf

LeFevre, K., Agrawal, R., Ercegovac, V., Ramakrishnan, R., Xu, Y., & DeWitt, D. J. (2004). Limiting disclosure in Hippocratic databases. In *Proceedings of the 30th International Conference on Very Large Databases (VLDB 2004)*. Toronto, Canada.

LeFevre, K., DeWitt, D., & Ramakrishnan, R. (2005). *Incognito: Efficient full-domain k-anonymity*. In ACM SIGMOD International Conference on Management of Data, June 2005.

LeFevre, K., DeWitt, D. J., & Ramakrishnan, R. (2006). Mondrian multidimensional k-anonymity. In *Proceedings of ICDE* (pp. 21-28).

Lerner, R. M. (2006). Amazon Web services. *Linux Journal, 143*, 20–24.

Levitin, A. (2003). *Introduction to the design and analysis of algorithms. Pearson*. Addison-Wesley.

Levy, S. E., & Gutwin, C. (2005). *Improving understanding of website privacy policies with fine-grained policy anchors*. Paper presented at the 14th International Conference on World Wide Web.

Li, N., Li, T., & Venkatasubramanian, S. (2007). t-Closeness: Privacy beyond k-anonymity and l-diversity. *ICDE, 2007*, 106–115.

Li, H., Ahn, D., & Hung, P. C. (2004). Algorithms for automated negotiations and their applications in information privacy. In *Proceedings IEEE International Conference* (pp. 255-262). e-Commerce Technology, 2004. CEC 2004.

Li, X., Yang, Y., Gouda, M., & Lam, S. (1999). Batch rekeying for secure group communications. *WWW10, 99*(7), 525-534.

Lieber, R. (2008, May 24). Heading off new account fraud. *New York Times*. Retrieved from http://www.nytimes.com/2008/05/24/business/yourmoney/24moneyside.html

Lieber, R. (2009, November 2). A free credit score followed by a monthly bill. *New York Times*. Retrieved from http://www.nytimes.com/2009/11/03/your-money/credit-scores/03scores.html?_r=1, Maine Bureau of Financial Institutions. (2008). *Main data breach study*. Retrieved from http://www.maine.gov/pfr/financialinstitutions/reports/pdf/DataBreachStudy.pdf

Liew, P., Kontogiannis, P., & Tong, T. (2004). *A framework for business model driven development*. Paper presented at the 12 International Workshop on Software Technology and Engineering Practice (STEP).

Lin, T. (2006). Managing information flows on discretionary access control models. *2006 IEEE International Conference on Systems, Man., and Cybernetics*, (pp. 4759-4762).

Lin, T. Y. (2000). Chinese Wall security model and conflict analysis. *24th IEEE Computer Society International Computer Software and Applications Conference (COMPSAC 2000)*, (pp. 122-127). Taipei, Taiwan.

Lindell, Y., & Pinkas, B. (2000). Privacy preserving data mining. *Proceedings of the Advances in Cryptology* (pp. 20-24), *LNCS 1880*. Springer-Verlag.

LinkedIn. (2011). *Relationships matter*. LinkedIn. Retrieved April, 2011, from http://www.linkedin.com/

Lioudakis, G. V. (2007). A middleware architecture for privacy protection. *Computer Networks, 51*(16), 4679–4696. doi:10.1016/j.comnet.2007.06.010

Lioudakis, G. V., Gaudino, F., Boschi, E., Bianchi, G., Kaklamani, D. I., & Venieris, I. S. (2010). Legislation-aware privacy protection in passive network monitoring. In Portela, I. M., & Cruz-Cunha, M. M. (Eds.), *Information communication technology law, protection and access rights: Global approaches and issues*. New York, NY: IGI Global. doi:10.4018/978-1-61520-975-0.ch022

Lioudakis, G. V., Gogoulos, F., Antonakopoulou, A., Kaklamani, D. I., & Venieris, I. S. (2009). Privacy protection in passive network monitoring: an access control approach. In *Proceedings of the IEEE 23rd International Conference on Advanced Information Networking and Applications (AINA-09)* (pp. 109-116). Washington, DC: IEEE Computer Society.

Lischka, M., Endo, Y., & Sanchez, M. (2009, November). *Deductive policies with XACML*. Paper presented at the Workshop on Secure Web Services, co-located with 16th ACM Conference on Computer and Communications Security (CCS-16), Chicago, Illinois, USA.

Lischka, M., Endo, Y., Torroglosa, E., Perez, A., & Gomez-Skarmeta, A. F. (2009, November). *Towards standardization of distributed access control*. Presented at the W3C Workshop on Access Control Application Scenarios, Luxembourg.

List, B., & Korherr, B. (2005). *A UML 2 profile for business process modelling*. Paper presented at the 1st International Workshop on Best Practices of UML (BP-UML) at ER-Conference, Klagenfurt, Austria.

Liu, X., & Eskicioglu, A. (2003). *Selective encryption of multimedia content in distributed networks: Challenges and new directions. IASTED Communications, Internet & Information Technology*. CIIT.

Liu, K., & Terzi, E. (2009). A framework for computing the privacy scores of users in online social networks. *Proceedings of the IEEE International Conference on Data Mining* (ICDM). Miami, Florida. USA.

Liu, Y., & Chen, X. (2004). A new information security model based on BLP Model and BiBA Model. *In Proceedings 7th International Conference on Signal Processing (ICSP'04)*, (pp. 2643-2646).

Lodderstedt, T., Basin, D., & Doser, J. (2002). *SecureUML: A UML-based modeling language for model-driven security*. Paper presented at the UML, 5th International Conference, Dresden, Germany.

London Economics. (2010). *Study on the economic benefits of privacy-enhancing technologies*. Final Report to The European Commission, DG Justice, Freedom and Security. Retrieved April 8, 2011, from http://bit.ly/heQNQT

Loong, L. H. (2009). Preparing for an aging population - The Singapore *experience. The Journal: AARP International*, (Winter), 12-17. Retrieved April 4, 2011, from http://www.nus.edu.sg/nec/InnoAge/ documents/ AARPjournalwinter09_PMLee.pdf

Lopez, G., Canovas, O., Gomez-Skarmeta, A. F., & Sanchez, M. (2008). A proposal for extending the eduroam infrastructure with authorization mechanisms. *Computer Standards & Interfaces, 30*(6), 418–423. doi:10.1016/j.csi.2008.03.010

Lopez, G., Reverte, O. C., Gomez-Skarmeta, A. F., & Girao, J. (2009). A swift take on identity management. *IEEE Computer, 42*(5), 58–65.

Lopez, J., Montenegro, J. A., Vivas, J. L., Okamoto, E., & Dawson, E. (2005). Specification and design of advanced authentication and authorization services. *Computer Standards & Interfaces, 27*(5), 467–478. doi:10.1016/j.csi.2005.01.005

Loukides, G., & Shao, J. (2008). Data utility and privacy protection trade-off in k-anonymisation. *Proceedings of the First International EDBT Workshop on Privacy and Anonymity in the Information Society* (PAIS), Nantes, France.

Lysyanskaya, A., Rivest, R. L., Sahai, A., & Wolf, S. (2000). Pseudonym systems. *Selected Areas in Cryptography -. Lecture Notes in Computer Science, 1758*, 184–199. doi:10.1007/3-540-46513-8_14

Machanavajjhala, A., Gehrke, J., Kifer, D., & Venkitasubramaniam, M. (2006). l-diversity: Privacy beyond k-anonymity. In *Proc. 22nd Intnl. Conf. Data Engg.* (ICDE), (p. 24).

Mackey, S. (2000). Towards a definition of wellness. *Journal of Holistic Nursing Practice, 7*(2), 34–38.

Mackinnon, S. J., Taylor, P. D., Meijer, H., & Akl, S. G. (1985). An optimal algorithm for assigning cryptographic keys to control access in a hierarchy. *IEEE Transactions on Computers, 34*(9), 797–802. doi:10.1109/TC.1985.1676635

Maes, S., Verhoeven, C., Kittel, F., & Scholten, H. (1998). Effects of a Dutch work-site wellness-health program: The Brabantia Project. *American Journal of Public Health, 88*(7), 1037–1041. doi:10.2105/AJPH.88.7.1037

Malkhi, D. Nisan, N., Pinkas, B., & Sella, Y. (2004). Fairplay - A secure two-party computation system. In *Proceedings of the 13th USENIX Security Symposium,* (pp. 287-302).

Maña, A., Ray, D., Sánchez, F., & Yagüe, M. I. (2004, Septiembre 2004). *Integrando la ingeniería de seguridad en un proceso de ingeniería software.* Paper presented at the VIII Reunión Española de Criptología y Seguridad de la Información, RECSI, Madrid. España.

Manasdeep, A. S., Jolly, D. S., Singh, A. K., Srivastava, M. A., & Singh, M. S. (2010). A proposed model for data privacy providing legal protection by e-court. *International Journal of Engineering Science and Technology, 2*(4), 649–657.

March, S. T., & Smith, G. F. (1995). Design and natural science research on information technology. *Decision Support Systems, 15*(4), 251–266. doi:10.1016/0167-9236(94)00041-2

Martin, K., & Plataniotis, K. N. (2008, August). Privacy protected surveillance using secure visual object coding. *IEEE Transactions on Circuits & Systems for Video Technology: Special Issue on Video Surveillance, 18*(8), 1152–1162. doi:10.1109/TCSVT.2008.927110

Marx, R., Fhom, H. S., Scheuermann, D., Bayarou, K. M., & Perez, A. (2010). *Increasing security and privacy in user-centric identity management: The IdM card approach.* Presented at the First International Workshop on Securing Information in Distributed Environments and Ubiquitous Systems (SIDEUS 2010), Fukuoka, Japan.

Masoumzadeh, A., & Joshi, J. B. D. (2008). PuRBAC: Purpose-aware role-based access control. In *Proceedings of the On the Move to Meaningful Internet Systems: OTM 2008* (LNCS 5332). Berlin, Germany: Springer.

Massacci, F., Mylopoulos, J., & Zannone, N. (2006). Hierarchical Hippocratic databases with minimal disclosure for virtual organizations. [New York, NY: Springer-Verlag.]. *The International Journal on Very Large Data Bases, 15*(4), 370–387. doi:10.1007/s00778-006-0009-y

Massacci, F., Mylopoulos, J., & Zannone, N. (2005). Minimal disclosure in hierarchical Hippocratic databases with delegation. In *Proceedings of the 10th European Symposium on Research in Computer Security (ESORICS 2005).* Milan, Italy.

Massey, A. K., Otto, P. N., Hayward, L. J., & Antón, A. I. (2009). Evaluating existing security and privacy requirements for legal compliance. *Requirements Engineering, 15*(1), 119–137. doi:10.1007/s00766-009-0089-5

Maximilien, E. M., Grandison, T., Sun, T., Richardson, D., Guo, S., & Liu, K. (2009). Enabling privacy as a fundamental construct for social networks. *Proceedings of the Workshop on Security and Privacy in Online Social Networking* (SPOSN), Vancouver, Canada.

McKeay, M. (2008). *Look to the acquiring banks, not the PCI Security Council.* May 30. Retrieved from http://www.mckeay.net/2008/05/30/look-to-the-acquiring-banks-not-the-pci-security-council/

McLean, J. (1990). The specification and modeling of computer security. *IEEE Computer, 23*(1), 9–16. doi:10.1109/2.48795

Menezes, J., van Oorschot, P. C., & Vanstone, S. A. (1997). *Handbook of applied cryptography.* CRC Press.

Mens, T., & Van Gorp, P. (2006). A taxonomy of model transformation. *Electronic Notes in Theoretical Computer Science, 152,* 125–142. doi:10.1016/j.entcs.2005.10.021

Meyerson, A., & Williams, R. (2004). On the complexity of optimal k-anonymity. In *Proc. of the 23rd ACM-SIGMOD-SIGACT-SIGART Symposium on the Principles of Database Systems,* (pp. 223-228). Paris, France, 2004.

Meziane, H., & Benbernou, S. (2010). A dynamic privacy model for Web Services. *Computer Standards & Interfaces, 32,* 288–304. doi:10.1016/j.csi.2010.02.001

Microsoft Corporation. (2006). *A technical reference for the information card profile V1.0*. Retrieved October 26, 2010, from http://download.microsoft.com/download/2/7/c/27c16ebb-bf83-4abd-8002-21fa111ba7ac/infocard-profile-v1-techref.pdf

Mie, X.-W., Feng, D.-G., Che, J.-J., & Wang, X.-P. (2006). Design and implementation of security operating system based on trusted computing. *International Conference on Machine Learning and Cybernetics*, (pp. 2776-2781).

Mills, D., & Martin, J. (Eds.). & Kasch, W. (2010). *Network time protocol version 4: Protocol and algorithms specification*. RFC5905, Internet Engineering Task Force (IETF). Retrieved March 15, 2011, from http://datatracker.ietf.org/doc/rfc5905/

Ministerio de Administraciones Públicas. (2005). *MAGERIT – versión 2. Metodología de análisis y gestión de riesgos de los sistemas de información*. Retrieved June 15, 2005, from http://www.csi.map.es/csi/pg5m20.htm

Minnesota Department of Health. (2010, July 22). *Disclosure to public health under the HIPAA privacy rule*. Retrieved October 16, 2010, from http://www.health.state.mn.us/divs/idepc/ immunize/registry/hipaa.html

Mokbel, M. F. (2007). Privacy in location-based services: State-of-the-art and research directions. *Proceedings of The International Conference On Mobile Data Management*, Mannheim, Germany.

Monahan, T. (2009). Identity theft vulnerability: Neoliberal governance through crime construction. *Theoretical Criminology, 13*(2), 155. doi:10.1177/1362480609102877

Moore, G. C., & Benbasat, I. (1991). Development of an instrument to measure the perceptions of adopting an information technology innovation. *Information Systems Research, 2*(3), 192–222. doi:10.1287/isre.2.3.192

Moreno, A., Sanchez, D., & Isern, D. (2003). Security measures in a medical multi-agent system. *Frontiers in Artificial Intelligence and Applications, 100*, 244–255.

Mueller, S. G., Weiner, M. W., Thal, L. J., Petersen, R. C., Jack, C., & Jagust, W. (2005, November). The Alzheimer's disease neuroimaging initiative. *Neuroimaging Clinics of North America, 15*(4), 869–877. doi:10.1016/j.nic.2005.09.008

Murdoch, S. J., Drimer, S., Anderson, R., & Bond, M. (2009). Chip and PIN is broken. *Proceedings of the 2010 IEEE Symposium on Security and Privacy*, (pp. 433-446).

Najera, R. (2009, November 4). *Records show case of dystonia is psychogenic and not related to flu vaccine*. Retrieved October 13, 2010, from http://www.examiner.com/disease-prevention-in-baltimore/records-show-case-of-dystonia-is-psychogenic-and-not-related-to-flu-vaccine

Nakamura, D. (2010). *Fat in Japan? You're breaking the law*. Retrieved April 4, 2011, from http://www.globalpost.com/dispatch/japan/091109/fat-japan-youre-breaking-the-law

Nalebuff, B., & Brandenburger, A. (1997). Co-opetition: Competitive and cooperative business strategies for the digital economy. *Strategy and Leadership, 25*(6), 28–35. doi:10.1108/eb054655

Naraine, R. (2007). Sensitive government e-mails leak through Tor exit nodes. *ZDNet*. Retrieved April 8, 2011, from http://zd.net/f68r72

National Computer Security Center – NCSC. (1987). *A guide to understanding discretionary access control in trusted system*. Report NSCD-TG-003 Version1.

National Health Statistics Group. (2010, October 28). *National health expenditure data*. Retrieved November 6, 2010, from http://www.cms.gov/NationalHealthExpend-Data /02_NationalHealthAccountsHistorical.asp

Nazir, A., Raza, S., & Chuah, C.-N. (2008). Unveiling Facebook: A measurement study of social network based applications. *IMC '08: Proceedings of the 8th ACM SIGCOMM conference on Internet measurement* (pp. 43-56). Vouliagmeni, Greece: ACM.

Nehf, J. P. (2007). Shopping for privacy on the Internet. *The Journal of Consumer Affairs, 41*(2), 351–375.

NEMA. (2009). *The DICOM standard*. Retrieved October 14, 2010, from ftp://medical.nema.org/medical/dicom/2009/

Nerenberg, L. (2006). *Preying on elders: A session on financial abuse*. Joint Conference of the National Council on the Aging and the American Society on Aging. March 15. Retrieved from http://www.lisanerenberg.com/media/preyingOnElders.pdf

Ni, Q., Bertino, E., Lobo, J., Brodie, C., Karat, C. M., Karat, J., & Trombetta, A. (2010). Privacy-aware role-based access control. [New York, NY: ACM.]. *Journal of ACM Transactions Information System Security*, *13*(3), 1–31. doi:10.1145/1805974.1805980

NIST Smart Grid Interoperability Panel – Cyber Security Working Group. (2010). *NIST guidelines for smart grid cyber security*. NISTIR 7628. Retrieved April 8, 2011, from http://1.usa.gov/dlAJhx

Norris, C., McCahill, M., & Wood, D. (2004). The growth of CCTV: A global perspective on the inter-national diffusion of video surveillance in publicly accessible space. *Surveillance & Society. CCTV Special Issue*, *2*(2/3), 376–395.

Novella, S. (2009, October 30). *The dystonia flu shot case*. Retrieved October 12, 2010, from http://theness.com/neurologicablog/?p=1152

NTIA. (2010). Information privacy and innovation in the internet economy. *Federal Register*. Retrieved April 2011 from http://www.federalregister.gov/articles/2010/12/21/2010-31971/information-privacy-and-innovation-in-the-internet-economy

Nurmi, D., Wolski, R., Grzegorczyk, C., Obertelli, G., Soman, S., Youseff, L., & Zagorodnov, D. (2008). The eucalyptus open-source cloud-computing system. *Proceedings of Cloud Computing and Applications* (CCA), Chicago, Illinois, USA. Retrieved April 4, 2011, from http://www.cca08.org/papers/Paper32-Daniel-Nurmi.pdf

Nyre, Å. A., Bernsmed, K., Bøe, S., & Pedersen, S. (2011). A server-side approach to privacy policy matching. Paper presented at the Sixth International Conference on Availability, Reliability and Security.

Nystedt, D. (2009).Taiwan to host IBM's first joint healthcare IT research unit. *PC World*. Retrieved April 4, 2011, from http://www.pcworld.com/article/185193/taiwan_to_host_ibms_first_joint_healthcare_it_research_unit.html

O.J. C 128/33. (2009). *Second opinion of the European Data Protection Supervisor on the review of Directive 2002/58/EC concerning the processing of personal data and the protection of privacy in the electronic communications sector (Directive on privacy and electronic communications).*

Object Management Group. (2003). *MDA guide version 1.0.1*. Retrieved from http://www.omg.org/docs/omg/03-06-01.pdf

Object Management Group. (2005a). *OCL 2.0 Specification, Version 2.0*. Retrieved from http://www.omg.org/docs/ptc/05-06-06.pdf

Object Management Group. (2005b). *Unified modeling language: Superstructure*. Retrieved from http://www.omg.org/docs/formal/05-07-04.pdf

Odlyzko, A. (2003). *Privacy, economics, and price discrimination on the Internet*. Paper presented at the 5th International Conference on Electronic Commerce.

Odlyzko, A. (2007). *Privacy and the clandestine evolution of e-commerce*. Paper presented at the Proceedings of the Ninth International Conference on Electronic Commerce Out-Law. (2009). *Privacy policy tool failed because of browser rejection, says W3C lawyer*. Retrieved March, 2011, from http://www.out-law.com/page-10437

Office of Civil Rights. (2008, December 15). *Personal health records and the HIPAA privacy rule*. Retrieved September 6, 2010, from http://www.hhs.gov/ocr/privacy/hipaa/ understanding/special/healthit/phrs.pdf

Office of Civil Rights. (2008, May 7). *Summary of the HIPAA privacy rule*. Retrieved October 18, 2010, from http://www.hhs.gov/ocr/privacy/hipaa/ understanding/summary/index.html

Office of the Information and Privacy Commissioner of Ontario. Canada & The Netherlands Data Protection Authority. (1995). *Privacy-enhancing technologies: The path to anonymity* (volume I). Office of the Information and Privacy Commissioner of Ontario, Canada. Retrieved April 8, 2011, from http://bit.ly/fw55Dj

Office of the Information and Privacy Commissioner of Ontario. Canada & The Netherlands Data Protection Authority. (1995). *Privacy-enhancing technologies: The path to anonymity,* (volume II). Office of the Information and Privacy Commissioner of Ontario, Canada. Retrieved April 8, 2011, from http://bit.ly/ihllwd

Office of the Information and Privacy Commissioner of Ontario. Canada & Advanced Card Technology Association of Canada (ACTA). (1997). *Smart, optical and other advanced cards: How to do a privacy assessment.* Office of the Information and Privacy Commissioner of Ontario, Canada. Retrieved April 8, 2011, from http://bit.ly/hoxPKL

Office of the Information and Privacy Commissioner of Ontario. Canada & The Netherlands Data Protection Authority. (1999). *Intelligent software agents, turning a privacy threat into a privacy protector.* Office of the Information and Privacy Commissioner of Ontario, Canada. Retrieved April 8, 2011, from http://bit.ly/hNrINH

Office of the Information and Privacy Commissioner of Ontario. Canada, Guardent, & PriceWaterHouseCoopers. (2001). *Privacy diagnostic tool workbook and FAQ.* Office of the Information and Privacy Commissioner of Ontario, Canada. Retrieved April 8, 2011, from http://bit.ly/gAhbsN

Office of the Information and Privacy Commissioner of Ontario. Canada. (2002). *Seven essential steps for designing privacy into technology.* Office of the Information and Privacy Commissioner of Ontario, Canada. Retrieved April 8, 2011, from http://bit.ly/fxt4oF

Office of the Information and Privacy Commissioner of Ontario. Canada & Canadian Marketing Association (CMA). (2004). *Incorporating privacy into marketing and customer relationship management.* Office of the Information and Privacy Commissioner of Ontario, Canada. Retrieved April 8, 2011, from http://bit.ly/gqELYD

Office of the Information and Privacy Commissioner of Ontario. Canada & The Ponemon Institute. (2004). *Cross-national study of Canadian and U.S. corporate privacy practices.* Office of the Information and Privacy Commissioner of Ontario, Canada. Retrieved April 8, 2011, from http://bit.ly/hZQxxs

Office of the Information and Privacy Commissioner of Ontario. Canada & IBM/Tivoli. (2005). *EPAL translation of the Freedom of Information and Protection of Privacy Act.* Office of the Information and Privacy Commissioner of Ontario, Canada. Retrieved April 8, 2011, from http://bit.ly/dGw5P9

Office of the Information and Privacy Commissioner of Ontario. Canada & Advanced Card Technology Association of Canada (ACTA). (2007). *Contactless smart card applications: Design tool and privacy impact assessment.* Office of the Information and Privacy Commissioner of Ontario, Canada. Retrieved April 8, 2011, from http://bit.ly/fy3k5b

Office of the Information and Privacy Commissioner of Ontario. Canada & Hewlett-Packard. (2008). *RFID and privacy: Guidance for health-care providers.* Office of the Information and Privacy Commissioner of Ontario, Canada. Retrieved April 8, 2011, from http://bit.ly/hN6KY3

Office of the Information and Privacy Commissioner of Ontario. Canada & Liberty Alliance. (2009). *The new federated privacy impact assessment (F-PIA) building privacy and trust-enabled federation.* Office of the Information and Privacy Commissioner of Ontario, Canada. Retrieved April 8, 2011, from http://bit.ly/f89UMs

Office of the Information and Privacy Commissioner of Ontario. Canada & Ontario Lottery Gaming Corporation & YMCA Canada. (2009). *Privacy risk management: Building privacy protection into a risk management framework to ensure that privacy risks are managed by default.* Office of the Information and Privacy Commissioner of Ontario, Canada. Retrieved April 8, 2011, from http://bit.ly/gGMA4r

Office of the Information and Privacy Commissioner of Ontario. Canada & NEC Computing. (2010), *Modelling cloud computing architecture without compromising privacy: A privacy by design approach.* Office of the Information and Privacy Commissioner of Ontario, Canada. Retrieved April 8, 2011, from http://bit.ly/fqnA8v

Office of the Information and Privacy Commissioner of Ontario. Canada & Nymity. (2010). *A pragmatic approach to privacy risk optimization: Privacy by design for business practices.* Office of the Privacy Commissioner of Ontario, Canada. Retrieved April 8, 2011, from http://bit.ly/hl0ws8

Office of the Privacy Commissioner of Australia (OPCA). (2010). *Privacy impact assessments (PIA) guide.* Retrieved April 8, 2011, from http://bit.ly/hRQu0a

Office of the Privacy Commissioner of Canada (OPCC). (2004). *A guide for businesses and organizations: Your privacy responsibilities.* Office of the Privacy Commissioner of Canada. Retrieved April 8, 2011, from http://bit.ly/fRKncL

Office of the Privacy Commissioner of Canada (OPCC). (2007). *Fact sheet on PIAs.* Office of the Privacy Commissioner of Canada. Retrieved April 8, 2011, from http://bit.ly/dTZ8Aj

Office of the Privacy Commissioner of Canada (OPCC). (2010). *Privacy, trust and innovation – Building Canada's digital advantage.* Submission to the Digital Economy Consultation, Office of the Privacy Commissioner of Canada. Retrieved April 8, 2011, from http://bit.ly/gJPihD

Ohm, P. (2010). Broken promises of privacy: Responding to the surprising failure of anonymization. *UCLA Law Review. University of California, Los Angeles. School of Law, 57,* 1701–1776.

Organization for Economic Co-operation and Development – OECD. (1980). *Guidelines on the protection of privacy and transborder flows of personal data.* Retrieved November 29, 2010, from http://www.oecd.org/document/18/0,3343,en_2649_34255_1815186_1_1_1_1,00.html

Organization for the Advancement of Structured Information Standards – OASIS. (2004). *OASIS eXtensible access control markup language (XACML) TC.* Retrieved November 29, 2010, from http://www.oasis-open.org/committees/xacml/

Organization for the Advancement of Structured Information Standards – OASIS. (2004). *OASIS privacy policy profile of XACML v2.0.* Retrieved November 29, 2010, from www.oasis-open.org/committees/access-control

Osborn, S. (2002). Integrating role graphs: A tool for security integration. *Data & Knowledge Engineering, 43,* 317–333. doi:10.1016/S0169-023X(02)00130-1

Oxford English Dictionary. (2010.). *Privacy.* Retrieved March 15, 2011, from http://www.askoxford.com

Ozminkowski, R. J., Ling, D., Goetzel, R. Z., Bruno, J. A., Rutter, K. R., Isaac, F., & Wang, S. (2002). Long-term impact of Johnson & Johnson's health & wellness program on health care utilization and expenditures. *Journal of Occupational and Environmental Medicine, 44*(1), 21–29. doi:10.1097/00043764-200201000-00005

Ozturk, C., Zhang, Y., & Trappe, W. (2004). Source-location privacy in energy-constrained sensor network routing. *Proceedings of The 2nd ACM Workshop on Security of Ad Hoc and Sensor Networks* (pp. 88-93). New York, NY, USA.

P802.1X/D11. (2001). *Standard for port based network access control.* LAN MAN Standards Committee of the IEEE Computer Society.

Paillier, P. (1999). Public-key cryptosystems based on composite degree residuosity classes. In *Proceedings of EUROCRYPT,* (pp. 223-238).

Palen, L., & Dourish, P. (2003). Unpacking privacy for a networked world. In *Proceedings of the ACM Special Interest Group on Computer-Human Interaction (SIGCHI) Conference on Human Factors in Computing Systems,* Florida, USA.

Park, J. S., Chen, M. S., & Yu, P. S. (1995). An effective hash-based algorithm for mining association rules. *Proceedings of the 1995 ACM SIGMOD International Conference on Management of Data* (pp. 175-186).

Pauley, W. A. (2010). Cloud provider transparency – An empirical evaluation. *IEEE Security and Privacy,* November-December 2010, 32-38.

Pearson, S., Shen, Y., & Mowbray, M. (2009). A privacy manager for cloud computing. *Lecture Notes in Computer Science, 5931,* 90–106. doi:10.1007/978-3-642-10665-1_9

Pearson, S. (2009). Taking account of privacy when designing cloud computing services. *Proceedings of the ICSE Workshop on Software Engineering Challenges of Cloud Computing* (pp. 44-52).

Peffers, K., Tuunanen, T., Rothenberger, M. A., & Chatterjee, S. (2007). A design science research methodology for information systems research. *Journal of Management Information Systems, 24*(3), 45–77. doi:10.2753/MIS0742-1222240302

Pettersson, J. S., et al. (2005). *Making PRIME usable.* Paper presented at the Symposium on Usable Privacy and Security.

Pfleeger, C. P. (1997). *Security in computing.* New Jersey, USA: Prentice-Hall PTR.

Pfleeger, C. P., & Pfleeger, S. L. (2003). *Security in computing.* New Jersey: Pearson Education, Prentice Hall.

Podesser, M., Schmidt, H., & Uhl, A. (2002). Selective bitplane encryption for secure transmission of image data in mobile environments. In CD-ROM *Proceedings of the 5th IEEE Nordic Signal Processing Symposium (NORSIG 2002),* Tromso-Trondheim, Norway.

Pohlig, S., & Hellman, M. (1978). An improved algorithm for computing logarithms over GF(p) and its cryptographic significance. *IEEE Transactions on Information Theory, 24,* 106–110. doi:10.1109/TIT.1978.1055817

Polat, H., & Du, W. (2003). Privacy-preserving collaborative filtering using randomized perturbation techniques. In *Proceedings of the 3rd IEEE International Conference on Data Mining,* (pp. 625-628).

Pollach, I. (2007). What's wrong with online privacy policies? *Communications of the ACM, 50*(9), 103–108. doi:10.1145/1284621.1284627

Ponemon, L. (2000). *Privacy risk management.* Long Beach, CA, USA: Presentation for The National Council of Higher Education Loan Programs.

Ponemon Institute. (2009). *Fourth annual US cost of data breach study: Benchmark study of companies.* Retrieved from http://www.ponemon.org/local/upload/fckjail / generalcontent/18/file/2008-2009\%20US\%20Cost\%20 of\%20Data\%20Breach\%20Report\%20Final.pdf

Ponemon Institute. (2010). *Benchmark study on patient privacy and data security.* November 9, 2010.

Ponemon Institute. (2011). *2010 annual study: U.S. cost of a data breach.* March.

Ponemon, L. (2005). *What do data breaches cost companies? Beyond dollars, customers are lost.* Ponemon Institute Report.

Ponemon, L. (2008). *Consumers' report card on data breach notification.* Ponemon Institute, April 15. Retrieved from http://www.ponemon.org/local/upload/fckjail/generalcontent/18/file/Consumer\%20Report\%20Card\%20 Data\%20Breach\%20Noti\%20Apr08.pdf

Porter, M. E. (1998). *Competitive strategy: Techniques for analyzing industries and competitors* (1st ed.). Free Press.

Poullet, Y. (2006). EU data protection policy. The directive 95/46/EC: Ten years after. *Journal of Computer Law & Security Report, 22*(3), 206–217. doi:10.1016/j.clsr.2006.03.004

Privacy and Innovation Symposium. (2010, May). Washington, D.C. Retrieved April 8, 2011, from http://1.usa.gov/hBdIrt

Privacy International. (1998–2003). *Privacy and human rights, annual reports.* Retrieved April 8, 2011, from http://bit.ly/hjKLSe

Privacy International and Electronic Privacy Information Center (EPIC). (2007). *Privacy and human rights 2006: An international survey of privacy laws and developments.* Retrieved April 8, 2011, from http://bit.ly/g9wOAh

Privacy International, the Electronic Privacy Information Center (EPIC) and the Center for Media and Communications Studies (CMCS). (2011). *European privacy and human rights 2010.* Retrieved April 8, 2011, from http://bit.ly/gnFZoC

Privacy Rights Clearinghouse. (2010, September). *Fact sheet 8a: HIPAA basics: Medical privacy in the electronic age.* Retrieved October 17, 2010, from http://www.privacyrights.org/fs/fs8a-hipaa.htm

Python Software Foundation. (2010). *Socket — Low-level networking interface — Python v2.6.4 documentation.* Retrieved March 15, 2011, from http://docs.python.org/library/socket.html

Qiao, L., & Nahrstedt, K. (1997). A new algorithm for MPEG video encryption. In *Proceedings of The First International Conference on Imaging Science, Systems, and Technology (CISST'97),* Las Vegas, Nevada, July 1997, (pp. 21–29).

Quirchmayr, G. (2004, January 2004). *Survivability and business continuity management.* Paper presented at the ACSW Frontiers 2004 Workshops, Dunedin, New Zealand.

QVT. (2005). *Meta object facility (MOF) 2.0 query/view/transformation specification.*

Radner, R. (2000). Costly and bounded rationality in individual and team decision-making. *Industrial and Corporate Change, 9*(4), 623–655. doi:10.1093/icc/9.4.623

Radner, R., & Marschak, J. (1954). Note on some proposed decision criteria. In Thrall, R. M. (Eds.), *Decision processes.* John Wiley.

Ravari, A. N., Jafarian, J. H., Amini, M., & Jalili, R. (2010). GTHBAC: A generalized temporal history based access control model. [Netherlands: Springer.]. *Journal of Telecommunication Systems, 45*(2), 111–125. doi:10.1007/s11235-009-9239-9

Ravari, A. N., Amini, M., Jalili, R., & Jafarian, J. H. (2008). A history based semantic aware access control model using logical time. In *Proceedings of the 11th International Conference on Computer and Information Technology (ICCIT 2008)* (pp. 43-50). Khulna, Bangladesh.

Reagle, J., & Cranor, L. F. (1999). The platform for privacy preferences. *Communications of the ACM, 42*(2), 55. doi:10.1145/293411.293455

Reding, V. (2010, January). *Privacy: The challenges ahead for the European Union.* Keynote Speech at the Data Protection Day, European Parliament, Brussels. Retrieved April 8, 2011, from http://bit.ly/fCRTK9

Reed, D., & Strongin, G. (2004). *The Dataweb: An introduction to XDI.* A White Paper for the OASIS XDI Technical Committee. Retrieved October 26, 2010, from http://www.oasis-open.org/committees/download.php/6434/wd-xdi-intro-white-paper-2004-04-12.pdf

Reeder, R. W., et al. (2008). *A user study of the expandable grid applied to P3P privacy policy visualization.* Paper presented at the 7th ACM Workshop on Privacy in the Electronic Society.

Reid, J. (2010, August 5). *Redskins insider.* Retrieved October 22, 2010, from http://voices.washingtonpost.com/ redskinsinsider/3-4-defense/shanahan-albert-haynesworth-to.html

Ren, K., & Lou, W. (2007). Privacy-enchanced, attack-resilient access control in pervasive computing environments with optional context authentication capability. *Mobile Networks and Applications, 12,* 79–92. doi:10.1007/s11036-006-0008-7

Reports, C. (2007). Costly credit-monitoring services offer limited fraud protection. *Consumer Reports,* April. Retrieved from http://www.consumerreports.org/cro/money/credit-loan/costly-credit-monitoring-services-offer-limited-fraud-protection-4-07/overview/0704_costly-credit-monitoring-services-offer-limited-fraud-protection_ov.htm

Retailer, I. (2006, December 14). Visa sets new fines, offers incentives to encourage PCI compliance. *Internet Retailer.* Retrieved from http://www.internetretailer.com/internet/ marketing-conference/87667-visa-sets-new-fines-offers-incentives-encourage-pci-compliance.html

Rights, P. (n.d.). [*A chronology of data breaches.* Retrieved from http://www.privacyrights.org/ar/ChronDataBreaches.htm]. *Clearing House (Menasha, Wis.).*

Rissanen, E., Parducci, B., & Lockhart, H. (2010). *eXtensible access control markup language* (XACML) Version 3.0. Retrieved October 26, 2010, from http://docs.oasis-open.org/xacml/3.0/xacml-3.0-core-spec-cs-01-en.pdf

Rjaibi, W. (2004). A multi-purpose implementation of mandatory access control in relational database management systems. *In Proceedings 30th VLDB Conference,* (pp. 1010-1020). Toronto, Canada.

Rodríguez, A., Fernández-Medina, E., & Piattini, M. (2007b). A BPMN extension for the modeling of security requirements in business processes. *IEICE Transactions on Information and Systems. E (Norwalk, Conn.), 90-D*(4), 745–752.

Rodríguez, A., & García-Rodríguez de Guzmán, I. (2007). *Obtaining use cases and security use cases from secure business process through the MDA approach.* Paper presented at the Workshop on Security in Information Systems (WOSIS), Funchal, Madeira - Portugal.

Rodríguez, A., Fernández-Medina, E., & Piattini, M. (2006, September 4-8). *Towards a UML 2.0 extension for the modeling of security requirements in business processes.* Paper presented at the 3rd International Conference on Trust, Privacy and Security in Digital Business (TrustBus), Krakow-Poland.

Rodríguez, A., Fernández-Medina, E., & Piattini, M. (2007a, September 3–7). *Analysis-level classes from secure business processes through models transformations.* Paper presented at the 4th International Conference on Trust, Privacy and Security in Digital Business (TrustBus), Regensburg, Germany.

Rodríguez, A., Fernández-Medina, E., & Piattini, M. (2007c, October 14-16). *CIM to PIM transformation: A reality.* Paper presented at the IFIP International Conference on Research and Practical Issues of Enterprise Information Systems (CONFENIS), Beijing, China.

Rodríguez, A., Fernández-Medina, E., & Piattini, M. (2007d). *M-BPSec: A method for security requirement elicitation from a UML 2.0 business process specification.* Paper presented at the 3rd International Workshop on Foundations and Practices of UML, Auckland, New Zealand.

Rodríguez, A., Fernández-Medina, E., & Piattini, M. (2007e, 24-28 September). *Towards CIM to PIM transformation: From secure business processes defined by BPMN to use cases.* Paper presented at the 5th International Conference on Business Process Management (BPM), Brisbane, Australia.

Romanosky, S., Telang, R., & Acquisti, A. (2011). Do data breach disclosure laws reduce identity theft? *Journal of Policy Analysis and Management, 30*(2). Retrieved April 8, 2011, from http://bit.ly/heVW6q

Rosson, M. B., & Carroll, J. M. (2002). *Usability engineering: Scenario-based development of human-computer interaction.* Morgan Kaufmann Pub.

Rowland, K. (2010, September). Privacy by design, or privacy by disaster? *Intelligent Utility.* Retrieved April 8, 2011, from http://bit.ly/gS2Fz1

Rungworawut, W., & Senivongse, T. (2005). A guideline to mapping business processes to UML class diagrams. *WSEAS Trans. on Computers, 4*(11), 1526–1533.

Rungworawut, W., & Senivongse, T. (2006). Using ontology search in the design of class diagram from business process model. *Enformatika, Transactions on Engineering. Computing and Technology, 12*, 165–170.

Ryssdal, R. (1991). *Data protection and the European Convention on Human Rights.* 13th Conf. Data Protection Comm'rs, 39.

Ryutov, T., Zhou, L., Neuman, C., Leithead, T., & Seamons, K. E. (2005). Adaptive trust negotiation and access control. *2005 Symposium on Access Control Models and Technologies* (pp. 139-146). Stockholm, Sweden: ACM.

Samarati, P. (2001). Protecting Respondents' Identities in Microdata Release. *IEEE Transactions on Knowledge and Data Engineering, 13*(6), 1010–1027. doi:10.1109/69.971193

Samarati, P. (2001). Protecting respondents' identities in microdata release. In *Proceedings of IEEE Trans. Knowl. Data Eng.* (pp. 1010-1027).

Samarati, P., & Sweeney, L. (1998). Generalizing data to provide anonymity when disclosing information (Abstract). In *Proc. of the 17th ACM-SIGMODSIGACT- SIGART Symposium on the Principles of Database Systems,* (p. 188). Seattle, WA, USA.

Samuel, A., Ghafoor, A., & Bertino, E. (2008). A framework for specification and verification of generalized spatio-temporal role based access control model. *CERIAS Technical Report 2007-08.* Purdue University.

Sandhu, R. S., Coyee, E. J., Ferinstein, H. L., & Youman, C. E. (1996). Role-based access control model. *IEEE Computer, 29*(2), 38–47.

Sandhu, R. (1988). Cryptographic implementation of a tree hierarchy for access control. *Information Processing Letters, 27*, 95–98. doi:10.1016/0020-0190(88)90099-3

Sandhu, R. (1993). Lattice-based access control models. *IEEE Computer, 26*(11), 9–19. doi:10.1109/2.241422

Savage, L. J. (1954). *The foundations of statistics* (2nd ed.). New York, NY: Wiley.

Savolaine, J., & Granello, P. F. (2002). The function of meaning and purpose for individual wellness. *The Journal of Humanistic Counseling, Education and Development, 41*, 178–189.

Scavo, T., & Cantor, S. (2005). *Shibboleth architecture: Technical overview*. Retrieved October 26, 2010, from http://shibboleth.internet2.edu/docs/draft-mace-shibboleth-tech-overview-latest.pdf

Schilit, B., Adams, N., Want, R., et al. (1994). Context-aware computing applications. In *Proceedings of the Workshop on Mobile Computing Systems and Application*. Santa Cruz, CA, (pp. 85–90).

Schlesinger, F. (2009, July 3). Hundreds of men wrongly convicted of being paedophiles after becoming victims of identity theft. *Daily Mail*. Retrieved from http://www.dailymail.co.uk/news/article-1197224/Hundreds-men-wrongly-convicted-paedophiles-victims-identity-theft.html\#ixzz0WDgSXOSg

Schneider, J. W. (2009). Preventing data breaches: Alternative approaches to deter negligent handling of consumer data. *Journal of Science and Technology Law*, *15*, 279.

Scholl, M., Stine, K., Hash, J., Bowen, P., Johnson, A., Smith, C. D., et al. (2008, October). An introductory resource guide for implementing the health insurance portability and accountability act (HIPAA) security rule. *NIST Special Publication 800-66 Revision 1*. National Institute of Standards and Technology. US Department of Commerce.

Schunter, M., & Ashley, P. (2002). The platform for enterprise privacy practices. In *Proceedings of the Information Security Solutions Europe (ISSE 2002)*. Paris, France.

Schunter, M., & Waidner, M. (2007). *Simplified privacy controls for aggregated services: Suspend and resume of personal data*. Paper presented at the 7th International Conference on Privacy Enhancing Technologies.

Schwartz, A. (2009). *Looking back at P3P: Lessons for the future*. Retrieved April 2011 from http://www.cdt.org/files/pdfs/P3P_Retro_Final_0.pdf

Schwartz, P. M., & Janger, E. J. (2007). Notification of data security breaches. *Michigan Law Review, 105*, 913. Brooklyn Law School, Legal Studies Paper No. 58. Retrieved April 8, 2011, from http://bit.ly/hQjHT0

Sedky, M. H., Moniri, M., & Chibelushi, C. C. (2005). Classification of smart video surveillance systems for commercial applications. In *Proceedings of the IEEE Conference on Advanced Video and Signal Based Surveillance (AVSS)*, (pp. 638-643).

Shabtai, A., Fledel, Y., Kanonov, U., Elovici, Y., Dolev, S., & Glezer, C. (2010). Google Android: A comprehensive security assessment. *IEEE Security & Privacy, 8*(2), 35–44. doi:10.1109/MSP.2010.2

Shamir, A. (1979). How to share a secret. *Communications of the ACM, 22*, 612–613. doi:10.1145/359168.359176

Shannon, C. E. (1949). Communication theory of secrecy systems. *Bell System Technical Journal, 28*(4), 656-715. Retrieved March 15, 2011, from http://netlab.cs.ucla.edu/wiki/files/shannon1949.pdf

Shelat, A. (2006). *Project Higgins: User-centric identity meta system and privacy*. IBM Research. Retrieved October 26, 2010, from https://www.prime-project.eu/events/standardisation-ws/slides/Higgins.pdf/download

Shen, V., & Chen, T. (2002). A novel key management scheme based on discrete logarithms and polynomial interpolations. *Computers & Security, 21*(2), 164–171. doi:10.1016/S0167-4048(02)00211-0

Sheppard, B. H., Hartwick, J., & Warshaw, P. R. (1988). The theory of reasoned action: A meta-analysis of past research with recommendations for modifications and future research. *The Journal of Consumer Research, 15*(3), 325–343. doi:10.1086/209170

Shokri, R., Freudiger, J., Jadliwala, M., & Hubaux, J. P. (2009). A distortion-based metric for location privacy. In *Proceedings of WPES'09, ACM Workshop on Privacy in the Electronic Society* (WPES), Chicago, IL, USA.

Shostack, A. (2009). *$450 per account? No*. Feb. 10. Retrieved from http://www.emergentchaos.com/archives/2009/02/450_per_account_no.html

Simmons, G. J. (1990). *How to (really) share a secret. Advances in Cryptology, Crypto'88 Proceedings* (pp. 390–448). Springer-Verlag.

Simmons, G. J. (1990). *Prepositioned shared secret and/or shared control schemes. Advances in Cryptology, Eurocrypt '89 Proceedings* (pp. 436–467). Springer-Verlag.

Simmons, G. J. (1992). *Contemporary cryptology: The science of information integrity.* IEEE Press.

Simon, H. A. (1959). Theories of decision-making in economics and behavioral science. *The American Economic Review, 49*(3), 253–283.

Simon, H. A. (1987). Bounded rationality. In Eatwell, J. (Eds.), *The New Palgrave.* London, UK: Maemillan.

Slattery, B. (2010, March 31). *Facebook flub leaks private e-mail addresses.* Retrieved October 28, 2010, from http://www.pcworld.com/article/193009/facebook_flub_leaks_private_email_addresses.html

Slicer. (2010). Retrieved October 13, 2010, from http://slicer.org/

Smari, W. W., Zhu, J., & Clemente, P. (2009). Trust and privacy in attribute based access control for collaboration environments. *International Conference on Information Integration and Web-based Applications & Services* (pp. 49-55). Kuala Lumpur, Malaysia: ACM.

Smith, A. M. (2007). *Data governance best practices: The beginning.* Retrieved from http://www.eiminstitute.org/library/eimi-archives/volume-1-issue-1-march-2007-edition/data-governance-best-practices-2013-the-beginning

Smith, C. L., & Robinson, M. (1999). The understanding of security technology and its applications. In *Proceedings of the IEEE International Carnahan Conference on Security Technology,* (pp. 26-37).

Social Security Administration. (2009). *Identity theft and your Social Security number.* SSA Publication No. 05-10064, August, ICN 463270. Retrieved from http://www.socialsecurity.gov/pubs/10064.html

Soghoian, C. (2009). Manipulation and abuse of the consumer credit reporting agencies. *First Monday, 14,* 8–3.

Solove, D. J. (2003). Identity theft, privacy, and the architecture of vulnerability. *The Hastings Law Journal, 54,* 1227. Retrieved from http://ssrn.com/abstract=416740.

Solove, D. J. (2006). A brief history of information privacy law. In Wolf, C. (Ed.), *Proskauer on privacy: A guide to privacy and data security law in the information age* (pp. 1–46). New York, NY: Practising Law Institute.

Sparrow, M. (1991). The application of network analysis to criminal intelligence: An assessment of the prospects. *Social Networks, 13,* 251–274. doi:10.1016/0378-8733(91)90008-H

Spiekermann, S., Grossklags, J., & Berendt, B. (2001). *E-privacy in 2nd generation e-commerce: Privacy preferences versus actual behavior.* Paper presented at the 3rd ACM Conference on Electronic Commerce.

Srikant, R., & Agrawal, R. (1995). Mining generalized association rules. In *Proc. of the 21st Int'l Conference on Very Large Databases,* August 1995.

Štolfa, S., & Vondrák, I. (2004, June 2004). *A description of business process modeling as a tool for definition of requirements specification.* Paper presented at the Systems Integration 12th Annual International Conference, Prague, Czech Republic.

Störrle, H. (2005). Semantics and verification of data flow in UML 2.0 Activities. *Electronic Notes in Theoretical Computer Science, 127*(4), 35–52. doi:10.1016/j.entcs.2004.08.046

Straub, D., & Welke, R. J. (1998). Coping with systems risk: Security planning models for management decision-making. *MIS Quart., 22*(4), 441–469. doi:10.2307/249551

Sun, X., Wang, H., & Li, J. (2008). On the complexity of restricted k-anonymity problem. *APWeb, 2008,* 287–296.

Sun, X., Wang, H., Li, J., & Truta, T. M. (2008). Enhanced p-sensitive k-anonymity models for privacy preserving data publishing. *Transactions on Data Privacy, 1*(2), 53–66.

Sweeney, L. (2002). k-anonymity: A model for protecting privacy. In *Proceedings of International Journal of Uncertainty, Fuzziness and Knowledge-Based Systems* (pp. 557-570).

SWIFT. (2008). *Secure widespread identities for federated telecommunications.* Retrieved October 26, 2010, from http://www.ist-swift.org

Szeto, M., & Miri, A. (2007). *Analysis of the use of privacy-enhancing technologies to achieve PIPEDA compliance in a B2C e-business model.* Paper presented at the Eighth World Congress on the Management of eBusiness, 2007. WCMeB 2007.

Tanenbaum, A. S., & Steen, V. (2007). *Distributed systems: Principles and paradigms*. Upper Saddle River, NJ: Prentice Hall.

The Ponemon Institute. (2010). *2009 annual study: Cost of a privacy breach sponsored by PGP Corp*. Retrieved April 8, 2011, from http://bit.ly/eRxyMK

The Ponemon Institute. (2011). *The true costs of compliance: A benchmark study of multinational organizations*. Independent Research Report. Retrieved April 8, 2011, from http://bit.ly/e13LZT

Thomas, R. K., & Sandhu, R. S. (1997). Task-based authorization controls (TBAC): A family of models for active and enterprise-oriented authorization management. In *Proceedings of the IFIP WG11.3 Workshop on Database Security* (pp. 166-181).

Thompson, J. D. (1967). *Organizations in action: Social science bases of administrative theory*. McGraw-Hill Companies.

Thomson, I. (2007). Hushmail turns out to be anything but. *ITNews*. Retrieved April 8, 2011, from http://bit.ly/gePNsZ

Tibken, S. (2010). Salesforce CEO touts mobility, social networking. *Dow Jones Newswires*. Retrieved April 4, 2011, from http://www.totaltele.com/view.aspx?C=4&ID=459551

Toft, T. (2007). *Primitives and applications for multiparty computation*. Unpublished doctoral dissertation, University of Aarhus, Denmark.

Tøndel, I. A., Nyre, Å. A., & Bernsmed, K. (2011). Learning Privacy Preferences. Paper presented at the Sixth International Conference on Availability, Reliability and Security.

Traian, T. M., & Bindu, V. (2006). *Privacy protection: p-sensitive k-anonymity property*. International Workshop of Privacy Data Management (PDM2006), In Conjunction with 22th International Conference of Data Engineering (ICDE), Atlanta, 2006.

TRUSTe. (n.d.). Privacy seals & services. Online Trust & Safety from TRUSTe. Retrieved February 17, 2011, from http://www.truste.org

Tversky, A., & Kahneman, D. (1974). Judgment under uncertainty: Heuristics and biases. *Science*, *28*(5), 1124–1134. doi:10.1126/science.185.4157.1124

Tzeng, W.-G. (2002). A time-bound cryptographic key assignment scheme for access control in a hierarchy. *IEEE Transactions on Knowledge and Data Engineering*, *14*(1), 182–188. doi:10.1109/69.979981

U.K. Information Commissioner's Office (ICO). (2006). *Data protection technical guidance note: Privacy enhancing technologies*. ICO. Retrieved April 8, 2011, from http://bit.ly/e36Upn

U.K. Information Commissioner's Office (ICO). (2007). *An international study of PIA law, policies and practices*. ICO. Retrieved April 8, 2011, from http://bit.ly/hB381i

U.K. Information Commissioner's Office (ICO). (2008). *Privacy by design report*. ICO. Retrieved April 8, 2011, from http://bit.ly/gZ4CYm

U.K. Information Commissioner's Office (ICO). (2008). *Privacy by design – An overview of privacy enhancing technologies*. Enterprise Privacy Group. Retrieved April 8, 2011, from http://bit.ly/hquBBQ

U.K. Information Commissioner's Office (ICO). (2008). *Privacy by design report recommendations: ICO implementation plan*. ICO. Retrieved April 8, 2011, from http://bit.ly/hpjWhw

U.K. Information Commissioner's Office (ICO). (2008). *Privacy by Design Conference (website)*. Manchester. Retrieved April 8, 2011, from http://bit.ly/f6MbGq

U.K. Information Commissioner's Office (ICO). (2009). Protecting people: A data protection strategy for the Information Commissioner's Office. ICO. Retrieved April 8, 2011, from http://bit.ly/gi5vW1

U.K. Information Commissioner's Office (ICO). (2009). *PIA handbook*, ICO. Retrieved April 8, 2011, from http://bit.ly/eEKU06

U.K. Information Commissioner's Office (ICO). (2010). *The privacy dividend: The business case for investing in proactive privacy protection*. ICO. Retrieved April 8, 2011, from http://bit.ly/eF2fM1

U.S. Federal Trade Commission (FTC). (2001). *Remarks by Tim Muris, FTC Chairman at the Privacy 2001 Conference*. Retrieved from http://1.usa.gov/eupYzF.

U.S. Federal Trade Commission (FTC). (2010, December). *Protecting consumer privacy in an era of rapid change: A proposed framework for businesses and policymakers*. Technical report. Retrieved April 8, 2011, from http://1.usa.gov/eupYzF

U.S. Federal Trade Commission (FTC). (2010). *Testimony regarding consumer online privacy by John Liebowitz, FTC Chairman before the Committee on Commerce, Science, and Transportation, U.S. Senate*. Washington, D.C. Retrieved April 8, 2011, from http://1.usa.gov/gFLtDw

U.S. Secretary's Advisory Committee on Automated Personal Data Systems. (1973). *Records, computers and the rights of citizens*. HEW Report. Retrieved April 8, 2011, from http://bit.ly/e63jZ6

U.S. White House. (2010). *Draft national strategy for trusted identities in cyberspace: Creating options for enhanced online security and privacy*. Retrieved April 8, 2011, from http://1.usa.gov/hNs1jw

United Nations. (1948). *Universal declaration of human rights*. Retrieved November 29, 2010, from http://www.ohchr.org/EN/UDHR/ Documents/60UDHR/bookleten.pdf

US Department of Health & Human Services. (2009). *Health information privacy*. Retrieved October 14, 2010, from HHS.gov: http://www.hhs.gov/ocr/privacy/

US. (2011). Welcome to the U.S.-EU & U.S.-Swiss safe harbor frameworks. Retrieved April, 2011, from http://www.export.gov/safeharbor/

USA.gov. (n.d.). *USDA possible personal information breach*. Retrieved from http://www.usa.gov/usdainfo.shtml

Venkatesh, V., Morris, M., Davis, G., & Davis, F. (2003). User acceptance of Information Technology: Toward a unified view. *Management Information Systems Quarterly*, *27*(3), 425–478.

Verma, M. (2004, October). *XML security: Control information access with XACML*. Retrieved from http://www.ibm.com/developerworks/xml/ library/x-xacml/

Vila, T., Greenstadt, R., & Molnar, D. (2003). *Why we can't be bothered to read privacy policies - Models of privacy economics as a lemons market*. Paper presented at the 5th International Conference on Electronic Commerce.

W3C. (1997). *Platform for internet content selection (PICS)*. Retrieved March, 2011, from http://www.w3.org/PICS

W3C. (2006). *Platform for privacy preferences*. Retrieved April, 2011, from http://www.w3.org/P3P/

W3C. (2007). *The W3C privacy page*. Retrieved March, 2011, from http://www.w3.org/Privacy/

Wacks, R. (2010). *Privacy: A very short introduction*. New York, NY: Oxford University Press.

Wang, S.-Y., & Laih, C.-S. (2006). Merging: An efficient solution for time-bound hierarchical key assignment scheme. *IEEE Transactions on Dependable and Secure Computing*, *3*(1), 91–100. doi:10.1109/TDSC.2006.15

Wang, F. (2009). *Online dispute resolution: Technology, management and legal practice from an international perspective*. Oxford, UK: Chandos Publishing.

Wang, F. (2010). *Law of electronic commercial transactions: Contemporary issues in the EU, US and China*. Oxford, UK: Cavendish-Routledge Publishing.

Wang, F., & Griffiths, N. (2010, July). Protecting privacy in automated transaction systems: A legal and technological perspective in the EU. *International Review of Law Computers & Technology*, *24*(2), 153–162. doi:10.1080/13600861003748243

Wang, J., Zhao, Y., Jiang, S., & Le, J. (2009). Providing privacy preserving in cloud computing. *Proceedings of the International Conference on Test and Measurement* (pp. 213-216).

Wang, K., Yu, P. S., & Chakraborty, S. (2004). Bottom-up generalization: A data mining solution to privacy protection. In *Proceedings of ICDM* (pp. 249-256).

Warren, S. D., & Brandeis, L. D. (1890). The right to privacy. *Harvard Law Review*, *4*(5), 193–220. doi:10.2307/1321160

Webster, J., & Watson, R. T. (2002). Analyzing the past to prepare for the future: Writing a literature review. *Management Information Systems Quarterly, 26*(2), xiii–xxiii.

Weiser, M. (1998). The future of ubiquitous computing on campus. *Communications of the ACM, 41*(1), 41–42. doi:10.1145/268092.268108

Weiser, M. (1999). The computer for the 21st century. *SIGMOBILE Mob. Comput. Commun. Rev., 3*(1), 3–11. doi:10.1145/329124.329126

Welsh, B., & Farrington, D. (2002). *Crime prevention effects of closed circuit television: A systematic review.* London, UK: Home Office Research, Development and Statistics Directorate.

Westin, A. F. (1967). *Privacy and freedom.* New York, NY: Atheneum.

WfMC. (1999). *Workflow management coalition: Terminology & glossary.*

White, S. A. (2004). *Process modeling notations and workflow patterns.* Retrieved from http://www.ebpml.org/bpmn.htm

Wikipedia. (2010, November 20). *Domain model.* Retrieved November 25, 2010, from http://en.wikipedia.org/wiki/Domain_model

Wikipedia. (2010, October 27). *Facebook.* Retrieved October 28, 2010, from http://en.wikipedia.org/wiki/Facebook

Wikipedia. (2010, October 28). *MySpace.* Retrieved October 28, 2010, from http://en.wikipedia.org/wiki/MySpace

Willenborg, L., & De Waal, T. (1996). Statistical disclosure control in practice. Springer-Verlag, 1996.

Wilson, R. L., & Rosen, P. A. (2003). Protecting data through perturbation techniques: Impact on the knowledge discovery process. *Journal of Database Management, 14*(2), 14–26. doi:10.4018/jdm.2003040102

Wilton, R. (2009). What's happened to PETs? *Information Security Technical Report, 14*(3), 146–153. doi:10.1016/j.istr.2009.10.010

Winkler, W. (2002). *Using simulated annealing for k-anonymity.* Research Report 2002-07, US Census Bureau Statistical Research Division, 2002.

Wolf, W., Ozer, B., & Lv, T. (2002). Smart cameras as embedded systems. *IEEE Computer, 35*(9), 48–53. doi:10.1109/MC.2002.1033027

World Wide Web Consortium. (2004). *Web ontology language (OWL).* Retrieved November 29, 2010, from http://www.w3.org/2004/OWL/

World Wide Web Consortium. (2006). *Extensible markup language (XML) XML 1.1* (2nd edition). Retrieved November 29, 2010, from http://www.w3.org/TR/2006/REC-xml11-20060816

Wright, T. (1995). *Eyes on the road: Intelligent transportation systems and your privacy.* Office of the Information and Privacy Commissioner of Ontario, Canada. Retrieved April 8, 2011, from http://bit.ly/fxaVpv

Wright, T. (1995). *Privacy protection models for the private sector.* Office of the Information and Privacy Commissioner of Ontario, Canada. Retrieved April 8, 2011, from http://bit.ly/hXnEmV

Xiao, X., & Tao, Y. (2006). Personalized privacy preservation. In *SIGMOD '06: Proceedings of the 2006 ACM SIGMOD International Conference on Management of Data,* 2006.

Xu, J., & Chen, H. (2005). Criminal network analysis and visualization. *Communications of the ACM, 48*(6), 100–107. doi:10.1145/1064830.1064834

Yang, C., & Li, C. (2004). Access control in a hierarchy using one-way functions. *Elsevier: Computers and Security, 23,* 659–664.

Yao, D., Frikken, K., Atallah, M., & Tamassia, R. (2008). Private information: To reveal or not to reveal. *ACM Transactions on Information and System Security, 12*(1), 1–27. doi:10.1145/1410234.1410240

Yao, A. (1982). Protocols for secure computations. In *Proceedings of the 23rd IEEE Symposium on Foundations of Computer Science,* (pp. 160-164).

Yao, C., Wang, S., & Jajodia, S. (2005). *Checking for k-anonymity violation by views.* In International Conference on Very Large Data Bases, Trondheim, Norway, August 2005.

Yi, X. (2005). Security of Chien's efficient time-bound hierarchical key assignment scheme. *IEEE Transactions on Knowledge and Data Engineering, 17*(9), 1298–1299. doi:10.1109/TKDE.2005.152

Yi, X., & Ye, Y. (2003). Security of Tzeng's time-bound key assignment scheme for access control in a hierarchy. *IEEE Transactions on Knowledge and Data Engineering, 15*(4), 1054–1055. doi:10.1109/TKDE.2003.1209023

Yu, W., Sun, Y., & Liu, R. (2007). Optimizing the rekeying cost for contributory group key agreement schemes. *IEEE Transactions on Dependable and Secure Computing, 4*(3), 228–242. doi:10.1109/TDSC.2007.1006

Zane, R. (2009). *IBM research collaborates with leading Taiwanese institutions to deliver wellness-centric healthcare via cloud computing.* Press Release. Retrieved April 4, 2011, from http://www-03.ibm.com/press/us/en/pressrelease/29086.wss

Zeng, L., Hsueh, P., Chang, H., Chung, C., & Huang, R. (2010). GreenOlive: An open platform for wellness management ecosystem. *Proceedings of the IEEE/INFORMS International Conference on Service Operations and Logistics, and Informatics* (SOLI), Beijing, China.

Zhang, G., & Parashar, M. (2004). Context-aware dynamic access control for pervasive application. *In Proceedings of the Communication Networks and Distributed Systems Modeling and Simulation Conference* (pp. 21-30). Society for Modeling and Simulation International.

Zhao, W., Chellappa, R., Phillips, P. J., & Rosenfeld, A. (2003). Face recognition: A literature survey. *ACM Computing Surveys, 35*(4), 399–458. doi:10.1145/954339.954342

Zhong, S., Yang, Z., & Wright, R. N. (2005). *Privacy-enhancing k-anonymization of customer data.* In ACM Conference on Principles of Database Systems(PODS), 2005.

Zou, X., & Ramamurthy, B. (2004). A GCD attack resistant CRTHACS for secure group communications. *In Proceedings International Conference on Information Technology: Coding and Computing (ITCC'04)*, (pp. 153-154).

Zuccato, A. (2004). Holistic security requirement engineering for electronic commerce. *Computers & Security, 23*(1), 63–76. doi:10.1016/S0167-4048(04)00065-3

Zwingelberg, H., & Storf, K. (2010). *PrimeLife dissemination report V2.* Retrieved October 26, 2010, from http://www.primelife.eu/images/stories/ deliverables/ h3.1.2-primelife_dissemination_report_v2.pdf

About the Contributors

George Yee is a Consultant and an Adjunct Professor with the Dept. of Systems and Computer Engineering, Carleton University, Ottawa, Canada. He was previously a Senior Research Officer for over 7 years in the Information Security Group, National Research Council Canada (NRC). Prior to the NRC, he had significant experience as a member of scientific staff and manager at Bell-Northern Research and Nortel Networks. George received his Ph.D. in Electrical Engineering from Carleton University and is a member of Professional Engineers Ontario. In addition, he is a Certified Information Systems Security Professional (CISSP) and a Certified Software Development Professional (CSDP). George's research interests as an Adjunct Professor lie in the engineering of reliable systems, involving security, fault tolerance, performance, and correctness.

* * *

Selim G. Akl is the Director of the School of Computing at Queen's University, with a cross- appointment in the Department of Mathematics and Statistics. Dr. Akl's research is in applied theory of computation and algorithmics, with a particular focus on parallel computation, computer security, digital signal processing, and unconventional computing (including quantum and biomolecular computers, sensor networks, and nonstandard computational problems). He has published over 150 papers in academic journals and numerous book chapters. He is the author of three books and the co-author of two monographs. Currently, Dr. Akl is Editor in Chief of *Parallel Processing Letters* and an editorial board member of *Computational Geometry, International Journal of Parallel, Emergent and Distributed Systems, Journal of Scalable Computing and Communications,* and *International Journal of High Performance Computing and Networking.*

Anna Antonakopoulou is a PhD candidate of the Intelligent Communications and Broadband Networks Laboratory (ICBNet) of the National Technical University of Athens (NTUA), Greece. She received her diploma in Electrical and Computer Engineering from the University of Patras in 2006. As a research fellow of the NTUA since 2007, she has participated in several European and national research projects. Her research interests include Internet technologies, information security & privacy, Semantic Web, object-oriented software design and development, QoS in IP networks, transport and control protocols; she has seven publications related to these fields.

Karin Bernsmed received her MSc degree from Linköping University in 2003 and her PhD in Telematics from the Norwegian University of Science and Technology (NTNU) in 2007. She worked as a Research Scientist at Telenor R&I until 2010, after which she joined SINTEF ICT. Her research interests include network security and privacy, security in cloud computing, and stochastic modeling and analysis.

Riccardo Bonazzi is a PhD candidate at the Information Systems Institute of the University of Lausanne, Switzerland. He has been working with multinational firms, international organizations, and SME (Small and Medium Enterprises) in the financial, telecommunication, transportation, and logistics industry sectors. His main research interests are requirement engineering for IT GRC (Governance, Risk and Compliance) and privacy management.

L. Jean Camp is a Professor of Informatics and Computer Science at Indiana University Bloomington. She has recently completed one year on Capitol Hill, where she served as military and technology Legislative Assistant for North Carolina's Second District. Professor Camp is the author of "Trust and Risk in Internet Commerce" (MIT Press), "Economics of Identity Theft" (Springer), and the Editor of "Economics of Information Security" (Kluwer Academic). She has authored over one hundred additional works, including more than ninety peer-reviewed works and two dozen book chapters. She has made scores of invited presentations on six continents. Her patents are in the area of privacy-enhancing technologies. Her core contributions are in the area of the social and economic implications of technologies of security and privacy. See http://www.ljean.com/cv.html for more detailed information.

Aniello Castiglione joined the Dipartimento di Informatica ed Applicazioni "R.M. Capocelli" of Università di Salerno in February 2006. He received a degree in Computer Science and his Ph.D. in Computer Science from the same university. He is a reviewer for several international journals (Elsevier, Hindawi, IEEE, Springer) and he has been a Member of international conference committees. He is a Member of several associations, including: IEEE (Institute of Electrical and Electronics Engineers), ACM (Association for Computing Machinery), IEEE Computer Society, of IEEE Communications Society, of GRIN (Gruppo di Informatica), and IISFA (International Information System Forensics Association, Italian Chapter). He is a Fellow of FSF (Free Software Foundation) as well as FSFE (Free Software Foundation Europe). For many years, he has been involved in forensic investigations, collaborating with several law enforcement agencies as a consultant. His research interests include data security, communication networks, digital forensics, computer forensics, security and privacy, security standards, and cryptography.

Ann Cavoukian is recognized as one of the leading privacy experts in the world. Her concept of *Privacy by Design*, now a global privacy standard, seeks to proactively embed privacy into the design specifications of information technology and accountable business practices, thereby achieving the strongest protection possible. An avowed believer in the role that technology can play in the protection of privacy, Dr. Cavoukian has been involved in numerous international committees focused on privacy, security, technology, and business, with a focus on strengthening confidence and trust in emerging technology applications. Dr. Cavoukian is also a member of several boards including, the *European Biometrics Forum, Future of Privacy Forum,* RIM Council, and has been conferred as a Distinguished Fellow of the Ponemon Institute. Dr. Cavoukian has also been honoured with the prestigious *Kristian Beckman Award* for her pioneering work on *Privacy by Design* and privacy protection in modern international environments.

Henry Chang is the Collaboratory Director of IBM Research Collaboratory in Taiwan, and a Senior Technical Staff Member in the Healthcare Transformation Department at the Thomas J. Watson Research Center. He received a B.S. degree in Electric Engineering from National Taiwan University in 1979, and

M.S. and Ph.D. degrees in Computer Sciences from the University of Wisconsin at Madison in 1982 and 1987, respectively. He subsequently joined IBM at the Thomas J. Watson Research Center, where he has worked on parallel operating systems, mobile file systems, model-based B2B interchange systems, and sense-and-respond business monitoring systems. In 2001, he received an IBM Innovation Award for his work on a model-based B2B collaboration solution. He is an author or coauthor of 10 patents and 70+ technical papers. Dr. Chang is a member of the Institute of Electrical and Electronics Engineers and the Association for Computing Machinery.

Yi-Hui Chen received the BS and MS degrees in Information Management from the Chaoyang University of Technology, Taichung, Taiwan, in 2001 and 2004, respectively. Afterwards, she got her PhD degree in Computer Science and Information Engineering from National Chung Cheng University, Chiayi, Taiwan in 2009. From 2009 to 2010, she worked for Academia Sinica with Prof. De-Nian Yang as a postdoctoral fellow. Later on, she served in the IBM Taiwan collaboratory research center as a research scientist. She is now an Assistant Professor in the Department of Applied Informatics and Multimedia, Asia University, Taichung, Taiwan.

Alfredo De Santis received a degree in Computer Science (cum laude) from the Università di Salerno in 1983. Since 1984, he has been with the Dipartimento di Informatica ed Applicazioni of the Università di Salerno. Since 1990 he is a Professor of Computer Science. From November 1991 to October 1995 and from November 1998 to October 2001 he was the Chairman of the Dipartimento di Informatica ed Applicazioni, Università di Salerno. From November 1996 to October 2003 he was the Chairman of the PhD Program in Computer Science at the Università di Salerno. From September 1987 to February 1990 he was a Visiting Scientist at IBM T. J. Watson Research Center, Yorktown Heights, New York. He spent August 1994 at the International Computer Science Institute (ICSI), Berkeley CA, USA, as a Visiting Scientist. From November 2009 he is in the Board of Directors of Consortium GARR (the Italian Academic & Research Network). His research interests include algorithms, data security, cryptography, information forensics, communication networks, information theory, and data compression.

Eduardo Fernández-Medina holds a PhD. and an MSc. in Computer Science from the University of Sevilla. His research activity is in the field of security in information systems, and particularly in security in business processes, databases, datawarehouses, and web services. Fernández-Medina is co-editor of several books and chapter books on these subjects, and has papers in international conferences (BPM, UML, ER, ESORICS, TRUSTBUS, etc.). He is author of several manuscripts journals (*Decision Support Systems, Information Systems, ACM Sigmod Record, Information Software Technology, Computers & Security, Computer Standards and Interfaces*, etc.). He leads the GSyA research group of the Department of Computer Science at the University of Castilla-La Mancha, in Ciudad Real, Spain. He belongs to various professional and research associations (ATI, AEC, AENOR, IFIP WG11.3, etc.).

Daniel Funke received his Bachelor's Degree in Applied Computer Science from the State University of Cooperative Education Baden-Württemberg Karlsruhe and is currently undergoing his Master's studies in Theoretical Computer Science at Karlsruhe Institute of Technology. His research interests include secure computation, evolutionary algorithms, and the combination of the two.

Simon Ganière (CISA, CISSP) is Manager within the Security and Privacy practice of Deloitte Switzerland. He has a wide experience of information and IT security particularly in the areas of software development, database, server, network and application security, security management, data protection, and privacy. He has lead and delivered several engagements related to data protection and privacy for large international companies in the financial industry.

Elena Torroglosa Garcia is a researcher in the Department of Information and Communications Engineering of the University of Murcia. Her research interests focus on identity management, privacy, and security. She received her MS in Computer Science from the University of Murcia.

Fotios Gogoulos is a PhD candidate of the Intelligent Communications and Broadband Networks Laboratory (ICBNet) of the National Technical University of Athens (NTUA), Greece. He received his diploma in Electrical and Computer Engineering from the NTUA in 2007. As a research fellow of the NTUA since 2007, he has participated in several European and national research projects. His research interests include information security and privacy, Semantic Web, IPTV, service discovery protocols, system modelling and simulation, P2P networks; he has six publications related to these fields.

Antonio F. Gómez-Skarmeta received his MSc degree in Computer Science from the University of Granada and his BSc (Hons.) and PhD degrees in Computer Science from the University of Murcia, Spain. Since 2009 he has been Full Professor at the same department and university. He has worked on various national and international research projects, including Euro6IX, 6Power, Positif, Seinit, Deserec, Enable, and Daidalos. His main interest is in the integration of security services at different layers such as networking, management and web services. He is Associate Editor of the *IEEE SMC-Part B* and reviewer of several international journals. He has published over 90 international papers and has been a member of several program committees.

Tyrone Grandison received his B.Sc. and M.Sc. degrees in Computer Studies from the University of the West Indies and a Ph.D. degree in Computer Science from the Imperial College in London. Currently, he is the Program Manager for Core Healthcare Services. Dr. Grandison is a Distinguished Engineer of the Association of Computing Machinery (ACM), a Senior Member of the Institute of Electrical and Electronics Engineers (IEEE), a Fellow of the British Computer Society (BCS), has been recognized by the National Society of Black Engineers (as Pioneer of the Year in 2009), the Black Engineer of the Year Award Board (as Modern Day Technology Leader in 2009, and Minority in Science Trailblazer in 2010), and has received the IEEE Technical Achievement Award in 2010 for "pioneering contributions to Secure and Private Data Management." He has authored over 70 technical papers and co-invented over 20 patents.

John Hale is a Professor of Computer Science at The University of Tulsa (TU) and member of the Institute for Information Security. He has published approximately 65 refereed articles and one book in the area of computer security. In addition to scholarly research, his responsibilities in iSec include curriculum development and outreach activities. In 2000, he received a NSF Early Faculty Career Development award for research and educational contributions in the field. Dr. Hale's research in this area explores secure operating systems, cyber attack modeling and analysis, network security, and cryptographic protocol verification. Dr. Hale is also a research scholar in the Institute of Bioinformatics and Computational Biology at TU. His research interests in this area include medical informatics and privacy, executable formalisms for cellular behavior, and neuroinformatics.

Pei-yun S Hsueh is a member of the Healthcare Transformation Group at the IBM T.J. Research Center. She received her Ph.D. degree and Master degree from the University of Edinburgh and University of California, Berkeley, respectively. Before joining the Services Research Department, she was working on social media analytics at the department of Business Analytics and Mathematical Science. Her research focuses on active personalization analytics for collaborative care solutions and cloud-based services. Dr. Hsueh is also a Google Anita Borg scholar award recipient.

Martin Gilje Jaatun received his MSc degree in Telematics from the Norwegian Institute of Technology in 1992, and has been a research scientist at SINTEF ICT since 2004. Previous positions include Scientist at the Norwegian Defence Research Establishment (FFI), and Senior Lecturer in information security at the Bodø Graduate School of Business. Mr. Jaatun has experience in computer and communications security, electronic privacy, and security evaluation. His current research interests include security in cloud computing and security of critical information infrastructures. He is vice chairman of the Cloud Computing Association (cloudcom.org) and a Senior Member of the IEEE.

Dimitra I. Kaklamani is a Professor at the School of Electrical and Computer Engineering (SECE) of the National Technical University of Athens (NTUA). She has received the Diploma and Ph.D. degrees from the SECE, NTUA. She has published over 150 journal and conference papers and led and participated in several EU and national research projects. Her research interests span across different fields and include the use of object-oriented methodologies and middleware technologies for the development of distributed systems and privacy-aware infrastructures, and the development of visualisation and real-time simulation techniques for solving complex, large scale modelling problems of microwave engineering, and information transmission systems.

Anne V.D.M. Kayem is a Senior Lecturer at the University of Cape Town, South Africa. Prior to joining the University of Cape Town in 2010, she was a post-doctoral scholar at the German Research Centre for Artificial Intelligence (DFKI Bremen, Germany). She holds a BSc and MSc in Computer Science from the University of Yaounde I, Cameroon, and a PhD degree in Computer Science from Queen's University (Kingston, Canada). More recently, she co-authored a monograph entitled "Adaptive Cryptographic Access Control" with Prof. Selim G. Akl and Prof. Patrick Martin. Her research interests lie in the area of information security with a focus on access control, adaptive security, information flow control, and privacy.

Florian Kerschbaum is a Senior Researcher and project lead at SAP Research in Karlsruhe, Germany. Before SAP he has worked for Siemens, the San Francisco-based startup Arxan, Intel, and Digital Equipment in the job functions of project manager, software architect, and developer. He holds a Ph.D. in computer science from the Karlsruhe Institute of Technology, a Master's degree from Purdue University, and a Bachelor's degree from Berufsakademie Mannheim.

Mary Kuehler earned a Master's degree in Computer Science from The University of Tulsa (TU). While at TU, her emphasis of study was in Medical Informatics with specific interests in digitizing medical records and creating functional and user-friendly software for use by medical personnel. These interests developed during several years spent grossing surgical specimens at a pathology laboratory.

Ci-Wei Lan is a Research Scientist at the IBM Taiwan Collaboratory. He received the Ph.D. degree from the Department of Computer Science and Information Engineering, National Central University, Taiwan in 2008. He is the co-organizer of IEEE Technical Committee on Business Informatics Systems (TCBIS), the co-organizing chair of IEEE International Conference on E-Business Engineering (ICEBE), and the co-workshop chair of Service-Oriented Applications, Integration and Collaboration (SOAIC). His research interests include data mining, multi-objective optimization, and service-oriented technology.

Min Li received her B.Sc. degree in Department of Mathematics, Hebei Normal University and her M.Sc. degree in Department of Mathematics, Ocean University of China in 2006. She received her PhD from the Department of Mathematics & Computing at University of Southern Queensland. She is a student member of IEEE, and her research interests lie at the intersection of databases, data mining, security, and privacy.

Georgios V. Lioudakis is a Senior Research Associate of the Intelligent Communications and Broadband Networks Laboratory (ICBNet) of the National Technical University of Athens (NTUA), Greece. He received his Dr.-Ing. degree in Electrical and Computer Engineering from the NTUA in 2008. As a research fellow of the NTUA since 2000, he has participated in several European and national research projects. His research interests include privacy protection, mobile networks and services, software engineering, middleware, and distributed technologies; he has several publications related to these fields. Since 2009, Dr. Lioudakis is also an Adjunct Lecturer at the Department of Telecommunications Science and Technology, University of Peloponnese, Greece.

Zhan Liu is a PhD candidate at the Information Systems Institute of the University of Lausanne, Switzerland. He is also currently working as a Research Assistant at HES-SO Valais. His main research interests are mobile business, mobile technology development, and privacy management.

Patrick Martin is a Professor of the School of Computing at Queen's University. He holds a BSc from the University of Toronto, MSc from Queen's University, and a PhD from the University of Toronto. He joined Queen's University in 1984. He is also a Visiting Scientist with IBM's Centre for Advanced Studies. His research interests include database system performance, Web services, autonomic computing systems, and cloud computing.

Alejandro Pérez Méndez is a Ph.D student in the Department of Information and Communications Engineering of the University of Murcia. His research interests are focused on network security, access control, and identity management. He received his MS in Computer Science from the University of Murcia.

Gabriel López Millan is a full time Assistant Professor in the Department of Information and Communications Engineering of the University of Murcia. His research interests include network security, PKI, identity management, authentication, and authorization. He received his MS and PhD in computer science from the University of Murcia.

Åsmund Ahlmann Nyre received his MSc degree in Communication Technology from the Norwegian University of Science and Technology (NTNU) in 2005. He worked until 2007 as Security Engineer at the Norwegian road-tolling company Q-Free, after which he joined SINTEF ICT. As of July 2009, Mr. Nyre additionally holds a position as PhD candidate at NTNU. His research interests include information control, privacy and network security.

Hao-Ting (Howard) Pai has been in the doctoral program in Department of Information Management at National Chung Cheng University, Taiwan (R.O.C.) since 2007. In 2010, he was sponsored by Taiwan's National Science Council (NSC) and IBM. He was a visiting researcher at IBM Thomas J. Watson Research Center (located in Hawthorne, NY) for one year on the security & privacy issues of cloud computing. The preliminary research results are embodied in two American patent applications and were accepted for publication in an international journal, the *IBM Journal of Research and Development*. His interest and research areas include the issues of security & privacy on mobile commerce, health care, non-infrastructure wireless networks, and cloud computing. He now is a student member of the IEEE.

Francesco Palmieri is an Assistant Professor at the Engineering Faculty of the Second University of Napoli, Italy. His major research interests concern high performance and evolutionary networking protocols and architectures, routing algorithms, and network security. Since 1989, he has worked for several international companies on networking-related projects and, starting from 1997, and until 2010, he was the Director of the Telecommunication and Networking division of the Federico II University, in Napoli, Italy. He has been closely involved with the development of the Internet in Italy as a senior member of the Technical-Scientific Advisory Committee and of the CSIRT of the Italian NREN GARR. He has published a significant number of papers in leading technical journals and conferences and given many invited talks and keynote speeches.

Andrew Patrick is an IT Research Analyst at the Office of the Privacy Commissioner of Canada examining the privacy implications of technologies and services. He is also an Adjunct Research Professor in the departments of Psychology and Computer Science at Carleton University where he conducts research on usable security and trustable privacy protection. Dr. Patrick has worked at the National Research Council of Canada (NRC), Nortel, and the Communications Research Centre (CRC). He has over 20 years of experience in conducting and managing advanced research on a variety of information technologies, including Voice over IP (VoIP), multimedia collaboration systems, e-commerce trust, advanced Internet services, social network analysis, and natural language interfaces. See http://www.andrewpatrick.ca for more information.

Mario Piattini has an MSc and a PhD in Computer Science from the Polytechnic University of Madrid. He is a Certified Information System Auditor from the ISACA (Information System Audit and Control Association). The author of several books and papers on databases, software engineering and information systems, Piattini leads the ALARCOS research group of the Department of Computer Science at the University of Castilla–La Mancha. His research interests are: advanced database design, database quality, software metrics, object- oriented metrics, and software maintenance.

Yves Pigneur is head of the Information Systems Institute of the University of Lausanne, Switzerland. He has served as the principal investigator for many research projects involving information system design, requirements engineering, information technology management, innovation, and e-business. Dr. Pigneur is the Swiss representative of IFIP TC 8 as well as being chairperson and program chair of several conferences (IFIP, ISDSS, AIM). He is editor-in-chief of the academic journal Systèmes d'information & management *(*SIM*)*. Dr. Pigneur has had his research published in over fifty books, refereed journals and conference proceedings, including JMIS, Comm. AIS, Electronic Markets (EM), Electronic Commerce Research and Applications (ECRA), Information Systems and e-Business Management (ISeB), *and* Int. J. Learning and Intellectual Capital.

Alfonso Rodríguez is PhD in Computer Science from the University of Castilla-La Mancha (Spain), and he is MBA from the University of Bio-Bio (Chile). He is Associate Professor at the Computer Science and Information Technology Department in University of Bio-Bio (Chillán, Chile). His research activities are security in business process and information systems.

Nakeisha Schimke is a Researcher with the Institute of Bioinformatics and Computational Biology at The University of Tulsa (TU). Dr. Schimke's research interests include health information privacy and neuroinformatics.

Xiaoxun Sun received his B.Sc and M.Sc. degree in Department of Mathematics, Ocean University of China in 2006. He received his PhD from the Department of Mathematics & Computing at University of Southern Queensland. His research interests include access control, data privacy and security, data mining, and applied cryptography.

Inger Anne Tøndel received her MSc degree from the Norwegian University of Science and Technology in 2004, and has since been employed at SINTEF ICT. Mrs. Tøndel's research interests include electronic privacy, access control, threat modeling, and security requirements engineering. She has been a staff member of the Norwegian Centre for Information Security, and also participated in several national and EU-funded research projects.

Li-Feng Tseng is a Senior Software Engineering Consultant with 12 years of software development and management experience. He possesses extensive skills in distributed client/servers, Internet, object-oriented, process control, and database technologies. In addition, his experience includes business requirement analysis, system analysis and design, system testing and deployment, automatic software engineering solution implementation, and software package evaluation. He has a proven ability to learn new skills, mentor developers, and instruct end-users.

Iakovos S. Venieris is a Professor at the School of Electrical and Computer Engineering of the National Technical University of Athens since 1994. He received the Dipl.-Ing. degree from the University of Patras, Greece in 1988, and the Ph.D. degree from the National Technical University of Athens in 1990, all in Electrical and Computer Engineering. His research interests are in the fields of distributed systems, service engineering, agent technology, multimedia, mobile communications and intelligent networks, internetworking, signalling, resource scheduling and allocation for network management, modelling, performance evaluation, and queuing theory. He has over 150 publications in the above areas. Prof. Venieris has received several national and international awards for academic achievement. He is a member of the IEEE and the Technical Chamber of Greece.

Faye Fangfei Wang is a Senior Lecturer in Law at Brunel University and convenor of the Cyberlaw Section at the Society of Legal Scholars in the UK. She specialises in cyberlaw, international trade law, private international law, and online dispute resolution. Dr. Wang is the author of the books: Internet Jurisdiction and Choice of Law: Legal Practices in the EU, US and China (Cambridge University Press, 2010); Law of Electronic Commercial Transactions: Contemporary Issues in the EU, US and China (Oxford Routledge-Cavendish, 2010); and Online Dispute Resolution: Technology, Management and Legal Practice from an International Perspective (Oxford Chandos Publishing, 2009).

Liangzhao Zeng is a Research Staff Member Department at the Thomas J. Watson Research Center. He received a Ph.D. degree in Computer Science from the University of New South Wales, Australia. He works in the areas of event-based system, cloud computing, data management, and services engineering, with a focus on software infrastructure and data management issues. His work has been incorporated into several products, including IBM's WebSphere Business Monitor™ and WebSphere Business Modeler™. He is a recipient of IBM's Outstanding Technical Achievement Award, a co-inventor of over twenty issued or pending patents and a co-author for over thirty technical publications. His recent research interests include complex event processing, semantic data management, cloud service, and service composition.

Index

CPSIA information can be obtained at www.ICGtesting.com
Printed in the USA
BVOW051733021211

276863BV00002BA/1/P

9 781613 505014